Sociology

A Liberating Perspective

Second Edition

Alexander Liazos

Regis College

Allyn and Bacon

Boston London Sydney Toronto

Series Editor: Karen Hanson
Series Editorial Assistant: Susan S. Brody
Production Administrator: Annette Joseph
Production Coordinator: Susan Freese
Editorial-Production Service: Kailyard Associates
Cover Administrator: Linda K. Dickinson
Cover Designer: Christy Rosso
Manufacturing Buyer: Tamara McCracken

We acknowledge the following for permission to reprint:

pp. 120, 228–229, 253 From Marjorie Shostak, *Nisa: The Life and Words of a !Kung Woman.* Harvard University Press, 1981.
pp. 155–156, 179 From Kai T. Erikson, *Everything in Its Path*, Simon & Schuster, 1976. Reprinted with permission.
p. 255 From Myra Sadker and David Sadker, "Sexism in the Schoolroom of the 80s." *Psychology Today*, March 1985, pp. 54–57. Reprinted with permission.

Acknowledgments continued on page 547

Library of Congress Cataloging-in-Publication Data

Liazos, Alexander, 1941–
    Sociology, a liberating perspective / Alexander Liazos.—2nd ed.
        p.   cm.
    Bibliography: p.
    Includes index.
    ISBN 0-205-11896-8
    1. Sociology.   2. Marxian school of sociology.   3. Equality.
I. Title.
HM51.L485   1989
301—dc19

For my brothers and sisters—
Christo, Vangeli, Kleoniki, and Ifigenia—
with love and affection.
For all the days I have been with each of you,
may we all be together soon.

Contents

Preface

Two simple but conflicting realities have guided my work on this book. First, as human beings, we find meaning and fulfillment in our lives through other people, in our work and play, and in our families, communities, and cultures. Second, our social existence, this shared experience of creating meaning in our lives, is threatened by social inequalities and by the exploitation and control of the many by the few. For many of us, and I hope for you as well, sociology is a field that seeks to understand the relationship between these two realities: shared experience and social injustice.

Philosophy and Methods

In *Sociology: A Liberating Perspective*, I maintain that sociology uses both disciplined and objective methods and personal and subjective insights. It is a personal and professional search to understand the world around us and our place in it. Although this search gives us some answers, albeit tentative ones, it often poses more questions and possibilities. It is guided by a sense of curiosity, wonder, questioning, and examination of our preconceptions and perceptions of social reality.

Sociology: A Liberating Perspective has a bias—no book is completely objective. But unlike most authors, I acknowledge my bias, and I present and explain it openly. I do not pretend to present all points of view. Rather I invite you, the student and the teacher, to debate, reflect upon, and challenge my arguments and to compare this text to others that present different points of view.

This text is presented from a Marxist socialist perspective, one which is deeply committed to democratic principles and to the struggle for an egalitarian society, a society without classes and free of sex and racial oppression and exploitation. We cannot understand modern societies if we do not examine class differences, the exploitation of most people by small ruling classes, and the struggle to create a just society. These are the fundamental social realities of our time. But this is not to say I subscribe to a mechanical, dogmatic, and simplistic Marxism (one Marx would certainly have rejected himself). I use Marxist concepts to understand a changing world, not to fit the world into a preconceived and rigid dogma.

One of the most constant themes running through *Sociology: A Liber-*

ating Perspective is that while we can, and do, shape our society, we are also limited by traditions and conditions that define the context in which we live. Social reality does limit and shape us; there is a social script we follow. But we—individually and collectively—choose how to interpret and re-interpret this script. We are not robots. We do change and shape social reality as much as it shapes us. There are limits, but there are also choices and possibilities.

One other strong theme in this text is that we live within a natural environment, and if we are to survive, we must recognize that its protection is essential. We must develop an environmental consciousness that pervades all of our decisions. We must live in harmony *in* nature and understand that, in the words of Robert Finch, "Nature is not something to coexist with, but [is] existence itself."

Although this text includes approaches, views, concepts, research, and literature from traditional sociology, I have also relied on a wide range of fields and sources: humanistic anthropology, ecology, history, the print media (mostly newspapers and periodicals), and my own life experiences.

I make extensive use of studies of other societies. These studies offer us a view of human and social realities vastly different from our own yet similar in the essential humanity we share with people everywhere. Inherently fascinating and intellectually stimulating, they offer comparisons and contrasts of different people—their behaviors and attitudes. They show us what past human societies were like, and they expand our vision of what they may be in the future. If sociology is to be more than a study of society as it exists in modern industrial societies (especially capitalist ones like the United States), if it is to be a study of human societies in general, we need to study societies in many places and in different times. For example, my understanding of human evolution, of inequalities and egalitarian conditions, of norms, roles, and the relationship between individuals and societies, of sex roles and childhood, and of other issues and debates has been profoundly shaped by my study of the Mbuti, the !Kung, and other preindustrial societies.

In many chapters I refer to and discuss personal and family experiences in Albania, Greece, and the United States. Personal experiences illuminate social reality. They are part of the information in our study of the world, but they are never sufficient by themselves. They provide a starting point, an essential beginning, but they should never be an ending. I use examples from my life in this spirit. All of us need to *begin* with our own lives, but we cannot stop there. We need to explore other social scenes—those near us in space and time *and* those removed in space and time.

At the end of the book, just before the index, you will find a short autobiography. You may want to read it before you proceed to Chapter 1. It may help you understand the strengths and weaknesses of the sociological perspective I present here.

Organization and Revision

I have organized the text in the following manner. Part I introduces sociology, the different perspectives, methods, and problems within the field. Part II presents what I see as the fundamental realities of our natural and social worlds and the conditions that make us social human beings: the evolution of human societies and the natural world around us, culture, community, family, and socialization. Part III explores the three fundamental social inequalities that divide us from each other and diminish our humanity and social existence: class, race, and sex inequalities.

As I explain above, the emphasis in this text differs from most sociology texts. Social evolution, the environment, nuclear war, and community are either absent from or only briefly discussed in most other texts. On the other hand, since this is not intended to be an encyclopedic tome, I have de-emphasized topics that are frequently discussed elsewhere, such as crime and deviance, health, education, and so on.

Aside from the normal updating and revisions that go into a second edition, I have added a new chapter on work, as well as new material on how the working class is changing, on what effects AIDS and sexual repression have on society, and on how anthropology has viewed women. There are several topics that have been substantially expanded: American values, norm conflicts, the role of the mass media, urban problems and diversity, delayed marriages, and environmental ethics and consciousness.

Acknowledgments

When I first began working on this book some five years ago, I knew I wanted to try to communicate to my readers my understanding of the human journey. Since I have experienced so little of what I write about, however, I undertook this task with trepidation. Even my reading does not begin to cover the massive amount of literature that is relevant to such an understanding. Working on this text has been a truly humbling experience. So it is with pleasure, gratitude, and thanks that I acknowledge my debt to so many people who have helped and supported me through this effort.

Janet Casey deserves my first and foremost thanks. She typed the entire manuscript for the first edition and the revisions for the second, which were in longhand. I could not have completed this work on time without her careful and prompt typing.

Al Levitt, former sociology editor at Allyn and Bacon, was twice coura-geous, perceptive, or foolhardy (depending on one's viewpoint) in agreeing to publish two very unusual textbooks. He provided me the opportunity to organize and develop my social and political perspective and to present it to students and others. I am deeply grateful to him.

The comments, suggestions, criticisms, and critical support of the six reviewers for this edition were invaluable in improving and updating the text. I want to thank Jim Messerschmidt (University of Southern Maine), Bob Ross (Clark University), Leonardo Salamini (Bradley University), Jane Shaw (The University of Connecticut), Jerrold Starr (University of West Virginia), and Michael Weichbrod (Montgomery College). I followed most of their suggestions. I am especially indebted to Jane Shaw and Bob Ross for their many suggestions and comments that forced me to clarify many points.

Rebecca Davison deserves a special thanks for the unenviable task of editing a textbook. Writers are attached to their work and reluctant to change it, so it takes a very patient and skillful person to edit a book. Her suggestions, questions, and clarifications improved the text immensely. Where I thought my meaning was clear she showed me how it was not, and the changes have improved my argument. In some places where she suggested different phrasing, I chose to keep the original wording, and the responsibility is mine for any remaining deficiencies.

Any text is the combined product of the writer's work and perspective and of his or her knowledge gathered from the labors of thousands of writers and researchers. All these people, many of whom would not agree with my conclusions, are listed in the bibliography. I thank them all.

I am also deeply indebted, as all of us are, to the millions of people, dead and alive, who have struggled for their liberation and the liberation of all humanity. They have given us hope and a better world. Among them have been the Americans, black and white, who struggled for racial justice and equality since the 1950s; the Vietnamese who fought against imperialism and those Americans who protested against the Vietnam War; the women who bravely started and created the feminist movement, liberating both women and men; the poor and exploited who have given their lives in liberation wars on all continents; and those everywhere working to prevent nuclear war, to create justice for all, and to shape societies where all people can live together without exploitation, hunger, and inequality.

I end with some personal acknowledgments. For three years, George and Aleka Michelis, who are now living in Greece, helped me relive my Greek past. Chris and Helena have been present and supportive during very difficult times. Melissa and Ariane have shared my jobs, have taught me about childhood and awakened the buried child in me, and have shown me their love in surprising and touching ways. And a very special friend for three years gave me her love, tenderness, companionship, and support.

Finally, I am grateful to my friends who supported me through some very difficult days in 1985. You were always there.

PART I

Approaches and Methods

CHAPTER 1

Sociological, Social, and Personal Issues

Personal and Social Journeys

As we go about our daily lives, we tend to focus mostly on our immediate surroundings and ignore much of what happens in the world beyond. Perhaps we must do so, if we are to avoid being overwhelmed by events seemingly so much beyond our control.

Yet, we cannot ignore the larger world for long. Sooner or later it touches us, our families, our friends, our communities. A company moves its plant to another location or closes a factory down. Thousands of people become unemployed. Individuals, families, and communities are devastated. A nuclear power plant leaks or disintegrates, and radiation is blown across nations and continents, poisoning food and people. The poor, who struggle for food and shelter while the rich exploit them, rise in protest, strike, and even revolt. We need to understand why such events happen, why such conditions exist, how they touch and shape our lives, and what we can do about them.

Although problems abound in our world, life goes on, with all its joys, sorrows, and complexities. We are part of the life cycle: we are born, grow up, struggle to survive, get old, and die. We all seek to create joy and happiness in our lives. We dance, sing, tell stories, joke, make love, play, contemplate the meaning of life, gently rock babies to sleep, remember and reminisce, and cry tears of joy and sadness. We enjoy our families and friends. We marvel at how a baby grows, the beauty of a tree, a sunset, the sea. We enjoy a meal that provides nutrition and sociability. We are both unique beings *and* participants in the eternal cycle of life. But this personal part of our lives is set within larger frameworks—families, communities, nations, and the globe. Within these spheres, we face many challenges.

Unprecedented devastation, death, and destruction are minutes away because of the nuclear weapons in the United States, Soviet Union, and elsewhere. We may try to block out of our consciousness the threat of nuclear war and the end of life because these thoughts and realities are both terrifying and incomprehensible. How can life end? How have we come to this madness? How can supposedly sane people rationally discuss *winning* a nuclear war? How can governments contemplate using nuclear weapons to win wars and control other nations?

Annihilation in a war is not the only threat we face from nuclear technology. Three Mile Island in 1979 and Chernobyl in 1986 demonstrated the dangers of even the so-called peaceful uses of nuclear power. At Chernobyl, some people and animals died immediately food was poisoned. But the long-term genetic damage to future generations in both accidents is still being debated and remains unknown. No one questions that there will be damage, just how much.

The environment around us is under constant assault. (See Chapter 3.) Acid rain, produced from industrial emissions released in the atmosphere, is killing trees and forests, and all aquatic life in many lakes. The ozone layer, which protects us from the harmful effects of sunlight, is being depleted because of emissions from spray cans and other products of modern industrial economies. Everywhere we are polluting or exhausting water supplies. Even the seas are not safe. Students who visited Boston Harbor were shocked by what they found. The *Boston Globe* (May 9, 1987) reported that "the deformities, evident in almost every fish pulled out of the water, were a shocking surprise to the students. . . . The flounder were covered with parasites and tumorous boils. . . . High, unexplained levels of the pesticide DDT and other related chemicals were measured in the waterway." (p. 2)

Meanwhile, millions of workers, in factories, fields, and offices, are exposed to dangerous working conditions and dangerous chemicals. According to government estimates, fifteen to twenty million people work in jobs that expose them to chemicals that can cause reproductive injuries. All types of workers are exposed to harmful chemicals and dangerous working conditions: farmworkers pick grapes that have been sprayed with pesticides; secretaries sit before video display terminals that emit radiation; miners breathe coal dust and asbestos fibers. (See Chapter 9.)

Our culture presents challenges to us, as well. It is undergoing many changes. What is expected, accepted, tolerated, supposedly normal? Is cohabitation of unmarried couples acceptable? Can high school students publish papers uncensored by the administration? How are we to react to people who think and act differently than we do, both in our culture and from other cultures? (See Chapter 4.)

Many communities are threatened by economic and social developments. Flint, Michigan, and other cities and towns have seen plants close and move. Family violence, suicides, people moving to find work elsewhere, and other events have shaken the life of many communities. The sense of community built over time declines as people move away from family, friends, and neighbors they love. Why do these plants move and close down? Who makes these decisions? Why? (See Chapter 5.)

People feel their families threatened, too. Students come to college convinced by the media that the American family is disintegrating because of high divorce rates, children left alone for a few hours as both parents work, and so on. Is the family falling apart or simply changing? Why is it changing? In most two-parent families, both parents work, yet real (after inflation) family incomes have not increased since the early 1970s. Why do both parents need to work to make the same income one worker used to make? How are families adjusting to this new condition? Is anyone helping families? There are more one-parent families than ever before. How are they managing financially and socially? (See Chapters 6 and 7.)

This financial picture of families gives us an idea of what the new economy looks like. Jobs that paid living wages in the 1940s, 1950s, and 1960s have been exported to other countries where workers get paid much lower wages. Other jobs have been eliminated for many reasons. Millions of new jobs in service occupations, sales, and clerical work have been created, but these jobs pay much less than those lost or exported. Millions of people who lose jobs never find another one, or they work at much lower wages. Others, especially minority youths, never find jobs. How is this new economy affecting people? Lower paying jobs, unemployment, tax changes that decreased the taxes paid by the rich few and corporations, accompanied by reduced government spending for housing, nutrition, health, and other programs have led to poverty, hunger, and homelessness for the many. (See Chapters 8 and 9.)

Many more people pay a much greater proportion of their income for housing than they did a few years ago. Hunger, almost eliminated by federal programs in the 1960s and 1970s, reappeared in the United States during the 1980s. Many studies have shown the existence of extensive and increasing hunger in America. Children have died of starvation; millions of others are malnourished. Many old people must spend most of their income on housing; many eat only one meal a day—a meal brought to their homes by meals-on-wheels programs. Many families turn to nonprofit food pantries or shelves in their own neighboring towns to avoid hunger.

How can hunger exist in a country so rich with food? People pay outrageous sums of money for frivolous luxuries—$1,000 for mink coats for dolls, $1,500 for video phones, gourmet food for pets—while thousands go hungry. While millions of families must choose between paying the rent or buying a badly needed pair of shoes, others live in homes "with a marble-floored foyer that soars at least two stories, a master bedroom that comes straight out of *Dynasty*, . . . and a living room suitable for full-court basketball" (*Dollars and Sense*, July/August, 1987:5). (See Chapter 8.)

The new economy has increased inequalities and class differences. The gap between the rich and affluent professionals and managers, on the one hand, and the working class and the poor, on the other, is widening. More people have low-paying jobs; more people are jobless. Why are class differences increasing? How can we assure the necessities of life to all people?

While inequalities between classes are increasing, various groups face their own specific problems. Women, blacks, Chicanos, Asians, the handicapped, and other minority groups still face discrimination and prejudice at work, in housing, in the media. We have made some headway. But even though we are more conscious of discrimination, discrimination still exists in overt and subtle forms.

Some blacks have made gains, but millions more are poor and unemployed. And one wonders what it means when during the 1988 presidential primary, the press constantly said that Jesse Jackson could not possibly become the Democratic nominee for president—this despite the fact that he received millions of votes. Why couldn't he? Very few people said *they* would not have voted for him because he is black, only that they believed other people were not ready for a black president. Who are these other people? (See Chapters 11 and 12.)

Even as women achieve many gains, they face unyielding traditions. More and more women need to work to support their families. Many women are losing ground as they try to support families with jobs that pay very little. This, coupled with the fact that more and more women need to work, means that women and children make up the majority of the poor in the United States. Most women in our economy make much less money than men, even when the work is comparable. Why? Who decides that the work women do is less valuable than what men do? (See Chapter 12.)

Men and women within the United States and throughout the world are protesting the kinds of injustices we've described above. Protests and revolutions in various stages of development have mushroomed everywhere. Within recent years, students in Italy, France, China, Mexico, South Korea, and Spain, among other places, demonstrated against their governments. They protested government corruption, repression, unemployment, and other injustices (Riotta, 1987).

In Brazil, supposedly one of the less poor countries, absolute poverty is widespread. United Nations workers have estimated that ten to twenty-five *million* children have been abandoned by their families, or their families cannot support them adequately. They roam the streets and peddle peanuts, or sell drugs, or resort to prostitution. Families live in shacks on hillsides that are washed downhill when torrential rains fall, drowning hundreds of people. Such abject poverty rules the lives of billions of people throughout the world. Why? (See Chapter 10.)

In other places, abject poverty may not reign, but individuals, families, and communities are undergoing profound social changes. In Greece, for example, the lives of millions of people have been disrupted when they leave their villages and stream into crowded cities. Others leave Greece and look for work in Germany and other northern European countries where they become *guestworkers*—temporary workers who are expected eventually to return to their homelands. They work in mines and generally hold the most menial jobs. They often live in barrack-like housing and save some of their wages to send to their elderly parents, wives, and children who are left behind in the villages. Fathers remain strangers to their growing children. Young people are scattered like leaves by the winds of social and economic changes. For all of them, the memories of their communities, their country, and their culture remain vivid and alive—and yet, gone forever.

Profound social changes are also taking place in the Soviet Union. In politics, the economy, and the media—from the top leadership down—people are raising questions, posing challenges, proposing alternatives.

This is but a small sample of the enormous variety of human and social conditions, changes, and problems that exist in the world today. Each of us sees and experiences but a few of these realities. Nevertheless, it is not now possible, nor desirable, for any of us to be concerned with *only* our own private lives. We live in a world where what happens in one part of it will sooner or later affect all of us. We need to understand the world around us, past and present.

Social Structure

All of us know our behavior and the behavior of others is, for the most part, organized, repetitive, regular, and predictable. Indeed, we take this predictability for granted. We could not survive if we did not develop the ability to tell what is and what is not usually predictable. Human social life is only possible because we can assume others will act much the same way as they have in the past. In other words, people in a society assume roles. A *role*, the expectations, obligations, and rewards of a social position (see Chapter 4), implies that a person in a social position (police officer, teacher, bank teller, and so on) can be expected to perform certain acts and avoid others.

Looking beyond these social interactions, we find other predictable social elements or social structures. *Social structure* refers to the fundamental assumption of sociology that society and social behavior are patterned, orderly, predictable, and organized and that there is a social network composed of norms, roles, and institutions. In short, society is structured as an organized entity; it is not a random and chance activity. Workplaces open and close at certain hours and operate by certain rules; schools open and close at appointed hours and teach certain skills, knowledge, and attitudes; trains and buses (usually) run on time. These and many other social regularities make life possible. In short, somewhat like a machine, we find society is composed of different parts that function in predictable ways.

Besides these obvious examples, there are subtler forms of social structure. Organizations and social groups often express their structure through formally appointed or elected leaders and rules, thus insuring the functioning of the organizations. Sociologists and others have shown, however, that even informal and apparently unorganized social settings and groups, if they continue to exist over a period of time, develop structures. Informal leaders and unwritten but clear rules develop. Think of groups of friends, work groups, an informal discussion group, all with no appointed leaders. When we closely observe these situations, we notice certain roles and norms (appropriate and expected behaviors) develop. For example, most such groups seem to have one or more members who try to help the group function more easily through joking, which eases tension and enables the members to work together. (For examples, see William F. White's *Streetcorner Society* and Elliott Liebow's *Tally's Corner*.)

Contemporary societies carry out their functions through institutions. An *institution* is a stable form of social organization developed over time to meet some need or want. Some of the institutions in modern societies are economic, religious, political, educational, military, medical, and family. (See Chapter 4.)

Formal and informal social structures regulate our lives, and they shape how we live and how we die. Emile Durkheim's book *Suicide* is an excellent illustration of the influence of social structures. He observes that suicide rates vary from group to group. After discounting many popular explanations for the differing rates, he concludes that groups with low suicide rates are characterized by close, supportive, and intense social lives. The community provides the members of these groups with regular social contact. They are not isolated and individualistic. Groups without such a close social life, however, tend to have higher suicide rates. Thus, we find that even a private act such as suicide is shaped by social structure and social interaction.

Giving birth is also a universal, natural, and private act. Yet, women and men experience it differently, depending on the assumptions, norms, and practices of the society in which they live. In Greek peasant society, women used to stay home for forty days after they gave birth. Years ago in the United States, the usual hospital stay for a birth was a week. More recently, women who had a normal birth went home in three days. Currently, thanks to better prenatal care, many women go home in one or two days. Among the !Kung, a tribe in southwest Africa, the norm is for the woman to give birth unaided. When she knows the time for birth is close, she will go to the bush and prepare a place to deliver. Afterwards, she will return to the camp. The same natural phenomenon, but with different understandings and expectations of how incapacitated a woman may be after delivery, results in different experiences.

Social structures change. Indeed, as they change, so do our lives—sometimes profoundly. In 1850, the typical American worker was still a farmer. His or her life was very different from the typical 1950 urban American worker who worked in factories and other blue-collar occupations. Today, such manufacturing jobs are being exported to places where labor is cheaper (Southeast Asia, Philippines, and so on), and American workers are shifting to low-paying service and clerical jobs (see Chapter 8). In many communities when factories close down, the unemployed workers must move away, losing family and community ties.

Our lives, our personal and social existence, are influenced and shaped by these social structures regardless of whether they are stable or changing. This is one of sociology's most important contributions to the understanding of individual and social existence. Sociologists devote much of their time to the study of social structures.

Sociology as Liberation

Our lives are influenced and shaped by social conditions and structures but not totally controlled by them. It is tempting either to see our existence as totally dominated and controlled by the roles within our social structures or to deny all influence and claim we can do as we please. Both of these positions negate reality and experience. Two examples illustrate how social structures control our lives and how we exercise control over them at the same time.

It is obvious that a classroom is a very structured environment, with many written and unwritten norms and roles. The teacher speaks most of the time, students listen (or pretend to), tests are given, and some learning goes on. Most classes are tolerable but not very engaging or lively experiences. The social structure of the classroom insures that they are usually dull and no more than tolerated. Yet I have had classes where students, because of their interest and determination, have managed to transform the classroom into an exciting and informative setting. The students and I looked forward to coming together. The deadening social structure of the classroom makes such happenings difficult but not impossible.

According to Shostak (1981), the norm of private delivery among the !Kung also turns out to be not so automatic or desirable. Young women are raised with this model and aspire to it. But older women know the danger and pain of being alone during delivery and encourage young women to be in another woman's company. The norm, after all, is not automatically adhered to. (See Chapter 4 for a more extended discussion of roles.)

These two examples illustrate an important sociological insight: People construct social structures and people can change them. It is dangerous to believe that social structures are unalterable, stable entities; it leads to fatalism and acceptance of oppressive social conditions. Social structures are human creations. Once they arise, they push us to act in certain ways. Many times they help us to meet our needs and desires and to enrich our lives. But at other times, structures can be harmful. We must then realize that we are not prisoners of society; we are creative participants. We can change society.

Even under the most oppressive social conditions, dreams of freedom and fulfillment linger on. Many books written in the past few years show that most workplaces in the United States are alienating and destructive. People hate their jobs. Because of considerations of profit and power, many managers create and perpetuate monotonous, mindless, and dangerous jobs. While this is depressing, it is equally as inspiring to see workers who are searching for ways to resist the monotony and control and who dream of useful and liberating work. Garson (1975) describes this spirit in this way: "It was the positive things I saw that touched me the most. Not that people are beaten down (which they are) but that they almost always pop up. Not that people are bored (which they are) but the ways they find to make it interesting. Not that people hate their work (which they do) but that even so, they try to make something out of it" (p. xiii). Studs Terkel (1974), in his preface to *Working* (110 people talking about their jobs), mentions the "extraordinary dreams of ordinary people." His book is a warning that sociology, which deals too often with the typical and the average, does not always accurately reflect what people experience. People are not replicas of factory models.

Social structures can be liberating tools that we can use to develop individual and group potentials. They should be like good cookbooks that direct and guide us to refine and express our skills. Cookbooks are liberating and enriching—social structures should be too. When they are not, it should be our task to study and change them. (For the argument that culture and social structure enable us to become individuals, see *Freedom and Culture* by Dorothy Lee.)

Sociological Perspectives

So far I have presented my view of what sociology is and the questions it asks. Other sociologists would ask different questions, or they would approach the same questions differently. Even though all sociologists are generally concerned with society, social groups, and social processes and seek to understand why and how societies exist, they each come to this task with differing biases, interests, views, and personal histories. In short, there are different *sociological perspectives,* different ways to view facts, conditions, people, and their relationships to each other. Because of this, sociologists differ greatly in the activities they are involved in and the questions they study in the name of sociology.

Sociologists have differing perspectives on the nature of society and differing opinions about the questions they should raise about social life. Here is an illustration. A person can look at a small hill full of trees from near or far or even while he or she stands in the middle of it, on the ground, or in a tree. Or the person could use an airplane or helicopter and fly over the hill. Depending on where the person views the hill, he or she will notice some particular feature of it, the forest or the individual trees, but each position will obscure some of its other features. Flying over the hill gives the person a good view of the hill as a whole but not a very good view of individual trees. To do that, the person needs to stand on the hill and among the trees. In other words, the position from which a person observes the hill seems to enhance or limit what aspect of the hill he or she sees. The problem is that a person must stand somewhere.

In observing society, a sociologist must also stand somewhere. Unfortunately, he or she is even more limited than the person on the hill. When sociologists look at social life, they always do so with a life history, certain knowledge, questions they have come to consider significant, and so on. All of this makes up their position—their view of the hill. But, unlike the observer of the hill, they cannot move as easily from one observational post to another. A person can examine the hill from a mile away, from a hundred feet, from the ground, from the tops of various trees, from a helicopter overhead. In fact, to get a total understanding of the hill, the observer could study it from all these points. This is impossible for sociologists. They have invested too much of themselves in learning and making social and political commitments to be able to change their positions that easily. So you are warned that in sociology (I would argue in all fields of study), there are differing perspectives.

Below we shall examine three perspectives that are dominant in sociology. Keep in mind that there are many others and many variations of these three. Studying these will not make you an expert of the many sociologies being practiced, but it will give you an appreciation of some important differences and debates in the field. (See Table 1.1.)

TABLE 1.1
Schematic Comparison of the Three Perspectives

	Image of Society	Illustrative Questions
Functionalist	A system of interrelated parts that is relatively stable; each part has functional consequences for the operation of society as a whole	*How is society integrated?* •What are the major parts of society? •How are these parts interrelated? •What are the consequences of each for the operation of society?
Conflict	A system characterized by social inequality; any part of society benefits some categories of people more than others; conflict-based social inequality promotes social change	*How is society divided?* •What are major patterns of social inequality? •How do some categories of people attempt to protect their privileges? •How do other categories of people attempt to improve their social position?
Interactionist	An ongoing process of social interaction in specific settings based on symbolic communication; individual perceptions of reality are variable and changing	*How is society experienced?* •How do human beings in interaction generate, sustain, and change social patterns? •How do individuals attempt to shape the reality perceived by others? •How does individual behavior change from one situation to another?

From John J. Macionis, *Sociology,* © 1987, p. 21. Reprinted by permission of Prentice Hall, Inc., Englewood Cliffs, NJ

The Functionalist Perspective

From sociology's inception early in the nineteenth century, many sociologists have found it useful to study society as if it were a living organism. The human body is a delicate system of many parts or elements (organs) that work together enabling us to survive. In many ways, society can be seen as a similar system where different elements (families, schools, religious organizations, work settings, communities, roles, norms, and so on) exist and work in relation to each other in order for the society to function.

A *functionalist* sees society as an independent entity, greater than the individuals who compose it. In order to survive and perpetuate itself, society has needs that must be met. These needs may and often do override the needs of individual people. For example, raising children may be a burden to many people, but no society can survive without new members, so it has rules about raising children that must be obeyed. All societies must create means to get enough food for their people, raise children, find some shelter, keep minimal harmony between their members, and protect themselves from human and nonhuman attackers. To meet these needs, societies develop institutions, roles, and norms. Families come together to grow or gather food and to raise children; rules develop on what people may or may not do; work settings are created for making tools, raising food, and so on. Other social structures develop, such as community organizations and governments that are aimed at meeting societal needs.

Functionalists tend to assume social structures arise and continue because they benefit the whole society. Social structures function for the common good and common survival, not just for some people in the society. All parts of the society tend to contribute to the maintenance and proper functioning of the society. (In fact, some functionalists have argued that some institutions and some social structures may at times be harmful to the society, but the tendency still is to see most elements of a society as functional to its existence.)

In a live organism the functioning (or malfunctioning) of one organ (heart, liver, etc.) affects the functioning of other organs and of the body as a whole; so it is in society. When one part of it functions well (a school system, for example), then other parts (workplaces, for example) and the society as a whole function well. When problems arise in schools, students who will later become workers do not get the proper training or have the motivation to do a good job. People who are unhappy at work will also often be unhappy family members. And so it goes.

Because society is a system of highly interrelated parts functioning to meet societal needs, a delicate balance exists. Too much change in the structure, especially if it happens too rapidly, unbalances the society and causes severe problems. Societal needs are not met; institutions do not function properly; and people are unsettled in such stressful situations. Thus, functionalists tend to emphasize the need for and importance of stability, continuity, and harmony. Only if these exist, they maintain, can there be well-functioning societies. In this sense, functionalism may be considered a conservative perspective on society. (On functionalism, see Abrahamson, 1978.)

The Conflict Perspective

Conflict sociologists fundamentally disagree with functionalism. When they look at society, they do not make the assumption that it is a well-integrated organism where all the different parts contribute to a functioning system.

The disagreement between the two perspectives is not total, of course. Conflict sociologists share many of the insights of functionalism. For example, they too find that social institutions are related. What happens in the family affects the school system and vice versa, or what happens at work affects the family. It is also obvious that when people gather in functioning groups (societies of all sizes), they must develop ways to raise their children, feed themselves, get along with each other, protect themselves, and so on. On these issues conflict sociologists do not disagree with the functionalists.

Conflict sociologists, however, challenge a number of other assumptions and arguments. First, and perhaps foremost, is the definition of and emphasis on society. Society is not an independent entity greater than the people in it; it does not have its own needs. Rather, a society is a group of people who agree and disagree with each other, who cooperate and compete, as they struggle to make a living, provide for their families, and participate in their communities. Society does not dictate and have needs; groups of people do. Society does not tell us to cover our bodies, for example; parents (some parents) do. They are carrying on customs handed down to them by their parents. To say society does this is to exclude protesting children and parents and other adults who do not feel embarrassed when they see a nude body.

A second important disagreement between functionalist and conflict sociologists is over the claim that institutions, traditions, roles, norms, and other elements of social life arise and continue to exist *because* they benefit society as a whole. Some social elements, for example, general norms against murder or reckless driving, do benefit all of society. But other elements may, and in fact do, benefit only some people and harm others, often a majority of others. The present educational and economic systems have existed for over a century, and it is tempting to argue that they benefit society as a whole. Conflict sociologists dispute this claim, arguing that many people suffer material, psychic, and social losses from these systems in our society.

Harmony, balance, agreement, and cooperation may be ideals and may have largely existed in primitive societies, but they do not characterize modern societies. Competition, conflict, and disagreement are the daily realities of the societies in which we live. Since the resources we need to survive—land, water, food, trees, oil, and so forth—are limited and often scarce, there is competition and disagreement about who will control their use and who will benefit from them. For example, beaches may be privately owned or open to the public; the profits from a corporation may go toward higher wages for workers or higher dividends for stockholders; the taxes on corporations may go up or down; taxes may go to build nuclear missiles or to build schools. The list of conflicts over the use of limited resources and over appropriate or inappropriate behavior is endless. The conclusion is obvious: In many, if not most, areas of social life there is little agreement, little consensus. Institutions, roles, and norms often benefit some people at the expense of other people.

As often as there is harmony and agreement in societies, there is coercion and disagreement. It may not have been so in the past, and it may not be so in future societies, but in modern societies there is conflict between groups on how the systems should function, how resources should be used, and who should benefit from social arrangements. Moreover, some groups are much more powerful than others and have many more resources in this struggle for control of the society and its institutions.

One particular version of the conflict perspective argues that in capitalist societies today it is the managers and stockholders of large corporations, industries, and banks who are the dominant and controlling group in society (see Chapters 8, 9, and 10). While they may not be in total control of the economy, the political system, and other institutions, they benefit more from the way the society functions than do the rest of the people. This ruling class is a very small portion of the population. (This is a Marxist perspective; see the end of this chapter.)

Interactionist Perspective

Interactionists do not so much disagree with functional or conflict sociologists as they ask somewhat different questions and focus on different issues.

The *interactionist perspective* studies ordinary daily social interactions intensively. In social situations such as schoolrooms, relationships between men and women or children and parents, or social gatherings, people shape and alter their actions in response to the actions of others. All of these social situations acquire meaning for us as we interpret our behavior and the behavior of others. We learn, for example, to become students as we react to, interpret, and understand the meaning of teachers' actions. To some degree, we create reality as we interact with other people. Reality is not a given, it is a process where we constantly interpret our own and others' actions and shape our actions in response to others' expectations and actions. By the words we use and how we use them, by body movements and gestures, by the subtle changes and redefinitions of what we and others mean, we define social reality.

The Three Perspectives on Education

The differences and similarities between the three perspectives may become clearer after we examine how they would study and interpret the educational system in a modern industrial society.

Functionalists consider this system necessary and desirable for industrial society. People need to read and write, to possess mathematical reasoning, and to develop attitudes, like punctuality and self-discipline, necessary for the work in this kind of society. These abilities are absolutely essential for the economic system to work. In addition, schools teach other values, beliefs, and skills basic to the culture of the society. Modern industrial society is hardly imaginable without its educational system, which arose and continues in order to fulfill absolutely essential functions.

Conflict sociologists agree that schools teach many essential skills and much useful knowledge, but they point to features of the educational system that benefit some people and work against the interests of others. From their very beginning, public schools have taught only limited skills to minorities, poor people, and until recently women. All these groups are taught some skills—especially the necessity of obedience—but they are discouraged from aspiring to leadership positions and managerial jobs. Private boarding schools and elite universities on the other hand train ruling class children for their powerful positions in later life. Children from the lower classes do not receive such an education. Schools prepare these people to adjust to and accept menial and limited jobs. The educational system does teach many skills necessary for the functioning of industrial society, but it also perpetuates class differences and class inequalities. Some people clearly benefit more from the educational system, others less, and many not at all.

Interactionists study the various interactions in classrooms and other school settings. For example, how do students learn to be deferential towards their teachers? How do they react to the expectations that they be deferential? What happens when they are not deferential? Do teachers direct questions and comments as much to boys as to girls? To good-looking students more than to the rest? What roles develop in the classroom?

For example, repeated and close observations show teachers directing their questions and comments to only a few students, whom we will call the talkers. If this is confirmed by observation, an interactionist may ask why it is so, how do other students react to this situation, and so forth. These and many similar concerns of the interactionist regarding education are of a different quality than are the issues raised by the other two approaches.

Conclusion

These perspectives are not mutually exclusive. The insights and concerns of all three can be applied to understanding human societies. Functionalist and conflict sociologists share certain assumptions and concerns, and the interactionist's approach can be used by both of the other types. (See Table 1.1 for a comparison of the three approaches.)

My own perspective, the perspective of this book, is clearly conflict oriented. I will argue, especially in Part III, that our society is dominated by and run largely for the benefit of a small ruling class. When I examine education, for example, I raise the issues and concerns outlined above. But I am also interested in what goes on in the classroom. In seeking to show how the education system perpetuates class inequalities, I use interactionist questions and techniques. Two sociologists in fact studied elementary schools in two different neighborhoods, and by describing the directions and actions of the teachers and the students' reactions, they showed the class bias in the schools. In schools attended by poor and working-class students teachers taught obedience. In schools attended by children of wealthy classes, they encouraged the students to take initiative and be creative. One class was being prepared for menial jobs by being taught obedience, the other class was being prepared for managerial jobs by being taught independence, leadership, and self-control. Thus, the interactionist perspective can be used to show how the educational system works. (See Wilcox & Moriarty, 1976.)

Although the three perspectives are not in total disagreement with each other, most sociologists espouse one view more strongly than another. In this book, I examine most traditional sociological concepts and issues (culture, family, socialization, social classes, minorities, and others) from a conflict-Marxist perspective. Most sociological textbooks have their own perspective; some books tend to have one of the three views presented here; others try to integrate them, but all of them have a perspective. Few, however, openly and explicitly identify their point of view.

Capitalist Society

Within each of these three perspectives, there are differing emphases and interests, just as there are different theologies within Christianity. Marxism is a particular school within the conflict perspective. More than other conflict theorists, Marxists focus on class inequalities, class conflicts, and the power of a ruling class as the fundamental features of contemporary capitalist societies. In this section I present a very brief version of a Marxist perspective, which also serves as an outline of the entire text. (See Beaud, 1981; Sweezy & Magdoff, 1985b; and Ollman, 1986, for a Marxist history of capitalism and the essence of Marxist thought.)

The Rise of Industrial Capitalism

Social Evolution
Until about ten thousand years ago people lived in societies that were small, egalitarian, and in harmony with their natural environment. They made their living by hunting animals and gathering plants, roots, and berries; they did not cultivate plants or raise animals.

For reasons anthropologists do not fully understand, some societies began to cultivate the soil and grow their own food. With this agriculture came a surplus of food. Growers raised more food than they could consume. This allowed a few people to become nonfood-producing specialists. Some people began to slowly acquire more possessions than others, and land became private property. In short, inequalities began to appear. Power, wealth, and work differences began to separate people, and sex-role and power differences between men and women became pronounced.

In later societies these inequalities and differences increased even more. In agricultural or peasant societies animals were vital to food production. Oxen and other animals pulled plows. Animal fertilizers were used, and technological innovations were made. As food surpluses increased, more specialists arose. These people began to control much of the wealth without doing any physical labor.

Industrial Capitalism

Beginning in the twelfth century, many social, political, technological, and economic changes occurred in some European societies. These changes gradually led to the political and economic domination of and forced social changes in societies in Europe, the Americas, Africa, and Asia. These changes also led to the rise of capitalism and industrialism, which began to dominate from the mid-1700s on.

Machines were introduced during this period, replacing many of the workers who had produced goods, raised food, and erected buildings. The machines and the resources that fueled the industrial societies were owned by a few people. Karl Marx, one of the architects of socialism, called these people the *bourgeoisie.* (Marxists now call them the *ruling class,* and most sociologists refer to them as the *upper class.*) The bourgeoisie were a new class of people in Europe, who gradually took over power from the aristocracy who had previously owned most of the land and had profited from the labor of peasants. To this day, in all capitalist societies a small ruling class controls and profits by the major means of production—the land, raw materials, industries and businesses, and other resources used by people in a society to produce the goods and services they need to survive.

Obviously most people own their own clothing, furniture, cars, and usually homes. But these possessions are not income producing, whereas the means of production owned by the ruling class produce income and wealth for them. Most people make their living by selling their labor to corporations that in turn exploit and profit from their labor.

Here is a hypothetical illustration. A worker works for eight hours a day making a product that the corporation sells for $200. The corporation pays the worker only $80 and uses another $70 for materials and other operating costs. The $50 that is left then goes to the shareholders who own the corporation—people who have not physically worked to produce that $50 profit.

Two ways corporations can increase their profits is to pay workers less or to keep their wages low while raising the price of a product or service. Thus, there is an inherent conflict in capitalist society. On the one hand is the ruling class, which owns the means of production and gets or increases its wealth (and thus power) by exploiting the labor of the working class. On the other hand are the workers who do not wish to have their labor exploited, who do not want to work for lower wages so that the ruling class profits. This antagonism between the two classes is inherent in capitalism, and it affects all of life, as we shall see.

This description of classes and life in capitalist societies is obviously too simplistic. Nevertheless it is not an exaggeration to claim that the fundamental social reality of capitalist societies today is the existence of social classes, of ruling class domination and control, and their effect on family, community, culture, work, and the environment. Many societies are still largely not industrialized. Of those that are, some have reached this condition through noncapitalist (socialist) development. (Socialist development raises its own issues and problems, only a few of which can be discussed in this book.)

Classes in the United States

The Ruling Class and the Working Class

Although there are at least four social classes in the United States (and probably in all advanced capitalist societies), the ruling class and the working class are at the center of the class struggle—the ruling class because it dominates and the working class because it is the majority of the population that is exploited.

The *ruling class* constitutes a very small portion of the population that owns the major means of production and controls the government. The *managerial class* are business managers, some lawyers, and other professionals who do not control the means of production but who work for the corporations or who provide services that stabilize capitalist society. They are the new middle class. The *poor* are those near or below the official poverty line. The poverty family income, as adjusted yearly by the government, does not allow for a living standard that even approaches the minimal consumption requirements necessary for social respect in the United States. The poor, people on welfare, the long-term unemployed, and those working for minimum wages, suffer from material, psychic, and social deprivation. Most Americans comprise the working class. They work for others at wages clearly below what could be considered affluent. They do not suffer materially, but their work is often alienating, and they often face unemployment.

Ruling-Class Domination

The ruling class clearly dominates the economy. The few thousand people who run the five hundred or so large corporations that shape the economy, corporation presidents and those on the corporate boards of directors, belong to the ruling class. Moreover, these few corporations are increasing their power and dominate the United States and even the world economic system.

The ruling class (almost entirely older white males of northern European descent) also dominate the national government. Most U.S. presidents and cabinet secretaries belong to the ruling class or have served as presidents of major corporations. U.S. senators and representatives, most of whom come from the professional class, have their political campaigns largely financed by ruling-class money, and their ideas shaped by ruling-class institutions.

The educational system, the mass media, and the culture in general are dominated or heavily influenced by ruling-class men and institutions. (See Chapters 8 and 10 for the composition and power of the ruling class.)

The Impact of Ruling-Class Domination

Social class differences and inequalities pervade capitalist societies. All aspects of life are affected, shaped, or dominated by the existence of classes and ruling-class power and control. As corporations and the ruling class seek to control the society, to maintain and increase their wealth, to make and increase their profits, to dominate production and sales, to compete with capitalists from other societies, and to stop socialist revolutions, they affect our daily lives. Let us outline briefly some ways in which our lives are shaped by ruling-class power.

Family and Community

Large corporations frequently relocate, close plants, and move their managers to new jobs and places. As men and women lose jobs or change jobs, family lives are disrupted. Families move and family and community ties are broken. Those who lose their jobs because of a corporate decision cannot support their families, and their hopelessness and despair poison family life. Alienating work inevitably affects workers' spirits and their relationship to their spouses and children.

Work and Alienation

Most people work for other people. They work at jobs over which they have little or no control. They perform tasks that others have designed for them and that deprive them of self-motivation and self-esteem. Many workers perform minute and repetitive tasks that tire both mind and body; others work at physically hard and sometimes dangerous jobs. In short, many people find their work alienating. Alienation means that a person feels estranged from others and from their own emotions.

Culture

Advertising, the mass media, and corporations are constantly trying to convince people that they need and want products or services. Food, clothing, and most products are controlled by or made to create profits for corporations—not to fulfill human needs. Since people derive their identities of who they are from the surrounding culture, and since that culture is increasingly controlled by the ruling class for profit, people's self-images are shaped by ruling-class institutions and needs. Low wages do not allow people to buy all the commodities they are told they need; family and community lives are disrupted by work or lack of work as corporations move plants to where they find cheaper labor; communities are poisoned by chemicals dumped illegally by corporations; dangerous materials at work threaten workers' health. Daily life and culture, and thus self-image and mental health, are shaped by corporate needs and actions. People have little or no control over these corporations. People can often resist (sometimes successfully) the control corporations have over their lives, but for the most part they initiate and determine even the rules by which people resist them.

Daily Life and Personal Relationships

Capitalist societies are driven by competition and the profit motive. Corporations and politicians and others produce dangerous or useless products, poison the air, ground, and water, bribe each other, pay few or no taxes, and make it clear that profits are more important than people. In such a climate, trust and honesty in people's daily transactions with each other become difficult. When profits are more important than people, human relationships go awry. Business people find ways to cheat their customers by performing unnecessary work or overcharging; students cheat on their exams and papers; landlords torch their buildings to collect fire insurance. Who can trust whom? How can people conduct their daily lives when they must suspect everyone and every transaction?

Racism

Throughout history people have been exploited. Cheap, or free in the case of slaves, labor made profits for plantation owners, factory owners, and others. Blacks, Chicanos, ethnic groups from Europe, and others have made the profits and fortunes for many capitalist enterprises. To justify this exploitation, there arose beliefs and laws claiming that certain groups of people are inferior and deserve lower wages and discrimination. Capitalism may not have created all the beliefs in the inferiority of other races and ethnic groups, but it used some and encouraged others in order to justify its exploitation of minorities.

Sexism

The ideology that women are inferior to men predates capitalism. But as capitalism developed it used and fostered this idea to justify the lower wages and limited job opportunities for women. Corporations such as insurance companies make huge profits by paying low wages to their mostly female employees. So long as capitalism dominates, so long as profits are paramount, the complete liberation of women will be almost impossible. Certainly most women cannot gain equality in a society where most men are exploited by a ruling class. For women to be liberated, all people must be liberated.

The Environment

Industrial development damages the environment. Chemicals dumped into the waters or buried in the ground, the smoke of burning coal that creates acid rain and kills lakes and trees, fertilizers that pollute groundwater and rivers are forms of industrial development that harm the environment in all industrial societies.

But industrial *capitalism* is even more dangerous to the environment. Because the basic tenet of capitalism is to compete for an ever-larger share of the marketplace, thus a larger share of the profits that can be gained, companies are constantly creating new products regardless of the effect these products might have on the environment. Nowhere is this more evident than in the chemical industry where new toxic substances are continually being developed. These products seriously damage the environment and threaten the health of workers. Dangerous working conditions are allowed to exist because they are profitable. Laws that protect the environment are opposed because they would lower corporate profits. The destructiveness of capitalism is clearly seen in its assault on the earth, air, and water that sustain our very lives.

Health

Environmental pollution and highly processed food damages our health. Corporations give us processed foods filled with chemicals because they produce more profits than do natural foods. In addition, our health is affected by a medical system that is increasingly profit oriented. Poor and working-class people find they cannot afford the cost of medical care. With many inner-city hospitals closing and federal health care programs losing funding, the poor have been especially hard hit.

War, Imperialism, and Nuclear War

War, as an organized activity of one group seeking to conquer and dominate another, did not exist in early human societies. With few possessions and no ownership of the land, there were no incentives for war. War first appeared with class inequalities and ownership of the land.

Capitalist nations conduct wars to dominate and exploit societies all over the world. The current world economic system is one where the ruling class of a rich nation exploits the people in a poor nation. Wars have been conducted to create, expand, and now preserve imperialism—the world capitalist system that benefits the ruling classes of the capitalist nations.

Nuclear war is a logical extension of war and imperialism. Nuclear weapons are meant to insure imperialist domination by the world's capitalist powers. If a nuclear war happens, it will happen because the United States fears it will lose control of the imperialist world order or because the Soviet Union fears an attack on itself or threatened loss of its power (or a combination of these events). Nuclear war is the last stage in the long history of class development, inequalities, and ruling-class control. The capitalist system, and the opposition to it by socialist societies (which contain their own forms of classes and inequalities), is the current stage of this development. Classes dominate classes, men dominate women, stronger nations dominate weaker nations, and ruling classes compete internationally. Nuclear war is the latest weapon in the effort to dominate the world. It may destroy its makers even as it destroys all of life.

Conclusion

It is not true that the ruling class in a capitalist society has total control of all aspects of the society and of our lives, nor are there human societies where everyone is exactly equal. Ruling classes, however, do exercise control most of the time over major decisions and institutions. That is the major reality of our lives today. We may, and we do, have control over parts of our lives, and on occasions we may and we do resist, limit, and even take away ruling-class domination. But these facts do not deny the predominant power of the ruling class and the effect it has on family, community, and the environment.

Socialist Values and Socialist Society

The rest of the book discusses my vision of a socialist society. Here I present a very concise statement of the qualities, values, and conditions I think are necessary for a humane society.

■ Everyone would have the basic necessities of life: food, shelter, and clothing.

■ Beyond that, people would lead simple lives and focus on social relationships, on being with people, on families and communities, not on material possessions.

■ Sharing and cooperation would be more important than competition.

■ People would live in harmony with the environment. There would be limits on how much we could take from the environment. Pollution in all its forms would stop.

■ Work would be a fulfilling, not alienating, experience. This could only happen if all workers shared equally in planning and carrying out the work they do.

■ Beyond personal items, there would be no private property. All work-places would be owned and run collectively.

■ Class differences would be reduced and eventually eliminated. There would be no great differences in material possessions and opportunities available to people. We would express our individuality through our work, hobbies, and interests.

■ There would be complete gender equality. Women *and* men would change. Both would be caring *and* assertive; both would do work *and* house-work. Men would not dominate women, nor women men.

■ Domination, power differences, hierarchies, and control would diminish and disappear. In a humane society, people only *persuade* others, never control them. To eliminate domination, new forms of political, educational, economic, and other institutions would be created.

■ All forms of inequalities and control would disappear, whether based on class, sex, race, ethnicity, sexual orientation, age (*any* age), physical condition, or any other difference or condition.

Even though it is hard to imagine we could ever achieve such a perfect society, each generation must have a vision of a more humane world and work toward it. We cannot hope to improve our society without the work of each generation. Only through struggle and determination (and a sense of humor) can we create a socialist and humane society. All people must partake in this task.

We need to change social institutions, structures, and material conditions, *and* our consciousness. This means, for example, that we need laws and regulations to stop pollution and the overuse of the natural resources. But we also need, each one of us, to become conscious of how our actions affect the environment and to change our actions willingly.

No society existing today, socialist or otherwise, approaches the socialism I describe here. It is an ideal far from reality. But steps are being taken in some societies to begin the journey toward the ideal even though progress is uneven. Societies may reduce class differences, for example, but pollute the environment and oppress women. Or they may enact legislation to protect the environment but perpetuate and increase class differences. And no contemporary society has yet undertaken to reduce, let alone eliminate, all forms of domination and control.

Finally, a word about the Soviet Union, Cuba, China, and other existing socialist societies. (They are socialist more in the expressed ideals and goals than in existing conditions.) Each contains many contradictions, problems, and inequalities. But far too many people point out these societies' problems and ignore their achievements. With all its problems, Cuba *is* preferable to Brazil, for example. There is political repression and domination in both societies, but there are not millions of starving children in the streets of Cuba, unlike Brazil. Education, medical care, and housing may be modest in Cuba, but they are far more accessible to most people there than in Brazil. Cuba feeds, clothes, and educates its children; capitalist Brazil, part of the so-called free world, has condemned millions of them to the streets and misery. The prospects of achieving a just and humane society are far greater in Cuba and Nicaragua than they are in Brazil, El Salvador, or Chile.

Summary

Sociology is the study of human societies and the changing social world around us. It studies groups and societies. It is both a personal search and journey and an organized discipline of a body of knowledge.

There is organization, pattern, and predictability in social behavior and in the structure of society. There are social conditions and rules in society that shape individual and group behavior. But *society,* or social reality, is a human creation of individuals and groups of various sizes. People shape and change it as much as it shapes and changes them.

Most sociologists share some common assumptions about social groups and society, but they have different opinions and preconceptions, ask different questions, and examine different issues. Three perspectives—the functionalist, conflict, and interactionist—are described and compared. A Marxist perspective, one form of the conflict perspective, is described in greater detail.

CHAPTER 2

Practicing Sociology

As sociology has become an established profession, sociologists have developed and refined methods and techniques for investigating the social world. These methods and techniques are tools that the sociologist decides how to manipulate. Like any tool, they are useless without a goal and a plan in mind. So before we can look at the tools and how to use them, we must develop a frame of mind, an approach.

Being Critical and Curious

Sociology, indeed, life itself, requires a critical and questioning mind and an intense curiosity. Without these qualities sociological inquiries or learning of any kind cannot take place.

Being Critical

Bertrand Russell (1961), the famous British philosopher, once wrote an essay entitled "An Outline of Intellectual Rubbish." In it, he listed many once-believed facts that in time have been shown to be false. Among them was Aristotle's belief that men have more teeth than women. Russell quipped, "Why didn't he count his wife's teeth?" (p. 73) Facts need to be questioned. Many facts people once believed true have been debunked as misconceptions or prejudices, and many things people now (often passionately) believe to be true will in time be shown to be incomplete, untrue, or nonsense.

Let us look at some past truths. During the nineteenth century, women were discouraged from getting too much education or from pursuing intellectual or professional careers. To do so, it was believed, would interfere with their womanly functions—having babies and caring for a family. The explanation for this lay in what the medical profession then considered a basic physiological law: *conservation of energy*. According to Ehrenrich and English

(1973), this theory said that "each human body contained a set quantity of energy that was directed variously from one organ or function to another. This meant that you could develop one organ or ability only at the expense of others, drawing energy away from the parts not being developed." (pp. 27–28) Thus, if a woman developed her mind, she was drawing energy away from her reproductive organs and making herself deficient and weak for having babies. This was considered a medical fact.

Another medical and scientific fact of the nineteenth century connected insanity with masturbation. People clothed a religious conviction with scientific trappings and warned of the dire consequences of masturbation. Many doctors argued that it caused deterioration of eyesight, impotence, insanity, begetting insane children, epilepsy, and a host of other misfortunes. We may laugh at such claims now, but doctors wrote these warnings as scientific facts. One assumes most people believed their own observations and ignored the doctors. (See Szasz, 1970.)

People still make such unwarranted claims. In fact, the typical book (this one included) surely makes claims that in time will be unsupported by evidence. One recent example is a book on work that opens with the argument that primitive gathering and hunting people worked long hours and were always on the edge of starvation. Kranzberg and Gies (1975) state, "For some two million years . . . the life of all mankind, except in a few favored locations and times, consisted mostly of work. Man was born, he worked, and he died." (p. 4) Until ten thousand years ago, when people began to cultivate crops, there was "an unceasing struggle to escape starvation." (p. 4) No evidence is given for such an extravagant claim; it must have seemed so obvious to the authors that they felt no need for documentation. Yet recent observations of still surviving gatherers and hunters, including the existing !Kung of the Kalahari desert, suggest the exact opposite: primitive people worked many fewer hours than we do and had an adequate, balanced, and steady diet. Lee's (1984) detailed observations of the !Kung, for example, reveal that they average 17.1 hours per week of "subsistence work" (gathering and hunting for food, what we call work); 6.3 hours for "tool making and fixing"; and 18.9 for housework, for a total of 42.3 hours a week. (p. 53) People in industrial societies today average at least forty hours a week at work, plus thirty to forty hours of housework, shopping, washing, and other domestic duties in addition to their paid work. Some anthropologists have called gathering and hunting societies the original leisure society. (See Kranzberg & Gies, 1975, and Friedl, 1981.)

We need to question facts and truths. We must always carefully examine our cherished beliefs and truths. But today, as in the past, people who question established so-called truths encounter ostracism and rejection. For example, Chandler (1987) shows that "maverick scientists" who propose new explanations for scientific phenomena have trouble finding research money and usually cannot get their findings published in science journals. Some of these scientists whose theories were initially rejected have seen, in time, their work accepted by the scientific community.

Being Curious

An intense curiosity and interest in the social world around us is a prerequisite for sociological work. Something must puzzle us, excite us, indeed, leave us restless until we know more about it. Without such an intense interest and curiosity, even in examining the supposedly obvious, there is no sociology.

To illustrate what I mean, let me pose some questions we could investigate. Something very familiar may make us wonder. Why *do* men and women tend to have such different jobs? Or someone may tell us that women smile more than men. *Do* they? How can we document this claim? And if it is true, why?

The questions we can pose may vary from direct and personal to large and historical. How close do people in the United States stand to each other before they begin to feel uncomfortable? How and when do we learn what is a proper distance? Or, we may wonder if women have been equal to men in any past societies. Equal in what sense? If we find that in every society men and women's roles have been different, is it still possible that the two sexes are equal? How can we study the question? We can study historical and anthropological reports of other times and places, but we may realize that almost all of these reports were written by men. Men who were raised in Western societies are commenting on societies much different than those in which they live. Can we trust their observations and conclusions?

Or we may notice some unsettling social conditions. If, for example, two men are convicted of robbing a bank and killing the guard, they will probably be given a life sentence or possibly be executed. On the other hand, if an automobile company builds a car that has a badly designed gas tank, one which the company's executives know is faulty and dangerous, and if eventually the cars produced by this company kill hundreds of people, it is very likely that nothing will happen to those who are responsible. The company could have fixed the defect, but doing so would have postponed production of the car, meaning a loss of business to the competition. The consequence is that many people are needlessly killed from exploding gas tanks. The company might have to pay monetary damages, but no one will ever spend time in prison for murder or even manslaughter. Why aren't these people treated the same under the law? Why do they get away with crimes that most people would be tried and convicted for?

Most of us have been bothered by questions like these and have wanted to know why people and groups function as they do. When that curiosity becomes intense, we are ready to undertake sociological research.

Methods and Techniques

Some sociological research is largely descriptive. For example, we may show how many families are composed of a father, a mother, and children; how many of a mother and children; how many of a mother, her children, and some other relative of the mother; how many of a father and children; and how many of other combinations of relatives. Or, we may describe the activities of a group of teenagers who spend a lot of time together. Such research is useful and necessary.

Usually, however, we go beyond description to search for causes or associations. We want to know why a social condition exists or why a new one has appeared. For instance, once we know that there are more divorced women who support their children largely alone (female-headed families) than there have been in the past, we may want to find out why such a change has come about. At this point we may make a *hypothesis,* a tentative statement about the association between two or more social conditions. For example, we may suspect that as more women work and feel less economically dependent on their husbands, they are more likely to divorce them if their marriages are unhappy. This hypothesis has two conditions, or *variables* that may be related to each other: Women's financial independence (first variable) leads to a higher divorce rate (second variable). This is not put forth as a fact, simply as a hunch, a possibility, which we have yet to investigate. Once we do, we may find it not to be true, and we may in fact find that another condition (say, women having fewer children, or women getting more education, etc.) is more associated with divorce.

In forming our hypothesis we must have clear definitions of the terms we use. In the above example employment, education, and divorce may be easily defined and quantified. Suppose, however, we are concerned with happiness. How do we define happy? Is it what people define as happiness, and if so, does this mean happiness varies widely from person to person? Vague terms like happiness, love, and so forth, present many problems. Consider "delinquency." Most teenagers shoplift or drink alcoholic beverages while still under the legal age or are truant from school a few times. All these acts are illegal. Are, therefore, most teenagers delinquents? If the answer is no, then *who* is a delinquent? When we use a term we must set out its definition. This is called an *operational definition*. These definitions are often very arbitrary and simplistic. Some people, for example, define "religiosity" according to how many times people attend church (Sanders, 1981).

Once we have formulated a hypothesis, which guides us in our search, there are three techniques used to collect the data we need (Deutscher, 1973): "(1) We can observe it [behavior] in process; (2) we can view the records [people] leave behind, written or otherwise artifactual; and (3) we can ask questions and listen to answers." (p. 12)

The following five research methods use one or more of these three data collection techniques. In all data collection it is essential for researchers to be critical, cautious, careful, and tentative of their ability to collect reliable data. There are problems and uncertainties in the interpretation of what we see, hear, and read. Nevertheless, we can believe in sociology as a worthwhile and useful field of study, and we can use data and findings if we can constantly keep in mind the limitations of sociology and the inherently tentative nature of our findings. We should search for better methods and be modest about our ability to reach firm conclusions about social realities and societies. But these things should not keep us from engaging in a lifelong search for answers. We may even think of the search itself as sociology.

Sample Surveys

Sample surveys ask people questions and count and interpret their answers. This sociological research method has been the most practiced (and most prestigious) for many years. While I am very critical of it (a bias you should beware of), I still think surveys have provided us with some essential and important data and findings.

If we want to know what Americans in general, or college students, or women between the ages of twenty and forty-nine, or men who watch football, or any other group of people think about some issue, or how they behave in certain social situations, we could interview all of the people in that group. But since that often means millions or hundreds of thousands of people, that is clearly an impossible task. The U.S. census comes closest to surveying the total population, even though it misses many people who refuse to return the census sheet. Researchers, on the other hand, must choose a portion of the whole, a *sample* of people, who will be interviewed. This sample, if we are to trust our findings, must be typical or representative of the whole population.

Let us look at an example. If college students is the group or population we want to study, our sample must have the same percentage of men and women as the percentage who attend college. If men are 52 percent of the college population, our sample, let us say 5,000, must have 2,600 men. If 30 percent attend community college, 25 percent attend state colleges, and so on, our sample must reflect these percentages. And our numbers of freshmen, sopho-mores, juniors, and seniors must also be representative. In other words, all of the factors that describe a college population must be represented in the sample.

Samples are usually small. Public opinion polls reporting what Ameri-cans think of some issue usually interview fifteen hundred to three thousand people; TV rating services sample at most 5,000 families from whom they conclude what programs Americans watch. One of the largest samples is the 110,000 Americans over twelve who are interviewed about crimes of which they were the victims. Even if we design our sample with utmost care and conscientiousness, there is always the problem of people who simply refuse to respond or are not available.

Once the sample has been chosen, we can proceed to interview the participants by mail, phone, or in person. People are asked factual questions about themselves, and one or more of the following types of questions: be-havioral, attitudinal (opinion), and hypothetical.

Factual questions are those that ask people their sex, age, religion, income, education, and so on. Responses to these questions should be fairly straightforward, but even in factual areas there are problems in trusting people's responses. For example, in a study cited by Levine (1976) in which people reported the amount of money in their savings accounts, 47 percent either did not report the savings account or failed to report the amount within one thousand dollars of the correct figure. We often cannot or we will not report the correct facts about ourselves.

Behavioral questions are those that ask people to report on their behaviors: how they vote, their sexual activities, how much time they spend with their children, how long they talk with their spouses, and so forth. Some of these items would be clearly known to the participants. For example, how they voted or how sexually active they were the previous day or week. If they give incorrect responses it is because they choose to do so or because they are embarrassed or for some other motive. Levine concludes that people who may not want to admit they did not vote in a recent election may report they did vote.

But reluctance is not the only reason people fail to report their behavior correctly. In many cases, people have forgotten or really do not know how they behave. They may remember how they voted last month but not whether or how they voted ten years ago. Generally, the longer the period of time that has lapsed, the more untrustworthy people's responses are. For many behavioral questions the problem is simply that the participants do not know how they behave. How long *do* people talk to their spouses? Informal surveys I have taken in my classes show that most people think at least half an hour a day, many saying one or two hours. But one study that observed and recorded the conversations of couples married fifteen or more years, and who claimed to be happily married, showed they talked an average of 27.5 minutes a *week* (Birdwhistell, 1970).

Wooden (1976) cites another study that shows a similar discrepancy between actual and reported behavior. "One study done of fathers who claimed to spend an average of at least 15 to 20 minutes a day playing with their one-year-old infant, revealed that the actual average was only 37.7 seconds per day." (p. 83) We should be careful and wary when we ask people to report on their actions, since much of what people do they will not or cannot report accurately. Rathje (1984), in a study comparing the amounts of cigarette boxes and beer containers people threw away with what they said they threw away, concluded that "garbage data recorded significantly more drinkers and smokers and higher rates of consumption than reported in interviews in the same neighborhoods." (p. 70)

In a long and careful review of the "validity of retrospective data," Bernard and others (1984) examine studies of people's reporting of their behavior in child care, health care, communication and social interaction, sick leave from work, voting, signing a petition, and other areas. They conclude that "on average, about half of what informants report is probably incorrect in some way." (p. 503)

We should be careful and wary when we ask people to report on their actions. Much of what people do they will not, or, more commonly, they cannot report accurately because of cultural preferences, personal biases, lack of interest, memory loss over time, and so on.

Attitudinal surveys ask for people's opinions, judgments, and attitudes. Do you approve of the death penalty? Do you think it will decrease crime? Do you approve of teachers going on strike? Do you think the President of the United States is doing a good job? Do you approve of mothers of preschool age children holding jobs?

Most people have many opinions, but not everyone has an opinion on every topic possible, nor are the opinions people have always based on much evidence or reflection. People may argue that the death penalty is a deterrent to crime, but how much have they actually studied the evidence? On many issues people simply have no opinions, but in trying to accommodate the interviewer, they offer an opinion. It is not necessarily an opinion they have considered or discussed, however. The significance of these kinds of responses is questionable.

Hypothetical questions are probably the most dangerous questions. This type of question asks people to say how they would act under hypothetical conditions. What would you do if your child married someone of another race or religion? What would you do if your child told you he or she was homosexual? To unmarried women: What would you do if you became pregnant? How would you feel and what would you do if you lost your job? The relationship between what people say and what they do—between sentiments and acts—has been investigated at length (Deutscher, 1973). Can we predict how people will act in certain situations by what they tell us they will do if they find themselves in a particular situation? Not necessarily.

Attitudinal surveys can compare two different situations. One is a verbal hypothetical situation. (The respondent does not have a real life choice.) An unmarried woman who is not pregnant does not have the difficult choice of abortion or raising a child without a partner. The other situation is an actual one. For example, a person who detests homosexuals may be told that his or her child is gay. These two conditions—hypothetical and actual—cannot be compared; we cannot use one to predict the other. It is not that people never, or always, do what they say they will do. Sometimes they do, sometimes they do not. There is some similarity between sentiments and actions, but they are not the same.

Let us examine one study that shows that there is no relationship at all between saying and doing. For two years, from 1930 to 1932, LaPiere (1934) traveled ten thousand miles, "twice across the United States, up and down the Pacific Coast," with a young Chinese couple. (p. 232) They stopped in 251 hotels, motels, restaurants, and campgrounds. LaPiere, who was white, stayed in the background when the young couple requested service. In all but one establishment they were served. Six months after they had visited an establishment, LaPiere mailed a questionnaire asking "Will you accept members of the Chinese race as guests in your establishment?" One hundred and twenty-eight of the 251 replied: 118 said no, 9 were undecided, and only 1 said yes. In other situations, of course, people who are prejudiced against people of other races and religions do indeed carry out and act on their prejudices.

Question Problems

It is important that questions be worded carefully and thoughtfully. Consciously or unconsciously we may bias questions to get the results we want. Let us look at three examples.

Duboff (1974) studied three different surveys on abortion that were carried out in 1973—each yielding different results. In a poll conducted by George Gallup, this question was asked: "The U.S. Supreme Court has ruled that a woman may go to a doctor *to end pregnancy* at any time during the first three months of pregnancy. Do you favor or oppose this ruling?" (p. 9) (emphasis added). Forty-seven percent approved, 44 percent disapproved. A pro-abortion group did a similar survey, replacing the phrase "to end pregnancy" with "for an abortion." Here, 41 percent approved, 48 percent did not. A third group asked, "As far as you are concerned would you say you are for or against abortion, or what *do* you think," and found 36.2 percent in favor and 59.4 percent against. (p. 9) Assuming the samples were similar and chosen carefully, it seems that the wording affected the percentages of people who approved or disapproved.

Another survey (*Dollars and Sense,* February, 1980) presented participants with this statement: "Since Henry Kissinger failed to make peace between Egypt and Israel, it looks as though he is losing his touch as a peacemaker." (p. 19) People were then asked if they agreed or disagreed with the statement. It seems to be a simple enough question. But read it again. There is a large assumption embedded within it: You must first believe that Kissinger was a peacemaker in order to answer the question.

Interviewees were caught in a similar double bind in a survey concerning the Massachusetts bottle bill. A group opposing the bill conducted the survey. One question they asked was: "Would you favor legislation to protect the environment even if such legislation meant a loss of jobs?" If someone believes, as I do, that laws protecting the environment create more jobs than they eliminate, it is impossible to answer the question accurately. Whatever he or she said would be accepting an assumption that he or she thinks is mistaken. Consciously loaded questions like this one or questions with large assumptions or slanted wording must be avoided. Questions must be worded very carefully.

Interviewer Problems

With rare exceptions (most notably the Kinsey surveys on sexuality) the people who conduct a survey are not the ones who do the actual interviewing. Researchers hire interviewers. Being hired hands, interviewers often act like other workers who work under someone else's control and who have little control over their jobs. Especially if the interview is long, they may simply skip some questions and fill in (guess at) the responses later. Or if they fear going into some neighborhood, they may say they went, but no one was home. The best solution is for researchers to do their own interviewing. Even then there are problems. As we mentioned before, people may offer opinions they do not have or report actions they did not perform. (See Roth, 1965; Deutscher, 1973; and Levine, 1976.)

The class, race, ethnic group, sex, age, and other characteristics of interviewers may also affect the responses people give. For example, a number of studies since the 1940s have shown that black respondents are more likely to say what they really think to black interviewers. They are less likely, for example, to tell white interviewers their perceptions of discrimination and prejudice. Black writers (Wright, 1966) have shown that generally blacks do not reveal their views, emotions, and thoughts to whites. Both Wright and Gwaltney (1980) conclude that those in subordinate social relationships (women, workers, blacks, students, others) learn that it is not safe to communicate openly and freely with their social superiors.

Similarly, when Hyman (1954) asked, "Do you think Jewish people in the United States have too much influence in the business world, not enough influence, or about the amount of influence they should have?", 50 percent of the gentiles said "too much influence" to interviewers they assumed were also gentile, but 22 percent gave that response to interviewers they assumed were Jewish. (p. 162)

Other studies show that low-income people feel more rapport with low-income interviewers and tend to express more radical, class-conscious issues with them rather than with middle-class interviewers.

Finally, women also respond differently to female and male interviewers. Many studies have shown that communication and interaction between women and men reflect and reinforce women's subordinate social position. For example, men tend to interrupt women in conversation much more than women interrupt men; men invade women's personal space more often than the reverse; and women are trained to make gestures of submission (the tendency to apologize, for example). These realities of male dominance interfere during interviews. Men and women do not stop being men and women simply because one is interviewing the other. (See Sapiro, 1986, and Henley & Freeman, 1984. For a general discussion of interviewer problems, see Bailey, 1982.)

Cause and Correlation

After the data have been collected, we can begin to test our hypothesis. Let us suppose our hypothesis is that the way people vote, Democratic or Republican, is affected by their race or ethnicity. The information collected from the survey on race-ethnicity and on voting in Table 2.1, which is purely imaginary as are Tables 2.2a, 2.2b, and 2.2c, would seem to confirm our hypothesis.

TABLE 2.1
Race, Ethnicity, and Voting in the
19– Presidential Elections (Imaginary Data)

	Voted Democratic	Voted Republican
Blacks	85%	15%
Italians	70%	30%
WASPs	40%	60%

But while we are considering these findings and discussing them with others, someone suggests that people's income is a more important determinant of how they vote, not their race or ethnicity. Since blacks do have lower incomes than whites, this is a plausible argument. We can thus construct Tables 2.2a, 2.2b, and 2.2c, which divide each of the three groups by income. These findings still show some difference by race and ethnicity. That is, more blacks than Italians making under $10,000 vote Democratic, and the same for the other two income categories. But the largest explanation seems to be income. White Anglo-Saxon Protestants (WASPs) making under $10,000 are much closer to blacks and Italians of the same income bracket than they are to WASPs making $30,000 and over.

When we notice (or suspect) that people of lower income vote Democratic and people of higher income vote Republican (this is an actual finding, but the percentages in my tables are imaginary), we would probably want to know why they do so. We might ask questions that reveal each group votes for the party they think best serves their economic interests and needs.

TABLE 2.2a
Income and Voting by Blacks, in the
19– Presidential Elections (Imaginary Data)

Annual Family Income	Voted Democratic	Voted Republican
$10,000	95%	5%
$15–20,000	85%	15%
$30,000 +	50%	50%

TABLE 2.2b
Income and Voting by Italians, in the
19– Presidential Elections (Imaginary Data)

Annual Family Income	Voted Democratic	Voted Republican
$10,000	90%	10%
$15–20,000	75%	25%
$30,000 +	45%	55%

TABLE 2.2c
Income and Voting by WASPs, in the
19– Presidential Elections (Imaginary Data)

Annual Family Income	Voted Democratic	Voted Republican
$10,000	85%	15%
$15–20,000	65%	35%
$30,000 +	30%	70%

Generally, survey data are analyzed in this manner. (Sociologists also use very complicated statistical techniques and formulas that we cannot discuss here.) One set of variables—age, sex, religion, income, and ethnicity—is related to another set—voting, opinions on abortion, child-rearing practices, and so on. The assumption is then made that variable *A* (income) affects or causes variable *B* (voting).

We have used various terms here that imply causal connections: cause, association, and effect. These terms usually mean that there is something in one variable, *A,* that gives rise to another variable, *B.* Cause means that there is a necessary connection between the two. But we must be careful. How can we tell if *A* brings about *B,* or *B* brings about *A* ? Does poverty cause broken homes, or do broken homes cause poverty? Or does some third condition cause both broken homes and poverty, say, sexual discrimination in jobs?

Let us be clear about what we are saying here. We claim, for example, that people who make over $30,000 a year are in some way compelled by that condition to vote Republican. But how does that compulsion come about? And how much of a compulsion is it when there are so many exceptions? There are hardly any sociological generalizations that apply to all members of a population. Statements that claim social conditions compel people and groups to behave in certain ways should be made with care and thoughtfulness. There is some truth in such claims, of course, but the nature of the cause is not the same as that of a lit match causing a piece of paper to burn. That causal connection always occurs—not so with causal connections in human social behavior. The connection is intricate, uncertain, and often changeable. Causal statements in the social sciences are only probable tendencies. For example, the higher a person's income, the more he or she is likely to vote Republican.

Advantages of Surveys

Surveys offer us three advantages. First, we can include many people in our study. If our resources allow it, thousands of people can be interviewed. Thus, we have a large sample. Second, we can ask people directly about the issue we are studying. And third, surveys allow us to conduct the study when we are ready. We do not need to wait for social phenomena to occur.

Participant Observation

Instead of asking people questions about their behavior and thoughts, we can choose to observe their behavior and the expression of their thoughts in actual social situations. This is called *participant observation*. We are not precluded from asking questions and carrying on discussions. We can and must engage in conversations, but we do so as we observe people in social settings.

Varieties of Participant Observation

Let us suppose that we want to know how being in a mental hospital affects people. We could interview present and past mental patients, but we could also choose to explore this question by spending time in a mental hospital with the patients. This could be done in different ways. We could actually be a mental patient and use our own experiences as evidence. A more conventional approach, however, is to find a way to enter the setting so that we can make careful and systematic observations. We could pretend to suffer from some mental illness and commit ourselves into a hospital. (Rosenhan et al., 1973, actually did this.) Or, either with or without telling the patients or the staff, we could get a job in a mental hospital that would enable us to spend time on the grounds so we could observe hospital life. For example, Goffman (1959) became an athletic director in a mental hospital. We could, finally, do none of these things and simply get permission to observe people, talk with them, and participate in some of their activities. I did this in the late 1960s, in a rest home, a group home for emotionally disturbed girls and one for boys (Liazos, 1970).

Different settings usually require different approaches. If we want to conduct participant-observer research among workers on an assembly line, we could get an assembly-line job without revealing our identity (Pfeffer, 1979), or we could work there but let people know we are studying the setting and people in it (Balzer, 1976). Or we could simply stand around, observe, and talk with people. (This last technique, however, could become a nuisance for workers.)

Conducting Participant Observation

As sociologists, we observe people with or without their permission or knowledge, but we also participate in their lives. This participation may be minimal or almost total. The latter is mandatory for anthropologists who visit another society and live there for a year or more. (See Turnbull, 1961, and Shostak, 1981.) Sociologists participate and observe in an effort to see the world as the people they are studying see it. We cannot, of course, ever fully know how prisoners, mental patients, or members of another society feel or think, and we cannot even observe all their behavior. But we can try to approximate that ideal. We can try to participate in every possible situation. In the year I spent in the boys' group home, I had dinner with them, we played cards, we attended sports activities together, and so on. There were only three activities I consciously avoided: accompanying any of them on their visits home, visiting the public school they attended, and going with them to dances and other social activities.

Participant observation is not easy, but it is satisfying and fulfilling in many ways. The relationships sociologists establish with the people they are studying are often profoundly meaningful and personal. Participant observation is also emotionally taxing and time consuming. For example, it is a necessity to write detailed notes of one's observations and reflections at the end of each day. Such notes are the only data and must be regular, detailed, and complete. They can run into hundreds of thousands of pages. But it is by careful study of these notes that we begin to see the patterns and social structures of the setting, people's reactions to these structures (formal and informal ones), and how people use and avoid them.

Whenever possible, participant observers also use interviews, existing records, statistics, and any and all other possible sources of data. But the primary sources of information are the observations the observer makes and the daily informal talks he or she engages in. So Goffman (1959), for example, tells us in detail the many ways by which mental hospitals degrade patients, strip them of their privacy and identity, and stigmatize them. But he also shows patients resisting and fighting against the hospital, its rules and regulations, and how they manage to find or create some private space, some dignity, and meaning in their lives.

Advantages of Participant Observation

By being with people in their own natural environment, we are able to see how they actually behave and feel, not how they may report their actions and emotions. In survey research there are, as we mentioned previously, a number of problems that arise when we ask questions about behavior and thought.

Let us look at two examples that compare survey and participant observation research. When Shostak (1981) talked with adult !Kung about their childhood, they remembered frequent physical spankings by their parents. But she saw very little of it actually happen. She might have had a problem in explaining this discrepancy, but at least she did not state as fact that the !Kung hit their children frequently. Turnbull (1961) is another example. He was told that if a Mbuti commits incest he is forever banished from the group. When a man did commit incest, he was indeed banished—for two or three days. He came back and no one ever mentioned the incident again.

Another advantage participant observation has over survey research is knowing the setting. If we have never known a situation, or if we know it only slightly, we cannot even think of the right questions to ask. Rosenhan's (1973) study of a mental hospital is an excellent illustration. Some of the researcher-patients at various times approached a staff member (psychiatrist, nurse, or attendant) and asked for some information. A common question was, "Could you tell me when I will be eligible for grounds privileges?" A direct and simple request, it would seem. Sixty staff members were approached with such requests 1,468 times. In well over 80 percent of the cases, there was either a "brief response to the question, offered while they were 'on the move' and with head averted, or no response at all." For example, when asked about grounds privileges, a doctor responded, "Good morning, Dave. How are you today?" and moved on without waiting for a response. (p. 255)

Such treatment of patients denies their humanity. They are treated as if they were nonpersons. It also reveals something of the true nature of mental hospital life. Had the researcher known of this social interaction and had he or she asked the staff about it, most would have been unaware of their behavior, or, if aware, would not have admitted it. Participant observation allows us access to such important social interactions.

More generally, participant observation allows us to study people in their total environment. We see people whole, we see them live, and we get closer to seeing their real behavior, thoughts, and emotions. If we only ask questions we miss the totality of the situation, we see it out of context.

Problems of Participant Observation

As I have said, participant observation is very time consuming and demands emotional and social commitment. We do not interview people and then walk away. We live, work, play, argue, laugh, and cry with them. It challenges our total being.

There is also an ethical problem. If we want to assure that our presence does not alter people's behavior, we may not want to reveal our identity. But by doing so, we are invading people's privacy without their consent or permission. We are spying on them, simply. Does the knowledge we may gain outweigh such a violation of privacy?

On the other hand, if we tell people our reason for being there, they may change or hide their behavior. If for no other reason than to retain our self-image, we do not open ourselves totally to anyone, especially to a stranger. The problem is partly (and only partly) overcome by spending a long time in the setting and in effect becoming part of it. In this way, we hope people will eventually relax and act naturally.

As with a survey sample, a participant observation situation should be typical or representative. The problem is that we can only study one hospital (or perhaps a few), or one factory, or one school. Even if we could trust what we found out here, could we conclude that *all* hospitals, factories, or schools function in the same way? A partial way out appears if many people each study a school and come to similar findings and conclusions. But what if they differ?

A more serious problem is the bias of the observer. Sociologists know (both from studies and personal experiences) that when different people look at the same event or place they notice different aspects of it. With the best of intentions and the most detailed observations, the observations will still be biased.

When we begin a study (any study, using any method), we begin it with certain biases, predilections, and interests. The study of Tepoztlán, a Mexican village, by two anthropologists is an excellent example. Redfield (1930) studied this village in the 1930s. In his early writings he describes such communities as warm, close, and desirable places for people to live in. Lewis (1951) also studied Tepoztlán about fifteen years later in the 1940s. In his early work, he describes small communities like Tepoztlán as places where people are suspicious of each other and not very warm and friendly.

Such biases are weaknesses, but they are also strengths. Perhaps Redfield had positive feelings about Tepoztlán and so the people showed him that aspect of themselves. Indeed, our personality is an important part of participant observation. We can understand people and their social worlds to the degree that we are compassionate, sensitive, open, and deeply caring. Such qualities enable us to get close to people and see how they experience their world. (Turnbull's *The Forest People* is an excellent example of how one's personality allows others to reveal their world to him or her.)

Modified Participant Observation

Some research falls somewhere between participant observation and survey interviews. In order to find out the quality of working-class life in America, Rubin (1976) interviewed fifty couples. She went to their homes and had long, intimate, and personal discussions with them. The interviews often required several visits and lasted up to a total of ten hours. Rubin did not live with the people in their neighborhoods, but neither did she conduct a quick survey interview. The report she wrote is more complex and rich than are survey reports, but less detailed than true participant observation.

Records of Human Behavior

When surveys are conducted, people are asked about their past and present actions, emotions, and thoughts. With participant observation, sociologists watch and ask about people. A third method uses *records of human behavior*—records people leave (on their own or collected by others) of their actions, emotions, and thoughts.

Here are some common types. Government records are the best example of records we use to study social behavior and social structures. The income records collected yearly by the U.S. Internal Revenue Service; arrest, trial, conviction, and prison records collected by various police and court agencies; birth and death records; and, of course, the decennial census taken by the Bureau of the Census—all these, and many others, have been used by social scientists. (The best single source of government records is the annual *Statistical Abstract of the United States,* published annually by the U.S. Department of Commerce and available in most libraries.)

But people leave other records behind: diaries, newspaper reports, the garbage they throw away, telephone connections and disconnections (which reveal family and community disruptions), biographies and autobiographies—indeed, the list is only limited by our imagination. The following humorous account gives us some idea of just how many kinds of records can exist (Deutscher, 1973):

> *While cleaning cesspools in suburban Long Island in the summer of 1949 (one of the few occupations then available to a college graduate with a major in philosophy), I was impressed with the number of condoms found in the sewage of a large apartment house, the mailboxes of which carried only Irish surnames. This might be taken as an unobtrusive measure of the use of birth control by Roman Catholics. However, it requires the assumption that all persons with Irish surnames are Catholic. Furthermore, there is no indication of*

the distribution among apartments; conceivably all of the condoms could have come from a small minority of tenants. (p. 133)

This example shows both the rich possibilities in the kinds of records of human behavior available to us and the problems we face in interpreting their validity and significance.

Let us look at two other examples of the use of records. Demos (1970) studied family life in the Plymouth Colony, and one aspect he investigated was the relationship between men and women. Sermons and other pronouncements of the times "assumed that woman was 'the weaker vessel' and that 'subjection' was her natural role." (p. 95) But when Demos examined court records, he found out that husbands and wives (unmarried men and women too) were equally likely to accuse each other in court of physical abuse. Public admittance by men that women were abusing them is an indication that women were hardly the weaker sex, the sermons of ministers notwithstanding.

Court records must be used with great care. They often tell us as much about the biases of the system that collects them as they do about crime in the social world. To begin with, at least 50 percent of the crimes committed are never reported. Of those reported to the police, most do not result in arrest. Of the people arrested, not all of them are prosecuted in the courts. Of people prosecuted, about 10 to 20 percent are not convicted. And of those convicted, most are not imprisoned. Now, depending on where in this process we choose to use records, we may encounter serious problems of credibility. If we want to find out, for example, the income and race of people who commit crime, and we study the records of court prosecutions, there is the possibility that poor and black people are more likely to be reported, to be arrested, and to be prosecuted for committing crimes than are wealthier, white people. Records here may tell us less about who commits crimes and more about the people who collect the information. (Because of such problems with government statistics on crime, sociologists and criminologists have sought to collect their own. They have conducted surveys in which people are asked about the crimes they commit or about offenses committed against them. Most delinquency or criminology textbooks discuss the uses and problems of these different kinds of data on crime.)

Income tax returns, which tell us the annual incomes of individuals and families, may underreport some incomes; diaries may be conscious efforts to create a certain self-image as much as they are reports of actual behavior; newspaper accounts may reflect the biases and prejudices of the reporter, or the editors, or of the times. For example, during January–March, 1973, there were 215 murders in Chicago, of which 51 were given some coverage in the *Chicago Tribune*. Of these 51, almost half were about white victims, whereas only 20 percent of the 215 victims were white. Blake (1974) reports, "Up front in the paper, where readership is high, the imbalance was even stronger—two-thirds of the murder stories on pages one through five involved white victims." (p. 593) But the reality was that most murder victims were black people.

All records must be used with great care and must be seen in light of the biases of the reporters and collectors. With such care, they can be very helpful. Often they are indispensable and the only evidence we can use. In this book, and all sociology texts, we resort to government statistics many times. For example, in the discussion of social classes (see Chapter 8), we use government statistics on incomes, wealth, and so on.

Content Analysis

Content analysis is a technique for interpreting the information contained in documents and other existing records of human behavior. A few examples will illustrate this technique.

Let us suppose we are studying the changes in race relations over the last fifty years. Magazine advertisements could be used as one index of the change or lack of change. We could decide to take the years 1930, 1940, 1950, 1960, 1970, and 1980 and select the three bestselling weekly magazines in those years. Then we could examine twelve issues a year (the first issue of each month), looking at all advertisements and counting the percentage of ads each year that picture black people. If we find 1 percent in 1930, 2 percent in 1960, and 3 percent in 1980 (when black people were almost 12 percent of the population), we would have one sign of some, although not very significant, change in race relations.

Another topic we may be interested in is the portrayal of sex roles in children's books. If we can determine the ten (or some such number) bestselling children's books for the years 1950, 1960, 1970, and 1980, we could analyze their portrayal of the two sexes. We could count the percentage of leading characters who are girls and those who are boys; we could also analyze the words used to describe boys and girls. For example, boys could be described in terms of strength and accomplishments, girls in terms of being pretty and well behaved. Such studies have been done (my students have done some), and they reveal that books, as one item in our culture, still largely exclude girls from leading roles in stories, although not as totally as in the past.

Content analysis is a systematic count and detailed discussion of images, perceptions, and stereotypes in newspaper stories, magazine ads and stories, books of all kinds, and TV and radio shows. They may not show us how the media audiences are affected nor how they receive the message, but they are an indication of the nature of that message. For example, subtle and open sexual messages in liquor advertisements (and many other product advertisements) can be analyzed, counted, and described. In this way we can document the commercial exploitation of human sexuality.

At times it is possible to use content analysis to compare perception with reality. For example, if we know that in 1986 over 47.5 percent of women with children under six were working outside the home (U.S. Department of Labor, 1987f), we could analyze all the children's books published in 1986 that contain stories that include mothers with young children. Do these stories show about 47 percent of the women holding jobs? If only 10 or 20 percent of the stories show this, we can document a misrepresentation of reality.

The spoken and implied images and messages of many forms of communication can be analyzed in a similar manner to find out social perceptions, changes of perceptions, cultural ideals, and so on. If the average American woman weighs one hundred forty pounds and is five feet six inches tall, but ads for clothing and related products show women who are one hundred twenty and six feet tall, we know there is a discrepancy that needs to be discussed and its significance analyzed.

Experiments

Experiments differ from the four previous techniques because they are situations that are *created* by social scientists. The person conducting an experiment is in control of the events and social interactions being studied.

Let us begin by examining a well-known experiment that studied the effects of people's actions and thoughts on other people. Asch's (1956) experiment involves ten people judging the length of two lines, an A line (say seven inches long) and a B line (say nine inches long). There is no doubt that B is longer than A. But the first nine people are instructed to say that A is longer. The tenth person, ignorant of the instructions given to the previous nine people, is asked to compare the lines after he or she has heard them claim A is longer. Will the tenth person believe his or her eyes, or will he or she give in to the others' reported perceptions? This experiment has been run many times, and it has been found that 36.8 percent of the uninformed subjects give in to perceived group pressure and report A to be longer. When one of the other nine is instructed to report line B longer, then a smaller percentage of the uninformed subjects give in and report line A longer. The percentage is further reduced when two and then three people are instructed to make the correct observation. Two comments should be made on this experiment. If 36.8 percent mistrust their own perceptions, 63.2 percent do not and resist group pressure. Deutscher (1973) reports studies that show uninformed subjects not making the same mistake and reporting the longer line correctly when they are interviewed alone later and are asked to compare the lines. This seems to show that what people say in a group is often not what they actually perceive and think.

Group Composition

In conducting experiments, the researcher must control the composition of the group carefully. In Asch's experiment, the tenth person could not differ in age, education, class, and so on, from the other nine. (Asch's subjects were college students, as are most experimental subjects.) If participants in experiments differ too much, their responses might be affected by these factors. Also, the lengths of the lines must be the same each time the experiment is run; the instructions and the setting must be exactly the same; and all other conditions must be alike. The only variable Asch changed was the number of people giving the incorrect answer, from nine to eight to seven. This was done to test whether at least some group support affected the response of the tenth person.

Variables

Experiments test the effect of one condition, called the *independent variable,* on another condition, called the *dependent variable.* How do changes in the independent variable affect the dependent variable? In order to conclude with confidence that changes in the dependent variable are caused by the independent variable, all conditions of two or more experiments must be kept as much alike as possible.

Let us imagine an experiment. Suppose that we suspect people with more education defend their opinions more vigorously than people with less education. What kind of an experiment could we set up? We could locate people of different educational backgrounds (less than high school, high school diploma, college degree), all of whom oppose capital punishment. We could then place each of them with a group of five people who favor capital punishment. If this were to be a perfect experiment, the only variable that should vary each time we ran it should be people's education. What should be held constant?

Age, sex, social class, and many other factors of the opponents of capital punishment should be similar. If their sex varied, for example, the results could mean men (or women) are less likely to defend their opinions. What about the defenders of capital punishment? Should they be the same five people in all fifty times we run the experiment? If they are, would they become weary and indifferent over time? If we have different groups, how can we assure they are socially the same, and, even more important, that they all hold equally firm views? We also need to measure the strength of their opinions. How can we make sure that the proponents of the death penalty argue that view equally strongly each time we run the experiment? Probably the most difficult problem we face is the definition and measurement of what constitutes the defense of a person's opposition to the death penalty. Should we count the length of time a person speaks, the number of times, the rationality of his or her arguments? If we consider the last, will not our own views on the death penalty affect what we consider rational arguments?

Advantages

The appeal and strength of an experiment is the ability for someone to precisely create a situation. To ask people about the influence of others on their behavior only invites gross misperceptions and false reports; to wait for such situations to occur naturally is too time consuming and problematic. It seems easier and more precise to conduct experiments. (For a well-run experiment, see Milgram, 1965.)

Problems with Experiments

There are three major problems in experimental research. We have already seen the difficulties researchers face when they must keep all variables (but the independent variable) alike each time they run the experiment.

There is also an ethical problem. In almost every experiment, people are not told the real purpose of the experiment. If people are told that group influence on their behavior is being studied, they will be too self-conscious. Thus, the experimenter disguises the real purpose by telling people there is another purpose for what he or she is asking them to do. At the end of the experiment people are told the real purpose. (See Milgram, 1965.)

The most serious problem with experiments is their artificial nature. Even if they do not know the real purpose of the experiment, people know that *it is* an experiment. With such knowledge, can people be expected to act as they would in actual social situations? By definition, experiments are artificial social settings and can rarely, if ever, approximate the intensity, urgency, significance, and importance of peoples' daily lives. People do not behave in experiments as they do in real situations. To demonstrate this, Orne (1962) conducted an experiment that involved a meaningless activity that in daily life people would refuse to perform. One time he gave each person 2,000 sheets, each with 224 additions on it. "After the instructions were given, the subject was deprived of his watch and told, 'Continue to work; I will return eventually.' Five and one-half hours later, the *experimenter* gave up!" Variations of the experiment demanded even more meaningless tasks, for example, instructions to add up the numbers on the same sheet over and over. People "tended to persist in the task for several hours with relatively little sign of overt hostility." Orne comes to a discouraging conclusion: "Thus far, we have been singularly unsuccessful in finding an experimental task which would be discontinued, or, indeed, refused by subjects in an experimental setting. Not only do subjects continue to perform boring, unrewarding tasks, but they do so with few errors and little decrement in speed." (p. 188) (For a discussion of the problems of experiments, see Deutscher, 1973.)

Each of the five methods presents possibilities and opportunities for the study of human social behavior, but they also each contain severe problems and limitations. To overcome a limitation, a researcher could use more than one method in the study of an issue. Ideally this should be done, but in reality it is not done by many sociologists. Each person has his or her preferred method (in my case participant observation and the careful use of documents and records). If someone studies the effects of mental hospitals on the patients by carrying out a survey, becoming a participant observer, using documents, and possibly even conducting an experiment, and the study conclusions from each method were similar, there could be more confidence in the findings. But such agreement of findings is not common. Different methods often produce different conclusions about the same issue (even the same method often produces different conclusions). If this is the case, which findings do we believe?

The Limits of Sociological Research

Sociologists and other social scientists have made large claims for their fields. They have argued that unlike the ignorance and biases of past generations, we can begin to achieve a scientific and more valid understanding of social and individual behavior. As a sociologist I share some of that optimism and hope. But like some other sociologists I have some reservations about the pronouncement of a new day for the study of people, groups, and societies. There are existential, political, ethical, and philosophical conditions and realities that should temper this zeal.

Existential Issues

In the early 1960s, when I began to study sociology at Clark University, three people influenced my intellectual development. David Lindsay Watson, a chemist and author of *The Study of Human Nature,* was the first. Albert Camus, a French philosopher, novelist, playwright, and political activist, was the second. James Agee, an American novelist, reporter, movie critic, and poet, was the third. Their thoughts and observations help us keep a proper perspective on the nature of our study: the meaning and context of our daily lives.

Watson (1953) argues passionately against the social scientists' tendency to categorize, measure, and objectify human experience. The numbers, responses, and categories of data do not describe human social experiences in all their richness and variety.

> *The world of our fellow men [and women] is like the surging of the ocean—turbulent, alluring, treacherous, and lovely. (p. 18)*
>
> *The richness of reality can never be wholly trapped—in words or symbols. (p. 71)*
>
> *Social scientists are not sufficiently awake to the urgency, confusion, uncertainty and fragmentariness of the settings in which impulses are stimulated, actions initiated, or decisions made. (p. 129)*
>
> *We must be ceaselessly aware that the dwelling of every man or woman is not the physical or social setting which are to be mapped by the camera or by "objective" study, but is a strange, teeming landscape of secret sorrows and hidden beauties like the one we ourselves know so well in the silence of the night. (pp. 93–94)*

James Agee and Walker Evans, a photographer, went to the South in the 1930s to report on the lives of poor sharecroppers. As Agee (1941) sat up late one night in the home of one of the families, alone in the stillness of the house, he reflected on the meaning of human existence.

> *All that each person is, and experiences, and shall never experience, in body and in mind, all these things are differing expressions of himself and of one root, and are identical: and not one of these things nor one of these persons is ever quite to be duplicated, nor replaced, nor has it ever quite had precedent: but each is a new and incommunicably tender life, wounded in every breath, and almost as hardly killed as easily wounded: sustaining, for a while, without defense, the enormous assaults of the universe. (p. 56)*

Agee warns us that each person is unlike every other person. Individuals are unique. To the extent he is describing an unalterable human condition, a social science that generalizes about all or most people becomes a precarious undertaking. I do not fully agree with Agee, but I am aware that we have to live and study in the tension created by the essential similarity of all of us, as people living in groups, *and* by the essential uniqueness of each of us. We are alike, and we are different. This may seem like a contradiction, but I think it is an accurate description of our existence. We are shaped by the social world around us *and* free of it; we are like all other people, *and* unlike all other people.

Albert Camus (1960) made me aware of the need (the unchangeable reality) to live in, create, and study in opposites. In the essay "Create Dangerously," he is referring to art, but his reflections apply to sociology and the other social sciences. "Art is neither complete rejection nor complete acceptance of what is. It is simultaneously rejection and acceptance, and this is why it must be a perpetually renewed wrenching apart. The artist constantly lives in such a state of ambiguity, incapable of negating the real and yet eternally bound to question it in its eternally unfinished aspects." (p. 264) Artists paint or write novels; they get their material from the world around them. But their art, while it is rooted in reality, is not a perfect replica of that reality. It focuses on and accentuates certain parts of that reality, seeking to transform that reality, or at least our understanding and perception of it.

As sociologists, we also engage in a denial and acceptance. We seek to portray and explain social reality, but we must always do so with the awareness that our portrait is incomplete. And it is incomplete because reality is always changing and is both universal and unique to each person and because our biases, loves, concerns, and passions are essential parts of the reality we seek to describe and transform. The sociologist is an involved person, struggling in the same world as those he or she claims to study.

Philosophical Issues

In discussing the five methods, I raised many warnings about the validity of each. Here I want to return to two problems common to all of them: the *observer effect* and the definition of concepts.

Observer Effects

By the very act of studying and observing situations we alter them in some way. We cannot study social settings as they are without us present. (When we use records and documents, we are assuming the biases of previous observers. We also change these documents by the categories in which we place them.) Whether we interview people, use participant observation, or conduct experiments, we are part of the situation. We are asking people to reflect upon and recall their behavior or tell us their opinions. Their family and friends might make similar requests but not as sociologists. The responses in those contexts are different.

As participant observers we become new members of social groups. Our very presence alters the situation. It is naive to think that people act, think, and talk openly in front of us. They may lie to us or simply avoid us. Or, if we are especially kind, compassionate, and caring, people may tell us deeply held secrets they have never revealed. Whatever happens, we, by our presence, have modified the preexisting social situation.

A somewhat humorous but very revealing example of observer effect was reported on "The Johnny Carson Show." A man who was skeptical of product endorsements in advertising thought people would not report their real views of the product if they thought they might appear on television. His experiment consisted of taking pure lemon extract (pure lemon juice) and pouring it in bottles that were labeled. He then asked people to taste the "new soft drink" he was planning to market. People drank it but struggled to hide the sour taste. When asked for their evaluations of the drink they called it "tangy," "different," "interesting," and so on. Not one said it was sour and not drinkable. He then told people it was not a soft drink, and they would not appear on TV. They all admitted the drink was not drinkable. So long as they thought they might appear on TV, they hid their real reaction, which had it been evident would not have gotten them on TV.

Definitions of Terms

Whatever issue or hypothesis we are studying, we use terms and concepts that need to be defined. In the study of the family, for example, we may be concerned with the quality of married life. The easy path is to define unhappy marriages as those that end up in divorce, a simple and fairly easily verifiable and quantifiable solution. But if we want to explore a meaningful question, say, what are the elements of a happy and satisfying marriage, we have a more difficult task. How do we define marital happiness? To ask people to provide their own definitions would mean grouping together very different experiences. One study (Bradburn & Caplovitz, 1965) on the mental health of Americans never defined what "happiness" was. People were simply asked, "Taking all things together, how would you say things are these days—would you say you are very happy, pretty happy, or not too happy?" (p. 7) Such definitions avoid all the moral, existential, and political issues necessarily present when we study the quality of life, married or otherwise.

Sociologists typically define concepts that can be measured and quantified, but in the process they lose essential aspects of social existence. Religiosity is more, and different, than just church attendance. Social classes are more than income categories and more than the ratings of a few chosen people (common techniques of defining social class). What is measurable and quantifiable is not necessarily the social and psychic reality we experience. A long and complicated philosophical discussion on the meaning of happiness may not help us to measure it, but it may awaken us to the human experiences that make for happiness.

Ethical and Political Issues

Social science studies also raise issues about the use and goals of social science research.

Ethical Problems

Most sociologists assume that the interference with and invasion of people's lives in the course of a study are justified by the resulting knowledge that is attained. This is especially so when researchers study people without their consent or knowledge, but it is also true when people do know of our activities. Especially if the person is persuasive, it is difficult for most people to refuse. Consent is not always fully and willingly given (Humphreys, 1975).

Many sociologists, to avoid the problems of observer effects, partially or wholly disguise their aims. Some have pretended to join religious sects, faked mental illness, gotten factory jobs, and even placed themselves in settings where sexual acts occur. The goals and motives of these people are, for the most part, laudable: to expose oppression or to show that deviant people are in fact normal. But do their means justify their ends? Such justification may exist under extraordinary conditions, but researchers should always be wary that they are not the sole judges of conditions that justify deception. This is an issue that needs careful thought and discussion. (See Festinger, Riecken & Schacter, 1956; Rosenhan, 1973; Pfeffer, 1979; and Humphreys, 1975.)

Studying the Powerless

Much of social science research studies powerless people: mental patients, prison inmates, students, poor people, prostitutes, minorities, and so on. It is difficult or impossible for them to refuse to be studied. A researcher may get permission from a person's superior (psychiatrist, prison warden, school principal), but in doing so make it impossible for the powerless person to refuse permission. The three settings I studied as a participant observer in the 1960s (an old-age rest home and two group homes for delinquents) are examples of situations where people have no choice. In each case I received the permission of the administration, but it never occurred to me that first I should ask the people living in these institutions for *their* permission. I think professionals many times assume certain prerogatives and cannot even imagine that they need the permission of the people who they are actually studying.

At the same time, few sociologists would dream of asking similar permission to study the lives of the powerful such as politicians, corporation executives, college presidents, boards of directors, and boards of trustees. Could Henry Kissinger and the CIA have been studied as they planned the overthrow of the government of Chile? Would corporate boards of directors allow someone to sit in on their deliberations to close down a factory or move it to a foreign country with cheap labor?

The Uses of Knowledge and Information

Social research is expensive and uses many resources. This is especially true of survey research. Since most sociologists cannot fund their own research, they turn to the government, foundations, and corporations for money. By funding most social research, these institutions are able to control, limit, and select the kinds of issues that are studied. Money gives them power. Few people would sponsor research that threatens their power and interests. Indeed, much of the research that is sponsored serves the interests of powerful groups and institutions and controls and manipulates powerless people. Its aim is to manipulate workers to produce more, pacify restive populations (prisoners, students, mental patients), persuade people to buy certain products, and stop revolutions in poor societies. Such research is not liberating or enlightening. It serves the interests of certain groups at the expense of millions of people. In short, we always need to ask, who benefits from the research we conduct? (For an extensive debate on this issue, see Weaver, 1973, and Babbie, 1986.)

Is Sociology Common Sense?

Many writers, students, and other people argue that sociology (the social sciences in general) does no more than belabor the obvious. It tells us what we already know, in more detail than we care to have. Many sociologists have responded that common sense is wrong and obvious truths are not so obvious. Common sense, they reply, in fact makes no factual sense.

Some Not So Obvious Truths

Watson (1953) and Goodman (1974) cite examples where they think social scientists tell us what we know already.

> Dr. Argelander has "established," by the methods of research, that intimate friends see a person in a more favorable light than do mere acquaintances. Poor Dr. A. must have very few friends if he needs the assistance of "research" to convince him of this. (p. 93)

> *At the University of California, researchers have found, through their academically approved methodologies, that dumb people are happier than smart people. The smart are less happy, they confess, because they think too much about whether they are happy or not.*

Goodman (1980a) offers other examples of what seem to her unnecessary research proving "what we already know." Doctors from Cleveland went to Guatemala to study women in labor and delivery. They found that those women who had someone with them constantly while they were in labor, holding their hands and talking with them, had a shorter and easier labor and delivery than the women who were alone. Goodman (1980a) thinks any woman could have told the doctors that "it's better for women not to go through labor alone." (p. 11)

Sociologists' Critique of Common Sense

Most sociology textbooks, and other works, describe common sense in very negative terms (they equate common sense with proverbs, for example, "Absence makes the heart grow fonder"). They see it as biased, subjective, incomplete, crude, and so on. For example, two recent textbook authors, Shepard (1981) and Stewart (1981), cite a number of what they think are statements believed by most people as obvious common sense but which sociology has shown to be mistaken. Here is an example: "People with little formal education are more likely to obey orders than college-educated people." Research (not cited in the text) supposedly shows the statement is wrong, but Shepard thinks most people, using common sense, would think the statement true. (See Landis, 1986; Liazos, 1976; and Pease, 1981.)

The approach taken by critics of common sense is to show that it is wrong and contradictory. Examples of supposedly wrong common sense abound. Common sense is shown to be contradictory by citing proverbs making opposing claims: out of sight, out of mind, *and* absence makes the heart grow fonder; look before you leap, *and* he who hesitates is lost. (Baldridge, 1975, cites ten more examples.)

Sociology and Common Sense

But sociological writings also abound with wrong statements and contradicting claims. There have been many beliefs long held as factual by sociologists that have proven to be wrong or unsubstantiated. As late as 1986, Landis (1986) stated that in nineteenth-century America the extended family (grandparents, children, and grandchildren living under one roof) was the norm. Many texts stated this as fact for years. Recent historical research seems to show, however, that at no time in American history were extended families more than 6 percent of all families. (See Pease, 1981, for more examples of wrong facts.)

There is hardly any issue or area of life about which sociologists are in agreement. On most important issues there are two or more theories and statements, often contradicting each other. Sociologists, for example, do not agree about the causes for and the nature of social classes. There are many theories about the causes of crime and delinquency, all citing facts to substantiate their claims. Sociological knowledge is no less contradictory than is common sense knowledge.

Some texts include tests for students to take. By failing them, students show they are ignorant about the social world. Could sociologists do better? Is there a test most of them would fail? Pease (1981) cites a study where only 25 percent (20 out of 80) of the sociologists and economists asked about "the relative household savings of blacks and whites" gave the correct answer. (p. 264) Critics of common sense compare the worst in common sense with the best in sociology. In reality, both sociology and common sense are correct some of the time and wrong some of the time. (Also see Landis, 1986, and Thio, 1986.)

If we think about it with an open mind, we will realize that common sense (proverbs and other knowledge based on our observations of ourselves and others) must be correct at least some of the time. People who are not sociologists could not survive if their knowledge and understanding of social life were incorrect. Valid, empirical knowledge of individuals, groups, and societies is indispensable for social life, for societies to endure and to function. Some people possess more valid knowledge than others, but just about everyone must have some understanding of psychology and sociology. Common sense is often wrong, of course, but that does not prove all common sense wrong, any more than the many mistakes sociologists make prove all sociology wrong.

There are many examples of people who are not sociologists who have a profound understanding of the social world. They have gained these insights through careful, repeated, and varying observations of the world—in the same way any good sociologist would. Through a careful study of her life experiences, Hannah Nelson, an elderly black woman who did not finish elementary school, came to some of the same conclusions many sociologists have come to (Gwaltney, 1980):

> We are the kind of people we have to be. I believe that is true of every group of people in every culture. I think that ancient Egyptians put in the Georgia and Carolina lowlands under conditions of slavery would be Geechees. I think that German tribesmen under the conditions which produced Japanese or Zulus would be Japanese or Zulus. White people would be the same kind of people we are if they had had our historical portion. We would be the kind of people they are if we had had theirs. People with the same blood, by which I mean the same biological heritage, are living in different ways from us in Africa and Europe. So I think that our way of living is different because of what you could call historical reasons. But our history is our history and it makes us the kind of people we are. I have known children of the same father to grow up in different races and think of themselves as very different from each other. (pp. 5–6)

(For more examples, see Liazos, 1976, and Pease, 1981.)

Hannah Nelson has learned that the social, economic, and historical conditions in which we live, and our reactions to these conditions, shape the kind of people we become. This is one of the most important insights in sociology, if not the most important one. Sociologists have documented, debated, and sought to understand it, but it is not an insight unique to sociology. It would be shocking if people over the course of human history had *not* come to this understanding. They may have expressed it differently, but the insight remains essentially the same.

Good sociology, like good common sense, is organized, systematic, inquiring, and curious. Sociologists should use all possible sources of information: personal experiences, the experiences of others, novels, biographies, dreams, songs and poetry, any and all human expressions and experiences. All of these sources are useful, provided we consider each of them carefully and know the biases and limits of each.

As sociology has become a profession, we, as the practitioners, have the time to devote most of our energies to the study of individuals, groups, and societies. We have more time, an advantage over most other people who must work at other endeavors in order to make a living. But by being professionals, by making our living as students of society, we divorce ourselves somewhat from that society. It is doubtful, for example, that we can know the alienation of work better than the workers who must hold alienating jobs.

I think there is value to sociology as a field of knowledge. It can help us understand the world and our place in it. But I do not see sociology as a superior and scientific avenue to that knowledge. It is a human endeavor, part of the world it seeks to understand. It does not hover above that world, but stands in its very midst. It continues the long tradition of people struggling to make sense of the world around them. Sociological methods, techniques, and theories offer possibilities, but each is also partial and limited.

It may seem that a defense of common sense is a call for an uncritical acceptance of current social conditions. As teachers and sociologists, we take it as our mission to help students think critically. A defense of common sense should not be interpreted as accepting the inequalities, prejudices, preconceptions, and discrimination all around us.

Rather, I want to avoid an uncritical acceptance of sociology (and the other social sciences) as well as an uncritical acceptance of common sense. Economists, sociologists, political scientists, and other social scientists can be obstacles to a clear and critical understanding of the social and political conditions in which we live. Struggles against oppression and injustice are led and engaged in not by social scientists but by people who live and come to experience, understand, explain, and criticize that oppression. Living, thinking, and acting are inseparable (Ollman, 1986).

Ordinary people are not ignorant. All of us can and do understand the societies in which we live. All of us can be—all of us are—mistaken, biased, prejudiced; all of us often see what we *want*, not what *is;* all of us must struggle against these tendencies.

Conclusion

When sociology first became established as an academic discipline early in the twentieth century, sociologists had great expectations that their studies would make sociology a *scientific* field similar to the natural and physical sciences. They developed methods to emulate those sciences.

But while sociologists try to be objective and observe human behavior and human societies as they actually exist, they cannot pretend to have created research methods that result in fully reliable findings and conclusions. Each sociological method has its promises and possibilities, but each also has its major limitations.

This conclusion should not be discouraging but rather should make sociologists more cautious and more willing to critically examine their methods and findings. Everyone needs to develop some basic understanding of how societies function. Sociology is only another and more recent tool that enables people to find that understanding. It is not a totally new nor a vastly superior one. After all, it is ourselves we are studying; objectivity can only be approached, never fully attained.

Summary

Sociological research presupposes a curiosity and a critical questioning of the social world around us. Sociologists explore relationships between different social conditions. They seek to show how one condition (an independent variable) affects another one (a dependent variable).

Sociologists collect data by observing human behavior, by asking questions, and collecting records people leave behind. There are five methods used in social research. These methods and the resulting findings must be used with caution. They present many problems and raise many issues.

In survey research (sample survey), researchers choose a representative sample of a population and ask questions. The responses are used to show a relationship between two or more variables (such as the effect of age on one's religious views). The kinds of questions that are asked, the wording of the questions, and the interviews present problems that need careful consideration.

Participant observation involves observation of and participation with people in a social setting, in contrast to a survey that asks questions. It allows the researcher to see how people actually behave, not how they think they behave. There are two major problems with this method. One is the effect the observer's bias has on the people being studied (observer effect). And two is the question of how representative one setting can be.

Another method is the examination, organization, and analysis of records people have left behind. Such records, in official documents, newspapers, and other places, provide the researcher with a rich variety of information. But here, too, there may be a bias in their recording and collection. They also may not be typical or representative.

Content analysis is a technique to organize and analyze communication, specifically the contents of books, magazines, television programs, movies, and other media. This method reveals biases and hidden messages in the material, for example, the sexism in children's books, but it does not tell us how such material affects the recipients of the messages.

Finally, experiments are controlled social situations created by researchers. By manipulating an independent variable, a researcher seeks to show its effects on a dependent variable. Experiments allow researchers to create and control a condition they wish to study, but the artificial nature of experiments may restrict the application of the findings to real settings.

There are four limits to sociological research: the inability of the researcher to understand people's actions in all their richness and variety, the observer effect, limited and arbitrary definitions of terms, and the ethical issues of privacy and political questions of the uses and abuses of sociological research.

There has been a long debate on whether sociology is more than common sense. The best of sociology, as well as the best of common sense, offer us valid and useful understandings of social behavior and societies. It may be that sociology is more systematic and more organized than common sense is, but it cannot claim superior expertise and more useful knowledge.

Suggested Readings

Babbie, Earl (1986). *The practice of social research* (4th ed.). Belmont, CA: Wadsworth. A detailed discussion of the philosophy, problems, and methods of social research.

Becker, Howard S. (1986). *Writing for social scientists: How to start and finish your thesis, book, or article.* Chicago: University of Chicago Press. A very readable, sometimes humorous, and very useful account of how sociologists do and should organize and write their research.

Bernard, Russell; Killworth, Peter; Kronenfeld, David; & Sailer, Lee (1984). The problem of informant accuracy: The validity of retrospective data. *Annual Review of Anthropology, 13,* 495–517. A review and discussion of studies that show that much of what people tell researchers is often incomplete or inaccurate. The authors present some possible solutions to overcome this problem.

Deutscher, Irwin (1973). *What we say/What we do.* Glenview, IL: Scott, Foresman. An outstanding discussion of the debate on whether people do what they say they will do. Deutscher reprints most of the classical studies of this debate.

Levine, James P. (1976, November). The potential for overreporting in criminal victimization surveys. *American Criminologist, 14*(3), 307–330. Levine concludes that the potential is significant.

Pease, John (1981, November). Sociology *and* the sense of the commoners. *American Sociologist, 16*(4), 257–271. Both sociology and common sense can be mistaken, and both can help us understand social reality.

Rosenhan, David L. (1973). On being sane in insane places. *Science, 179*, 250–258. By faking mental illness, eight people each committed themselves to twelve mental hospitals and through participant observation they describe conditions in mental hospitals.

Russell, Bertrand (1961). An outline of intellectual rubbish. In Robert Egner and Lester Denonn (Eds.), *The basic writings of Bertrand Russell* (pp. 73–99). New York: Simon & Schuster. A humorous, satiric, and devastating critique of all the so-called facts people have believed through the ages.

Spradley, James P. (1980). *Participant observation*. New York: Holt, Rinehart & Winston. A detailed discussion of participant observation: finding the setting, making observations, organizing the data, and so forth.

Turnbull, Colin (1961). *The forest people*. New York: Simon & Schuster. A moving and vivid example of participant observation by an anthropologist. Turnbull comes as close as possible to feeling and telling us what it is like being an Mbuti of the Ituri Forest.

Watson, David Lindsay (1953). *The study of human nature*. Yellow Springs, OH: Antioch Press. Watson, a chemist, argues that by trying to be scientific and objective, social scientists tend to miss the essence of human and social experiences.

PART II

Social Life

CHAPTER 3

People in the Natural Environment

Today we live in a society where people move and travel extensively. Yet few people ever spend long periods of time in another society, even one that is similar to theirs. Even fewer people visit or live in third-world countries. Past societies are inaccessible to direct experience, but few people ever read in any depth about the societies that existed before the industrial era. In time, space, and daily experience we are limited to knowing one society well at one point in history.

My purpose here is to help you cross a bridge into the vast history of human societies. In addition to presenting some known facts about economic and social conditions in these societies, we will explore what it might have been like living in them. We should never forget that people live in both a natural and social environment and experience these realities in their minds and spirits. (Turnbull's *The Forest People* is a superb account of a people and their natural, material, social, and spiritual totality.)

In order to understand our present societies and our future possibilities, it is imperative that we remember two fundamental realities of our existence. First, we live in a natural environment that has limits and possibilities we ignore only at our gravest peril. And second, our industrial society is only a recent development in human history. We still carry with us remnants and influences of our past, collectively as human beings and individually as members of societies, groups, and families. The past is in the present —we are still natural beings. We cannot know who we are unless we know our past and our place in the natural world.

This chapter is divided into three parts. The first part presents some basic aspects of social evolution. It describes the economies and social conditions of different types of societies. In the second part I argue that contemporary industrial societies, the latest stage of human evolution, have exploited and abused the environment and may destroy the social and physical worlds as we know them. I end with a discussion of nuclear weapons and war, the ultimate threat to our existence.

The Evolution of Human Societies

In the five hundred thousand years human beings have inhabited this earth, they have lived in four main types of societies.

■ *Gathering and hunting societies.* Until about ten thousand years ago, people lived by hunting animals and gathering wild fruits and vegetables.

■ *Horticultural societies.* At about ten thousand years ago, some people began to cultivate gardens, where they grew their own fruits and vegetables. They used digging sticks, and later metal hoes, to prepare these gardens. Gradually horticulture spread.

■ *Agricultural societies.* About five thousand to six thousand years ago, people began to use the plow and animals to cultivate grains, which enabled them to grow much more food on the same piece of land than they could by horticulture.

■ *Industrial societies.* Around the mid-1700s, the western European countries began to industrialize. Gathering-hunting and horticultural societies became more rare, and agrarian societies in other parts of the world began rapidly industrializing. But in many parts of the world millions of people still practice traditional agriculture.

Each of these four types of society is discussed below. In each case, we shall explore their size, economic system, social and political organization, men and women and their lives in families, social equalities and inequalities, and people's relationship to the environment. These societies differ in the means they use to make a living from their environment, but they also differ in other, equally significant respects.

We have no written records from the distant past, so we do not know how gatherers-hunters lived ten thousand years ago. But limited archaeological evidence and observations of still existing gathering-hunting and horticultural societies provide us with enough evidence to speculate about these very early societies.

The types of societies described here are generalizations and abstractions of many societies throughout human history. Many societies are combinations of these four types. When Europeans came to America around 1500, most Indian societies in what is now the northeast United States and southeast Canada were horticultural, but they also engaged in considerable gathering and hunting. The changes from one type to another are usually slow and gradual. They occur over hundreds and thousands of years.

Gathering and Hunting Societies

Approximately ten thousand years ago people gathered their food—wild roots, berries, vegetables, honey, and other wild edible plants—and hunted animals. About two thousand years ago, only about half the people on earth lived in such societies. About five hundred years ago, only 15 percent were still gatherers and hunters, and today of the 5 billion people on earth, under thirty thousand still live this way (Friedl, 1981).

Population

Hundreds and thousands of people may share the same language and culture and belong to the same tribe, but functioning social and economic groups of gatherers-hunters are small. The average size is twenty-five to forty, and on rare occasions up to one hundred people live together.

Because the people in these societies only use resources that exist naturally in their immediate vicinity, the population density ranges from one person per square mile in desert areas, Australia, for example, to three people per square mile in more favorable climates and conditions. In environments rich in natural resources the density reaches ten people per square mile. (Population density in the United States is about seventy people per square mile. In many countries of the world it reaches three hundred and over.) Generally, gatherers-hunters do not exhaust the animal and plant resources of their lands. They move to a new area before the resources in an area have been exhausted. (See Lenski & Lenski, 1978, and Friedl, 1981.)

Making a Living

Before anthropologists carried out detailed investigations of existing gathering-hunting societies, people in these societies were described as living on the edge of starvation, their food supply always precarious. But many recent studies show that their diet is varied, plentiful, and nutritious, and that they do not work long hours to procure the food they need (Lee, 1984, and Shostak, 1981). They hunt animals or gather plants three to four days a week, for about fifteen hours. Even the !Kung, who live in the Kalahari Desert in southwest Africa, have a plentiful supply of food and devote fifteen to twenty hours a week to procure this source. They spend about twenty more hours a week making and fixing their tools and doing domestic work. They know about five hundred species of plants and animals, which to eat and which to avoid. Indeed, gathering-hunting societies are self-sufficient, providing for all their needs: food, clothing, shelter, tools, and entertainment.

In both the Lee (1984) and Shostak (1981) studies, the men hunt animals and the women gather roots, berries, and other plants. This division is not rigid: men on occasion gather plants and women kill animals (usually not large ones) that they come across during their gathering. Among the !Kung, as among most gathering-hunting societies, the food gathered by women constitutes 60 to 80 percent of the diet. (Recent studies by Leacock, 1981, and others, 1981, show that women in gathering-hunting societies in general supply more than half of the food.)

Lenski and Lenski (1978) point out that in order not to exhaust the food supply in any one area, groups move frequently, usually every one to three months, but their movements are within "fairly well-defined territories." (p. 118) Indeed, eventually people return to the same spot.

In our society an important element regarding food is whether or not it is nutritious. We might think that because gatherers-hunters had less complicated (some would say less sophisticated) means for obtaining food that they probably would be less nourished. But this does not seem to be the case. Paleontologists are studying the bones of ancient people and are gathering evidence that shows that gatherers-hunters had a healthier, more nutritious diet than did later peoples. One study by Diamond (1987) found that gatherers-hunters who lived in what are now Greece and Turkey averaged heights of five feet, nine inches for men and five feet, five inches for women. Agriculturalists in the same areas around 3000 B.C. averaged five feet, three inches for men and five feet for women. Another study showed that farmers who succeeded gatherers-hunters in Ohio and Illinois around 1150 A.D. showed a "four-fold increase in iron deficiency anemia . . . and an increase in degenerative conditions of the spine, probably reflecting a lot of hard physical labor." (p. 85)

Their nomadic existence prevents hunting-gathering groups from accumulating material objects. The Mbuti of the Ituri Forest have a minimal and utilitarian material culture—few clothes and a few tools (bows and arrows, knives, etc.). The only exception to this are the elaborate belts they make (Turnbull, 1961).

In short, we can guess from observing existing gatherers-hunters, that early peoples worked only a few hours, had an adequate diet, kept their needs few and simple, and, when not touched by outsiders and their illnesses, they lived long lives. Today the people who live within these societies do not lead precarious existences (Bodley, 1983).

Social Organization

Gatherers-hunters live in societies organized on very different principles than agrarian or industrial societies. Division of labor is simple, mostly along sex lines. Cooperation and reciprocity are guiding norms. Most social activities take place within families and kin relations. There are no specialists, and everyone but the very old and children contribute to the food supply and other needs. There are no powerful leaders, no one who can coerce others' behavior, and class differences do not exist. The differences that do exist are the result of different temperaments, interests, and abilities. A careful reading of the literature about gatherers-hunters and their societies shows they are free individuals bound by no powerful leaders and only by a few necessary norms.

As was mentioned, men do the hunting, with some occasional exceptions when women capture and kill smaller animals. At times men are absent for up to four days to capture larger animals (giraffes among the !Kung). Women stay closer to home to gather roots and berries and to care for the children. In some societies more than in others, men participate in raising the children, but it is primarily the women who are responsible for their care. The division of other work, for example the building of huts, varies from society to society. In some it is men's work, in others women's work.

Cooperation is a fundamental social expectation. In order for the hunt to be successful, cooperation is necessary. Those who violate this norm are ostracized and severely criticized. Turnbull (1961) gives us an illustration of this in the case of Cephu, one of the tribesmen, who went ahead of everyone else and took the animals for his own use. Severe ostracism forced him to distribute the catch among the rest of the group. Cooperation and sharing of the catch assures that the hunt will be successful and that everyone will get a share. No one goes without food. And when people do hunt as individuals there is the expectation of reciprocity. The hunter shares a good catch and others will in turn share theirs.

In our society we have schools, workplaces, hospitals, churches, government offices, courts, police, and many other institutions. Specialized institutions exist for our many needs. Not so among gatherers-hunters. There, family and kin (immediate and extended) provide for all the needs of the people. All of one's social activities—work, play, eating, worship—take place with the same small group of kinfolk. The family is the focus of all social activities; it is the most essential characteristic of gathering-hunting peoples.

An equally important characteristic of these societies is the absence of social hierarchies and leaders, or, rather, the presence of autonomy and individuality. Not only is there no leader, no central authority, for the tribe as a whole, but within each group of twenty-five to forty there is also no leader. People respect and listen to those who possess a skill or knowledge, for example a good hunter, but they are not coerced to follow any commands. People choose to follow a person's advice, suggestion, or example because they respect and recognize his or her accomplishments and knowledge. Someone may try to persuade others to a course of action, but he or she has no way to coerce those who resist. At worst, if disagreements become strong and continuous, the group splits up. No one can be forced to do what they clearly reject and dislike. (See Friedl, 1981, and Leacock, 1981.)

The few norms of social conduct that exist are not rigid. Turnbull (1961) concludes that the Mbuti are bound by very few rules, and they have great latitude in following general patterns of behavior. Cooperation in the hunt is one essential rule for survival, but even those who persist in violating it may only face disapproval, not formal punishment. In time, such people may be forced to leave, but few such clear rules exist.

It is impossible for people to live so closely and constantly with each other without having conflicts and disputes. They do occur. But they are settled in a cooperative, communal manner. Various expressions of social disapproval usually suffice to deal with most cases. Contempt and ridicule worked effectively against Cephu who violated the expectation of cooperation. And when private disputes are not settled by the two parties themselves, the community as a whole has the authority and responsibility to settle it. This ensures the survival of the group and its smooth functioning. Turnbull (1961) gives many examples. Serious crimes, such as theft, "were dealt with by a sound thrashing which was administered co-operatively by all who felt inclined to participate, but only after the entire group had been involved in discussing the case. Less serious offenses were settled in the simplest way, by the litigants themselves either arguing out the case, or engaging in a mild fight." (pp.110–111)

Finally, gathering-hunting societies have no social classes, no concept of the land as private property, and no warfare. The three are related. The land is owned by no one, not even the group. It exists for the common use. Different groups do have a general area that they use exclusively. Other groups are told to stay away. There are no fences and no clear demarcations, and groups often share water-holes and other sites. Certainly no individuals own land. With no ownership of land, with limited material possessions (necessitated by the frequent moves), and with the need for everyone to work, share, and cooperate, no social classes arise in these societies. This is not to say that every person or family is forced to own only so many possessions and no more, or that everyone is exactly the same. Rather, with the land equally available to everyone, and with a clear limit to the amount of material possessions, there is no need, opportunity, or desire for anyone to have substantially more than others. Warfare, therefore, makes no sense. Since war is usually waged to capture other people's land and confiscate their material possessions, it cannot arise where land is owned by no one and where no one owns very much.

The natural, economic, and social environments create values and practices that differ significantly from those in later societies. Turnbull's (1983b) comment on the Mbuti applies to gatherers-hunters generally:

One of the most dramatic things, for me, that emerges from any study of the Mbuti is their preoccupation with values, and their relative lack of concern with the material world, or, rather, with the world of material well-being. And lest it be said that this is implying that they are somehow more virtuous, or "better" than we are, let me deny that at once. They are whatever they are, like most of us, not because they are better or worse, but because of the context in which they live, and for survival in which they have developed the most satisfactory way of life they could devise. If there is little mendacity and virtually no crime, little attachment to material wealth and great attachment to moral values, it is not because they are "good" or consider these qualities to be virtues, but rather because this is what they have to be in order to survive. To lie and steal, to connive and cheat, to amass private wealth, power, and prestige, are simply dysfunctional in their context—or have been up to the present. In societies where they, or similar actions, become essential for survival, they are on their way to becoming accepted modes of behavior, if not virtues. (p. 11)

The future of the few contemporary gathering-hunting societies is uncertain. The !Kung, the Mbuti, and others face enormous pressures to become farmers and urban workers. Governments, corporations, and others want to take over and exploit their lands. Some who left the gathering-hunting way of life are returning to a modified form of it (for example, they use modern medicines) (Bodley, 1982). Others have changed significantly but still retain some of their traditions. The Mbuti still hunt, for example, while they use more food from the outside (Turnbull, 1983b). Lee (1984) says most !Kung no longer live in the bush and no longer gather or hunt much.

Horticultural Societies

The advent of horticulture led to many significant social, economic, and political changes in human societies. Populations became larger and denser. There was more division of labor and specialization. Inequalities and warfare made their appearance. Human settlements became more permanent and urban. People had more material possessions. The changes were gradual but definite.

Population

Horticultural communities average one hundred fifty to two hundred people, compared to twenty-five to forty in gathering-hunting groups. In some advanced horticultural societies there are larger communities, what we now call towns and small cities. Since people cultivate a plot of land for two to four years, sometimes longer, settlements are more permanent. Houses are built and possessions amassed. The larger population and permanent settlement are a result of the larger food supply made possible by the cultivation of gardens. (See Friedl, 1981, and Lenski & Lenski, 1978.)

Making a Living

Gardens were cultivated with a digging stick in early horticultural societies, and in the advanced horticultural societies, people use hoes. (In contrast, agriculture involves the use of plows driven by animals and the use of fertilizers.) People manually clear the land of trees (often by burning them), cultivate the soil, seed it, and harvest the crops. Corn, yams, and other root plants are often the staples in horticultural societies. Usually a plot is cultivated from two to four years until the soil nutrients are exhausted. It is then abandoned and another field is cleared. In ten to twenty years, after the soil has been replenished, a plot is used again.

In a horticultural society, it is not necessary for everyone in the community to secure the food supply. People produce a little more than they need, and, in time, this surplus is used to support nonfood producing specialists (religious and political leaders, craftspeople, etc.).

Early horticultural societies had mixed economies: people cultivated gardens but they also hunted, fished, and gathered wild plants. The transition to almost complete dependence on horticulture probably took thousands of years (see Johnson, 1978, for a description of a surviving society with such a mixed economy).

The permanent settlements that horticulture necessitates require the accumulation of material possessions: houses, tools, weapons, pottery, and so on—thus the rise of private property. People own the land they use, houses, and many more artifacts that gatherers-hunters do not need or want (Bodley, 1983). But we should note that compared to industrial societies, people in horticultural societies have very few possessions. Johnson (1978) provides a vivid description of the immense differences in possessions.

Social Organization

Some horticultural societies resemble gathering-hunting societies in their social organization. The family is still the dominant institution. It is the producing and consuming social unit. Specialists do arise and some functions are taken outside the family, such as religious worship, but most social activity still largely takes place within the family. As with the gathering and hunting societies, there are no leaders and no centralized authority, but there are a few social class differences.

Lenski and Lenski (1978) distinguish between *simple* and *advanced* horticultural societies. The advanced societies use metal weapons and/or tools that make it possible to produce more food and wage wars. In addition, they have more centralized authority and larger populations. There are clear class differences and powerful rulers who exploit the population. Lenski and Lenski cite Egypt and early China as examples.

Many horticultural societies are tribes. A tribe is a group of people who share a common language, common ethnic and culture traditions, and who believe they are descended from the same ancestor. They are not ruled by a leader and do not live together most of the time, but instead live in communities of one hundred fifty to two hundred people. The entire tribe only comes together for ceremonial and other important occasions (dances, religious festivals, etc.).

Other horticultural societies are structured as chiefdoms. The leaders or chiefs have authority and power and rule over larger populations, more land, and more food production than we find in tribes. Their authority comes from kinship ties, and their rule supposedly benefits everyone in the chiefdom. The exploitation of the masses that characterizes agricultural societies seems largely absent (Friedl, 1981).

A stable food surplus supports a larger population that has a few nonproducers of food. Some are craftspeople, who make pottery and other goods. Others, chiefs and religious specialists, produce no food or material goods. They are supported by the work of others. Thus, class differences and inequalities make their appearance. Inequalities in sex roles also become more pronounced. As we will see in Chapter 12, men and women may play different roles in gathering-hunting societies, but they are largely equal to each other.

Both men and women make essential contributions to the survival of the group, both obtain food, and no one owns land. In horticultural societies, some men own land and control the food raised on it. Men begin to dominate. This is a significant but by no means desirable change in human societies.

So horticultural societies, especially the later, more advanced ones, are significantly different from gathering-hunting societies. They differ still more profoundly from industrial societies. Johnson (1978) lived among the Machiguenga, in the Amazon jungle of Peru, and compares their life to life in France. These people practice horticulture and also gather and hunt. They are less hurried than the French, have more free time, and possess and need few material goods. There is no frantic production or consumption within the Machiguenga society.

> *Each time I return to their communities, after a period of two or three days, I sense a definite decrease in time pressure; this is a physiological as well as a psychological sensation.*
>
> *This feeling of a leisurely pace of life reflects the fact that among the Machiguenga daily activities are never hurried or desperate. Each task is allotted its full measure of time, and free time is not felt to be boring or lost but is accepted as entirely natural. These feelings last throughout the field visit, but when I return home I am conscious of the pressure and sense of hurry building up to its former level. (p. 53)*
>
> *Once, after a long rainy period, I laid my various footgear side by side in the sun to dry. There were a pair of hiking boots, a pair of canvas-topped jungle boots, and two pairs of sneakers. Some men came to visit and began inspecting the shoes, fingering the materials, commenting on the cleats, and trying them on for size. Then the discussion turned to how numerous my shoes were, and one man remarked that I had still another pair. There were protests of disbelief and I was asked if that was true. I said, "No, that's all I have." The man then said, "Wait," and went inside the house, returning with an "extra pair" of sneakers that I had left forgotten and unused in a corner of the room for months. This was not the only occasion on which I could not keep track of my possessions, a deficiency unknown to the Machiguenga.*
>
> *My feelings about this incident were compounded when I discovered that, no matter which pair of shoes I wore, I could never keep up with these men, whose bare feet seemed magically to grip the slipperiest of rocks or to find toe holds in the muddy trails. (p. 55)*

People in horticultural societies, especially the simpler ones, do not work long hours. In a recent study Werner (1984) shows that adult Mekranoti Indians in Brazil work an average total of about fifty hours.

8.5 hours Gardening
6.0 hours Hunting
1.5 hours Fishing
1.0 hours Gathering wild food
33.5 hours All other jobs.

> *Altogether, the Mekranoti need to work less than 51 hours a week, and this includes getting to and from work, cooking, repairing broken tools, and all other things we normally don't count as part of our work week. (p. 160)*

People in industrial societies work much longer: at least forty hours on the job, *plus* commuting and doing domestic chores for a total of seventy to eighty hours a week easily.

The following incident shows the same lack of interest in material possessions that Johnson found among the Machiguenga (Werner, 1984):

> *Despite their fascination with manufactured goods, the Mekranoti were not ready to accept everything civilization had to offer. Once, while sitting in the men's house, 'Omexti asked for a tool to fix an arrowhead. I dug into my pockets and pulled out an elaborate Swiss army knife I had brought along. By the time I opened it and handed it to 'Omexti, he had already fixed his arrow with a twig he pulled from a tree. Out of curiosity he examined my knife for a few minutes, then handed it back. "What good is this?" he asked. "Did you work to get it?" He then spent the next few minutes patiently explaining that some of the things kuben made were just not worth the trouble. "It's better to have more time to talk to your neighbors," he lectured. (p. 269)*

It is important to note here that some social scientists consider *pastoral societies* an important variant of human societies. Friedl discusses them but Lenski and Lenski do not. Pastoralists domesticate and raise cows, sheep, or other animals, whose meat, milk, and other products they rely upon for food, clothing, and so on. Friedl (1981) describes them socially resembling horticulturalists in all their variety.

Agricultural Societies

Agricultural societies, unlike those of gatherers-hunters and horticulturalists, are still very much in existence today. By the mid-1700s most people in the world, especially in Asia and Europe, were peasants making a living off of ancestral farms. Industrialism began to change these societies after 1750. In many respects the peasant society is a cherished ideal for many people. The more positive aspects of the peasant culture, such as tightly knit communities, vivid ethnic traditions like folk dances, and even food, are much sought after and revered. Most people who have come to the United States left peasant villages for life in industrial and urban communities. Albania and Greece, where I lived the first fourteen years of my life, are still adjusting to the momentous changes occurring as they make the transition from agriculture to industrial societies. The peasant traditions and institutions are at the same time co-existing with and struggling against the new order. In India, China, Latin America, and elsewhere, millions of people still live in peasant villages. The plow and the oxen still cultivate the land as airplanes and satellites fly overhead and radio and television blare out music and information. The transition from one society to another society is usually long and often painful.

Population

Agricultural societies support much larger populations than either gathering-hunting or horticultural societies. Early agricultural societies numbered in the millions and supported cities of up to 100,000 people. Advanced societies today are often ten times larger than earlier ones, and their cities have reached populations of a million, with total populations of well over ten million. Some parts of Russia and China are still largely agrarian. In these societies, the urban population never exceeds 10 percent of the total population: cities are supported by the production, labor, and taxes of the peasants (Lenski & Lenski, 1978).

Making a Living

It is estimated that between five and six thousand years ago some societies began to plant grains. Plows pulled by oxen or other animals prepared the land for planting. Food was produced on less land. Plows brought up more nutrients from deeper in the soil, and farmers began to use fertilizers from cows, horses, and other animals. People were then able to cultivate the same piece of land for generations (although wise peasants usually allowed different plots to lie fallow every two to four years). Since grains can be stored, agrarian societies had surpluses of food. So, with a plow and two oxen a family could work a much greater area than horticulturalists could. Besides the plow, agricultural societies made other changes and inventions. Animals not only pulled plows but they also transported goods; the wheel was invented for use on wagons and to make pottery; windpower was used to sail ships and boats and later to draw water from the ground; and writing and the calendar were invented. These and other changes changed life and social relationships.

In today's agrarian societies, peasants do all the work on their farms. They plant and sow, take care of the animals, and build their houses and barns. Most peasant families live in the same village and work the same piece of land for generations. They have a deep attachment to land, house, and village. My family on my father's side has been in the same Albanian village for sixteen generations or about four hundred years. My father was born in the same house in which he now lives, and he has lived all of his life in this village, except for the years away at school and time in the army.

Social Organization

The differences between an agrarian society and the other two types of societies are not limited to population size, food production, and other material and mechanical devices. There are profound differences in institutions and social relations. Power is more concentrated, social classes are more pronounced, and the peasants who work the land are more exploited by the ruling classes and urban residents. Civilization with its advances in food production and machinery is a mixed blessing.

The rise of the state as a form of government is one of the most significant changes that took place in the early transition from horticultural to agrarian societies. A state is a large, centralized form of government. Gatherers-hunters and simple horticulturalists have no leaders and no central governments. Chiefdoms feature some centralized power and control, but, in theory at least, there are kinship ties between the chief and the people. A state, on the other hand, is not based on kin ties, or necessarily a common culture or ethnic heritage among the people. The Roman empire contained many cultures and ethnic groups; Britain joined into one state at least four different ethnic groups: English, Scottish, Welsh, and Irish. Moreover, the rulers are not bound by obligations, they need not reach a consensus with those they rule. They can, and often do, act on their own will alone (Friedl, 1981).

Peasants in agricultural societies have been tied to a centralized authority (the state) whose laws they must obey and to whom they must pay taxes (often in the form of large portions of their harvests). Experts and officials from urban centers have dictated policies that have governed these people who make their living from the land. Peasants have come to rely heavily on manufactured goods and the services of specialists (Friedl, 1981).

The history of agricultural societies is strewn with examples of extreme exploitation of the peasants. Landowners, primarily the aristocracy, levied heavy taxes on the peasants—so heavy, in fact, they were often barely able to feed themselves. In contrast to horticultural societies, where those who worked the land were able to provide for themselves, peasants in agricultural societies were very likely to be serfs or slaves. The Russian aristocracy, most of whom lived in opulence, owned millions of serfs who were regarded as little more than human machinery and who lived in abject poverty and misery. It is little wonder that peasant revolts were commonplace. Lenski and Lenski (1978) note that "internal struggles occurred in all advanced agrarian societies." (p. 196) From 1801 to 1861, there were 1,467 uprisings in Russia.

Poverty, exploitation, and inequality has not been limited to the countryside, however. They have been prevalent in cities, too. Begging, poverty, crime, and prostitution have been the fate of thousands of urban residents. Some historians estimate that from 10 to 30 percent of city populations are beggars (Lenski & Lenski, 1978).

Inequality and exploitation pervade agricultural societies. According to Lenski and Lenski (1978), there are three "social cleavages" in these societies: between a small ruling class and the masses of people; between a small urban minority and the majority of peasants; and between a tiny literate minority and the illiterate masses. It is obvious that the exploited group in all three instances is composed mostly of peasants.

In addition to exploiting the peasant masses, the ruling class has turned to conquest and warfare to increase its wealth and power. Over two thousand years of European history show this kind of conquest and theft by the ruling class. The soldiers who fought and died to increase the wealth and prestige of the various royalties in Europe were peasants for the most part. Lenski and Lenski (1978) think that later agrarian societies saw no major inventions because the ruling class spent its wealth and energy waging war, instead of using it for advancing agricultural methods to increase production.

Social class divisions became more complex in later agrarian societies. In addition to the ruling classes (usually royalty in Europe), there arose a middle class, usually merchants and various skilled laborers. For the most part, these people led more comfortable lives than most peasants. It was the more wealthy merchants, and later industrialists, who fought the old landed aristocracy for control of the state in many European societies.

Monetary systems, which were created in the latter part of the agricultural period, made the activities of merchants, middle people, and traders more possible. Merchants generated and created a demand for their goods. Columbus was looking for a shorter route to India to expedite and advance trading by merchants (Lenski & Lenski, 1978).

As the urban centers of agricultural societies grew so did the kind and number of specialists. In Barcelona, Spain, in 1385 there were one hundred occupations, among them: sailors, shoemakers, tailors, fishermen, weavers, tanners, inn-keepers, carpenters, brokers, bakers, butchers, silversmiths, spicers, notaries, and bargemen. Specialization of work today is much more developed, of course, but in the context of human history, Barcelona in 1385 was profoundly different from the lives of gatherers-hunters (Lenski & Lenski, 1978).

Finally, the family was transformed in agricultural society. It no longer dominated as totally as it did in the two earlier societies. The state partly supplanted it. Laws and regulations, outside institutions, and occupational specialists took away some family functions. The family was no longer the sole basis of social organization, but it was still probably the most important institution in the lives and experiences of most people. It was still the production unit. Peasant families worked together to raise their own food and other needs. Even in cities, businesses were often family enterprises. The fact that arranged marriages were still the rule in many peasant societies clearly shows the predominance of family ties and family considerations (Lenski & Lenski, 1978).

Industrial Societies

Industrial societies have existed for only a small portion of human history —about two hundred fifty years. Industrial civilization, characterized by a capitalist economic system and profound national and international class conflicts and exploitation, has brought humanity to the brink of extinction. Class conflicts, exploitation, the assault on the environment, and impending nuclear war make it possible (some argue, probable) that virtually all life on this planet will become extinct. We now live with the real threat of sudden and total catastrophe, where the few survivors will envy the dead. During a celebration of Martin Luther King's birthday, my daughter's third-grade class was asked to write down their dreams or hopes (after King's famous speech, "I have a dream"). Melissa, my eight-year-old daughter, wrote her two dreams: no more pollution and no more nuclear weapons.

Population

Industrial and industrializing societies have very large populations that are concentrated in urban centers. Today, cities with a million or more inhabitants are common; a few have populations of ten million or more. In Greece, over one-third of the people live in and around Athens. In fully industrialized nations over 75 percent of the people live in and around cities. In industrializing societies, a majority of the people still live in peasant communities, but there are increasing numbers who are leaving and going to the cities. Shantytowns and shacks are found in all large cities in Latin America, Asia (with the exception of cities in socialist societies like China), and Africa. In India, people are literally living on the streets. We are now seeing homeless people in the United States, perhaps up to two million of them. Before 1900 no nation had more than half of its people living in urban sites. Britain and the United States were the first to become urbanized, with many other countries joining them.

Making a Living

In fully industrialized societies, such as the United States, only 2 to 3 percent of the people are food producers. These people rely on other workers who make the machines used to raise the food and manufacture the clothing and other necessities. The industrial era has produced an immense number of machines, inventions, and specializations (the U.S. Department of Labor lists about twenty thousand different jobs in the United States). Initially, when people left the land they went to work in factories making clothes, machines, and later cars, radios, televisions, washing machines, and other durable and nondurable goods. Since World War II, in the United States at least, about two-thirds of the population work in offices and service industries—they neither raise food nor manufacture products.

Today's industrial societies use much more energy than any of the other societies we have discussed. Some estimates show that primitive hunters and farmers used 4,000 to 12,000 kilocalories per capita daily; early industrial society used about 70,000, and the United States, in 1970, used approximately 230,000 (Bodley, 1983; citing the work of Cook, 1971). The machines, electricity, heating, mechanized food production, and so on mean that industrial societies use from twenty to fifty-six times more energy per person than earlier societies, and there are many more of us using this energy.

In a superb chapter, "Industrial Food Systems," Bodley (1983) shows that industrial food production is much more wasteful than it was in earlier economies. Machines that cultivate the land use many more calories than people recover from eating the food. In addition, energy is expended in transporting the food long distances and processing and packaging it. We are using up energy faster than it gets replaced (Bodley, 1983).

In contrast, Werner (1984), points out that "for every hour of gardening one Mekranoti adult produces almost 18,000 kilocalories of food. (As a basis for comparison, Americans consume approximately 3,000 kilocalories of food per day.)" (p. 159) Using no machines and much less energy, in one hour one Mekranoti produces enough food to feed six Americans for a day.

Social Organization

This book, like many sociology texts, focuses largely on the social organization of the United States and other industrial societies. It stresses the profound differences between earlier forms of social organization and those we find in industrial societies today. Family, community, childhood, old age, work, the environment, leisure time, all of these and more are shaped by industrialism and capitalism. Class divisions and class conflicts are increasing throughout the world; exploitation of the many by the few continues and grows; crime, poverty, and unrest are common; nuclear war is possible—probable. Three of the most important differences that separate the industrial societies from agrarian, horticultural, and gathering and hunting societies involve the family, work, and the focus of power.

Our families are very important to us. Regardless of whether we are close to our relatives, or whether we consider them uncaring, dominating, or destructive, emotionally and socially families are at the center of our existence. Yet it is also true that families today differ profoundly in structure and function from families in earlier societies. Family members simply do fewer things with each other. Most family functions we find in the other three types of societies have been taken over by other institutions. Work, education, leisure and entertainment, health care, and so on, are now the province of specialists and specialized institutions. Families may be no less important to us, but they are different.

Work has also changed dramatically. Our skills and control over work have diminished. People are doing smaller and smaller tasks, under the direction and control of others, in factories and offices away from their families. The history of industrial societies shows that people do resist, often violently, the loss of skill and control over their work. In gathering and hunting societies people have worked fifteen to twenty hours a week at their own pace and for their own consumption; horticulturalist societies have not seemed to have worked much more. Peasants may have worked more, but many of them have at least set their own pace and controlled the work process. Industrial workers have improved their lot especially in comparison to the early years of industrialization, when they worked long hours under horrible working conditions, and received low wages. Most people, however, still do not have control over their work.

Finally, power and control over others have increased. New technologies and increased production seem to be used more to control and exploit people, than to liberate and help them. As we shall see, a few nations, and within them a few people and corporations, control the political and economic institutions. In many parts of the world revolutions are occurring against national and international exploitations, against the hunger and misery millions experience. The achievements of these revolutions are uneven and uncertain. While socialist societies are creating liberating conditions, they are perpetuating old problems and creating some new ones. One thing is certain: technology, population growth, class conflicts and exploitation, and revolutions and class struggles everywhere are increasing the threat of nuclear war. Humanity will either have to survive united or fall divided.

The Conquest of the World

It must be noted that gathering and hunting, horticultural, and agrarian societies have not embraced industrialism voluntarily. Around 1800, industrial capitalists in Europe and the United States began to exploit people in Africa and Asia, as well as people within their own societies, such as the Irish in Britain. As we will see in the discussion on imperialism (Chapter 10), these people were forced to contribute land, labor, and raw materials to the factories and industries of capitalist nations. Military force, violence, criminal laws, and heavy taxes, as well as changes in local cultures, began to drastically change traditional economies and customs. Millions of people were bought as slaves or forced to relocate to work the land to raise cotton, sugar, cocoa, tea, coffee, and other cash crops for use by European and U.S. industries. Millions of acres of land were used to grow cash crops for trade and consumption in capitalist societies and were thus unavailable for raising corn, wheat, lentils, and other crops local people used to feed themselves. Lands everywhere were mined for the metals and minerals used to supply capitalism's factories. Few people and societies chose willingly to enter this capitalist world economy, which benefitted only a few and exploited many. (See Bodley, 1982; Wolf, 1982; and discussion of imperialism in Chapter 10.)

A Summary of Social Changes

The following summary lists the important changes in human societies that have taken place since the earliest gathering-hunting societies.

■ More and more functions have been taken away from the family and given to other institutions. Families are also smaller.

■ Inequalities have appeared and intensified: men over women, one class over another, rulers and specialists over everyone.

■ The division of labor has intensified. Most people's work is controlled by others, and some of their product is taken away by others.

■ Warfare has appeared, spread, and intensified and may culminate in the destruction of humanity. According to Bodley (1983), warfare appears and intensifies as a result of social inequalities and specializations. (See Chapter 8.)

■ Societies have increased the exploitation of the natural world, using resources beyond the capacity to replace them and damaging and destroying environments. We have sought mastery, control, and exploitation of the environment, not peaceful coexistence with it.

Society and Its Relationship to the Natural World

One moonlit night, toward the end of his stay with the Mbuti, Turnbull (1961) heard a noise from the nearby woods. He went over to see what made it.

> *There, in the tiny clearing, splashed with silver, was the sophisticated Kenge [Turnbull's friend], clad in bark cloth, adorned with leaves, with a flower stuck in his hair. He was all alone, dancing around and singing softly to himself as he gazed up at the treetops. [Turnbull asked Kenge why he was dancing alone.] He stopped, turned slowly around and looked at me as though I was the biggest fool he had ever seen; and he was plainly surprised by my stupidity.*
>
> *"But I'm not dancing alone," he said. "I am dancing with the forest, dancing with the moon." Then, with the utmost unconcern, he ignored me and continued his dance of love and life. (p. 272)*

The !Kung, in addition to their knowledge of 500 species of animals and plants, are attuned to their environment in other ways. For example they can look at footprints in the sand and identify the specific person who made them. According to Shostak (1981), "The !Kung can easily recognize the tracks of any person they know well, as well as a number of others, and they can tell much about a person's circumstances and behavior by reading this record in the sand." (p. 379)

Native North Americans are also close to and respect and revere the earth (McLuhan, 1971).

> *They speak with courtesy and respect of the land, of animals, of the objects which made up the territory in which they lived. They saw no virtue in imposing their will over their environment: private acquisition, almost without exception, was to them a way to poverty, not to riches. The meaning of their life was identified through their relationships with each other and their homelands—all of which was given depth and resonance by memory. (p. 1)*

McLuhan goes on to quote Indians and Indian sayings that show this reverence for the land.

> *Holy Mother Earth, the trees and all nature, are witnesses of your thoughts and deeds. (p. 5)*
>
> *We love quiet: we suffer the mouse to play; when the woods are rustled by the wind, we fear not. (p. 5)*

What is life? It is the flash of a firefly in the night. It is the breath of a buffalo in the winter time. It is the little shadow which runs across the grass and loses itself in the sunset. (p. 12)

Ohiyesa (Charles Eastman), a native American who lived in the early 1900s, tells of burial places where "the outward signs of burial had been long since obliterated," which his grandmother would point out to him and his brother. He always found bones in such places. He attributed her ability to locate such graves to "remarkable powers of concentration and abstraction" and to a spiritual community with nature. (p. 7)

Bodley (1983) argues that primitive people, especially gatherers-hunters, see themselves as part of nature. They recognize that nature must not be exploited and abused, and their conception of the good life assumes *limited* material wants and desires but rich human relations. Primitive people see themselves as "part of nature and may name [themselves] after animals, impute souls to plants and animals, acknowledge ritual kinship with certain species, conduct rituals designed to help propagate particularly valued species, and offer ritual apologies when animals must be killed." (p. 56)

Increasingly, as societies have supposedly advanced, people have sought to dominate nature rather than share it with other living species; they have sought to transform it, rather than seek to understand it and live within its limits. Frank DiLuzio (Steiner, 1976), the former director of the Los Alamos Scientific Laboratories, commented that when Indians see a running brook they appreciate the sound and beauty of the scenery, unlike industrial people who see it as a way of making electricity.

The following discussion examines in detail how industrial societies in the last one hundred years have changed, damaged, and in some cases even destroyed environments. It will also discuss how individuals, groups, and governments are working to stop the damage and to return to the ecological wisdom of our ancestors.

A Growing Threat to the Environment

Ecology is not a narrow area of study. It deals with more than polluted rivers and lakes. As Barry Commoner (1976) has shown, ecology refers to the totality of our relation to the environment (which includes people), the quality of life, and how we manage to make a living from the earth, water, and air around us. The problem of modern ecological disaster arose out of the imbalance of the three systems in which we live.

The ecosystem—the great natural interwoven, ecological cycles that comprise the planet's skin, and the minerals that lie beneath it—provides all the resources that support human life and activity.

The production system—the man-made network of agricultural and indus-

*trial processes—converts these resources into goods and services, the real
wealth that sustains society: food, manufactured goods, transportation, and
communication.*

*The economic system—the recipient of the real wealth created by the pro-
duction system—transforms that wealth into earnings, profit, credit, savings,
investment, taxes; and governs how that wealth is distributed, and what is
done with it. (pp. 2–3)*

The economic system depends on the productive system, which depends
on the ecosystem. Without the ecosystem we cannot survive. Therefore, to
insure our survival we should understand, respect, and protect the air, earth,
and water around us. The environmental crisis has arisen because the economic system and the production system no longer operate within the bounds
of the ecosystem. To insure high profits for corporations (the capitalist economic system), technologies have been created, such as gas-guzzling cars that
both deplete the earth's limited resources and pollute air, earth, and water
(Commoner, 1976).

Our relationships to the environment are many and are affected by
many aspects of our life style. Besides the pollution caused by auto emissions,
pesticides, and other chemicals, the kind of food we eat (sugar and processed
foods) may affect us. The energy we use for transportation and the manufacture of products exhausts nonrenewable, limited natural resources and pollutes the environment. Our use of land is still another aspect of how we relate
to the environment. The noise of cars, planes, and industry; the additives in
our food; the amount of waste we throw away—all these are aspects of
ecological imbalance. Ultimately, these destructive ways of relating to the
environment take their toll on our physical, emotional, and social health.

Exhausting Natural Resources

Industrial and capitalist societies have yet to understand that there are *limits*
to the earth's natural resources. Everywhere we look we find this profound
lack of wisdom. Our bodies are made mostly of water; three-quarters of the
earth is covered by water. Water is the stuff of life. Yet we pollute and waste
it. Herbicides, pesticides, chemical dumps, leaking gasoline storage tanks,
garbage—these and more abuses poison our water and threaten our health.
Daily, it seems, one more city or town finds its water polluted.

But we also waste water. We use great quantities of it. Opie (1981)
estimates that in the early nineteenth century city residents used two to three
gallons of water per person per day; in 1980, New Yorkers used 190 gallons
of water per person per day. Between 1940 and 1980, total per capita consumption of water in the U.S. doubled (*Statistical Abstract,* 1987:188). In the
southwestern United States, where the water is pumped up from underground
supplies, the groundwater level is rapidly getting lower, and many area wells
will be dry by the year 2000 or soon after. Yet we still are not conscious of the

need to preserve water, not only in our homes but in our factories, farms, and offices. "Draining America dry" and "water, water, running out" are accurate descriptions of our problem. (See also Powledge, 1982, and *Sanctuary,* January, 1982.)

The land that grows the food we eat is also threatened. As the number of family farms decreases and the size of the remaining corporate farms increases, land will be treated with less respect and more as an investment for profit. Connecticut, for example, went from 9,000 farms (1959) and 1.3 million acres of farmland (1949), to 3,800 farms (1974) and 400,000 acres (1982). Most of the food people eat on the east coast is now shipped from California, Florida, and Mexico. These areas have the right climate but often lack water. So at the public's expense water systems are built usually for use by large corporate farms. Food is grown with enormous amounts of fertilizers, pesticides, and other chemicals. Such farming practices damage the soil, as does erosion. Bradlee (1983) notes that "each year, an average of five tons of soil per acre of farmland is lost due to erosion." Farming for profit is simply destructive to the land. Yet more ecological farming techniques, to feed everyone on earth, are possible. (See also Kitron & Schultz, 1983; Zwerdling, 1978; and Lappé & Collins, 1977.)

Wetlands and salt marshes are crucial ecological areas. Rosenbaum (1977) points out that "Wetlands are valuable breeding grounds for waterfowl and fish; they recharge groundwater supplies and filter pollution." (p. 215) Salt marshes also are necessary and productive. Rosenbaum further states that they are "among the most productive environments on earth. Their output of plant material equals that of tropical rainforests; they are twice as productive as ordinary farmlands." (p. 215) But these valuable and irreplaceable lands are being lost at a rate of 400,000 acres a year to highways, shopping malls, hotels, and other construction (Williams, 1986, and Williams, 1984b).

The great forestlands of the world are also essential for our survival. They provide the oxygen we breathe, wood, habitats for animals, and peaceful places to walk and hike. Yet they are constantly abused by corporations and governments seeking to dig out coal and other minerals. The U.S. Congress in the early 1980s passed a wilderness bill protecting some forests, but the law is limited and the pressure to exploit the land is constant. Turning to forests for energy through burning wood could also be catastrophic. New technologies to use wood for heating homes and other energy uses demand vast clearcutting of forests (all trees are cut down), causing permanent damage to the environment. To save oil we may be turning to wood, but we cannot afford to consume wood at the same rate we have been consuming oil just to perpetuate our present life styles. We have yet to learn that there are limits on us, everywhere. (See Harris, 1981, and Reid, 1982.)

The tropical forests in the Amazon and Central America are destroyed to raise cattle for beef exports to the United States and elsewhere. After five to eight years, the cleared land, often cleared with poisonous herbicides, is hard and unproductive, and often abandoned. But for those few years it makes profits for the rich cattle ranchers and corporations, at enormous cost to the environment. Skinner (1985), in his article, "Big Mac and the Tropical Forests," chronicles the rape of these forests.

> *These are the harsh facts: the tropical forests are being leveled for com-mercial purposes at the rate of 150,000 square kilometers a year, an area the size of England and Wales combined.*
>
> *At this rate, the world's tropical forests could be entirely destroyed within seventy-three years. Already as much as a fifth or a quarter of the huge Ama-zon forest, which constitutes a third of the world's total rain forest, has been cut, and the rate of destruction is accelerating. And nearly two thirds of the Central American forests have been cleared or severely degraded since 1950.*
>
> *Tropical forests, which cover only 7 percent of the Earth's land surface (it used to be 12 percent), support half the species of the world's living things. (p. 25)*

Most people have been, and still largely are, ignorant of the problems of water, farmland, and forests. But we have known for over ten years about the energy crisis. In the short run, we have curbed the increase in the consumption of oil and other energy sources.

As we mentioned before, industrial societies use much more energy than did earlier societies. There are more people using the earth's nonrenewable resources (oil, coal, gas) for energy instead of renewable resources like wood. U.S. per capita energy consumption went up 62 percent from 1950 to 1973, declined slightly in the mid 1970s, reached the 1973 level in 1978 and 1979, and by 1985 had declined by 12 percent compared to 1973. Even though 59 percent of energy used in the United States is lost because of inefficiency, the government policy still focuses largely on increased production of energy sources, not on conservation. The historical development of human societies clearly shows that if we use nonrenewable energy sources at our present rate, sooner or later we will exhaust them. (See *Dollars and Sense,* July-August, 1980, and *Statistical Abstract,* 1987:543.)

This brief look at our natural resources and our use and abuse of them should make us aware of the need to conserve and to change our basic life styles. Industrial and capitalist societies cannot continue their wasteful and excessive use of the world's natural resources, nor can the developing societies expect to be able to follow this pattern. Wood, unlike oil, gas, or coal, is renewable but needs to be cultivated and harvested properly and used wisely. It cannot be used as a replacement for oil. Moreover, burning wood, especially in airtight stoves, also causes air pollution. Solar energy can be used, but we need to use minerals (limited resources) to collect the sun's energy if we are to use large quantities of energy to support present consumption rates. Other alternative energy sources have their own risks. There is no escaping the need to reduce energy consumption, to protect and wisely use our resources (*Boston Globe,* December 27, 1982).

Polluting Air, Earth, Water

We are not only exhausting and destroying food and natural resources, we are polluting the air, ground, and water where these resources are found. The air we breathe, the water we drink, the food we eat are poisoned and polluted. The byproducts of the capitalist life style, one that is driven by profit and the domination and exploitation of nature, pollute the world around us. Examples of this abound.

The ozone layer in the upper atmosphere protects us from the dangers of ultraviolet radiation. For sometime it has been suspected that chlorofluorocarbons (CFCs) are destroying the ozone. In 1981, government scientists published data that supported this theory. CFCs were banned in 1978 from aerosol sprays, but Kristof (1981) reports "800 million pounds of CFCs continue to be produced in the United States each year and used in foam products, refrigerators, air conditioners, and solvents." (p. 13)

Study after study keeps warning that ozone depletion poses a serious and widespread threat to the ozone layer. One study forecast an estimated 1.44 million cancer cases (*Boston Globe,* September 4, 1986:6). Worldwide production of chemicals that contribute to ozone depletion is growing by 3 percent a year. The United States produces a third of these chemicals. Scientific conferences keep warning of the problem. (See *Boston Globe,* March 10, 1987:3, and Greenbaum, 1986a.) Finally a treaty to reduce the use of ozone-depleting chemicals was signed in Montreal on September 16, 1987. Twenty-four nations, the United States among them, and the European Community agreed to reduce their use of these chemicals by 50 percent over the next twelve years. Some environmentalists worry that the reduction may be too little, too late. Another concern is that developing (poor) nations are allowed to increase their use of chlorofluorocarbons (CFCs) up to 10 percent a year over the next ten years, if they consider it necessary for their economic growth (*Guardian,* October 7, 1987:5).

Power plants and industries produce sulfer dioxide emissions that once in the atmosphere mix with nitrogen oxides and water and create acid rain. Sangeorge (1982) discusses a massive twelve hundred page study by the Environmental Protection Agency that shows acid rain is formed by emissions from the industrial midwestern parts of the United States and Canada. According to Sangeorge the report states that acid rain "is killing fish, destroying lakes and damaging man-made structures in the northeastern United States and southeast Canada." It may also be "slowing forest growth and threatening human health." (p. 1) In addition, it is eating at pipes and affecting drinking water. (See also *Sanctuary*, January, 1982:12, and Williams, 1983.)

In the middle and late 1980s, reports and studies showed acid rain and its effects spreading throughout the United States and the world. An EPA study concluded that New England has serious problems with acid rain waters. Another showed that it is spreading throughout the United States. It is found in Canada, much of it blown from smokestacks from U.S. factories. German and other European forests are affected and many trees are dead or dying. And fourteen third world (poor) countries are also showing the effects of acid rain pollution, which results from traffic congestion and heavy reliance on fossil fuels. (See *Boston Globe,* July 2, 1985:20; Williams, 1984a; Bird & Holland, 1984; Connel, 1984; Hansen, 1984; and Gould, 1985.)

Acid rain, like other kinds of pollution, threatens the very existence of many species. Mitchell (1982) reports that in parts of New England, the blue-spotted salamander is close to extinction because the waters it inhabits are poisoned by acid rain.

> *The ancestral form of the blue-spotted salamander developed sometime during the Carboniferous period, some 300 million years ago. In its time on this earth, it has survived the upwelling of continents, periods of intense volcanic activity, innumerable glacial advances and retreats, a 12-million-year drought, whatever it was that killed the dinosaurs, and any number of similarly cataclysmic events. It is certainly a testimony to the insidious effects of that relative latecomer, Homo sapiens, that the blue-spot may not survive the rain that once gave it life. (p. 2)*

In addition to sulfur dioxide emissions from factories that create acid rain, industrial societies release other substances into the air that are causing the Earth's temperature to increase. According to Dumanoski (1988), scientists at a June 1988 conference in Toronto concluded that "increases in carbon dioxide from fossil fuel burning, as well as other gases released by industrial and agricultural activity, are trapping the sun's heat like the glass in a greenhouse and causing temperatures to climb." (p. 13) There are estimates that the Earth's temperature will rise as much as nine degrees Fahrenheit in the next half century, something unprecedented in human history. But even a rise of one degree can cause the sea level to rise and flood many areas, decrease rainfall and alter rainfall patterns thus reducing food supplies, increase pollution in urban areas, and so on.

Our cars, factories, and mines produce other pollutants. Lead pollution is one of the most dangerous. For years it was thought to be only a problem for poor children who ate chipping paint in old city buildings. We now find that lead is everywhere. It is found not only in paint and gasoline (where its use is slowly being phased out) but also in fertilizers, cosmetics, ammunition, plaster, ceramic glazes, printing inks. The lead, naturally buried deep in the ground, has been mined and released in the air, water, and soil, where it stays. It does not disintegrate or disappear. At most, it moves around. It gets deposited in our bones as we breathe it in the air or eat it in food. Vegetables absorb it from the soil. It is a major health hazard for children. It kills a few children each year, causes major brain damage in others, and affects millions by lowering their intelligence, causing difficulty in concentrating and behavioral problems. In 1986, two thousand children were poisoned by lead in Boston, and in 1984 two million were poisoned throughout the United States. (See *Boston Globe,* June 30, 1985:25, 42; June 23, 1987:18.)

The risk is widespread, affecting children everywhere. Babies and toddlers get lead on their hands from crawling indoors and outdoors, and then put their fingers in their mouths. The *Boston Globe* (February 2, 1987) reported that "lead in dust comes from the weathering and flaking of old lead paint, paint removed in renovations and, sadly, from de-leading projects themselves. Lead gets into soil from paint flaking or being removed from a house, from leaded gasoline fumes and from industrial pollution." (p. 41) Three recent studies have shown that lead is also a threat to the fetus. Even at very low levels, levels three times lower than safety limits for young children, lead slows mental development during the early years of life, "impairing the child's ability to learn and perform simple manual tasks." Some lead is being removed, including contaminated soil, but people who deal with the problem claim that lead removal is very slow. (See also *Boston Globe*, January 20, 1987:1, 10; April 23, 1987:24.)

Many sources of water are being polluted—lakes, rivers, the oceans —and our major source of drinking water, groundwater. Lead is but one source. Chemicals from illegal dumps or improperly constructed waste sites seep into groundwater. Wastes from city sewers are emptied into lakes and the ocean, and radioactive wastes have until recently been dumped into the oceans, where the barrels are rusting and will eventually release the waste into the sea. Oceans, like lakes and rivers, are also being poisoned by the runoff of pesticides, chemical fertilizers, and other chemicals (Foster, 1981).

Water resources continued to be contaminated into the late 1980s. In Massachusetts, forty-one communities closed down some of their water supplies because of contamination from municipal dumps, chemical dumpings, and other pollutants. Municipal dumps in New Hampshire contaminated groundwaters (Greenbaum, 1987c). Fertilizers, herbicides, and pesticides are poisoning waters under and near farmlands throughout the United States. Toxic wastes have created a serious problem in Canadian rivers. In 1986, a chemical spill in Switzerland virtually destroyed the Rhine River, which also flows through Germany, leaving long stretches of it lifeless for many years into the future. (See also Fruhling, 1986, and *Guardian*, December 17, 1986:17.)

Love Canal in 1978 made us acutely aware of the problem of chemical wastes. In 1983 the entire community of Times Beach, Missouri, had to be closed because of dioxin in the ground and water. These are only two of the most publicized cases; there are thousands of similar cases of chemical dumping across the country. In Missouri, officials estimated that dioxin (a very carcinogenic chemical found in herbicides and other products) may be in one hundred other sites in the state. Hooker Chemical Company, which became infamous in Love Canal, New York, has buried chemicals throughout the United States. The state of Michigan is filled with PCBs and faces a major disaster. Vietnam veterans are fighting yet another war, this time against the defoliants (many containing dioxin) the U.S. military used to destroy forests. The veterans are claiming that they are suffering genetic damage because of its use. With fifty-two million tons of toxic wastes produced each year by industry, most of it buried in the ground, the United States is indeed "drowning in chemical garbage." (*Guardian*, November 12, 1980:9, provides many details on the extent and dangers of toxic chemical wastes; for more details see also the *Guardian*, May 12, 1982:2; July 28, 1982:7; February 2, 1983:5; March 2, 1983:12; Gibbs, 1981; Tallmer, 1981; and *Boston Globe*, January 19, 1983:4; November 4, 1985:41.)

We are, in fact, a society based on garbage. Marinelli and Robinson (1981) estimate that the United States produces about 160 million tons of solid waste every year, about three and a half pounds per person per day. And that is only solid municipal wastes. If we add industrial wastes, sewage sludge, junked cars, and construction and demolition rubble, we could indeed have three to four *billion* tons a year. And there are also the hazardous chemicals dumped illegally everywhere. (See also *Guardian*, May 13, 1987:11.)

In his study of garbage thrown away in Tucson dumps in the early 1970s, Rathje (1984) found that the "average household each year discards 1,800 plastic items, both wraps and containers; 850 steel cans; 500 recyclable all-aluminum cans; and more than 13,000 individual items of paper and cardboard (largely packaging)." (p. 74) They also discarded five hundred glass bottles a year. It is estimated that a hundred million pounds of plastic trash each year kill thousands of "sea birds, fish, and marine animals by entanglement and choking" (*Sanctuary,* May/June, 1987:19; see also Rathje, 1984).

Most American communities are running out of room and money to dispose of garbage. More and more municipalities are resorting to recycling, which does help. The ultimate solution, however, is to produce and consume fewer garbage-producing items. (See *Guardian*, May 13, 1987:10–11; May 20, 1987:2.)

Dangers in the Workplace

Factories, fields, offices, and other workplaces are polluted by chemicals and other substances that injure and kill many people each year. Vinyl chloride, asbestos, cotton dust, lead, and other substances abound in many factories. Some of these substances are new, others have been around but kept secret from workers for many years. Asbestos received some publicity in the late 1970s and early 1980s. This highly dangerous substance causes asbestosis, a disease of the lungs that has no known cure. Cotton dust and coal dust also damage health, as do the thousands of chemicals to which workers are exposed. It has been estimated that one hundred thousand people die each year from diseases they contract at work, and millions of others get various ailments. (See Dumanoski, 1983, and *Guardian*, September 17, 1980:6.)

Farm and field workers are not exempt from dangerous chemicals. A study of Florida farmworkers found that "48 percent of them had been directly sprayed with chemicals at least once in the previous year." Aerial cropdusting and other uses of pesticides expose these workers to chemicals daily and lead to "skin disease, sleeplessness, fatigue, and more significantly, cancer, liver damage, and birth defects." (See Zacovic, 1980, and *Guardian,* July 1, 1981:7.)

According to studies by the National Cancer Institute (Greenbaum, 1986b), "farmers who mixed or applied the herbicide 2, 4-dichloro-phenoxyacetic acid, or 2, 4-D, were eight times as likely to develop lymphatic cancer as farmers who did not use the chemical." (p. 21) Farmworkers who pick grapes and other fruit and vegetable crops in California are continually exposed to dangerous pesticides. (See the monthly magazine *Food and Justice,* published by the United Farm Workers, for the workers' side on pesticide use. April and November 1986 are two typical issues.)

We are now discovering that office workers are no safer than those in factories and fields. Well-insulated office buildings with poor ventilation systems keep in and circulate toxic substances like asbestos, carbon monoxide, formaldehyde, and ozone. Office workers often complain of headaches, dizziness, and tiredness. According to Makower (1982) some scientists think indoor air pollution may be more dangerous than outdoor pollution. Computers, photocopiers, word processors, and other technologies have "introduced a whole range of problems, from tired eyes and bad backs to cataracts and cancer" and psychological stress, sometimes leading to heart disease. (pp. 1–2) Video display terminals (VDTs) may be linked to pregnancy problems. Eight workplaces with VDTs were studied, and of ninety-four total pregnancies of women in these offices, fifty-six resulted in miscarriage or infant death. More reports add to the debate on VDTs and pregnancy. "Clusters of problem pregnancies continue to surface among VDT workers: so far 13 such clusters have been identified in the U.S., Canada, and Europe." (pp. 1–2) The low-level radiation emitted by VDTs may harm developing embryos (*Guardian,* March 12, 1986:6).

Health Problems

The many toxic substances in our environment are dangerous to adults but even more dangerous, in smaller doses, to our children. Norwood's *At Highest Risk* (1980) documents and explores the many risks the unborn and young children face in a chemicalized world. We have barely begun to find out the effects. Pregnant mothers who were given the hormone DES in the 1950s gave birth to girls who fifteen to twenty years later have a much greater possibility of getting cervical cancer, and 25 percent of these women's sons sustained genital abnormalities. Not only are many pregnancies terminated by miscarriages because of exposure to or use of various toxic substances or drugs, but many adverse health effects, such as cancers, general ill health, and lower mental development, have a greater likelihood of occurring—even though they may not appear for many years.

Mother's milk itself may not be safe. South Vietnamese mothers, exposed to dioxin from the herbicide Agent Orange, sprayed by American forces during the Vietnam War, are passing on to their nursing children in one year one hundred to four hundred times the estimated *lifetime* allowance of dioxin. A study, cited by Hart (1987), of two hundred pooled samples of North American breast milk concluded: "There is no doubt whatsoever that in one to two years, the average North American nursing infant will be given more exposure to dioxin than the CDC [Center for Disease Control, a U.S. government agency] considers allowable in a lifetime." (p. 33) DDT and other chemicals found in mothers' milk also typically exceed allowable levels. Among its other effects, dioxin has been found to effect the immune system.

Exposure to asbestos fibers also takes between twenty-five and thirty years to appear. Lung cancer and other illnesses show up in people who have breathed these fibers. Some scientists think asbestos fibers damage the body's immune system, which makes a person susceptible to illness (Cooke, 1983).

However it works in the body, asbestos is dangerous and pervasive. It first became noticed in factories, shipyards, and other workplaces, but homes and schools also contain it. Asbestos is such a reliable fire retardant and insulator that it has been used on ceilings and walls, home furnaces, and about three thousand other uses in the home. In some homes it is everpresent in the air. Between 1946 and 1972, asbestos was used extensively in schools and other buildings for fireproofing, insulation, soundproofing, and decoration. Now it is difficult to locate the source of the fibers. As of September 1982, many schools were not yet inspected, largely because various government bodies did not show much urgency in their efforts. (See Dobbin, 1983, and Stoffel & Phillips, 1986.)

Carcinogenic substances are everywhere. Hundreds of new chemicals are introduced every year, and for most of them, we will not know what their effects will be for years. The chemical industry has created two million chemicals that do not occur in nature. In 1984, according to a National Academy of Science report, 65,725 of these were heavily used in the United States. There is no information or studies on the toxicity of 78 percent of them. Even when evidence does surface, it is often suppressed. Asbestos is a classic case. At least as early as the 1930s it was known that it injures and kills, but it was only in the 1970s that workers found out the dangers they were being exposed to. A report on benzene and its effects was suppressed in 1982. Some 500,000 workers had been exposed to benzene, but it was not until seventeen workers died after being exposed to the legal (supposedly safe) limit that concern was raised. (See *Boston Globe*, August 9, 1982:9; *Dollars and Sense,* October 1982:13–15; Bale, 1983; and *Guardian*, January 21, 1987:2.)

The food we eat may also cause illness. New evidence seems to show that the antibiotics given to the animals used for food may affect our health. Heavy use of such antibiotics leads to the creation of bacteria resistant to any antibiotics. This bacteria may be transmitted to humans. Much of the food we eat is sprayed with pesticides. Some of these pesticides are banned in the United States, but corporations export them to other (poorer) countries, where they are used on food exported to the United States. In the same way, pesticides, herbicides, and other chemicals find their way into lakes, rivers, and the ocean and into the fish we eat. Chemical pollution knows no national boundaries.

(See Weir & Shapiro, 1981 for a general discussion of pollution; on food irradiation, see *Guardian,* February 26, 1986:6; on pesticides sprayed on cranberries, lawns, and elsewhere, see the entire issue of *Sanctuary,* April 1987; and on pesticides and other chemicals in our food, see Powledge, 1984a and 1984b, and especially Silverstein, 1984.)

Other items in our homes, in addition to the food we eat, may affect our health according to an article in the *Boston Globe* (April 14, 1986).

> *The American home is under attack.*
> *Noxious fumes ooze from walls filled with formaldehyde foam insulation. The toll is recorded in tearing eyes, irritated noses and throats, dizziness, nausea, headaches and rashes.*
> *Radioactive radon seeps in from underground soil and rocks, reaching dangerous levels in as many as 7 million homes, many of them in New England. The federal government says the gas may be responsible for up to 20,000 deaths a year from lung cancer—second only to cigarette smoking.*
> *And an array of exotic toxic chemicals, including cancer-causing agents such as benzene and carbon tetrachloride, escape from such seemingly harmless household products as air fresheners, furniture polishes, paints and cleaning solvents. Tests on 40 typical homes turned up 20 to 150 of the chemicals, at levels up to 45 times higher than levels outdoors.*
> *Indoor pollution isn't new but in recent years the problem has intensified as more dangerous products have been brought into homes and more pollutants have been trapped in energy-efficient buildings.*

Pollution causes psychic as well as physical injury. Three months after the accident at the nuclear power plant at Three Mile Island, women near the area exhibited three times the normal rates of clinical depression or anxiety. Three years later, their rate was still twice that found in the general population. The psychic trauma of having lived in a highly polluted area has killed some people. Three teenagers who had lived in Love Canal, New York, committed suicide because they feared they would get cancer, they would conceive abnormal children, or have health problems. (See Ackerman, 1982, and Freedman, 1981.)

The Nuclear Age

Some radiation occurs naturally. Exposure to this radiation may be no problem for most of us, but industrial societies have added greatly to the amount found in nature. Radiation from nuclear power plants, X-rays, radiation from atomic weapon tests, and wastes from these three sources present a danger to all of us. It is becoming increasingly evident that there may be no safe level of exposure to radiation. Nuclear energy and atomic weapons workers, soldiers, and civilians who were exposed to fallout from atomic tests are now seeing the effects of radiation on their health. During the 1950s, people in Utah and Nevada were encouraged to watch the atomic explosions. These people now have high rates of cancer and other illnesses—much greater than the average population. No longer trusting their government, they sued for damages in 1982. In 1984, a lower court ruled that the government was at fault for conducting the tests and causing the higher rates of cancer. But in 1987 a federal appeals court overturned the 1984 decision. The plaintiffs are planning to appeal to the U.S. Supreme Court. Birth defects and other illnesses have also increased near the Harrisburg, Pennsylvania, Three Mile Island nuclear power plant after an accident in March of 1979. The evidence is accumulating that radiation from any source is dangerous, often deadly. (See Wasserman & Solomon, 1982; Sternglass, 1981; Walters, 1982; and *Boston Globe,* April 22, 1987:13.)

Many other people have been exposed to dangerous levels of radiation without their permission or knowledge. A study by the Government Accounting Office (GAO), contradicting Pentagon claims, found that 17,000 of the 42,000 servicemen "who took part in the two atomic tests at Bikini Atoll in 1946 were probably exposed to dangerously high radiation" (*Boston Globe,* October 25, 1986:3). Others did give consent to radiation exposure, but they were assured there was no danger to them. But the 131 prisoners whose testicles were systematically exposed to large doses of x-rays from 1963 to 1973 had to consent to vasectomies at the end of the experiment. Patients at the Massachusetts General Hospital in Boston, and others, were also exposed to radiation with partial or no knowledge of what was happening to them. (See also *Boston Globe,* December 5, 1985:68, and *Progressive,* November, 1986:12.)

Three Mile Island, as frightening as it was, released relatively little radiation compared to that released from nuclear weapons. Yet it had dramatic and clear effects. Let us look at the findings (Wasserman & Solomon, 1983):

> *Dr. Ernest Sternglass, a professor of radiology at the Pittsburgh Medical School, has charged that the death rate among infants in Harrisburg skyrocketed in the three months immediately following the T.M.I. [Three Mile Island] accident to triple what it had been for the same period in 1977 and 1978. The State of Pennsylvania and Metropolitan Edison—owner of T.M.I.—at first denied there was such a rise, and when the state's own figures confirmed it they argued it was merely a "coincidence." But an increase from 8.1 per thousand in the spring of 1977 and 11.5 in 1978 to 29.7 per thousand in 1979 is too great to dismiss as a coincidence. Moreover, the neonatal death rate—infants dying before one month of age—was even more striking, jumping from zero per thousand in the spring of 1977 and 7.6 in 1978 to 29.7 per thousand in 1979.*
>
> *Dr. Gordon MacLeod, who was Pennsylvania secretary of health at the time of the T.M.I. incident, has also used state statistics to demonstrate a marked rise in hypothyroidism among children born in southeastern Pennsylvania—downwind from T.M.I.—after the accident. The disease is common among Marshall Island children born downwind from the bomb tests there. (p. 16)*

Nuclear energy has many problems. Plant construction often has design errors and defective material. Safety precautions are lax. Above all, there is yet no safe method or place to dispose of the wastes from nuclear power plants (and other users of radiation). No one wants the dumps in their backyard. These radioactive wastes will continue to be dangerous for thousands of years, up to half a million years from now. The oceans have been used to dump nuclear wastes, but they offer no long-term solution. Even if no more nuclear power plants and weapons were produced, we would still have waste that we cannot dispose of properly. (See Claffey, 1982; *Guardian,* April 21,1982:9; and Polsgrove, 1983.)

Since 1983, it has been obvious that nuclear power is on the way out. Construction of proposed power plants has been cancelled, and no new orders for plants have been placed since 1978. There are at least four reasons for this: the escalating construction costs, the problems of safety and of disposal of wastes, the drastic decrease in demand for electricity from projections of the 1960s and 1970s, and citizen opposition to nuclear power. Many people protest against nuclear power because of the dangers to health and environment; others refuse to finance the construction of such plants by refusing to pay electric companies for their construction costs. In Washington state, citizens revolted against paying for failed nuclear plants. The Pilgrim plant in Plymouth, Massachusetts, was shut down in April 1986 because of numerous safety problems and violations and may never open again. As of summer 1988, the newly built plant in Seabrook, New Hampshire, had not been given the license to begin operating because nearby communities and the government of Massachusetts argue that it would be impossible to evacuate nearby residents in the event of an accident at Seabrook. It may never open. Many people have struggled since 1976 to prevent it from ever operating. It may be premature to announce the end of the nuclear power industry, but it is clearly on the wane. (For further discussion of nuclear power see Wasserman, 1982; *Dollars and Sense*, January 1983:12–17; Gould, 1984; Alpert, 1987; and *Guardian*, August 6, 1986:10–11.)

The debate about the safety of nuclear power reached new levels following the accident at the reactor at Chernobyl in the Soviet Union on April 26, 1986. An accident that the Soviets had claimed had only one in ten thousand chances of happening, did happen. An accident that U.S. nuclear power interests argued immediately after Chernobyl could not happen in the United States, may indeed happen: the Nuclear Regulatory Commission has estimated that in the next twenty years there is a 45 percent chance of an accident in the United States similar to the one at Chernobyl. In fact, about half of the U.S. nuclear reactors are very similar to the one at Chernobyl, and no U.S. reactor could have withstood the force of the explosion at Chernobyl. As more U.S. nuclear reactors are being shut down for numerous safety violations, we cannot feel at all safe that Chernobyl is impossible in the United States. Many accidental releases of radiation have occurred, and there *was* Three Mile Island in 1979.

The accident at Chernobyl apparently resulted both from human error and technical deficiencies. Its effects have been drastic. In the months after the accident thirty-one people died from radiation poisoning and 237 others are seriously ill. There is a continuing debate about the long-term effects, which have been and will be followed closely in the next few years. There are estimates of between five thousand and forty thousand deaths from cancers due to radiation exposure (the forty thousand estimate comes from Soviet scientists). Genetic effects, in the Soviet Union and surrounding countries, may never be fully known. In the months following the accident, food, such as milk, meat, and cheese, was contaminated in the USSR, Poland, Sweden, Germany, and other places.

The area around Chernobyl was devastated and remains empty. Twenty-seven communities were emptied—135,000 people were evacuated. It will be years before it is safe for people to return. It may be many decades before people may safely live near the area immediately around the plant.

Despite the devastation, supporters of nuclear power in the United States, Soviet Union, and elsewhere, still insist that nuclear power is safe and must be developed. But Chernobyl has had a sobering effect on millions of people. Since Chernobyl, resistance to nuclear power has grown everywhere. People can no longer be dismissed when they raise concerns and questions about nuclear power and its safety. (See *Guardian,* May 14, 1986:3; June 11, 1986:13; June 18, 1986:18; August 20, 1986:21; September 24, 1986:17; April 29, 1987:19; *Boston Globe*, April 27, 1987:41, 43; June 19, 1987:1, 28; *Progressive,* October, 1986:10; Egger, 1987; Rudolph & Ridley, 1986; and Scarlott, 1986.)

Struggles to Protect the Environment

The probable end of nuclear power is one of a number of gains made in the struggle to protect the environment. Laws to prevent pollution and conserve energy have been enacted and some gains have been made. Because of strong air pollution control laws, there is now less lead and other pollutants in the air. More and more former supporters of nuclear power are opposing it. A *Dollars and Sense* (March, 1983) survey shows 78 percent of the respondents would not grant exemptions to air pollution rules even if those rules cost some people their jobs. Union members were the most opposed to any exemptions.

But business opposition to laws and regulations limiting their polluting practices has been unremitting. They see protection of the environment as a threat to their profits and control. Large corporations have an enormous amount of control and influence over the government (see Chapter 10), but their power became especially obvious and their destruction of laws protecting the environment notably more blatant during the Reagan administration. Any compromise, moderation, and appearance of protecting the environment were abandoned and an assault was launched against most protections of workers, the public at large, and the environment. The catering to business interests finally outraged even the conservative Congress. Members of Congress put pressure on the administration, and in early 1983, several top administrators of the Environmental Protection Agency (EPA) resigned. According to Clay-brook (1984) these officials made no attempt to camouflage their service to business interests over the environment.

Even as bad as the Reagan record has been, it is a mistake to think things were better before his administration. Gains for the protection of the environment have been at best minimal and more appearance than reality. The longterm trend of industrial capitalism has been one of destruction and degradation of the environment.

There is no need here to present the details of the assault on the environment and workers that has occurred during the early 1980s. The budget of the EPA, inadequate even before 1981, was cut by more than a third. EPA officials who tried to enforce the laws were fired, harassed, and made ineffective. Reports critical of business practices were changed or never published. Regulations to remove chemicals or other dangers from workplaces were ignored, changed, or not enforced. Any policy, regulation, or law that meant corporations would have to spend money to protect workers or the environment was judged too costly. Capitalism at its worst—profits over people—triumphed. (See *Guardian,* July 22, 1981:2; August 26, 1981:4; September 2, 1981:2; September 23, 1981:9; May 26, 1982:1,10; June 9, 1982:4; and July 14, 1982:3.)

Generally speaking, our industrial capitalist society has been and continues to be harmful to the environment. But despite this trend there have been some efforts to check pollution and protect the environment. In the 1970s, a number of laws were passed to protect people and the environment. The 1970 Occupational Safety and Health Administration (OSHA) is a limited tool for workers to protect themselves from dangerous chemicals and other conditions. The 1970 Clean Air Act has helped reduce air pollution. With 1975 serving as a baseline of 100, standard measurements in 1984 show carbon monoxide was down to 66, sulfur dioxide to 67, nitrogen dioxide to 90, and lead to 30. (See *Guardian,* December 3, 1986:5, and *Statistical Abstract,* 1987:190.)

The Reagan administration's efforts to dismantle environmental programs have been somewhat mitigated by environmentalists who have kept the pressure on Congress. The Congress was able to pass regulations that impose stricter regulations for monitoring hazardous waste sites. It defeated attempts to weaken clean air regulations, and gas and oil exploration in wilderness areas was limited or prohibited. (See *Guardian,* January 27, 1982:1; September 1, 1982:6; December 15, 1982:3; and *Boston Globe,* October 19, 1982:3; January 1, 1983:49.)

Environmental gains, some limited and some more significant, are being made. Residents of Woburn, Massachusetts, won a suit against a corporation whose chemical dumping had polluted groundwater and caused a large increase in the leukemia rate in Woburn. The bald eagle and other rare and endangered species have begun to show some recovery since the pesticide DDT was banned. Despite the continued loss of wetlands, the courts and the EPA will probably stop the building of a shopping mall in Attleboro, Massachusetts, that would destroy wetlands. As landfills become more scarce, and as people realize the burning of trash to produce energy is polluting (it emits dioxins and other matter), more and more cities and states will require recycling. Some states are buying farmland and keeping it permanently for farming, to prevent its commercial development. Although President Reagan vetoed a bill requiring appliance manufacturers to build more energy efficient appliances, Massachusetts passed such a bill in 1986. Finally, Congress overrode President Reagan's veto in early 1987 and passed a clean waters bill. Over eight years, $20 billion will be spent, mostly for sewage treatment plants. Much remains to be done, but these gains reduce pollution, save energy, and protect the environment. (See *Guardian,* February 11, 1987:9; *Boston Globe,* December 28, 1985:36; Greenbaum, 1987b; *Sanctuary,* May/June, 1987:19; Moore W., 1987; Greenbaum, 1987a; and *Guardian,* February 4, 1987:2.)

We may also be witnessing the emergence and growth of a new consciousness, a realization that all of us must wage a long-lasting struggle against the destruction of industrial capitalism. Such a struggle involves many groups organizing, educating, and resisting on many fronts. Poor blacks in Afton, North Carolina, are trying to stop a chemical dump site in their town. Workers are insisting that chemicals be removed from their workplaces. Farmers and others are organizing and banning herbicides in Oregon. People on Long Island, New York, are finding out about and working to stop the use of pesticides that are poisoning their waters. Native Americans are continuing their centuries-long struggle to resist the exploitation of their homelands. Thousands and millions of people are protesting against nuclear power and nuclear weapons. As I stood among the almost one million people who were demanding nuclear disarmament in New York City on June 12, 1982, I was filled with a hope that finally we may be witnessing the reappearance of an environmental consciousness. The banners and the pamphlets passed around spoke not only of the opposition to nuclear weapons, but they also celebrated mother earth, pleaded for human needs over corporate profits, urged jobs not weapons, and proclaimed life over death. The destruction visited upon the earth has been profound and pervasive; the effects will be felt for hundreds of years. Industrial capitalism will not give up easily. The hope that a new consciousness is arising may be quixotic. Nevertheless, it is a hope that is based on the struggles of many groups now fighting for a new ethic, a new society based not on profit, not on the interests of corporations, not on more and more material possessions but on respect for each other and the environment, on meeting all people's basic needs, on the realization that we must live with the natural world, not against it. (See *Guardian*, October 20, 1982:8; Jackson & Wright, 1981; Goldfarb & Wartenberg, 1983; Day, 1983; Freudenberg, 1984; and Polsgrove, 1984.)

One of the obstacles to protecting the environment has been people's fear that jobs would be lost as a result of laws regulating air and water pollution, exploitation of wilderness areas, and other environment protection measures. Environmentalists and workers have seemed to oppose each other at times, but recently there have been signs of recognition on both sides. I have mentioned the *Dollars and Sense* (March 1983:19) poll that shows 78 percent of those interviewed oppose weakening of anti-pollution laws, even if some jobs would be lost. But over and above this, there is an emerging alliance of workers and environmentalists that is arguing that air pollution and other dangers affect all people, workers especially, and that protection of the environment means more jobs, not fewer. (See also Dumanoski, 1983.)

Clean water, clean air, offices and factories free of dangerous chemicals, forests and farmlands free of herbicides and pesticides, energy conservation, freedom from the dangers of radiation—all these concerns, and more, are aspects of one issue. The short-term fear of losing a job cannot compensate for the threat to our lives and health.

The fear of losing jobs because of laws protecting the environment is not based on facts. Decentralized solar energy companies create jobs; reforesting lands and cleaning up rivers create jobs; energy conservation creates jobs. But jobs *are* lost when corporations move out of the United States to places where labor costs are lower (over a million jobs from 1966 to 1973). Jobs are lost when corporations invest in new technology that reduces the workforce. Jobs are lost when the United States government develops military weapons rather than programs for meeting human needs. Corporate control and profits, and a militarized society, would decline from protecting the environment—jobs would not. (See Dumanoski, 1983, and Anderson, 1980.)

Towards an Environmental Consciousness

An environmental consciousness requires a sense of limits and reduced consumption. (People in poor countries, of course, need to increase their consumption of food and other basic needs.) We need to understand that the environment imposes limits on us—we cannot exploit and pollute it without serious consequences to ourselves. We need to recapture the sense of limits and respect for the environment that pre-industrial people had (Bodley, 1983).

Technological progress usually brings undesirable consequences. As an example, Levins (1986) mentions the Aswan Dam in Egypt, which brought more than electricity.

> *The Aswan Dam was an engineering success in that it retained the water it was intended to retain. But by stopping the seasonal flooding that provided renewed soil fertility, the dam made farmers dependent on imported chemical fertilizers; the reduced flow of water into the Mediterranean Sea increased salinity and adversely affected fisheries; the outflow of the Nile was reduced to the point that it could no longer offset the erosion of the coastline; the irrigation ditches became the habitat for snails that transmit liver flukes. (p. 18)*

Many disasters in 1985 and 1986 were warnings that technology and progress bring mixed blessings. The gas poisoning and death of over two thousand people from the accident at the Union Carbide plant in Bhopal, India, the Challenger and Chernobyl disasters, and the spilling of the deadly chemicals into the Rhine River in 1986 all remind us of the limits and consequences that accompany technology. (See Engler, 1985, and Chandler, 1986.)

We resort to pesticides because we want more perfect-looking fruit, and we encourage pest infestation by growing vast fields of one crop instead of alternating rows of different crops. But despite the use of more pesticides, some pests develop a resistance to the chemicals used to kill them, and they continue to multiply profusely. We then use more and even stronger pesticides, polluting the environment even more. We need to use known organic methods to control pests and put more effort and money toward developing organic farming. (See Slater, 1986; *Boston Globe,* April 19, 1986:1, 15; and *Sanctuary,* April 1987:15.)

To deal with the enormous amounts of plastic and other garbage we produce, corporations have built high-technology incinerators that burn garbage to produce energy. That seems an easy and profitable solution, but some people argue that these incinerators emit dioxins and other dangerous substances. The solution to too much garbage is much less garbage and recycling, not technological miracles. We cannot consume and waste resources without a price. (See *Guardian,* May 13, 1987:10–11.)

Some people think that renewable energy is the solution to resource depletion. Instead of heating our homes with oil or coal, which are not renewable, they suggest we use wood, for example. But the world could never replace wood and forests fast enough for us to consume at present energy levels. There is simply not enough land and time. And, furthermore, wood smoke pollutes the air when burned on a large scale.

Solar energy is nonpolluting and should be used. But there are not enough minerals (needed for solar collectors), sunny days (at least in some places), and earth surface to collect enough solar energy so we can consume energy at present levels. *All energy sources have their limits and consequences.* We cannot escape the fundamental reality that people in industrial societies need to use less energy and use it wisely, need to avoid pollution of the environment, and need to use all resources carefully and frugally. (See also *Boston Globe,* December 27, 1982:3.)

Capitalism and the Environment

As societies throughout the world become more industrialized, whether capitalist, socialist, or a variation of one or both, people will demand more material goods. The production of these goods will deplete energy sources and add pollutants to the air, land, and water. In capitalist societies, the corporate search for profit and wealth makes pollution and resource depletion even more pervasive and destructive. Industrial capitalism is inherently dangerous and destructive because it fosters profits over the environment and people.

Let us review some examples. Dangerous substances are used in workplaces and often are not removed even after their danger is known because corporate profits would be reduced. Chemical wastes are dumped in the ground (usually illegally) because this is the cheapest disposal method. In a capitalist society profits are the first and foremost consideration of corporations. Unsafe drugs are invented and sold; dangerous pesticides are sold in poor countries; fields are sprayed with pesticides to decrease costs and increase profits. In the short-run those corporate actions may save money, but in the long-run they cost workers and citizens their health (Commoner, 1971, 1976). (For more details, see Liazos, 1982.)

The dominance of the private car over public transportation has led to more energy consumption and more pollution. Compared to trains and electrified trolleys, cars use much more energy per rider, and they emit more pollutants.

Americans in urban areas once had and used a public transit system. In 1947, 40 percent of Americans took public transportation to work; today only 6 percent do so. Why? According to some studies, the automobile corporations bought out and systematically destroyed private public transit systems in order to increase the market and use of the cars they made. They increased their profits at the cost of much higher energy consumption and pollution. (See Snell, 1973, and *Guardian,* January 8, 1986:10–11.)

The search for more corporate profits also leads to more garbage. In order to expand their markets, corporations create more throwaway products. Plastic cups, spoons, and plates, however, become garbage that pollutes the environment since they are not biodegradable (they do not decompose). The latest product, polysterenes (Styrofoam), widely used in the fast food industry, "now provides one of the quickest-growing markets for the stagnant polymers industry. Of course, most of the polysterene is quickly converted into trash." Unlike paper products, however, Styrofoam cups and plates do not decompose —they stay garbage. Corporate expansion leads to pollution. (See *Guardian*, May 20, 1987:2; May 13, 1987:11.)

Tropical forests are also being destroyed for corporate profits. Corporate ranchers cut down the trees to create grazing lands for cattle. They make quick profits in a few years, but in many places have abandoned the land leaving it now largely barren. American fast-food corporations also profit by buying cheaper beef—$1.47 per kilogram versus $3.30 per kilogram for U.S. beef. (See Skinner, 1985; Williams, 1985b; and *Guardian*, November 5, 1986:2.)

Finally, food that is highly processed uses greater amounts of energy and chemicals than unprocessed, fresh food. Because of our life style, our work schedules, and our propensity toward the quick and easy, huge food conglomerates have developed a plethora of processed food products. These companies play on our harried lives—offering us a so-called solution to our lack of time. But the time we think we save must be counterbalanced with the energy we waste and the pollution we create. For example, in 1980 a pound of potatoes sold for sixteen cents a pound; canned, it sold for thirty-three cents. A pound of frozen french fries sold for fifty-nine cents, and as Pringle potato chips, $1.91 a pound. The more processing, the more energy and chemicals used, the higher the price. But this price merely covers the cost of production and the needed profit. It does not cover the cost of waste and pollution. (See Silverstein, 1984, and Bodley, 1983.)

Other societies, socialist and nonsocialist alike, that seek to raise their material well-being also pollute and destroy the environment. Socialist societies, in their rush to industrialize, pollute rivers and lakes just as much as capitalist societies. Poland is an example of a socialist society that sought to industrialize, but took few measures to prevent the degradation of the environment and the effects on people. A *Boston Globe* (August 12, 1984) article reported the following from Poland:

> The daily press sounds alarms about drinking milk, eating cottage cheese, ice cream or canned food. We are warned against feeding chicken to small children because chickens are fed female hormones. We are warned against feeding our kids carrots or cauliflower or soft fruit because chemical fertilizer is being misused by both the state farms and the individual farmers. . . .
>
> Huge factories and plants were built, but no funds were allotted for the installation of filters and waste disposal appliances. Waste and dirt of every kind and description were drained into rivers, lakes and the sea: gases and fumes of every kind and description were released into the air. The fact that those who were supposed to benefit from this gigantic industrialization effort would be drinking the water and breathing the air was somehow overlooked. . . .
>
> The Vistula River, known as the "Queen" of Poland's rivers, sports only 10½ miles of drinkable water. The other 640 miles of its waters are so contaminated that even a swim is a serious health hazard. The same applies to the two "Princesses," the rivers Bud and Odra. Warsaw is the only capital in Europe that does not have a sewage purification plant. Out of Poland's 500 large lakes, 300 are completely devoid of biological life. (p. A1, A4)

Kenney (1988) found that four years later environmental conditions in Poland had deteriorated even further. The city government of Wroclaw was "considering a ban on the growing of any vegetable crops because of the environmental contamination of the Silesian region." (p. 19) A protest movement has arisen to stop the pollution. For example, two thousand people marched to stop a chromium plant from polluting nearby wells.

The search for corporate growth and profits is a major cause of environmental and health problems, but not the only one. Any society that seeks technological and material growth without an environmental consciousness, without an understanding of the limits and costs of growth, sooner or later meets the consequences (Liazos, 1982).

Nuclear War

We must now live with the realization that we cannot eliminate nuclear weapons, at least not in the foreseeable future. Even if it were possible to totally deactivate and bury all present nuclear weapons, the knowledge, technology, and resources to build them would still exist and still threaten human existence. It would take little time, at most a few years, for the weapons and the means to deliver them to be manufactured again. Until and unless we change the social, political, and economic conditions that led to the creation and use of nuclear weapons, their presence will continue to haunt life on earth. These conditions, as outlined and discussed in this chapter (and later chapters), stem from social inequalities: men dominating women, one class of people dominating another class, leaders dominating the masses. These inequities create conflict between groups and nations for control and exploitation of other groups and societies. It may be difficult to realize that nuclear weapons were created and that national leaders still see them as *weapons* to be used to defeat the enemy, to control and exploit the resources of other people. The irony is that if these weapons are ever used, no one will win—the whole world will lose.

The United States government, and the corporate interests it represents (see Chapter 9), built the atomic bomb to gain military superiority. Since then it has been used as a threat (often successfully) when the United States has been losing a conventional war. For example, Ellsberg (1981) examined government documents that show President Nixon made "secret threats of massive escalation, including possible use of nuclear weapons, conveyed to the North Vietnamese by Henry Kissinger, 1969–72." (p. 6) We do not know whether the Soviet Union ever made similar threats.

I am writing these words on Easter Sunday. This holiday not only celebrates the rebirth of Christ but in a larger sense the rebirth of life as it reappears in spring. Nature everywhere is signaling the start of another season of life and growth. Shall we have many more springs? Is life close to devastation and extinction? How can it be that at the very moment I am writing, at the moment you are reading this, we are only minutes away from a potential virtual destruction of life, where the survivors will envy the dead? If we are to have any chance of survival, we must understand the real causes of the impending catastrophe, but before we examine the causes, let us look at the effects.

The Effects of Nuclear War

A paper in *The New England Journal of Medicine* by Abrams and von Kaenel (1981) describes the destruction that would occur in a nuclear attack on the United States. (The effects would be the same and even more destructive upon the USSR after an attack by the U.S.) The Federal Emergency Management Agency estimates that if a 6,559 megaton attack (about 523,720 Hiroshima bombs) occurs this is what will happen:

> *Moments after the attack, 86 million people—nearly 40 percent of the popu-*
> *lation—will be dead. An additional 34 million—27 percent of the survi-*
> *vors—will be severely injured. Fifty million additional fatalities are anticipated*
> *during the shelter period, for a total of 133 million deaths. Many of the mil-*
> *lions of surviving injured will have received moderate to high radiation doses.*
> *Approximately 60 million may survive and emerge from the shelter period*
> *without serious injury and with relatively limited radiation exposure. (p.*
> *1226)*

Those sixty million survivors will emerge into a devastated world. Fall-out radiation will be all around them for weeks, months, even years. Suffocation and heat prostration will threaten them for up to four weeks, as will dehydration. Medical care will be limited or unavailable for months and probably years. Radiation will lower disease resistance and the lack of sanitary conditions will accelerate the spread of communicable diseases. Two recent studies (*Boston Globe,* January 6, 1986), in 1985 and 1986, concluded that of all the catastrophes that will take place on earth, starvation will be the major killer. This will be due not only to the immediate devastation of land, machinery, and seed but also to the weather conditions. A 1983 conference of top United States and Soviet scientists concluded that an all-out nuclear war would first devastate the northern hemisphere of our planet and then, eventually, the southern hemisphere. In addition to the effects described above, the scientists warned that the soot and dust released from the fires of the blasts would lower world temperatures drastically by blocking out the sun. Urquhart (1984) says "For example, New England might experience temperatures of minus 20 or 30 degrees Fahrenheit in July, if the war occurred in summer." Among the effects of such drastic temperature reductions would be the impossibility of growing food. Finally, if there are future generations, most scientists believe they will be genetically damaged and have high cancer rates.

History of Nuclear Weapons and War

The United States first developed nuclear weapons in 1945. It used them that same year on two cities in Japan—Hiroshima and Nagasaki. In 1949, the USSR developed its own nuclear bombs. France, England, and China developed their own weapons in time, and other nations now have the capacity to develop them. Israel, South Africa, and India have this capability of developing nuclear bombs. Some people also suspect that South Africa has tested a bomb in the early 1980s. It is clear, however, that the United States and the USSR are *the* major military powers—each with a large arsenal of atomic weapons and delivery systems. (Delivery systems are airplanes, submarines, or land-based missiles.)

Until the late 1960s, the United States was clearly ahead in the number of atomic weapons and in its capacity to deliver them. The U.S. government used that superiority as a threat against the USSR and other nations. It is also a fact that as of 1988 the United States has refused to pledge that it will not be the first to use nuclear weapons. To do so, in the view of the U.S. government, would be to lose an important strategy position. In June 1982, at the United Nations disarmament conference, the USSR pledged not to be the first to use nuclear weapons. The U.S. government is now seeking to regain nuclear superiority. (See Ellsberg, 1981; Thompson & Smith, 1981; Sweezy & Magdoff, 1982; *Guardian,* June 17, 1982, the entire issue; and Kaku & Axelrod, 1987.)

After lagging behind for years, the USSR gained parity with the United States in 1970. Many studies came to that conclusion in the early 1980s. Each nation had more than enough weapons to kill each person on earth many times over. The means of delivering these bombs were also extensive. "The U.S. currently has 348 intercontinental bombers [airplanes], 2152 ICBM warheads [intercontinental ballistic missiles, which are land-based], and 4656 SLBM [submarine launched ballistic missiles] warheads. The Soviet arsenal is composed of 156 bombers, 5354 ICBM warheads and 1334 SLBM warheads." Herbert Scoville, a former Central Intelligence Agency deputy director, is one of many people who have concluded that in 1982 the two nations had reached nuclear weapons equality. (See *Guardian,* February 3, 1982:4, and *Statistical Abstract,* 1987:325.)

But during the years the United States had superiority, and even during the years of parity, the United States frequently threatened to use nuclear weapons—the Korean War and the Vietnam War are two examples. President Nixon was prepared to drop atomic bombs on Hanoi in late 1969, and, according to his own memoirs, he was deterred only by massive anti-war demonstrations in Washington, D.C., on October 15 and November 15, 1969. He feared he would not have enough public support for such an action (Ellsberg, 1981). (I was at that Washington demonstration on that sunny November Saturday. None of us even suspected that our presence may have helped to deter Nixon from using nuclear bombs on Hanoi. We should never underestimate the effects of resistance and demonstrations.)

The threat of using nuclear weapons may have had little effect during the Vietnam and Korean Wars, but it did notably during the Cuban missile crisis when the United States ordered the Soviets to remove their missiles from Cuba. Ellsberg (1981) lists twelve occasions when U.S. presidents threatened to use nuclear weapons. The American public did not know of these threats, but the USSR and other nations did. Every president since Truman, with the exception of Ford, apparently engaged in such threats. Reagan was not the first president to make first use of nuclear weapons part of a military strategy. This history of the use of the nuclear threat is carefully documented by Ellsberg; it is one we cannot forget. (See also Thompson & Smith, 1981.)

War, Imperialism, and Nuclear War

Some people argue that in order to reduce the possibility of nuclear war, we should increase the size of our armed forces and improve the quality and quantity of conventional weapons. Two fallacies underlie this argument. The first fallacy is that conventional wars have been very destructive and will become more so. As Klare (1982) shows in detail, cluster bombs are incredibly lethal. When they were used by Israel in Lebanon, they caused many injuries and deaths as the bomblets exploded and spread over areas of up to seventy-five city blocks. Other, old and new, conventional weapons are equally or more destructive. Millions have died or been permanently injured in conventional wars. (See *Progressive,* June 1982:4.)

But the second fallacy is even more fundamental. History shows us that the most likely use of nuclear weapons will arise during a conventional war. U.S. presidents have threatened to use nuclear weapons and continue to do so, in cases where actual or hypothetical U.S. interests (in reality corporate interests) are being threatened by the loss of a conventional war. President Carter repeatedly refused to exclude first use of tactical nuclear weapons if he saw a threat to oil resources in the Middle East. This oil is crucial to the West and was seen as being threatened by the USSR and its armed forces. President Nixon wanted to win and end the Vietnam War by visiting a devastating nuclear weapons blow upon North Vietnam. It cannot be stressed enough that the U.S. government and its corporate interests have contemplated the use of nuclear weapons in many places in the world where social revolutions have sought to overthrow exploiting governments allied with the U.S. government and corporate interests. (See *Guardian,* April 7, 1982:19; *Nation,* June 12, 1982:706; Ellsburg, 1981; Klare, 1982; and Gerson, 1985.)

It is within this context that increases in the U.S. military budget and the reassertion of nuclear superiority of the 1980s must be examined. Western imperialism has suffered significant setbacks since the 1970s. Revolutions have been waged around the world. Within the last twenty years, Vietnam, Iran, Nicaragua, and Zimbabwe have overthrown United States-supported governments. Central America is now the battlefield of the 1980s. South Africa is ripe for a long revolutionary war, and revolutions are imminent elsewhere. People everywhere are struggling against exploitation and social class injustices. As long as the United States and its allies seek to stop change and revolutions, preparations for and the willingness to use nuclear weapons first will continue to threaten us. Nuclear weapons are seen as the ultimate defense against people who are perceived to threaten corporate and imperialist interests (Sweezy & Magdoff, 1982).

The USSR has its own imperialist interests, its own concerns with domination. Afghanistan in 1979 and Poland in 1981 are constant reminders of that reality. But we cannot ignore the history that shows the U.S. government began, continues, and is escalating the proliferation of nuclear weapons. Thompson (1983) and others argue that war and nuclear war will continue to threaten humanity as long as oppression and injustice exist anywhere in the world. Solomon (1983) argues that the United States has been the main cause of the arms race. The USSR presents as much of a threat to the world as the United States and its allies. Democracy, socialism, and equality must be achieved everywhere. (See Thompson, 1983, and *Guardian*, April 20, 1983:19.)

The huge increases in the military budgets of the 1980s are an indication that the United States is trying to reassert its nuclear superiority. The U.S. government is preparing to fight and win a nuclear war. That reality is undeniable, no matter what we are told. According to an article in *The Progressive* (June, 1982), "The MX and Trident missiles now in preparation are more accurate than anything the Soviets have or expect to have soon. Thousands of small, cheap, highly accurate cruise missiles, capable of evading radar, will soon be coming off the assembly lines . . . the Russians have no defense against them and no weapons to match . . . The United States is lusting, as never before, after nuclear *superiority*." (p. 9)

Pershing missiles can reach the Soviet Union, Lens (1982) points out "within four to six minutes of launch . . . The Trident submarine will be able to direct its warheads at Moscow from a distance of 4,000 miles." (p. 25) The escalation of the nuclear arms race is obvious. And as the U.S. government rearms to dominate the world, life in the United States is deteriorating.

Wars and nuclear wars will continue to exist as long as national and international inequalities and oppression exist. This is a fundamental lesson we must learn and keep ever-present in our consciousness and daily lives. We have not learned this yet, but at some level we are beginning to glimpse some of this reality. At the very least we are beginning to understand the insanity of preparing for a nuclear war, even if we do not understand the causes for such preparations.

Demonstrations, like the one on June 12, 1982 in New York City and those in Europe, are signs of the resistance and new consciousness. Unlike the 1950s, people and even city governments are refusing to prepare for nuclear war by rejecting and ridiculing any talk that civil defense and shelters would protect people during nuclear war. The rejection is based on simple common sense. It is a revolt against the idea that a nuclear war is survivable. *Prevention* is the only possible salvation (Morrisey, 1983).

In 1987, some optimism is possible. There is increasing talk of a reduction in missiles. The Soviet Union has made a number of proposals to reduce and eventually eliminate most missiles. Moreover, in August 1985 the Soviet Union unilaterally stopped the testing of nuclear weapons and repeatedly asked the United States to join in that test ban. But the Reagan administration never joined and the Soviet Union resumed testing in February 1987.

After the huge anti-nuclear rally in 1982, the disarmament movement has been somewhat quiet. But it did succeed in getting the Reagan administration to soften its provocative behavior and join the Soviet Union in arms control talks. Tony Palomba (1987) points out that we may have made no progress in removing specific missiles and weapons, but we have raised our consciousness. With a long-term view and understanding of nuclear war and weapons, we can end the threat if we continue the struggle. During the Reagan years "we have built the largest movement opposing nuclear war that has existed to date . . . one of the most critical lessons about changing U.S. foreign policy is that the struggle is long-term. It demands consistency, commitment, and a belief that what you do today will make a difference several years later." (p. 4) People in many places are working to end the specter of nuclear annihilation. (See also Farren, 1983; *Nation,* April 9, 1983; *Boston Globe,* May 11, 1984:13; and Levene, 1985.)

Conclusion

It is an illusion to think we can dominate and control the material world around us. The history of human societies, the recent use of industrial capitalism, the destructive effects on the environment, and the potential nuclear holocaust facing us all argue for egalitarian societies that live in harmony with all plant and animal life and with the air, earth, and water. In the long history of life—human, plant, and animal—industrialism and capitalism are but very recent developments. But ironically they may also be the very elements that destroy all life unless they are changed.

Summary

People are social beings living in a natural environment. How people relate to each other and to their natural environment has slowly changed over time. Historically, people have lived in four basic kinds of societies. Gathering and hunting societies are small. People live by gathering plants and hunting animals. They are in harmony with their environment and are largely egalitarian. Horticultural societies plant gardens and support somewhat larger populations than do gathering and hunting societies. There are a few specialists (people who do not raise food), but the societies are still largely egalitarian. Agricultural societies cultivate the land using plows and fertilizers. Their larger food supplies support larger populations and more people who do not produce food. There are clear class differences and inequalities, powerful leaders and states. Warfare is common. Industrial societies substitute machines and nonhuman energy for human labor. Increased food production supports very large populations. Social inequalities are present. In industrial capitalist societies the search for wealth, profit, and power leads to the exploitation of workers and of the environment.

Five major social changes have occurred in human history: the family has lost most of its functions; inequalities have appeared; work has become specialized; warfare has appeared; and the environment has been damaged, polluted, and exploited.

In industrial and capitalist societies, the production and economic systems are in imbalance with the natural world, which gave rise to and sustains all life.

Natural resources—water, energy, air, land—are being used up faster than they can be replenished. Industrial societies pollute rivers, lakes, oceans, the land, and the air with wastes and byproducts of the production system. Pesticides used to raise crops, food additives, and so on, all pollute the environment and our bodies. Factories, offices, and fields also endanger people's health. Chemicals, asbestos, pesticides, sophisticated machines (such as video display terminals), and other substances and machines are responsible for many diseases and adverse health effects.

Nuclear power, another element in industrial societies, is also a serious threat because of dangers from the radiation produced by nuclear energy wastes that cannot be disposed of safely.

There has been limited and uneven progress in protecting the environment.

The primary threat to the environment and to life today is industrial capitalism and its search for wealth, power, and profit.

Many studies show that an all-out nuclear war would be devastating, quite probably destroying most or all life on earth. The United States has initiated and accelerated the nuclear weapons race. Presidential administrations have used nuclear superiority to threaten enemies during conventional wars or when they perceived a threat to the country's economic, political, and military power.

Warfare appeared when inequalities, private property, and powerful leaders and societies appeared. Nuclear war is the latest weapon in the history of warfare. The threat of nuclear war will exist as long as inequalities and imperialism exist.

Suggested Readings

Bodley, John H. (1983). *Anthropology and contemporary human problems* (2nd ed.). Palo Alto, CA: Mayfield. Bodley argues that gatherers-hunters and horticulturalists understood their natural and social environments well, and we can learn from them.

Claybrook, Joan (1984). *Retreat from safety: Reagan's attack on America's health.* New York; Pantheon.

Farren, Pat (Ed.) (1983). *What will it take to prevent nuclear war? Grassroots responses to our most challenging question.* Cambridge, MA: Schenkman. People of all ages and walks of life offer their views and hopes.

Kaku, Michio & Axelrod, Daniel (1987). *To win a nuclear war: The Pentagon's secret war plans.* Boston: South End. Based on recently declassified Top Secret documents, the book shows how the Pentagon has planned to fight and win a nuclear war.

Lappé, Frances Moore & Collins, Joseph (1978). *Food first: Beyond the myth of scarcity.* New York: Ballantine. The authors argue that the earth can feed all people, but it does not because only a few people who control the land and raise crops for profit, not to feed people.

Lee, Richard B. (1984). *The Dobe !Kung*. New York: Holt, Rinehart & Winston. An outstanding description of a contemporary gathering-hunting society and the changes in their culture and economy.

McLuhan, T. C. (1971). *To touch the earth: A self-portrait of Indian existence*. New York: Pocket Books. Native Americans through the centuries tell of their reverence for the land, their reflections on life, and their reactions to conquest.

Radin, Paul (1953). *The world of primitive man*. New York: Henry Schuman. Respect for the individual, irrespective of age or sex, an amazing degree of social integration, and a concept of personal security are positive features of gathering-hunting and horticultural societies.

Shostak, Marjorie (1981). *Nisa: The life and words of a !Kung woman*. New York: Vintage. A lively and absorbing story of Nisa's life from the 1920s to the 1970s in a gathering-hunting society. She is a strong, assertive, and resourceful person.

Silverstein, Brett (1984). *Fed up: The forces that make you fat, sick, and poor*. Boston: South End. The increasing corporate control of food production and increasing use of pesticides and chemicals make our food unhealthy and expensive.

Thompson, E.P. & Smith, Dan (Eds.). (1981). *Protest and survive*. New York: Monthly Review Press. Papers on nuclear war and the disarmament movement.

Turnbull, Colin (1983). *The Mbuti pygmies: Change and adaptation*. New York: Holt, Rinehart & Winston. The Mbuti of the Ituri Forest in Zaire seek to retain their gathering-hunting life as the outside world invades their forest. Like the *Forest people,* the book is a moving account of a people Turnbull has come to know well, understand, and love.

Turnbull, Colin (1984, June). "Interview with Colin Turnbull." *Omni*, pp. 87–90, 124–134. In a very personal and intense statement, Turnbull argues that we can learn from the Mbuti and other pre-industrial people; they can help us understand ourselves and the value and meaning of life.

Wasserman, Harvey & Solomon, Norman (1982). *Killing our own: The disaster of America's experience with atomic radiation*. New York: Dell. A history of radiation from nuclear bombs, nuclear energy, x-rays, and other sources—the effects of radiation, the people affected, and their struggles to protect themselves.

Two Periodicals

Peacework: A New England peace and justice newsletter. American Friends Service Committee, 2161 Massachusetts Ave., Cambridge, MA 02140. An excellent journal of people, philosophies, strategies, and resources for peace and justice. The May 1987 issue has statements by nine peace and justice activists on the state of the nuclear disarmament movement.

Sanctuary, published nine times a year by the Massachusetts Audubon Society (South Great Rd., Lincoln, MA 01773). An outstanding magazine on the environment, environmental destruction, and struggles to protect the environment. The April 1987 issue is devoted to pesticide use and its dangers; the May/June 1987 issue discusses family farms in Concord, Massachusetts, their problems and how they manage to survive.

CHAPTER 4

Culture and Humanity

I grew up in Albania and Greece during the 1940s and 1950s. Although many things that most people in the United States take for granted—cars, radios, telephones, recorded music, refrigerators—did exist, they were not part of my daily life nor part of the lives of most people I knew. I also spoke Greek, a language that has a somewhat different conception of life than does English. In American movies and from an occasional tourist, I heard English spoken, but it sounded strange and unnatural to me.

Growing up as a Greek was different from growing up in the United States because of the language and material possessions (or, lack of them). The games I played, the way I related to people, the foods I ate and enjoyed, the music and songs that aroused feelings and emotions within me, the religion and history I was taught, all these experiences made me a Greek and different from people my age growing up in the United States and other parts of the world. When I arrived in the United States in 1955, at the age of fourteen, I was intensely lonely and longed for the familiar people, places, experiences, material objects, foods, and so on that had lent meaning to my life. I swore that I would return to Greece within five years.

But I did not return to Greece. In time, my elder brother and I became Americans. We learned to use American material possessions, to enjoy American food, and to watch TV. We also gradually learned English and most of the nuances and intricacies of the language. Our grandmother, who also came to the United States in 1955, at the age of 75, did come to use a stove, refrigerator, telephone, and other items and to eat some American foods. But she never learned to speak English, she could never understand most American customs and values, and she longed to return to her village. She never made it. She died in the United States in 1965. Despite her large family that was here, two daughters and thirteen grandchildren, despite the easier material life, she was lonely for the people, places, sounds, smells, customs, routines, foods, and language she grew up with.

A Definition of Culture

Culture is the most basic and general concept used by sociologists and anthropologists. It refers to a total way of life shared by a people in a society. It is their customs, traditions, beliefs, norms, roles, skills, knowledge of the natural and social world, and, above all, their values. Our culture is the totality of our experience as human beings. Although cultures may have similar qualities, it is the totality of each culture that gives it its uniqueness, that makes me Greek, you American, and others Navaho, Chinese, French, Ibo, Mexican, Algerian, and so forth. Before we examine this definition more closely, let us look at five other definitions of culture.

In 1871, Edward Tylor, an early anthropologist, defined culture as "that complex whole which includes knowledge, belief, art, morals, law, custom, and any other capabilities and habits acquired by man as a member of society" (Harris, 1983, p. 5). According to Friedl (1981), this definition calls attention to three qualities of culture: that it is "a whole, integrated unit"; that it is socially acquired by people and not inherently biological; and that it is a "group phenomenon," something we acquire, share, and change with other people in human groups.

Harris (1983) defines a culture as "the learned, socially acquired traditions and life-styles of the members of a society, including their patterned, repetitive ways of thinking, feeling, and acting." (p. 5) To Friedl (1981), culture is "a way of life that is common to a group of people, a collection of beliefs and attitudes, shared understandings and patterns of behavior that allow those people to live together in relative harmony, but set them apart from other peoples." (p.88)

Sociologists define culture in similar ways: Landis (1986) says it is a ". . . complex set of learned and shared beliefs, customs, skills, habits, traditions, and knowledge common to the members of a society." (p. 75) Light and Keller (1982) say it is ". . . a set of traditions and rules that shape the feelings, thoughts, and behavior of a group of people." (p. 59)

Let us look briefly now at the wide variations among cultures. In American society, a newly married couple would establish their own household. In Greek peasant society a couple would live with the groom's parents. Among the Navajo they would live with the bride's family. American teenagers learn to drive cars. Eskimo youths learn about the many kinds of snow. A young person in a gathering and hunting society learns to use a bow and arrow and the habits of many animals. Each of these skills is vital for physical and social survival within each of these societies. Americans learn to compete in play, in sports, in school, and at work; the Hopi and the !Kung are taught to cooperate and share. Some people eat pigs, others get physically ill at the mere *thought* of eating them. Ariane, my seven-year-old daughter, grimaces in disgust at the thought of eating horses. Some people worship a personal god (Christians and others), others believe in many gods (ancient Greeks among them), and others revere and worship the nature around them (the Mbuti of the Ituri Forest, for example). Among Native Americans, children are nursed up to the ages of three and four, and even up to the age of six; in industrial societies, many babies are bottle fed from the day they are born, and, if they are nursed, they are usually weaned by five to six months.

Hundreds of other examples can be cited that all point to the tremendous variety of behaviors, values, and experiences among cultures. As we shall see, people in each culture are usually convinced theirs is the best and natural one.

Culture as Life Itself

As a way of life, culture gives meaning to our existence. It is, in a fundamental way, life itself. Without culture we are not human. Without our own unique culture we are bereft and lonely. To lose one's culture is to lose something equal to life itself. We may survive physically, but we will feel lonely and empty.

Let us look at three examples. My grandmother lived for ten years in the United States. Materially she led a much more comfortable life than she ever had in Albania or Greece. Yet during all those ten years she was terribly lonely and unhappy. She missed talking in Greek, she missed the daily trips to the vegetable marketplace, she missed the long talks with neighbors, she missed all the daily and seasonal routines of her life. She was alive, but only in a physical sense.

In the *Lonely African,* Turnbull (1962) describes the predicament of African people and tribes whose cultures and economies were forcibly and violently changed and exploited by European colonizers. Many native people tried to acquire the culture of their conquerors as a way to survive. Most were rejected by the white people. They realized that they were a people without a culture—rejected by the new and unable to return to the old tribal ways. One of them, Masoudi, told Turnbull, "I died the day I left this village and went to Matadi [a nearby town where Europeans lived]—there is no point going back there. I am an old man [only in his late thirties] and I have only one worry. I believed in your world at one time, even if I did not understand it, and I tried to follow your ways. But in doing this I lost my spirit. It left me somewhere . . . and I am empty." (p. 53)

Ramon, the chief of the Digger tribe of California, in his talks with Benedict (1934), also lamented the loss of his culture. He had become a Christian and had adopted modern agriculture and life style. But he talked of the old traditions, of the dances his people performed and foods they ate, with excitement and emotion. One day he told Benedict his thoughts. "In the beginning, God gave to every people a cup, a cup of clay, and from this cup they drank their life. They all dipped in the water, but their cups were different. Our cup is broken now. It has passed away." (p. 34)

I do not know whether most of you can understand what it means to lose your culture. Most of you have never known any other culture. Few, if any, people choose to leave their culture. Wars, poverty, and other changes beyond their control have forced millions of people to leave behind family, community, and culture.

For years, I felt an intense longing for my life in Greece. I eventually became busy with studies, work, and family, and gradually forgot what I had lost. Or I thought I had forgotten. But now I realize that I did lose something and that I can never forget it. I can never be fully an American. This loss is not of any one experience, tradition, or quality of life—it *is* a total way of life, one I had led for fourteen years and one I had to abandon to start a new way of life. I can never return to the old one, but the new one is also not fully satisfactory to my spirit. In talks with other Greeks, reflecting on my own experience, and reading about other people's experiences, I have come to know that to lose your culture is to be forever incomplete.

About 1:00 A.M. on a cold February night, a friend who left Korea at age fourteen and I were talking about our lives. He said that when he goes to visit his family in Korea he always feel homeless. He has changed from the person he was when he left Korea, and to some degree Korea changed from what it was during his youth. But when he returns to the United States, even though most of his family, friends, and life are here now, he feels homeless here too.

Feeling homeless is a widespread human experience, especially in the recent past after changes brought about by industrialism, colonialism, and imperialism. As people leave their traditional cultures, voluntarily, by force, by need, or some combination of these, they never belong fully to the new culture, but they can never return to the old one. Robert Park and other sociologists from the Chicago school (1910–1930) used the term "marginal" (Stein, 1960). *Marginal people* (the marginal man) live in two worlds yet are strangers to both; they relate to two cultures but belong fully to neither. Park thought that this marginality enabled them to have a more detached and objective view towards both cultures. It may be that social marginality gives people a sharper, clearer, and more objective understanding of the society around them, but as a human and emotional experience, there is a sense of homelessness, a loss never replaced.

Culture as Human Nature

All the habits, traditions, tastes, values, social relations, and routines we learn as we grow up are natural, automatic, comfortable. It is almost inconceivable to us that people could live, think, and act differently than we do.

Culture Shock

We can learn about other cultures in a variety of ways. We can read about them, visit them as tourists, live there as visitors for a while, or settle there permanently. If we read or visit as tourists, it is likely that we will not experience the intense difference in thought, feelings, emotions, and traditions. But prolonged contact, especially with societies radically different from our own, can lead to *culture shock,* which is the emotional, intellectual, and even physical shock we experience when we encounter another culture. All the habits, assumptions, routines, and daily smells and sights we take for granted are absent. It is almost like starting life anew. But unlike infants who have no culture, we already possess one that resists the new culture around us.

When I arrived in the United States in 1955, I was surrounded by relatives who spoke Greek. But newspapers, radios, people on the street caused me daily anxiety as I struggled to understand English. But language was hardly my most serious problem. The pace of life in the United States was much more hurried than it had been in Greece. Also, Greeks walked more. The streets were always full of people, whereas here most streets are empty. It took me a long time to understand and accept the quick-paced life style dominated by the car.

I remember vividly the time a cousin tried to explain football and baseball to me. All I understood about baseball was that people held sticks that they waved at a thrown ball. For one who had grown up with soccer, these American sports were one more piece of evidence that nothing made much sense in American life. I despaired that I would never understand this new culture. (Now I know all the finer points of both sports, and I cannot understand why I was baffled by them.)

Most people who live with people of another culture experience culture shock. It threatens everything a person values and feels comfortable with. Historically, most immigrants who arrive here settle with people of their own ethnic group. Irish, Italian, Greek, Polish, Puerto Rican, and others have neighborhoods with stores and other institutions catering to their needs. In a sense, people avoid culture shock by selectively using some parts of the larger American culture and keeping some of their own. They struggle to keep the traditions, habits, language, and values of the old country. (For a moving and often humorous account of Italian immigrants in Rochester, New York, early in the twentieth century, see Jerre Mangione's *Mount Allegro.*)

But if someone moves alone to a different culture, he or she must relate to that culture. Avoiding it by living with other people from his or her past culture is not possible. Anthropologists experience intense culture shock in the first few months of their stay with native people. Living in peasant villages, among gatherers and hunters, or in tribes of horticultural people, anthropologists are often forced to survive in cultures with vastly different values, traditions, and material comforts. In time, most come to understand and even appreciate the culture of the people, but the anxiety of surviving without the tools and habits of one's culture is severe. When anthropologists report their final conclusions about the cultures they are studying, they omit any mention of the long period of adjustment they underwent. A few researchers have written of their personal experiences, and through these we have come to realize that even those people who are trained to understand and accept different cultures cannot avoid the intensity of culture shock. (For an excellent discussion, see Friedl, 1981, pp. 95–98.)

Ethnocentrism

It makes sense, of course, to feel comfortable with and prefer the foods, traditions, habits, and values of our own culture—they have become second nature to us. But in contacts with other cultures we sometimes not only declare a preference for our own culture but often we also judge other cultures as inferior to ours. They seem threatening to our own values and traditions, and they sometimes seem incomprehensible, unnatural and inhuman, and disgusting. *Ethnocentrism* is not merely preferring our culture over other cultures, it is declaring that our culture is superior to all others. Human history is replete with examples of ethnocentrism. Religion, a strong element in most cultures, has stark ethnocentric strains. Most nations seem to assume that a god (or gods) has chosen them as the blessed people and is on their side in wars and conflicts. Converting other cultures to Christianity, for example, has been accomplished by wars, propaganda, and other direct and indirect means of force. In the Americas, Africa, and Asia, the religions of the local people have been considered inferior. These people have been seen as pagans and heathens condemned to eternal hell unless they convert to Christianity. African tribespeople have been taught by Christian missionaries to be ashamed of nudity and to cover their bodies. Such fervent belief in Christianity as the only correct religion, combined with the economic exploitation of the people and their lands, has led to the destruction of tribal cultures throughout the world. (See Turnbull, 1962, and Bodley, 1982.)

A remarkable and vivid example of religious ethnocentrism is found in the *Jesuit Relations* (1896–1901). During the seventeenth and eighteenth centuries, Jesuit missionaries left France to convert to Christianity and save the souls of people in native societies of what is now southeastern Canada and northeastern United States (the Montagnais, Micmac, Iroquois, and others). Their annual reports to their superiors in France are filled with ethnocentric statements. While they note repeatedly the hospitality, generosity, gentleness, cooperation, sharing, even temper, and similar qualities of these people, they continually refer to them as "savages" and "uncivilized." They were savages, it seems, because they were not Christians, because they placed no value on material possessions, because they enjoyed sex without guilt, because they were highly individualistic, and because they were not driven to work hard to amass possessions. In short, they were not fully human because they were not French Catholics.

A few words from the *Jesuit Relations* (1896–1901) says it plainly:

> They are, I say, savage, haunting the woods, ignorant, lawless, and rude; they
> are wanderers, with nothing to attach them to a place, neither home nor rela-

tionships, neither possessions nor love of country; as a people they have bad habits, are extremely lazy, gluttonous, profane, treacherous, cruel in their revenge, and given to all kinds of lewdness, men and women alike, . . . (Vol. 1, p. 173)

Their licentious and lazy lives, their rude and untutored minds, able to comprehend so little, the scarcity of words to explain our mysteries, never having had any form of divine worship, will tax our wits. (Vol. 4, p. 219)

In their 1925 study of Muncie ("Middletown"), Indiana, Lynd and Lynd (1929) found many people who believed Christianity to be the only true religion. In a survey among high school students, 92 percent of the girls and 83 percent of the boys agreed that "Christianity is the one true religion and all peoples should be converted to it." (p. 316) In the late 1970s, Muncie teenagers seemed to be less intolerant—only one-third agreed with that statement.

Fear, criticism, rejection, and destruction of other cultures are widespread. When we do not understand other cultures, we seek to destroy them. Indeed, we often see other people and their cultures as less than human. Many societies refer to themselves in terms that mean "people" or "the people," and by implication people in other societies are nonhuman. The word *barbarian* comes from the Greeks, who thought other people were dogs (*bar-bar* to Greeks is how dogs bark, the equivalent of English *bow-bow*). Today, by referring to contemporary industrial societies as "modern" and "civilized," we imply that tribal societies are inferior. Indeed, early Europeans referred to tribal societies as "savage" and "primitive."

We have discussed ethnocentrism on a large and total scale, but it is also prevalent in judging specific areas of other cultures: food, clothing, family traditions, child-rearing practices, sexual habits, music and art, and so on. We can be threatened by any differences we confront. We may be disgusted by the !Kung who eat lizards and other animals, but they would be shocked that people in the United States are starving while others gorge themselves and food rots in storage bins. The sharing of all food with relatives and neighbors is a strong norm in !Kung society. They would be even more shocked, I think, to learn that we have restaurants serving expensive cuts of meat to dogs. My relatives and friends in Albania were shocked when I told them that married children in the United States do not live with their parents. They see this as callous and uncaring behavior toward parents. The list is endless. When people do not understand, they disapprove of the practices and values of other people (Friedl, 1981).

Conflicts and wars over cultural differences co-exist with theft and economic exploitation. Europeans who colonized America were not only shocked by the supposedly heathen practices of native Americans (who were even more shocked by the Europeans' materialism and destruction of the environment) but also stole the Indians' lands and often killed them. Indian religions and values were attacked as morally wrong, economies were changed, and lands taken away. It is unclear whether the lands were taken away because Indians were seen as inferior and unworthy of them, or Europeans declared Indian cultures inferior in order to justify their own theft, plunder, and killing.

What is cause and what is effect? Whatever the case, we should be aware that economic exploitation of a people often co-exists with a criticism and rejection of their culture as inferior.

Ideology is a concept related to ethnocentrism. As used in politics, philosophy, and sociology, an ideology usually refers to a set of beliefs, ideas, and statements held by a group of people that explains and justifies their interests and actions. It is usually implied that ideologies are justifications and rationalizations of a group's interests; thus, "ideology" and "ideological" are pejorative terms. Many ideologies may exist in a society, but usually there is a dominant ideology that supports and legitimates the existing social order. For example, people justified slavery by arguing that slaves were inferior people who could not manage on their own; the belief that Indians were lazy, heathen, and savage was used to justify the theft of their lands and the destruction of their cultures.

But Otten (1981) insists that ideologies are more than mere rationalizations:

> *Quite often, ideology* suggests hypocrisy, lies, and deliberate manipulation, but the term is more subtle. All of us like, and perhaps need, to believe that our position is explainable and justifiable. The term *ideology* builds upon the fact that our social position shapes our mental outlook and that human beings constantly seek explanations and justifications. Although ideological explanations may be self-satisfying, they are not necessarily hypocritical or deliberately manipulative; they are sincere, though limited, views, which grow out of our social placements. For example, given that fact that I am a teacher, I am predisposed to think that learning is important. (p. 211)

Ethnocentrism is not only preferring our own culture over others, it is the belief that other cultures are inferior to ours.

Cultural Relativism

Ideally, of course, we should be able to understand that cultures are simply *different,* not better or worse. For any people, their customs, values, and life styles are correct for them and make sense for their society. The essence of *cultural relativism* is the ability to understand any cultural item as proper and good for a given people and their culture and society. For example, arranged marriages may make no sense in industrial societies today, but we can come to understand how and why they are necessary in peasant and other societies (see Chapter 6 on the family). We would perhaps not choose such marriage practices for ourselves, but we can accept them as appropriate for other people who practice them.

Anthropologists and others have sought to educate themselves and others on the importance of understanding each culture on its own terms. Imposing our values and standards on other cultures blinds us to seeing the world as they do, to understanding their values and traditions.

Speaking very personally, I still do not know how to think about cultural relativism. On the one hand, it is clear to me that we must totally reject the religious bigotry that condemns people of other religions to eternal damnation. Nothing has shocked me as much as the history of the Christians' forced conversion of others. The intolerance and bigotry of many Christians through the centuries, and their economic exploitation and destruction of tribal societies, is a sorry chapter in human history.

In addition, I have come to admire the values of many other cultures: the sharing and cooperation of the !Kung and the Mbuti, the respect for nature and for the individuality of children by native Americans, the communal spirit of tribes throughout the world.

As one who has lived in two different cultures, I have a deep appreciation of the logic and reasoning for different traditions and practices. Indeed, I enjoy them. I still relish certain Greek dishes, but I also enjoy many American foods. I do not like but understand the relative isolation of family members from each other.

But I see aspects of many cultures of the world I neither understand nor accept. No amount of explaining and studying can make me understand the Nazi's murdering of millions of Jews and others. Nor, in all honesty, can I understand the long history of the oppression of women in many societies. I came from a peasant society where women are controlled and limited in many ways. Not only do I reject this condition, I do not even understand it from the perspective of the people who practice it.

There are many other practices and values I cannot accept or understand. Nevertheless, I reject ethnocentrism and see the need for relativism. I do make judgments and hold certain values, but I also see the danger of imposing them on other people. I more than accept cultural differences—I celebrate and delight in them. I know I can learn from other cultures thereby enriching my own life. Yet I am offended, shocked, and hurt by people imposing their values on other people whose values are different. How can I disapprove of people passing judgments on other cultures when I do so? I think my values are based on respect for nature and for all people (men, women, children), on the dignity and equality of everyone, on the right of all people to have enough to eat and live. Using these values I pass judgment on the practices and values of cultures. Yet the early Christians who forcibly converted people to their religion must have thought they espoused moral and ethical values that were beneficial to all people. Did they deceive themselves? Did they use such explanations for their material benefit, whereas I do not? I think my values are based on universal principles for human survival and the dignity and respect of all people, but if I allow myself to make judgments on other cultures, how can I stop others from doing the same? It is a dilemma with which we all must struggle.

In his review of the first edition of this text, Bob Ross (personal communication) makes the following observation about the discussion of cultural relativism:

Some issues cannot be properly raised until they can be solved. If they can be solved, then historical judgement is harsh. But they are not. Slavery, burning of wives at husbands' death, and female circumcision are examples. Scratch a relativist and you find an ignoramus, a wimp, or a person who agrees with the practice under question. As between rock and opera I don't care much. As between the Eskimo practice of deserting the infirm elderly and our own, it depends entirely on society's resources, and I and Liazos know ours is humanly preferable.

Cultural relativism does not say that today we should emulate the Eskimo (although in the eyes of many people in other societies we do abandon our elderly when we allow or force them to live alone). It simply asks that we make an effort to see whether the Eskimo practice of leaving behind the infirm elderly was an economic and material necessity for them.

The dilemma of cultural relativism is simply stated but profound. Once we allow for some judgements of other people's cultures, of their values and traditions, how can we avoid ethnocentrism? We cannot say that we can never judge others, but we can insist that before we do so we should make every effort to understand their culture in terms of *their* conditions, needs, and possibilities, their values and norms.

The Influence of Culture

Experience, reflection, and reading teach us that our existence in the world is shaped and influenced by our culture. As we shall see, the language we use in our culture shapes our thoughts, observations, and orientations. The food we like or abhor, the experiences that move us or leave us indifferent, the sex acts we prefer or detest, how we choose our mates and raise our children, all these, and much more, our culture teaches us. Cultures do change, of course, and within cultures there are disagreements and conflicts on values and practices, but at any given time a culture as a whole and total way of life provides us with guidelines, resources, and orientations.

Health, illness, and death also are shaped by culture. How people live and how and when they die are different cultural experiences. Let us look at three examples.

The Abkhasians of the Soviet Union are among the longest living and healthiest people in the world. What accounts for such health and longevity? Different parts of their culture seem to combine to help create a healthy life style that leads to a long life. They eat moderately and drink a glass of wine each day (no more and no less). In addition, they walk everywhere and breathe clean mountain air. They work all their lives, reducing their hours as they age but continuing to work into their eighties and nineties. Their work provides them with exercise, a routine in their life, and a feeling of being useful. Their families are close and supportive, as is their community. When they get old they are respected and cared for, so they do not dread aging. All these elements seem to form a culture that provides support and meaning for people and leads to a long life (Benet, 1974).

Roseto, Pennsylvania, is a town of 1,600 people, 95 percent of whom are of Italian origin. From the early 1960s to the early 1970s, the town's heart attack rate increased from one-third the national average (in 1961) to three times the national average. Their diet had not changed: during both periods people ate the same large, rich meals. But the culture of the town, its life style, traditions, and values, had changed. In the early 1960s, Roseto had been a town with close family and community ties and supports. The easy-going pace, which had included long, leisurely family meals and gatherings, had given way to a faster life, where people ate and ran. Long commuting to jobs, concern with money to keep up with others, and social isolation had become common by the early 1970s. The stress, pressure, and declining family and community life produced heart attacks (Chambliss & Ryther, 1975).

The same phenomenon of different life styles and cultures leading to different heart attack rates was observed among the Japanese in the United States. Those Japanese who kept their traditions, which focus on family life and support, had low rates, but Landis (1986) reports "those Japanese who adopted the American life style (or personality) and became impatient, aggressive, harddriving, competitive go-getters were five times as likely to have heart attacks as those who maintained Japanese ways." (p. 78)

Culture conditions both social and physical existence.

Language and Culture

A culture and its language are inseparable. Language reflects and shapes a people's values, biases, perspectives, concerns, history, and (in many societies) social inequalities.

Language Reflects Social Reality

On one level, a people's language reveals their concerns, values, and activities. To people in the United States and other societies, snow is not important. Our language contains no more than two or three words referring to snow. To the Eskimo, however, snow is very essential. Their language has twenty-two different words that refer to it. It is important for them to know the kind of snow to which the speaker refers. If we were interested we could learn the differences between the twenty-two types of snow, and we could even use combinations of English words to describe them. But Eskimo children learn these terms easily and naturally as they grow up, and they can easily identify and tell the differences between the twenty-two types, whereas to an English speaker they must be pointed out and explained carefully.

On the other hand, the English language has many more words for colors than most other languages (Barnouw, 1982).

*The Navaho have a word that covers a range from green through blue to pur-
ple, while the Zuni have a term that includes both orange and yellow. Cultures differ in the numbers of colors differentiated. Our own language is rich
in color terms, partly through the influence of the fashion business and traditions of the arts. The largest collection of English color terms has over 3,000
entries, although only about eight terms are commonly used. Some languages,
on the other hand, have only three color terms, generally corresponding to our
black, white, and red. (p. 36)*

And within our culture some people are more color-conscious than others
(Friedl, 1981). "To you or me, red may simply be red, whereas to an interior
decorator there are important differences among scarlet, vermillion, crimson,
maroon, murrey, magenta, and cerise."(p.15) It is not that the Zuni and the
Navaho, or most Americans, are physically incapable of seeing these color
differences, but rather, the cultures and groups in which we grow up do not
choose to focus upon all the possible color differences, so we do not develop
terms and consciousness for them.

Kinship terms also reflect cultural values and differences. Americans call
the woman who gave birth to them "mother." The Navaho and many other
people, however, use one term to refer to both the woman who gave birth to
them and to her biological sister (in our culture this would be our "aunt"). We
cannot translate their word into the English "mother" nor our word "mother"
into their word. It would violate both linguistic and social reality to do so. The
Navaho relate to their "mother" and "aunt" in similar ways, and their language reflects this reality. They are clearly aware of the biological facts, but
their language focuses on the social reality. Linguistic differences in kinship
terminology reflect different social realities.

Language Shapes Thought, Experience, and Perception

Most of us would agree that a people's language reflects their concerns, values,
and activities. But some linguists and anthropologists go beyond this claim
arguing that each language shapes and determines its user's thought, experience, and perception of the physical and social world. (See Whorf, 1941, and
Sapir, 1949, 1959.)

A child is born in the United States or in a European country where an
Indo-European language is spoken. She speaks no words and knows nothing
of the principles of the language spoken in her family or community. But she
learns the language, she understands fairly soon (usually with little or no
explicit instruction) that she can use words to refer to past, present, or future
times. She is forced to think in such terms of time. Another child is born among
the Hopi (a tribe in the southwest United States). He is not forced to direct his
speech and thought to past, present, and future. There are linguistic construc-
tions he can use to refer to events that took place before today, but the
language does not focus on time as English and other Indo-European languages do.

Do these two children experience the world similarly? Do the two languages force them to develop different values, concerns, and perceptions? If people speaking different languages experience and conceive the world around them differently, is language the *cause* of these differences? Or, do people have values and concerns that in time they come to include in their language? These are questions that linguists, philosophers, anthropologists, and others have debated for a long time. No final answers have been (and probably will never be) found. At most, we can say that language may not *determine* or *totally shape* how people in different cultures experience the world, but there is no doubt that it *influences* and *encourages* us to perceive and think along certain lines. It is probably true that the Hopi are more conscious of the present and are less future oriented; they value the present and focus on it. A child born into their society comes to experience social and physical reality largely through the language he or she speaks; indeed, his or her language is part of that reality. Reality is experienced through language. So, the Hopi language leads to a different consciousness of time than does English. Language is also used to pass on cultural behavior from one generation to the next. For example, many Latin American parents sleep with their children until they are four or five years old. In North American culture, on the other hand, parents are often told that sleeping with their children is not a good thing, that a child needs to learn to sleep alone. For each person born into a culture, behavior, ideas, and the physical world are presented to him or her through language.

The Evolution of Culture

That we have culture in human societies means that our behavior is largely learned rather than instinctive. Other primates also learn from experience and from each other, but not on the scale and quality human beings do.

How have human beings come to develop culture and to become so different from other species? Scientists have no definite answers, but scattered evidence and speculation seem to indicate that about five-hundred thousand years ago certain physical changes in our physical evolution enabled us to develop culture. Four important changes took place in the human body: the brain became larger, we developed the opposable thumb on our hands, our posture became more erect, and we gained better eyesight. These four changes, in turn, both made possible, and to some degree necessitated, changes in how our ancestors lived and developed as a species. About half a million years ago our ancestors took three important steps that dramatically changed their relationship to each other and to the natural world around them: they began to use tools, they developed language as a system of communication, and they started to organize themselves into families and other institutions (Friedl, 1981).

Tools

A tool is a part of nature that we alter for use in relating to the environment. A club, a spear, a knife, a bow and arrow are examples of tools that our ancestors used in order to get their food and protect themselves. Today, of course, we have almost totally transformed our environment so we alter it at will through the use of machines (a type of tool); we know of no other way to relate to the environment. It is important to remember, however, that in the distant past our ancestors had to invent the concept of tools; they had to imagine changing and using wood, stone, and metal in their struggle to survive.

For a long time it was thought that only humans use tools. But Oliver (1981) writes about several studies that carefully observed some primates, such as chimpanzees, and have shown that these animals make use of primitive tools. Chimps have been observed to cut off a tree branch, clean it of leaves and other protrusions, and then insert it in an ant hole to remove ants out of it. When one end could no longer be used, they then used the other end of the stick. Such primitive tools are used by other primates. However, it is clear that tool usage among people is inordinately more extensive and of a very different quality.

Language

All species seem to communicate in some manner: fish, insects, mammals, and birds all have means of getting messages and information to each other. But human language seems to be a vastly different, more intricate, and more developed system of communication.

This may only be our own anthropocentric view. Dolphins and primates do not have the physical apparatus to *speak* human languages, but they are able to use up to two hundred words of *sign language*. Indeed, they have been able to *create* new words (new for them) by combining words they already knew. One chimp knew the words for "water" and "bird," but not for "duck." When it saw a duck, it named it a "waterbird" (Oliver, 1981).

Studies of chimps learning human languages seem to show they simply do not have the capacity to use human languages. But these studies have always seemed to me to be showing the obvious. Chimps are not people. We do not learn their system of communication. Why should they want and need to learn ours?

Leaving aside the question of whether human languages are superior systems of communication when compared to the communication of other species, it seems clear that language has enabled the human species to develop along a different path than other species. Language enables us to transmit knowledge, skills, and ideas from one generation to the next. It means we learn from each other, including all past generations, and it has made our behavior learned rather than instinctive. Language is an indispensable part of our being and our existence. For better or for worse, we cannot think of being human without it.

Families and Institutions

Human infants have the longest period of dependency on their parents of any other species. Some anthropologists have speculated that in the evolution of our species those females and males who cooperated in the upbringing of infants had a greater chance of survival. Families enabled the females to raise the children while the males provided protection and some of the food, notably by hunting larger animals (as was noted before, women also gathered plants and even captured smaller animals). For physical survival, and probably for companionship and other psychic and social benefits, people gradually developed the family. (Anthropologists who speculate on the rise of the family do not indicate when larger cooperating groups and communities arose.)

As human beings came to live in groups, they developed stable and organized social structures that they could use to meet their basic needs. Food, shelter, clothing, procreation and raising children, learning basic survival skills, caring for the sick, and a basic understanding of the world are needs all of us must satisfy.

In gathering and hunting societies most of these needs were met by the family, and the rest were met by all the families together, a small band of twenty-five to one hundred people. But as societies evolved, special organizations, which we call *institutions,* were gradually created to meet the needs once met by the family. An institution is a stable form of social organization developed over time to meet some need or want. Within institutions, people have different functions and roles, and usually someone has more authority. For example, in economic institutions an owner, a boss, or a manager directs workers who plant or harvest food, or make cars, or build houses.

Economic institutions produce our food, clothing, shelter, and offer us services. Religious institutions provide us with answers to the mystery of life and lead us in worship. Political institutions organize the legal system that governs our lives. Educational institutions train the young (and not so young these days) in basic and more advanced skills. Military institutions claim to protect us from outside threats, and are likely to invade other societies in the name of national security. Medical institutions aim to cure illness and safeguard health. New types of institutions may be developing, for example entertainment institutions that claim more and more resources and occupy more and more people in order to provide distractions, diversions, and thrills to occupy our leisure time. And of course, the *family* survives, still procreating and socializing, still providing warmth and security, and integrating us with all of the other institutions. Specialized institutions have taken functions away from the family, but in some ways families still educate, entertain, protect, feed, and clothe us. Tools, language, family, and institutions seem to have gradually led to the development of human cultures and societies.

Values

We have discussed briefly the physical and social changes that led to the evolution of culture. People within cultures also make choices and values about their relation to the natural world, about their relationships to each other, and about all matters of life and death. All cultures have values, but different cultures often have different kinds of values.

Basic Values

Our culture is like the water that surrounds a fish. The fish is probably not conscious of the water because it is all it sees, feels, and knows. Our culture surrounds us everywhere; it is our life, so we do not become conscious of living in it. It guides and enables us to live, think, and experience life. Certain unspoken assumptions, ideals, and choices color each culture and act as guides for people. These we call *values*.

Values guide and give meaning to our lives (Lee, 1976):

By human values, by a value or a system of values, I mean the basis upon which an individual chooses one course rather than another, judges as better or worse, right or wrong. We can speak about human values, but we cannot know them directly. We infer them through their expression in behavior. . . .

We experience value when our activity is permeated with satisfaction, when we find meaning in our life, when we feel good, when we act not out of calculating choice and not for extraneous purpose, but rather because this is the only way that we, as ourselves, deeply want to act. (p.5)

Since these values are so basic and taken so for granted as part of human nature, we may not be aware that they are values. Nevertheless, they represent choices we make about our lives. Below we will examine some basic American values, but first let us look briefly at the values of some other cultures.

The !Kung value cooperation. In order for cooperation and sharing to be possible, it is important that power and domination do not arise. People cannot feel superior to others; they cannot think of themselves as better than other people and still cooperate. The emphasis on cooperation, sharing, and equality pervades all !Kung life. It is a basic value. Lee (1969) lived among the !Kung for over a year, yet he was ignorant of this value until the end of his stay when he accidentally learned of it.

Lee went to the Kalahari Desert "to study the hunting and gathering subsistence economy of the !Kung, and to accomplish that it was essential not to provide them with food, share my own food, or interfere in any way with their food-gathering activities." (p. 22) But at the end of his year's stay, to compensate for his stinginess, he decided to provide a feast for the whole group. He bought what he knew they considered a delicacy: a big, fat cow, obviously full of meat. But when he told some !Kung which cow he had bought, people responded in dismay. "Do you expect us to eat that bag of bones?" they said. They warned Lee that "there are many fierce ones here, and with such a small quantity of meat to distribute, how can you give everybody a fair share?" (p. 26) Fights would inevitably ensue.

Lee could not understand what was happening. When the feast day arrived, he feared for the worst. The cow had at least two inches of fat on it and was full of meat. Everyone laughed and had a great time. But Lee did not see the joke.

After a while he asked a !Kung friend (/gaugo) for an explanation:

> "Why did you tell me the black ox was worthless, when you could see that it was loaded with fat and meat?" "It is our way," he said smiling. "We always like to fool people about that. Say there is a Bushman who has been hunting. He must not come home and announce like a braggart, 'I have killed a big one in the bush!' He must sit down in silence until I or someone else comes up to his fire and asks, 'What did you see today?' He replies quietly, 'Ah, I'm no good for hunting. I saw nothing at all (pause) just a little tiny one.' Then I smile to myself,"/gaugo continued, "because I know he has killed something big . . ."
>
> "But," I asked, "why insult a man after he has gone to all that trouble to track and kill an animal and when he is going to share the meat with you so that your children will have something to eat?"
>
> "Arrogance," was his cryptic reply.
>
> "Arrogance?"
>
> "Yes, when a young man kills much meat he comes to think of himself as a chief or a big man, and he thinks of the rest of us as his servants or inferiors. We can't accept this. We refuse one who boasts, for someday his pride will make him kill somebody. So we always speak of his meat as worthless. This way we cool his heart and make him gentle." (pp. 28–29)

Shostak (1981) also found the same emphasis on promoting cooperation and criticizing competition—this is as true for children as it is adults.

> Most childhood games involve little or no competition. Children play beside one another, sharing activities, but group rules are rarely established. Each child attempts, through repetition, to become more accomplished, not to defeat or outshine someone else. It is likely that the small number of children playing together and the lack of others the same age against whom to judge themselves encourage this attitude. But !Kung adults also actively avoid competition and the ranking of individuals into hierarchies. In fact, the cultural constraint against drawing sharp differentiations among people leads the !Kung to shun such determinations as winner, prettiest, and most successful, or even best dancer, hunter, healer, musician, or bread-maker. People are aware, of course, of the often impressive talents of others around them, and they derive great benefit from those talents; but it is considered extremely bad manners to call attention to them. (pp. 108–109)

As a basic value, cooperation pervades many cultures beside the !Kung: the Hopi and other native American tribes, the Mbuti of the Ituri Forest, and others. In contrast, competition is a basic value of American and other cultures. All games American children play seem to have winners and losers. When Melissa, my first daughter, was three, she and another child began going up a jungle gym. Almost immediately they began to shout at each other, "I can climb higher than you can!" School grades, sports, material possessions, awards giving all have an element of competition.

Comparisons and competition are found everywhere in American society. Let me cite a very revealing example. When people are first introduced to my children Melissa and Ariane, some say, "My, what pretty names you have," and some others say, "Ariane, that is such an unusual and pretty name." On some occasions Ariane told me that she is tired of people commenting about her unusual name. But Melissa also seems to have been affected by that unspoken comparison. Melissa once complained that people think her name is "ugly." Since I had never heard someone even hint that they thought Melissa is an ugly name, I asked what she meant. She explained that people often comment how pretty and unusual Ariane's name is, but no one ever says that about her name. I reminded her that many people say that both their names are pretty. But I could see her point. By singling out Ariane's name for praise, people imply that it is somehow better or prettier. I told her I was sorry, and I wished some people would not go out of their way to comment on her sister's name only. The spirit of comparison and competition invades our consciousness and actions, even if only by unspoken comparisons. Excessive praise of one person implies others are inferior, or so we have come to perceive such praise, even if there is no such intention.

Some cultures stress equality more than social differences, the present rather than the future, acceptance more than conquest of nature. We know a culture by the values it espouses.

The Origin of Values

Ideals and beliefs shape our values, which guide our daily conduct. But where do values come from? How do people in different cultures choose their values? Harris and Lee provide two different answers.

Harris (1974) examines one of the most basic values of Hindu culture: the sacred nature of the cow and the taboo against killing it and eating its flesh. Hindus believe the cow is sacred, and this belief shapes their lives. Harris argues, however, that whatever Hindus may believe about the sacredness of the cow, the taboo against eating it has a rational, material, practical, and economic explanation. Hindus do not eat cows because they are vastly more useful to them as sources of fertilizer and fuel and beasts of burden in the fields. Harris shows in detail how the Hindu economy depends on the cow for the oxen it provides to work the fields, the manure it produces, which is used to fertilize the land and when dried is energy for cooking, and also for the milk it gives. Literally, the cow is the source of life for the Hindus. They get much more protein and energy by keeping it alive. In order to insure that cows were used economically, Harris argues, Hindu culture declared it sacred. Economic use and necessity are the source of the Hindu value on the sacredness of the cow. (Harris makes a somewhat similar analysis of the Hebrew taboo against eating pork.)

Lee (1959), on the other hand, argues that values are ultimate sources of human behavior. Values are not derived from material considerations. If the Hopi thought strictly materially, they would work for money and buy more corn than they can raise themselves. But the planting and growing of corn is part of their culture. It symbolizes the relationship to the land they love; it provides more than nutrition. Store-bought corn is only nutrition. Although physical survival and material considerations are important, are they the ultimate sources for the choices we make and values we espouse? Lee believes that "human physical survival" is assumed to be the ultimate goal, but that there is no proof for this assumption. It is survival in the context of a culture we value and esteem that is the ultimate goal.

Both Harris (1974) and Lee (1959) make us aware of important issues. To ensure physical survival, people will develop practices, traditions, and values that make this possible. In a sense, cooperation is a value among the !Kung and the Mbuti because it is more efficient and practical for individual and group survival. More game is caught cooperatively, and everyone gets some of it. Sharing too ensures survival—you share with me when I do not make a catch, and I with you when your catch is poor. As Turnbull (1983b) says about the Mbuti and their emphasis on sharing and cooperation, they do not hold them for their own sake "rather because this is what they *have to be* in order to survive. To lie and steal, to connive and cheat, to amass private wealth, power, and prestige, are simply disfunctional in their context—or they have been up to the present." (p. 11) Values are created in specific economic and material conditions.

But Lee (1959) reminds us that physical survival is not the only or ultimate goal of life. Other considerations matter. These considerations also lead to choosing values that do not have strictly material motives. Our culture and all it means to us is equally significant for physical, psychic, and social survival.

American Values

Through the years I have asked my students to list what they consider the basic values are of American society. They name success—an expensive car, fashionable clothes, a high paying job, and other values that generally mean two things: money and material possessions. They list freedom, democracy, and family less often. A student rarely mentions friends, and I have yet to hear community as an American value.

In their study of Muncie, Indiana, in 1935 Lynd and Lynd (1937) found the commitment to making money pervading all of Muncie's institutions. Everywhere they turned—schools, churches, businesses, voluntary associations—they ran "upon the culture's commitment, implicit and explicit, to the necessity for and goodness of hard work in the acquisition of property." Newspapers did not advise marrying for money alone, but "there is probably nothing more important to domestic happiness in the world" than money (p. 242).

In a long chapter, "The Middletown Spirit," they list and discuss the values of the Middletown (and one assumes American) culture. Whereas honesty, kindness, the family, and similar values are listed, the two dominant values are materialism and money, and a belief in the primacy of the "American Way" and Christianity.

Later writers have pointed to similar values. Williams (1970), in *American Society,* lists success, work, progress, efficiency, practicality, and other materially oriented values. In addition, according to Williams and others, Americans profess to believe in freedom, equality, democracy, science, individualism, and so on. Lynd and Lynd (1937), and others later, include religion, at least in terms of church membership and attendance, and a professed belief in God.

Competition and material possessions are indisputable American values. If we can judge a culture by what people do and by who receives the highest rewards and prestige, not by what they profess to believe, we can say these values dominate American culture. They have been evident from the beginning of our history, as wise Indians quickly realized. In 1877, Sitting Bull bemoaned that "the love of possession is a disease" with white people. European settlers, on the other hand, considered the Indians lazy because they were not driven to work long hours to amass material possessions. The Europeans' secret admiration of the Indians' lack of avarice and ambition attested to the presence of these values in white culture.

Even though capitalist culture socializes us to value material success, and even though we do internalize it to a large degree, often we feel uncomfortable and ambivalent about its effects on our lives. For example, in a 1985 survey 70 percent of a quarter million college students agreed that "a major reason for attending college is to be able to make more money" (*Boston Globe,* November 1, 1986:2). But when 150 adults throughout the United States were interviewed in 1987, "overwhelmingly, people worried about the state of American values, voicing concern about private selfishness and immorality as well as public corruption" (*Boston Globe,* June 21, 1987:1, 16). Many worried about a declining social consciousness. They thought people should be concerned with the common good, not only their own advancement and success.

Others express the same concerns. Bellah and others (1985) lived and talked with two hundred middle-class Americans (almost all white) in four communities in the early 1980s. In their book, *Habits of the Heart: Individ-*

ualism and Commitment in American Life, they conclude that individualism and self-interest (social, monetary, and material advancement) "may have grown cancerous" and may be threatening freedom and democracy.

Success, freedom and justice are the values people strive to integrate in their lives. *Success,* economic and social achievement, is at the core of their lives. Often, as people work long hours, are away from their family, and often move away from family and friends to higher positions in other places, they may have nagging doubts about whether success will bring the promised happiness. But usually such doubts are repressed, even as family life suffers and therapists provide no answers for troubled souls.

Freedom (Bellah et al., 1985) often means no more than being left alone by others and this "freedom to be left alone is a freedom that implies being alone." (p. 23) Freedom is seen as the absence of something, often meaning the absence of relationship with and responsibility for others. According to Lee (1959), we want freedom *from* rather than freedom *for.* Such a conception of freedom is logical in a culture and an economy that worship individual success as the highest good, instead of social and communal responsibility.

Justice, the third value, often is warmly supported but it remains vague and general. Individualism and a confused sense of freedom prevent people from defining and committing themselves to justice. Without a sense of commitment and community, it is difficult to imagine programs and groups that we can create or join to bring about justice for all pepole. Parks, better schools, affordable housing for all people, jobs for everyone that pay a living wage, and so on, cannot be achieved if we seek only individual success and the freedom to be left alone.

The authors of *Habits of the Heart* say little about the economic and social conditions that made self-interest the primary value in American culture. In its long development, capitalism has destroyed communities (see Chapter 5) and has created a culture that promises happiness if only we buy, own, and consume and if we work long hours. In addition, in his review of *Habits of the Heart,* Eden (1986) argues that working-class people, minorities, many women's groups, and others have looked beyond individualism and self-interest. In their struggles for justice and equality, they have created and joined social movements that sought to improve the common good, not just individual self-interest. They have worked for changes, for laws and institutions, that benefit all people and their communities.

Freedom as an American value is also problematic. As we have discussed, part of the problem is that it implies only freedom *from,* or being left alone. Freedom also means the ability to think and speak freely with other people, to say and write what we believe, to challenge our and others' ideas in open debate and discussion. We espouse this notion of freedom. But the actions of the U.S. government, corporations, and the culture they help shape make such freedom more an appearance than a reality. People whose ideas and beliefs have opposed government policy and powerful groups have not fared well in the United States. In recent history, since the 1950s, the FBI, the

CIA, and other government agencies have spied upon, infiltrated, sabotaged, even killed people who have sought to use their legal right to protest against government actions or for social change. Civil rights are supposedly inherent in the idea of freedom, but violations of these rights have been massive and pervasive. A 1976 U.S. Senate study documents the persecution of dissenting individuals and groups. It cites women's groups, civil rights and other black organizations, Martin Luther King, Jr., the Black Panthers, even U.S. politicians, and many others who have been spied on, have had false rumors spread about them, have had their offices broken into, and have had FBI agents infiltrate their group and steer it toward violence. On occasion people have been shot and killed. (See Skolnick & Currie, 1979.)

Freedom continues to be attacked and limited from government agencies. The Supreme Court, which since the 1950s has protected and promoted freedom, in recent decisions has allowed government limitations on our freedoms. Consider the following case. In 1958, a sergeant "volunteered to test gas masks and protective clothing. Instead, he was secretly administered LSD. Afterward, he had hallucinations, beat his wife and suffered a loss of memory. He was discharged from the service and his marriage dissolved" (*Boston Globe,* June 26, 1987:3). The government admitted that this man and other soldiers were given LSD without their knowledge or consent. Yet, the Supreme Court ruled that the soldier could not sue the government. Are we free if we lose control of our persons and bodies?

The freedom to think and speak freely is curtailed when government agencies spy on people. The *Progressive* (December, 1985) reported that thirty-five U.S. government agencies "have compiled computerized records on 114 million of us." (p. 12) According to the Office of Technology Assessment, "twenty-five Government agencies employ closed-circuit television cameras; twenty-one use night-vision systems; nineteen utilize miniature radio transmitters; . . . and seven listen in on telephone conversations." (p. 12) The FBI, the CIA, and police agencies continue to spy on and harass groups and individuals that criticize the government. (For a general discussion of government spying, see McGehee, 1985; Donner, 1985; and *Guardian,* March 4, 1987:6.)

Other institutions also assault and limited freedom of speech. Hentoff (1984a) shows that high school principals deny the right of student journalists to question school authorities by censoring school newspapers, despite a 1967 Supreme Court decision that guarantees such freedom. In another case reported in the *Boston Globe* (April 21, 1986), a student who wore a black armband to protest the bombing of Libya by U.S. planes in April 1986 was called names, sworn at, and threatened by other students. And for years various groups have sought, with some success, to censor school textbooks.

Both Chomsky (1985) and Hentoff (1984b) show that by their action and example, governments, corporations, school authorities, churches, and others have shaped a culture that restricts and limits freedom. At work, in schools, and elsewhere people are afraid to speak freely. They fear, often with good reason, that they will be penalized if they express their views and beliefs publicly. Even democratic systems limit what is thinkable and allowable. A careful reading of the sources I cite here, and many others that are available, shows that if freedom is an American value, it is so only because through the years many people have dared to speak out despite opposition and repression.

These statements represent my understanding of American values. It is, however, more important for you to explore and question the issue of values. What do you profess to hold dearest? Do your actions support your statements? Whose actions and whose words represent American values? Are some professed values contradicted by other values and by actions? Can a society with over two hundred million people who constitute many different groups ever agree on what values all or most of us should hold and live by? Can we co-exist holding different values? Are some values more important than others?

Religion

Most sociologists and anthropologists think that religion is a universal phenomenon. They define it as a belief in some power, entity, or being above and beyond human beings. Some anthropologists point out, however, that the essence of religion is not a belief in a supernatural entity, but the daily conduct of our lives in a culture that embodies our most basic values. According to Lee (1959), to describe a people's way of life (their culture) *is* to describe their religion. The Mbuti, for example, worship the forest, which provides their food and shelter. It is unclear whether they see it as a supernatural being or whether they believe in any kind of afterlife. To many social researchers, these beliefs are essential aspects of religion (Turnbull, 1961).

A distinction can also be made between religion as the experience of human beings relating to the world versus religion as an institution. The power and coercion of religions and religious leaders arose with the coming of horticultural, and even more with agricultural, societies. It has been an institution that often controls people's lives and uses power to exploit them. Religious intolerance is everpresent. Some churches and some religious leaders, for example those who worked for civil rights in the 1960s, have worked for human liberation and equality, but more often than not religion is an oppressive force. In some ways, it has been the opiate of the masses—a promise of a happy afterlife to compensate for present exploitation and misery. The religion of early human societies; the personal, emotional, spiritual, and intellectual experience of many people; and religion as an institution in the past and present—these are three different realities. People need to understand the world around them and their place in it; they do not need the power, control, and repression some religions practice.

Subcultures

Behavioral and value variations exist in all contemporary societies. Groups of people within larger societies often hold values that differ to some degree from the values of the society around them. A group of people that shares some or most of a culture within a society but also has some unique values of its own is called a *subculture*.

The degree to which a subculture differs from the main culture varies considerably. Professional groups with their mannerisms and argot are barely subcultures. Baseball players and sociologists may talk a language unintelligible to outsiders, but their basic values are no different from the rest of their society. On the other hand, ethnic and racial groups, especially recent arrivals, are clear examples of subcultures. Other examples are evangelical Christian churches, the Amish, and the Hare Krishna, political groups that seek to change American society, and people in communes and collectives.

At some point, the differences may be so deep and extensive that a subculture may be a separate culture. The Amish and some Indian tribes on reservations probably are entirely distinct cultures that historically came to be within the political and geographical boundaries of another culture. Cars, electricity, and other necessities of industrial society are absent from Amish communities. They value family and community life much more than do most Americans. Some Indian nations hold values and lead lives vastly different from the world outside the reservations. Many native Americans, for example, have a deep respect for the individual. In contrast to most nonnative Americans, many tribal cultures do not interfere with their children's development. From infancy on, children have very few limits set for them. (See Chapter 7.)

Some groups seek to *change* basic American values. They continue or renew dissenting traditions that seek to redefine how we should live. People whose consciousness was shaped by the civil rights, anti-war, and feminist movements of the 1950s and 1960s are the most recent example. They want to direct Americans away from self-interest and the obsessions with material success, towards a commitment to community, justice, and social responsibility. Also, they want to create true democracy and insure freedom by changing the economic and political institutions that permit a few people to hold most of the power. (See Chapter 10.)

Most subcultures, especially ethnic groups, in time diminish or even disappear. In *Mount Allegro,* Mangione (1981) describes vividly, movingly, and humorously the conflict between the immigrant Italian parents, who insisted their children speak only Italian at home and keep Italian traditions, and their children, who wanted to be American, like their friends. In time, most subcultures blend into the culture around them. But new ones enter or arise.

Cultural Integration

Ideally *cultural integration* should prevail in a society. Values, norms, and roles should fit together and be consistent, and basic values should be expressed in all social behavior. They should not contradict each other, and they should be present and expressed throughout the whole culture. For example, competition as an American value should not be contradicted by cooperative practices, and it should be present everywhere. It does exist, as I said, in sports, education, work, and other areas of American life. But is cooperation totally absent from American culture?

Probably no culture that has ever existed has been fully integrated, unified, and consistent. Since culture is an abstraction, what really exists are people behaving, contradictions, inconsistencies, and disagreements. Cultural integration becomes even more of an impossibility in contemporary industrial societies.

Indeed, frequently the contradictions become pronounced. In American society today, the values of success and materialism diminish the opportunities of family and community. People who move to new locations for better jobs and more money, for example, put family and community second because employment mobility disrupts family and community ties.

In the political arena, democracy and freedom are the expressed values. But as we saw above, the government often violates these values. In addition, freedom and democratic control are absent from other institutions. For example, schools and most workplaces are highly authoritarian settings. People there must follow the orders of teachers, administrators, bosses, and managers. How can we teach people to believe in and practice democratic values when these values are contradicted in their daily lives?

Socialist societies also face severe problems with contradictory values. Many of them arose from peasant societies, where patriarchal and authoritarian traditions had been held for centuries. It takes generations to plant the new values of equality and freedom. In the old societies, older men were clearly dominant while women were clearly subordinate. All socialist societies believe in the equality of women, but the implementation of this value has been uneven.

During the turbulent decade of the Chinese Cultural Revolution (1966 to 1976) some Chinese leaders attempted to lessen cultural contradictions between the old and new societies. In politics and economic affairs the society worked toward equality, but in art and literature from China's past there was clearly a perpetuation of authoritarian and anti-egalitarian values. Operas, plays, and literature extolled obedience to the emperors and reflected patriarchal attitudes. How can a new society truly arise when values so antithetical to it are still perpetuated in art and literature? Is there no need for new forms of plays and fiction that express the values of the new society? The contradiction of the Cultural Revolution itself, however, was that instead of educating people to understand and appreciate a new culture, it simply banned the products of the old one—thus, partly creating a new authoritarianism (Liazos, 1982).

In varying degrees, all cultures probably contain contradictions and conflicts in their prevailing values, and the implementation of expressed values is usually incomplete. Values express ideals that we usually do not fully achieve. At times we may come closer to achieving them than at other times, but full implementation may be an unachievable goal.

Norms

A *norm* is the expected and accepted behavior for a given social situation. We should laugh when watching a TV comedy show, but laughter is not common at funerals. Norms, in other words, apply to specific situations—what is appropriate and expected in situation *A* is not in situation *B*.

In our daily lives, we are constantly following (and occasionally violating) norms. We do not often attend church in bathing suits. Bathing suits also are not usually worn when we walk down the street during the winter. But on hot summer days we can wear them on streets, in supermarkets, and other places. We do not usually attend class in pajamas (a student who once did so at Regis College was sent back to her room), but shorts, perhaps even bathing suits, would be allowed on hot days. Upon first meeting our teachers, and for most of us for ever after, we do not address them by their first name. (What would happen if you did? Try doing this as an exercise.) We eat most foods with silverware; we wear shoes to church but not to bed; we make love in bedrooms, in cars, and isolated places, but not usually in the presence of others; men in the United States do not wear skirts, and, at one time, women could not wear pants (in some situations women still are not allowed to wear pants). When I was growing up in Greek society, if I dropped a piece of bread on the ground, I was expected to pick it up, kiss it, make the sign of the cross, and then place it where people could not step on it; also, whenever I met a priest in the street, I was expected to kiss his hand (I am told that norm has now disappeared). The examples are endless.

Everywhere we go, everyday, there are norms of expectation and norms of prohibition. In a sense, social life is possible because of norms. They allow us to predict fairly accurately what people will do in most situations. Could we lead our lives if most of the time we had no clue or idea how others will behave toward us? Imagine a society with few or no norms. Think of some norms that guide our behavior; if they were constantly violated, what would happen to social life?

How do we learn norms? By now, most of us do not remember when and how we learned most of the norms we follow. When and by whom were you told that you could not appear nude in public? At what age is it no longer permissible for children to appear nude at public beaches, their own backyards, their homes? You know that by age fifteen or twenty you cannot appear nude on public beaches, and, for most of you, nudity is even prohibited in your own homes in front of your relatives. But when did these prohibitions arise—at the age of one, two, three, five, ten? And what would happen if you did appear nude at five on a public beach, or your backyard, or your own home? When my daughters were about two, on hot days they freely walked naked in our home and in the yard. But one day visiting relatives told one of them, in pretend (but not really pretend) shock, "Shame on you!"

It is difficult to tell how we learned most norms. We usually cannot recall when they first entered our lives. All my students clearly know the incest taboo, but not one has been able to recall ever being told that incest is immoral or wrong. It seems that many norms simply are there.

Apparently, we follow most norms more or less automatically. We may not even know that a norm exists. When talking to most people, how close can you get to them? One-and-a-half to two feet is the distance most of us seem to prefer and feel the most at ease. What would happen if, when standing next to someone, you got six inches away from them—or stood six feet away? Until someone violates this norm (and many other norms), we may be unconscious that one exists. (Perhaps sociologists exaggerate that many unspoken norms exist. Can you think of other examples? Can you argue that there are very few such norms?)

Finally, it should be obvious that norms regulating given areas of life vary widely from society to society. In Latin American societies, people do not feel comfortable talking to others at one-and-a-half to two feet distances—they need to get closer. Messenger (1969) notes that in 1960, the people in an Irish village had "an obsessive fear of nakedness which permits them, after infancy, to bathe only their feet, hands, and face and precludes bathing in the sea and the use of bathtubs." (p. 45) In the United States and other industrial societies today much of the human body can be revealed in public, and in many gathering and hunting and tribal societies people are nude or semi-nude all the time. Imagine the horror of the British when they met people they considered naked savages—and the amusement of the tribal people when they saw the overdressed British (especially in hot tropical areas). The examples are endless, but the point is simple. Norms vary widely from culture to culture. Indeed, it is this variation that accounts for culture shock and ethnocentrism.

Folkways and Mores

A common distinction made by sociologists is between folkways and mores (pronounced "mor-ays"). A *folkway* expresses an expectation but not an obligation. In the United States, you could eat rice with your fingers; you could start your meal with your dessert (Ariane, when she was in the first grade, told me that on occasion she did just that at lunch in school—her form of rebellion); you could attend church in sneakers. There are many such norms you could violate. People might gossip about you and disapprove of your actions, but no specific sanction would be attached to such violations. For example, in Europe women do not shave their underarms; in the United States most women do. What happens if you do not? Your husband or parents, or someone, will probably make a comment of disapproval—even scream and yell at you, perhaps. A waitress was fired from a job for not shaving her legs. (She took her case to court and eventually won.)

Mores are obligatory norms that have severe sanctions and disapproval attached to them. Incest, eating human flesh, murder, rape, total public nudity, and others are commonly given as examples of mores. When on occasion these actions take place, they usually provoke horror, disgust, and strong disapproval (but on occasion all do happen).

Norms in daily life cannot always be neatly separated into folkways or mores. For example, is the norm that American women should shave their legs and underarms a folkway or a more? If you get fired from a job for violating this norm, or if a relative expresses clear disapproval, it would seem to be more than a folkway. Wearing a tie is clearly not a more, but organizations often have rules that male employees have to wear them. And if no explicit rules on ties exist often there are clear unspoken norms. No one may openly criticize you, but if you persist in not wearing a tie, you may eventually lose your job or not be promoted. In reality, there is wide variation in people's commitment to norms and in the strength of the negative reactions and sanctions against those who violate them. If we wish, and if we are willing to pay the price, we could violate many norms. In time, repeated violations of a norm may bring about a new norm.

Law, Crime, and Deviance

In agricultural and industrial societies, many norms are written into law. *Laws* are norms with specific sanctions attached to them and that are enforced by representatives of the government—police, courts, and others. Gathering and hunting societies have no laws and no institutions or personnel to enforce them. The Mbuti Turnbull studied are an excellent example. In chapters 5 and 6 of *The Forest People,* Turnbull describes a society with clear norms, with community enforcement of those norms considered essential for the group's survival, but the group has no laws, no police, no courts, or prisons.

According to some anthropologists, laws only arise in societies characterized by class differences and other social inequalities. They represent the attempt of the higher classes to impose their will and views on other people. So long as the community agrees on the norms for daily conduct, there is no need for law and law enforcement. Many laws are written precisely because people do what the law forbids. In Chapter 3, I showed that in societal evolution social classes and other forms of inequality did not exist in earlier societies and only appeared with the rise of agriculture and industry. Laws and law enforcement may be seen as mechanisms by which the higher classes impose their control on the rest of the population (Diamond, 1971).

To make this discussion more concrete, let us look at some laws in the contemporary United States. Sometimes the actions of some people cause the death of others. Here are some examples: during a domestic argument a wife shoots at her husband and kills him; while robbing a bank the robbers shoot the guards and kill them; warring street gangs beat or shoot at some of their rivals who then die; corporations dump dangerous chemicals in the ground or in bodies of water, causing some people to get cancer and die; other corporations do not tell their workers that breathing asbestos is highly dangerous, which results in many workers dying from lung cancers twenty to thirty years hence; an automobile manufacturer knowingly produces a car with a gas tank too close to the rear and thus increases the chance of an explosion after a crash, which could burn passengers to death; a coal company is repeatedly warned by the government that it must fix a dam on its property, or it may soon burst and drown people downstream (this actually happened on February 26, 1972. The flood killed over two hundred people). All these are conscious and knowing actions that result in other people's deaths. But only some are considered murder under the law. Only some people are tried for murder and spend time in prison. It seems that powerful individuals and institutions can kill without their actions being considered murder by the law. Indeed, for many years now over five times as many people (about one hundred thousand versus twenty thousand) die yearly from accidents at work and diseases they contract at work, than do from shootings, stabbings, and beatings. But only the latter actions are considered murder. Why?

Or think of theft. If you or I were to take an item or money from a store or a house, we would be considered criminals—we would be violating the law. But deceptive and misleading advertising steals more money than do the actions of individuals. If and when corporations are found lying, however, at most they get a slap on the wrist, perhaps pay a small fine, and promise never to do it again. But no one goes to prison, no one is seen as a criminal.

Clearly, in capitalist societies today laws are written and laws are changed to serve the interests of corporations and the rich and powerful. This segment of society may not always succeed in its efforts to use the legal system for its interests (people sometimes do change laws so they benefit all people), but the legal system largely serves the interests of only a few people. (See Chambliss & Seidman, 1982, and Simon & Eitzen, 1986, and Chapter 10 for the discussion on corporate crimes.)

Norm Conflicts and Norm Changes

Norms are not independent entities that hover over us and control our behavior. They are the views, biases, and interests of past and present individuals and groups. As such, they are subject to disagreements and differing interpretations. Whereas it would be a mistake to assume we are totally free to follow or reject norms, it is also a mistake to assume that there is complete agreement about and acceptance of all norms. Rarely, if ever, and not for very long, are norms universally accepted in any culture. Conflict and disagreement over norms is a constant reality of life.

Historians and anthropologists persuade us that past societies or other societies have or had universally accepted norms. Or, at the very least, those who rejected the norms kept their opinions to themselves. As I read, think, and reflect more about this throughout the years, I find such views of consensus and agreement misleading and dangerous.

Let us look at some examples. The mid- and late-nineteenth century is known for the control and repression of sexuality. It is believed by many people that women were convinced by society during this period that by nature they were asexual beings. Orgasms and sexual pleasures were unnatural. At most they were to consent to sex in order to have children and to satisfy their husbands, whose nature did allow for sexual pleasure. The ideology held not only that women *should not* enjoy sex, but that by nature they *do not*.

Such is the popular view of sexual norms of that time. We have come to think that these norms were universally accepted by *all* people living then. Degler (1974), however, shows convincingly that this view was only one side of a controversial issue. Some doctors and others wrote that women did not enjoy sex, but just as many doctors wrote that sexual pleasure is normal, desirable, and necessary for women. One doctor wrote in 1870, "Passion [is] absolutely necessary in woman . . . That female passion exists is as obvious as that the sun shines." Those arguing for the asexual nature of women were not reporting a norm, rather, they were trying to *create* one. They were *prescribing* what women should do, not *describing* what women in fact do.

Degler (1974) cites a survey on women's sexuality conducted by Dr. Clelia Duel Mosher (1863–1940) in the early 1890s over the course of about twenty years. It has never been published. Forty-five middle-class married women took part in the survey. Most were born around 1870 and were married by 1900. Thirty-five out of the forty-five "testified that they felt desire for sexual intercourse independent of their husband's interest, while nine said they never or rarely felt any such desire." (p. 416) To the question "Do you always have a venereal orgasm?," two did not respond; five said "no" (possibly meaning they experience orgasm some of the time); nine said "always"; seven said "usually"; eighteen said "sometimes," "not always," or "no" but noted exceptions; and four said "once" or "never." (p. 416) This is hardly a portrait of sexually repressed women.

The ideology of the asexuality of women may have left a legacy of guilt. Women may have normal sexual feelings, but they may also feel guilty about them. Rubin (1976) argues that in fact women, especially working-class women, continued to experience guilty feelings into the 1950s and even into the early 1970s. The fifty working-class women she interviewed in 1973 reported more frequent, and more varied, sexual activity than the sex surveys of the 1940s and 1950s showed. The norm of the frequency and nature of sexual activity, for men and women, began to change in the 1960s. But Rubin claims that the women she interviewed still felt ambivalent about what they did: guilt and uneasiness surrounded their sex life. An old ideology dies hard, apparently.

This discussion should warn us that we should avoid definite conclusions about norms. Often we cannot be certain what the norm is for a given action, accurately determine how many people follow the alleged norm, or even know accurately how people who follow it, or do not follow it, *feel* about it. These uncertainties exist because often one side of a controversy may succeed in establishing its view as the dominant one, and because (as we saw in Chapter

2) people may be unwilling or unable to tell us what they do, think, and feel. In addition, people change their views and opinions about others' actions. What they disapprove of today they may accept tomorrow and vice versa.

It may be safer to assume that controversies and conflicts over norms are the rule rather than the exception. We may in time forget these conflicts, but when they occur they are often intense and even violent. In the late 1960s and early 1970s the length of boys' and men's hair became a very controversial issue. As more and more young men wore their hair longer, some people reacted with anger. "Long-haired hippy" and "radical" became terms hurled at political protesters and youth in general. Long hair did become, for many people (on both sides), a sign of social and political protest. High-school and college athletes were thrown off teams because they refused to follow their coaches' orders to trim their hair. Even professional teams had specific rules about beards, mustaches, sideburns, and long hair. Parents and sons often argued about hair length. In time, the controversy subsided. Generally, by the 1980s hair had become shorter again, though not as short as the almost universal crew-cut and near-crew-cut of the 1950s. Even today, however, very long hair is not acceptable to many (most?) people. Certainly men who want to succeed in business and the professions realize early enough the wisdom of trimming their hair.

Cohabitation (unmarried men and women living together) is another changing norm. While it is tolerated more now, it is not universally acceptable, nor was it totally absent in the past. About 425,000 unmarried couples lived together in 1960; 523,000 in 1970; 1,589,000 in 1980; and 1,983,000 in 1985. The 1985 group was composed of: never married, 1,064,000 men and 1,021,000 women; divorced, 679,000 men and 747,000 women; and married, spouse absent, 151,000 men and 163,000 women (*Statistical Abstract,* 1987:42). These official data collected by the U.S. Bureau of the Census probably underestimate the actual number. Many people will not reveal their living arrangements to the government. A study by Watson (1983) suggests that cohabitation may be much more widespread than official statistics suggest. Of eighty-four couples who had announced their impending marriages in the press in Victoria, British Columbia, thirty-seven (44 percent) said they had "shared a 'bedroom and/or bed' for four or more nights a week for three or more consecutive months" before their marriage. (p. 142) Seventeen more said they had lived together in some less involved arrangement, for a total of fifty-four out of eighty-four couples (64 percent). We can conclude that some form of premarital cohabitation may be exercised by a majority of people in North America in the 1980s.

But do parents and people in general approve of cohabitation? And what does "approval" mean? Blessing of the event, realistic acceptance, or grudging resignation? How many parents virtually disown their children for practicing cohabitation? And do we think differently of never-married people in their early twenties who live together unmarried than we do of divorced people in their thirties or older who do so? And how do the cohabitors feel? It seems that most tell their friends but not their parents. Jackson (1983) found that many cohabiting couples engaged in elaborate cover-ups to deceive their parents, although most are found out sooner or later. And at least some parents are aware of the deception and choose to feign ignorance. Actions, feelings, and reactions have changed over time.

Recent developments may indicate a growing acceptance of cohabitation. Goodman (1980b) wrote about a divorced woman with her three children who was living with a man without having married him. The children were "comfortable and happy in this new 'family'." (p. 10) Her ex-husband agreed that she was a good and loving mother, but he sued for custody of the children, and the court awarded it to him. The judges concluded that "she had created an immoral atmosphere for the three daughters by living 'in sin'." (p. 10) But in 1987, the *Boston Globe* (January 30, 1987) ran an article about a report from the Newark, New Jersey diocese of the Episcopal Church (with three million members in the United States) urged that the church "should recognize and bless committed nonmarital sexual relationships between homosexuals, young adults, the divorced, and the widowed" (in the words of the news story). (p. 8) And in Massachusetts, where cohabitation had been a crime since 1784, couples were punished by standing them "at the gallows for one hour with a noose around their necks" and inflicting thirty-nine lashes on each (*Boston Globe,* May 9, 1987:17–18). Cohabitation became legal in 1987.

Disagreement and conflict over appropriate and expected behavior are common. A particularly dramatic and vivid example is found in Davis's (1982) study of Hamilton, Ohio, in the late 1970s. Sam Shie had been a very effective and popular music teacher at the high school for ten years. A male department store detective accused him of sexual solicitation in the men's room. Shie vehemently denied the accusation and claimed that the detective had misinterpreted his actions. The school department fired Shie. A hearing about the firing, which amounted to a trial, was held over the next few months.

The principal and other school administrators argued that even if he were innocent, Shie could not longer be an effective teacher. The accusation and the publicity had destroyed his credibility. Teachers testified that the school department was mistaken in this conclusion, and over a thousand students signed a petition in support of Shie. The administration did not rescind its decision.

Some people argued that even if Shie were guilty of the charge, what he did in his private life was his own business. All that mattered were his effective teaching and his actions while he taught. The basketball coach was praised by his church for testifying in support of Shie, but the man who kept score at the games for him quit in protest. People in Hamilton were sharply divided over what Shie did or did not do, over the appropriateness of the firing of Shie, and over people's testimony. Davis (1982), Shie's colleagues and students, and it seems many or most Hamiltonians did not think Shie was guilty of the charge; and even if he were, many said, it did not detract from his effectiveness or popularity. The school administration disagreed and refused to rehire Shie even after the hearing officer recommended they do so (but he also concluded that Shie probably was guilty of the charge). Shie sued in court and after losing at lower levels eventually won. (Davis's work was published before Shie won his court case. See the Hamilton *Journal News*, March 20, 1982:5.)

What do Hamiltonians believe about appropriate sexuality and its consequences? What is the norm? Whose norm?

As a final example, let us look at the case of a teacher who had a child out of wedlock. It may be safe to say that some years ago an unmarried woman teacher would lose her job were she to have a child. Many people would agree with such an action today. The *Guardian* (January 12, 1983) reported that in 1982, in East Hampton, Long Island, New York, a controversy arose concerning an unmarried woman teacher who became pregnant and decided to have and keep the baby.

> *When the pregnancy of Patricia Hope, a biology teacher, became obvious this fall, a number of outraged parents and citizens drew up a petition to have her dismissed. One father likened her pregnancy without benefit of clergy to "an X-rated movie." The opposition drew a large number of students, former students and parents to Hope's support, and a counter-petition was presented to the school board. All insisted that what counted were Hope's abilities as a fine teacher able to succeed with rebellious and troubled youngsters. Hope's union, the New York State United Teachers, insisted that her case was one of sex discrimination. After an informal public hearing the East Hampton school board refused to fire Hope, who has tenure. (p. 2)*

There is an increasing incidence, and probably acceptance, of childbearing by unmarried women. In 1960, there were 225,000 babies born to unmarried women; 400,000 in 1970; 655,000 in 1980; and 770,000 in 1984 (35 percent of women nineteen and under; 54 percent to women twenty to twenty-nine; and 11 percent to women thirty and over) (*Statistical Abstract*, 1987: 61). Even though there is still debate and controversy, and even though most children in 1984 (79 percent) were born to married women, news stories, people we know, and statistics indicate that childbearing outside marriage is becoming more acceptable.

Many anthropologists believe that in small gathering-hunting and horticultural (tribal) societies there is general agreement about and acceptance of norms. (Such a view may tell us more about the limits of anthropological observation than about social reality in these societies.) This observation, however, may constitute only the views of those people who spoke with the anthropologists, not a careful observation over a long period of time. In societies where women's virginity is the reported norm, whose norm is it? All of the people? All of the women, many women, or some women? Men mostly? Do we know how women really feel, how willingly they accept the stated norm? Given our discussion about the nineteenth century, we must be careful in our conclusions about virginity as a norm in any society. It may be only some people's norm; it may represent the triumph of patriarchal authority rather than universal agreement.

Even in societies where sharing is an accepted norm because it contributes to group survival, there may be some people who resist it. As a child, Nisa one day spotted a wildebeest in the desert that had recently been killed by lions (Shostak, 1981). Her parents brought it back to the !Kung village where they proceeded to share it. Nisa, however, protested long and loudly.

> But I didn't want any of it given away. I cried, "I was the one who saw it!" Whenever I saw them give some away, I followed the person to his hut and took it back, saying, "Did you see the wildebeest? Mommy and I were together and I was the one who saw it!" I took the meat away and hung it again on the branch beside mother's hut. People said, "Oh! This child! Isn't she going to share what she has? Is she a child who sees something and doesn't give any of it to others?" But I said, "Did you see it? I myself saw it with my very own eyes, and this wildebeest is mine. I'm going to hang it up by my hut so I can eat it all."
>
> Later, I went to play. While I was away, mother took the meat and shared it with everyone. When I came back, I asked where all the meat had gone because I couldn't see it anywhere. (p. 94)

Another stated norm among the !Kung is solitary childbirth (Shostak, 1981). When a woman is ready to deliver she goes into the bush by herself, delivers her baby, and then returns to the camp. But !Kung women feel ambivalent about this. Older women, knowing the dangers and pains of childbirth, in fact, encourage new mothers not to deliver alone. Nisa, as a new mother, decided to follow the stated ideal norm. But other women scolded her when they went to her after her delivery; they told her she was "without sense" to endanger herself. However the norm came about, !Kung women do not accept it uniformly.

Conflict over norms may be the rule, not the exception. In time, such conflict often leads to modifications and changes in norms.

Norms and Values

Most sociologists think that values are general guidelines and ideas for behavior, whereas norms pertain to specific situations and actions. According to Hewitt and Hewitt (1986), "Norms help establish the minute-to-minute and day-to-day definitions of what people expect others to do and what they think others expect of them." (p. 63) Competition and success, for example, are *values* we internalize as we grow up, but many and different social situations embody these values. There are many ways to get rich, some not quite legitimate.

Roles

Statuses

Each society and culture has many social positions. There are positions in the family, the economic system, and in institutions. There are parents and children, wives and husbands, farmers, carpenters, bakers, priests, police, teachers, students, and many others. As we move from earlier to later societies in human evolution, the number of social positions increases. Moreover, the meaning of any particular social position is not the same within all cultures. As we saw above, a "mother" in the United States is not the same position as a "mother" in some other societies. Even the universal social positions of men and women, children and parents, and age categories have different definitions from culture to culture.

A social position is called a *status*. A few of these statuses are automatically assigned to us: sex, age, and kin (such as son or daughter). These are called ascribed statuses. Others are achieved: husband or wife, worker, student, athlete, and so on. Our ascribed statuses, of course, often influence the types and quality of statuses we may achieve. For example, in some societies women cannot hold a job outside the home; or, if they can work, only certain jobs are open to them. Men on the other hand, have the status of breadwinners in many societies. They *must* work outside the home. In our society, a man who stays home and takes care of the house and children although still rare is more frequent and more accepted today. There is, however, still a heavy stigma placed on this man by most people in our society. In this case, the line between ascribed and achieved status seems blurred.

Of all the statuses we occupy, one often dominates over the rest; it is the one that shapes all others. Sex, race, and work statuses can become master statuses. Being a woman, a black person, a corporation president, or a farm worker, can and usually does determine the nature and quality of all other statuses. A corporation president in the United States is more than likely a white man; a farm worker is likely to be a black or Chicano (Mexican-American) man or woman. But if you are a black woman doctor, what is your master status?

A Status Is Occupied, A Role Is Played

Roles are the expectations, obligations, and rewards of any given status. As sociologists have traditionally defined them, statuses are occupied and roles are played. The role of college teacher requires that a person meet classes, give grades, advise students, usually belong to committees, engage in some scholarly activity, and so on. The rewards are the pay, medical and retirement benefits, and a degree of prestige and respect. But a moment's reflection will tell us that the thousands of people who occupy the status of "college teacher" behave very differently in their roles: they teach with many different styles, give many types of tests and assignments, advise students with varying degrees of interest and care, do a lot, a little, or no research and writing, and so on. And furthermore, the pay and prestige vary widely from college to college.

Roles are related to but not the same as norms. Some norms are specific to given roles: judges wear black robes, teachers give tests, women wash dishes and men take out the garbage (traditionally, anyway), and so on. Moreover, roles have many norms associated with them. Among other things, a mother cooks, cleans, makes beds, and goes shopping (nowadays, some fathers share these duties). But many norms are not specific to any role or roles. They are general expectations: using utensils when we eat, not appearing nude in public, driving on the right side of the road, and others apply to everyone in the United States.

Roles are also played in relation to other roles. Teachers and students, parents and children, husbands and wives, workers and bosses, each is possible only so long as the other exists. You cannot be a student if there are no teachers, and teachers need students to exist.

Role Conflicts

We play more than one role. I am a teacher, father, son, brother, political activist, and sometimes a writer, among others. Each of these roles has expectations and obligations. Sometimes meeting the expectations of one role makes it difficult or impossible to meet the expectations of the other role. This is called a *role conflict*.

Work and family roles often conflict with each other. Successful executives, doctors, lawyers, business owners, and people in demanding jobs may need (or think they need) to devote most of their time to their work. In doing so, however, they have less time for their spouses, children, and other relatives. For parents and spouses in our country today, this is one of the most severe role conflicts. Time given to work often is time taken away from family.

There are many role conflicts. Teachers whose children are also their students; police who stop a speeding car driven by a relative; doctors who treat relatives—all these, and more, pose conflicting demands. A police officer is supposed to enforce the law fairly but also give special consideration to relatives. If you were a police officer, which would you give priority to?

You may want to explore this issue further. How are most of your role conflicts resolved? Does your family or your work receive the most time, or do you balance both of these? One possible solution is to redefine the expectations of one role. For example, work should require less of our time, especially professional jobs. People could begin to complain that it is too destructive to family life for some jobs to demand long working days.

Role Conformity and Uniformity

The concept of people having roles originated from the stage. Actors and actresses step into a character and into a story. In this way, roles are like performances, with scripts, directors, and scenery.

Berger (1963) among others, has developed the argument that roles are played largely in conformity with a social script. In playing a role, we not only perform the actions associated with it, we also come to develop feelings and emotions that accompany the role. "In other words, one becomes wise by being appointed a professor, believing by engaging in activities that presuppose belief, and ready for battle by marching in formation." (p. 96) In time, we become the roles we play: judges, professors, priests, farmers, and so on. "The role forms, shapes, patterns both action and actor. It is very difficult to pretend in this world. Normally, one becomes what one plays at." (p. 98)

Reflect upon the many people you have seen play roles. Do women become mothers? Do they develop motherly emotions as they play the role of mother? Do men become fathers by the same process? Do people who are judges become somber, serious, and wise because the role expects such qualities? How do you take on the role of student? You have been playing it for at least thirteen years. Has the role shaped you so that now you *are* a student? And what does that mean?

Are Roles Automatic and Imprisoning?

We cannot deny that social positions carry with them certain expectations and limits. If you flout too many of these expectations you may lose your children (lose the parent role), or you may be thrown out of school (a student no more). But do we *become* the roles we play? Along with the action, do we always or usually *develop* the associated emotional commitment? Are we not often *coerced* into playing at least some roles?

Blacks, women, and many workers have played roles more out of coercion and need than out of any commitment to them. Slaves, freed blacks, and women have been expected to smile in the presence of the people controlling them. Subservience and politeness have been clear requirements for blacks and women. To survive, they have complied. Some, as Wright (1966) observes, have made smiling and subservience automatic parts of their lives. Others have obliged but with a seething resentment. And some have rebelled against such expectations. Wright lost many jobs because he did not smile in the presence of his white employers. Can we say that blacks and women develop the emotions that accompany their roles? Or, that they even willingly become these roles? To be sure, many probably did to some degree. But many others resisted, pretended, and scarcely hid a boiling anger. The autobiographies of Frederick Douglass (1855), Richard Wright (1945), and many other blacks and women clearly show that commitment to roles is not automatic, that how we act is not necessarily how we feel.

I am not saying that roles never shape people, or that they never develop the proper emotions for the roles they play. Rather, we cannot *assume* that roles usually shape people or that they play them with commitment. How roles are played depends on the person, the time, and the place. These things should be considered when investigating how roles are played. Indeed, the role as a sociological concept distorts reality. Very few people and very few statuses ever resemble roles in the theater. Are the smiles of workers serving the public genuine? Is the politeness shown to bosses and managers really felt, or is it staged so a person keeps his or her job? Do prostitutes enjoy sex with their customers?

In order to survive the monotony or degradation in many jobs, people develop strategies. They do things bosses and managers prohibit or disapprove of, but they do them to survive. Workers may mess up an assembly line so it will stop, and they can rest for a few minutes. Or, as a challenge, they might perform their tasks with their eyes closed. They look for anything to break the monotony and resist authority. For millions of people, their jobs are prisons, they are *doing time*. They can't wait for the next break, the end of the day, the weekend, their vacation, or retirement. Are these people willingly performing and becoming their roles? In reality, we are often forced to play roles and to pretend emotions and commitments. (See Terkel, 1974; Garson, 1975; and Pfeffer, 1979.)

Most roles are also not precisely defined. We have options, alternatives, and freedom in our actions. Parents, teachers, police, and others do not behave exactly alike within their roles. From observation we learn that the same roles are played differently and that violating stated expectations does not bring automatic sanctions.

Many of us overconform in our roles. We think we have little freedom and will suffer greatly if we deviate from perceived expectations. Frequently, when we do deviate we find that little or nothing happens to us. This is not to deny that people sometimes lose their jobs and suffer other losses because they did not fulfill the expectations of their roles. These things do happen, which explains why people play roles they have no internal allegiance to. In order to survive we pretend and go along. But at the same time, when there are role duties and expectations that are demeaning, degrading, and otherwise harmful, we may be able to change them.

Changes in Roles

History shows that many roles have changed over time. They have changed because people, individually and in groups, have struggled against prevailing definitions. Along the way many people have suffered for their resistance. Nevertheless, they have marched, defied superiors, organized, rebelled, and spread visions of different roles and conditions.

Workers have organized, gone on strike, and struggled in other ways in order to redefine what a boss or manager could do to and demand from workers. Workers now have rights they did not possess in the past; they cannot be terrorized. (As we shall see in Chapters 8 and 9, there is an ongoing struggle over the expectations bosses have of workers. They seek to undo the gains workers have attained through long struggles.) Role expectations of mothers, fathers, wives, husbands, women, men, and others have been changing. Mothers now work outside the home. They are not expected to stay home and define themselves only in relation to husbands and children (of course, many husbands are unhappy over these changes).

As norms have changed, so have roles. At any given time there are different understandings of what roles entail, and these differences often lead to changes. Few roles today, if any, are the same as they were fifty or one hundred years ago. Even in my own lifetime I have seen roles change. Mothers are more likely to work, and fathers now share more of the housework and caring for children. People my age were not raised with these expectations, but they have become realities for many of us. In your own lives you may have already seen roles change. By the time you are old and reflect back to your childhood you will surely notice some role changes.

Cultural Change

The preceding discussion on norm and role changes may lead you to think that cultural change is constant and total. To some degree, all cultures are stable. The three Middletown studies, which encompass the years from the 1890s to late 1970s, reveal that Muncie, Indiana, experienced both change *and* continuity. The change has been most noticeable in technology: telephones, cars, refrigerators, stoves, washing machines, radios, TVs, and now computers. Values and institutions, norms and roles, also have changed, but more gradually and not totally. Competition and success still prevail. Sex roles have changed, but many differences between men and women persist.

Each generation feels threatened by change. Lynd and Lynd (1929) point out that many people in Muncie, Indiana, during the 1920s felt an impending doom. Cars allowed young people to date outside their parents' presence, divorce increased, mothers began working outside the home, and other changes seemed to signal the end of the world as they knew it. Fifty years later, not far away, in Hamilton, Ohio, people whose grandparents survived the 1920s still complained about the rising divorce rate and the young who show no respect for their elders. They considered the 1920s the good old days, but the adults of that time saw them as unstable.

Sources of Change

Cultures change because of internal conditions, from conflicts and developments within them. They also change because technology, norms, and customs are imported and adapted (in part or in whole) from other cultures.

In the United States, we have seen changes in technology, farming techniques, manufacturing, clothing styles, values, norms, roles, and customs. We do not replicate and reproduce the exact culture passed on to us. As we live and expand our experiences, as individuals, in families and communities, we come to desire or demand changes in our lives. Gradually, for example, we have come to redefine what proper sexuality is, as we discover through our individual and collective experiences that existing norms leave us unhappy and unfulfilled. In our work, as we accumulate a history, we may find that the money and our daily experience are inadequate and alienating. If this happens, we can organize and demand change. Change comes about through individual and collective challenges, questioning, and struggles.

Change also comes about through *cultural diffusion*. Except possibly for some very isolated groups, the histories of human societies abound in the diffusion of technology and ideas from culture to culture. In a now famous essay, Linton (1937) shows that most items we take for granted as American and part of our daily lives we have actually borrowed from foreign cultures. Clocks, toilets, chairs, umbrellas, silverware, coffee, shoes, and many others were first made or grown in other places in the world.

Today, cross-cultural exchanges occur constantly. Modern technology has spread from a few cultures to most others. Televisions, radios, and cars began in the United States but now exist everywhere. Ideas in science, clothing, furnishings, foods, and all areas of life are spreading, more or less rapidly, from one society to another.

Linton and others, however, have confused the spreading of material items and nonmaterial cultural ideas. The former spreads much easier and faster than the latter. What Linton (1937) described were material objects, conveniences, and technology. Sports, music, and other artistic ideas also spread but not as fast as telephones and cars. Norms, roles, values, customs, and traditions spread even more slowly and not quite so easily. People keep their own values and norms and resist outside influences.

Whether we look at internal or external sources of change, we may wonder how material and nonmaterial changes interact. How have the telephone and the car, for example, changed our norms and values? Some sociologists argue that these technological items have drastically changed our courting and dating customs. Young women and men can now meet and talk and move about without parental presence and control. Sex and social interaction are different in cars and by telephone than in the past. Other material changes are also thought to have caused changes in norms and traditions (Lynd & Lynd, 1929).

Logically and experientially, however, material changes may precede and cause normative change; or, both changes may arise at about the same time; or, finally, changes in the culture, in its values, norms, institutions, and economy, may lead to the invention or acceptance of material items. The clock illustrates the last condition. The clock had been in existence from at least the fifteenth century, but it was not prevalent in peasant societies for at least another one hundred years. Industrialism and capitalism, with their demand for control, order, and predictability, surely led to the emergence of the clock as a dominating force in our lives. Pre-industrial people did not use nor need to use clocks. A technology can only be introduced to and accepted by a culture that is ready for it. A clock would have made no sense to the Tikopia (horticulturalists living on a Polynesian island) (Firth, 1936).

> *The sun, moon and stars do serve as their guides and the coordination of ac-tivities can be effected by reference to their position. But the period spent in bringing certain physical processes to completion—the period needed to con-vert raw food into cooked, to walk from one side of the island to the other, to take out a canoe, paddle the length of the reef and return, or sweep the bay with a seine net, to carry through half a dozen dances, also gives a useful measure of time. When a man is out fishing the length of his stay is governed not so much by the position of the sun, but by the state of the tide, the amount of his catch, and the degree of his interest in the pursuit. The concep-tion of time as an infinite number of units of equal length, mathematically di-visible and inexorably passing by is one that is quite foreign to the Tikopia. They allow their activity to be governed by their intrinsic requirements and not by any external regulator other than the alternation of day and night and of the seasons. (pp. 98–99)*

Cultural Imperialism

For at least the last forty years, American culture has been the most dominant and pervasive in the world. It is probably true that in any period in history when one society dominates others politically, economically, and militarily, its culture also spreads and dominates. France, Spain, and England have at times dominated other societies. These are examples of *cultural imperialism,* the more or less forced change of a culture to standards of a more powerful society.

If you travel throughout the world today, you will see that U.S. life styles and norms are spreading. American clothing, music, all sorts of products and machines, and other items are evident everywhere. Coke, Pepsi, and ham-burgers are replacing native foods and drinks in many places of the world. In Mexico, the rich, wishing to emulate a culture they consider superior, eat pancakes instead of native dishes. When growing up in Greece, I learned through American movies and other sources how to chew gum and emulate other American mannerisms. American television shows rule the airwaves of the nonsocialist world. Indeed, even during the three years (1970–1973) of the socialist government in Chile, the most popular television channel in the country was dominated by American shows. Eighty percent of the films and over 50 percent of the shows were U.S. productions. Directly and indirectly, they espoused capitalist values (Halley, 1981).

In addition, English (first spread by the British) is becoming an interna-tional language. During Spain's conquest of South America, Spanish replaced native languages wherever colonies were built. Moreover, wherever Euro-pean and American countries built colonies, missionaries followed to spread Christianity and other western values. People everywhere have resisted such cultural imperialism, some more successfully than others.

Ross (personal communication) points out that cultural imperialism does not explain fully the changes that come to local cultures. "Native elites buy and broadcast American media products. When a British franchiser buys a MacDonald's store who is to 'blame': American capitalism, British capitalism, or capitalism?" (All three, I think.)

Force—military, economic, and social—indeed caused much cultural change in the past. New norms, products, economic institutions, religions, and so on were imposed on local peoples by foreign powers. European colonialists used military power, stole and killed, and denigrated local traditions wherever they went (Bodley, 1982).

Today, however, military violence is not necessary. Foreign corporations and local capitalists join to destroy local products and traditions and introduce new ones. In Greece, for example, European and U.S. corporations sell products, some of which they make in their Greek plants. Greek capitalists cooperate in the destruction of traditional Greek culture by buying, emulating, and pushing foreign products. Most TV shows come from America, all soft drinks are American brands, and so on. Foreign imperialism, local capitalists, and the desire to emulate the culture of powerful nations drastically changed Greek culture, replacing traditional Greek products, fashions, and entertainment with ones from the United States (and Europe to a lesser extent). (See Chapter 10, on imperialism.)

All societies change, but at what speed, by whom, and for whose benefit?

Cultural Manipulation

Ideally, a culture represents a people's deepest and most treasured values, traditions, customs, and life styles. It is a way of life—*their* way of life—which they espouse and which gives their lives meaning. Culture is a people's life. People create, develop, and change it to fulfill their dreams and meet their needs.

Historically, however, a group or a social class may culturally manipulate people to meet its interests and reflect its values. Over the last hundred years, American culture has been increasingly manipulated and shaped by capitalist and corporate interests and values. Advertising and television have been used to sell corporate products and the capitalist ideology. Is it an exaggeration to say as Halley (1981) says that "culture no longer expresses human hope, but rather ratifies the logic of capitalist exploitation and meaningless consumption?" (p. 140) *Cultural manipulation,* then, is the use of mass media by powerful corporations to induce people to buy and use their products.

Food, Toys, Cars, and Other Products

One of the most distinctive and pleasurable aspects of any culture is its food. Food is necessary for nutrition, of course, but it is also for sharing, emotional satisfaction, and celebration. For people who have moved from one culture to another, cooking and eating dishes from their homeland enables them to perpetuate the memory and pleasures of their past life.

Increasingly, what we eat in the United States is less the expression of our needs and traditions and more the product of profit-seeking, corporate capitalism. Some new foods may be better, tastier, and more convenient. More and more food, however, is being produced by corporations that use chemicals and technology in order to increase profits. Bodley, Zwerdling, and others have shown that profit is the sole consideration for the tasteless chemical dishes found in supermarkets. Not only are they tasteless, but they waste energy through processing and packaging, and their chemicals often damage our bodies. White (1983) offers us a vivid and satirical picture of our corporate eating habits.

> *Durkee Lemon-Butter Sauce Mix for Fish. The label reads, "Enjoy the classic flavor of melted butter, freshly squeezed lemon, and chopped parsley without all the work." Gosh, you know how much work it is to melt butter, squeeze a lemon and chop parsley. I get tired just thinking about it. Instead, you can purchase this handy product and follow the eight, count 'em, eight, steps listed on the back of the package. Before you know it, in only 40 minutes or so, you have fish in a lemon-butter sauce full of lots of interesting chemical additives and preservatives you wouldn't have gotten if you'd used those troublesome, time-consuming fresh ingredients. (p. 13)*

Using fresh ingredients saves energy and money, and surely tastes better. But corporate profits demand that we learn to pay more, forego the pleasure of cooking it ourselves, and convince ourselves that the chemical concoction is the same as real lemon, parsley, and butter.

Who demands these products? Do they meet consumer wants and needs? A commission appointed by President Johnson in the 1960s to study food marketing found that "only 3 percent of the suggestions for 127 new products in a sample . . . actually came from future consumers. Consumers simply are not clamoring for new products" (Marple & Wissman, 1968, cited in Bodley, 1983, p. 132). When I arrived in the United States in 1955, there were no disposable containers for beer, soda, and other drinks; they were all returnable. By the 1970s there was nothing but disposable bottles and cans. I saw no consumer riots demanding them. Corporations imposed them on the public because it was in their business interests. Energy was wasted and streets, playgrounds, and other spaces were polluted by litter. Now, state by state consumers are fighting to force the corporations to use returnable bottles. Corporations are spending millions of dollars to persuade people to keep disposable containers, but voters are no longer swayed by their arguments.

The search for corporate profits extends to infants and children. A federal food program for poor mothers and their children has existed for some years. In 1982, food corporations persuaded the government to change the program and include infant formula and sugar cereals in the foods available. Healthy and nutritious foods are now being replaced with products that have large amounts of sugar. Indeed, Saturday morning television, when children watch cartoons, is glutted with ads for cereals and other foods that list sugar as their first ingredient.

Children's toys and games are also found in every culture. They are fun, they prepare children for their adult roles, and they express important values. But as every parent knows, corporations are forever searching to persuade children they must have some new toy, or they will suffer social ostracism and endless boredom. Last year's doll, TV or movie plastic hero or heroine, competitive or destructive war game, these and more must be replaced with new models. Do our children need or even really want them? Or, are they persuaded to want them? Furthermore, many toys and games are teaching violence, sexism, and competition. Most of the newer video games involve violence, destruction, wars, and competition.

The search for supposedly new products and profits never ceases. Jeans are one of the most useful and durable items of American clothing. Unable to improve on them, some enterprising companies are using social striving and snobbery as a way to charge two to five times the price of ordinary jeans. People pay higher prices for designer jeans because they believe it will give them some kind of social distinction.

No item is more characteristic of the American culture than the car. It has become much more than a mode of transportation (albeit an inefficient one, burning much more energy than trains or buses). It is a status symbol, a dating place, even a sexual symbol. It has separated home and work. People can now live far away from where they work. People can also shop far and wide; they are not limited to neighborhood stores. But it also means a decline in social relations and community (see Chapter 5). How has the car become so dominant in our culture? Did we as consumers choose it willingly? Perhaps. But corporations have made sure that their desire for profits and our will coincided. According to Snell (1973), heavy advertising, lobbying of Congress and the President to build highways, and some outright destruction of public transportation, have all combined to create the triumph of the automobile. It is evident in Lynd and Lynd (1937) that even by the 1930s the car had become so important that in the midst of the Great Depression it was the last of all their possessions people gave away. No wonder most of the largest U.S. corporations make cars or car products.

TV and Advertising

The effects of television and advertising on individuals (children and adults), and on the culture in general, have been and will be debated for years. Whatever else we may say, both are pervasive in our culture. By the time an American youth graduates from high school, he or she will have watched about 350,000 commercials and many hours of TV. Four to six-year-old children average a little over two hours of TV a day; ten-year-olds three and a half; twelve-year-olds four; and by twenty the number is down to slightly over three hours. (See *Newsweek,* February 21, 1977; Liebert et al, 1982.)

Advertisers spend enormous sums of money to persuade us that we need their products. Fifty billion dollars were spent on advertising in 1979, fifty-five billion in 1980, and ninety-five billion in 1985 (*Statistical Abstract,* 1982–1983:566; 1987:537). This includes all sources: newspapers, television, direct mail, radio, and magazines (in that order). We are surrounded by ads. My children playfully sing commercials they see on TV.

Advertising *creates* a demand for corporate products. Sometimes it only informs us, but its primary intent is to manipulate us, to appeal to our insecurities to create needs, wants, and expectations. Corporations make products with nonexisting consumer interest and then seek to convince us we need them. Cosmetics manipulate women's fear of getting old (or, do they also create that fear?); automobile companies sell gas guzzlers by inciting male fantasies of the power and control that may be lacking in their lives; sex and sexuality are constantly implied, promised, and depicted to sell cars, cosmetics, clothes, alcohol, and many other products. Our images of ourselves and our material culture are partly corporate creations. (But not entirely. Witness the electric toothbrush, which surely ranks among the most useless products ever made. People simply refused to buy it, so it never became part of our culture.) (See Henry, 1963; Ewen, 1976; Schrank, 1977; Halley, 1981; and Gitlin, 1986.)

Advertising corporations have created the Advertising Council, a non-profit corporation that makes and distributes public service announcements, reminding us not to litter, not to start forest fires, to buckle our seat belts, and so forth. Its messages are on radio and television stations and appear in newspapers and magazines. In the early 1980s, about $650 million worth of time and space were donated by the media. There would be no objection to such public-spirited announcements except that they contain hidden messages. One message blames individuals, not corporations. Pollution is largely caused by the actions of corporations: energy-wasting cars that pollute the air with lead and other substances, chemicals dumped in the ground or water are a few examples. But the Ad Council seems to tell us that all we need do is to dispose of litter properly and pollution will disappear. Individuals, not corporations, are told not to pollute (Peck, 1983).

Christmas is the annual occasion for an orgy of advertising and consumption. Sharing and giving, basic human motivations and pleasures, are exploited to their utmost. We are badgered to buy expensive and often useless products. Small fortunes are spent to buy expensive presents for relatives and friends. For many people, the joy of Christmas has become a chore and a depressing experience. Corporations and merchants consider the season a failure unless consumers spend more money than the previous year. We now have books written to help us "tame the monster that's become Christmas." They contain suggestions and advice on inexpensive gifts we can make ourselves. We have moved very far from the joy of sharing and giving; these human impulses now serve the interests and profit ledgers of corporations.

The mass media and advertising reach every corner of our culture. They touch every aspect of our lives and seemingly penetrate deeply into our consciousness. They celebrate and promote consumerism, self-interest, corporate profits, capitalism, and the acceptance of the status quo. Often, as Rapping (1987) shows, television programs appeal to and exploit deeply felt needs and emotions. Sometimes they help us understand the world around us, help and enlighten us. More often, however, they simplify and distort social reality. For example, local news and other programs focus so much on individuals, on helping a few people find jobs (as one example), that they take attention away from the real causes of unemployment: corporations and the capitalist economy that are primarily concerned with their profits and growth, not creating jobs. (See Chapter 9 for details.)

Advertising *creates* needs and corporations profit by meeting them. News on television and newspapers is incomplete, biased, and trivial. All media promote a patriotism that is synonymous with capitalist and corporate interests. The exploitation of the Statue of Liberty centennial celebration is a recent example. It became a symbol of home and freedom for millions of people who sailed by it as they approached the United States. But television and corporations, in an orgy of consumerism, exploited and manipulated this important symbol of our culture to sell their products and ideology. The Statue of Liberty, like other values, symbols, and traditions, fell victim to commercialism. Thus, capitalism and the corporations that pollute the environment and destroy communities (see Chapter 5), also seek to manipulate our consciousness by controlling the mass media. (See Gratz & Fettman, 1985; Gitlin, 1986; Parenti, 1986; and Rapping, 1987.)

The mass media do not shape our consciousness totally. Advertisers and corporations would like us to be human robots who can be directed to enhance their power and profits. Their aims and partial success in manipulating cultures and lives cannot be denied, but such manipulation is not total. We should not overestimate the power of advertising, the mass media, and capitalist ideology. The changes and political resistance we see all around us would be impossible if the mass media were all-powerful.

Conclusion

By the time my daughter Melissa was two years old she had been talking for about a year. Like all children, she found language perplexing, fascinating, and liberating. One day, as we were having tea, the two of us had the following conversation.

As she took a knife, I asked: "Why do you want the knife?"
She replied, "I want to cut the table in half."
"Why do you want to cut the table in half?"

"Because I want to cut my tea in half."

"Why do you want to cut the tea in half?"

"Because I like it blue."

That was the whole conversation, which I wrote down verbatim immediately after we had it. What does it mean? Was it no more than a playful use of words? Was she simply trying out new meanings, new ways to use the language? She was smiling and clearly enjoying herself.

I begin my concluding comments with this example of childish language to indicate the creative and liberating potentiality and actuality of language and culture. Culture is what makes us human. It is the history we create with others. It is the tool, which we adapt and change as we go through life, that enables us to learn, grow, and create. Like a good cookbook, it provides us with education and skills to express ourselves, to be creative (Lee, 1959).

We do not always agree about the meaning, significance, and truth of the culture we share with others. Disagreements about and changes in culture indicate that it does not have to imprison us; it can be liberating and creative. We shape it—the "we" includes each of us as individuals, in families, communities, and nations. Together we struggle to create the meaning of our existence.

In the previous section of this chapter we examined evidence that showed how corporations manipulate American culture for their own profit and interest. In many, possibly all, cultures individuals and groups probably experience similar manipulation by powerful interests. This manipulation is not always successful. Part of the struggle of being human, of living in and creating cultures, is working against the manipulation of dominating groups. In the United States today, and probably throughout the world, culture is a complex reality of what people need and want, of what people must do to survive under their social conditions (for us, capitalism and industrialism), of what is imposed on them and what they are persuaded to do, of past history and present reality, of dreams and realities, of fears and hopes. Corporations may seek total control, but they cannot attain it. Our culture and our humanity are ours. We cannot hope to keep them without a struggle, but with a struggle we can liberate ourselves to build a culture for us all—as individuals, families, communities, and nations.

Summary

Culture is the total way of life that is shared by a people in society. It refers to their customs, traditions, beliefs, norms, roles, skills, knowledge of the physical and social worlds, and values. There is wide variation between cultures. Culture is life itself, it provides meaning and satisfaction, and to lose it is to lose part of life.

Our culture is human nature for most of us. The actions and values we learn as children become automatic and easy. Culture shock, which is the emotional and physical shock we experience when we encounter another culture, and ethnocentrism which is the assumption that our culture is superior to all others, show how natural culture becomes. Cultural relativism, the ability to judge other cultures by their standards and in their contexts, is very difficult.

Culture conditions and shapes not only our actions and values, but these actions and values shape even our physical well-being: how well we live and how long we live.

A culture and its language are inseparable. Language reflects the values and social realities of our culture. Some writers argue language shapes and directs our thoughts, experiences, and perceptions of the world around us.

Physical changes—such as erect posture and a larger brain—led to the evolution of culture. Our ancestors invented tools, developed languages, and created families and other institutions, which are the essentials of human culture.

All cultures have values—some actions are emphasized and others are repressed. Certain values, such as cooperation or competition, are basic to each culture. Values partly reflect a society's adjustment to its material conditions, but they also express a people's commitment to relationships and conditions they cherish for themselves. What Americans say and do show they value materialism, possessions, and competition. There is currently a serious debate over basic American values. Freedom is often given as a highly esteemed value, but in reality governments often repress people who exercise their right to speak and protest.

Ideally, the basic values of a society are integrated throughout the society. In reality, they often are not. Subcultures, groups espousing values that differ from those of the larger culture, show that cultural integration is incomplete.

Our daily behavior is guided by norms, which are usually unspoken and unconscious. Norms vary widely from culture to culture. Mores are more obligatory norms than are folkways. Laws are written norms found in class societies. They usually express the effort of a small powerful group to impose its norms on others. Generally, there are conflicts between individuals and groups on what the norms should be, and in time norms do change.

People have a social position, or status, in most societies. A status entails a role, which has expectations and rewards. As we play our various roles the expectations of some roles conflict with the expectations of other roles. There is also a debate whether roles shape us, whether we play a script, or whether we write the script and direct the action. Changes in roles over time would indicate that roles are not automatic.

Cultures can change because people find the present culture unsatisfying or because other cultures introduce foreign elements. In recent world history, some cultures have greatly influenced other cultures, by example and by force. The United States is the most recent example.

American culture is manipulated in many ways, often successfully, by corporations for their own economic and political benefit.

We create culture in cooperation with, and struggle against, others. It is a human creation that enables us to become human. It can be limiting, but it is also liberating.

Suggested Readings

Bellah, Robert N.; Madsen, Richard; Sullivan, William M.; Swindler, Ann; & Tipton, Steven M. (1985). *Habits of the heart: Individualism and commitment in American life*. New York: Harper & Row. Self-interest and individualism are the basic values of middle-class Americans.

Bodley, John H. (1982). *Victims of progress* (2nd ed.). Palo Alto, CA: Mayfield. Bodley argues that gathering-hunting and horticultural peoples led ecologically and socially balanced lives. While, on the other hand, our so-called progress (industrialism), threatens to destroy life on earth.

Davis, Peter (1982). *Hometown: A portrait of an American Community*. New York: Simon & Schuster. Davis evokes the values, emotions, and life styles of a supposedly typical American community.

Gitlin, Todd (Ed.). (1986). *Watching television*. New York: Pantheon. Seven writers explore the impact of TV on the United States by examining network news, soap operas, children's television, music videos, car commercials, and other programming.

Harris, Marvin (1974). *Cows, pigs, wars, and witches: The riddles of culture*. New York: Random House. Harris looks for the material and objective reasons behind values and traditions.

Lee, Dorothy (1959). *Freedom and culture*. Englewood Cliffs, NJ: Prentice Hall. And also (1976) *Valuing the self: What we can learn from other cultures*. Prospect Heights, IL: Waveland. In both books, Lee argues that freedom and individuality are possible only in communities of people who value both individuality and social responsibility.

Lee, Richard B. (1969, December). Eating Christmas in the Kalahari. *Natural History* Reprinted in Richard A. Gould (1973) (Ed.), *Man's many ways* (pp. 22–29). New York: Harper & Row. Lee describes vividly the !Kung value of humility and lack of arrogance.

Lynd, Robert S. & Lynd, Helen Merrell (1929). *Middletown*. And also (1937) *Middletown in transition*. New York: Harcourt, Brace. Two monumental and richly detailed studies of Muncie, Indiana, in the 1920s and 1930s. The Lynds describe and analyze work, family, education, religion, leisure, and politics.

Mangione, Jerre (1942, 1981). *Mount Allegro*. New York: Columbia University Press. An autobiographical novel of Mangione's youth in an Italian family in Rochester, New York, during the 1910s and 1920s. It is a nostalgic, warm, humorous, and loving story.

Parenti, Michael (1986). *Inventing reality: The politics of the mass media*. New York: St. Martin's. The mass media, dominated by capitalist institutions and values, distract us from understanding social reality.

Rapping, Elayne (1987). *The looking glass world of nonfiction TV*. Boston: South End. News, game shows, and other programming appeal to real human needs and emotions, but ultimately television distorts reality and prevents us from understanding social conditions.

Silverstein, Brett (1984). *Fed up: The forces that make you fat, sick, and poor*. Boston: South End. These forces are the corporations that control food, processing it with chemicals and polluting the environment to increase their profits.

CHAPTER 5

Community

A culture is shared by people living in many communities of varying sizes. The Mbuti culture is shared by many small bands of people living throughout the Ituri Forest. The Navaho people share the same culture but live in small towns and villages throughout the southwestern United States. Americans share a culture and live in both small towns and large metropoli. We share a culture with many people, few of whom we ever meet. Our community, however, is different. It is made up of our family, neighbors, friends, people we work with, people who serve us, and others whom we see and interact with frequently. People have always lived in communities. A *community,* in a traditional sense, means a small group of people who occupy a given space, live there a long time (usually all their lives), have frequent social contact with each other, and share a culture. The following discussion expands on this definition and discusses the condition of community and communities in today's societies.

There are three concerns and themes in this chapter:

1. How we define community and what community means to us as a basic human experience;

2. The effects of urbanization on community, social relations, and the human experience; and

3. The social conditions and the social, political, and economic changes that are diminishing the sense of community.

The Meaning of Community

American Communities

In 1965, Cox (Baltzell, 1969), an American theologian, described the small town where he grew up in the early twentieth century.

Having lived both as a villager and as an urbanite I know just what these terms mean. During my boyhood, my parents never referred to "the milkman," "the insurance agent," "the junk collector." These people were respectively, Paul Weaver, Joe Villanova, and Roxy Barazano. All of our family's market transactions took place within a web of wider and more inclusive friendship and kinship ties with the same people. They were never anonymous. In fact, the occasional salesman or repairman whom we did not know was always viewed with dark suspicion until we could make sure where he came from, who his parents were, and whether his family was "any good." Trips to the grocery store, gasoline station, or post office were invariably social visits, never merely functional contacts. (p. 3)

Emergencies often create a sense of community. Neighbors share and help each other. I lived through such an emergency in the winter of 1978. Within a forty-eight-hour period about thirty inches of snow fell in eastern Massachusetts. Drifts piled the snow over six feet high in places. Streets were impassable, and the whole region closed down for a week. People were caught without food and many people found themselves stranded or without electricity. Radio and television stations stepped in to give helpful advice. For example, emergency numbers for medical care, fuel, and food were constantly read over the air. People were reminded to call on any elderly neighbors and make sure they were safe.

People who called radio stations with comments and questions were put on the air. I remember one caller from Lexington saying over the radio that she had extra food and that any of her neighbors who needed it could have it. This story served as a shock of recognition: People realized that there was both an absence of community *and* a longing for it. For in any real community, people from Lexington would not need to call radio stations in Boston, ten miles away, to offer food to neighbors. Such assistance and caring would be done automatically if people knew their neighbors and had ongoing ties with them.

The storm emergency caused an outpouring of the communal spirit repressed by modern social conditions. People helped each other in unprecedented ways. Forced to stay out of cars, people began to walk and discovered neighbors whom they rarely saw or never met. Many people said how satisfying it was to rediscover their neighbors and the pleasures of walking. The emergency ended in a week, and people went back to their old routines, left with a pleasant memory. Community became unreal once more.

People from Buffalo Creek, West Virginia, describe their communities before they were destroyed by a flood on February 26, 1972 (Erikson, 1976).

We all just seemed, in that vicinity, like one big family. We raised our children with our neighbor's children, they was all raised up together, and if your children wasn't at my house on a weekend from Friday to Sunday, mine was at your house with your children. And that's the way we raised our children, we raised them together, more or less like brothers and sisters. The whole community was that way. (pp. 146–147)

What's a neighbor? Well, when I went to my neighbor's house on Saturday or Sunday, if I wanted a cup of coffee I never waited until the lady of the house asked me. I just went into the dish cabinet and got me a cup of coffee or a glass of juice just like it was my own home. They come to my house, they done the same. See? (pp. 187–188)

If my car wouldn't start, all I'd have to do is call my neighbors and they would take me to work. If I was there by myself or something, if my husband was out late, the neighbors would come over and check if everything was okay. So it was just a rare thing. It was just a certain type of relationship that you just knew from people growing up together and sharing the same experiences. (p. 190)

Some of you may still live in small towns or urban neighborhoods where ethnic or other ties create close relationships. You know most, perhaps even all, of the people who live near you; you shop in the same stores where the people serving you are friends or acquaintances; most people have probably lived in the same area for many years, some all their lives. Most or all of your family lives in the same house, or on the same street, or at least, nearby. Most daily contacts are with people you know. Such communities have existed and still exist in many parts of the United States. Gans (1982) describes an Italian community in Boston that existed until the late 1950s when it was razed by urban renewal.

An English Community

Young and Willmott (1957) studied Bethnal Green, a working-class neighborhood in London, England. In the early 1950s, they found that 54 percent of the people had been born and had lived all their lives there. Of the rest, over half had lived in Bethnal Green for more than fifteen years. As a result, people felt at home wherever they went. "Whenever they go for a walk in the street, for a drink in the pub, or for a row on the lake in Victoria Park, they know the faces in the crowd." (p. 116)

One local resident described her feelings about Bethnal Green. "Well, you're born into it, aren't you? You grow up here. I don't think I'd like to live anywhere else. Both my husband and me were born here and have lived here all our lives." Another resident said, "You asking me what I think of Bethnal Green is like asking a countryman what he thinks of the country. You understand what I mean? Well, I've always lived here, I'm contented. I suppose when you've always lived here you like it." (p. 113)

Bethnal Greeners had close family lives, and their relatives served as connections to the community. Parents, siblings, spouses, and children introduced people to their friends. Because people lived in the community for many years, over time they built many ties: school, workplace, street, and family each provided opportunities to meet and know people, to talk, play, and socialize with them. Few strangers exist in Bethnal Green. Almost every-one one saw in the street was someone one knew or knew about.

A Community in Albania

Once in 1980 and again in 1985, I spent a month in my home village of Llongo, Albania. It is a village of 110 families. In July 1980, at seven-thirty one evening I was standing in the center of the village, talking to my father, who was sixty-eight, and my brother-in-law, who was forty-two. As we talked, people kept passing by, on their way to or from home, returning from work or the village store, or going to visit family or friends. Some children were playing nearby. After we had been there for fifteen or twenty minutes, I noticed that my father and brother-in-law either exchanged greetings or talked briefly with *every* person who walked by us. I asked my father if he knew all the people in Llongo. He replied that he did know everyone—about five hundred to six hundred people, even babies. He went on to tell me that he also knew many people in neighboring villages. My brother-in-law told me only some babies and young children were unknown to him. Indeed, everyone knew everyone else with the only exception being some of the young children. I lived the first six years of my life in Llongo, but I do not know nor can I imagine the experience of living in a community where there are no strangers.

When my brother Chris returned to the United States from a visit to Albania, he invited family and friends over to tell them about his time there. Our father's two sisters, who were seventy-one and eighty-two and who were living in the United States with their families, were among the people present. They had been born in Llongo, but they emigrated to the United States in 1930 and had not been back to their village since. Their husbands, children, grandchildren, and other relatives also lived in the United States. That evening, however, they returned to Llongo, to a world and a part of them-selves they had left behind, forever it seemed. Frequently with tears in their eyes, they asked about people and places. Is the village well still where it was? What about our house, how does it stand? How large is it? Is the village square still frequented by people? Where is the schoolhouse? How is so and so doing? Is that fig tree still standing? They asked question after question revealing a deep attachment to a place, a people, a memory, a *community*. I was moved to see them express such emotions, emotions I was unaware they still held and cherished. Their family and lives were in the United States, but a part of them would stay forever in Llongo.

A Definition

A community is a people, a place, an experience, and a common culture. Let us look at some definitions and some issues that revolve around the meaning of these definitions.

Iwańska (1963) defines community in a traditional sense: "a group of people living on the same piece of land, sharing the same aspirations and interests, participating in the same activities, feeling the same pride, love, and fears, and united by a strong sense of loyalty."(p. 205)

Most sociology textbooks have little or no discussion of community, yet it is one of the most central ideas in sociology. During the development of sociology in nineteenth-century Europe, community and the decline of community were the focus of much writing and research. The community continues to be an important social structure for sociologists to examine (Nisbet, 1966).

The word *community* is used in many contexts. Bands of gatherers-hunters, villages, towns, cities, neighborhoods are all called communities. So are ethnic or racial groups, business and professional organizations, religious groups, political organizations, communes, and many others. These usages refer minimally to community as a shared experience or interest. In the following discussion, Iwańska's and Taylor's definitions of community will be used, in the older sociological sense that goes beyond just a shared experience.

Taylor (1982) provides us with one of the more detailed and careful definitions and discussions of community. He finds "three attributes or characteristics possessed in *some* degree by *all* communities," *community, anarchy and liberty*.

"The first and most basic of these 'core' characteristics is that the set of persons who compose a community have beliefs and values in common." (p. 26) This does not mean that each person holds all beliefs with an equally strong commitment. It does mean that there is a general acceptance of some basic values. The second characteristic of a community is the "relations between members should be *direct* and they should be *many-sided*." (p. 29) We meet directly, often, and on many occasions with the people who share our community. Such frequent contact is difficult (I would say impossible) unless we live in close physical proximity. The third characteristic of community is reciprocity. There is cooperation, sharing, mutual aid, and other types of exchanges and relations. In the long run, reciprocity benefits the community as a whole and each member in it.

Taylor (1982) adds three more characteristics on which the above characteristics depend. In order for a community to exist, for relationships to be frequent and direct, for people to share values, and for reciprocity, a community must be small, stable, and have rough economic equality between members. There is no exact number for how many people there should be in a community, but surely no human group can possess the characteristics we are discussing if it numbers in the many thousands. We can get to know only so many people, and we can only have frequent interaction with a few. Stability is important because the bonds that allow for trust and sharing are only developed over a long period of time. Large inequalities in wealth and power lessen the chances for reciprocity and social contact, and create differences in interests and values. Great social and economic inequalities cannot create strong common bonds. (p. 157)

Some social scientists take exception to the preceding definition. For example, Bender (1978) does not think that social reality allows us to restrict community only to a place or a locality. A community can exist even if its members do not live in physical proximity to each other. He cites and disputes the common sociological definition that sees a "community as an aggregate of people who share a common interest in a particular locality." For Bender, a community is an *experience,* not a *place.* "There is an expectation of a special quality of human relationship in a community, and it is this experiential dimension that is crucial to its definition." Preoccupation with space, locality, and territory draw attention away from the basic trait of community, which is "a network of social relations marked by mutuality and emotional bonds." These bonds exist among a "limited number of people" who form a restricted social network and are "held together by shared understandings and a sense of obligation." (p. 5)

Certainly people who simply live near each other but share no values, activities, and expectations do not make a community. The world today abounds with neighborhoods that are not communities. But if we carefully examine the characteristics Bender and others posit as essential to a community, we will see that they cannot exist easily (if at all) within a group of people scattered far and wide. Frequent interaction, shared activities, obligatory exchanges, and sharing only happen when people live in a common space.

The following are the essential aspects of a community. Although they may exist in different degrees within different communities, they *must* exist. One is not more important than another, and each reinforces the others.

- The population is fairly small.
- People within a community live on the same piece of land.
- This same group of people have lived on this piece of land for a long time (stability).
- There is frequent, direct, and many-sided social contact between the people in the group.
- The members share common values, beliefs, interests, traditions, and activities (a common culture).
- There is sharing, cooperation, and exchange, a sense of obligation and reciprocity.
- People are relatively equal to each other, economically, socially, and otherwise.

What Community Is and Is Not

We shall see below that societies are gradually but steadily moving away from the characteristics of community existence. This does not imply, however, that in some golden past there were communities free of all conflict and filled with harmony between people, or that all traces of community have disappeared. There was no paradise then, and there is no hell now.

Conflict and Cooperation

Communities are like families; they vary widely. Even in the best and closest of families there are conflicts and disagreements; all is not unity and harmony. Conversely, in all functioning families, even those rife with discord and turmoil, there may be a basic sense of trust, love, sharing, and expectation. If these qualities disappear, the family will probably not exist as a structure. Communities also have conflicts and disagreements between their members. Redfield (1960), in comparing his study with Lewis's (1951) study of Tepoztlán (carried out seventeen years apart), concludes that both he and Lewis present the true social reality of the community. He found cooperation, common values, and friendliness; Lewis found tension, suspicion, and conflict between the people. They are different aspects of the same reality. Nor are relations between members necessarily loving, emotional, or intense. Even friendships are not universal. But Taylor (1982) argues that deep and meaningful relationships and friendships are more possible in communities for reasons we discussed above. (Turnbull's book *The Forest People* gives an outstanding example of a functioning community. This is a community where loving relationships and cooperation co-exist with tension and conflict, where people are always supported by a sense of a common destiny and existence.)

Social Control and Conformity

No society, no social group anywhere, can last long without adherence to some norms. To exist as a social entity, a group of people must have some common norms they follow.

Many social scientists characterize small communities as oppressive and stifling, where people lose all individuality (a point that will be explored below). We cannot deny that community members do experience some coercion and social control, but, as Taylor (1982) argues, so do people who do not live in communities. But in communities people *participate* in forming norms and in enforcing them; they are not enforced by an external authority such as the police or the courts. (Again, an example of communal social control are the Mbuti in *The Forest People*).

Human groups, which approximate the closest ideal of community, enforce their own social control. As we saw in Chapter 3 when discussing the Mbuti, and as Taylor (1982) points out, there are four types of social control in these communities: "(i) the threat of 'self-help' retaliation, (ii) the offer of reciprocity and the threat of its withdrawl, (iii) the use of the sanctions of approval and disapproval, the latter especially via gossip, ridicule and shaming, and (iv) the threat of witchcraft accusations and of supernatural sanctions." (p. 91) These informal means of social control exist in all human societies. But they are more possible and more effective in communities. Smallness, stability, reciprocity, shared values, and direct and many-sided interaction allow gossip, shaming, and withdrawal of reciprocity to function effectively. Where people need and value each other, where reciprocity is necessary and appreciated, only there can the threat or actuality of its withdrawal end dangerous and offending behavior. People we know can shame us; strangers cannot.

Community and Individuality

But is not such a personal and constant social control oppressive? Aren't people forced to conform fully, to become replicas of each other, in order to survive? Many social scientists have come to such conclusions, and we cannot deny that some conformity does exist in communities. It must exist everywhere. But there is just as much evidence that a community also allows for individuality, for the growth and expression of different and distinct personalities.

The Mbuti retain their individuality within their tightly knit community (Turnbull, 1961). They are shy or confident, boastful or reticent; some are more artistic than others, some better storytellers; they debate, argue, and fight among themselves over the meaning of and need for norms. You could not mistake one for the other. Each is a distinct, free, and expressive person. Nor were the Mayan people Redfield (1960) studied all alike; indeed, "each was a distinct individual, a unique combination of personal traits." (p. 66) He found as much difference between them as he found between the people of any other society he studied or lived in.

Colonial towns in the United States also allowed for differences and divergencies. Studies of the New England and mid-Atlantic states have shown considerable religious diversity, for example. Up to 50 percent, according to Bender (1978), of these communities had "permanent dissenting congregations." (p. 75) Despite (or because of?) fundamental religious differences, residents of these towns felt a common bond, a community spirit.

Established communities exhibit respect and tolerance for differences. People make allowances for individual quirks and traits that seem deviant to strangers. If people know another person deeply, they are not bothered by apparently deviant acts. This point is also made by Erikson (1976).

Indeed, in a community we can be known for our character rather than for external appearances and material possessions. We are known by our actions and qualities, not by appearances. People who know us long and well *know* us and respect our true being. As Young and Willmott (1957) suggest, we are judged as *whole* persons "with the usual mixture of all kinds of qualities, some good, some bad, some indefinable." (p. 161) Here, we can develop and practice habits, abilities, and preferences. The community provides us with psychic, social, and material resources.

Some historians, sociologists, and novelists, however, have criticized small-town America. Novelists like Sinclair Lewis (1920) in his novel *Main Street* depict life in small communities as oppressive, suffocating, narrow-minded, and conforming. They see no benefit to life in small towns. Their writings are part of an ongoing debate on the nature and life in communities.

The Urbanization of Societies

We have seen in Chapter 3 that human societies have become increasingly larger. So have the groups in which people live. We have moved from bands to villages to towns to cities, and now to megacities composed of cities and their suburbs in unbroken continuity. Indeed, much of the eastern United States and two or three other regions are continuous cities or megalopoli. Some historians and sociologists think *urbanization,* the process by which people live in or near large cities, has created social isolation and destroyed communities. It has been accelerating and spreading throughout the world during the last century.

Growth and Change

Throughout history the vast majority of people have lived in small communities. Redfield (1960) characterizes communities as small, distinctive, homogeneous, and self-sufficient. They are places where people are born, live, and die. Bender's (1978) study of communities in fifteenth-century England showed that 90 percent of the people "died within ten miles of their places of birth." (p. 63)

Up to about 1900, the United States was rural society. People lived in small communities. Bender (1978) argues that as a sense of nationhood became more pronounced from 1800 on, a sense of localism also persisted. After the Civil War the United States began a long social revolution that transformed it into an urban society. Although industrialism had begun long before this, it grew tremendously after 1865. As the United States industrialized, as factories flourished in cities, rural people and immigrants moved there. Transportation systems expanded with new roads, the transcontinental railroad, and canals. Socially, politically, and economically communities were becoming less isolated, less local, less self-sufficient. As cities grew and industrialism expanded, so did the concentration of economic power. By 1900, there were monopolies or oligopolies in steel, oil, banking, and other industrial and commercial areas. Fewer people and businesses dominated the U.S. economy. Inmigration to the cities continued unabated. For example, poor blacks began to leave the rural South when their labor was replaced by machines, and they were thrown off farms. This flow of people from the country was augmented by a stream of immigrants from other countries. By 1920, more than half of the U.S. population lived in urban areas.

Let us look at some numbers that show the growth of American cities and the change in communities. In 1840, Chicago was a small town, but by 1890, it had exceeded one million (see Table 5.1). By 1980, the Chicago metropolitan area (the city and suburbs) exceeded seven million people.

Tables 5.2 and 5.3 show the drastic changes in the U.S. population. From a population slightly over 5 percent urban in 1790, we became over 50 percent urban by 1920, and 73.7 percent urban in 1980. Moreover, the total

TABLE 5.1
Population Increase of Chicago

City Proper	Metropolitan Chicago
1860– 110,000	1960–6,221,000
1880– 500,000	1970–6,977,000
1890–1,000,000	1980–7,104,000
1900–1,700,000	
1910–2,180,000	
1920–2,700,000	
1930–3,370,000	
1970–3,369,000	
1980–3,005,000	
1984–2,992,000	

Stein (1960) and *Statistical Abstract* 1982–1983:
17,22; 1987:31

TABLE 5.2
United States Rural and Urban Residents, 1790–1980 (by thousands)

Year	Urban	Rural
1790	202	3,728
1810	525	6,714
1830	1,127	11,739
1850	3,544	19,648
1870	9,902	28,656
1890	22,106	40,841
1910	41,999	49,973
1920	54,158	51,553
1930	68,955	53,820
1950	96,468	54,230
1960	125,259	54,054
1970	149,325	53,887
1980	166,965	59,539

Statistical Abstract 1982–1983:26

population increased dramatically from 1850 to 1920, the years of highest immigration to the United States.

Mobility and Instability

Americans not only live in larger municipalities, in huge congregations of cities and their adjacent suburbs, but they also move from community to community fairly frequently. So two characteristics of community—small size and stability—are becoming more uncommon.

Table 5.4 shows that every five years over 40 percent of all Americans

TABLE 5.3
U.S. Urban and Rural Population
by Size of Place, 1960 to 1980 (by percentage)

	Percentage of Total Population		
Class and Size	*1960*	*1970*	*1980*
Urban	69.9	73.5	73.7
Places of 1,000,000 or more	9.8	9.2	7.7
Places of 500,000–1,000,000	6.2	6.4	4.8
Places of 250,000–500,000	6.0	5.1	5.4
Places of 100,000–250,000	6.5	7.0	7.5
Places of 50,000–100,00	7.7	8.2	8.7
Places of 25,000–50,000	8.3	8.8	10.4
Places of 10,000–25,000	9.8	10.5	12.1
Places of 5,000–10,000	5.5	6.4	6.8
Places of 2,500–5,000	4.2	4.0	4.1
Places under 2,500	.4	.4	.6
Other urban	5.5	7.5	5.5
Rural	30.1	26.5	26.3
Places of 1,000–2,500	3.6	3.3	3.1
Places under 1,000	2.2	1.9	1.7
Other rural	24.3	21.3	21.4

Statistical Abstract 1982–1983: 21

TABLE 5.4
Mobility Status of the United States Population:
1970–1975 and 1980–1985 (by percentage)

1970–1975

Same house (nonmovers)	51.5%
Different house in United States (movers)	41.3
Same county	24.2
Different county	17.1
Same state	8.4
Different state	8.6
Abroad or not known	7.2

1980–1985

Same house (nonmovers)	58.3%
Different house in United States (movers)	39.1
Same county	22.1
Different county	17.8
Same state	9.1
Different state	8.7
Movers from abroad	1.8

Statistical Abstract 1977:37; 1987:25

move to a different house or apartment, often to a different city or town. Only 20 percent of adult Americans settle in a house within a fifty-mile radius of where they were born. Eighty percent move over fifty miles away from their community of birth. The contrast to the stability of small communities (see above) is striking (Kimble, 1970).

Each time we move we sever community ties, and we must form new ones. The physical environment of a community stays the same, but the comings and goings disturb the network of social relationships. Neighborhoods within cities can become local communities, but not when people move every few years. For decades people moved to cities; after 1945 people began to move from cities to suburbs, and the exodus continues. But metropolitan areas are becoming larger. People are also moving from suburb to suburb: for a house in a more affluent comunity, to a new job, and for many other reasons. This movement weakens community bonds since it takes time to know, trust, and like people.

Effects of Urbanization

Philosophers, social reformers, novelists, anthropologists, sociologists, and many others have explored the effects of urbanization on the human condition. What happens to our values, our spirits, our social relationships when we live in large human congregations?

In their well-known essays, Simmel (1903) and Wirth (1938) argue that urban conditions promote alienation, social isolation, mental illness, rootlessness, and other destructive conditions. People can be isolated in the midst of thousands and millions of other people surrounding them; neighbors are strangers to each other; lonely old people, poor people, victims of crimes receive no help and human comfort from their neighbors. Frequently we hear about victims of crime who receive no help from neighbors or bystanders. Since people are strangers to each other, they seem unable or unwilling to offer assistance. It seems that we are becoming less social and more isolated. Study after study of large cities, Chicago especially, show increased social isolation, loneliness, mental illness, crime, and other forms of personal suffering and deviance (Stein, 1960).

Several studies summarized in Bender (1978) argue, however, that urban life is not as isolating and disorganized as Wirth and others claim, that communities do exist within cities. People have strong and ongoing social networks. The people they observed, lived with, and interviewed had connections with family (immediate and extended), friends, neighbors, coworkers, and others. Although communities in America are being assaulted constantly, many functioning communities have existed and continue to exist in urban America.

The truth lies neither with Simmel and Wirth nor with their critics. In dramatizing the changes our society has undergone, Simmel and Wirth overreport the amount of isolation, loneliness, estrangement, and threat to our psyches and social life caused by urbanization. To be sure, some parts of each large city are populated with people who are almost totally bereft of any social contact. Although the seeming indifference to and isolation from our fellow citizens, even in suburbia, cannot be denied, most people are not social isolates regardless of where they live.

The absence of total social isolation, however, does not imply the existence of community. While people retain and struggle to retain family and community ties, social conditions in modern cities and suburbs make such ties more precarious, more tentative, more unstable. We simply live under much different conditions than the people in African tribes, colonial New England, or in unindustrialized countries. Our social contacts *are* different. The data presented earlier in this chapter and those presented below leave no doubt that for the last few centuries our relationships with our neighbors in places we inhabit have been changing. The changes may be seen as better or worse. We may or may not conclude that community exists in modern societies. But the change is indisputable. Most people in the United States no longer live in small, stable, and frequently interacting groups.

At least some of these changes are harmful. What to some people is more privacy, freedom, and individuality in modern society, is to others a denial of social contacts—perhaps also a denial of human nature, for *we are social beings*. More and more studies are beginning to show what experience has taught many people: decreasing social contact causes illness and death. According to Knox (1982), "Cardiac death and mortality from all causes" are two to four times higher among people "with fewer friends and contacts." (p. 11) It does not even seem to matter whether these human contacts are satisfactory or happy—any human contact is better than none, it seems. A later study, cited in the *Boston Globe* (August 30, 1984), concludes that following a first heart attack, men whose lives are beset by stress and social isolation are four times more likely than those not isolated to die from a second attack. (Isolated people were those who belonged to no social group and rarely visited friends or relatives.) For social and physical survival, we need to be with other people, and we need to be with them often.

Urban Diversity

Generally speaking, the larger a group of people, the more diversity it offers. As bands gave way to villages, villages to towns, towns to cities, and smaller cities to ever larger ones, people have lived in increasingly diverse and heterogeneous settings. A large city contains a greater number of groups of people that are different and many more human activities than does a small town. Many types of social and political groups, theater, music, dancing, sports, and other forms of entertainment, many ethnic and racial groups, hundreds of special jobs and thousands of job openings—the variety and diversity of human experience are impressive in any large city. These are among the reasons people have been attracted to cities during the last century.

Many social scientists have thought that urban life allows for and encourages people to be different and individualistic. In a small town everyone knows you, and you can never escape watchful eyes. In a city, you can escape such close observation. But the price of escape from others' eyes is often social isolation. Furthermore, as I argue above, small communities do not necessarily repress individuality.

The Problems of American Cities

Along with the opportunities and excitement of urban life also come some poverty, a polluted environment, more crime, and other problems. Cities have always been beset with some of these conditions.

Since the 1940s, when middle-class families, economic opportunities, and money moved out of large cities and to the suburbs, these cities have experienced serious economic and social problems. Housing has deteriorated, poverty has increased, city services have declined, and poor blacks and other minorities have inherited deteriorating environments. The cities in the United States face numerous problems, but among the most intractable are poverty, discrimination of minorities, and lack of affordable housing.

The Move to Suburbia and Back to the Cities

There was a large population migration from cities to suburbs immediately after World War II. Sparked by federal and bank housing policies that encouraged people to buy single-family houses in the suburbs, the dominance of the car (see Chapter 3), bank and corporate decisions to invest money and create jobs outside cities, and other trends, people left cities by the millions. Small towns near large cities expanded in population, and new towns were built where once apples, potatoes, and tomatoes grew. From the 1950s to 1980s large U.S. cities lost population while surrounding metropolitan areas were booming (see Tables 5.1 and 5.3). Total U.S. population was expanding but large cities were declining.

Urban population decline may have stopped during the 1980s (*Statistical Abstract,* 1987: 31–33). Some large cities even show some population increase. Neighborhoods that had been left to the poor and minorities are now desirable. Housing developers and speculators have begun to invest money in urban marketplaces, condominiums, and conversion of apartments to condominiums. The invasion of yuppies is upon us.

The Decrease in Primary Relationships

Small communities provide their members with a variety of social relationships. Not everyone is everyone else's intimate friend, but no one is a stranger.

Members of my family who live in Llongo, Albania, the Mbuti of the Ituri Forest, Americans who live in small towns—all have daily contacts with people they know. They occasionally meet outsiders, but almost all their contacts are with people they know (Bender, 1978). Increasingly in modern society the people we meet or see in stores and supermarkets, government agencies, on the street, everywhere, are people we are unlikely to know. A supermarket differs radically from a village store, and others like it that are steadily going out of existence. All of you, I assume, have shopped at some sort of establishment whose owners and employees you know, where you can chat, gossip, joke, or reminisce.

Even if you shop regularly at a supermarket, it is diffcult to get to know the employees—leisurely chatting is not encouraged on the fast check-out counter (some people, especially isolated old people, do attempt to carry out social talks). Supermarket shopping is unlike shopping at the small corner store of fifty years ago. Such stores not only provided socializing opportunities, they sold on credit to regular customers because people were more than just customers: they were friends and neighbors who could not be turned away in time of need (Terkel, 1970).

A group of psychologists observed activity in twenty-eight supermarkets and twelve outdoor farmers' markets in the same cities. Here are some of their conclusions (Rubenstein, 1981):

> *Only about one out of every 10 supermarket customers shopping alone or with small children chatted socially with other customers; two out of every three farmers' market shoppers who came without other adults had social chats.*
>
> *While half of all supermarket shoppers made perfunctory remarks like "have a nice day" to employees, each farmers' market shopper asked about two questions for specific information and half discussed topics other than food, such as buying beehives and farms. (p. 19)*

Think of lunch at one of the many diners, neighborhood restaurants, and other eating places still populating our towns and cities, and then contemplate eating at McDonald's or any other fast-food place. Could you chat or joke with the harried and rushed service people? Some of you may have eaten at a neighborhood cafe or restaurant whose owners, employees, and many customers you know. Compare the human experience of eating there with eating at McDonald's.

While most of us still have many personal contacts, they are fewer and decreasing. If you speak with an older person, someone who is at least sixty years old, you may see that even in their lifetime they have seen personal contacts become impersonal. Before long, gas stations will be unstaffed. People will drive to a gas station where they will insert cards in a computer and then fill their own gas tanks. Another small element of social life will have vanished. The loss of social contact is not welcome, it is bemoaned. We often struggle against this trend, but stores and bureaucracies want speed and efficiency, not leisurely chats.

The phone company urges us to "reach out and touch someone"—family and friends. It exploits our longing to be near those we love and whose lives touch and enrich our lives. Telephones and cars are seen by many people as liberating: we can make friends in many places, and we can keep in touch with people we love. But it seems that phones and cars replace (rather poorly at that) what communities used to provide. And unlike phone talks, talks with family, friends and neighbors in small communities allow us to see, touch, and smell other people (Goodman, 1983b).

A number of sociologists, anthropologists, and historians have examined the profound transformation of social relationships within human communities. They have all done so by developing opposite types of communities, the first reflecting the small community we are discussing here, the second reflecting the more impersonal nature of urban living. The following lists some of these typologies and their authors. We will discuss in detail Cooley's (1909) primary and secondary groups.

Social Relationships
within Human Communities

Small Communities	*Modern Societies*
Status (Sir Henry Maine)	Contract
Community (*Gemeinschaft*) (Ferdinand Tonnies)	Society (*Gesellschaft*)
Folk society (Robert Redfield)	Urban society
Communal relationships (Max Weber)	Associative relationships
Mechanical solidarity (Emile Durkheim)	Organic solidarity
Primary groups (Charles Horton Cooley)	Secondary groups

These authors and their community types are discussed in Nisbet (1966) and Bender (1978).

In his book *Social Organization,* Cooley (1909) argues that *primary groups* exist in all human societies, and they shape our nature. They make us human. Primary groups are "characterized by intimate face-to-face association and cooperation," and they form "the social nature and ideals of the individual." The most important, but not the only ones, are "the family, the play-group of children, and the neighborhood or community group of elders." (p. 23) In these and other primary groups, we relate to people as total human beings. The relationship is an end in itself, it exists for itself, not for some other end. We see these people often, we have known them for a long time, we feel a closeness and common destiny with them, and we will probably grow old with them.

The term *secondary group* is not used explicitly by Cooley, but his writings seem to imply it. In secondary groups, the relationship is not an end unto itself, but rather a means to an end. In these groups we do not relate to others as whole human beings. Relationships are limited and often temporary. There is no deep identity with the group or its members. Most work groups in contemporary societies are examples of secondary groups. So, it seems, are many clubs, associations, and other organizations. Members have limited relationships. Many secondary groups—work groups, sport teams, political organizations, and others—may and do become so important, involving, and all-encompassing to their members that in time they become primary groups. Many groups fall somewhere between the two types; their members may feel a common bond and they may have frequent contacts, but they do not approach the intimacy of family and close friends. In small communities there are more primary group relationships. In the recent past in Europe, the United States, and elsewhere, there were many daily relationships that were not primary (as Cooley defines the term) but which were still more personal than many of our daily contacts today. Not only are primary relationships weakening, but other contacts with people we know are also declining.

The two types of human societies in the list above do not imply a total contrast between older communities and present ones. They refer to a *relative change*. More human relationships were primary in colonial America and in other small communities, but primary relationships still exist. Indeed, without them there is social and physical death, as studies on loneliness show. We are referring to a *decrease* in primary relationships and to fewer daily contacts with people we know, not to their total absence.

Industrialism, Capitalism, and Community

We have seen that in today's world, community is changing, if not declining and disappearing. What has caused this transformation in the basic form of our social existence? Some social scientists argue that industrialization, urbanization, centralization and enlargement of institutions, technology (cars, phones, computers, and so on), and other social changes, alone or in various combinations, have diminished community. To these social processes I would add *capitalism*.

In recent U.S. history, capitalism has been the primary cause for the decline of the community. The search for profit, growth and control by corporations and the ruling class (see Chapters 8 and 10) has created, encouraged, and added to urbanization, industrialization, bureaucratization, and technology. These in turn have diminished the conditions that a community needs in order to survive, thus leading to the decline, and sometimes the abandonment, of the social structure. Let us look at some examples that will help to illustrate and support this conclusion.

Corporate Decision Making and Community Well-Being

Chapters 8 and 10 describe in detail the control large corporations and the ruling class have of the economy, government, and other social institutions. This control has not always been so dominant and pervasive. It began to expand after the Civil War and has continued to grow. As corporations have grown and their power has increased, local community autonomy has decreased. Local control of communities has been increasingly removed from the hands of the people who live there. Many sociological studies of the last fifty years have documented the decrease in control communities have over their own economies and institutions, and how this has affected community life. Community politics is now controlled by local powerful banks, real estate firms, and other businesses. (See Chapter 10.) Outside institutions, run for profit and controlled by the ruling class, now influence and shape American communities. (See Lynd & Lynd, 1929, 1937; Warner, 1963; West, 1945; Vidich & Bensman, 1958; Gallaher, 1961; Stein, 1960; Olson, 1963; Bender, 1978.)

Mechanization
Corporations make decisions solely on the basis of how to increase their power and profit—this kind of decision making has destructive effects on local communities. People lose their lands and jobs, are forced to relocate, and thus break their community ties.

Caudill's (1963) history of coal mining in Appalachia shows graphically how corporations and capitalism can destroy a community. Beginning in the late nineteenth century, coal mining companies moved to Appalachia and began to exploit the people. Over time these companies have used their power to force their workers to accept unjust contracts. They have taken the local wealth out of the region. As the companies increased profits by mechanizing the mines and by extracting coal by stripping it from the surface (not mining it underground), they created massive unemployment. Their mining practices have destroyed the land and caused flooding since treeless land cannot hold water.

Unwittingly, people practically sold their lands through leases which they thought allowed companies only to dig for coal underground. Courts have ruled that coal companies can do whatever they wish to land—even totally strip it—in their search for coal (Caudill, 1963). When one man sued the company that had plowed up his land, the judge told him, "The truth is that the only rights you have on your land is to breathe on it and pay the taxes. For all practical purposes the company that owns the minerals in your land owns all the other rights pertaining to it." (p. 308)

By the 1950s, poverty and unemployment in Appalachia were widespread. During the Depression of the 1930s, despite poverty, people stayed on because "they felt a powerful attachment to the familiar hills, valleys and institutions surrounding them." (p. 177) But in time the continuing poverty forced people to leave. In many counties, over 75 percent of the high school graduating class left within a year. The effects were drastic. Caudill writes, "In community after community one can visit a dozen houses in a row without finding a single man who is employed. Most are retired miners and their wives who live on social security and union pension checks. Hundreds of other houses are occupied by aged widows, some of whom have taken in a grandchild or other youngster for 'company' in their old age. . . ." (p. 333) One may walk the streets of camps and wander along winding creek roads for days and rarely find a young man or woman.

According to Caudill, in many Appalachian counties today, most people survive on some form of public assistance. They feel degraded and dispirited. Any sense of community will erode when many of its inhabitants leave and those left behind must survive in abject poverty. These are effects of corporate plunder, the creation of a new local economy, and the brutal dismissal of workers in order to increase profits through mechanization.

In the late 1950s, Swados (1959) visited a town where the coal mine had closed. Most workers were determined to stay on, but, without jobs and money, their lives began to change. They had once gone fishing and socialized with each other, but they now kept to themselves or moved away. They were discouraged and felt their world was falling apart. The company had closed the mine purely for economic considerations without concern for people's lives and how it would effect them.

What happens to those who leave? Do they find better lives? Hardly. As discussed above, they long for their old home, neighbors, and community. "And in the taverns of Northern industrial cities former hillbillies for months sipped beer to the lament, 'I wanna go home, I wanna go home.' " (Packard, 1972, p. 5) Gitlin and Hollander (1970) talked with many people who had moved from Appalachia to Chicago. These people told of enduring severe poverty and exploitation in the city. They were only able to obtain the lowest paying jobs, lived in crowded slums, had little (or inadequate) health care, and many—much to their horror—had to go on welfare. Thus, these Appalachian people were exploited twice: Corporations ruined their land and communities and forced them to move, and business in the big city exploited them as cheap labor. There is hardly any sense of community possible under these conditions.

Corporate Relocations and Plant Closings

Corporations continue to shut down plants and offices in communities and move to other places (mostly foreign countries today) where cheap labor and low or no taxes enable them to increase their profits. Local communities are often devastated as a result. Thousands lose their jobs, family lives are disrupted, stores close as people have no money to shop there, and community life diminishes. It cannot be stressed strongly enough that corporations make decisions based solely on interest and profit, and affect the lives of thousands and millions of people everywhere.

For example, in the mid-1970s five rural communities in the western United States and Hawaii experienced severe unemployment. According to Young and Newton (1980), their "economic survival depended on one company or one industry [mining, timbering, growing pineapples, farming] which had made decisions to leave the areas." It is not that the companies were losing money but rather, they expected to make more profits in their new locations because of cheaper labor. The people who lost their jobs, many in their forties and fifties, did not want to move away to look for new jobs, but in time some were forced to move elsewhere. Of those who stayed on, many became depressed losing their pride and self-confidence as they remained without work. In time, of course, their children will have to move away. The profit imperative leads not only to "human obsolescence," it also eats away at community life.

During the 1970s and 1980s, steel companies closed down many of their mills in the East and Midwest. The companies say they closed them because they could not compete with foreign steel companies that pay their workers much lower wages than American workers receive, and for other reasons. Laid-off workers and others disagree; they think that the steel companies failed to modernize their operations, and they decided to invest their money in buying oil and other nonsteel corporations.

Whatever the explanation, many communities, such as Clairton, Pennsylvania, have been devastated (Marquis, 1986). They have become ghost towns. Thousands of people are unemployed and many leave. Others desperately hang on to their houses and communities. Seventy-three-year-old Wayne said, "I've lived here all my life. I know everyone. Walk out on the street and there isn't anyone I don't know. If I go to a strange place, I'll miss that." (p. 26) The divorce and suicide rates have increased to twice the national average. Young people are leaving to find jobs Clairton no longer has. "A town can't survive without young blood." (p. 26)

Urban Renewal and Gentrification

Many city neighborhoods have a sense of community. People who have lived in these communities for many years have created ties and traditions that bind them together. Corporate policies that have as their most important goals expansion, profit, and control, tend to destroy these neighborhoods. Through urban renewal and gentrification usually involving condominium conversion, long term residents are forced out and replaced by people who can afford expensive apartments and stores that cater to professional people.

In the 1950s and 1960s (and to a smaller degree in the 1970s and 1980s), large parts of many American cities underwent a process known as urban renewal. Usually a city, using federal and city money and special legislation, forced out residents and businesses. The monetary compensation for their property was usually considerably below fair market value. Most, especially poor blacks, moved to slum areas making them even more crowded. Almost all paid considerably higher rents. Gans (1982) estimates that over a million people have been displaced by urban renewal since 1950. People suffered by moving to worse housing or by paying considerably higher rent; they also lost neighbors, friends, and community. Gans summarizes many studies that show the majority of displaced people grieved for a lost home, neighborhood, and community. Depression and a sense of loss were prevalent among the displaced people of Boston's West End, for example. Many may still be suffering from lost friends and neighbors.

Housing Almost thirty years after the destruction of the West End, the memories and anger of former residents are still strong. About seven hundred of them held a reunion in 1986. They spoke movingly, nostalgically, and angrily about a diverse and close community that was destroyed (*Boston Globe*, November 17, 1986:20).

"[The West End] was fantastic. I can't tell you how much I miss it."

"What I miss most about it is how close the people were. No one ever locked their doors."

"It didn't matter if you were black, Jewish, Irish, Italian, Lithuanian, Albanian, Polish. We were the only neighborhood in the city that had such a multi-ethnic group."

The official explanation for urban renewal has been that the areas were slums. Some were, but most were ethnic and working-class communities that did not fit city planners' designs of desirable neighborhoods and stood in the way of corporate expansion and profits. After existing buildings were torn down with public money, the land was sold cheaply to private developers. But the new apartments and businesses were not rented to old residents. People from the upper class paid the high apartment rents and higher prices at the new stores. Urban renewal has meant the forcible removal of poor, minority, and working-class people from their communities to provide profit for business and convenient homes for the upper class.

Gentrification and condominium conversion has replaced urban renewal. Gentrification refers to the displacement of older residents by professional and more affluent people. They rent or buy homes in traditional working-class areas that are becoming desirable locations, thus raising property values and forcing residents out. Gentrification is happening across the United States, and is fueled by real estate developers in search of profits. With suburban growth probably at its limit, developers have turned to renovating urban buildings and neighborhoods. They cater to younger, often childless professionals. The former residents—working class, poor, and minorities—are displaced.

Where do they go? No one knows, or seems to care. One study cited in the *Guardian* (March 6, 1985) estimated that seventeen thousand families in New York City public housing have doubled up (two families in one apartment). The neighborhoods from which they were displaced have been *devitalized,* not revitalized. Former ethnic communities in Philadelphia, now gentrified, are lifeless. "Summer chairs on the sidewalk, televisions out on the stoop and children's street games are replaced with a . . . deathly hush on the street." (p. 10)

Where urban renewal once destroyed the West End of Boston, gentrification is destroying the North End, a neighborhood long known for its close and deep community ties. It has become attractive to developers and affluent people who want the charm of city life. It is close to Boston attractions and adjacent to the Quincy Market, a renovated area with many shops catering to tourists and professionals.

Rents are increasing rapidly in the North End, some up to $1,000 a month in 1987. Most residents cannot afford them and are moving out. Apartments are converted to condominiums. Much of the change is caused by outside developers and newcomers, but some is fueled by a few North End residents and merchants who see an opportunity for large profits. Once 90 percent Italian, it is now under 50 percent. Butcher shops, small markets, bakeries, and other small stores are giving way to upscale stores catering to more affluent newcomers and tourists.

Iida's (1985) study comparing the North End with the already gentrified Back Bay shows the differences. People who enter a bakery or market at the North End do more than shop. They chat, exchange information and gossip, laugh, and leave emotionally richer. Even an observing sociology student is not allowed to simply shop and walk out. The owners inquire about her health, her reasons for being there, and are helpful and friendly. Shopping in Back Bay stores, on the other hand, is quick, formal, and businesslike. A life-long resident said of her local butcher shop: "If he closed I'd be heartbroken." Another commented: "A young professional doesn't come here with the intent to raise a family. You lose the family, you lose the community. You just have people living here" (*Boston Globe,* May 9, 1987: 41).

The loss of community for greater profits knows no boundaries; it happens in suburbs as well as cities. Wellesley, an affluent suburb west of Boston, in 1987 lost a theater, the Community Playhouse. The building will be converted to stores and make much more profit for its owners. One resident wrote in a letter to the *Boston Globe* (March 9, 1987) that "another gathering place is eliminated. . . . The Playhouse was a place one could go and see people one knows. It was a place that gave us a sense of community. . . . But the purchaser and the trustees [of the property] felt there was something more important than happiness and a sense of community here. To them, and to our society at large, the bottom line is profits." (p. 13)

One form of displacing local residents and promoting gentrification is condominium conversion. When rental apartment buildings are converted to condominiums the present occupants are usually forced to move out since they cannot afford to buy the apartments they occupy. From 1971 to 1980 about 360,000 units were converted to condominiums, with about 150,000 of those in 1980 alone. Condo conversion is speeding up. Dreier and Atlas (1981) show there is a good reason for this: profits are huge in condo conversion. A thirty-story apartment building in Chicago was bought for $10 million in 1973. After spending $250,000 on remodeling, the developers sold the units for a total of $14 million—a 44 percent profit. Another apartment complex was bought for $50 million, slightly renovated, and the co-ops were put on the market for $100 million. Condominium conversion has continued and even accelerated in Boston and other cities (*Boston Globe*, June 2, 1987: 1).

Residents of buildings that are to be converted often resist removal. They use laws that protect them and give them time before they must move out. But the profits to be made are too great and landlords often provide residents with the motivation. They increase their rents, shut off heat and utilities, do not make needed repairs, and harass them in many other ways (*Boston Globe*, April 1, 1981: 1, 17).

If all else fails, one way to force residents out is to burn them out. There have been cases where landlords have let a building run down, harassed the occupants, insured their buildings at values much higher than the market values, and then hired arsonists to set them on fire. They have renovated the buildings with the insurance they collected (usually still standing and structurally sound after the fire) and sell the units as condominiums. Arson for profit has swept many U.S. cities since the late 1970s. Some neighborhoods have organized and stopped it, but it remains a serious problem in many cities. Some experts have estimated that about half of the 600,000 arson fires in 1979 were set for profit. (See *Guardian*, December 9, 1981: 6; March 6, 1985: 10–11.)

Condo conversion, urban renewal, and other forms of displacing long term neighborhood residents displaced 500,000 to 800,000 people yearly in the late 1970s (Gans, 1982). When people are forced to move out, community life is disrupted. Bob Lee, a sixty-four-year-old man, was forced out of his room in a Cambridge, Massachusetts, neighborhood because of condo conversion (*Boston Globe*, October 17, 1980). On his last day before he left, his neighbors came by to wish him a sad goodbye and bemoan the loss of a person who created a sense of safety and community.

> For 17 years, Lee has been surveying the neighborhood from his favorite chair on the porch, with his radio tuned to a Red Sox game, or with a game of checkers or cribbage in progress, all the neighborhood news to tell, and a bucket to spit in.
>
> "We were all crying when we got the news that they were moving Bob Lee out," said Soifer, who shares an apartment with several other young women. "He makes us feel safer. He's always out on that porch, day and night. Last October he called the police on a guy who was trying to break into my apartment. And then there was an attempted rape on the street last year. Bob was instrumental in getting new street lights turned on and in putting on a big block party for safety. He's the center of the street. He makes this a neighborhood."
>
> Mary Denros, a native of Greece, dropped by with a bag of groceries on

her way to her food service job. Silver-haired Frances O'Hare, who has been greeted by Lee on her way to church every day for 17 years, dropped by with a carefully wrapped gift shaped like a bottle. (p. 51)

Because they stand in the way of greater profits, long-time residents in many neighborhoods are losing ties with neighbors. This is the human meaning of condo conversion, arson-for-profit, and urban renewal. Many of them, especially old people, will not have the money, strength, or will to re-create what they lost. Community, fragile as it is, becomes even more fragile. (For more on the housing crisis, see Chapter 8.)

Stores   Among the institutions that have provided some sense of community have been neighborhood stores where people meet people they know and exchange greetings and news. Increasingly, however, shopping centers and malls are replacing neighborhood businesses.

The profits are high. "The Draper Company reports clearing 21 percent annual profit on its $1.2 million investment in a Monterey, California, mall." In 1977, shopping centers represented $60 billion worth of investments and 44 percent of the retail trade. They are safe and profitable investments, so insurance corporations, banks, and others happily invest in them (*Dollars and Sense,* July-August 1978: 8–9).

They are a controlled environment. The music, physical arrangement, and total atmosphere encourage shopping. "The mirrors, the music, and the sound of rushing water create a sense of distortion. There is never a clock to remind one of the world outside the mall" (*Dollars and Sense,* July-August 1978: 8–9).

Malls are places where teenagers and some elderly people congregate. Some young people are known as "mall rats" and "the mall is the only community they know." But it is a controlled and artificial setting, existing only for greater corporate profits. A mall manager lamented the fact there is no "community feeling" in his mall (Preston, 1982).

In *The Mall: An Attempted Escape from Everyday Life,* Jacobs (1984) studied people who frequent malls. He concluded that malls impoverish their social life and provide no sense of community. If people seek "a more meaningful and hospitable place," they do not find it in malls. They are bland environments that filter out people who are different. They create a homogeneous environment. There is little in malls to "stimulate one, and to help provide life with greater meaning." (pp. 111–113) There is no variety, no street life, no long-term relationships, no people who care. Malls are *businesses,* not communities.

Expanding Institutions

Hospitals, colleges and universities, museums, and other large institutions have also destroyed neighborhoods. In *The Rape of Our Neighborhoods,* Worthy (1976) shows both the determination of institutions to expand at any cost and the strategies to fight them. (This book is an education for all of us who have been socialized to believe in the benevolence of hospitals and universities.)

Institutions expand not for the benefit of the community, but for glamour, prestige, and power. With an excess of hospital beds, hospitals still seek to buy whole city blocks, tear down the houses, and erect new buildings and garages. They try to buy up property quietly; they proceed secretly, never announcing the whole expansion plan. Unless community residents catch on to the game early and oppose expansion vigorously, it is soon too late (as in the area near Boston's Symphony Hall, where the Christian Science Church forced out old residents and businesses). Institutions, bureaucrats, and experts fear popular resistance and try to keep things quiet with an aura of expertise, authority, and benevolence.

When residents begin to oppose expansion, institutions have a three-step plan. First, ignore the opposition. When it will not go away, blame the conflict on radicals and outside agitators. When that does not still opposition, resort to dirty tricks. The apartments of residents who will not move out are often burglarized, set on fire, deprived of heat, and so it goes. Most of us find it difficult to believe that hospitals and universities resort to such tactics to force residents out; however, Worthy's (1976) documentation is detailed and overwhelming. When people get in the way of powerful institutions, war is declared upon them. Wars involve sly tactics as well as force and violence.

Harvard University is a prime example of an institution that wrecks neighborhoods as it expands. Worthy (1976) provides extensive information on its tactics. For example, when the state of Massachusetts was stopped by three thousand demonstrating residents from buying a city block to use for a mental health center, Harvard moved in quietly and bought the homes one by one. In 1982, some Boston residents fought Boston University (B.U.) from expanding into their neighborhood. B.U. and the city government ignored the residents' protests and more than twenty buildings were bought by B.U. and converted into dormitories. Gradually, a stable neighborhood is being taken over and changed by an institution (*Boston Globe,* September 27, 1982: 36).

Genocide

For millions of people throughout the world, the destruction of their cultures and communities has been the direct result of European and U.S. imperialism. We need to look no further than our own country to see this. Native Americans were killed, starved, and otherwise decimated when their lands were stolen from them by expanding capitalist nations in the seventeenth and eighteenth centuries. Their economies were forcibly changed and their cultures and communities undermined. When they did not die from slaughter, starvation, or disease, native peoples were removed from their lands, forced to work on plantations or in construction. Native Americans living in the Great Plains died by the hundreds when Europeans killed the buffalo indiscriminately, thus destroying their whole culture and economy, which had depended on the buffalo. (See Bodley, 1982, 1983; and Vidich, 1980.)

Genocide is the destruction of a community by killing or forcibly moving its people, or by destroying the community's economic base. Genocide still happens today and is not limited to Indians. The incident described below shows how the lives of the poor—regardless of race or creed—are dismissed.

Erikson (1976) in his book *Everything in Its Path* relates the story of a number of small communities in West Virginia. On February 26, 1972, a number of communities in Buffalo Creek, West Virginia, were destroyed. Five thousand people lived in Buffalo Creek in a number of small communities. At the top of the creek, a coal company had created a forty-acre lake, about forty feet deep. It was dammed with wastes of "mine dust, shale, clay, low-quality coal, and a vast assortment of other impurities." (pp. 21–48) For years government inspectors had warned the company that the dam was unsafe and could burst. For years the company did nothing to improve the dam's safety. Following heavy rains, the dam simply collapsed on the 26th and the sludge and water poured downstream. Company officials had seen that it was dangerously porous and ready to go, but did not warn the people in the communities below. In the few minutes following the dam's collapse, over two hundred people died, many more were injured, and houses and buildings were totally demolished.

The survivors experienced a keen loss of community. We saw earlier in the chapter the rich community life that had existed in Buffalo Creek. Below some of the survivors tell about their loss.

> *It's kind of sad around there now. There's not much happiness. You don't have any friends around, people around, like we had before. Some of them are in trailer camps. Some of them bought homes and moved away. Some of them just left and didn't come back. It's like teeth in an old folk's mouth down there now. (p. 196)*
>
> *The people who are here don't get out and do things like they used to. Before the flood, the men worked on old cars or got together and talked for hours at a time. Now it's just a few minutes at a time, and it seems everyone wants their children to stay close home. (p. 224)*
>
> *All I can call the disaster is murder. The coal company knew the dam was bad, but they did not tell the people. All they wanted was to make money. They did not care about the good people that lived up Buffalo Creek. (p. 183)*

The destruction of Buffalo Creek is but an extreme case of how capitalism affects communities. The search and demand for profit, growth, and control diminish and destroy communities.

The Struggle and Search for Community

Since culture and community are the essence of human existence, people resist and struggle against the assault on these aspects of their lives.

More and more localities and states are contemplating and passing leg-islation to prevent corporations from closing shop and moving away. And if they do move away, they are being forced to pay the workers and the com-munity so that the devastation will be minimized.

Arson-for-profit and gentrification are becoming controversial political issues. People demonstrate, picket, lobby for laws, and otherwise seek to protect and preserve their neighborhoods (*Guardian*, June 2, 1982: 9).

Thousands of people create and join communes, cooperatives, free schools, counseling centers, political groups, and other groups that are meant to create a sense of community. In such groups, relations are to be direct and personal, open and spontaneous. Participation by and equality of all are cherished values. Most do not succeed and fade away, but their appearance attests to the quest for community (Starr, 1979).

Liebert (1983) says that in Calfornia, "a nonprofit group has proposed building 36 apartments, with shared livingrooms, kitchens and bathrooms." (p. 3) In part, such a community will reduce the cost of housing, which in the 1980s is rapidly becoming astronomically high (in 1983 the average home in Marin County cost $187,000) and beyond most people's reach. An equally important motive, however, is the creation of a community by forcing people to share livingrooms, dining rooms, television rooms, and other common fa-cilities. As one of the founders claims, "through physical proximity you meet people. You don't have to drive twenty miles across town to see a friend." (p. 3) We cannot tell how well such a communal arrangement will work; it may be forced and partly artificial. But it does express the longing for human associ-ation.

Other people are joining various religious cults. These groups raise serious social and political issues, but they do indicate the need and desire for people to belong to an intimate group.

As individuals and in groups, through struggles of various types, people continue to preserve, search for, and create communities. Without community we are not fully human.

Conclusion

This discussion of community has been shaped by my life in a village in Albania and a town in Greece. My grandmother who raised my brother and I in Greece and lived with us until she died in 1965 had intermittent contact with relatives through the years, and my recent visits to Albania and Greece have kept alive in me the memories, images, values, emotions, conflicts, and dilemmas of a peasant community.

Community, as I've described it here, exists in all societies. Since I am the most familiar with peasant communities from my experiences growing up in Llongo, some may find nostalgia and perhaps even a little romanticism, in the discussion of these communities. Undoubtedly there is, but I have also tried to balance these sentiments with an honest picture of some of the repression and negativity that occurs in community life, especially in peasant communities. I am aware that inequalities and repression do exist. Women, for example, are oppressed in many ways, individuality is often discouraged, and family life can be suffocating. On the other hand, communities such as the gathering-hunting and horticultural variety seem to be largely egalitarian. From what researchers have been able to gather from studying the few communities that still exist and from those that once existed, there was (is) freedom and individuality along with equality and social responsibility. (See Chapter 3.)

The passing of communities represents a very profound social transformation. Life in gathering-hunting bands, villages, and small towns was *different*. That difference became vivid for me on my visit to Albania and my home village. What I had read in history and sociology became concrete when I realized that every person *knows* every other person in Llongo. Then I experienced and felt some of the emotional, social, and daily meaning of community. I still cannot imagine what it must be like to literally *know* everyone where you live. My experience, like that of almost all of us in industrial societies, is of knowing a few neighbors, and of seeing scattered relatives and friends now and then, but mostly seeing people I know barely or know not at all.

It takes some imagination and empathy to understand the concrete human experience of people in small communities. People whose communities are destroyed feel empty, and the loss is equal to life itself. We cannot impose our views on what they live and value. In their nostalgia my grandmother, former West Enders, and people in Buffalo Creek surely forget the negative aspects of life in these places. But the nostalgia is for something very real—for people and places and experiences and memories that enriched their lives.

That July evening in Llongo will live in my consciousness and emotions forever. It gave me a sense of what community has been, and what it can be.

Summary

In this chapter, we have described communities in the United States, England, and Albania. Community, above all, is a group of people who have lived in the same place for many years and who have frequent and direct contact with each other. There is both cooperation and conflict in communities. Even though conformity is usually fairly strong, people can express their individuality in communities.

The United States, and the world at large, has become more urbanized as people have moved into and near cities. In addition, people are moving more frequently, with very few people living all their lives near where they were born. Some sociologists and historians argue that urbanization and mobility have led to social isolation and the loss of community, others see community as strong as ever. Actual conditions are probably somewhere in between. American cities have been experiencing population losses, increasing poverty, and other problems. In the 1980s, some people have been moving back to cities.

Relationships among people today are becoming more impersonal. Business transactions are with strangers, whereas in the past they were with people we knew. Increasingly, we live our lives more in secondary groups, although we still have ties with primary groups.

Captalism and industrialism have been destroying communities for centuries. Some communities have been destroyed when people were killed or forcibly moved. Local economies have been taken over by national corporations. Some regions, such as Appalachia, have been exploited economically and left to suffer the consequences as people have had to leave their communities to escape the poverty. Other communities have suffered when corporations moved their plants, leaving their workers unemployed and forcing them to become poor or move on. Arson, urban renewal, condo conversion, and gentrification are destroying urban communities, as are shopping malls and expanding institutions that force people to leave communities.

Many groups are engaged in struggles against the forces that are destroying communities. They seek to preserve and re-create communities.

Suggested Readings

Bender, Thomas (1978). *Community and social change in America*. Baltimore: Johns Hopkins University Press. A history of social change and its effects on community.

Erikson, Kai (1976). *Everything in its path: Destruction of community in the Buffalo Creek flood*. New York: Simon & Schuster. Erikson describes the community that existed before the flood, and the effects its destruction had on people and families.

Gans, Herbert (1982). *The urban villagers* (2nd ed.). New York: Free Press. The people in this small Boston community led a rich family and community life, until the West End was destroyed by urban renewal in the late 1950s.

Lewis, Sinclair (1920). *Main street*. New York: New American Library. In his classic novel, Lewis portrays small-town America as narrow-minded and suffocating.

Simmel, Georg (1903). The metropolis and mental life. In Kurt H. Wolff (Trans. and Ed.), *The sociology of Georg Simmel* (pp. 409–424). New York: Free Press. Simmel believes that urban life causes alienation and destroys social ties.

Stein, Maurice (1960). *The eclipse of community*. New York: Harper & Row. Stein summarizes and discusses some classic community studies that describe social changes in American communities.

Taylor, Michael (1982). *Community, anarchy, and liberty*. New York: Cambridge University Press. Taylor thinks community is possible only where there is freedom and social equality.

Wirth, Louis (1938). Urbanism as a way of life. *American Journal of Sociology, 44*(1), 1–24. Urban life promotes social disintegration, mental illness, and other physical and social problems.

Worthy, William (1976). *The rape of our neighborhoods*. New York: Morrow. Hospitals, universities, and urban renewal destroy communities when they buy and tear down homes and apartment buildings for their own expansion.

Young, Michael & Willmott, Peter (1957). *Family and kinship in East London*. Baltimore: Penguin. Family and community ties are strong in this working-class neighborhood of London.

CHAPTER 6

Families:
Changes and Continuities

In the Spring of 1987, I taught a course on the family to two groups of students. One was a day class of forty-five women ages nineteen to twenty-two. The other was an evening class of twenty-eight students (eighteen day students, twenty to twenty-two years old, and ten continuing education students, ages ranging from the mid-twenties to the late fifties). Before I said anything, I handed out a questionnaire. Among the eight questions were "What does your family mean to you?" and "What do you think is the condition of the family in the United States today?"

To the first question, all but four people wrote positive, glowing, and moving comments. The people who felt negatively about their families said that they wanted to create loving and close families of their own. Most people said they could not imagine life without their families. They said they find security, comfort, love, and acceptance within their families and insisted that they are close to their parents, siblings, and other relatives, and they see them often. With one or two exceptions, they reported no major conflicts or disagreements. A few others wrote that there are occasional arguments, but they do not diminish the essential love and care people feel for each other. Over 90 percent of the single people said they intend to marry and have children.

But while people gave a glowing account of their own families, they found the family in general in deep trouble. They were all worried that people no longer are close to their families. Increasing divorce, parents too busy to spend time with their children, and working mothers are some of the conditions they mentioned as leading to the decline and demise of the family. Compared to the supposedly good old days the students felt that people just no longer care that much for their families.

The discrepancy is obvious. How can the family be in such deep trouble if everyone claims that her or his family is in splendid condition? Where is the misperception?

Later in the semester most students wrote a paper that outlined and discussed the history and current situation of their families. Everyone wrote that they found researching and writing their papers a moving and a joyful experience. The enthusiasm and the revelation were obvious. Most people learned new details and stories when they talked to relatives they had not seen for years. Someone discovered a strong, lively grandmother who as a young mother went out to work in the 1930s. Another person found a hidden divorce, and some people found an aunt or an uncle they never knew existed. For some students, the research for the paper *created* a stronger sense of family.

Most ruefully noted that they no longer see cousins, uncles, aunts, grandparents, or even siblings who married and moved away as often as when they were younger. They insisted, however, that they *feel* as close to them as they ever did. They attach as much emotional significance to relatives now as ever; indeed, many noted that as they grow older they appreciate and care for their families more than ever. The students showed me the intense, deep, and universal desire for and commitment to the family and taught me that it is the most important of all human experiences.

In anonymous written comments at the end of the year, about half of the students said that in the course they learned that the family is surviving and doing better than they had believed when they started the course. I certainly had no intention to convey that message. Indeed, I had no message. Rather, I wanted to expose them to the debate between those who argue (from different social and political perspectives) that the family is declining, and those who find the family in splendid and vibrant condition. Also, I wanted to carefully explain the enormous difficulties of finding out what *is* happening to the family, as distinct from what we would *like* to be happening, or what we would like to *believe* is happening. Finally, I wanted to describe the wide variety of family types in the United States today, throughout history, and across cultures.

Families are changing in many ways and not changing in others. Some of the changes represent a lessening and decline in the commitment to the family. Other changes, such as the gradual liberation of wives and mothers, are positive and needed. But whatever sociologists, historians, and others say, whatever statistics we may offer, whatever misperceptions we may think people have—the seventy-three people who debated and studied the family with me convinced me that the vast majority of Americans want to be and believe in families. For most people, life is empty without a family.

Although most people abide by the belief that the family is all important. The family as a social structure is an ideal that doesn't necessarily match reality. Even though we say we want close family ties, we are constantly striving for economic independence, and when there is no economic imperative family kinship becomes more tenuous. Government and corporate policies also often split up families, destroying what little cohesion they had. And, finally our strong strain of self-interest and individualism is a characteristic that contradicts the commitment to the family.

Difficulties in the Study of the Family

It is an enormously difficult undertaking to understand the family in one's own society, let alone in another society or another period of time. The following biases, presuppositions, and misperceptions contribute to the difficulty.

Interpreting Data

The same facts may be interpreted differently. For example, even if we agree that divorce has increased dramatically in the last few decades, how do we interpret that increase? Most people assume that the higher divorce rate shows the family is losing its strength and importance. But others argue that people who divorce do value the family, but find their spouse and their specific relationship unfulfilling, oppressive, or destructive. If wives leave abusive husbands, do they devalue family life, or, do they value a happy and egalitarian marriage? Other conditions and changes within marriage and the family are equally susceptible to differing interpretations. As you read further in this chapter (and in reading of your own), remember that few facts speak for themselves.

Personal and Theoretical Perspectives

Few, if any, of us can avoid imposing our biases, needs, personal histories, and theoretical predispositions on the material we read. We cannot do otherwise. Such imposition is most notable when we explore family life, which is significant to us and emotionally loaded.

Sociologists and historians are of two minds: Some feel the family is in serious trouble, that its bonds are weakening and it is withering away; others believe that it is very stable and vibrant. (Caplow et al., 1982, present the second perspective.) I have taught a course on the family for seven years, and I have found that everyone comes to the study of the family with one of these biases, or some variation of one of them. For years I believed that the family was declining. I am no longer convinced this is true, but I also do not think that the family is in splendid condition.

The family is changing, no doubt. Some of the changes I find liberating and desirable. The trend toward egalitarian marriages and people's unwillingness to stay in unhappy marriages are just two examples. Other changes disturb me, for example, the relative isolation of old people, the trend of living alone, the geographical separation of relatives, and government and corporate policies that disrupt family life. How do we weigh these changes and arrive at a conclusion about the current state of the family?

Ethnocentrism: The Ideal Family

As we shall see later there is no definition that encompasses all the human groupings that have been called families throughout history. We assume that our experience and (what we take to be) our culture's values are universal. Although it may be changing, for decades most Americans believed that the normal family is (or should be) composed of a mother who stays home, a father who goes to work, and their children. Even in the 1950s, those supposedly happy, golden days, millions of Americans did not live in this ideal family. Today, even if we exempt childless families, parents whose grown children have moved out, and others, most families with dependent children do not fit the 1950s model. With over 50 percent of mothers with children under six working outside the home, and millions of single-parent families (see below), the ideal nuclear family of the 1950s television family shows is not the norm. There are millions of families composed of a father who goes to work and a mother who stays home until the youngest child is eight to ten years old. But we seriously misunderstand American families if we believe that most of them fit this description.

Furthermore, if we assume that our family norms do or should apply to other societies, we fail to understand their family experiences. Societies where parents choose their children's spouses, where married children live with their parents, and where other customs and norms different from ours exist, will seem strange. But these customs are neither right nor wrong—they are merely different. Ethnocentrism will prevent us from understanding, appreciating, and learning from the vast variety of human families. We should always keep in mind that no one family type is more or less natural or useful than any other.

Assumptions about Family Life

We distort reality if we imagine families as unitary entities. Each family is composed of individuals; some are born into it and others join it by marriage. Each person may experience the same family life differently. Many studies have shown that husbands and wives have different perceptions and experiences of their lives together (Rubin, 1983). A student once conducted separate interviews with a couple both of whom worked. The husband told the interviewer that they managed their jobs, housework, and children well; he was happy. But the wife said she felt burdened, tired, and rushed since she did most of the housework.

Other assumptions may also blind us from seeing the reality of family life. We cannot assume that families are or ought to be harmonious and peaceful. Some sociologists and historians, in fact, argue that conflict, disagreement, and some violence are normal to family life. A setting so intimate, so intense, and so important to us is bound to have tension and problems along with love, care, and cooperation. On the other hand, we may come to expect conflict and violence in families—an assumption that may blind us from seeing the underlying love and cooperation. Or if child abuse includes occasional slaps, we could conclude that abuse is endemic to families. All assumptions need to be examined and challenged.

Longing for the Good Old Days

We constantly idealize the past. In the midst of our daily conflicts and compromises, we would like to think that in the past people led more stable and less troubled lives. Older people nostalgically recall a past that never existed. Some young people become convinced by television shows and other cultural mythmakers that there once was a golden past. The show *The Waltons* is a good example. For people growing up in the 1970s families in the 1930s appeared to be united, loving, and always able to solve their problems. In the late 1970s and early 1980s, *Happy Days* recalled the 1950s as innocent and amusing. Until recently, historians and sociologists stated as a fact that in the past Americans lived in extended, three-generation families (Landis, 1986). We know now that at most only 6 percent of families in the United States have ever been extended. (See Demos, 1970, and Zinn & Eitzen, 1987.)

Family conflict has always existed. People tended to hide their conflicts, but we are gradually discovering that family problems are not a new phenomenon. (For a historical perspective on divorce, see Lynd & Lynd, 1929 and 1937.) We must be careful, however, that in our efforts to debunk the myth of the good old days, we do not also miss some conditions in the past that were desirable and perhaps preferable to what we have today. Not all change is an improvement.

The Evolution and Functions of the Family

In Chapters 3 and 4 we discussed Gough's (1971) theory on the origins of the family. In the evolution of our species, because of the long period of dependency of the young, the *family* enabled humans to survive and evolve. Men and women cooperated with each other, sharing the responsibility for protection, food, and nurturing the young.

In gathering and hunting societies, families cooperated and shared the food men and women procured: women roots and fruits and some game, men the animals they caught and killed. Later, men and women began to work the land—clearing, digging, plowing, sowing, and reaping the harvest. In these very early societies, the family was the social *and* economic unit. It was the source of all the necessities for survival: food, clothing, tools, housing. As we saw in Chapter 3, specialists gradually appeared, but until the arrival of industrialism, the family remained the prime economic institution. Families gathered, grew, or made all of their food and material objects. Very few families in industrial societies can be considered self-contained production units. Some families may work together to produce various items, a few may raise food, but most families acquire their necessities by having individual members work in offices and service industries. Families make very little of what they use, such as food, clothing, houses, and appliances. Regardless of whether we praise or bemoan this recent transformation of the family, we must try to understand the reasons for it.

Families have always had many functions and meanings. Families not only add new members to society, but they nurture and socialize them as well. People acquire the culture of their society through their family. It also provides intimacy, sharing, and security for children and adults. Especially today, families seem to be havens, refuges away from the competitive and impersonal world outside. Breines (1981) notes that parents, spouses, and children provide "the space for and possibility of personal life for adults." (p. 24)

Family Types

Families vary from society to society, from one historical period to another, and often within the same society.

Nuclear, Extended, and Modified Extended

Sociologists and anthropologists see two basic types of families: nuclear and extended.

A *nuclear family* is composed of two generations—parents and children —who reside in one household. Husband and wife cooperate in providing the basic necessities for living and in raising the children. In industrial societies the nuclear family has been, or is becoming, an ideal family type. It is unclear whether it has actually been the norm in our society.

Unlike the nuclear family, the *extended family* is composed of three or more generations living together in one household. A brief history of my family will illustrate how the extended family operates in one particular society. I should note here that despite frequent quarrels and resentments, people in extended families have a strong sense of obligation and responsibility. For example, even though in practice people often find it burdensome to care for their elderly parents, very few ever shirk that obligation. Indeed, in 1980, when I told people in my parents' village that in the United States elderly parents do not live with their married children, they were shocked. They thought Americans were uncaring and selfish.

My knowledge of my family extends to my father's grandparents. My grandfather was their only child. When he married he brought his wife to live in the same household with his parents and grandmother. My paternal grandparents, Christos and Afroditi, had six children, two sons (Nicholas, and my father, Theodore) and four daughters (Theodora, Eleni, Vasilo, and Sophia). As the daughters married each one moved in the household of her husband's parents. Two of them eventually emigrated to the United States with their husbands and children.

When my uncle and father married, each brought his wife to live in the same household with their parents and grandparents. At the age of fifteen, when my mother married my father in 1930, she moved into a family that shared one kitchen and other common facilities. Four generations lived together: my father's grandmother, her son and his wife, their two sons (my father and uncle) and their wives, and my uncle and aunt's children. Over the course of ten years my father's grandmother and his father died and my parents had children. As the families of the two brothers became larger, and as various family conflicts grew, my father and uncle separated. A new house was built, adjoining the old one, where my uncle moved his wife and four children. Their three daughters got married and moved out; their son married, and he and his wife have been living with my aunt since his marriage in the early 1950s (my uncle died in 1946).

My parents had five children (actually eight, but three sisters died when they were young), three sons and two daughters. My older brother Chris and I left home in 1947. Our two sisters—Kleoniki and Ifigenia—were married and moved to their husbands' parents' homes in the 1960s. My older sister now lives with her mother-in-law, husband, and four children. My younger sister lives in the same building with her parents-in-law, and her husband's siblings, but they have their own separate household (their own kichen and other rooms). The family members, however, do see each other daily. My brother was married in 1964, and I was married a year later. We both established our own nuclear families in the United States.

My parents still live in Llongo, Albania, in our ancestral family home. In 1988, they were seventy-six and seventy-three years old. My younger brother, his wife, and their three children (two daughters, sixteen and ten, and a son, six) live with them. They live as one family, using all the same cooking and other facilities. While I was visiting, my mother did most of the cooking, and my sister-in-law did most of the cleaning (she ran the village day care but was not working during my visit). My father and brother (a teacher most of the year) worked the vineyards and garden, but they mostly catered to their visiting son and brother.

These three generations—seven people—live as an extended family. Most other families in the village also are extended. Members of these families share income, work, and social activities as one unit. There are conflicts, disagreements, and feelings of resentment, as there are in most families everywhere. My brother and his wife have two daughters and a son. They intend to continue the tradition of having their son and his wife live with them after he marries, but he may or may not wish to do this. By the time he marries norms may have changed. (For a description of peasant families in Greece in 1960, similar to my family in Llongo, Albania, see Friedl, 1962.)

Families are not only nuclear or extended—there are many variations. In the United States today, there are three generation families, families with one parent, and so on. In Llongo older people do not always live with their married sons: some come to violent disagreements and separate, some had only daughters who moved in with their in-laws, occasionally a husband will move in with his wife's parents, some live alone because their sons have moved to the city, and they want to stay in the village, and some never had or lost their children.

Messenger (1969) studied an Irish village, Inis Beag, that had a "predominance of the nuclear family." But the following description of the seventy-one households reveals the tremendous variation that can exist within a society (late marriage and celibacy account for many of the households).

Number of Households	Personnel
30	Husband, wife, and offspring
5	Husband, wife, offspring, and the husband's widowed mother
4	Husband and wife who are childless
4	Husband, wife, offspring, and both parents of the husband
3	Husband, wife, offspring, and the husband's unmarried sister
2	Husband and wife who are childless and both parents of the husband
1	Husband, wife, offspring, and the husband's father who is a widower
1	Husband, wife, offspring, and both parents of the husband and his unmarried sister
1	Husband and wife whose offspring have emigrated
7	Widow and her unmarried offspring
5	Single man (bachelor)
2	Brother and sister both of whom are unmarried
2	Two brothers and a sister all of whom are unmarried
2	Widower and his unmarried offspring
1	Two bachelor brothers
1	Bachelor and his widowed sister-in-law (p. 71)

Many societies in the world have a third family type—a *modified extended family*. It is neither composed of three generations living under one roof nor is it an isolated and independent unit with only parents and children. This family type consists of married children who live next to or very near their parents. While they may have their own separate households, they see and socialize with each other frequently. They help each other and share their daily lives. There is much and frequent social contact. The Mbuti, !Kung, and other gathering-hunting societies have what I call modified extended families. This family type also exists in the United States, England, and probably many other societies.

Family Variations

Ethnic Families

Modified extended families have existed among ethnic groups in the United States for some time. Mangione (1981), in an autobiographical novel, described the family life of his Italian-speaking relatives in Rochester, New York, from 1910 to the 1930s. Gans (1982) became a participant-observer and studied the working-class Italians in Boston's West End in the late 1950s. Both studies reveal much socializing and frequent contact between parents and children, siblings, cousins, and others.

Mangione's parents emigrated to the United States leaving their parents in Sicily. So only parents and chidren lived in his home in Rochester. But his uncles, aunts, and other relatives, who lived nearby, were an integral part of his daily life. Any excuse sufficed for a large family gathering. Parties, celebrations, and other occasions brought many relatives together for talk, food, and singing. His Sicilian relatives had "a magnificent talent for gregariousness and a pathetic dread of being alone." They "seemed happiest when they were crowded in a stuffy room noisy with chatter and children." (p. 23)

When Mangione decided to go away to college, his relatives were shocked.

> When I broke the news that I was going to an out-of-town university—
> Syracuse—my relatives were plainly horrified. Could it be that I was becoming a calloused American? The idea that I could bear to leave them behind
> offended some of them. They began to regard me as a heretic. A good Sicilian
> son stuck near his family; the only time he left it was to marry, and even then
> he lived close by so that he could see his relatives often. Life, after all, was
> being with each other. You never left your flesh and blood of your own free
> will. You left only when it was impossible to earn a living near them, or when
> you died. (p. 227)

On some Sunday nights, after his aunts and uncles had left following a big Sunday family gathering, they would return late at night and serenade the Mangione household. "They stood under our bedroom windows and sang gently until some member of the household awoke; and when they saw a light go on their singing became louder and more joyous, breaking into an uproarious crescendo as the door was opened to them." (p. 21) On one occasion his parents gave a banquet for some relatives who were leaving for California. When they changed their minds and stayed in Rochester, his parents gave another banquet to celebrate their staying. (p. 127)

The intense closeness and socializing also created violent family squabbles at times. For example, not all relatives could fit in at any one social gathering, and those who were excluded sometimes vocalized their discontent. The arguments would be bitter and people would not speak to each other for months and even years. Other relatives would set in motion elaborate plans to reconcile the disputing parties. In addition, the frequent gatherings and intense socializing seemed suffocating and oppressive to some people.

Gans (1982) found somewhat similar family life among the Italians of the West End. Relatives saw each other frequently. Women and men rented apartments in the same building, same street, or near their parents' apartments and homes. Women saw their mothers usually daily. Formal and informal gatherings on Sundays and evenings were frequent.

Many Greeks in the United States have modified extended families. My aunt Theodora, a widow at ninety, lives with an unmarried son. All five of her married children live within a mile or less of her house, three within walking distance. She sees each of them at least two to three times a week, and she sees at least one child at least once a day. My aunt Helen, seventy-eight and a widow, has an unmarried son living with her. A married son lives on the second floor, and a granddaughter (daughter of the people on the second floor) lives on the first floor. Her other three children live three to five miles away. But she sees all of them frequently, and most Sundays they all gather for dinner at her house.

Young and Willmott (1957) found that the working-class people of Bethnal Green in East London, England, had extended families similar to the Italians and Greeks in the United States. Most couples settled in the vicinity of their parents' home and continued to see them frequently, usually daily. Daughters were especially close to their mothers, turning to them for help and advice on raising children on occasion, asking them to take care of children after school, shopping together, having afternoon tea, and so on. The older mother ("Mum") was the social center of family life. Siblings and their families met each other at her house for family gatherings. Table 6.1 shows that the physical proximity to the parents' home led to continuing, close family ties.

The ideal in Young and Willmot's study was to live *near* one's parents, especially the wife's. But a severe housing shortage often forced young couples to live *with* one set of parents. In a sample of forty-five, twenty-one couples began their marriage by living with in-laws. The housing shortage also meant that some people had to leave Bethnal Green and settle in a London suburb some fifteen miles away. Most of the people who left, however, missed their families and the community life of Bethnal Green.

Black Families

Black families in the United States vary in their composition and life styles. Middle-class black families seem to resemble their white counterparts. They

TABLE 6.1
Contacts of Women According to Distance of Mothers
(General sample—133 married women
with mothers alive and not in the same dwelling)

Residence of mother	Number of married women	Women who saw their mother in previous twenty-four hours
Same street or block of flats	23	23
Elsewhere in Bethnal Green	49	33
Adjacent borough	25	4
Elsewhere	36	3

From Michael Young and Peter Willmott, *Family and Kindship in East Long,* © 1957 Routledge and Kegan Paul. Used by permission of publisher.

live similarly and emphasize similar values (for example, education for their children). There is little difference between their homes and activities and those of middle-class white families (Willie, 1981).

Working-class and poor black families must cope under difficult conditions. In Chapter 11 we shall discuss in detail the economic and social conditions of black people in the United States. For purposes of this discussion it is only necessary to point out that unemployment is high among blacks (up to 50 percent in some cities), that their housing is poorer on the average, that healthcare and other services are inadequate or nonexistent, and that discrimination persists in many areas. These conditions often make it difficult for families to survive as nuclear units and for men to hold jobs and help provide for their families. Thus, an extended family, a domestic network in which women are more central than men, has arisen. Some men—husbands, brothers, friends—are present, but it is mothers, daughters, and sisters who maintain the extended family. They run families with cooperation, sharing, imagination, and resourcefulness—they must in order to survive under the conditions imposed upon them. (See Liebow, 1967; Stack, 1974; Gutman, 1976; Valentine, 1978; and Kenyatta, 1983.)

Blacks also have modified-extended families with many relatives living close to each other, sometimes sharing homes. Relatives count on each other. They cooperate to meet emergencies. For example a family may take in relatives who have lost their apartment. There is extensive sharing of responsibilities, some adults care for children while others work. In times of need, children, parents, kin, and friends are the only sources of help and assistance. Stack relates one story of a woman who inherited some money from a relative who died and spent most of it on relatives. She bought them shoes and clothes and helped them in other ways. (See Stack, 1974, and McCain, 1983.)

There are other ethnic family variations in the United States, of course. Chicanos or Mexican-Americans, Puerto Ricans, native Americans, and many other groups carry on some of their own traditions and live under different social conditions.

Variations in Family Composition

Today, there are many families that are not composed of father, mother, and children. Single-parent families are the largest variation. Millions of women, and some men, whether through divorce, the death of a spouse, or because they never married, are raising children alone (see discussion of single parents, below). But there are other variations. Lesbian and gay couples live as families and raise children, their own or adopted ones. There are foster families, children raised by their grandparents (for whatever reason), and elderly parents whose children have moved away.

There are what we may call *intentional families*. They may be a group of unrelated elderly people (same sex or both sexes) who live together in a house for companionship and affordability. Or, they may be a number of parents living communally and raising their children jointly. Some of these groups may not be families in the eyes of some people, but they *function* as families. They share and cooperate, they provide comfort, to make life richer and more meaningful than it would be if members lived alone. (See LeMasters & DeFrain, 1983, Chapters 6 and 9, for some of these variations.)

Families and Cultures

Any typology of families will not totally capture the rich variety of family experiences. I have presented some types here as a means of bringing some order and coherence to the discussion, but the social and existential realities of family life are not so easily categorized. In closing this discussion, I want to present a brief description of families in two societies. These families are not strange variations of what our society sees as normal. On the contrary, they are normal to the people who experience them.

About 3 percent (close to one hundred thousand) of the Israeli population live in *kibbutzim* (plural for *kibbutz*). Each *kibbutz* has about three hundred people. Except for personal possessions, all property is communally owned, and the community provides for everyone's needs. All major decisions affecting the *kibbutz* are discussed and made by all the adults. Most meals are eaten in a common cafeteria, and laundry and other services are provided by the community. Men and women who marry have a room of their own, but other rooms are communal. Soon after birth, children go to a community nursery where they are raised by trained nurses. They eat, sleep, and play there. But parents and children do develop a common bond. Children know who their parents are. Parents and children spend two to three hours with each other each evening. In the last few years, children have begun to spend even more time with their parents (weekends, some evenings, when they are ill). Nevertheless children are still not raised by their parents. In a *kibbutz* the family includes everyone. There have been some changes in the kibbutzim during the last twenty years, and by the late 1980s, many of the children were living with their parents. (See Talmon, 1965; Rabkin, 1976; *Boston Globe,* April 5, 1981:17, 22; and Queen, Habenstein, & Quadagno, 1985.)

The Nayar lived in India. Their family structure, as practiced in the nineteenth century, was one of the most unusual in the annals of anthropological literature. In this society, the men were warriors who had no responsibility for their wives or children—in fact, they did not live with them. A woman married a man of the same caste (social class) as her own. On the night of the wedding they might or might not have had sexual relations. The next day the man would leave. From that point on the husband and wife were free to have short- or long-term sexual relationships with other people. They did not live together or have any obligations to each other, except that when the husband died, the wife and her children performed the death ritual for him. Children were raised and cared for by women, their mothers and brothers and sisters who lived in the same household. Thus, there was a stable institution in which children were raised. There was order, not chaos.

People who write about the Nayar argue that this system freed the men to be warriors. It also provided for the procreation, care, and socialization of new members and for the sexual needs of the adults. (See Gough, 1959; Friedl, 1981; Oliver, 1981; and Harris, 1983.)

These are two of many examples of the diversity of family structure. For whatever reasons of either necessity or choice, people in any culture must create a system for having and raising children and for providing for sexual and emotional needs. Oliver (1981) argues that whatever the family is (or, in some people's eyes, is not), "men must marry women, or vice-versa, children must be produced and cared for and placed in a recognized social network, and families must perform the tasks that will enable the society to continue." (p. 271) (See Queen, Habenstein, & Quadagno, 1985, for descriptions of families in many different types of societies.)

Marriage

The Nayar represent the weakest, and rarest, form of marriage. Most societies expect and make more of marriage than the Nayar. Thus, a family's experience in any society is shaped also by who a person marries and how mates are chosen.

In most societies one cannot reach adult status without marrying. Marriage is a universal social expectation. It is incomprehensible that anyone would choose to stay single. Such people are pitied. Single anthropologists are beyond the understanding of the people they study. In a Mexican village, Chiñas (1983) found that "anyone who lives alone by preference, as I did for a time, is completely beyond comprehension; a person without kin is to be pitied. When I was introduced to someone for the first time it was always with the expectation that 'she is all alone, far from her family.' " (p. 89) Turnbull (1961) came to his hut one evening to find a tall, beautiful woman from a neighboring nonpygmy tribe waiting for him. His Mbuti friends had arranged a wife for him. (Turnbull tactfully vetoed the marriage.)

Henry (1941) had a similar experience. "The women who did not want to interest me in themselves or in their children besought me to marry someone else—anyone . . . 'Why? Why?' she kept repeating, 'why do you live alone thus without a wife? Get a wife.' 'Whom shall I marry?' said I. 'Marry anybody. Why go around unmarried.' Even the children found it hard to understand that I was single and they used to ask me interminably: 'Have you a wife in your country?' . . . 'Do you intend to marry?' " (p. 25)

How Many Partners?

Within human societies there are four types of marriages. Some societies have only one kind, others have more.

Contrary to what we may think today, *monogamy,* or one woman married to one man, is not the universal human experience. It is, however, becoming more prevalent as societies industrialize. Societies that allow men and women to have more than one spouse are becoming monogamous. Moreover, even in industrial societies people often marry more than one person, but they do so sequentially, not simultaneously. With divorce becoming more prevalent, many people will marry more than one person before they die.

A majority of societies in the past allowed *polygamy,* or people marrying more than one person. Usually, it meant one man marrying two or more women (*polygyny*). A woman marrying two or more men (*polyandry*) has been much more rare. Polygamous marriages usually represent a status attained by the wealthier people of society. A man who marries many women has prestige. But we should note that in polygamous societies most people still marry one person for the simple reason that the numbers of men and women do not allow most people to have more than one spouse.

It is unclear whether any society ever sanctioned *group marriage*. In at least one society, the Kaingang tribe in the highlands of Brazil, group marriage has been practiced. Indeed, as Henry (1941) shows in Chapter 4 of his book, one tribesman, Wanyeki, lived in all four types of marriage. At different times of his life he had one wife, then three wives, then two other men and he had three wives, then he and two men had one wife. Such a sequence was rare, but its existence does show the variety of marital arrangements. Henry shows that each arrangement has its own advantages and problems, and some arrangements are better than others. Wanyeki could share a wife with other men, but other men objected to a polyandrous marriage.

Who Chooses Mates?

In the United States, people find their own mates. Many students are horrified when I suggest that their parents could choose their spouses. Indeed, in many societies people are free to find their own mates, but in other societies, parents find their children's spouses. This is not so cruel and arbitrary as it may seem. In Greek peasant society the married couple lives with the husband's parents; thus the new wife is not only married to him, but also to his family. She must be compatible with and acceptable to others beside her husband. When parents choose a spouse for their child they look for someone who is compatible with the family and who has a common background.

Arranged marriages happen in many ways. In some societies parents may arrange marriages when children are still infants (even unborn). The potential couple may not see each other before the day they marry. India has had such arrangements. In other cases the couple may meet a few times before they marry but only for introductory purposes, not to approve or disapprove. My father's mother told me that at age fourteen she met her husband for the first time (they were from different villages) and soon after they were married. My parents too had an arranged marriage.

Some arrangements are more flexible than others. Often, as among the Cheyenne, the young people see and like each other, then ask their parents to arrange a marriage. If the two people strongly object to the proposed marriage, they can often resist and argue against it, making the parents drop it. How marriages happen is much more varied than the two simple alternatives of falling in love or having parents arrange a marriage.

Who Marries Whom?

Even in societies where people "fall in love" and marry, most people tend to limit the groups where they look for love. Social class, race, ethnicity, and religion restrict people's choices. Most people marry people close to their own age, race, religion, social class, education, political views, and other factors. It is difficult to marry outside one's class. In India, to this day, few people marry outside their caste (a rigid class system). People who marry outside their group often are disowned, at times even ritually buried.

In the United States, there are few interracial marriages. In 1970, less than 1 percent (.7) of all married couples were interracial, 1.3 percent in 1980, and 1.55 percent in 1985. Also, the vast majority marry someone in the same social class or close to it. In neighborhoods, friendship groups, clubs and associations, college life, and so on, people meet mostly people of the same class as their own. (See *Statistical Abstract*, 1987:39; *Boston Globe*, July 6, 1984:3; Gilbert & Kahl, 1987; and Zinn & Eitzen, 1987.)

Where Do People Live?

In our society, most newly married couples begin their own households. How close is it to the relatives? In some groups, as we learned, people prefer to live very near their parents. In class discussions, I have been told the ideal is "close but not too close," which means a few miles away. Certainly professional people in the United States move hundreds and thousands of miles away, wherever their jobs take them, while working-class people tend to live closer to their parents.

As in all matters, societies vary widely. In some a couple may live with or next to the wife's parents, as among the Navaho; in some they may live with the husband's parents, as in some peasant societies; and in others they live wherever they choose. But in all societies there is the expectation and hope that children will continue to associate with their parents.

Marital Happiness

Sociologists have avoided the trap of trying to define *love*, but they have not hesitated to study *happiness* in marriage. Sometimes they may not define it at all but simply ask people if they are happy in (or satisfied with) their marriage and give them various degrees of happiness from which to choose. Sociologists may try to deduce marital happiness or unhappiness (sometimes compared to being single) from responses to various questions.

By some ideal standard of total communication, continuing romance, and intimate sharing of many interests not many couples are happy. Also, happiness and satisfaction seem to decline with the arrival of children and increase with their departure. Couples who are interviewed frequently have stated high expectations for spouses, but at the same time they report that they know few couples who meet these expectations within their marriage (Melville, 1983).

Data show that married people are healthier and have lower mortality rates. Lynch (1977) reports findings that cancer rates, heart disease rates, and other illnesses are two to three times higher for unmarried people. In 1973, it was found that Canadian single men twenty-five to sixty-four years of age had a mortality rate over 80 percent higher than that of married men; for single women twenty-four to forty-four years of age, it was 90 percent higher; and for single women forty-five to sixty-four years of age it was 36 percent higher. Single men and women over sixty-five also had higher mortality rates. Interestingly, widowed and divorced people had even higher mortality rates than single people. (See also Smart & Smart, 1976.)

Mental health studies, however, show that marriage is better than singlehood for men but not for women. Married men are healthier than single men, but single women are healthier than married women. Melville (1983) mentions that "although women describe themselves as being happier when married, single women report fewer neurotic symptoms, are less fearful, and have fewer feelings of inadequacy, depression, and passivity" than do married women. (p. 164)

Changing Families

In the last twenty years sociologists, historians, and other observers have been debating the nature and significance of changes in family life. Some see profound changes in family life and feel it is declining; others see no changes, or they see improvements. Let us look at some of the data and arguments.

Household Size

Table 6.2 clearly shows that households have been getting smaller, especially in the twentieth century. The decline has come about partly because people have fewer children, but also because unmarried adults no longer live with their parents or married siblings. Fewer people live in families than ever before, and those people who do, live in increasingly smaller ones. Table 6.3 provides further evidence of these changes. In 1790, only 3.7 percent of households consisted of only one person, but 23.7 percent did so in 1985. In contrast, 11.1 percent of households contained five or more members in 1985, whereas 63 percent did in 1790.

American families have never been largely extended, contrary to a still

TABLE 6.2
Average size of U.S. Households, 1689–1986

Year	Number of people	Year	Number of people
1689	6[1]	1970	3.14
1790	5.8	1975	2.94
1900	4.8	1980	2.76
1950	3.37	1986	2.67
1960	3.33		

Demos 1970; Kobrin 1976; and *Statistical Abstract* 1982–1983:43; 1987:42
[1] Only for Bristol, Massachusetts

TABLE 6.3
Households by Number of Persons, 1790–1985 (by percentage)

Year	1 person	2 persons	3–4 persons	5–6 persons	7 or more
1790	3.7	7.8	25.5	27.1	35.9
1900	5.1	15.0	34.4	25.1	20.4
1950	10.9	28.8	40.4	15.1	4.9
1960	13.1	27.8	36.5	17.2	5.4
1970	17.0	28.8	33.1	16.0	5.1
1975	19.6	30.6	33.0	13.3	3.5
1980	22.7	31.4	33.2	10.6	2.2
1985	23.7	31.6	33.5	9.6	1.5

Kobrin, 1976; *Statistical Abstract* 1982–1983:44; 1987:45

persisting belief. Throughout United States history about 6 percent of all families have been extended. Demos (1970) describes a late seventeenth-century Plymouth plantation as basically nuclear, but at times it was altered by the presence of aged parents no longer able to care for themselves, unmarried adults (siblings and others), and sick and homeless relatives and nonrelatives.

Functions and Responsibilities

The Plymouth family study suggests that the family in the past differed from today's in more than size and composition of the household. The family then performed many more functions than it does today. The Plymouth plantation study shows in detail what families did. Families grew their own food, made their shoes and clothing, and provided for almost all their other material needs. Families continued to provide for all or most of their needs well into the nineteenth century. A New England farmer wrote that he spent only ten dollars in the course of a whole year, "for salt, nails and the like. Nothing to eat, drink or wear was bought, as my farm produced it all." (Ewen, 1976, p. 114) Wives, husbands, and children were complete production units.

But Plymouth Plantation families did much more than provide for their material necessities. Children were taught reading, writing, and trades, either within their own family or as apprentices to other families. Ill family members were cared for. The community placed aged and ill people who had no relatives with other families. People even served criminal sentences by working for a family (who bought their services from the town). Thus, the family functioned as a school, a job training center, a hospital, a penal institution of sorts, as well as an economic unit that produced everyone's needs. Special outside institutions perform these functions today (Demos, 1970).

The Family and Industrialization

Why have families become smaller, and why have they lost many of their functions? Industrialism, which began around the mid-eighteenth century and accelerated in the nineteenth century, has been the primary cause.

Oakley (1974), in her book *Woman's Work* describes family and women's lives in pre-industrial and industrial England. Blau (1984) explores a somewhat similar social history in the United States. Oakley (1974) cites three changes brought about by industrialism: "separation of the man from the intimate daily routine of domestic life. . . . The economic dependence of women and children on men. . . . [and the] isolation of housework and childcare from other work." (p. 59)

When the family was a whole production unit, men, women, and even children all worked to provide for their own needs. They worked together, in or near each other's presence. Women, according to Oakley, were not dependent on their husbands, they contributed equally to their families' survival. A man was not expected to be the sole provider of his family; the whole family provided for itself. As the husband and wife worked, their children were near them. As children got older, they gradually joined their parents.

But as industrialism gradually developed (at least in England and the United States) men were removed from the family presence. First in factories (initially for twelve to fourteen hour days, six to seven days a week) and later in offices men toiled away from their families. Most women, until well into the twentieth century, were confined to the home, isolated from husbands at work and children in school. They cleaned and cooked, but they made no clothes, candles, and other products, nor did they help raise the food. Women and children became much more dependent on men, and the entire family spent much less time in each other's presence. (See Oakley, 1974; Blau, 1984; Ewen, 1976, and for a documentary history of American families, see Scott and Wishy, 1982.)

These historical changes have worried and alarmed many people because they see them as causing the decline of the family. These fears have also been expressed by sociologists, historians, religious people, and many others. Over the last twenty years other social observers have responded to these fears. They find the family as strong as, if not stronger than, ever. (See Bane, 1976; Caplow et al., 1982; and Hareven, 1983.)

They argue that there was no family utopia in pre-industrial societies. Families were not extended, contrary to popular belief, and not unlike today, families had conflicts. Mothers and fathers were busy too and did not necessarily devote more time to their children than parents do today. With a shorter life span, families were often without parents or grandparents. As a people, Americans have always been mobile, restlessly looking for new opportunities, so family stability has not been pronounced. Indeed, Hareven (1979) argues

> *In many ways, industrialization strengthened families. It enabled them to leave the isolation of rural life, and, by affording sons and daughters new occupational opportunities in cities, it encouraged children to stay in their parental home much longer than they had in rural areas. Nor did industrialization destroy traditional kinship ties. Even though they did not live in the same household, most people depended on their relatives for assistance in migrating, in finding housing and jobs, and in childcare especially in the absence of public welfare agencies. (p. 16)*

Although these critics agree that families and households are smaller and that families perform fewer functions, they do not see the family structure as weakening or less important in people's lives. But even given this, what emotional and social meanings *do* families have for us today?

The Family as Refuge

When I teach a course on the family, I begin by requesting students to write (anonymously) what their families mean to them and to list the members of their families. Seventy-five percent of them always list only their parents and siblings as their family. The rest include grandparents, uncles and aunts, cousins (in rare cases do these people live with a student's nuclear family), and an occasional pet, usually a dog.

Love, Security, Warmth

Family means love, acceptance, and security. These words appear in all descriptions. Here are some examples of student comments:

> *My family means my world to me. Without my family, I wouldn't be who I am today. I can't imagine existence without them. My family is 'love'.*

> *My family to me means security, love, understanding, and a sense of belonging. I know that no matter what I do, they'll always be there for me.*

To me my family means love, security, and protection. They mean under-standing, comfort, and help to each other.

Most of my students' comments are positive, accepting, loving, and glowing. It is a very rare student, on this first meeting of the class, who refers to family conflicts and problems. These come later. When people respond to family, they recall positive experiences and emotions. For many, if not most, this description of family may be a hope and a fantasy more than it is a reality, but hopes and fantasies are parts of our lives.

Some working-class parents turn to family camping to recapture or create the close and intimate family life they feel is missing in their lives. Cerullo and Ewen (1982) went camping with some of these families near Worcester, Massachusetts. They saw and were told that camping was an escape from all the conditions that make family life difficult. While camping, parents and children are freed from work, housework, and school demands, and all the time becomes family time.

Family camping had in it a distant image of family—one in which men and women and children performed the tasks that had to be done as they came up, in sight or within the experience of the others, a kind of family in which work and men had not yet departed from women and the home. (p. 28)

The separation of work and home, and the increasing demands of family survival, have wrought havoc in family life. Many people turned to camping in response to wanting some time to "be together" and to "be a family." "Camping is a way to keep the family together." "This is the only time to really be a family. At home everybody's off in their own direction. . . ." (p. 32)

Families relax, cook, and talk with other campers. The intense family experience they seek is a public event, in rather crowded campsites, outside the tents in the presence of fellow campers. Thus, family and community are joint experiences. One enriches the other, it seems.

Community and Family

Community and family unity characterize pre-industrial societies. Studies (Bender, 1978) of America before 1900 have shown that "the wall between the family and the town was highly permeable." (pp. 114–115) Family life and community life co-existed. People in families related to other families and jointly celebrated community events and participated in community projects (Demos, 1970).

Caplow and others (1982), who studied Muncie, Indiana, in the late 1970s, think that there has been a shift away from the community to the family. Comparing 1900 to the present, they find that in 1900 the important holidays were Washington's Birthday, Memorial Day, Independence Day, and Labor Day. On those days there were parades and other community activities, with the emphasis on community celebration. Now, however, these holidays get short notice. Except for July 4, these holidays have been shifted to Mondays, thus shifting their emphasis to three-day weekends for family outings, instead of their traditional community meeting. It is Thanksgiving, Christmas, and Easter, among others, celebrated mostly as family occasions, that have replaced community holidays.

At first glance this interpretation seems eminently rational. Yet closer reflection throws some doubt on the rise of the family over the decline of community. Since in every human society family activity co-exists with community activity, how can we interpret the claim by Caplow and others? For example, in New England, families often gathered on porches. These porches were open to the community. It was where family and community met. Now families have become more private. But in this private state, is family life richer? Has it compensated for the decrease in community relations? Or, are hope and fantasy mixed in with the reality of family intimacy to compensate for decline both in community and family?

Family Life in Muncie

Muncie, Indiana, is a city of 80,000 people. When Caplow and others (1982) moved to Muncie in the late 1970s to carry out an updated study (two earlier ones had been done in 1925 and 1935), they focused on family life. Their conclusions are unambiguously optimistic. Family life in Muncie is vibrant and thriving. The family is "in exceptionally good condition," and "it is *not* isolated." (p. 323) And "although we cannot give an entirely clean bill of health to the nuclear family, the composite family [which includes parents, siblings, and other relatives with whom people associate] . . . is in splendid condition in Middletown [Muncie]." (p. 340)

In Muncie surveys, people stated they felt obligated to keep in touch with relatives: 73 percent with parents, 58 percent with brothers or sisters, 36 percent with cousins, and 60 percent with grown children. In addition, "most Middletown [Muncie] people feel good about their parents, love them, and make sacrifices for them when necessary. They see them often and enjoy doing so." (p. 220)

Sentiments and norms clearly encourage strong and close family ties. But do actions reflect and fulfill these sentiments? Let us look first at where family relatives live. Beyond the nuclear family, how many people have relatives in Muncie? Forty-three percent of the parents, 31 percent of the brothers and sisters, 54 percent of the grown children, and 20 percent of other kin live in Muncie. Eighteen percent more of the parents, 16 percent more of the siblings, 14 percent more of the grown children, 14 percent more of the other kin live within fifty miles of Muncie. (p. 381)

How often do relatives see each other, and what do they do when they meet? Forty-eight percent of the adults see their parents at least weekly and 80 percent at least monthly. Brothers and sisters are seen half as frequently.

The closer people live to relatives, the more frequently they see them. Of adults whose parents live in Muncie, 83 percent visit them weekly; of those adults whose parents live fifty to a hundred miles from Muncie, only 6 percent see them weekly.

What do relatives do when they get together? In a 1977 Muncie survey, people were asked, "In the past two years or so . . . how often have you and your parent(s) engaged in the following types of activities together?" A majority reported that they have picnics, play cards, drop in for short talks, and share birthdays or other happy occasions with their parents several times a year. For example, 66 percent of the men and women said they pay "brief drop-in visits for conversation" with their parents, 55 percent of the women and 47 percent of the men play cards and have picnics with them, and 22 percent of the men and 51 percent of the women shop together with their parents (Caplow et al., 1982). Also, parents help their children and (less often) children their parents.

Generally, Muncie people are in more contact with their relatives than with their friends, their friends than with their neighbors. Clearly, family predominates over community. (p. 221)

A word of caution on the meaning of these survey findings. The reported frequency of family visits and shared activities may exaggerate the actual behavior. As we discussed in Chapter 2, people are not always accurate observers of their behavior. They become especially unreliable in family life, where people's values of what should be (close and frequent ties) may exaggerate the amount of actual family contact. We cannot accept the reported behavior on family life as the absolute truth.

What do these reports on family life and family values tell us? Undeniably, most Americans want their parents, siblings, children, and other relatives to be in their lives. They talk warmly about relatives. They report frequent visits and shared activities. The campers and most people who try to salvage family life from the routines and demands of the larger world turn to spouses, children, and others for the love, acceptance, security, and intimacy that is lacking outside the family. Fantasy, hope, reality, and behavior intermingle as the family becomes a haven from the turbulent seas of work, economic insecurity, and declining community. (See Lasch, 1977, and Cerullo & Ewen, 1982.)

Indeed, even though the family has lost many of its pre-industrial functions, even though the socialization of children has become more and more the domain of outside institutions, the family's function as a place of intimacy, solace, and support has probably increased. With community life less vibrant, with the loss of friends as people move from community to community, the family probably has become more important than ever.

There are no data on frequency of family contacts in the past, and those from Muncie and other places today cannot be wholly accepted. So we cannot make any comparisons of decline, increase, or stability in family contacts, except to say with some certainty that the family is no longer a production unit. What, then, *can* we conclude about the meaning of the family as reflected in behavior? Not much, I fear. We can only know what the emotional and social meaning of family is for ourselves. We can rejoice when we realize our hopes for our family and feel disappointment when reality does not meet our hopes.

Families Today

In previous sections, we have explored the long historical development and changes of family life. We have also discussed some of the emotional and psychic meanings we attach to our families. We shall now present some data and details on some fairly recent changes: the increase in the numbers of working mothers, economic conditions of families, singlehood, divorce, and others.

Working Mothers

One of the most significant changes in the family over the last fifty years has been the increase in the number of working mothers. In 1950, only 11.9 percent of the women with children under six worked; 34.4 percent in 1974, 47.8 in 1981, and 56.8 in 1987 did so. (See Table 6.4.) For married mothers, husband present with children six to seventeen years old the increase has been dramatic: from 28.3 percent in 1950 to 70.7 percent in 1987. Even more revealing is that 84.5 percent of divorced women with children six to seventeen worked in 1987. Lastly, the most telling statistics may be that in March 1987, 51.9 percent of mothers with the age of the youngest child *one or under* were in the labor force (compared to 31.6 percent in 1977), and 63.1 percent

TABLE 6.4
Married, Separated, and Divorced Women—Labor Force Status by Age of Children, 1970, 1981, and 1987

	Percent in Labor Force		
	1970	1981	1987
Married, husband present			
Children under 6	30.3	47.8	56.8
Children 6–17 only	49.2	62.5	70.6
Separated			
Children under 6	45.4	51.0	55.1
Children 6–17 only	60.6	70.0	72.6
Divorced			
Children under 6	63.3	65.4	70.5
Children 6–17 only	82.4	83.4	84.5

Statistical Abstract 1982–1983:382, and U.S. Department of Labor, 1987h

of mothers with a youngest child of five were in the labor force, compared to 50.6 percent in 1977. (See Szymanski, 1976, and U.S. Department of Labor, 1987h.)

We should note here that poor mothers (black, white, and others) have always worked in great numbers. The ideal of the mother who stays home has never applied to most poor women. The problems of child care and balancing work and home are new for mothers of upper classes but not for poor and working-class women. (See McCain, 1983, and Rubin, 1976.)

In Chapter 12, we will explore the meaning of paid work in women's lives. Here, we need only to say that as mothers have returned to work, fathers and children have been affected too. For example some have begun to take over more of the housework. A comic strip, "Sally Forth," explores some of the tensions and issues that arise in families of working mothers.

For working parents of pre-school age and school-age children, child care is a major problem. Organized day care and other forms of child care do not meet the needs of most families in the United States. Parents alternate working hours, a relative or neighbor cares for the children, or other arrangements are made. Parents in other countries have similar concerns, but some countries (East Germany is the best example) provide many more day-care facilities than does the United States. In some societies, Albania, for example, most grandparents care for the children while parents work. In the United States, various groups are working to increase day-care facilities. (See McCain, 1983; Adams & Winston, 1980; Foreman, 1980; Curley et al., 1981; and *Dollars and Sense,* March 1987: 6–9.)

Family Incomes

The financial condition of families varies considerably, depending on who and how many people provide income. According to U.S. Department of Labor Statistics (1987d), in 1987, married-couple families with one earner had a median weekly income of $395 ($469 if the earner was a husband, $219 for the wife). Where both husband and wife worked, the weekly median increased to $737. Families maintained by women, with the woman (usually the mother) working, had a much lower weekly median income, $257. As we saw above, most mothers work. All but a few families need two incomes in order to manage. Those with one income, for whatever reason, face hardships.

As we shall see in Chapter 8, most American families do not earn enough to reach the intermediate family budget published by the U.S. government, which may be seen as the beginning level of a middle-class life style. By U.S. standards, most families do not seem to lead a comfortable life. I do not mean that most families starve or are otherwise deprived, but they experience stress in trying to reach what the culture holds to be the ideal material level of existence. (See Rubin, 1976, and *Statistical Abstract,* 1987:431.)

And during the 1980s, social policies that had provided supports for families changed radically and thus lowered the incomes of millions of families, especially black families and those headed by women. (See Chapters 8, 11, and 12 for details.)

Work and the economy cause other stresses. The following anecdote illustrates the stress families can go through. A couple was separated when the man lost his job and could only find another one a thousand miles away. The woman stayed behind with their three children until she could sell the house and find a job in the city where her mate had found work. Both the man and woman had to work to pay off college loans and meet other expenses. Their family life was completely disrupted. Millions of families experience deprivation, dislocation, tension, and stress because of economic conditions and social expectations (Goodman, 1982).

Delayed Marriages

In the first edition of this text, I called this section "Singlehood." Upon reflection, however, I realized that I had been caught in the myth making of the media. In fact, there is no evidence that there has been any increase in the number of people who never marry. The fact is that people are marrying later and divorcing more often. But as many people as ever try marriage at least once.

Let us look at some statistics. (See Table 6.5.) The percent of single (never-married) people, eighteen years old and over, has increased steadily. In 1985, women's median age at first marriage was 23.3 years, men's 25.5. It was the highest since this statistic was first kept in 1890. The lowest median age at first marriage came in the 1950s, after the age had decreased from a higher median in the 1930s. It has increased steadily since the 1950s.

But the numbers for never-married people are more revealing when we examine specific age groups. For men twenty-five to twenty-nine, the percent of never-married increased from 19.1 in 1970 to 38.7 in 1985; for women, from 10.5 to 26.4—a significant increase, obviously. But when we compare forty to forty-four-year-olds in 1970 and 1985, we see little difference. For women, it increased from 4.9 percent to 5.3 percent, and for men it rose from 6.3 to 8.6. (Remember, we count only those who have never married. People

TABLE 6.5
Percentages of Single (never-married people), 1970 and 1985

	1970		1985	
	Men	*Women*	*Men*	*Women*
18 years old and over	18.9	13.7	25.2	18.2
25–29 years old	19.1	10.5	38.7	26.4
40–44 years old	6.3	8.6	4.9	5.3

Statistical Abstract, 1987:39

who have married and divorced are excluded from these figures.) (See *Statistical Abstract,* 1987: 39, and *Boston Globe,* December 10, 1986: 17.)

These are averages, including people from many classes, regions, and ethnic groups. I suspect most of the people who delay marriage, and thus raise the median age for first marriages, are college graduates. Most wait until they reach their late twenties, some their thirties, before they marry. They wait to establish themselves in better jobs and save some money. Most women especially are in no rush to marry as soon as they leave college. (Stories I hear and newspaper accounts tell of an increasing number of young, single adults who live at home with their parents, instead of renting or buying their own places, in order to save money.)

As more people graduate from college, the median age at first marriage may increase even more. But I suspect that working-class people, those who do not attend college, those who work in blue-collar and service occupations, may still marry in their late teens and early twenties. (See *Boston Globe,* June 18, 1987:1, 26; Stein, 1981; and Melville, 1983.)

Cohabitation

As we saw in Chapter 4, the number of unmarried couples who live together has increased dramatically, from about 425,000 in 1960 to almost two million in 1985. These statistics surely underestimate the real number of cohabiting couples. (See *Statistical Abstract,* 1987:42, and Watson, 1983.)

Melville (1983) points out that people have different motives for cohabitation: as a trial marriage with the person they hope to marry, as a convenient way for having sex, cooking, and sharing expenses, and as a substitute for marriage because they object in principle to the legal obligations and restrictions of marriage. Sometimes people have different perceptions of their relationship. Men are more likely to see cohabitation as a convenient arrangement, women as a trial marriage with emotional commitment.

Most couples who cohabit seem to *drift* into the arrangement according to Jackson (1983). As they become more involved, they spend more time together, often staying overnight with each other. More and more such nights follow, and one day they realize they are living together. At that point, they must decide who to tell and who not to tell. Is there any difference in marital happiness or divorce rates between couples who cohabit before marriage and those who do not? Most studies carried out so far have concluded that there is no difference. (See Watson, 1983; Newcomb, 1984; and Zinn & Eitzen, 1987.)

Fewer Children

Couples face three choices about children: whether to have any at all, when to have them, and how many to have. There has been little change on whether to have children. As many couples as ever have at least one child during their marriage. But people now delay parenthood and have fewer children compared at least to the 1950s. (Even the baby boom of the 1950s was an exception to a trend of having fewer children that began in the 1800s, according to some studies.) Ninety-five percent of a class of 45 women at Regis College said in 1987 that they plan to have children. Table 6.6 shows the dramatic decrease in the birth rate from 1950 to 1984. The rate has stabilized from 1975 to 1984, with a slight increase in the rates for women in their thirties.

The number of childless couples has not increased. Indeed, in the 1970s "the percentage of child-free couples in the United States was less than one-quarter what it had been in the 1920s." Of women who have ever married, ages forty to forty-four, 14 percent were childless in 1960, 6.6 in 1980, and 8.0 in 1985. Most married women still have children. But some couples choose to remain childless. People who choose not to have children do so for many reasons: Some feel they would not make good parents. Others feel there are plenty of children already to take care of and take an active part in the lives of other people's children. Yet others feel that children would interfere with their work. Although there is still tremendous pressure for people to have children, voluntary childlessness is more acceptable now than in the past.

The number of childless couples has not changed as dramatically, however, as the number of children people are having. Never-married women, twenty-five to twenty-nine years old, who are childless have increased from 15.8 percent in 1970 to 28.7 in 1985. Clearly, married women are having fewer children, and they are having them later in life. (See *Statistical Abstract,* 1987:64; Melville, 1983; and Veevers, 1973.)

Single Parents

Because of rising divorce rates and other reasons, there has been an increase in the number of families with one parent. In 1970, 84.9 percent of children under eighteen lived with two parents, 10.7 percent with only their mother,

TABLE 6.6
Birth Rates, 1950–1984

	1950	1960	1970	1975	1979	1984
Per 1,000 population	24.1	23.7	18.4	14.8	15.9	15.5
Per 1,000 women, 15–44	106.2	118.0	87.9	66.7	68.5	NA
Per 1,000 women, 20–24	196.6	258.1	167.8	114.7	115.7	107.3
Per 1,000 women, 25–29	166.1	197.4	145.1	110.3	115.6	108.3
Per 1,000 women, 30–34	103.7	112.7	73.3	53.1	61.8	66.5
Per 1,000 women, 35–39	52.9	56.2	31.7	19.4	19.4	22.8

Statistical Abstract, 1982–1983:60–61; 1987:58–59
NA—not available

1.1 with only their father, and 3.3 with neither parent (*Statistical Abstract,* 1982–1983:52; 1987:48). By 1985, 74 percent of the children under eighteen lived with both parents, 21 percent with only their mother, 2.5 with only their father, and 2.7 with neither parent. For blacks, the rate of single-parent homes is about three times that for whites.

There may be some emotional and social consequences for the fifteen million children who live in one-parent families, but two practical problems predominate—child care and very low income. Most single mothers work. As we have seen, the United States provides few facilities for day care, and working single parents must improvise arrangements for their children. In addition, because of the continuing sex discrimination in jobs and pay (see Chapter 12), women who support their families face severe financial problems. (For the men who are single parents, about 600,000 of them, see Greif, 1985.) In 1987, families maintained by women had a median weekly income of $309, compared with the median of $620 for married-couple families. The United States, compared to some other nations, provides little support for single-parent families. At a time when these families are increasing, this lack of support is a major problem. (See U.S. Department of Labor, 1987d; Schorr & Moen, 1979; and Adams & Winston, 1980.)

Divorce

Divorce is one of the most controversial, debated, and misunderstood issues in family life. Its apparent dramatic increase is cited as an indication of social breakdown. But how much divorce is there, and what are its causes and consequences?

Divorce exists and is common in almost all societies. The European peasant background of many of us, and the low divorce rate in the United States until early in this century, have hidden this reality from us. But by some estimates, about a third of all marriages are terminated in most societies. The Jesuits (*Jesuit Relations,* 1896–1910) noted (and decried) the prevalence of divorce in Indian societies in the seventeenth century. Lee (1984) found that among the !Kung half of all first marriages are dissolved, as are 10 percent of those that last five or more years.

In our society, the counting of the number of divorces is somewhat confusing. One way of counting lists the number of divorces per year per 1,000 people (usually eighteen years old and over). For example, from 1960 to 1981, the number for men increased from 2.0 to 5.7 per thousand, and from 2.9 to 7.6 for women. These figures show almost a tripling of the divorce rate (*Statistical Abstract,* 1982–1983:41).

A second measure of divorce compares the number of marriages and divorces in any given year. In 1950 there were 1,667,000 marriages and 385,000 divorces, a little over four marriages for every divorce. By 1970 the ratio was 3 to 1, and from 1975 to 1985, it had stabilized at 2 to 1 (see Table 6.7). Both of these methods may be misleading because the relative proportion

TABLE 6.7
Marriages/Divorces Ratios, U.S. 1910–1985 versus
Muncie, Indiana, 1910–1930

Year	United States	Muncie, Indiana
1910	11.4:1	3.8:1
1920	7.5:1	3.0:1
1930	5.8:1	2.2:1
1940	6.0:1	
1950	4.3:1	
1960	3.9:1	
1970	3.0:1	
1975	2.1:1	
1980	2.0:1	
1985	2.0:1	

Statistical Abstract, 1987:58, and Lynd & Lynd, 1937, p. 544

of people who are of marriageable age may differ from year to year, and so may the number of married people from whom divorces may result.

Another problem may be the accuracy of divorce statistics, especially in the past. For example, in Muncie, Indiana, in 1930, the divorce rate was almost three times the national rate (see Table 6.7). Can it be that Muncie couples, living in a small, midwest town, were more divorce prone than couples in the rest of the United States, including large cities? Caplow and others (1982) believe not and show the national statistics before 1930 were gathered very poorly, underreporting the divorces for those years. If this is so, dramatic increases in the divorce rate may be exaggerated. Indeed, it may be that from the 1920s on, divorce has remained stable, with some short-term increases (such as after World War II). For the present, if we extrapolate current figures into the future, we could predict that marriage in the United States has a 50 percent chance of ending in divorce. Other industrial societies have divorce rates one-third to two-thirds of the U.S. rate (Westhues, 1982).

A third, more accurate but more difficult and costly method would study the number of married people who become divorced over time. In 1985, 2,425,000 couples were married. If we could interview all of them periodically and record how many were still married, in fifty to sixty years we would know how many lived together till death parted them.

However we measure it, divorce has risen during the last hundred years. What explains this increase? There are four possible causes.

1. Men and women are less willing to stay in unhappy relationships. Marriage relationships probably have not worsened over the years. Rather, men, and especially women, are leaving marriages that they find empty and meaningless. Women especially are leaving oppressive marriages. Men and women have higher expectations of marriages, and they end them when they are unfulfilled.

2. Changing attitudes about divorce and changes in divorce laws have made it more acceptable. Divorce began to increase earlier in this century. Gradually, it has become more acceptable and laws have made it easier to get divorced. All states now have some form of no-fault divorce, where the couple can separate without one party having to prove the other is to blame for the divorce. People now find divorce regrettable but necessary in many cases. Many people argue that divorce is preferable to an unhappy marriage, for both parents *and* children. Divorced people are not stigmatized or ostracized. (See Lynd & Lynd, 1937, and Caplow et al., 1982.)

3. Women are less dependent on men. Women can leave unhappy marriages because more of them work and can support themselves financially. They may not do so in comfort, as we saw above, but they can survive. The divorce rate has been higher among poorer people; poor women have always worked and been less dependent on men whose income has not provided as much support for the family as has the income of men from wealthier classes. Also, during the Great Depression, when many men lost their jobs, divorce increased.

4. Economic and other historical conditions also affect the divorce rate. Looking at United States and Western history over the last one hundred fifty years, Westhues (1982) concludes that divorce has also increased because couples engage in fewer common activities and have fewer common interests. Westhues cites four specific changes: (a) Unlike the farm families of old, modern couples rarely work together. Thus, they have fewer common bonds and experiences. (b) Many couples do not share common ethnic, religious, and social class backgrounds. (c) "Shared parental involvement" in raising children has declined. (d) The more years a couple spends together in common activity or in building a "common past" seems to decrease the chance of divorce. Sex and romance, Westhues claims, do not suffice to create a long-lasting relationship.

Divorce raises many issues. One of the most important issues is children. In the past, parents have often said they would stay together "for the sake of the children." But gradually, more parents believe that divorce will not destroy their children. Some research is beginning to show that after the initial hurt and pain, most children adjust to the divorce and lead normal lives. Parents are coming to the conclusion that unhappy marriages harm children more than divorces do.

Still, children of divorce do face some problems, at least temporarily. Most obviously, one parent (usually the mother) has less money, time, and energy to give to the children. In addition, many or most children rarely see their fathers. According to Zinn and Eitzen (1987), half the children had not seen their fathers for a year or more. But on the other hand, some studies claim that in the long run children do better with one parent rather than two who do not get along. Most of my students whose parents are divorced have also come to that conclusion.

Another issue is remarriage. Most divorced people remarry. The 1980 census found that 78 percent of divorced men and 69 percent of divorced women remarry. But age, sex, class, and race affect the remarriage rates. The older a woman is at the time of divorce, the fewer her chances of remarrying. Seventy-six percent of women who divorce before age thirty, 56 percent who do so between thirty and thirty-nine, 32 percent who do in their forties, and 12 percent who do after fifty remarry. Men's chances of remarrying are higher. There are three times as many women as men in the forty-five to sixty-four year old age bracket who are single, divorced, or widowed. Also, white women are about three times more likely to remarry than are black women (Zinn & Eitzen, 1987).

Remarried people often claim that their second marriages are happy, happier than their first. Perhaps. But the divorce rates of second marriages are no lower than those of first marriages (Family Planning Perspectives, 1986). It would seem that divorced once, we would not make the same mistake twice. On the other hand, we could argue that people who divorce once may be less reluctant to leave their second marriage if it is unfulfilling. In addition, people who bring children into a marriage from a previous one face unique problems: children's divided loyalties, uncertainty by the stepparent on whether and how to discipline the children, and so on. I know of no study of the success of *third* marriages. (See Zinn & Eitzen, 1987, and Melville, 1983.)

Some Reflections on Divorce

As of this writing, I have been divorced seven years. During this time I have thought and worried about my life, my relationship with my daughters, and the effect of the divorce on their development. I have also talked with many people about divorce generally and about my divorce, and I have read a few studies and papers on divorce. The following are some reflections about my divorce, my children, and the experience of divorce.

There is no doubt that compared to 1900 and 1950 divorce has increased, although not as dramatically as we think (see data on Muncie, Indiana, in Table 6.7). It is much easier to obtain and is socially acceptable. Most children, in time, cope with it and go on to lead satisfying lives. Some even grow stronger from the experience.

But if divorce is not the devastating, disruptive, and negative experience we once thought it was, it is not entirely free of consequences, losses, and regrets either. First, and perhaps foremost, it is a financial disaster for most people involved. It is especially so for the women and their children (income is reduced to half or less), and to a smaller degree for many fathers. Second, at the same time that there is relief that the long years of conflict and estrangement are over, sadness, sorrow, anger, and regret also follow the separation. Third, many children grow apart from their fathers. Statistics show, and my students strongly argued in the spring of 1987, that most divorced fathers do not see their children regularly. Those of us who do, usually do so for a third or less of each week. The time is never enough. Often, I worry how my daughters must experience the commuting between two homes. They have accepted and adjusted to the divorce, but occasionally I detect hints of sadness that it had to happen.

Divorce is an accepted part of our society and of many of our lives. We cope with it, and some people even grow stronger in the process. But it is not easy. I wince when I hear people say or imply that people resort to divorce cavalierly and without much thought or care. Everyone I know who divorced a spouse did so after many years of conflict, hesitation, and a troubled mind. Few people divorce without sadness and regret. Most of us change permanently.

Family Violence

For some years now professional literature and the mass media have been publicizing various forms of family violence, child abuse, incest, spouse abuse, and elder abuse. (Child abuse will be explored in Chapter 7, spouse abuse in Chapter 12.) We do not know if family violence is increasing or if the media have just become more aware of it. Depending on how we define abuse, we could point to violence in the majority of American families. As Rivers (1980) cogently argues, there is a great deal of serious violence in the family, but it is greatly overdrawn when even a slap on a child's bottom counts as violence. One study cited in Rivers claims that in 50 percent of the American families surveyed there was "a scene of family violence at least once a year." The same study reports 2.3 million children were beaten up in one year, and 1.8 million were assaulted with a gun or knife (equally alarming numbers are given for older children who abused their parents). Others produce figures showing 28 million cases of wife abuse every year. These numbers are definitional and statistical creations. We cannot count family violence very precisely.

Indeed, statistical overkill may detract attention from the real and serious violence that does exist in families. Violence results when a society approves of physical punishment and control of children, when a society controls and oppresses women, and when an economic system makes work alienating and creates stress through monetary insecurity. (See Caplow et al., 1982; Elshtain, 1985; Wexler, 1985; Kempe & Kempe, 1984; *Boston Globe*, November 19, 1986:18; Pillemer & Wolf, 1986; Russell, 1986; and Terkel, 1974.)

Women in Families

Even though men, women, and children compose families, and even though families are profoundly important for men and women, in most (if not all) societies women perform most of the family work. While this is changing somewhat, the family is still women's domain. Even in industrial societies today women bear, raise, and socialize children, women cook and clean, women buy presents, women take responsibility for family gatherings. Historically (not biologically) women have made family life possible (Breines, 1981).

But this historical reality has been a mixed blessing for women (at least in Western societies). While women have done the work, men have held the power and reaped the prestige. This domination by men, called *patriarchy,* has been analyzed and criticized by feminists of various political persuasions. Breines (1981) says, "A male-dominant family system prevailed in precapitalist societies of the West in which the father controlled the labor of women and children and utilized his power over the capacity of the wife to bear children. This authority of men over women was supported by legal and property rights of the father, including the right to 'give away' his daughter, and continued in varying guises into the present." (pp. 27–28) This has meant that the oldest male has often had total control to choose his children's mates. In the United States in the nineteenth century, patriarchal power enabled men to legally commit their wives to mental hospitals without having to justify their confinement. They did not need to give proof that their wives were mentally ill, their authority sufficed. Well into the twentieth century the husband continued to have total control over community property—a wife's earnings or any inheritance from her family were his (Szasz, 1970).

Feminists recognize the ambivalent nature of the family. They understand and appreciate the support, nurturing, and social significance families have for their members. At the same time, however, they see that it oppresses women, at least in its patriarchal form in the West. Industrialism has contributed to the erosion of the patriarchal family structure. This decline has some positive aspects, at least from a feminist point of view. There are, of course, gains and losses with the deterioration of patriarchy (Gordon & Hunter, 1977–1978).

Feminists have challenged the traditional family in the West. They do not see it as natural or inevitable. Men's authority, power, and control, women's economic dependence on men, and women's exclusive responsibility for children and housework—all are oppressive to women and need to change. Women have been buried within the family and have served family functions, but in the process their needs and individuality have been submerged. Careers, jobs, lives of their own have been sacrificed to serve husbands and children. Women must be seen "as individuals within the family, rather than as mere components of it or anchors to it." Rather than ask, What do women do for their families? we need to ask, What does the family do for women and to them? Husbands and children have been nurtured, but women also need to be encouraged to assume their own identities. Families must do for women as much as they do for them. Women help men by giving them support, so men must help women. (See Thorne, 1982, and Bridenthal, 1982.)

No biological imperative demands that women raise children alone, cook, clean, and take care of the home by themselves. These necessary tasks should be shared equally by men and women just as the role of provider should be shared. Men and women should both have productive work inside and outside of the family. Men and women can share jobs and housework. (See Chapter 12 for more details on jobs and housework.) We need to realize that there is no family that is eternally unchangeable and universally the same. We also must understand that families are complex; they are neither totally good nor totally bad. They give sustenance and love, *and* they oppress some people. It is that oppression that feminists insist must end.

In "Family Ties: Feminism's Next Frontier," Walsh (1986) argues that feminists must put more emphasis on the nurturing and emotional sustenance that families provide for women as well as men. They must also work for affordable, quality day care, higher family income, and other policies that will strengthen all families.

The Political and Economic Context

In gathering and hunting societies, families exist in small communities. People experience their families and their communities as one. A few families compose the entire community. But as societies become larger, outside political, social, and economic influences intrude on community and family. They are not so isolated and independent. In peasant societies, decisions made by authorities in cities affect community and family. Taxes are paid to the state, wars are fought, and other legal and administrative decisions made that necessitate community and family responses.

Capitalism, Industrialism, and Families

In this and previous chapters I have often referred to the impact of political and economic institutions and changes on families. Economic conditions and values require people to move to new sites where jobs exist. Industrialism creates cities with factories and offices, and people leave their towns for the jobs in these cities. The emphasis on success and materialism, or, often, the need for physical survival, means family becomes secondary. Family lives adjust to economic conditions, not the reverse. People first find jobs, then they move or create families near their jobs.

This economic system, which dominates our society, community, and family, gradually is controlled and shaped by fewer and fewer people (see Chapter 10). This ruling class runs the economy, and also the government, largely for its own benefit, interests, and power. Decisons are made to build or move plants, to close offices, and so on, without consideration of the impact these actions will have on family and community. We have seen in the chapter on community the economic devastation corporate decisions can bring on families and communities. When people lose their jobs and must move to new communities for jobs, their family and community lives are changed. Grandparents, cousins, aunts and uncles, friends, and familiar faces are left behind. People's lives are disrupted.

But family life is shaped by more than corporate decisions to locate or relocate plants and offices. Urban renewal has also forced people to move. The mass media continue to influence family life, as well as experts and professionals. Doctors, psychiatrists, social workers, and others have gradually taken away authority from parents and family. They tell us how to raise children and how to experience family relationships. You may see these people's roles as benevolent. Perhaps they are. But benevolent or harmful, experts have diminished the family's autonomy. They now claim the knowledge and expertise that parents and families used to possess until very recently. You may wonder how mothers raised children without pediatricians and psychiatrists, who after all did not appear until around 1900. I assure you they managed, and with much less expert advice than parents have today. (For an elaboration of the rule of professionals and experts, see Liazos, 1982.)

Families in Socialist Societies

No major political, social, or economic change can arise without a profound impact on families. The transition to socialism, now affecting about half the world's population, has been the most profound social change in the twentieth century. How has it affected family life? I cannot generalize about all socialist societies, so I will use two societies, China and Albania, to show the impact of socialism on family life.

Socialism has sought to reduce patriarchal authority and liberate women, but it has also sought to keep and strengthen families as functioning units of society. It has not sought to destroy families. I saw in 1980 and 1985 that the family in Albania persists and thrives. People's lives center on family obligations, functions, and contacts.

Let us look at China as an example. For centuries, it had been a patriarchal society. The men ruled the family. When China was dominated, economically and politically, by the West in the nineteenth century, social and economic conditions deteriorated. There was much poverty and suffering. Most families were very poor and landless. They were exploited by local landlords, and China was exploited by Japan and the West. The ideal of strong, three-generation families was difficult to fulfill under these conditions.

When socialism began in 1949, the legal liberation of women also began. Today in China wives are equal to their husbands, and parents cannot arrange their children's marriages. This is more an ideal than reality. Stacey (1979) says both practices have been slow to change because there is so much resistance to the new laws. Women now work outside the home, they attend schools and are gaining equality. With economic stability, three-generation families are possible and family life has been strengthened. Most elderly Chinese live with their children and grandchildren.

Despite these advances, tradition is difficult to erase. Sex role differences have not disappeared for example. Even though they work full-time, women still do the housework. Sex-typed jobs continue. And, parents still prefer boy children. In traditional China, a son and his wife took care of his parents with whom they lived. Thus, for old age security, it was imperative to have a son. (In Albania, too, sons are important, for the same reason.) This need to have a son creates several problems: it perpetuates the male controlled families; it makes for actual, if not legal, patriarchy; and for China, it worsens the population problem because parents keep having children until they have a son.

With over a billion people, population is one of China's most pressing problems. The country is now engaged in an intense population control program. The need for families to have only one or two children is widely publicized; birth control is free and encouraged; and economic incentives are offered to people who have one child (monthly allowances, health benefits, preference in housing, which is still in short supply are some examples). Conversely, parents with more than two children are not given these benefits and must pay to the state a percentage of their wages. But peasant traditions persist. Economic security in old age, the perpetuation of the family name, and the continuing male domination make sons desirable. If a family adheres to the ideal of one child, and if it is a girl, who will care for them in old age? There are occasional abuses. For example, infant daughters are killed and fetuses are aborted late in pregnancy. But these are rare; the usual practice is just to have more children until a son arrives. It is here that both attitudes and economic realities must change. Chinese leaders realize that if they are going to change traditional values, they must also provide economic security in old age. Such profound changes in family life take generations. The country has a long struggle ahead. (See Stacey, 1979; *Beijing Review,* November 16, 1979; Sidel, 1982; and *Guardian,* May 4, 1983:18.)

In China, Albania, and elsewhere, socialism has meant a struggle against patriarchy and for the equality of women and the strengthening of the family. Indeed, China, by trying to combine industry and agriculture in the countryside, may avoid the effects of industrialization and urbanization on the family. Albania, too, by careful planning has avoided displacing people from villages to cities and has enabled families and communities to stay strong and vibrant. It may yet be possible to change the patriarchal family structure, encourage close and intimate family ties, *and* industrialize.

Conclusion

Despite its smaller size and fewer functions the family remains central in the lives of most people. In various surveys over 80 percent of the respondents claim that they value their families above everything else. In the spring of 1987 95 percent of sixty-three single college students (mostly women) wrote that they intend to marry and have children.

But as we as family members struggle to find ways to spend more time together and to maintain ties, as families try to provide a place of love, warmth, and emotional sustenance, as they attempt to raise and socialize children, economic and political conditions and pressures are constantly pulling at the structure. What does it mean that one-third of an average American family's food budget is spent on meals outside the home? What does it mean for families when both parents need to work full-time but they cannot find day-care facilities for their children? How can we change our economy so that it supports families, not disrupt them as it does now? We cannot ignore the many economic and social policies and conditions that disrupt and diminish family life.

Finally, for men, and even more for women, the family is a great paradox. It provides love, security, and warmth, it anchors our existence and helps us grow, but, to some degree in most societies, it also limits, controls, and even at times oppresses us. Our task, at least our hope, is to nourish, perpetuate, and strengthen all that is life-enhancing and positive in families, and to change the values, economic conditions, social policies, and traditions that oppress people. Feminists rightly exposed the oppression of women in patriarchal families. Now some feminists insist that we also pay attention to the qualities that women and men search for in the families where they were born and raised, and those they create. Let us imagine and create families without oppression. (See Walsh, 1986, and Pogrebin, 1983, especially Chapter 10, "Familial Friendships: Love and Time Are All We Have.")

Summary

Most people say that the family is the most important experience and institution in their lives. Thus, we need to understand and study the family carefully, but we face a number of difficulties in this study: interpreting the meaning of data (for example, the rising divorce rate); imposing our biases and perspectives on the material we study; perceiving the nuclear family as the ideal family; assuming that all family members experience and perceive family life similarly; and idealizing families of the past.

The rise of the family was an important development in human evolution. Throughout human history the family has been the basic production unit for food, other goods, and services. Perhaps even more importantly, it has socialized children and given social and emotional sustenance to all its members.

In addition to the nuclear and extended family, there is the modified-extended family. Many ethnic families in the United State still live in modified-extended families. Family members see each other often. Some poor black people in the United States live in extended families headed by the oldest woman of the family, and increasingly more people live in single-parent families. A brief discussion of families in the Israeli kibbutzim and other societies shows the great variety of the human group we call family.

Marriage has been a universal social expectation, the mark of adult status. Societies vary in the number of marriage partners a person is expected or allowed to have, in whom one is allowed to marry, and in the location of residence after marriage. In many societies the parents have chosen their children's mates. Many sociological research studies argue that married people generally are happier than unmarried ones.

Families have changed over the last three or four centuries. The average U.S. household is half the size it was in 1790. Also, many functions once performed by the family (food production, caring for the ill, job training, etc.) are now performed by special institutions. For the most part, industrialization has caused these changes, which some sociologists view as negative developments and others as positive. Families have also undergone significant changes in the recent past. Due in part to financial need more mothers now work outside the home. More people are delaying marriage or never marrying, more men and women live together who are not married, and most couples have fewer children (a few have none). The rise in divorce has led to more children being raised by one parent. Although the rise in divorce has not been as sudden and dramatic as some people think, it is real. The stigma of divorce has disappeared, and people are unwilling to stay in unhappy marriages. Also, there is less common experience to bind together men and women. Finally, more cases of family violence are being reported, but it is not clear whether this represents an increase in violence or just an increase in awareness.

Even though families today have fewer functions, for most people they remain important. Ideally, families are the source of love, security, and emotional sustenance. Families interact less with the larger community than they did, but family contacts are reported to be frequent and are an essential experience in our lives. In today's society people are struggling to find more family time as the pressures of the outside world infringe on family life.

While in one sense the family is women's domain, in another sense it is their prison since men still hold the control within the family. This patriarchal structure oppresses women by keeping them from gaining social, economic, and personal independence. Feminists recognize the nurturing aspects of family life and the important role women play in this regard, but they do not see this as a reason for women to be limited to domestic lives.

Political, social, and economic developments affect the family structure and functions. Corporate and government policies force families to move and affect families in many other ways. In socialist societies, economic and social changes seem to have strengthened family life.

Suggested Readings

Caplow, Theodore et al. (1982). *Middletown families*. Minneapolis, MN: University of Minnesota Press. The authors conclude that most Middletown families are stable, healthy, and in splendid condition.

Cerullo, Margaret & Ewen, Phyllis (1982, January–April). 'Having a good time': The American family goes camping. *Radical America, 16* (1–2), pp. 13–44. Working-class families go camping to share family time that daily life makes difficult to find.

Demos, John (1970). *A little commonwealth: Family life in Plymouth Colony*. New York: Oxford. Pre-industrial family had many more functions than it does today.

Mangione, Jerre (1942, 1981). *Mount Allegro*. New York: Columbia University Press. A nostalgic, warm, funny, and richly detailed autobiography of life in an Italian family.

Pogrebin, Letty Cottin (1983). *Family politics: Love and politics on an intimate frontier*. New York: McGraw-Hill. One feminist's critical and supportive discussion of what families are and can be for us.

Rubin, Lillian B. (1976). *Worlds of pain: Life in the working-class family*. New York: Basic Books. Rubin claims that working-class families are beset with conflicts and tensions, with some occasional joys.

Russell, Diana (1986). *The secret trauma: Incest in the lives of girls and women*. New York: Basic Books. Incest is more common, and more harmful, than we know.

Stack, Carol B. (1974). *All our kin: Strategies for survival in a black community*. New York: Harper & Row. Black families cope with poverty, discrimination, and other problems by building family networks of sharing and cooperation.

Walsh, Joan (1986, September). Family ties: Feminism's new frontier. *Progressive*, pp. 21–23. Walsh urges feminists to pay attention to the supportive functions of the family as well as its oppressive aspects.

Willie, Charles V. (1981). *A new look at black families* (2nd ed.). Bayside, NY: General Hall. Willie describes the life styles and values of middle-class, working-class, and poor black families.

Young, Michael & Willmott, Peter (1957). *Family and kinship in East London*. Baltimore: Penguin. The extended families of East London lead very close family lives.

Zinn, Maxine Baca & Eitzen, D. Stanley (1987). *Diversity in American families*. New York: Harper & Row. A thorough review of most aspects of American families in the 1980s.

CHAPTER 7

Socialization

Newborn babies are completely helpless. They cannot walk, talk, or feed themselves. They must be fed, held, and protected. At the moment of birth they begin a long process that will make them *human* beings. They possess certain biological potential—speech, walking, use of their hands, and so on— but these capacities must be carefully developed. Only when adults are paralyzed and must relearn every body motion do we realize how much learning babies must do. They do it apparently so automatically that we are unaware how extensive, detailed, and important that learning is.

Physical development is necessary for all newborns, but it does not in itself suffice to make us human. Language, values, skills, norms, and roles are also part of the process. The process of physical development and of learning and internalizing a culture is called *socialization*. It encompasses all the areas of culture and social living we discussed in the previous three chapters.

This chapter looks at how we become socialized and what socialization means to our lives. The elements of socialization—culture, community, and family—are the outside realities that provide us with resources and limits as we travel through life. We encounter them the day we leave our mother's womb. Indeed, we encounter them even while in the womb. Our mothers' diets, the environments in which they live, and other factors affect our physical development before we assume our existence separate from our mothers. For example, fetuses whose mothers have poor diets or have ingested lead or other toxic chemicals may experience insufficient brain development and are more likely to be born retarded.

Physical and Social Contact

As infants, in order to survive, we need to eat. We also need to be held, talked to and with, and in other ways receive stimulation and recognition from people around us. But there is considerable debate and disagreement on the amount and frequency of social and physical contact an infant needs to survive and grow properly. There is also some debate on the stage of life at which such contact is necessary for healthy growth. The following section will discuss some cases and studies relative to this issue and make some tentative conclusions.

Anna and Isabelle

In his study, Davis (1947) describes the results of two cases of extreme isolation. In 1938, in two different parts of the United States, two six-year-old girls were found to be raised by their mothers in relative isolation. Both had been born to single mothers and both families insisted that the babies be raised in relative secrecy and isolation in upstairs rooms.

Anna was brought to her grandfather's house at five and a half months. Until she was found at age six, she was "kept on the second floor in an attic-like room." Her mother worked on the grandfather's farm and gave Anna minimal attention. "Ordinarily, it seems, Anna received only enough care to keep her barely alive. She appears to have been seldom moved from one position to another. Her clothing and bedding were filthy. She apparently had no instruction, no friendly attention." When she was found at age six she "could not talk, walk, or do anything that showed intelligence. She was in an extremely emaciated and undernourished condition, with skeleton-like legs and a bloated abdomen." (p. 431)

For the next four years she lived first in a foster home and then a home for retarded children. By ten she could walk, feed herself, bounce and catch a ball, dress herself and had begun to talk at the level of a two year old. She also played with other children and was fairly sociable and pleasant. On August 6, 1942, she died of hemorrhagic jaundice.

Isabelle was raised in a dark room by her deaf-mute mother. Her mother fed and held her, but she could not teach her how to talk. They communicated by gestures. The sunless room and poor diet made Isabelle rachitic, and her legs were very bowed. She was afraid of strangers, especially men. At six, she behaved like an infant and "many of her actions resembled those of deaf children." (p. 435)

Isabelle, unlike Anna, received immediate and intense attention. She was soon taught how to speak and made rapid progress. By the time she was eight and a half she was normal. When Davis saw her in April 1940 she was a "very bright, cheerful, energetic little girl." (p. 436) She continued to grow normally.

What accounts for the different fates of Anna and Isabelle? Why did Anna make so little progress in speech and physical development compared to Isabelle? Davis presents two possible explanations. It may be that Anna was born mentally retarded or that Isabelle received immediate and intense instruction and attention and Anna did not. A third difference was that Isabelle's mother held her and gave her affection while Anna's mother rarely saw her and possibly never held her. More likely, all three factors account for the difference between the two girls.

The Wild Boy of Aveyron

Lane (1976a) wrote, "One day in 1797 . . . peasants in the region of Lacaune, in south-central France, spied a naked boy fleeing through the woods." (p. 32) He was seen again and captured briefly before he escaped. Finally on January 8, 1800 he was captured and began to live with a doctor and his maid. In the next five years Dr. Itard and Madame Guérin worked long and patiently to civilize Victor, whose age was estimated between ten and twelve years old. He did not speak or behave as a human. Despite the best efforts of his teachers, Victor never learned how to speak. He did learn to focus his eyesight on objects, to use utensils while he ate, to be aware of other people and their needs, and generally made some progress towards becoming a normal human being.

But he never progressed to the point that he was fully socialized. He never spoke. His intellectual facilities developed slowly and painfully. Emotionally, he remained in a stage of profound egoism. After five years, when Victor was in his late teens, his education ended. He was left to the care of Madame Guérin. Ten years later, a visitor found him "fearful, half-wild, and unable to learn to speak, despite all the efforts that were made." (p. 37) He died in that house in 1828, somewhere in his forties. It was never determined how and why Victor came to the woods, at what age, and how he survived. (See also Lane, 1976b.)

Some people who have studied Victor's history think he had been retarded or autistic when he went into the forest, perhaps abandoned there by his parents. Lane, after careful reading of Dr. Itard's diary, disagrees, and concludes that "man depends on society not only for morality and communication but even for the most rudimentary discriminations, concepts, and skills. Social isolation is disastrous, and if it's prolonged, its effects are in large part irreversible. Man outside of society is an ignoble savage." (p. 38)

Children in an Orphanage

In the 1940s, Spitz (Elkin & Handel, 1984), a psychiatrist, studied ninety-one children, three years old and younger, who had been raised in an orphanage. Six nurses cared for the forty-five children who were eighteen months and younger. Two years from the time he began his study a third of the children had died and those still in the orphanage were extraordinarily retarded. Even though after they reached fifteen months the children received more attention, they seemed unable to recover from the effects of the first months of life. Mentally, socially, and physically they remained underdeveloped. Minimal social stimulation and interaction seemed to have permanently damaged the children.

Motherless Monkeys

Harlow and others (1959) conducted experiments where they raised rhesus monkeys without their mothers. Two substitute mothers were provided, one made of wire and the other of wire covered with soft cloth. Invariably, the monkeys preferred the cloth mother for the comfort she seemed to provide, even when the other mother held the bottle. As adults, these motherless monkeys were hostile, withdrawn, apathetic, and generally very unhappy. They did not know how to mate with other monkeys, and females who were artificially impregnated could not care for their own babies and were often abusive towards them.

The conclusion drawn from these studies would seem obvious. Monkeys cannot grow up normally without the physical, emotional, and social care of adult monkeys. Raised in isolation when young (up to about six months), they remain unsocial and unhappy. But in a later experiment Harlow (Kagan, 1973) took a group of monkeys who had been raised in isolation for six months and "placed them with normal infant female monkeys three months younger than themselves for 26 weeks." (p. 56) After seven months they were as normal as monkeys raised by mothers. This seems to suggest that the effects of isolation are reversible, at least early in life.

(I have read many textbook summaries of Harlow's experiments. Not one raises the disturbing ethical implications of the cruel deprivation of the infant monkeys. Is any advance in scientific knowledge ever justified at the expense of living beings? Medical and psychological research often leaves physical scars on primate and other mammals. Can we justify the suffering, pain, and sometimes the death of these animals? I cannot.)

Guatemalan Children

Kagan (1973), who studied child development in Guatemala, concludes that children who are seemingly deprived in their first few years of life are by ten years of age physically, emotionally, and socially as normal as children anywhere else. Guatemalan "infants in the first years of their lives [are] completely isolated in their homes because parents believe that sun and dust and air or the gazes of either pregnant women or men fresh with perspiration from the field will cause illness." (p. 55) Parents love their children; "mothers nurse on demand and hold their infants close to their bodies." (p. 55) But they do not talk or relate to them socially in other ways. Nor do children have toys. Whereas in the West children begin to talk between twelve to eighteen months, Guatemalan children do so between two and a half to three years. By all indications, these children seem retarded and deprived, but they grow up to be alert, active, and fully developed.

What do these studies and cases of isolated children tell us? How much touching, holding, talking with, playing with, and other signs of attention do children need to grow up normal and happy? At what age must they receive this attention? How much deprivation, at what stage in life, causes irreversible damage?

Davis (1947) thinks that children who are isolated and deprived until they are fifteen years old "almost certainly" have no hope of ever being fully socialized. That latest age "might possibly be as low as . . . ten." (p. 437) Kagan (1973) comes to somewhat similar conclusions: "The first two years of life do not inexorably doom you to retardation and . . . there's much more potential for recovery than Western psychologists have surmised. . . . I can say with confidence . . . that an abnormal experience in the first two years of life in no way affects basic intellectual functions or the ability to be affectively normal—to experience gaiety and sadness, guilt and shame." (pp. 55–56)

There are no certain conclusions. *Total* deprivation of human contact would seem to leave lasting damage. Victor, who apparently spent most of his early childhood, up to the age of ten, totally without human association, attests to that conclusion. But some minimal contact, as we see in Isabelle's case, keeps the potential for human growth alive. Children seem to be tough and resilient. Spitz's findings (Elkin & Handel, 1984) do not justify gloomy conclusions on permanent psychic damage. Deprivation can be overcome.

But of course there is never any justification for depriving infants and children of human association, love, and care. Children may survive relative isolation, but surely they are happier if they spend their formative years with people who will talk with them and hold them. We also need to note that what constitutes "deprivation" is culturally relative. Parental practices that leave no lasting damage in Guatemala, if performed by individual parents in another society, could cause irreversible damage. If a child in the United States was raised like a child is raised in Guatemalan villages, he or she could be a misfit and suffer socially and emotionally. Cultural practices differ from the practices of individual parents.

Culture and Socialization

There is a seemingly infinite variety in childrearing practices, and what is required in one culture is forbidden in another. Let us look at some of these differences by examining certain areas of human development and then discussing what they seem to teach us.

Crying

Long before parents must deal with their infants' crawling, walking, talking, toilet-training, and anger, they must respond to their crying. According to Scheff (1976) "From the instant of birth, the infant makes known his [or her] feelings directly and compellingly. The cry and the scream make the parents' sleep problematic. . . . The parents must find some way of dealing with crying and screaming, and they must find it immediately." (p. 81) Scheff also says the parents' and the culture's response to the baby's crying shapes its personality as a child and adult. If parents hold and soothe the baby, comfort him or her and seek to remove the source of the distress, the child is more likely to be a warm, trusting, secure, and accepting person. The more punitive the reaction to a child's crying, the more parents seek to repress the crying and the emotions, the more likely the adult in that culture is to be punitive and repressive in his or her emotions.

Cultures vary widely in how they handle crying infants. Those that seek to repress it, however, are not necessarily punitive and unloving of their children, contrary to Scheff's implication. The Cheyenne love their children and care for them tenderly. But they will not tolerate crying, according to Hoebel (1960), and they stop it quickly and effectively. "Crying babies are not scolded, slapped, or threatened. They are simply taken out on the cradle-board away from the camp and into the brush where they are hung on a bush. There the squalling infant is left alone until it cries itself out. A few such experiences indelibly teach it that bawling brings not reward but complete and total rejection and the loss of all social contacts. On the other hand, the good baby is cuddled and constantly loved." (p. 92)

In the United States we do not banish crying infants out of our sight. But as an infant grows older it is left alone to cry itself to sleep, especially after it has been fed, diapered, and held for a few minutes. (Some parents, however, always or almost always hold a crying baby.) As they grow older, children, especially boys, are discouraged from crying. They are ridiculed by peers as crybabies,and they are surrounded by males who do not cry. Thus, Scheff (1976) would argue, men learn to repress their emotions. Other societies do not repress crying and other emotions, in contrast to the Cheyennes and American. (See also Nanda, 1980.)

Touching and Nursing

In varying degrees, American children are held by their parents and others. In some societies there is limited touching and holding of children. In others, however, children are almost constantly held and touched from the day they are born. Among the Arapesh (Mead, 1935), "During its first months the child is never far from someone's arms. When the mother walks about she carries the baby suspended from her forehead in its special small net bag, or suspended under one breast in a bark-cloth sling." (p. 40) Sleeping or awake, children are in constant physical contact with the mother or another adult. According to Mead, the constant holding, touching, and affection leads to a "warm and maternal temperament of both men and women" in Arapesh society. (p. 40)

!Kung children also are held and touched constantly (Shostak, 1981):

!Kung children spend their first few years in almost constant close contact with their mothers. The !Kung infant has continual access to the mother's

breast, day and night, usually for at least three years, and nurses on demand several times an hour. The child sleeps beside the mother at night, and during the day is carried in a sling, skin-to-skin on the mother's hip, wherever the mother goes, at work or at play. (This position is an ideal height for older children, who love to entertain babies.) When the child is not in the sling, the mother may be amusing her—bouncing, singing, or talking. If they are physically separated, it is usually for short periods, when the father, siblings, cousins, grandparents, aunts, uncles, or friends of the family are playing with the baby while the mother sits close by. (p. 45)

Infants and babies are nursed on demand not only among the !Kung, but in many (if not most) societies. Before industrial societies, nursing provided frequent touching between mother and child. Bottle-feeding at one point replaced nursing as the preferred method, but now more mothers are again nursing their babies, usually for only a few months. In contrast, in many societies children nurse until they are three or four years, occasionally until they are six years old.

!Kung children nurse until their mother gets pregnant with the next child, when she must stop (somewhere between two and four years). For children who nursed on demand, weaning is often a traumatic experience. Nisa persistently tried to continue to nurse, even after her brother was born. She recalls that one day when her mother and brother fell asleep, she secretly nursed from her. Shostak says, however, that because children are given so much love and attention as infants and babies, they survive the weaning relatively well and are left with no emotional scars.

Physical Punishment

"Spare the rod and spoil the child" goes the Biblical saying. In Greece and other peasant societies, physical punishment of children is normal and frequent. Corporal punishment was common in American schools, but today it is rare. The vast majority of American parents, however, do on occasion hit their children. Over 90 percent of my students have told me that they were hit (usually on their buttocks) when they were growing up. In some societies children are hit more often and harder than they are in the United States. In other societies, children are rarely or never touched in anger or for punishment.

The Cheyennes, who repress their children's crying, rarely punish them physically (Hoebel, 1960). Downs (1972) observed little spanking among the Navaho. "In seven months' close association with seven nuclear families with a total of twenty-nine children below fifteen years of age, I observed a child struck on only four occasions. . . . All the blows involved were rather mild, even when compared with the spankings of the most 'progressive' Anglo [white, non-Indian] mother. Disobedient children are often threatened that an uncle or older brother will be requested to spank them." (p. 24)

Physical punishment may not coincide with people's perception and memories. Shostak (1981) says in the case of the !Kung that "beating and threats of beating are almost universal in the childhood memories of !Kung adults," but anthropologists who have lived with the !Kung have "almost never" witnessed physical punishment. "It is probably that rare instances of physical punishment become exaggerated and vivid in the child's memory," and the *threats* of beating are remembered as actual beatings. (pp. 49–50)

Our society is currently grappling with the distinction between child abuse and discipline. How we define child abuse determines whether it exists as a social problem in the United States and how extensive it is. Almost all children are hit some time during their childhood, but many children are beaten. These children have been treated for everything from broken bones to internal injuries—some have died as a result of this kind of abuse. One wonders if our culture did not sanction spanking, whether it is likely there would be much less child abuse. Spanking is not abuse, but the sanctioning of spanking creates the social climate where it may gradually escalate to abuse.

Officially, in 1984 there were a combined total of 1.1 million reported cases of child neglect and abuse. There may have been many more unreported abused children. Moreover, it is likely that our perception and awareness of abuse, not its incidence, have increased in the last few years. Whatever the numbers may be, we should ask why parents beat their children leaving them with broken bones and occasionally killing them. (See *Statistical Abstract, 1987: 161.*)

When parents find themselves under great stress, they often lose their patience and their restraint. Constant worry about money, alienating work conditions or no work at all, feelings of deprivation and low self-esteem, all these exhaust parental strength and patience. Many parents (not only the poor) raise their children without any outside support, no family or community to take over some of the responsibilities and burdens of rearing children. Cultural, political, social, and economic conditions combine to create child abuse. We should not think that parents who beat their children are necessarily evil and do not love them. The culture and the economy place tremendous pressure on them (Gil, 1975).

If we focus not on parents who hit children but on children and conditions that harm, injure, and kill them, we see that outside political and economic forces threaten children much more than parents. An economic system that creates deprivation, degradation, and environmental poisoning truly threatens and harms children (Gil, 1975).

Noninterference

Parents often hit their children because the children will not obey them. But obedience and control of children varies widely from culture to culture. In the United States, Greece, and many other societies children are taught to obey. Obedience to authority is ingrained into their personality. When we are young, we are told what to wear, what and when to eat (or not eat), when and how to cut our hair, and so on endlessly. Because of this we learn to interfere in other people's actions and behavior. We offer unsolicited advice on what car to buy, where to go for dinner, and are, as Good Tracks (1973) notes, "always telling each other and everyone else what [we] should do, buy, see, sell, read, study or accomplish—all without any consideration of what the individual may want to do." (p. 31)

But consider the following examples from native American societies. Lee (1959) reported that an anthropologist observed an eighteen-month-old child "with hair so long that it got in his eyes and seemed to cause him discomfort." She asked the mother why she had not cut his hair, and the mother replied, "He has not asked to have it cut."(p. 7) The child could not yet talk, but the mother would not presume to act on his behalf without his consent. Another woman, when asked if a baby could talk, replied "yes." But the anthropologist was puzzled because the child only made "meaningless" sounds. The woman explained that the baby could talk, but she "could not understand what the baby said." (p. 12) She could only speak for herself, not the baby. She would not, as we would, say that the baby made meaningless sounds.

In the seventeenth century, the freedom native parents gave to their children shocked Jesuit missionaries and other Europeans. Champlain (*Jesuit Relations,* 1896–1901) wrote that among the Huron "the children have great freedom. . . . The fathers and mothers indulge them too much, and never punish them." (vol. 5, p. 197) In turn, the punishment given to European children shocked the Indians. They could not bear to see children spanked, and they tried to stop it. According to Father LaJeune, "they will not tolerate the chastisement of their children, whatever they may do; they permit only a simple reprimand." (vol. 5, p. 197) Later, he wrote: "These barbarians cannot bear to have their children punished, not even scolded, not being able to refuse anything to a crying child." (vol. 6, p. 153)

People who do not cut their children's hair or do not punish them are not unconcerned or ignorant. They are merely stating what they believe is profound respect for the autonomy of the individual, no matter what his or her age. As they grow up, children see that adults respect each other's autonomy and do not presume to speak or act for others; they see that adults do not coerce them, interfere with their person, or force them to obey; they see that adults will not tolerate interfering behavior from children. Even if children hurt themselves, they will not rush up and interrupt a parent who is talking or doing something. They will wait until the parent comes over and tends to them. Interfering behavior is not practiced or rewarded. According to Good Tracks (1973),

> *Indian adults do not respond to interfering demands, so the child does not learn coercive methods of behavior. This does not imply that Indian children are never aggressive, but only that the culture does not reward aggression when it interferes with the activity of others. Indian children are taught to be*

considerate through the example of their elders, and the adult treats the child with the same respect and consideration that he expects for himself. It is generally against the child-rearing practices of Indian people to bother or interrupt their children when they are playing or to make them do something against their will, even when it is in their own best interest. (p. 32)

(For noninterference among the Navaho, see Lee, 1959; Pelletier, 1970; and Downs, 1972.)

Culture and Personality

What does this review of different socialization practices tell us? Here are three conclusions.

The first is that any socialization process is effective and leads to well-adjusted and healthy adults, as long as it is consistent and accepted throughout the culture. There are limits, of course. Children cannot be brutally beaten or starved. But "cruelty" is a relative term. Are Cheyenne infants crying alone in the brush being abused? Does spanking in Greece and the United States cause irreparable harm? It seems not. As I said, it appears that if all (or most) parents in a society are consistent in their practices, children adjust to them and grow up healthy.

The second is that children are raised to fit into their society. The values, institutions, norms, and roles of the society provide a context in which they can grow, and socialization must prepare them to live in their society. Kagan (1976) argues that in a society where people live in close physical proximity and where they must also cooperate, anger and its expression must be suppressed. In the United States, where competition and individualism reign supreme, anger is allowed (even encouraged), within limits. Each society creates the personality and emotions suitable to its economy, institutions, and values.

And the third conclusion is that cultural relativism can only be carried so far (see Chapter 4, on culture). We can appreciate that children are raised in a variety of ways, and most children in any society survive, grow, and adjust. I cannot condemn Cheyenne parents for repressing their children's crying, or American parents for hitting their children (especially since I have hit mine on occasion). Neither can I say, however, that I feel comfortable with beating and coercion of children.

I admire the Navaho and other societies where hitting and coercion are largely absent from the lives of children and parents. I get exasperated when I am on the phone, and my children will not wait until I finish before they make a request (or, often, demand). But then I recall the constant demands I make on them: finish your meal, put on your jacket, go to sleep, and so on. As a responsible American parent I have no choice. It is in my personality and my culture to require my children to behave in ways that are in their best interest. I cannot, as one parent, raise my children the way the Navaho raise theirs.

They would be misfits and probably spoiled in American society. But I do weary of the constant demands they make of me, and I of them. As I try to show throughout this book culture, history, economy, and politics all shape the conditions in which we raise our children.

Sexuality

Can a society totally ignore biology? Many anthropologists argue that human behavior is totally determined by culture, but can we deny that we are also physical and natural beings? I think not. Our physical nature plays as much a role in our socialization as our culture. One aspect in particular exerts a heavy force on how we become socialized. Anthropologists point to the tremendous variety of sexual forms of expression and its near repression in some societies, and imply that all forms of sexual expression and repression are acceptable and human. I cannot share this relativism. Sexuality is one of the most misunderstood and complex human experiences, and in many societies it has caused people much suffering. We can appreciate the variety of its expression, but I think we must not neglect the suffering that results from its repression.

Limits to Our Knowledge

Sex and love-making are largely private acts. When mentioned publicly they evoke both embarrassment and secrecy. These reactions, of course, vary from society to society. In many societies sexuality is either not discussed openly or exaggerated, or, probably more commonly, both. This has certainly been the history in Western, Christian society. Therefore, our understanding of sexuality in our own society, both pre- and post-industrial, is biased, incomplete, and misleading. At least for now, it is obvious that we cannot accept current research and writing as approximating the truth. We must live with many doubts. Nimmo (1970) points to at least four problems anthropologists have faced in their study of sex. These problems apply as well to sociologists studying their own society.

1. Individuals willing to talk to us openly about a normally "delicate" subject may not be typical of the population.

2. A man or woman receives a one-sided view of sex, that of their own sex. Interviewing people of the opposite sex poses inherent problems in most societies.

3. More than in any other area, we depend entirely on people's reports of their actions. We cannot observe behavior—and if we do, our presence alters it.

4. In many societies, it is difficult to find a time and place to discuss sex.

I would add another problem. Since children's sexuality is supposedly nonexistent or evil in many societies, discussing it with children or adults is a touchy subject.

Culture and Children's Sexuality

Below we will present some data on cultural variation in sexual expression, but first we need to note that children's sexuality exists in a cultural context. Children see (or do not see), talk about, and experience sex within their culture, where norms and values dictate what is acceptable and what is prohibited in sexual expression. Generally, the more repressed sexuality is for adults, the more repressed it is for children.

Some societies are very restrictive, denying children any form of sexual expression. Some of them later allow considerable sexual freedom to adolescents. But restrictiveness does not eliminate sexuality, for in these societies children often engage in forbidden acts (masturbation, for example). Other societies permit and even encourage sexuality in children. Children hear adults discuss sex, often see them engage in it (in some contexts), and play-act their love-making (see the example of the !Kung below). Some evidence, from our own and other societies, clearly shows that irrespective of adult wishes, commands, and punishments, irrespective of adults forbidding children from hearing, discussing, and practicing sexuality, children do so nevertheless. They may feel guilty, receive wrong information, and perhaps not enjoy it, but sex is part of their lives (Barnouw, 1971).

!Kung families live in one hut. Therefore, young children often wake up and hear and see their parents making love. Nisa did not object seeing them when she was little, but she recollected as an adult that as an older child she began to resent their love-making when she was in the hut. Why did they not wait until she was out? In fact, Shostak (1981) claims that !Kung parents encourage their older children to sleep elsewhere at night.

Nisa and other !Kung see sex as a necessity of life. (Nisa at least made sure she was never without it.) So !Kung children see sex and hear it openly discussed and joked about. Sexual innuendos pervade much of !Kung conversation. Long before they reach ten, children play-act intercourse and other forms of sexuality. They disappear from their parents' sight and set up their own households, where boys and girls pretend to make love and play husband and wife. Adults often disapprove of their children's play, but Shostak (1981) says they do nothing to stop it.

The Bajau (Nimmo, 1970), the Kaingang, and other societies also encourage children's sexuality. Children are openly exposed to talk about sex, to sexual jokes, and to some sexual practices. There is no shame or punishment attached to these topics. While children do not have intercourse, the Kaingáng, according to Henry (1941), see everyone except the very youngest children as sexual.

Most historical literature on sexuality in the United States suggests that the United States has been largely restrictive until recently. In the last twenty to thirty years, some (many? most?) parents have begun to discuss sex more freely with their children. But children growing up in our society find themselves facing severe contradictions. On the one hand, they reach physical sexual maturity around the age of twelve or thirteen, compared to fifteen or seventeen in the past and in pre-industrial societies. There is also pressure from the inundation of sexual messages, stimulation, and advertisements in the mass media. On the other hand, the message from many parents is to postpone sexual expression, most notably intercourse. By the time most Americans marry in their early or mid-twenties, they are no longer virgins. There is, however, the long period of adolescence when they are physically mature, but socially they are neither children nor adults. Moreover, how much sexuality (touching, kissing, embracing) do most children see live at home? Seeing it in movies and TV differs from seeing it at home; the message is not the same (Melville, 1983).

Cultural Variation

The biology of sex is much the same for men and women in all societies, but cultures respond differently to it. There is variation in all aspects of human sexual behavior. In some societies people discuss, joke about, touch and kiss, and show their bodies openly, freely, and naturally. But some or all of these acts are forbidden in other societies where sex is a secret and forbidden subject. In some societies men and women are thought to be equally and fully sexual beings and both are expected to seek sexual partners and satisfaction. The !Kung, Kaingáng, and Bajau are some examples. In other societies, however, women and often men are discouraged from wanting sexual pleasure, with intercourse meant only for procreation. Christian and other societies have often viewed sex as a necessary evil. Finally, there is variation in how men and women enjoy (or do not enjoy) each other's love and sexual expression. In some societies kissing is essential to love-making; in others it is a disgusting thought. In some societies people touch, caress, and engage in foreplay and exploration, while in other societies people quickly engage in intercourse. And positions for intercourse vary: in many societies the only position used is the man on top of the woman, but in others various positions are mandated or offered as alternatives. Also, some homosexuality is found in all societies, but some societies punish it severely (even by death), others stigmatize homosexuals, and still others sanction it by providing approved roles for them (Barnouw, 1971).

But in no society that I know of (or that I can imagine) do all people completely assimilate cultural limits on sexuality. Even at the risk of death and other penalties people have premarital or extramarital sex, homosexual relationships, or behave sexually in ways other than those approved of by society. In general people go beyond the limits set by society.

The Irish of Inis Beag seem to be some of the most sexually repressed people yet observed (always keeping in mind that anthropologists never can find the absolute truth about sex). As Messenger (1969) presents them, they never reveal their bodies, except for hands and head; there are no sexual jokes; women are not to enjoy sex, only to endure it; there is much ignorance about women's ability to reach climax and other biological realities; and the separation of sexes begins early and continues for years, especially given the late marriage age. The Cheyenne also are sexually repressed. One of their cultural ideals is for a husband and wife to abstain for seven years after the birth of a child (Hoebel, 1960).

The Kaingáng, the !Kung, and the Bajau are among many societies that express sexuality openly, freely, and often. In all of them, it is a frequent topic of discussion. Men and women both seek and enjoy it. Henry (1941) was courted by many Kaingáng women who were not humiliated by his refusals; premarital sex is common, as is sex play among children. Shostak (1981) found that Nisa and other !Kung women were equal to men in their interest in and enjoyment of sex.

Mead's *Coming of Age in Samoa* (1928) is an anthropological classic that has shaped our understanding of human sexuality (especially among adolescents). She found the adolescent girls whom she interviewed were generally free of the turmoil of American adolescents. Specifically, pre-marital sex was common and accepted and the girls enjoyed it.

But in the spring of 1983 a controversy surfaced in the mass media, following the publication of Freeman's (1983) book, *Margaret Mead and Samoa—The Making and Un-making of an Anthropological Myth.* Since 1940, Freeman has spent a total of six years in Samoa, talking and associating mostly with men. He contends that the Samoan girls pulled a fast one on Mead. They lied to her about pre-marital sex in Samoa. Freeman says that the Samoans have one of the most developed cults of virginity known to anthropology. Furthermore, he claims Samoan society is as ridden with crime, deviance, and conflict as most other societies.

Freeman accuses Mead of going to Samoa with the intention of showing that culture shapes human behavior. Others, then and now, claim that our biology largely determines how we behave, so people in all societies largely behave similarly. By showing a trouble-free adolescence and pre-marital sex, Mead could make her argument of cultural influence on human behavior. But Freeman, who holds a view opposite to Mead's, ignores his own biases. For example, it is quite possible that the cult of virginity was introduced to Samoan culture by the Christian missionaries. When Freeman was told by Samoan men that Mead misrepresented adolescent sexuality in *Coming of Age in Samoa,* he might have been hearing a new norm on sexuality. He was told to please correct Mead's incorrect portrait of Samoan culture. And he set out to do that, ignoring that what Samoan men told him may be both a recent development and also only a male view. Samoan adolescents in the 1920s may have behaved as Mead told us, and what Freeman reports may only be a cultural ideal as told to him by Samoan men.

Sex in the United States

A simplified history of sex in the West would show sexual repression in the nineteenth and early twentieth centuries, and sexual freedom and liberation today. Some evidence does seem to show that sex now is more openly discussed, and probably practiced and enjoyed by more people, than it was in the past. But such a conclusion misrepresents both past and present. Surely there was more sexual expression in the past, just as there is some confusion, guilt, and abstinence today. (See Degler, 1974, and DuBois, 1982.)

Recent historical studies argue that the Puritans did not repress their sexuality, contrary to the long-standing belief, implied in the very use of the word "puritanical" to mean repression and denial of sexuality. In Chapter 4 we saw that in the nineteenth century women led a more active sex life than we had thought. Also, there may not be much difference between our times and earlier decades in this century. Behavior may not have changed as much as we think. The Lynd and Lynd (1937) survey of "more than two dozen young business-class persons in their twenties" in Muncie, Indiana, found "seven out of every ten of them, evenly divided as to sex, to have had sexual relations prior to marriage." (p. 169) Davis (1982) comments

> That was in the 1930s and hardly accorded with the public standards of the times. In the late 1970's, however, after the widely acclaimed "sexual revolution," slightly over fifty percent of those surveyed in the senior year at both Hamilton high schools still listed themselves as virgins. This figure will decline, of course, by the time the seniors reach the age of the Middletown [Muncie] sample, but the indication is strong that behavior has not changed nearly as dramatically as both radicals and hand-wringers claim. (p. 29)

(See also Thompson, 1986; *Boston Globe,* April 21, 1987:2; Degler, 1974; and DuBois,1982.)

Sigmund Freud, Kinsey and his associates, and Masters and Johnson have helped to change our views and knowledge of sex. Freud argued against the view of his time that children are born innocent of sexual interest and are only corrupted when adults introduce it to them. Indeed, Freud claimed that the reverse is more accurate: children are born sexual and sensual beings, and adults repress childhood sexuality. They teach children to be embarrassed by their bodies, to avoid sexual talk, to hide all expressions of sexuality. (Freud is obviously referring only to Western societies.)

Kinsey shocked many people by showing that there was more sexual activity, of different kinds, than official morality seemed to allow in the 1930s and 1940s. And Masters and Johnson corrected many long-held beliefs about the biology of sex, among them women's ability to have orgasms (frequency, kinds, etc.). These three findings changed our understanding of human sexuality and sexual practices in our society.

Most research and writing on sex in the United States today (and probably in other Western societies) concludes that more people engage in it (single and married) in a much greater variety than ever before in Western history. There is no doubt that it is talked about, written about, and depicted (in hard and soft pornography) much more than in the past. Legal restrictions on sex, for example against premarital or extramarital intercourse, have been repealed or are simply ignored. There is more sex in and out of marriage, at least when we compare survey findings of the 1940s with the 1970s and 1980s.

Surveys and personal experiences show that most American youth believe that premarital sex is normal and acceptable for women and men when it is with someone you care about (but do not necessarily intend to marry). Surveys in the 1970s and 1980s show that most women and men engage in premarital intercourse. A Harris poll which sampled 1,000 U.S. teenagers in September and October of 1986, found that 57 percent "of seventeen-year-olds had had sexual intercourse, 29 percent by age fifteen, and 20 percent by age fourteen. More boys than girls had had such experience at every age level, including 61 percent to 53 percent among seventeen-year olds." A 1984 study found that 65.6 percent of nineteen-year-old, never-married women said they had had intercourse, and 73.3 percent of those twenty to twenty-four said they had done so. (See *Boston Globe,* December 17, 1986: 12; *Statistical Abstract,* 1987: 66; and Melville, 1983.)

Young people may act and talk sexy, but most don't seem to discuss sex in any rational manner. Most don't have serious and long talks about sex with their parents and other adults. Over half of the women students I survey in my classes claim they have never done so. Much ignorance about sex persists. Very few teens use contraceptives during their first intercourse, and many continue not using them, accounting for the thousands of unwanted pregnancies. Girls are caught between their emotional and physical desires, pressures from boyfriends, and mixed messages that boys can but girls should not. (See *Boston Globe,* May 11,1984: 15, July 1, 1986: 13, December 17, 1986: 12; *Guardian,* January 21, 1987: 2; and Zinn & Eitzen, 1987.)

Some people think (or hope?) that we may be witnessing a new, conservative morality on premarital sex. Herpes, AIDS, and a growing belief that sex is more meaningful with commitment and intimacy may change sexual behavior. It will take a few years before we can tell how many people are changing their sexual habits, and how long such a change will last.

Marital sex has also increased. Sexual liberation had begun by the time Kinsey carried out his surveys from 1938 to 1949. The median marital coitus frequency per week was reported as 1.95 for ages twenty-six to thirty-five (men and women). Hunt's (1974) survey found a median of 2.55. But the most significant changes have been in variety, attitude, and pleasure. Hunt summarizes his findings this way:

> *Since Kinsey's time marital sex in America has become a good deal more egalitarian (with husbands being more considerate of their wives' needs, and wives assuming more responsibility for the success of intercourse); that husbands and wives are much freer in terms of the kinds of foreplay and coital*

positions they use; that the conscious pursuit of sensuous pleasure in marriage has become much more acceptable to both sexes; and that there is a considerable increase in the percentage of marital sexual experiences that yield genuine satisfaction to both persons. (p. 148)

There is still some confusion, guilt, and uncertainty. Rubin (1976) claims that many of the fifty working-class wives she interviewed in 1973 did enjoy sex but felt some guilt about it. Many still are not open and initiating in their sex life with their husbands. But the general picture is one of much change in attitudes and behavior. Surveys in Muncie, Indiana, in the late 1970s confirm the change in sexual behavior. (See Caplow et al., 1982; Hunt, 1974; Melville, 1983; and Westhues, 1982.)

AIDS and Sexual Repression

AIDS (acquired immune deficiency syndrome) may be one of the most dangerous health crises of our century. Unless we find a vaccine to prevent it and medicines to cure it soon, it may kill millions. Thousands have died from AIDS as of 1988.

Unfortunately, some people use AIDS to argue for sexual abstinence outside marriage. They exploit a serious health crisis to argue for their moral views and to punish those who disagree. One of President Reagan's domestic advisors said (Kochis, 1986): "The problem is that we have allowed the erosion of basic values and standards of decency in our society. The administration's message should be: abstain from sex now, wait for your future husband or wife, marry and remain faithful." (p. 16) Conservatives use the fear of AIDS to propagate a philosophy "whose main characters are guilt, shame, victim-blaming, homophobia, an obsessive fear of death, and a reflexive faith in the status quo." (p. 16) They argue that AIDS is God's punishment to gay people and those who engage in premarital sex, for the sins of the "sexual revolution."

But AIDS is a disease. Morality and religion have nothing to do with diseases. The cause is biological and AIDS can only be cured by a rational medical and research progam that offers treatment and prevents its spread. Whereas the government and most other institutions in the United States have done little or nothing to educate the public about AIDS prevention, other countries have encouraged and educated people to be careful while they enjoy sex. In a recent article, McLaughlin (1987) quoted the Danes' public education message: "Love is good for people, and sex is healthy as well as desirable. So do not forsake either love or sex because of AIDS. Just be careful." (p. 11) Use condoms and take other precautions.

Liberation, Repression, and Exploitation

Past cultural ideals and norms of human sexuality in the West were repressive. Some evidence (and common sense) would indicate that many people rejected these norms, although not always openly. Therefore, the recent freedom and discussion of sex has had a liberating effect. But much repression still exists. The long history of denial of sexuality, of creating guilt and ambivalence, lingers on. Repression also exists in the continuing contradiction that many adults cannot discuss sex with their children and disapprove of it when they do mention it. But at the same time, sex is openly manipulated and exploited in society. Pornography, which removes all emotion and tenderness from lovemaking, is one source of exploitation. As serious, if not more so, is the use of sex to sell products. Sexual symbols and sexual promises pervade advertising. Pornography and advertising debase men, women, and sexuality. They create ambivalence about the meaning and value of the liberation we are gaining.

Repression and exploitation coexist. It becomes difficult in our society to understand and experience sexuality in perspective. Indeed, exploitation and constant erotic stimulation, together with manuals on sexual happiness, seem to imply that the basic source of human happiness is frequent orgasms and an untold variety of sexual expressions. It may be, as Westhues (1982) argues, that as men and women lose control over their jobs and lives (since most of us have little or no say in what we do and how we do it), they seek to compensate for this loss by a compulsive search for sexual fulfillment. "Out of boredom and for want of challenge in their working lives, people shift their thinking away from the future toward the present and become more content to take pleasure just in one another's bodies." (p. 361) Commercial exploitation and stimulation, plus empty lives, cause us to search for more meaning in sexual pleasure than it can actually give us. Sex cannot compensate for loss of community, family, meaningful work, and control over our lives.

Sexual enjoyment is one of life's pleasures. It is also part of our biological heritage. Many societies have enhanced people's ability to partake of that pleasure. Others, however, have repressed it. In the West we have created a variation, it seems, by exploiting it while we are liberating it. Snitow, Stansell, and Thompson (1983) also explore many of the issues and controversies we face in seeking to liberate sexuality.

Agents of Socialization

In pre-industrial societies children were socialized by family and community. Parents, siblings, other relatives, neighbors, and friends taught children norms, values, and roles. These people still socialize children, but schools, the mass media, and other institutions have taken over some of this socialization. All of these groups are *agents of socialization* that prepare children for social life.

Among the Mbuti, !Kung, and other pre-industrial societies children can see the society that socializes them. The family and community, people who agree and disagree, are concrete and alive. They know who requires, expects,

encourages, and forbids actions and attitudes. Large industrial societies, however, do not offer such a concrete society to children. Elkin and Handel (1984)
tell us that "society specifies certain outcomes or ranges of outcomes of socialization." (p. 34) Among them are loyalty to the society and obedience of its
laws. But does society really present a real and unified front to children? What
is this society that tells poor and black children and girls that they are excluded from certain opportunities in the United States? And if children's
parents encourage them to cooperate instead of compete but the school encourages them to compete, which social instruction should they follow? Sometimes it may be obvious that a general expectation is societal, but a more
thorough examination of socialization should make it difficult to argue that
society determines how children get socialized. Poor children may be taken
away from their parents if the court finds the parents to be unfit, but equally
unfit rich parents do not lose custody of their children. Who within society
should judge the fitness of parents?

The Family

Despite its reduced functions, the family remains the first and primary group
that socializes us. Even in one-parent families it is the parent, the siblings, and
other relatives who introduce a person to life and his or her culture.

In the United States, we receive and keep for some years our family's
status. Until we go to work, our social standing is that of our parents and other
relatives. The values, norms, and roles of our culture are mediated and
translated for us through our family. The meaning of sexuality and human
contact are introduced to children by parents, grandparents, siblings, and
other relatives. We learn about intimate and personal relationships through
the people around us. Social relationships are developed first by our parents
feeding, holding, and talking to us. Then come brothers, sisters, and others.
Later, when we attend school, watch TV, play sports, hang around with
friends, we gradually grow more independent, but we stay primarily in our
family for many years (Elkin & Handel, 1984).

A family in the United States means parents and children, but other
relatives often play an important role. When grandparents or uncles and aunts
live close by they often partake in the socialization of children. Indeed, in
many societies other relatives are almost as important as parents. For example, when Nisa was in conflict with her parents over a number of issues, she
went to live with her grandparents or favorite aunts (Shostak, 1981). She
returned in a few weeks or months when emotions and feelings had cooled off.
In this way, relatives help raise children.

Society and the Generalized Other

When we were born we could not walk, talk, feed ourselves or provide for any
of our needs. We depended entirely on others. As we grew we watched other

people's actions and heard their words. Gradually, we came to imitate them. We became human and social, we acquired a self, as we grew up in our family and later in the wider community. During these years we came to view our actions, emotions, and thoughts as we understood others viewed them. This ability to judge, interpret, and regulate our actions and thoughts by the standards of others around us makes us *social* human beings.

George Herbert Mead (1934) contributed significantly to our under-standing of this process. He argues that as small children we simply imitate the actions of parents, siblings, and others near us. But soon after we begin to play *roles:* firefighter, carpenter, nurse, doctor, and so on. We act and talk as we have seen these people do, or as we are told they do, as as we imagine they do.

But in time we advance beyond the stage where we play single roles. We begin to participate in action and play with others; we are aware of, and take into account, the roles of many others in relation to our role. Like a game of baseball, we must know, anticipate, and coordinate our actions with the roles of all eight of our teammates and the opposition players. In life generally, as we grow older we begin to rehearse in our minds the reactions of others, of the community in general, to our proposed actions. Early in our life, our conduct is guided by those raising us, our significant others (as Mead calls them). We guide our actions according to their roles, models, and guidelines. But as we grow up, we gradually learn of the larger community and society, which guide our actions—what Mead calls the *generalized other*. When this happens we are fully social beings (Elkin & Handel, 1984).

Peer Groups

In all human societies children play with other children or what is called their *peer group*. As they grow older, their arena of action is away from adult supervision, apart from and often in opposition to adults. In the United States, we move about and rarely keep our childhood friends (in a survey I took in a sociology class, only three or four out of twenty students still saw childhood friends); in pre-industrial societies people went through life associating with their childhood playmates. Nisa played house with boys and girls who re-mained her friends for life (Shostak, 1981).

Neighbors, schoolmates, cousins, and others are our peers. In games and in just being together, we learn from our agemates how to relate to people, how to negotiate, how to protect ourselves, how to be with others. My daugh-ter, Melissa, rides bikes with her best friend. They ride slowly, and they talk and plan their day. Ariane, Melissa's younger sister, learns the ambiguities of fitting in. She tells Melissa she does not understand "what's so great about stickers. You look at them once or twice and that's it." But she goes on to note that you have to collect them since all other kids are doing it. So you learn how to get along, to be with others, and to cooperate, but you also learn that sometimes conforming to peer expectations involves action that may not be enjoyable or preferable.

With school, organized sports (led by adults), and other adult-directed activities children have less time away from adult supervision. Perhaps with exaggerated nostalgia, I remember my childhood free from adult presence. We ran our own track meets, played our own soccer games, and argued endlessly the finest details of the rules. I see my daughters play little league baseball, and it is the adults who make the rules and argue over them. Indeed, the players do not know most of the rules. One wonders for whose benefit the games are played. Adults scream and shout directions to six-year-olds who are only half-attentive.

Schools

Going to school is such an expected and automatic (if not always enjoyable) experience in our lives that we may forget how recent a development it is. It takes a major portion of our time and energies. In school, we supposedly learn skills and attitudes indispensable to living in modern societies. It was only about one hundred fifty years ago that mass public education first appeared in any society. Its existence has profoundly reshaped the experience of childhood.

Schools do, of course, teach us how to read and write, to count and solve arithmetic problems. They do impart information about the natural and social world. At their best, they inspire children, introduce them to the wider world, and liberate them. But their functions do not stop there. According to many education critics, they perform two other functions: they perpetuate social inequalities (class, sex, and racial) by favoring some children over others, causing those who fail to blame themselves (see next four chapters, especially Chapter 8); and they often create a culture of fear, obedience, and dogmatism. Children are controlled and taught to obey more than they are taught how to think on their own.

The first and foremost reality that teaches conformity and obedience is that by law children must attend school. While in school, children do learn reading, geography, science, and so on, but they also learn that they have no say in what they learn or how they learn it. Thus begins a lifelong process of learning obedience. Children must obey school rules and regulations. Some are eminently reasonable, but others seem designed mostly to show adult control, such as the rules of the length of boys' hair.

Finally, and perhaps most important, we learn a conception of ourselves. Competition and fear of failure convince us we are bright or stupid. Even bright students, however, develop what Holt (1964) thinks is dread and fear of failure. One day he asked his class, "What do you think, what goes through your mind, when the teacher asks you a question and you don't know the answer?" After a long silence, one student said in a loud voice, "Gulp!"

He spoke for everyone. They all began to clamor, and all said the same thing, that when the teacher asked them a question and they didn't know the answer they were scared half to death. I was flabbergasted—to find this in a school which people think of as progressive; which does its best not to put pressure on little children; which does not give marks in the lower grades; which tries to keep children from feeling that they're in some kind of race.

I asked them why they felt gulpish. They said they were afraid of failing, afraid of being kept back, afraid of being called stupid, afraid of feeling themselves stupid. Stupid. Why is it such a deadly insult to these children, almost the worst thing they can think of to call each other? Where do they learn this?

Even in the kindest and gentlest of schools children are afraid, many of them a great deal of the time, some of them almost all the time. (pp. 38–39)

Dennison (1969) after describing some public-school students whose interest in learning had been destroyed by the fear, shame, anxiety, and self-contempt they had felt in their former schools, concluded that "the school child's chief expense of energy is self-defense against the environment." (p. 85)

Schooling is not blatantly bad. Some schools and teachers promote liberating, inquiring, and democratic values. Control and conformity taught in schools is not obvious and direct, nor is it experienced constantly. But the underlying and basic structure of education leads more to conformity, acceptance, and obedience than it does to free thinking.

Historically schools have reproduced class inequalities. They have prepared students from the upper classes for the top jobs and positions, and they have directed students from the lower classes to menial and often dead-end jobs.

During the 1960s and early 1970s, there was a social movement to make education liberating rather than conforming and to make schools provide equal educational opportunities for all people, including the poor, minorities, and women. Since then, there has been a countermovement stressing discipline, the so-called basics, and less emphasis on programs to help the children of working class, poor, and minority families. Conservatives argue that the liberating changes of the 1960s ruined the schools. Students are performing worse and learning less than before. By getting strict and teaching the basics, we can educate our students better, they argue. They will become better-educated workers so the United States can catch up with the workers in other industrial societies.

This analysis distorts recent U.S. history and the U.S. economy today (see Chapter 9) for the following reasons:

1. The educational reforms of the 1960s were never implemented very deeply or widely. Little money, commitment, and motivation went to creating liberating schools.

2. Schools never performed better than they have in the last twenty years. Schools have always taught a few people well and prepared them for

bright futures (mostly white boys from the upper classes), and the rest were taught some basic skills and no more. They were asked to be realistic and settle for the jobs at the bottom of the economy. Drop-out rates have always been high. Children soon see that most jobs open to them require little education, so they leave school.

3. It was not more years of schooling, or any thorough education, that helped millions of Irish, Italian, and other immigrants get ahead. Rather, it was the availability of jobs (especially union jobs) in factories, construction, and so on that paid decent wages. These jobs never required much education. And as I show in Chapter 9, these kinds of industrial jobs are disappearing, replaced by jobs in hotels, stores, and other service businesses that pay much less than industrial jobs do. Service jobs require no higher education.

4. Another reason schools have not been liberating and have not helped students develop inquiring minds is because the rest of the society does not encourage the growth of inquiry. Democracy cannot exist in schools when it is absent in work and other settings. Corporations want obedient workers, not people who ask questions and examine everything critically.

5. Finally, professional and managerial jobs are not increasing.

Therefore, the conservative proposals to rebuild education with an emphasis on discipline, obedience, longer school hours, and more traditional teaching techniques will not improve the prospects of most students. We need to focus on the economy and the kinds of jobs available to students when they leave school (see Chapter 9). (See Pincus, 1984; Bastian et al., 1985; and Aronowitz & Giroux, 1985.)

Day Care

Because today's family is usually made up of only parents and children and because most mothers of pre-school-age children must work, day care has become a major problem for our society. The need for day care is one of the most recent social phenomena in industrial societies. There are millions of children who need child-care arrangements because their parent(s) work. In March 1987, of children one and under living in families, 50 percent had both parents or the single parent they lived with working. For those three to five, over 54 percent of the total had working parents. Thus, over half of the children five and under need some child-care arrangements because for some part of the day there is no parent home. In addition, millions of children six and over also need some child care after school ends. Clearly, the need for child care is great. (See Table 7.1.)

Who cares for the children whose parents are working? In Table 7.2 we see that only a relatively few children five and under are in day-care centers. Only 15 percent of these children were in one of more than thirty thousand

TABLE 7.1
Labor Force Status of Mothers, with Children under 6,
1977 and 1987 (by percentage)

Age of Children and Family type	Percent Mothers in Labor Force	
	1977	*1987*
1. All Mothers		
1 and under	31.1	50.2
2 years	38.4	53.6
3 years	38.4	53.6
4 years	42.3	54.5
5 years	43.0	56.2
2. Mothers in Married-Couple Families		
1 and under	31.2	52.1
2 years	37.6	55.5
3 years	37.3	53.8
4 years	40.8	55.5
5 years	41.4	57.2
3. Mothers in Families Maintained by Women		
1 and under	32.4	45.7
2 years	46.2	51.0
3 years	46.8	57.4
4 years	52.5	56.3
5 years	52.7	57.5

U.S. Department of Labor (1987h), adapted from Table 2

day-care establishments in 1982 (19 percent if we consider only mothers who work full-time). Fully 43 percent of working mothers had their children cared for by their husband or another relative in their own or another home; 27.5 percent by a nonrelative in their own or another home; and 9 percent of mothers care for their children while they work. (Table 7.2 does not account for the arrangements made by 5 percent of the mothers). (See *Statistical Abstract,* 1987: 367, 368.)

A few children who attend school stay on school grounds in some child-care arrangements ("extended day"), but parents must pay for this service. For example, such programs are run in some suburban Boston towns, but schools and municipal governments usually provide no leadership—the parents must set up the programs. Other school children come home to mothers who work part-time, or are cared for by other relatives (including older siblings), or go to neighbors, or care for themselves, or make other arrangements. There are few studies and statistics on younger school children and who cares for them after school.

Norgren (1984) points out that unlike other industrial societies (France,

TABLE 7.2
Child-Care Arrangements Used by Employed Mothers for Youngest Child under Five Years Old: 1982*

Principal Child Care Arrangement	Total	Employment Status		Marital Status		Race	
		Full-time	*Part-time*	*Married, husband present*	*Other*	*White*	*Black*
Number of mothers employed (1,000)	5,086	3,263	1,824	4,093	993	4,203	717
Percent Distribution							
Total	100.0	100.0	100.0	100.0	100.0	100.0	100.0
Care in child's home	30.6	25.7	39.3	30.4	31.6	30.8	26.7
By father	13.9	10.3	20.3	16.8	1.9	14.7	8.3
By other relative	11.2	10.3	12.7	8.8	21.0	9.7	16.5
By nonrelative	5.5	5.1	6.3	4.8	8.7	6.4	1.9
Care in another home	40.2	43.8	34.0	40.7	38.2	40.3	42.2
By relative	18.2	19.7	15.6	18.0	19.0	16.7	28.4
By nonrelative	22.0	24.1	18.4	22.7	19.2	23.6	13.8
Group care center	14.8	18.8	7.5	13.4	20.2	13.6	20.9
Mother cares for child while working	9.1	6.2	14.4	10.5	3.3	10.3	3.1
Other arrangements	.2	.3	.1	.1	.5	.1	.6

Statistical Abstract, 1987:367, table 626
* As of June. Covers employed women, 18 to 44 years old having at least one child under 5 years old. Based on Current Population Survey.

Sweden, East Germany, the Soviet Union, and others) the United States has no social policy to provide quality day care for its children. Although no country has been able to meet the total need for day care, many have policies that provide for a much greater percentage of children than does the United States. Many provide for over 50 percent of the children. East Germany provides for 90 percent of the children three to six years old.

In 1982, there were only 1.6 million places in licensed day-care centers, most in private institutions (profit and nonprofit). The government only grudgingly began to finance day care for the children of poor mothers in the late 1960s (Headstart programs mostly). That commitment has weakened since then, especially in the 1980s. The percent of mothers who work has increased steadily, but we have no social policy to provide quality day care for the children. Parents, mostly mothers, are left to make their own arrangements and pay for them. Economic conditions require that most mothers work, but they are punished for doing so by being given little or no help in caring for their children. A few corporations have begun to set up and run day-care centers for their own employees, usually on their premises. (See *Dollars and Sense,* November, 1982: 8–9, 12; March, 1987: 6–9; *Boston Globe,* January 15, 1987: 73; Berns, 1985; and Norgren, 1984 for an excellent history of day-care institutions, day-care policy and philosophy in the United States and a comparison with other countries.)

Most of the social and political indifference and opposition to day care comes from a long-held belief in the United States that children need to be raised entirely by their own mothers if they are to grow up healthy and happy. Much research and debate has focused on this belief. Most studies have found no evidence that day care harms children. Children in quality institutions, whose parents spend some time with them when they return home, socially and intellectually do as well as or better than children raised entirely by their own parents (mostly their mothers). Moreover, mothers who like their work and whose children are in quality centers tend to be happier and healthier than full-time mothers. (For research and summaries of research on the positive and negative effects of day care on children, see Kagan, 1978; Berns, 1985; Zinn & Eitzen, 1987; and Norgren, 1984.)

The best child-care arrangements we can make, for the happiness, growth, and liberation of children, parents, other family members, and the larger community should not only include day care but also other ways of seeing our work. Perhaps if both parents of young children work, they should work only part-time. And during this period our society should pay them enough to live without hardships. Children should attend well run, sufficiently staffed, and enriching day-care institutions, but for only part of each day. Thus, both parents and children would spend time outside the home, to see and play with others, but they would also have time for all to be together in leisurely and relaxing conditions. Parents who work full-time and children who are in day care eight to ten hours a day cannot find enough quality time in the evening. Everyone feels tired and rushed when dinner must be cooked, dishes washed, children bathed, and so on in two to three hours. People need to rest and relax. Long mornings or afternoons allow for the slow unfolding of play, meditation, and time together.

This arrangement would allow parents to have more time with each other, some time alone, and time to pursue hobbies and social or political interests. Some mornings or afternoons, when the children are not in day care or with either parent, a grandparent, uncle, aunt, another relative, a friend, or a neighbor could be and play with them. There are other possibilities. These different arrangements would enrich everyone's life. Children, parents, relatives, friends, the entire community would benefit.

I am not critical of parents whose children are in day care for the whole day (or in no day care at all). The children cope and may even thrive in well-run institutions. When run well, and carefully, they provide learning and enjoyable experiences for the children. For two years, both of my daughters attended a parent cooperative nursery school. They looked forward to being there. But according to *Dollars and Sense* (November, 1982), 40 percent of the almost nineteen thousand child-care centers in the United States are run by profit-making businesses. The staff (mostly women) in these centers are paid at or near the minimum wage, space is crowded, and the routine is rigid.

Observers have found "a degree of impersonality which critics consider detrimental to the child's development . . . Children are kept in groups, herded from one line at the swings to another for juice and crackers." (p. 8) In addition, most of the cost of child care is paid by the parents, with the government providing only tax breaks. Our government and society thus are ignoring an important development in the lives of millions of our children.

It is obvious that working parents of young children live under too much stress. We should work to create child-care arrangements and communities with all the options and alternatives I describe if we value our children and the quality of all our lives.

Television and Mass Media

People in their mid-thirties and under have lived with nuclear weapons and television all their lives. Unlike nuclear weapons, TV does not kill, but it is omnipresent and influences perceptions and attitudes.

During their first fifteen years of life, most American children spend more time in front of the TV set than they do in the classroom. Four-year-olds average over two hours of TV daily, six-year-olds, 2.5 hours; ten-year-olds, 3.5 hours; twelve-year-olds, almost 4 hours; and sixteen-year-olds, a little over 3. A survey in the 1960s found that 60 percent of the families said they had changed their sleeping patterns, and 55 percent their meal times, because of the TV. About 80 percent said they used it as a baby sitter (Liebert et al., 1982).

The theory that TV violence encourages violence within society is hotly debated. Much research, most of it sponsored by the government, tends to show that many children are affected adversely; they become more violent and aggressive after watching violence on TV. The violent effect is especially pronounced in conjunction with other factors. Most social scientists (Liebert et al., 1982) on whose research and papers a 1972 government report is based agreed that "viewing television violence increases aggressiveness." (p. 100)

Commercials on television also influence children, as they are meant to. They glamorize toys, present sugar cereals as nutritious, and are often misleading. (One example of this is the quick voice at the end announcing that the toy must be assembled.) Studies have shown, as have painful experiences, that children ask for the products they see advertised. (I have had modest success in explaining to my children that advertisements often lie, exaggerate, mislead, and sell useless or harmful products.) Parents' groups have not been as powerful as the industry lobbyists who have influenced Congress to stop the Federal Communications Commission (FCC) from regulating advertising directed to children. (See Liebert et al., 1982.)

Finally, many content analyses (Liebert et al., 1982) of TV programs have shown that women, blacks, and other minorities are absent from or stereotyped in the world of television. Leading characters are predominantly white males. Males play 66 to 75 percent of all TV roles, and are shown as more powerful, aggressive, and intelligent than women. Thus, TV reinforces and partially creates stereotypes.

While not wishing to excuse TV for its role in creating violence, we must note that violence existed long before TV ever appeared. Poverty, oppression, inequality, alienating work, and other conditions caused and still cause violence. The stereotypes TV creates are much more important. Corporate violence and crime are never shown; women, as noted, are stereotyped or absent, as are blacks; and, perhaps as important as any other effect, time spent watching TV is time taken away from other activities: reading, playing, and so on. TV encourages passivity. Even the best TV programs that inform and entertain stifle imagination if indulged in in excess.

Class, Race, Ethnicity

The family begins the process of socialization. Our lives as social beings begin here. While it is the most important group in society, it is not monolithic. It comes in many forms: poor, working class, or wealthy; Negro, Caucasian, or Oriental; Irish, Greek, or Jewish—to name a few of the economic, racial, and cultural forms.

Most of the research and writing on the effects of class, race, and ethnicity on socialization is pejorative against poor and minority parents. They are depicted as punitive, rigid, and somehow uncaring with their children. Since almost all of this research is based on interviews and little of it on observation, we cannot know how accurate it is.

Perhaps the most well-known research on class and socialization has been carried out by Kohn (Gilbert & Kahl, 1987). Parents of middle- and working-class children were given lists of characteristics and were asked to choose those they thought were desirable for children the same age as their child. Here are some of the statements: "good student," "popular with other children," "good manners," "curious about things," and "happy." Middle-class parents chose items that show they value "consideration of other people, curiosity, responsibility, and self-control." Working-class parents' choices reveal that they value "good manners, neatness, obedience, honesty, and being a good student." (p. 119)

The major difference here is between self-control and obedience. According to Kohn, middle-class parents work in occupations where initiative, self-control, and self-direction are desirable and necessary qualities (professionals, managers, etc.). Thus, they come to value these characteristics, and they teach them to their children, preparing them for similar occupations. Working-class parents work in factories and other occupations where they take orders and follow rules. To survive, one needs to be obedient. They teach obedience to their children, and they prepare them for their likely future occupations. To teach obedience, they are strict and rigid with their children, who must follow parental rules without explanation. Middle-class parents, on the other hand, explain rules to their children and try to teach them to be responsible for their own behavior.

While there may be some truth to these conclusions, we should temper them with some observations. First, most jobs, well over 90 percent, do not involve much autonomy and self-direction. Some jobs are more routine and mindless than others, but few people have control over their jobs. Therefore, it is unclear how many children are prepared for such jobs. Second, as I said, the data are responses to interviews, reporting what people *say they value*. We would need to observe whether parents teach self-direction or obedience to authority in their daily interactions with their children.

As we shall see in later chapters, however, people from the lower classes, women, blacks, and other minorities *are* socialized differently. But the expectations and messages they get come less from their parents and more from other sources: schools, police and courts, the mass media, the corporate world, and other institutions.

Autobiographies, novels, histories, and social science studies have described the childhood of black children. Most of them have had to grow up and live in two worlds: one of their families, neighbors, and friends, and the other the white world of schools, work, and television. They begin life in a black culture (or, subculture) with a somewhat different language, pastimes, and traditions. But soon, as they watch television, attend school, and move in other settings, they confront a world that variously stereotypes them, ignores them, discriminates against them, and denigrates their life styles. Often, television ignores or stereotypes black people. Teachers, often unconsciously, label them as slow students and do not help them learn. School systems segregate them and offer them fewer resources in those segregated schools. (See Gwaltney, 1980, and Hale-Benson, 1986.)

In their teens, they begin their association with the world of work. Lack of good jobs and poor education insure that they find low-paying or no work. Tempting them in American cities today is the drug world, with its deceptive promise of quick profits. An occasional youth makes money, some others become addicted to drugs, a few more resort to larceny and theft, and most of them face unemployment or very menial jobs. (See Williams & Kornblum, 1985.)

Growing up black has always been difficult. It leaves permanent scars. The self-esteem of many blacks is low, as psychologists and others have shown. Coles (1967) describes one young black child's view of herself. Ruby, a six-year-old, drew a self-portrait and a portrait of a white girl. The difference between the two portraits tells much about Ruby's self-esteem. Her self-portrait is clearly smaller and has fewer details. The sun over her head is smaller than the sun over the white girl. On the ground next to the white girl there are flowers, but none next to Ruby. How does a six-year-old girl internalize such deep feelings and emotions? (See Chapter 11 for the conditions under which most black children live. *Black Boy* by Richard Wright and *The Autobiography of Malcolm X* are two among many superb descriptions of black childhood.)

Children in America

If a child suffers it is not because his or her parents stress obedience over self-control or good grades over self-initiative. A child suffers because of neglect and abuse from his or her parents, but also—and perhaps to a much greater extent—from insensitive educational policy and crushing economic conditions.

In 1985, 23 percent of the children under six lived in poverty (as defined by the government, which uses a very low income); 50 percent of all black children did so. About half a million children were in foster homes and institutions. Finally, ten million had "no known source of health care." In 1985, 40 percent of one to four-year-olds and 30 percent of five to fourteen-year-olds were not immunized against polio. Other childhood diseases had equally high rates of unimmunized children. This is in a country with supposedly the best medical care in the world. (See *Boston Globe,* December 10, 1982: 19, and *Statistical Abstract,* 1987: 102, 446.)

Poverty, teenage unemployment, and other disadvantages black children suffer are especially high. From 1980 to 1981 the disappearance and death of twenty-eight black children in Atlanta received extensive publicity. But the running away, disappearance, and death of black children and youth are endemic in urban slums. No one usually pays attention to them. Runaways (white and black) could be half a million or two million, but no one knows because no one counts. Browning (1981) thinks black children leave home because of poverty and unemployment. Whatever the reason, they run away and many are never found.

In previous chapters we mentioned corporate ads and propaganda in schools, on television, and other media. Ads for expensive items undermine poor and thrifty parents and create tensions and conflicts.

Bottle feeding, environmental pollution, and the threat of nuclear war also menace our children. We have heard of the millions of children in poor nations who die each year (about ten million) or become ill or malnourished from infant formula. Poor parents, hooked on formula by aggressive advertising, cannot afford enough of it or do not know how to sterilize it properly. But hospital practices in the United States also encourage bottle feeding, and about five thousand infants a year die from illnesses related to bottle feeding. Under present conditions working mothers cannot nurse, of course, but workplaces and schedules could be changed to allow nursing. In many socialist societies nursing mothers, whose infants are in adjoining child-care centers, receive two, thirty to forty-five minute extra breaks for nursing. If we care for our children, we can arrange for their care.

In Chapter 3, we saw how environmental pollution is harmful to children. Here we can add that the recent dioxin contamination of Times Beach, Missouri, and other places has added another dimension to the problem. Internal documents of the Environmental Protection Agency (EPA) (Freedman & Weir, 1983) show an "estimate that some children playing in the dioxin-laden dirt in Missouri have as high as a seven-in-ten chance of developing cancer." (p. 601) Meanwhile, in the early 1980s EPA budgets were cut, thus reducing its ability to discover and eliminate such pollution.

Japan is the only nation thus far to have experienced nuclear war. But the threat and fear of it exists for all children. A majority of the 1,100 children who were interviewed by the American Psychiatric Association think there will be nuclear war within their lifetimes, and they do not think their communities will survive it. A filmmaker was told by many children, "I'm scared I won't grow up." (*Guardian,* December 8, 1982:18)

I doubt growing up has ever been without its conflicts, doubts, and fears (and its joys, discoveries, and pleasures). To these eternal problems we have added our own: poverty for some, dangerous environmental conditions for many or most, the threat of nuclear war for all. This too is the world that our children will inherit.

Sex Roles and Socialization

In Chapter 11, we will explore in depth sex roles and discrimination against women. We will also describe women's roles in pre-industrial and industrial societies. Below are some observations and comments on the sex role socialization of boys and girls.

!Kung Children

Shostak's (1981) study of !Kung boys and girls shows some gender differences, but the similarities in their play and interests are much more pronounced.

> *Our derisive terms "tomboy" and "sissy" seem to have no counterparts in !Kung vocabulary. !Kung children are not segregated by sex, neither sex is trained to be submissive or fierce, and neither sex is restrained from expressing the full breadth of emotion that seems inherent in the human spirit. . . . Because the !Kung impose no responsibilities on their children, place no value on virginity, and do not require that the female body be covered or hidden, girls are as free and unfettered as boys. . . . A closer look does reveal subtle distinctions in the kinds of activities engaged in by the two sexes. A study of !Kung children at play showed that boys were more physically aggressive than girls and that girls interacted with adults other than their mothers more than boys did. But, in contrast to studies of children's play in other societies !Kung girls and boys were found to be equally active, equally capable of sustaining attention to tasks, and equal in the amount of time they spent playing with objects. Also, !Kung children showed no preference for playing only with children of their own sex. (p. 109)*

Sex Roles in America

Children begin to learn *sex roles* (the different social expectations of boys and girls) at birth. Boys and girls are treated differently. For example, girls are perceived as softer and weaker. Parents tend to handle boys more vigorously. It is such treatment that makes boys tougher and better in sports and physical activity.

From the first few months of life, people respond differently to boys and girls. In Lake's (1975) experiment, five young mothers were given Beth "a six-month-old in a pink frilly dress for a period of observed interaction; five others were given Adam, a six-month-old in blue overalls. Compared to Adam, Beth was smiled at more, offered a doll to play with more often and described as 'sweet' with a 'soft cry.' Adam and Beth were the same child " (Oakley, 1981, p. 96).

At age two and a half, boys often are drawn to what are labeled girls' toys, but they are soon taught to hide such liking. Harrison (1974) tells of "a small boy who once went to the pathetic extreme of fashioning a stuffed airplane to take to bed to 'cuddle', thus, presumably, preserving his orthodox masculine image while satisfying his need to nurture and to be gentle." Harrison goes on to list some typical actions that foster sex roles:

> *A fire engine rushes past your house. Whom do you call to see it? Your daughter, or your son?*
>
> *You drive past a wedding party. Whose attention do you call to it? Your son's, or your daughter's?*
>
> *You are given flowers. Whom do you ask to arrange them prettily in a vase? Your son, or your daughter?*
>
> *Out walking with your children, you pass a woman with a small baby. With whom do you share your pleasure in the infant? Your son, or your daughter?*
>
> *A building is under construction. To whom do you point out the crane, the workers, the details of construction? Your daughter or your son?*
>
> *Relatives come to visit. Do they hug and kiss your daughter and tell her how pretty she looks? Do they shake hands with your son, toss him up in the air, and jocularly mess up his hair? Why?*
>
> *Your small son asks for a doll, a toy even, or a jump rope. How do you react?*
>
> *Your daughter and your son both ask for trucks for Christmas. Who gets the 29¢ truck in the Christmas stocking? Who gets the $9.95 truck under the tree?*
>
> *Would a stranger be able to tell the sex of each of your children from their respective Christmas list? (pp. 4–7)*

Further on Harrison describes some ways by which teachers in school reinforce stereotypes. For example, a teacher to whom a girl goes with her carpentry problem hammers in the nails properly for her, but the teacher tells a boy with the same problem to do it himself. (pp. 9–11) (Both my observation of my own daughters and reading convince me that sex roles become entrenched long before children go to the first grade.)

In the school she studied in 1970, Harrison found that second-grade girls were interested in rockets, but they hid this interest when they were with boys. Such fears begin with the use of toys and the reactions of others. They become reinforced at school where, for example, women are still almost entirely absent from history books.

Studies carried out in the 1980s show that schools still favor boys and socialize girls to be passive. Sadker and Sadker (1985) observed many classrooms and their observations and conclusions are disturbing.

> *We found that at all grade levels, in all communities and in all subject areas, boys dominated classroom communication. They participated in more interactions than girls did and their participation became greater as the year went on. . . . When boys call out comments without raising their hands, teachers accept their answers. However, when girls call out, teachers reprimand this "inappropriate" behavior with messages such as, "In this class we don't shout out answers, we raise our hands." The message is subtle but powerful: Boys should be academically assertive and grab teacher attention; girls should act like ladies and keep quiet. (p. 54)*

The following is a typical pattern.

Teacher: "What's the capital of Maryland? Joel?"
Joel: "Baltimore."
Teacher: "What's the largest city in Maryland, Joel?"
Joel: "Baltimore."
Teacher: "That's good. But Baltimore isn't the capital. The capital is also the location of the U.S. Naval Academy. Joel, do you want to try again?"
Joel: "Annapolis."
Teacher: "Excellent. Anne, what's the capital of Maine?"
Anne: "Portland."
Teacher: "Judy, do you want to try?"
Judy: "Augusta."
Teacher: "O.K."

> *In this snapshot of a classroom discussion, Joel was told when his answer was wrong (criticism); was helped to discover the correct answer (remediation); and was praised when he offered the correct response. When Anne was wrong, the teacher, rather than staying with her, moved to Judy, who received only simple acceptance for her correct answer. Joel received the more specific teacher reaction and benefited from a longer, more precise and intense educational interaction.*
>
> *Too often, girls remain in the dark about the quality of their answers. Teachers rarely tell them if their answers are excellent, need to be improved, or are just plain wrong. (p. 56)*

Teachers are ignorant of these conditions, even when they are plainly obvious.

When we showed teachers and administrators a film of a classroom discussion and asked who was talking more, the teachers overwhelmingly said the girls were. But in reality, the boys in the film were outtalking the girls at a ratio of three to one. Even educators who are active in feminist issues were unable to spot the sex bias until they counted and coded who was talking and who was just watching. Stereotypes of garrulous and gossipy women are so strong that teachers fail to see this communications gender gap even when it is right before their eyes. (p. 54)

Education, from kindergarten to college, creates and reinforces male domination and female passivity.

Children's books reinforce the image of women as unequal to men. For example, when I read books to my daughters who were five and three in 1979, I was astounded by the nearly total absence of women and girls. Not only were most human characters in the books male, but so were most animal characters. Cats, dogs, bees, butterflies, and birds either are given male names or are referred to as "he." So by the age of three, both my daughters had many times looked at a book they had not seen or heard of before, seen an animal whose sex is not obvious, and called the animal "he." Generally, both of them now use "he" when they want to refer to people in general. When I ask them why they do so, they can offer no explanation; like the air around them, sexism simply exists and is taken for granted. Two cases of sex role socialization will help illustrate this further.

Identical Twins: Boy and Girl

Money and Ehrhardt (1972) reported a case in the 1960s where one boy of a pair of identical twins underwent a sex-change operation. At seven months, while he was being circumcised by electrocautery, his penis was destroyed by an electrical current that was too powerful. His penis "was ablated flush with the abdominal wall." After much thought and many consultations, the distraught parents agreed to a sex-change operation. At seventeen months the infant received a female name, female clothing, and hair style. The first step of the operation took place at twenty-one months.

Over the next four years, up to the age of six, the mother wrote and reported regularly to the clinic. The girl had been socialized to behave in a manner "appropriate" to her sex. Unlike her brother, she was very neat. Also, "she seems to be daintier." She, unlike her brother, liked to do housework, and her mother encouraged such activity. For Christmas, she "wanted and received . . . dolls, a doll house, and a doll carriage," while her brother "wanted and obtained a garage with gas pumps and tools. . . . He chose very masculine things like a fireman or a policeman or something like that. He wanted to do what daddy does, work where daddy does, and carry a lunch kit, and drive a car. She didn't want any of those things." (pp. 118–123) She did have her "tomboyish traits" which her mother discouraged. The case speaks for itself. Identical biology, different sex role training, and we find a typical boy and a typical girl.

Body Movements, Separate Play

The sex-role training that begins at birth leaves unmistakable marks on children. Let us look at one manifestation of this training.

I was once invited, along with fifty other fathers of first graders, to a breakfast. Our children entertained us with music, dance, and play-acting. They pretended to be flowers, to be picking flowers and sowing, and to be riding the merry-go-round. I noticed that the boys' body movements were stiff. Girls moved with more ease, their bodies flowing. They also got into the spirit of pretending to be flowers and the up-and-down motion of horses on a merry-go-round. Not so the boys. They would not bend their knees and bodies to simulate the up-and-down movement of horses on a merry-go-round. They did not play as freely. They seemed much more self-conscious than the girls, unable to pretend and express themselves. The results of the process that socializes boys to be less emotional, less expressive, and less free with their bodies were pronounced throughout the performance.

As they get older, children begin to separate into groups of girls and groups of boys. Thorne and Luria (1986) observed fourth and fifth graders in Michigan, California, and Massachusetts schools in the middle 1980s. Their study showed this sex separation.

> When they [the children] choose seats, select companions for work or play, or arrange themselves in line, elementary school children frequently cluster into same-sex groups. At lunchtime, boys and girls often sit separately and talk matter-of-factly about "girls' tables" and "boys' tables." Playgrounds have gendered spaces: boys control some areas and activities, such as large playing fields and basketball courts; and girls control smaller enclaves like jungle-gym areas and concrete spaces for hopscotch or jumprope. . . .
>
> [There are] some groups with a fairly even mix of boys and girls, especially in games like kickball, dodgeball, and handball, and in classroom and playground activities organized by adults. Some girls frequently play with boys, integrating their group in a token way, and a few boys, especially in the lower grades, play with groups of girls. (p. 178)

Thorne and Luria (1986) note that boys and girls play differently. Boys are more competitive and aggressive; they play in larger groups; and they occupy more public space as they pursue sports and other activities. Girls, on the other hand, play in smaller groups, focus more on friendships with one or two others, and "more often engage in turn-taking activities like jumprope and doing tricks on the bars, and they less often play organized sports." (p. 179) (The authors refer to play as unsupervised and not organized by adults.)

Labeling and Self-Fulfilling Prophecy

The identical-twin brother and sister are a striking illustration of the *self-fulfilling prophecy* and *labeling*. Biologically they are identical (until the age of twelve when she will be given hormones to suppress male characteristics). But by being treated as if she were a "girl" she has become a *girl*.

Many years ago Thomas Merton (1957) wrote, "If men [people] define situations as real, they are real in their consequences." (p. 421) Later, Merton elaborated on this definition: "The self-fulfilling prophecy is, in the beginning, a *false* definition of the situation evoking a new behavior which makes the originally false conception come *true*." (p. 423)

We can say, then, that a self-fulfilling prophecy is a social condition that, though initially nonexistent, is created when people act as if it were true. It is a widespread phenomenon. A rumor that a bank is insolvent causes depositors to take out their money, making it insolvent. Tagging poor, black, or female children as stupid, slow, or inferior in time makes them inferior. At age ten girls are better than boys in mathematics, but the belief in the reverse, and a teacher's treatment of boys as more intelligent, in time makes girls inferior to boys.

Labeling is the identification of others (especially children) as people who possess certain traits and characteristics. We categorize, type, stamp, and tag individuals and groups. Such labeling does not always or automatically succeed in creating a previously nonexistent reality. But if it is done in the early years of life, and if many people label us consistently and repeatedly, and if these people are important and powerful, then in time we are likely to change—thus making the label true.

Labeling is pervasive. Parents, relatives, neighbors, teachers, police, doctors, psychiatrists, social workers, all are in the labeling enterprise. Sometimes it is explicit and intentional; more often it is implicit and unconscious. Consistent praise of one child as pretty (or handsome), intelligent, and polite may leave the unspoken message to other children that they lack these qualities. Studies have shown that teachers pay more attention to boys and "pretty" (or "handsome" children). They look at them more and address more comments and questions to them. Even a feminist teacher, when she listened to tape recordings of her class, found that she gave girls only 42 percent of her time, at best. "Both she and the boys experienced her efforts as favoritism to girls" when she struggled to give girls even this little attention. Gradually the children who receive more attention think of themselves as more intelligent and likable, thus they *become* more intelligent and likable (Snitow, 1983).

Rosenthal and Jacobson (1968) conducted a study that illustrates the effects of labeling. They told elementary school teachers in a California school that some of their students had been given special tests, which found some of them were bright and likely to bloom academically. In reality, the "bright" students had been chosen at random, but the teachers' "knowledge" that certain students were "bright" apparently made them bright. Their I.Q. scores and their grades improved dramatically in the following year. (Some other studies have confirmed these findings, but others have not.) Significantly, the effect was most dramatic in the first and second grades; in the fifth and sixth grades "bright" students' I.Q. scores and grades did not improve significantly.

The students in the school were mostly minority children (black and Chicano), and they had probably already been labeled as "slow." For them and their teachers, that label was a reality unlikely to change by the introduction of a new label. The self-fulfilling prophecy seems to function most effectively in the earlier years of life.

Labeling usually is assumed to be a negative social process. Children and adults are categorized as slow, mean, inferior, delinquent, and so on. But as the above study shows, there is also positive labeling. Children can be labeled positively as bright, friendly, and kind. As a parent and teacher, I have found myself constantly struggling to avoid positive and negative labels. In our society, where competition is fierce, comparisons seem natural. Children with low self-images and those who think themselves superior are the inevitable outcome of societies driven by sex, race, and class inequalities.

Socialization after Childhood

We do not cease to grow, learn, and change at the end of childhood. Socialization continues in adolesence, youth, adulthood, middle and old age. Indeed, we need to learn how to leave this world as much as we need to learn how to enter and survive in it.

New People, New Roles

Children in pre-industrial societies grow up in small communities. There are few people and few work roles. Among gatherers and hunters, for example, all boys and all girls learn skills directly from their parents and other adults, and as they grow older, they can easily imagine their adult work, family, and social relationships. Boys become men and hunt, girls become women and gather food and raise children. The transition to adulthood is smooth, continuous, consistent, and visible.

The transition is more difficult in industrial societies. If children move from community to community, always meeting new people, they might not always have the time to know about the jobs they would like to hold as adults. It is difficult for many of them to know or imagine what they will be. What does a social worker do? What do so many people do in offices? People who provide visible services or produce clothes, machines, and other items have clearly understandable jobs, but they are not very prestigious or desirable. People who dirty their hands are not models for children to emulate willingly (although they will do the work to survive). How does one learn to endure alienating work all day? How does one look forward to it? (See Chapter 9 for a discussion of work.)

In all societies, childhood socialization melts into later life. The language, values, norms, and skills we learned as children we continue to use as we learn new skills and meet new people. In this respect there is continuity from childhood to adulthood. But in industrial societies there are also discontinuities. All of us meet new people; some of these people alter our course in life as they introduce new possibilities, values, and perspectives. Many institutions require significant changes in our behavior: schools, workplaces, armed services, and voluntary organizations socialize us into new (or partly new) roles, norms, and expectations. In them, we often meet new people from distant places.

Some of us undergo dramatic and almost total change. Religious cults, mental hospitals, prisons, nunneries (in the old days), and other institutions strip off old identities and bestow new ones (some of these are more welcome than others). This is *resocialization,* a process we undergo as adults that radically changes the person we become during childhood socialization. Although we never completely erase previous learning, some (or much) of it is erased. As converts to a religious cult for example, we would acquire new and very different values and norms. Few of us undergo total transformations, however. And even fewer of us, perhaps, remain as we emerged from childhood. In different degrees and paces, we add to, subtract from, and modify our childhood experiences and identities (Goffman, 1959).

Stages of Life

Children are surrounded by people of many ages. At some point they understand that in the natural process of life they will move from one lifestage to another, from status to status. Peers, parents, and grandparents are clearly visible statuses in every society.

But industrial society has prolonged some stages and introduced new ones. People confront the reality of these many stages both as children and as they progress through the stages. For most of human history there was a short period of childhood, a longer period of adulthood, and a short period of old age. In our society there is now an extended childhood, adolescence, youth, adulthood, middle age, and old age, which is probably subdivided into two stages, retirement and infirmity.

Childhood   Many historians over the last twenty years have amassed evidence that shows that childhood in pre-industrial Western societies was fairly short, six to eight years. At that point children did not reach full adult status, of course, but they began to assume many more adult roles and responsibilities than children do today. They worked and played with older people (Aries, 1962).

Anthropolgists have shown that in gathering-hunting and horticultural societies people begin to assume responsibility early in life. Children are given animals to tend or other useful tasks to perform. Generally, they are gradually but consistently introduced to adult roles from the age of five or six. Work is like play for them, not a drudgery. Sun Chief (1942), a Hopi, recalls his childhood and how work and play melded into one activity.

By the time I was six . . . I had learned to find my way about the mesa and to avoid graves, shrines, and harmful plants, to size up people, and to watch out

*for witches. . . . I could help plant and weed, went out herding with my fa-
ther, and was a kiva trader. I owned a dog and a cat, a small bow made by
my father, and a few good arrows. . . . I could ride a tame burro, kill a kanga-
roo rat, and catch small birds, but I could not make fire with a drill and I was
not a good runner like the other fellows . . . and I had almost stopped running
after my mother for her milk. (p. 84)*

With local variations (and some few exceptions) Sun Chief's Hopi childhood resembles the lives of all children in pre-industrial societies. For us,
childhood is much longer. Only an exceptional American six-year-old could
match Sun Chief's range of accomplishments. Indeed, in the eyes of the law
we remain children until the age of sixteen, seventeen, or eighteen (seventeen
in thirty-four states), when we are finally emancipated. (See Benedict, 1938,
and Lee, 1959.)

Adolescence   The concept, the word, and the social reality of adolescence is
a very recent development in human societies. The concept of adolescence as
a stage in life has only been recognized since the turn of the century. It is not
a biological stage but one we *created*. Adolescence arrived legally with the
creation of the juvenile courts in 1899, the enactment of child labor laws (more
properly, the prohibition of child labor), mandatory school attendance (at first
until fourteen and later sixteen), and other developments. Adolescence as a
period between childhood and adulthood simply did not exist before 1900.
Fifteen-year-olds in 1800 were not yet full adults, but they were much closer
to adulthood than they are today. They performed useful, necessary, and
valued work.

In the 1980s, adolescence is a stage of hope and future promises, of
anxiety and potential dangers. Davis (1982) says, "If adolescence is anything,
it is winning and losing. Grades, dates, a driver's license, complexion, approval, graduation, scholarships, college admission—success and failure loom-
ing on all fronts. School becomes victory for brains, beauty, and jocks, defeat
for practically everyone else. It is especially a defeat for those from homes that
have not prepared them for books and literacy, a defeat passed through the
generations like watch fobs and lace doilies." (p. 42)

Many observers see the trends toward more single-parent families, more
families with both parents working, and less contact with extended family
members as detrimental to children. Hodges (1987) goes so far as to say that
these changes in the family structure are casting our "children into the wilderness." Young children receive some child care, but teenagers are too often
left on their own. Parents and relatives, out of economic necessity, or the drive
for more money, often have no time for them. In addition, corporations
manipulate their anxieties and loneliness to sell products. Teen call-in lines
("Phone-A-Friend" and others) is a fad promoted by various telephone companies to exploit teenagers' alienation, boredom, and loneliness by promising
instant social contact and friendship—at a good price for company profits
(Bartholomew, 1987).

Teenagers' frustration, loneliness, and alienation many times can lead to violence. Accidents (two-thirds of which are car accidents), homicides, and suicides account for 77 percent of all deaths. For black youths, homicides are the number one cause of death. In 1987, for a few weeks the mass media focused on a few teenagers who committed group suicides, then went on to other stories. Teenage suicide, however, has been increasing and is more common than a few media stories suggest. According to Kohl (1987), "The current annual rate is 400,000 attempts, 6,000 of which end in death. That averages out to fifteen teenagers a day." (p. 603) The 1983 suicide rate for people age fifteen to twenty-four was 12 per 100,000, close to 16 for people forty-five to sixty-four, and 19 for those over 65. (See also *Boston Globe,* June 26, 1987: 1, 84; and *Statistical Abstract, 1987:* 79.)

Why are so many young people rejecting life? What desperation drives them to end life just as it starts? How could they feel so hopeless? Kohl thinks many young people feel unwanted, unneeded, rejected. School and work have no place for them. Referring to four teenagers who committed suicide together in Bergenfield, New Jersey, Kohl (1987) writes that they were "depressed and, as teenagers, were considered sources of trouble and burdens to society. They were marginal and, what is worse, disposable. There was no attempt to reach out to them. There was no attempt to change school programs to meet their needs or change economic priorities to give them places in the world. It is easier to demand things of teenagers than to serve their needs." (p. 604) Kohl goes on to make some general observations:

> It is foolish to call adolescents a problem. Young people are as full of hope as of despondency. They are asking to be brought into the world, and too often they are turned away. . . .
>
> A sense that you are not needed, that no one is reaching out to help, can cause you to forsake all expectations of the future. Add to that scorn for your friends and your music and your way of dressing, the absence of economic hope, empty days to fill and the availability of drugs, and you have a formula for suicide. The final ingredient might be the lack of intimacy and the fear of never experiencing love. . . .
>
> What the schools and the media and the community never look at is the world these teenagers decided to abandon. (pp. 604, 606)

Youth   We may have created yet another stage before adulthood (the ages of which might be between eighteen and twenty five). College attendance and marriage delayed till the late twenties and even later may postpone the assumption of full adult status. This is a recent and ongoing development we need to explore. Most of you reading this book are eighteen to twenty years old. Can you claim to be full adults? In what ways are you and are you not an adult?

Adulthood   In our society, this may be a short period of life. It may correspond to the years when people marry and raise children. For most people, they assume the role and responsibilites, at this time, that they will retain for the rest of their lives.

Middle Age   Since people are having fewer and fewer children, and since they leave home in their late teens or soon after, many people are childless by about the age of forty. Men and women who reach mid-life may face many years of life with only their spouse at home or alone. Women especially, who have spent their lives taking care of families, suddenly have no families on which to bestow their nurturing. Thus, facing a mid-life crisis sometimes means starting new careers or returning to school. (Thus mid-life crisis seems less prominent now with more women having children later in life.)

Recently, some social scientists have begun to explore the lives of men at mid-life. Like women, they begin to reassess and evaluate where they have been and what they face ahead as they begin the latter part of life. Men and women in their forties, at least in our society, undergo a form of *adult socialization*. As they live alone or in couples, as jobs or careers for most of them offer no more prospects to grow and advance, as the body gives new messages, as they have more memories than future experiences, they confront new realities. Past socialization is inadequate in this existential crisis. People need to learn how to lead their lives in ways that are true to their past but flexible enough for the future. (See Tamir, 1982, and Farrell & Rosenberg, 1981.)

Old Age   People everywhere get old, but cultures define the experience differently. Among the Abkhasians people do not retire at any specific age. They continue to work, adjusting the amount of work to the changing capacities of their bodies. They work, dance, and enjoy life into their eighties, nineties, and later (a person must be ninety to join one of the dance groups). Not many societies provide people with such longevity and security in their old age. Pre-industrial societies did not define old age as rigidly as our society does, with a set retirement age and loss of status, income, and activity. Forced retirement is a crisis people must learn to survive, with little preparation. Even the people who have jobs that are alienating and difficult and who eagerly await retirement face the crisis of retirement. With life expectancy increasing, people have years of active life before infirmity sets in (we will discuss old age in Chapter 11).

As we move through the stages of life, we continue to be socialized, or rather, we undergo new socializations. But we also continue to be the same person. What we are as children remains with us, even though throughout life its memory is often repressed. We never cease recalling and evaluating our early years. It is true that our personalities are not set in concrete at age six or seven, but it is undeniable that all later learning, growth, and change take place in the context of experiences, memories, habits, and predilections molded in our early years. As I travel through my forties, and as I recall my childhood, I am impressed with how many of my patterns, moods, fears, longings, insecurities, and enjoyments reach back to the earlier me. Outwardly

I have changed. I have learned many things and had many experiences, but inwardly I seem to be the little boy in Llongo, Albania. When I was thirty-nine my mother told me her memories of me until the age of six (when we were separated), and I felt a shock of recognition that I am still as I was then. I want to draw no grand conclusion that we never change. Obviously we do. But there is an inward continuity from childhood on. Memories, dreams, longings, desires, loves, and hates linger on.

Death   As a human and social experience, the meaning of death has changed. We are born in hospitals and we die in them or in nursing homes. It was not always so. People arrived on and left this earth in their homes. Chiñas (1983) says that among the Zapotecs (in Mexico) "sick people are never isolated from other persons because they are sick. Indeed, there seems to be a conscious effort to include the gravely ill member in all of the household affairs by placing him [or her] in a central spot where he [or she] can observe and hear everything. . . . When death seems imminent, relatives and neighbors, including children except babies, crowd around the dying person. . . ." (p. 61)

People as Social and Individual Beings

I will conclude this chapter with some reflections, with a letter, and with a question and a hope. Many philosophers, moralists, psychologists, sociologists, and others have commented on the meaning of human existence. We are biological and social: we walk, eat, make love, *and* we learn roles, norms, and values. We are socialized. But what are we as a result of our biological-social-cultural existence? Who is the I, me, myself of which we speak? Is each of us a carbon copy of a typical personality in our culture? What makes us individuals, separate from others yet like them? How do we play social roles and follow social norms yet remain individuals? Are we acting staged performances, as the concept *role* implies? What do we *experience* as a result of socialization?

A twenty-six-year-old woman wrote the following letter to Ann Landers (*Boston Globe*, March 21, 1981: 7):

> *Dear Ann Landers:*
>
> *I have written this letter four times and never mailed it. It seems so childish. But I am particularly bothered by my problem tonight, so I am putting this one in the mailbox—come hell or high water.*
>
> *I'm not a flighty teenager, I'm a grown woman of 26. The problem: My looks. I am not overweight—in fact, I'm on the skinny side. But my hair is awful, my nose has a hump and is much too long. My eyes are too close together and my lips are too thin. I hate to look in the mirror because I am so ugly.*
>
> *Ever since I was a small child people have made fun of me because I look like a witch. When I was 14, I went crying to my favorite teacher. (Kids can*

*be so cruel.) She told me not to pay attention to them because I was beautiful
on the inside and that is what counts.*

*I have only had three dates in my entire life. None of the fellows asked me
out a second time. (Apparently they weren't interested in my beautiful
insides.) Am I going to be miserable all my life because I was cursed with this
ugly face? Please tell me what to do.*

Depressed and Lonely in Dallas

Frank Jones (Gerth & Mills, 1954) wrote, "It has been said that everyone is three persons: what he thinks he is, what others think he is, and what
he thinks others think he is. The fourth—what he really is—is unknown;
perhaps it doesn't exist." (p. 91)

We can hope there is a real person. And that we do know that person,
even if deeply buried within us.

Conclusion

In every society, children and adults are raised to fit into the culture and social
structures around them. Parents, neighbors, teachers, bosses, and others seek
to influence and direct their thoughts, values, and actions. The Hopi seek to
raise cooperative children, the Arapesh gentle children, the Americans aggressive and competitive children (especially the boys). Socialist societies
emphasize the group and cooperation, and capitalist societies emphasize individual self-interest.

But the fit and the molding are never perfect. As I grow older, I become
increasingly convinced that in all societies children do not faithfully follow the
paths laid out for them. Individual resistance, variation, and outright rebellion
are frequent. As much as we are impressed by the seeming uniformity in adult
character and personality of the typical American, Hopi, Arapesh, Chinese, or
other nationality, we need to be impressed by the variation and resistance
within each society. Culture and socialization are not physical molds that turn
out exact and identical replicas. The fact that cultures change, that norms and
roles vary in each given time and in historical time, is evidence that socialization is a human process, created and changed by people as they travel the
stages of life and historical eras. There are cooperative Americans and competitive Hopi, peasants who resisted the repression of their sexuality, American men who cry, and !Kung who do not share.

This is also true in capitalist societies. Socialization is not a uniform and
consistent process of unified society. The Mbuti and the !Kung may be seen
as teaching fairly consistent values and norms, but in the United States today
different groups have contradicting expectations of, and give different messages to, many children. Do black parents have the same expectations of their
children as do racist institutions? Do any parents really want to raise their
children to be happy and obedient workers for the corporations who will profit

from their labor? Schools and corporations may want obedient workers, but are their interests and expectations part of a general socialization process?

Different groups have differing interests and biases in the socialization of children. I have not stressed this issue in this chapter, but it is implied here and in the next four chapters. The social inequalities, contradictions, and struggles described there have a profound impact on the lives and growth of children.

A final philosophical reflection. It has been asked whether a society (or today, a powerful group) can totally shape and mold the personality of children and adults. Can people be raised to behave in a particular way that one group wishes? For example, can sex and sensuality be repressed totally? In all children raised by that group? For how long? Or, is there some human nature, some innate human quality, that will resist and rebel against such repression and control (of sexuality or other behaviors)? We cannot answer that question for all people, at all times, or for all societies. But sooner or later *some* people resist attempts at total control and repression, even at the cost of their lives. It is also clear that over time people and societies everywhere modify and change their norms, roles, and values. Socialization and culture are human processes of stability, order, *and* change.

Summary

Socialization is the process through which children acquire their culture and become fully human. Physical and social contact is required during this process, but there has been a long debate about how much contact is needed, what affect deprivation has on people, and at what age the effects become irreversible. A number of studies on this issue are discussed in this chapter.

Socialization varies from culture to culture. For example, there are different responses to crying, physical punishment, holding children and nursing infants, and the amount of freedom children have. Cultural differences in socialization lead to differences in personality.

Cultures also vary widely in what they allow and forbid in sexual expression for children and adults. Despite inherent limits in our ability to study sexuality, it seems obvious that some societies repress expressions of sexuality in children, and others allow or encourage it. Specifically, in the United States it seems people now engage in more and more varied sex, but at the same time there is still some sexual repression and considerable commercial exploitation of sexuality.

Children are socialized both by the society at large (the generalized other) and by specific groups: family, peers, schools, day care, and the mass media. Generally, today the family and the immediate community play a smaller role in socialization, replaced in part by schools, the mass media, and so on. Also, the experience of socialization differs according to one's race, ethnicity, and class.

The lives of many children in America are affected by poverty, racial problems, environmental pollution, the threat of nuclear war, and other social conditions.

Boys and girls among the !Kung and other similar societies are socialized more alike than in the United States, where from early childhood boys and girls are socialized to play different roles. The case of identical twin boys, one of whom became a girl, is a striking illustration that sex roles are cultural creations, not biological imperatives.

Two very important processes of socialization are labeling and the self-fulfilling prophecy. The treatment and expectations of others can be so strong as to create behaviors and personalities that did not exist before.

Socialization continues past childhood, although we could argue that our basic orientation to life is shaped in our early years. The lifecyle now has more distinct stages than it had in the past.

People in every society raise their children so they will fit into the existing culture and social structures, but that fit is never perfect, not all children are fully socialized into the culture. Resistance and change are historical and social realities.

Suggested Readings

Elkin, Frederick & Handel, Gerald (1984). *The child and society: The process of socialization* (4th ed.). New York: Random House. An overview of socialization and the effects of the mass media, the family, social class, and sex roles on socialization.

Harrison, Barbara Grizzutti (1974). *Unlearning the life: Sexism in school.* New York: Morrow. A description of sexism in a school in 1970 and of the parents' effort to eliminate it.

Hodges, Michael H. (Spring, 1987). Children in the Wilderness. *Social Policy*, 43–47. Hodges worries that as families, work, and other social elements change, children are forgotten and left alone.

Holt, John (1964). *How children fail.* New York: Dell. A passionate argument that schools control and teach obedience to children, instead of helping them think critically.

Norgren, Jill (1984). Child care. In Jo Freeman (Ed.), *Women: A feminist perspective* (pp. 139–153). Palo Alto, CA: Mayfield. An excellent review and discussion of the need for a day-care policy, U.S. attitudes about day care, the history of day care in the United States, and policies in other societies.

Sadker, Myra & Sadker, David (1985, March). Sexism in the schoolroom of the '80s. *Psychology Today*, 54–57. Schools at all levels still encourage male dominance and female subservience.

Shostak, Marjorie (1981). *Nisa: The autobiography of a !Kung woman.* New York: Vintage. The earlier chapters provide a vivid description of Nisa's !Kung childhood.

Turnbull, Colin (1983). *The human cycle*. New York: Simon & Schuster. Drawing on his experience and study of many societies, Turnbull explores the experience and meaning of childhood, adolescence, youth, adulthood, and old age.

Williams, Terry & Kornblum, William (1985). *Growing up poor*. Lexington, MA: Lexington Books. Poor teenagers in U.S. cities, black and white, face bleak futures because there are no jobs for them, schools do not educate them, and they face discrimination in many places.

PART III

Social Inequalities

CHAPTER 8

Classes and Class Struggles

Experiences, Perceptions, and Emotions

It is a sunny, warm, and quiet Sunday morning in late June. As I sit here writing, I want to tell you of the enormous and profound social class differences that exist in the United States and the world—about the rich and poor, about people who starve and people who have cooks who prepare them elaborate meals, about people who have no homes and others who have many homes worth millions of dollars, about people who despair they can provide for their children and people whose children will inherit so much money they will never need to work, and about millions of people who live somewhere between these extremes. But at this moment the pain of the millions of people everywhere who are suffering materially, socially, and emotionally seems very distant from the tranquil and lovely world outside my window. My mind is filled, instead, with reflections of the walk I took with my children, Melissa and Ariane, around Walden Pond yesterday afternoon.

As we neared the end of the two-mile path, we sat by the side of the pond with the wooded hills behind us. We felt calm, rested, and happy. Melissa, wistfully, kept saying how happy she was and how she wished she could build a house up on the hill so she could walk down to the pond every day. I kept thinking about when the Indians lived here, and Thoreau after them, and how they lived with nature, not against it. That tranquility is still with me this morning. How can there be such suffering, exploitation, destruction of woods and waters, such pervasive inequalities, in this lovely world I see around me? How can I *feel* at this moment the oppression and misery of millions, which make the opulence of others possible? How can those of us who do not experience this suffering and anxiety understand this reality? Can such reality exist? What does it mean? Why does it exist?

The inequalities among social classes, races and ethnic groups, and men and women are the essential realities of our lives today. In Chapter 3 we saw that there were no social classes in early human societies. Everyone was provided with the basic necessities of life but very little more. In the course of societal change, over the last ten thousand years, more and more inequalities have appeared; they have become profound and universal. At the same time, many people have been struggling to diminish and eliminate these inequalities and the suffering they cause.

Let us begin our discussion of social classes and social inequalities by looking at some personal experiences. We will then examine the underlying causes and the effects of class inequalities.

Childhood Memories

Our earliest experiences and memories are probably of being fed and held, of learning how to walk and play, of learning how to talk, feed ourselves, and experience life in all its rich variety. We notice differences among people in age, sex, size, and temperaments, to name a few. Somewhere in our development we begin to notice social inequalities. (Very few students in my classes can recall the age and circumstances when they first became aware of social classes.) Long before we reach the age of twenty, all of us know that inequalities exist, but most of us cannot recall when we became conscious of them. They almost seem to be part of nature, like air, earth, and water.

But some people can vividly recollect an incident or incidents that made them (often painfully) aware that some people have more than others—more money, more toys, more power, more prestige. My earliest memory reaches back to when I was six or seven in Greece. My grandmother, brother, and I lived in a two-room apartment. In a large house across the street lived a judge with his wife and a son my age. A little servant girl of six or seven also lived with them. I do not remember (or I never knew) how she came to be their servant, whether she was an orphan or the child of very poor parents who had to place her with a family. I do remember that the judge's family mistreated her, especially the son. I recall vividly one incident, when he picked up a pointed metal object and threw it at her in anger. It hit her on the buttocks and opened a cut that bled profusely. I cannot remember what happened next, but I still feel the shock and anger I felt then. That girl and her wound have stayed with me. They epitomize the essence and cruelty of social class inequities. Later experiences of being poor also left their impressions on my memory and emotions, but none are as clear and painful.

Lerner (1980) recalls her childhood that was filled with fear and humiliation.

> *The red clay of the foothills of the Blue Ridge was caked on her bare feet. The hand-me-down rag she called a dress was so worn her flesh was clearly visible in too many places. Her stringy hair framed her face, which was red from the ninety-degree heat as well as from embarrassment.*
>
> *She was standing at the back door of a large, two-story, white house. As the door opened, she asked to "borrow" some ice. This was the source of her embarrassment: Her family had no refrigerator, and she knew the "borrowed ice" would not be returned.*

Through the door she saw the landowner's daughter playing the piano, wearing a pink ruffled dress with a matching pink ribbon in her hair. The two girls were about the same age.

Clutching the ice, she ran home. At lunch she would have a wonderful treat—Kool-aid with ice; but after the treat, she would spend the hot afternoon in the fields.

1930? 1940? No, this was 1959. I was the little girl—I'm a sharecropper's daughter.

The South has many legacies. Mine was no running water, an outside toilet, a wood stove, worn-out parents, constant fear of disease and hunger, and a lasting, burning anger.

Throughout the South, families still live under the injustice of the sharecropping system. The landowner provides the land, and in some cases, the fertilizer. The sharecropper provides the labor, the seeds, and the extra hands in the form of his children. The sharecropper harvests the crops and receives a portion of the profits, never more than half and usually a lot less. It is a system of perpetual poverty for the sharecropper and easy profit for the landowner.

Sharecroppers are usually outcasts in the community. Landowners would rather not be reminded of the grinding poverty that provides their wealth. Although sharecropping is an extension of slavery, many sharecroppers are white, as my family was.

My father's hands, blistered and bleeding from the labor, were a common sight. My mother's toes often bled. When you don't have shoes, your toes are easy targets for a hoe that is swung under the influence of fatigue. (p. 66)

Today, millions of children live in poverty. They have little or no medical care, no adequate housing. They are often hungry and many suffer from lead poisoning. Schools do not teach them, and when they grow up, they can't find jobs. They grow up with little hope and few expectations (Williams & Kornblum, 1985).

Upper-class children, on the other hand, grow up with a sense of entitlement and self-assurance. They expect, much in the same manner we all expect the sun to rise and set, social position, wealth, and servants to care for them. They reflect what they see, hear, and experience. They hear their parents talk about making important decisions; they are surrounded by people who attend to their every need and desire; they are raised by governesses while their parents are out having fun, and they expect to do the same later. As children, they see and know of no other way to be. You are probably neither poor nor ostentatiously rich. What childhood experiences and memories do you have about class differences?

Poverty in America

In all class societies, there are many people who are poor and suffer materially, emotionally, and socially. Many poor people in the United States cannot work or cannot find work. What assistance they receive is barely enough to survive. Even those who can get work more often than not can't live on what they make.

The poor are caught in a trap. If they work, they cannot get public assistance, but the jobs they can get will not pay them enough to live on. Carla, a single parent of three children, is just one example (Kumin, 1983). She refuses to live in a slum so half her $718 monthly income goes for rent. How does one clothe and feed a family of four on $350 a month? No longer eligible for some food assistance programs, she and her children occasionally have toasted frozen waffles and water for dinner. With no cash on hand, Carla cannot buy food items that are on sale. How does she accept being poor? "I'm still from that middle-class upbringing that makes it very hard for me to say that I'm poor. To accept the truth, I am *poor*. The last week in August we ate oatmeal three times a day because that's what was left in the cupboard; can you believe that?" (p. 576)

In the United States, farmworkers, the people who harvest the food we eat, are among the poorest and most exploited. Thousands, perhaps over a million, work for minimum wages, put in long hours, are cheated and exploited by the growers, and live in miserable housing. The details may seem unreal for the 1980s. An article in the *Progressive* (August, 1982:12) described the conditions this way: "the roaches, the barbed wire, the corrugated tin shacks at 120 degrees Fahrenheit, the garbage rotting under the porches, the lines in the morning outside the woefully overtaxed privies. It's all there, and it is the norm, not the exception." Some live in virtual slavery. They are held against their will, beaten if they try to leave, and have deductions taken out of their checks for food, leaving them with little money left over. Crew leaders actually claim the workers owe *them* money. The federal government does little to stop this slavery, except for an occasional conviction (one crew leader received a life term in prison and another twenty years).

Some of the most desperate farmworkers live and work in California. Mexicans and other Central and Latin Americans enter the United States illegally and take any job available. For $200 a week, they work six ten-hour days. Injuries and illness plague them. Foster (1982) gives a vivid picture of one place workers call "Devils Canyon."

In the first clearing there is a shack made of twine, twigs, and old plastic fertilizer bags. Inside, an elderly, bootless man is hunkered on a worn crate and a teen-aged boy is wrapped in a blanket on the floor. The boy, Manuel Perez, flaps the blanket, as if to beat off the settling chill. Perez rubs his eyes, yawns, and apologizes. "We got up at 4:30 this morning. It takes until 6 to walk to the fields. We picked tomatoes—for nine or ten hours—and then we walked back." He is a boy of nineteen, but he says his joints ache like an old man's.

Perez talks softly about the legal, state-inspected farm labor camps where he has worked in other parts of California. At the other camps there was at least potable water, instead of irrigation pipes carrying the taste of fertilizer and pesticide residues. There was shelter instead of a strip of plastic stretched across two sticks. There was food. Here a fiyuquero, a "catering" truck-driver, sells moldy goods at inflated prices. (p. 45)

Meanwhile, some dolls and dogs live better than these people who feed us. During the height of the popularity of the Cabbage Patch Kids, a store in Brighton, New York, sold mink and rabbit fur coats for the dolls, at $150 to $1,000 each. In Chicago, Famous Fido's Doggie Deli "offers gourmet dinners for dogs and cats as well as $8-a-muzzle pet birthday parties and obedience school graduation celebrations." (*Boston Globe,* September 1, 1984:2).

The Working-Class Majority

Most Americans do not live under such degrading and debilitating poverty, but millions do, and their exploited labor enriches only a few others. Millions of other people live on the poverty line. Their days are filled with anxiety and worry. The so-called average Americans may be better off economically, but they too live with insecurity at their door. Their jobs are not satisfying; their incomes can barely pay their bills. Even those who manage to keep their jobs have unemployed relatives, friends, and neighbors. A minority of Americans lead a comfortable life, but they lead it in the midst of a society ridden with inequalities and class conflicts, a capitalist society where the pollution and destruction of the environment damage everyone's health and well-being, a society where a wealthy ruling class has created and perpetuates poverty, exploitation, economic insecurity, and a dying environment. This ruling class, about a million people, clearly dominates the society and its economy for its own benefit (see below and Chapters 9 and 10 for evidence supporting these conclusions).

Garbage and Class

In many ways, people's relationship to garbage starkly illuminates social class differences. Some people banish garbage from their sight. Heffman (1971) reported that at a cost of a million dollars, the Rockefellers built a subbasement "so that garbage trucks could enter a tunnel to pick up refuse without being seen." Generally, "anything that offended the eyes of the Rockefellers was removed." (p. 96) Some people dispose of the garbage of others. Ray Murdock (Lasson, 1971) talks about his work: "When it's cold out the cans feel heavier and harder; when it's hot the stench penetrates the lungs and nostrils, and stays there. . . . I been working around garbage all my life and it still makes me puke. If I have too much of it on a hot day, with the bouncing in the truck, I puke my guts out sure as hell by noon-time." (p. 17)

In many cities of the world, poor people look through other people's garbage for food to eat and old newspapers, clothes, and other items they can use. Their numbers, in fact, have multiplied in the United States, with the economic crisis and rising unemployment of the 1980s. I have seen an old man picking cigarette butts from the sidewalks of Cambridge. And some people are treated like garbage. In Calcutta, India, Chambliss and Ryther (1975) report that "carts go through the streets every morning and collect the dead bodies that have accumulated from the night before." Homeless people in many other cities end up as garbage. (p. 6)

Classes

We have just read a few examples of the most harmful affects of social inequalities. Millions of people are poor. Many more are not poverty stricken, but they barely manage to make ends meet. Some live comfortably, while a very few are rich. At some level, most of us are aware of this condition. We need to understand why such class divisions exist.

Classes and the Means of Production

Through the ages people have developed various modes of production (economies) to survive. We saw in Chapter 3 that our earliest ancestors gathered and hunted for their food and other material necessities. They were followed by horticultural, agricultural, and industrial societies.

In gathering-hunting and horticultural societies everyone owned the means of making a living (means of production). Land was not owned by anyone. People had equal access to it to gather or hunt or to cultivate their gardens. They did not own it individually. The group as a whole owned it. Thus, every child born into these societies inherited the land and could use it as much as any other child. With the exception of young children and old people, everyone worked and contributed to the subsistence of the group. Differences in material possessions were relatively small and due to one's temperament and interests, not to land or other wealth one inherited.

There is relative equality in gathering-hunting and horticultural societies, unlike peasant (agricultural) societies. In the peasant societies that exist today, some people own more land than others and pass it on to their children. Historically, a few people (the nobility) came to own vast tracts of land. Since they and their families could not work that land by themselves, they rented it to landless people. The usual arrangement was for the landless peasants to split their crops fifty–fifty with the landlords. The landlords, without doing any work, came to amass much wealth from the work of others. They profited from and exploited their labor.

Today, in industrial societies, only 2 to 3 percent of the people grow the food for all of us. Most of the rest of us work in factories, offices, or other workplaces. Only a very few people in our society own their place of work. The workplace owners pay our wages. If there are profits left over, these go to the owners. Objectively, then, the fundamental distinction in capitalist societies is between those who work for others and get paid enough (usually) to live and continue working, and the owners whose incomes come from the profits workers make possible.

According to Marx and people who follow his tradition, capitalist societies are divided into different groups or *classes*. Each class is composed of people who have the same relationship to the means of production. The large factories, offices, and other enterprises that produce most of the goods and provide most of the services are *owned and controlled by a very few people*. Managers and executives own little or nothing, but by virtue of their education, training, and appointment, they occupy positions in corporations that give them some control over the means of production. Still others have a small degree of control; they occupy lower management and technical positions. Most of the people are workers who follow the rules and orders of the managers above them. As we descend the order of ownership and control, people make less money. (This simplified picture will be discussed in more detail later on in this chapter.)

Our economic situation, then, is shaped by our relationship to the means of production. We may own a corporation, or we may own a large share of it. We may own stock in many corporations, or we may own no stock in any corporation, which is the case for most of us. With or without ownership, we may serve on corporation boards of directors, or we may be presidents of corporations, or we may hold other higher managerial positions. Some people are managers in government or other organizations. Most of us work in places with little or no control over what we do: in offices, factories, restaurants, stores, and thousands of other settings. We relate variously to the economy that provides our daily bread, but many more loaves go to a few people than go to the rest.

Generally speaking, we tend to marry and socialize with people whose place in the economy is the same or similar to our own. We share similar interests, values, life styles, and pastimes. Usually, owners and managers of large businesses socialize with each other, workers with other workers. The two groups rarely mingle. Workers drink beer in their neighborhood bars; owners and managers sip cocktails in their country clubs. And, of course, each group lives in its separate neighborhoods.

A social class (henceforth, *class*), then, is a group of people who have a common relationship to the means of production and who share interests, life style, pastimes, and values.

The preceding discussion clearly implies that the economic position we hold determines and shapes who we are, what we do and think, the people we marry, and the friends we make. Marxists have debated this idea with each other and with nonMarxists. (See, for example, the works cited at the end of this section.) The debate has been long, ongoing, lively, often stimulating, and sometimes acrimonious. Few, if any, Marxists ever argue that our economic position *completely determines* our action and thoughts. Such a position sometimes is wrongly attributed to Marx. Religion, personal interests, education, the unique set of circumstances each one of us finds and creates in life, our ethnic traditions, and other realities of our lives also affect what we do and how we think. We are not robots driven by economic position. But in the long run our relationship to the means of production, our occupation and income, play the primary role in our lives. Gender, culture, life experience, and other differences affect us and the classes to which we belong, but as Gilbert and Kahl (1987) state "classes develop out of relationships to the means of production." (p. 15)

Studies and our own daily observations confirm that for most of us, in the long run our economic position, occupation, income, wealth, residence and neighborhood, education, and general life style tend to converge. We tend to socialize with people on the same level in these spheres of life. Not every engineer who makes $50,000 a year leads the same life as every other engineer, but professionals who make, say, $40,000 to $60,000 as a group are different from people who have not attended college and average $15,000 to $20,000 in unskilled and semi-skilled jobs.

Before we outline and discuss classes in the United States, let us examine a more formal and detailed definition of class.

A class is composed of the following elements:

1. A group of families whose members intermarry,

2. People who have the same relationship to the means of production, similar economic positions,

3. People who share common economic and political interests that are in conflict with the interests of other classes, and

4. People who share common values and life styles that are different from the life styles and values of other classes (life styles include education, residence, speech, dress, leisure activities, and hobbies).

Historically, classes have been composed of groups of families, not individuals. We inherit our economic and social position from our families. Whether we stay in the same class, or rise or fall socially, we live in families who socialize with other families in the same general social position. Thus, classes are composed of groups of families. Usually the best indication that a group of families is a class is the willingness of people to marry others from that group.

For most of us our occupation is the single most important index of our class. Some people derive large annual incomes from their investments, but even most of these people hold top managerial positions, follow professions, or hold political office. Their investment holdings and employment positions indicate their class. For the rest of us, our occupation clearly tells others our class membership. Most sociologists who study classes use people's occupations to place them in different classes.

Classes, like roles, can only exist in relationship to each other, to other classes. A person can only be a teacher if there are students she or he can teach. Similarly, a class is only possible in relationship to other classes above and below it. The *middle class* is between a higher and lower class. But in addition, and this is essential to the very nature of classes, *the economic and political interests of a class are necessarily in conflict with the interests of some other class(es)*. Owners and managers make more or less profit as they pay their workers less or more. One class gains or loses at the expense of another. Often, but not always, people in a class are conscious of common interests with others in their class, and of conflicting interests with other classes. (See discussion of class conflict and class consciousness later in this chapter.)

Finally, it seems obvious that people in the same class follow similar life styles (see below), but perhaps we need to qualify this generalization. There are many individual differences in interests, tastes, and actions between people in the same class. People are not carbon copies of each other. What we mean is that people in class A, as a group, generally have similar life styles when compared to classes B, C, and D. This is not to say that people in two or more classes never share any interests. For example, music tastes often cross class lines.

Classes in the United States

We could identify any number of classes in the United States. We could begin with a division of two, the business class and the working class, as the Lynds (1929) thought they found in Muncie, Indiana, in 1925. The list could expand to three, upper, middle, and lower classes, or it could go to six by dividing each of these three into upper and lower. Further distinctions could be and have been made.

If we focus on people's relationship to the means of production, there is one basic division between those who own and control the means and those who do not. But this division oversimplifies reality. Individuals often border on both classes. Also, those who do not own the means of production vary enormously, from affluent managers and professionals to those on welfare. Nevertheless, starting with the basic division between owners and nonowners, we can make sense of classes in the United States (and probably other capitalist societies) by locating people in one of the four following classes.

1. The ruling class is the group of people who own and control the means of production. (Most sociologists call them the upper class.)

2. The managerial class is made up of the managers and professionals who do not own the means of production or who are not wealthy enough to live off their investments. Many help manage the enterprises owned by the ruling class. Professionals and managers get paid well. They are the group most sociologists call the middle or upper-middle class (these terms may be used interchangeably).

3. The working class is the majority of the population. They work for salaries and wages, own no income-producing wealth, businesses, stocks, or bonds (as distinct from owning homes, cars, and other personal possessions),

and have no control over the means of production. Millions border on the managerial class, but many more are not far from poverty.

4. The poor class is composed of people who may be unemployed, on welfare, or, more likely who work part or full-time in unskilled jobs for very low wages. Millions have relatives and friends in the working class.

The Ruling Class

They own and control the major means of production. *Most income-producing property is in the hands of the ruling class.* Families and individuals from the ruling class directly and indirectly exercise control over the economic, political, governmental, and educational institutions. That is, as we shall see in Chapter 10, their *power* extends beyond owning and profiting from the economic institutions to influencing and shaping the course of other institutions.

People who own small businesses, employ a few workers, and work hard to make a comfortable living are not members of the ruling class. Nor are high-level managers or professionals who get paid well. All these people could not live off their investments, they must work for most of their annual income. But even more essential is the fact that they do not exercise *control* over the means of production. Individuals from these groups, or even more likely their children, *may* move into the ruling class if they accumulate considerable wealth in the form of stocks, bonds, real estate, and other income-producing property. Then they could live off the income of such property. So long as most of their annual income comes from their salaries, however, small business owners, professionals, and managers are not members of the ruling class.

The ruling class, by definition, appropriates for itself the surplus value produced from the labor of the working class. When people work forty hours a week, and produce items or provide services that sell for $1,000, but they get paid only $400, whatever is left from the other $600 after paying for the materials, rents, taxes, and so on, is extra value that is profit for the owners. The ruling class lives off of the labor of workers.

Within the ruling class there is a distinction, or difference, between old money and new money. Families that have been wealthy for three to four generations stay somewhat aloof from and may not marry people from families whose wealth is more recent. But this is a social, not an economic, difference. People from both groups own and control the major corporations of the United States. In time new money ages, and people are accepted socially.

Estimates of the percent of Americans in this class vary from ½ to 2 percent. Some sociologists who have been studying this class estimate it closer to ½ percent. Let us settle for 1 percent, about 2.5 million people. They vary from the super-powerful and super-rich, the Rockefellers, DuPonts, Mellons, Kennedys, and a few others, to people barely above the managerial class.

The Managerial Class

As we said, people in managerial and professional occupations own little or no income-producing property. Managers derive most of their annual income from salaries, small business owners from their profits, and professionals from their fees. Managers hold very high level positions in corporations and banks and other financial institutions. They manage, direct, and control the middle managers and workers below them. Together with members of the ruling class, they decide what products corporations will make, where they will invest, and so on. They get paid well and some eventually come to own enough stocks and other property so they move up economically and socially.

Managers and professionals have had advanced training and education. Managers are presidents, vice-presidents, and consultants in corporations and government agencies. Oppenheimer (1985) says "The professions include, depending on authority, governmental classification system, time, and place, every occupation from upper-level manager to store-front lawyer; from surgeon and priest to student nurse and computer programming coder; from astronaut, athlete, and author to technician, therapist, and veterinarian." (p. 136)

But not all these people belong to the managerial class. Professors from famous universities who consult for corporations and the government who influence the decisions of these institutions, and get rewarded handsomely, do belong. Most college teachers, however, have no such influence and get paid much less. They are closer to the working class. Nor are all lawyers members of this class. They vary from senior partners in large law firms to small-town practitioners. There are engineers and other technicians whose skills are essential in running various enterprises and who work closely with top management, and others who carry out tasks assigned to them. A few psychologists, nurses, and social workers may hold decision-making positions (usually as administrators of social agencies), but most try to ease people's pains rather than gain any financial benefit from their labor. The examples are many. The essence of the managerial class is participation in managing and controlling the economic, social, and political institutions. The closer people are to top management levels, the more we can say they belong to this class.

Small business owners may also be members of the managerial class. A family with three to four hardware stores, for example, may make up to half a million dollars a year and are bordering on the ruling class. A restaurant owner with three to four employees, on the other hand, may clear about $30,000 a year. Socially, this person probably associates with people from the working class.

We saw that the ruling class profits by appropriating for themselves the surplus value produced by workers. The managerial class also profits since the owners pay them well from the profits they make from the workers. The two classes are close allies although they are not the same class.

Education, hard work, and perseverence are essential for members of this class, whether they are corporation managers, doctors, engineers, or famous university professors. But personal traits and accomplishments do not suffice for membership in the managerial class. Suitable employment must exist for people in this class. For example, the high administrative and technical positions of the flourishing computer industry have provided opportunties for a few thousand people. If the industry declines, however, some people will lose their jobs and may move down socially.

This class, which is also called the professional-managerial, upper-middle, coordinator, or simply the middle class varies in estimates from 10 to 20 percent of the population. Most writers estimate 15 percent.

The Working Class

This is the most troublesome class to define because included here are many people usually considered to be middle class. Members range from middle-level managers, most teachers, nurses, and social workers to blue-collar workers barely out of poverty. Many of these people would not associate with each other. Their life styles differ and their incomes and work situations vary widely. Why are they in the same class then?

The simplest reason is that they belong together not because of who they are but because of *who they are not*. They clearly are not in the ruling class. Some come close to poverty. People in this class may have been poor once, or they may fall into poverty in the future. Most hold steady jobs and meet minimal standards of economic survival and social prestige, as defined in the United States. On the other hand, there are people who work on the edge of the managerial class, but who do not occupy positions of control or decision-making. People in the working class, then, have no investments and live by their wages or salaries, exercise relatively little or no control where they work, and must follow the directions of others. There are exceptions. Teachers, for example, may run their classrooms with some measure of independence, depending on the school system and the level at which they teach.

The following list gives some specific examples of people who belong to this class:

most teachers	messengers
file clerks	office machine operators
nurses	payroll clerks
technicians	railway mail clerks
service workers	social workers
carpenters	insurance adjusters
police	postal clerks
firefighters	receptionists
automobile workers	secretaries
car mechanics	shipping clerks
library assistants	stenographers
bank tellers	storekeepers
bookkeepers	telegraph operators
cashiers	telephone operators
bill collectors	ticket agents
vehicle dispatchers	typists

The following are some examples of people who work in the ever-expanding service occupations:

hotel maids	practical nurses and nursing aids
janitors	airline stewards
bartenders	bellhops
cooks	barbers
dishwashers	elevator operators
waiters and waitresses	police and firefighters
dental assistants	school monitors

Finally, there are the traditional blue-collar workers. The percentage of blue-collar workers is shrinking, as millions of manufacturing jobs are exported to countries where workers are paid very little (see Chapter 9). Blue-collar workers operate the machines that make cars, appliances, and clothes; they build homes and buildings; they drive buses, trucks, taxis, and trains; they repair cars, machines, and houses; they extract coal, oil, and uranium from the earth; and they sow and harvest the food we eat (although most farm workers get paid so low that they are poor or on the edge of poverty).

Despite what we may have read and been taught to believe, people in these vastly different occupations do belong to one class. They may wear blue, white, or pink collars, and they may have greasy or clean hands. But the work they do is fairly monotonous, they follow the directions of higher authorities, and the range in income is clearly lower than what people in managerial positions make. In 1983, executives, administrators, managers, and professionals had a median income of about $30,000 a year. The median income of workers, however, was about $19,000. It was $20,000 for technical workers, $18,000 for craftspeople, $16,000 for machine operators, and $10,500 for service workers (Gilbert & Kahl, 1987).

These are *median* incomes, with half making over and half under these figures. Moreover, there is tremendous variation within each occupation. A cook may be a famous chef in a very expensive restaurant and may function as a manager, getting paid accordingly; or, he or she may be a short-order cook in a local diner. Nevertheless, the general tendencies and averages show very clearly that despite all the differences most people *are* working class, both in pay and occupational circumstances. If a woman attends college, becomes a social worker, and marries a high school teacher, do they belong to the same or a different class than their parents who are carpenters, car mechanics, and cashiers? The income and job autonomy of these occupations are fairly close. Objectively, the vast majority of people in the working class are more similar to each other than they are to people in other classes. (See Braverman, 1974, and Oppenheimer, 1985.)

By various estimates, 70 to 75 percent of Americans work in blue-collar, clerical, sales, service, and middle and low level managerial and professional occupations. They are the working class of the United States.

The Poor

Estimates show 10 to 15 percent of the American population lead financially precarious lives. Few are hungry and cold, but all have problems finding affordable and adequate housing, paying their bills, and buying any extras. Most work, but their wages are very low and unemployment is a constant threat. Others want work but cannot find it. Still others, mostly single and divorced mothers with children, exist on welfare. In *every* state, welfare benefits add up to an income well below the poverty level listed by the U.S. government.

Many poor people border on the working class. The two classes meld into each other. Some sociologists think that the poor are not a separate class, only a subcategory of the working class. Whatever we call them, poor people suffer materially, socially, and emotionally. They are the people others are terrified to become. People keep working in dangerous, boring, and dehumanizing jobs to avoid being poor.

Closing Comments on Classes

I end this discussion of classes in the United States with some qualifications and clarifications.

First, only the ruling class and the poor are easily and obviously identifiable. To a lesser extent, so are the wealthier members of the managerial class. There are no clear lines at either end of the working class, however. I have given a few examples that show classes merge into each other. Most American families float in the great middle, the working class. Those at the lower end struggle to avoid falling into poverty, and those in the higher end hope to reach the top.

Second, membership differs from, let us say, membership in an organization. Members of an organization are formally admitted, and there is a concrete membership list. Classes, on the other hand, are fluid, changeable, and approximate. One lawyer may make a million dollars a year (some corporation lawyers do); another may barely manage to make $25,000. One college teacher may work at Harvard University and consult with corporations and the government, another may teach at a community college for the same pay as police and firefighters (occasionally even less). A nurse may be married to a doctor or a high administrator, while another may have to perform the unpleasant task of emptying bedpans. The differences and complications of class are endless, but the conclusion is obvious: classes are not concrete entities where people are easily assigned. Subjective considerations and perceptions influence how we perceive classes and where we think we belong, where others place us, and where some objective criteria indicate we belong.

Third, while classes are not easily measured physical entities, they are real. They refer to human relations, to the way we relate to each other, as subordinates or as bosses, as employers or employees, as people who are prestigious or disreputable, as rich or poor, as powerful or powerless. They refer to the concrete experiences of Americans, those who eat oatmeal or frozen waffles for dinner or those who have a French chef prepare their meal.

Fourth, classes change over time. The number and the prestige of independent business owners have decreased while professionals and managers have increased. Small farmers and independent craftspeople have also almost disappeared. And since 1865, the ruling class in the United States has grown and expanded its control and wealth over more and more areas of the society. During the last two to three decades, the composition of the working class has been changing. As we shall see in Chapter 9, millions of manufacturing jobs that paid decent wages have been exported to other countries or have been eliminated, while service, sales, and clerical jobs, paying much less, have been expanding.

The fifth and final point is that some societies have a more rigid class system than do others. For centuries in India, people were born into a class (*caste*), and they could not leave it. They were obliged to marry and live within their caste, much as black and white people in the United States were once forbidden to mix. Despite its abolition, the caste system persists in India. Low caste people who refuse to stay within their caste are beaten and persecuted by higher caste people. In the United States, our classes are more fluid and people do move from one class to another, but most people stay within their parents' class. Mobility is the exception rather than the rule (Glass, 1982).

Other Definitions and Lists

Most sociologists think that occupation, income, and wealth are central to understanding and defining social classes. Most of them, however, do not think that people's relationship to the means of production is the primary factor. They focus as much or more on education, residence, leisure activities, dress, manner of speech, and life styles in general.

The following comment by Warner, Meeker, and Eels (1960) represents the thinking of most sociologists: "While significant and necessary, the economic factors are not sufficient to predict where a particular family or individual will be or to explain completely the phenomena of social position. Money must be translated into socially approved behavior and possessions, and they in turn must be translated into intimate participation with, and acceptance by, members of a superior class." (p. 11)

Most sociologists think that there are five to six social classes in the United States (and probably all other capitalist societies). There are three major classes, upper, middle, and lower, and each of those is subdivided into two.

1. *Upper-upper class.* These are the richest Americans whose wealth has been in the family for at least two or three generations.

2. *Lower-upper class.* The wealth of these families is more recent than that of upper-upper families. They have not yet assimilated into the upper-upper class in terms of behavior and life styles.

3. *Upper-middle class.*   These familes are not wealthy but live comfortably. They work as professionals, managers, and small business people.
They live in the so-called better suburbs.

4. *Lower-middle class.*   These families make less money than upper-
middle-class families. Their jobs usually do not involve manual labor; they
work as clerks, salespeople, teachers, police, middle-management people, or
other similar jobs.

5. *Upper-lower class.*   People here work in blue-collar jobs and make
modest incomes. (Classes 4 and 5 together make up the majority of the
American population.)

6. *Lower-lower class.*   These are the poor people of our society. Many
work, but the minimum wages they make and the frequent periods of unemployment, leave them constantly financially insecure. This group includes
retired poor people, people on welfare, and so on.

This is the typical social class breakdown of the United States. These
descriptions usually include life styles, personalities, and behaviors typical of
the people in each class. For example, people in the upper classes go to the
ballet and museums, those in the lower classes watch baseball games and TV;
or, parents in the lower classes are more strict with their children than are
upper-middle class parents. The list of social class differences is endless and a
great deal of sociological research focuses on them. (Warner initially developed these six classes. Many sociologists and textbook writers have elaborated
on them, but they have kept them essentially as Warner first conceived them
in his study of Newburyport, Massachusetts, "Yankee City," in the 1930s; see
Warner, 1963.)

The Two Lists Compared

There are three fundamental differences between the Marxist class categories
I propose and those given by most sociologists (see Figure 8.1). First, Marxists
think there is one class at the top, variously called the bourgeoisie, capitalist
class, dominant class, or ruling class. The upper-upper and lower-upper classes
may differ in life styles, but the essence of their class is power, control, and
wealth. The Kennedys, as newly rich people, were not immediately accepted
by the old aristocracy. But their wealth and power, and their effect on society,
has been no less than that of the older ruling-class families. New and old rich
together control the economy for their benefit. Second, I argued above at some
length that there is a large working class. There is no middle class, lower or
otherwise, below the managerial class. Third, there is a clear difference in the
criteria people use to define classes. Marxists think that the *primary,* but *not
the only,* criterion is our relationship to the means of production, whether we
own and control them, and the amount of power people possess. Other sociologists think that economic factors are important but not primary.

FIGURE 8.1
Comparison of the Two Lists of Classes

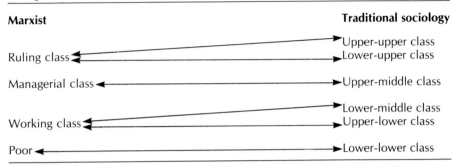

Arrows indicate the class(es) in each list roughly equivalent or synonymous with classes in the other list.

Life in Capitalist Societies

Our class, that is our relationship to the means of production, shapes our lives. The class to which we belong affects every aspect of our existence to some degree. Our parents' class determines their job and income, which affect where we live, the education we receive, our life style, the quality of our life. These experiences, in turn, shape how we think about ourselves.

Income and Wealth

In the United States, as in other capitalist societies, poor countries, and to some degree in socialist societies, there are vast inequalities in the annual incomes and the accumulated wealth of families.

Income

Before we examine the income of American families, let us first present some family budgets that show the income necessary for different levels of existence (see Table 8.1). Until 1981, these family budgets were compiled annually by the U.S. Bureau of Labor Statistics. To obtain 1985 figures, I added 18 percent, the increase in the Consumer Price Index from 1981 to 1985, to the 1981 figures. These family budgets were called the lower, intermediate, and higher. The lower, about $18,300 in 1985, is on the edge of poverty. The higher, about $46,000 in 1985, is the beginning of a modestly comfortable life style, where the working class merges into the managerial class (*Statistical Abstract,* 1982–1983:465).

In 1986, the median weekly earnings of families where both spouses worked was $706, an annual income of about $36,700. With the 1985 higher budget at $10,000 above that income, it is obvious that well over half of families (probably over 70 percent) where both spouses work do not make

TABLE 8.1
Budgets for a Family of Four in a Metropolitan Area 1981 and 1985

Family Class Status	Years	
	1981	*1985**
Lower	$15,481	$18,268
Intermediate	$25,893	$30,554
Higher	$39,117	$46,158

Statistical Abstract, 1982–1983:465 and 1987:463
* 1985 budgets estimated by adding 18 percent to 1981 budgets, which is the rise in the consumer price index, 1981–1985. See *Statistical Abstract,* 1987:463.

enough to live comfortably. If we add the families with one or no workers, even more than 70 percent of families do not reach the higher budget. Furthermore, these family budgets are for a family of four, including two children of thirteen and eight; no college expenses in this budget (U.S. Department of Labor, 1987d: Table 6).

Table 8.2 provides more detail on family incomes. In 1985, over 80 percent of families made under $50,000. In most of the United States in 1985, allowing for variations in family size, family needs, and local costs of living, $50,000 was the bare minimum for the good life as portrayed by the media and dictated by the larger society. Table 8.2 also shows that in constant 1985 dollars there has been no increase in the median family income from 1970 to 1985. Indeed, there was an increase in the percent of families making under $15,000, a corresponding decrease in families making $15,000 to $25,000, and a significant increase in those making over $50,000.

The higher the income, the more of it that comes from investments, not salaries (Gilbert & Kahl, 1987). The following figures exclude capital gains, which were not subject to taxation in 1978. People who made over a million dollars in 1978, on the average received 65 percent of that income from stocks, bonds, and other nonjob sources. Those who made between half and one million dollars, 52 percent; and those who made between $200,000 and

TABLE 8.2
Money Income of Families
Percent Distribution by Income Level, in Constant (1985) Dollars, 1970 and 1985*

	Under $15,000	$15,000–24,999	$25,000–34,999	$35,000–49,999	$50,000
1970	21.9	23.0	22.9	19.3	13.0
1985	23.5	20.8	18.6	18.8	18.0

Statistical Abstract, 1987:436
* Median income for all families for 1970 was $27,336 and for 1985 it was $27,735.

$500,000, 35 percent. The more money you make, the less likely you are to work for it. Most wealthy Americans inherit their money.

Table 8.3 provides an overview of the different life styles possible at different income levels. Study it with some care. In 1984, the richest 20 percent of Americans spent four times as much as the poorest 20 percent. They spent two and one-half times as much on food, three times as much on housing, and five times as much on entertainment. Perhaps the most revealing difference is the amount saved for retirement, pensions, and social security: an average of $196 for the poorest 20 percent, $1,174 for the third (middle) 20 percent, and $4,608 for the top 20 percent. Those accumulated benefits of the managerial class assure a comfortable old age.

Table 8.4 shows the national distribution of income in 1981 and 1986. It explains the different expenditures and life styles we just discussed. It also shows that the percent of total income that went to the richest people increased from 1981 to 1986. In order to manage, families are borrowing more money, which is increasing the amount of their debt (See *Dollars and Sense,* October 1986:20–22.)

Meanwhile, as the real incomes of the poorest families are decreasing, as more and more of the poor are working poor, welfare benefits are getting lower (they are increasing less than the rate of inflation). Evidence shows that most people stay on welfare about two years and that welfare does not decrease people's desire to work. The poor *are* getting poorer. (See *Dollars and Sense,* July/August, 1986:19; December, 1986:9–11; June 1987:6–8; and *Boston Globe,* March 21, 1987:3.)

Wealth

The vastly unequal annual incomes steadily accumulate and create even more unequal family wealth. In fact, very few people own most of the wealth, especially income-producing wealth.

TABLE 8.3
Quintiles (fifths) of Income before Taxes:
Average Annual Expenditures of All Consumer Units Interview Survey, 1984*

Expenditures	Lowest 20%	Third 20%	Highest 20%	Total complete reporting
Average annual expenditures	$10,831	$18,077	$39,246	$21,241
Food	2,064	3,049	5,165	3,278
Housing	3,688	5,476	11,161	6,313
Apparel and services	564	924	2,317	1,125
Health care	579	893	1,230	908
Entertainment	419	799	2,089	1,000
Life, other personal insurance	189	223	613	308
Retirement, pensions, social security	196	1,174	4,608	1,787

U.S. Department of Labor, 1986j: Table 1
* Partial list of itemized expenditures.

TABLE 8.4
Money Income of Families, by Each Fifth (20 percent) of
Families, and Top 5 Percent, 1981 and 1986
(Percent of Aggregate U.S. Income for 1981 and 1986)

Family Income Level	Percent of U.S. Income	
	1981	*1986*
Lowest fifth	5.0	4.6
Second fifth	11.3	10.8
Third fifth	17.4	16.8
Fourth fifth	24.4	24.0
Highest fifth	41.9	43.7
Top 5 percent	15.4	17.0

Statistical Abstract, 1982–1983:435 and *Dollars and Sense,* November, 1987:22

In 1983, according to a study by the Federal Reserve Board, 55 percent of all U.S. families had no wealth or were in debt, once liabilities are deducted (*Dollars and Sense,* April, 1985:8). A government survey of wealth in 1983 reveals profound inequalities. One half of one percent of families owned 35.1 percent of the wealth; the richest 10 percent owned 71.7 percent; and the rest, 90 percent, owned only 28.2 percent. These figures include homes. If we exclude homes and focus mostly on income-producing wealth, wealth is even more concentrated in a few families: 45.4 percent for the top one-half of a percent, 83.2 percent for the richest ten percent, and only 16.7 for the other 90 percent. Finally, the richest one-half of a percent of families own 58.2 percent of business assets. (More details are found in Chapters 9 and 10.)

Table 8.5 shows that the richest Americans own most of the nation's *income-producing property* (stocks and bonds). That is, if cars, homes, and other such property are excluded and only property that makes money is considered, the concentration of wealth is clearly seen. Other studies show that up to three-quarters of all stocks and bonds are owned by the richest 1 percent of Americans. The rich also manage to hide some of their wealth. As Green (1982) shows, for example, corporation presidents and others not only make half a million or more a year, but they receive many free benefits such as vacation homes, cars, and stocks at much lower prices than their real value.

Self-Conceptions

Mills (1982) chose two groups of four to seven year-olds in two day-care centers. Group A came from poor families, many on welfare. Group B lived in a fairly affluent community, with parents who were mostly in the managerial class. The children were asked: "If you could have three wishes, what would you wish for?"

The more affluent children responded quickly and easily. Their wishes rolled off their tongues. The poor children, however, "seemed very puzzled

TABLE 8.5
**Property and Assets of Richest ½ of 1 Percent and Richest
10 Percent of Americans, 1983 (in percent of totals)**

Assets	Top ½ percent of all	Top 10 percent of all
Corporate stock	46.5	89.3
Bonds	43.6	90.4
Real estate*	35.6	77.8
All wealth*	45.4	83.2

Kloby, 1987, and *Dollars and Sense,* April, 1987:10–11
* Private homes excluded

and many needed the question restated three or four times before answering."
(p. 5) Five children would not answer at all and were replaced by five other
children. Some could give only one wish. How can we explain this difference
in response? Perhaps poor children learn that wishing is futile. More than
likely they learn to repress and control their wishes for toys, food, and other
items because experience has taught them the frustration of wishing.

We saw earlier in this chapter that ruling-class children (and probably
most children of managerial families) grow up with a sense of confidence and
assurance. But as we descend down the class ladder, we find that growing up
in a class society leaves people with low self-esteem. Coles (1970) observes
that six-year-old children of poor parents (blacks, migrant farmworkers, and
others) reveal their self-images in the self-portraits they draw. They are small,
blurry, and indistinct, compared to the portraits drawn by children of the same
age but wealthier classes.

Poor people are not the only ones whose psyches are scarred. Most
working-class people also endure shame and a sense of failure. If people
survive spiritually, they do so only through struggle or through delusion (what
Longo calls "hoping, not living"). Collins (1978), writing about her father, a
commercial artist who never got the chance to paint the pictures he longed to
do, describes the destruction of the self that is so common among the working
class (this same phenomenon is portrayed in Arthur Miller's "Death of a
Salesman").

> *Year after year the disease got worse. Debilitated by the constant anxiety of
> personal inadequacy—the dominant mode of self-apprehension among men in
> a class-stratified society which yet appears permeable—my father became
> more and more irritable, harassed and despondent. His worry grew into an
> obsession. Most of the arguments between my father and mother erupted over
> money. They always ended with his shouting at her, "Well, somebody in this
> house has to worry about the bills!" and my mother collapsing in tears that
> were her strength. Soon my father's body conformed to the obsession, his
> shoulders becoming rounded, his wide chest, the symbol of manliness and
> pride, curving into a hollow.*

Yet in all those years I never saw him cry, never saw him get angry at any-one or anything else, except at members of the family as a kind of reflex, for he was a loving man. The brunt of his rage was turned in upon himself. In a society in which advancement and economic success appear to depend on merit, and respect hinges on advancement, to fail is to doubt the integrity of the self. (p. 86)

Read that passage two or three times. Consider its implications carefully, for here we see how capitalism and class inequalities invade and corrode the deepest sense of ourselves.

Childhood and Education

In the previous chapter we saw how the lives of children are affected by their class. We have seen above that young children's identities are shaped by their family's class. By five or six, most children know what the world around them thinks of them and their family, and they know what life awaits them.

The educational system is one of the institutions that shapes their future. How many years of schooling a child gets, the quality (or at least the prestige and reputation) of the school he or she attends, the amount of money spent on his or her education, the type of college he or she attends, all are largely shaped by the child's family's social class. The education children receive opens or closes doors and determines how much money they can earn (see Table 8.6). (I do not mean that people with more and "better" schooling necessarily know more or are more intelligent, only that it allows them to obtain many jobs closed to those with less schooling, merely by requiring longer school attendance, preferably at "better" schools.) While we cannot provide all the evidence for the above statements here, we can give some data. (For those interested, see Liazos, 1982; Gilbert & Kahl, 1987; and Pincus, 1980.)

Communities and states with higher average incomes spend more money per student than do those with lower incomes. In 1983, Mississippi, with per capita income of $6,801, spent $2,305 per student; New York, with per capita income of $10,183, spent $5,616 per student. In addition, parents in the higher classes reside in communities that spend more money on the schools, or they send their children to private schools (*Statistical Abstract*, 1987:130, 440).

When we compare college attendance we find that students in the highest ability group but different classes, have different rates of attendance. One study in the 1960s found 91 percent of the brightest students from the highest class (as defined in that study) entered college, but only 50 percent of equally bright students from the lowest class did so (Gilbert & Kahl, 1987).

The colleges people attend vary in the prestige and the opportunities

TABLE 8.6
Money Income of Households—Percent Distribution by Money Income Level,
by Educational Attainment of Householder, 1985

Educational Attainment of Householder	Money Income Level					Median Income (dollars)
	Under $10,000	*$10– 19,999*	*$20– 34,999*	*$35– 49,999*	*$50,000+*	
Less than 8 years	49.5	29.0	15.2	4.5	1.9	10,124
8 years	39.4	28.8	20.6	7.7	3.5	12,970
9–11 years	33.2	29.5	22.6	9.7	5.0	15,171
12 years (high school)	18.1	24.4	30.9	16.7	10.0	23,134
1–3 years of college	13.0	20.0	31.8	19.5	15.8	27,337
4 or more years of college	5.0	12.5	25.1	21.3	35.9	39,506

Statistical Abstract, 1987:432

they provide. Many poor and working-class youth attend community colleges, and the education and training they receive there does not seem to enhance their social class standing. Community colleges provide the appearance of equal educational opportunity for all people, but the reality contradicts that promise. Indeed, the educational system tends to keep students in their parents' class, not move them up socially. Data clearly show that the higher a family's income, the more likely a person is to attend college, finish college, and attend a more prestigious college. And as we showed, these realities hold even if we compare students of the same ability and achievement (see Pincus, 1980; Liazos, 1982; and Gilbert & Kahl, 1987).

Marriage

We saw in Chapter 6 that most people marry within their own class. They do so because they associate with others from the same class. Indeed, a social class is composed of freely intermarrying families.

In the following passage from Kahn (1973), we see how a poor Appalachian woman views marriage and social class. (See also Rubin, 1976 and Gilbert & Kahl, 1987.)

> *The kids from the rich families in Clay County don't date the poor kids. Their parents won't let them associate with poor kids. The rich boys marry the rich girls. The parents of the rich kids don't care anything about them anyway, and I can imagine how it would be if they came home and told their parents they were dating somebody from up in the hollow that didn't have much of anything. And some of the rich guys might try to give the poor girls trouble, take them out to see what they can get out of them.*

Behavior and Language

Class and social behavior are closely related. Our behavior reveals our class. Our family and neighbors (which *is* our class) shape much of our daily behavior. How we speak and dress, what we prefer and reject, are reflections of our class. Moreover, higher classes seek to impose their standards and actions as superior and preferred, and to label those of people from lower classes as inferior and undesirable.

In all class societies clothes become a status symbol. We judge others by the clothes they wear. People from higher classes dress to communicate their status and impress others. Lurie (1981) in *The Language of Clothes* gives many examples from Western history. Conspicuous consumption in dress continues today. "According to *Business Week*, some executives are extending their 'dress to success' look to eyeglasses, with frames made of African buffalo horn starting at $400 or a gold frame set with diamonds for $3,000" (*Labor Notes,* May 1987:4).

People dressed in work clothes, obvious symbols of their class, become invisible. Montgomery (1986), a newspaper columnist, dressed in dirty clothes while he was working in the garden of a social and charitable organization of which he is a member, is ignored by fellow members who do not recognize him. A worker tells him that people dressed in suits "look right through you." (p. 19)

Table 8.7 shows some differences in participation in outdoor recreation activities of people with different family incomes.

People from higher classes tend to speak differently, even to speak different languages, to distinguish themselves from people in the lower classes. Thus, around 1900 the Russian nobility spoke French to each other. The language spoken by most Russians was too common and vulgar for them.

TABLE 8.7
Participation in Outdoor Recreation Activities, by Family Income, by Percent, 1983

Activities	Family Income		
	under $5,000	*$15–25,000*	*$50,000 and over*
Walking for pleasure	45	54	62
Swimming	34	57	72
Picnics	36	53	58
Attending sports events	24	43	61
Fishing	24	38	35
Boating	16	27	43
Tennis	12	18	37
Golf	6	13	27
Snow skiing	5	7	21

Statistical Abstract, 1987:218

Professor Higgins (in the play and film *My Fair Lady*) struggles mightily until Eliza can pronounce "The rain in Spain falls mainly in the plain," in proper upper-class diction. In the play, she is accepted into the nobility—not so in real life, however. Language reflects people's social class upbringing, but merely learning the speech of the upper-class will not lead to joining it.

Let us close this section with an example from long ago. The power and preferences of the ruling class of the eleventh century have left their marks on our language. Here are a few examples: beef–cow, mutton–sheep, venison––deer, pork–pig. The words on the right are for whole live animals, those on the left for cuts of meat we cook and eat. Why the difference? Chambliss and Ryther (1975) explain it this way:

> *The words on the left are all of French origin; the words on the right are all Germanic. The contemporary English language reflects a long struggle between people for control of England. In 1066 A.D. the Normans conquered the island, and for some time after 1066, the ruling nobility spoke the French language of the Norman conquerors. The Anglo-Saxon peasants, who spoke a Germanic language, did the dirty work of caring for the animals. Their words came to signify the live animal. The French-speaking nobility ate the animals. Their words came to signify the animal as food. Embedded into contemporary English we can see the traces of an old struggle between social classes which was in turn the result of cultural imperialism, the attempt of the Normans to impose their ways on the Anglo-Saxons. (p. 83)*

Speech and all other behavioral differences between classes are not objectively superior or inferior. So long as we understand each other's intended meaning, all language, dialects, and words are equal. Invidious comparisons arise only when higher classes seek to judge their speech as superior, and sometimes to impose it on others.

Health

Poor people generally have a shorter life expectancy and a higher mortality rate than more affluent people. They also become ill more often. The hospitalization rate differs by class. In 1976, it was 24 percent higher for lower-income groups. According to a report in the *Boston Globe* (June 9, 1977:1), in 1972, a Boston neighborhood populated by poor (mostly black) people had a death rate 30 percent higher than the statewide average and 50 percent higher than nearby affluent suburbs. People died from respiratory diseases, cancers, heart-disease, pneumonia, and other causes at a rate two or more times higher than the rest of Massachusetts.

Many studies have shown that on the whole people in the poorer classes receive either inferior medical care or none at all. For example, poor women who undergo hysterectomies develop many more complications than middle-class women (*Guardian*, January 19, 1983:10).

Poor health and inadequate medical care tend to deteriorate even further during economic recessions. A rise of *1 percent* in unemployment leads to an increase of about 320 suicides. In areas of increasing unemployment, TB and the infant mortality rate increase. In Detroit in 1982, there were 33 infant deaths per thousand births, a rate as high as that found in poor countries of the world. Cuts in federal programs for health and nutrition in the 1980s led to a dramatic rise in infant death rates of poor people, especially blacks (see Chapter 11 for more details). (See *Progressive,* April 1983:20; *Guardian,* January 5, 1983:5; and *Boston Globe,* May 24, 1984:20; February 9, 1987:1, 5.)

Cuts in federal nutrition programs, higher unemployment, and lower incomes for poor people have led to an increase in hunger, compared to the 1970s. Twenty national studies have shown that up to twenty million Americans are hungry. They are people on welfare, retired people on fixed incomes, and full-time workers who receive low wages. Poor nutrition is directly connected with poor health. (See *Boston Globe,* January 10, 1986:8; December 10, 1986:58; Lupo, 1986b; and *Guardian,* February 18, 1987:2; March 27, 1987:1.)

City and county hospitals have traditionally provided medical care for many people. In the early 1980s many were closing or reducing their services. From 1950 to 1980, hospital beds in public hospitals in thirty-one large cities decreased by 40 percent, whereas in other hospitals they increased by 60 percent. Many profit and nonprofit hospitals refuse medical care to uninsured people who cannot pay when they enter the hospital. (See *Dollars and Sense,* November 1982:16; Guardian, July 29, 1981:7; Bale, 1985; and Downs, 1987.)

In addition, in 1986 almost thirty-five million Americans were without any health insurance (*Boston Globe,* September 24, 1986:7). Their numbers increased by 15 percent from 1982 to 1984, as more people were working in service occupations (see next chapter), which pay low wages and provide no benefits.

Therefore, the findings of the U.S. Public Health Service should not be surprising. Gilbert and Kahl (1987) report that in 1980 the Public Health Service conducted interviews and found that "those with incomes under $5,000 were four times more likely to report themselves in poor or fair health than those with incomes over $25,000." (p. 110) In mental health, too, people in the lower income categories suffer more and receive worse care.

How you live, how you die, and when you die are linked to social class.

Housing

In 1965, Kohl (1967) taught a fifth-grade class in Harlem, New York City. One day he took his thirty-six students (all poor blacks) on a tour of Park Avenue in lower Manhattan. Luxury stores and expensive apartments were everywhere. The children could not believe that this was the same Park Avenue that went through their neighborhood just a mile up the street. All their street had were dilapidated apartments and boarded up stores.

Spend an hour or two driving through the streets of any metropolitan area. In and around Boston, one sees the wide variety of housing and class of families who live there. Poor people live in deteriorating public housing or crowded slums. Slightly better off families live in two and three story deckers, three to four feet apart and with postage-stamp-size yards. Further up the class ladder distances between homes increase and yards get bigger. More affluent people live in single-family homes, and those that are still more affluent in larger homes and two-acre plots. The very wealthy live in fifteen to twenty room houses, many of them mansions, and they might own other houses. (Increasingly, wealthy people buy expensive condominiums in newly desirable city neighborhoods.) Where you live, perhaps more than any other sign, identifies your social class.

These traditional differences between the housing of different classes have intensified dramatically during the 1980s. Working-class and poor people face a housing crisis. Housing prices have doubled and tripled over the last five to six years in most urban areas, fewer people can afford to buy houses, and home ownership has declined. Rents have also more than doubled. There are fewer affordable apartments. Few new ones are built for working-class families and existing ones are converted to condominiums. Not only do people spend a much greater percentage of their income on housing, but many families and individuals are making less or are unemployed and cannot find any housing they can afford. As a result, millions are homeless, as many as three million people in the mid-1980s. Thousands of others—an estimated 230,000 people in New York City alone—stay off the streets by doubling in the homes and apartments of friends and relatives.

Let me support these conclusions with data, studies, and examples.

Housing for ruling-class and managerial families is abundant, albeit more expensive. In Atlanta, Boston, and elsewhere, for a million or two you can buy houses with plenty of amenities and luxuries in desirable (or newly desirable) places. For most people, however, owning a home, the middle class symbol of the American dream, has become more difficult. In Watertown, Massachusetts, an average town of 32,000 people, adjacent to Boston, the median price of a home increased from $85,000 in 1980 to $240,000 in 1987. The expensive homes available require a much greater proportion of annual income to meet mortgage payments, assuming people can find the money to make the down payment. "During the 1950s, about two-thirds of all families could have afforded the typical new house without spending more than 25 percent of their income on housing. By 1970, the proportion of households that could afford a new house [by spending no more than 25 percent of their income on housing] had declined to one half, by 1976 to just one fourth, and by 1981 to less than one-tenth" (*Dollars and Sense,* December 1985:5).

Working-class families in the 1980s spend 35 to 50 percent of their earnings on housing. Consequently, home ownership is declining for the first time since the 1940s. In 1977, 65 percent of all families and "unrelated individuals" owned their homes, but 60 percent did so in 1983. (See Center for Popular Economics, 1986:27; Kuttner, 1985; *Boston Globe,* September 30, 1985:1; and *Dollars and Sense,* March 1986:10–12; July/August 1987:5.)

Renting an apartment is no easier. As we learned in Chapter 5 conversion of apartments to condominiums, gentrification, and arson for profit have reduced the number of affordable apartments, leading to drastic rent increases. In the 1980s, as the federal government sharply cut funds to build and maintain low-income housing, the crisis has intensified. Cities that become gentrified push out working-class people. According to Kuttner (1987a), "The price of an average two-bedroom apartment advertised in the [*Boston*] *Globe* jumped from $515 in 1982 to $850 in 1985." (p. 15) When 50 low-income apartments were advertised in 1986 in Boston, 1655 families applied for them. Boston was one of the three or four most expensive areas in 1987, but rents are increasing everywhere. (See also Lupo, 1986d; *Statistical Abstract,* 1987:464, 469; and *Boston Globe,* September 20, 1986:17; May 6, 1987:1; June 2, 1987:1.)

Fewer apartments, less federal money for low-income housing, and the inevitable rent increases have increased the numbers of the homeless. Homeless people have existed for years, but their numbers multiplied with the economic crisis of the 1980s. The estimated three million homeless in 1987 may increase to eighteen million by 2003 if current policies and conditions do not change, according to a report by the Neighborhood Reinvestment Corporation, a non-profit group funded by Congress (*Senior Citizen News,* 1987:3).

Shelters for the homeless have sprouted in most U.S. cities, even as millions still sleep on the streets. Others, especially families with children, are "temporarily" housed in run-down hotels. There, children have no place to play and mothers no place to cook. Still others double up with relatives or friends. The homeless are the most visible reminder of the profound housing crisis. (The following are a few of the many sources that describe homelessness in the 1980s: Kozol, 1988; Hartman, 1985; Nelson, 1985; Dinkins & Wackstein, 1986; Fabricant & Kelly, 1986; Rivlin, 1986; *Boston Globe,* June 3, 1986:25; *Senior Citizen News,* 1987; and *Guardian,* February 4, 1987:10–11.)

Housing has become the largest concern and worry of millions of people. In polls taken in 1986 and 1987 in Boston, people were asked to choose their main concern from a number of different choices. Housing was the number one choice of 30 to 40 percent of them. People's lives are totally disrupted when housing becomes scarce and prohibitively expensive. Watertown, Massachusetts, where I live, is a good example.

Watertown has been a blue-collar, working-class community for decades. But the housing crisis now means that people who grew up here cannot buy or rent here. In the seven years I have lived here, prices of homes and rents have more than doubled. Young people who marry and want to stay near their relatives and friends cannot find housing. They must move twenty to thirty miles away, where prices are not low but less expensive than in Watertown.

Old people are forced out of apartments where they have lived for years because their rents have doubled. Everyone I talk with is worried about working-class people of all ages who cannot find affordable housing. Families are divided. Neighborhoods are changing. Rising housing prices are steadily forcing out working-class families.

Rents increase for many reasons. Speculators buy apartment buildings and turn them into condominiums. They sell them and make a huge profit for themselves, but there are fewer affordable rental units. In addition, the federal government now finances few low-income housing units (as it increases military spending). Kuttner (1987a) notes that "in 1986, in the entire country, the Department of Housing and Urban Development subsidized construction of just 25,000 new affordable housing units, compared with more than 200,000 produced yearly during the administration of Republican Gerald Ford and nearly 300,000 under Jimmy Carter." (p. 15) Even 300,000 units do not meet the need.

As home and rent prices increase, people have less money to pay them because incomes have not kept up with housing costs. Indeed, many are unemployed and others make less money as service jobs replace industrial ones (see next chapter for details). We now have the new phenomenon of homeless people who work full-time. (See *Guardian,* March 6, 1985:10–11; Lupo, 1986a; Bratt, Hartman, & Meyerson, 1986; Marcuse, 1987.)

The housing crisis symbolizes one of the fundamental conditions of class societies: *profits come before people.* It is the working class and the poor who struggle to pay for housing or are homeless. In the spring of 1987 a few Congresspeople slept with the homeless in the streets of Washington to dramatize their plight. Representative Ron Dellums (1987) of California said: "I got up in the morning angry, outraged; outraged at a society that forces thousands of human beings to live on the streets of American when we can put a damn MX missile in Minutemen silos to the tune of multi-billions of dollars." (p. 1)

Crime and Justice

In its majestic objectivity, the criminal justice system provides equal protection to all people who hire the best and most expensive lawyers available. Wealthier people are usually either found innocent or, if convicted, given lighter sentences than poorer people—this is true for all crimes from murder to theft. Balkan, Berger, and Schmidt (1980) state, "In California in 1976 . . . 100 percent [of those sentenced to death] had been unemployed or subemployed. The death penalty has never been applied uniformly to offenders from all strata [classes] of society." (p. 124)

In a well-known study Chambliss (1973) shows how the police, the school, and the community discriminated against working-class youth. The Saints (children of professional families) and the Roughnecks (working class) were two groups of high-school students both of whom engaged in delinquent behavior. Their actions were equally serious and dangerous. But the Rough-necks were often stopped and arrested by the police. They were labeled as troublemakers. Two of them received football scholarships from colleges and ended their delinquency. Of the other four, two ended up in prison for murder, one became a small-time gambler, and the fate of the other one is unknown. The police did not stop or arrest the Saints, and on the rare occasions they did, the Saints politely talked their way out of trouble. Seven of the eight Saints became successful professionals and businesspeople.

But the inequality and injustice of the law hardly stops at the prejudices of the criminal justice system. As we saw in Chapter 4, what the law defines as crime also discriminates in favor of the ruling class. Crimes committed by corporations are not defined as crimes. A bank robber or someone who breaks into a house may get fifteen years in prison, not so corporation executives who knowingly build lethal cars, dump dangerous chemicals, or commit other dangerous acts. (For an elaboration of the law's relation to social class, see Reiman, 1979; Balkan, Berger, & Schmidt, 1980; Chambliss & Seidman, 1982.)

The Quality of Life

The obsession with success, money, material possessions, and upward mobility debilitates people who cannot attain these things, but also profoundly affects the lives of families and individuals in the upper classes.

Corporation presidents, among the most successful Americans, often pay heavily for their success. They are so busy they do not reflect on their lives. Trausch (1981) quotes one president: "I hadn't thought about a lot of these things [power, success, family] for years. There's not much opportunity to do that." In addition, family life suffers when successful people work long hours and travel often, sometimes for days and weeks, missing birthdays and other occasions.

But families in the higher classes do achieve material success. They pay $500 for a diamond or a suit without undergoing an emotional and financial crisis. Most other Americans are caught in the experiential dilemma of life style expectations, on the one hand, and financial realities, on the other. They are exposed to a fantasy and a dream that is beyond their reach.

Drugs (legal and illegal), alcohol, and various faddist psychotherapies serve as escapes from this dilemma. Those who are unemployed feel the greatest threat to their self-respect and to their financial stability, which leads them to drugs and alcohol to kill the pain. "Take away a job, you take away identity—they're one and the same thing," said a drug and alcohol counselor in Detroit in 1981, when unemployment soared (Nyhan, 1981, p. 1). Drugs, alcohol, and other forms of escape exist everywhere in the United States. Workers with dangerous or boring jobs drink excessively or use legal and illegal drugs. In the 1980s, government officials and others argued that co-caine and other drugs were major problems in the United States. They were only partly correct. Legal drugs like valium and alcohol are much more widely used and cause many more deaths than cocaine does. The focus on cocaine and the demand for drug testing take attention away from the widespread abuse of legal drugs and the reasons that people use drugs. Dangerous and boring jobs, unemployment, financial crises, poverty, and racial discrimination, among others, are the social conditions that lead to drug abuse of all types. (Hills, 1980; *Guardian,* September 17, 1986:2; October 15, 1986:19; November 19, 1986:19.)

This suffering is not the same as that experienced by the poor. Millions of Americans are hungry and have inadequate housing, of course, but for most Americans life under capitalism means competition, insecurity, an unattainable life style, doubts about the adequacy of one's self. That is the quality of life under capitalism. Anxiety, competition, and materialism create mistrust and cheating and poison human relations. We expect people to cheat us. The *Chicago Tribune* (June 22, 1976:1) ran an article showing that most garages overcharge or do unnecessary work; we see corporations poisoning the air, earth, and water as they indiscriminately dump chemicals to save on disposal costs; we see corporations knowingly build unsafe cars; we see pervasive cheating everywhere; we see anxiety relieved by excessive drinking and drugs; we see families suffer from parents too busy at work or parents without work; we see people work at jobs that diminish their humanity because they are so mindless and routine; these too are the costs of social class inequalities. They penetrate our minds, spirits, and self-conceptions.

The class to which we belong has specific effects on our lives. Our health, education, marriage, where we live, and many other aspects of our lives are shaped by our class, as we have seen.

Class and Happiness

During discussions of social classes, I ask students whether people in one class are generally happier than people in another class. Do our chances to lead a happy life vary depending on the class to which we belong? Are people on welfare, those with unskilled jobs making poverty wages, craftspeople, sales workers, secretaries, firefighters, teachers, nurses, engineers, factory workers, lawyers, doctors, corporation executives at various levels, corporation presidents, and members of the wealthiest and most powerful families—all equally likely, or equally unlikely, to lead meaningful, fulfilling, and satisfing lives? If not, who is more likely to find happiness in life? Why?

Class Consciousness, Class Conflicts, and Class Struggles

We know that classes exist. We know that most aspects of our lives are shaped by the class to which we belong. But how do we react to their existence?

Class Consciousness

Class consciousness is the awareness that classes exist, that we belong to one of these classes, and that the interests of our class conflict with the interests of other classes. It means that we examine most institutions and traditions from a critical perspective that sees some people benefiting at the expense of other people. It can mean, for example, that if we visit an art museum housed in a stately home donated by a rich family, we realize that the home and the art objects were bought with profits made by exploiting poor peasants and workers (Montgomery, 1985).

Some observers say that most Americans do not think class differences matter to them or that the differences have grown smaller over the years. Gilbert and Kahl (1987) note, however, that whatever people may say, they act as if class differences are important. In a 1975 survey conducted by Jackman and Jackman (1983), people were interviewed about their "class awareness." The results indicate that people believe that classes exist and are important. Ninety-seven percent identified themselves with one of the five choices they were given.

Upper class	1 percent
Upper-middle class	8 percent
Middle class	43 percent
Working class	37 percent
Poor	8 percent

In assigning themselves to one of these classes, people used their income, occupation, and education as the main criteria, but they also included life styles, beliefs, and feelings. There was also widespread awareness that the middle class versus working class distinction made by government statisticians (see above) contradicts social reality. Fifty percent of all clerical workers and 58 percent of all craftspeople considered themselves working class. Clearly, Americans, especially those in the lower classes, are keenly aware that social classes are ever-present realities of our society.

Except for people in the ruling class, class consciousness is not strong in the United States (see Chapter 10). People do realize that different classes exist, and they usually resent people in the upper classes. But the educational system, the mass media, and the ideology that the United States is a society where anyone can succeed if only he or she strives hard, tend to reduce class consciousness. Most people, including most social scientists, deny or minimize the existence of classes and the conflicting interests between them (Davis, 1982.)

As we saw in Chapter 4, people who dissent (sometimes called "radicals"), who protest and argue that the system favors the higher classes, are dismissed, repressed, and persecuted. Organized strikes, protests, and struggles have been common in U.S. history, in the late nineteenth century, in the

1920s and 1930s, and more recently. But textbooks ignore most of this history. For example, few people know the history of International Workers' Day, May 1. It is celebrated throughout the world, except in the United States, to honor the history and struggles of workers. It commemorates an American event. On May 1, 1886, workers gathered in Haymarket Square, Chicago, following many days of strikes, to continue their demand for an eight-hour day. It ended when the police fired on the crowd, killing four people. (See Brecher, 1972; Lynd & Lynd, 1937; Szymanski & Goertzel, 1979; Domhoff, 1983; Kluegel & Smith, 1986; and Navarro, 1986b.)

Most people are not class conscious enough to challenge the legitimacy of the dominant ideology. They do not see the necessity to change the rules and the system that perpetuate classes and inequalities. But there are people who are aware and angry and who take action against social injustice. In one survey, reported by the Center for Popular Economics (1986), 61 percent of those interviewed stated that income and wealth inequalities in the United States are unfair and the gap between the rich and the poor should be made smaller. In another survey, two psychologists found that 78 percent of U.S. workers distrust management (*Dollars and Sense,* May 1987:4).

Class Conflicts

Since land and material possessions are limited in every society, if one group gains more of them, it will have to do so largely at the expense of others. This *class conflict* is the inevitable condition in capitalist societies, where one class can only benefit if another class loses. This is a fundamental social reality in all class societies. Without equality, the rich gain at the expense of the rest of the people, who must struggle against the rich in order to increase their share of the goods. Marx and Engels (1959) wrote eloquently in 1847 that "the history of all hitherto existing society is the history of class struggles. Freeman and slave, patrician and plebeian, lord and serf, guildmaster and journeyman, in a word, oppressor and oppressed stood in constant opposition to one another, carried on an uninterrupted, now hidden, now open fight, a fight that each time ended, either in a revolutionary reconstitution of society at large, or in the common ruin of the contending classes." (p. 7)

As we saw in Chapter 3, class differences began to appear in horticultural societies, but they became pronounced in agricultural societies. Industrial societies have developed their own versions of class systems.

In the United States, class differences have always existed, but they became greater and sharper when industrialism began to dominate after 1865, after which point large companies and the ruling class increased their power and wealth. As they did so, working people resisted through unions, legislation to curb ruling class power, taxes on the wealth of the ruling class, and government programs to benefit the poor and the working class. After long, bitter, and often bloody struggles working people succeeded during the 1930s to form unions and to pass social legislation (social security, minimum wages, nutrition programs, etc.). These gains have made substantial improvement in the lives of most people, although they have not changed the basic class divisions and the dominance of the ruling class. But beginning in the 1970s and even more in the 1980s, the ruling class (with the support and active leadership of the federal government) staged a counterattack, which now seeks to undo most of the social gains of the last fifty or sixty years. (See Lens, 1981, and *Guardian*, September 14, 1982:1, 4.)

During the 1980s, programs benefiting working people have been reduced or eliminated. Food programs, nutrition programs, Medicare and Medicaid, education programs, OSHA worker protection programs, these and many other programs have been attacked and their funding cut. For example, after-inflation cuts amounted to reductions of 80.7 percent in subsidized housing, 47.1 percent in housing assistance for the elderly, and 27.7 percent in legal services to the poor. Total cuts in all low-income programs amounted to 50.4 percent in that seven-year period (*Dollars and Sense*, April 1988:8). At the same time, Congress has passed tax cuts benefiting corporations and the rich (Center for Popular Economics, 1986).

The income data cited above show that there has been a shift, with the ruling and managerial classes taking a greater percentage of total income in the 1980s than they did in previous decades. During the 1980s, corporations have formulated and carried out a strategy to lower workers' real wages and to destroy unions, which have been the workers' main instrument to raise their wages. Real hourly wages (after we discount inflation) have fallen 8.7 percent from 1973 to 1986, 5 percent from 1979 to 1984. (See Center for Popular Economics, 1986:6, and *Dollars and Sense*, July/August 1987:6.)

The tax cuts of 1981, 1982, and 1983 mostly benefited corporations, the ruling class, and professional-managerial families. The 1983 tax cut gave an additional $36 *billion* to families making over $80,000 and took away $1.2 billion from those making under $10,000. The poorest families lost an average of $150 each since losses from spending cuts were greater than the minuscule tax cuts they were given. Families making $40,000 to $80,000 gained an average of $1,800 each, and those over $80,000 an additional $15,000. This is Robinhood in reverse. (See *Guardian*, December 22, 1982:2; *Dollars and Sense*, February 1983:7; and Center for Popular Economics, 1986:50–51, 145–146.)

Another working-class gain of the last fifty or so years, unions, is also being attacked. Union membership declined in the 1970s, from 30.8 percent of nonagricultural employment in 1970, to 25.2 percent in 1980, and 18 percent in 1985. Two reasons largely account for this decline. Manufacturing jobs, which have been a traditional stronghold of unions, have declined. As service and office jobs increase, management in these fields resists and sabotages workers' efforts to unionize. In 1983 there were 1,500 consulting firms that specialized in preventing new unions and destroying (busting) existing ones. They charged up to $200 an hour to prevent clerks and others from making $4 to $5 an hour. Hospitals, universities, computer corporations, chain stores, government agencies, and religious institutions hire them for advice on tactics to bust and prevent unions. They use psychological tactics to intimidate and frighten workers, such as isolating union leaders and union sympathizers in remote parts of the workplace. (See *Dollars and Sense,* March 1983:8–9; *Statistical Abstract,* 1987:409; and Koeppel, 1982, for union busting of migrant workers.)

The mass media generally give incomplete and negative coverage of workers' strikes. Problems at picketlines are shown, but the issues over which the workers are striking are barely mentioned. Because of worsening employment conditions and other reasons, there has been a drastic decrease in strikes. The number of strikes involving 1,000 or more workers, lasting one or more days, has declined from 381 strikes involving 2.5 million workers in 1970, to 187 involving 800,000 in 1980, and 54 involving 324,000 in 1985 (*Statistical Abstract,* 1987:410). (For a vivid description of a strike and biased news coverage, in Hamilton, Ohio, see Davis, 1982, Chapters 10 and 11.)

Unions have made a real difference in workers' wages. In 1985, in most occupations unionized workers earned 20 to 30 percent higher median weekly earnings than those not in unions. For example, unionized women clerical and sales workers earned 28 percent more, $380 versus $297. (See *Dollars and Sense,* September 1986:22, and *Statistical Abstract,* 1987:409.)

With the recession and increasing unemployment, corporations are threatening to close or relocate their plants unless workers take reductions in pay and other benefits. They have succeeded in a number of cases, notably in the auto industry. Some unions have refused to give back gains they earned after years of struggle, and have gone on strike. Corporations have also begun to use robots in many production jobs, both to save money and fight unions (*Guardian,* March 23, 1983:18; April 13, 1983:1, 11).

Class Struggles

It is clear that corporations and the ruling class are very class conscious, and that they are seeking to increase their profits and power at the expense of the working class. Data given in the next four chapters should leave no doubt that class conflict, even class warfare, is taking place. But as the ruling class and its allies seek to consolidate and increase their wealth and power, many working class individuals and institutions are waging struggles for greater equality.

Class struggle is being waged on many fronts. For example, many workers are organizing to stop the destruction of unions. By being determined, allying themselves with other groups, and using their imagination they are succeeding in forming new unions and keeping old ones strong. Hotel workers in Boston took a weak union, carefully prepared for a strike, and won both pay increases and other benefits. Homemakers also organized unions in Boston and other places. And in 1981, 400,000 people went to Washington to demonstrate against government policies that favored corporations and the rich.

(See Clawson, Johnson, & Schall, 1982; City Life, 1983; *Guardian,* September 30, 1981:1, 8; and Rubin, 1986.)

At the same time that many unions are losing members, workers in and out of unions are fighting to build, preserve, or strengthen unions. A small union local of 149 steelworkers was on strike for over half a year in 1986, refusing to accept wage cuts. Some family farmers facing bankruptcy because of declining food prices formed alliances with unions, civil rights, and anti-hunger groups to improve economic conditions for all people. And a group of poor and uneducated Chicano women struck a food canning company for eighteen months to prevent huge wage cuts. They won after a long and bitter struggle. More and more workers, white and black, men and women, are working to recapture wages and benefits they lost to corporations in the early 1980s. (See Downs, 1986; Wettstein & Gormican, 1987; Erlich, 1987; and *Guardian,* April 8, 1987:13.)

Renters in many cities have formed organizations to institute rent control and provide rights for renters. Neighborhoods are being organized to resist the destruction of their homes by profit-seeking builders and corporations. The Association of Community Organizations for Reform Now (ACORN) has chapters in forty cities in twenty-six states, with sixty thousand members and 130 full-time staff. ACORN and similar organizations organize working-class people to change conditions for and by themselves. For example, they have fought against raises in utility rates, to stop factories from polluting the area, and for improved housing. As people succeed in winning these fights they gain confidence to continue working for equality. A group in Pittsburgh organized a community to stop Nabisco from closing its local plant. (See Dreier, 1982; Fullinwider, 1983; *Guardian,* April 27, 1983:10–11; January 12, 1983:2.)

Finally, there are proposals and discussions for basic changes in our society. One such proposal would reduce unemployment in two ways. One, the government could put people to work doing a lot of the necessary work in our society: running day-care centers, reclaiming the land, building housing, and meeting other needs. The Works Projects Administration (WPA) of the 1930s is a successful precedent for this. Two, communities and unions could take over and run many of the plants that corporations are relocating or closing down. Jobs would be provided and communities reclaimed (Moody, 1983).

Throughout our land, throughout the world, people are working to create just societies. Sometimes they do so quietly and unobtrusively; at other times they burst into public view with demonstrations and other public acts. Many who are inactive support these struggles quietly. Others may not know they exist. (For a general discussion of equality and class conflict, see Ryan, 1981, and Zeitlin, 1980.)

Social Mobility

There are some people in the lower classes who know inequalities exist but do not protest against or resent the economic system that creates these inequalities because they hope to join those at the top of the hierarchy. President Reagan has argued many times that Americans want the opportunity to succeed—that, he said, is the heart of the American system. He is referring to *social mobility* or the ability of a person to move up or down within the class system. But how possible is it for people to move up socially? Can someone be poor but through hard work move up to the upper classes?

Gilbert and Kahl (1987) summarize a study by Featherman in which he conducted interviews with 33,600 men about their and their fathers' occupations. By comparing the sons' occupations with their fathers' we can make some conclusions on social mobility: how many move up, how many down, how many remain in the same class. Using occupation as the sole criterion of social class, Featherman's study found that 49 percent of the sons moved up, 32 percent remained in the same class, and 19 percent descended the class ladder. Fathers and sons were grouped into five occupational categories: upper white-collar, lower white-collar, upper manual, lower manual, and farm. These data, according to these categories, show considerable social mobility.

Gilbert and Kahl (1987) go on to argue that much of the mobility in the twentieth century has been the product of an expanding and changing economy. Farm, unskilled, and other manual labor jobs have declined, and white-collar jobs have increased dramatically. Thus, a father may work in a factory, but when his son reaches adulthood, the father's job will have disappeared and been replaced by a white-collar one. (pp. 161–165)

Seen in this light, Featherman's conclusions are not as sound as they might first appear. Sons of skilled factory workers and craftspeople may become school teachers, sales clerks, bank tellers, and social workers. But have they really moved up socially from their parents' class? I doubt it. The apparent social mobility is actually a *definitional* and *statistical* creature. If, by definition, a school teacher or computer operator belongs to a higher class than does his or her mechanic, carpenter, or farmer father, then we have social mobility. But in the real world all these people make about the same income and are members of the same working class. They do not socialize with corporation presidents, vice-presidents, managers, or doctors.

In a study by Featherman and Hauser (in Gilbert & Kahl, 1987), of all the sons of "construction craftsmen" 11.6 percent became "salaried professionals." This category includes teachers and social workers. Because they do not dirty their hands, unlike their fathers, they are considered to be in a higher class, but this is *not* social mobility.

A few societies have almost no social mobility, the caste system in India, for example. But the United States and other capitalist societies are much more open than India; people can and some do move up the social scale. Most of them do so as new job opportunities are created. When the occupational structure ceases to expand, people can only move by displacing the children of families in classes higher than their own. Nevertheless, significant social mobility is limited even in these countries. A few people can move up to the managerial class, even fewer up to the ruling class. A ruling class may change over a long period of time, say 200 years, and be almost entirely composed of different families, but from one generation to the next, people in the upper reaches are born there. For example, one study found that only 5 to 10 percent of the corporate rich rose from the working class; eight out of thirteen billionaires have inherited their wealth (Stevenson, 1982).

Are Social Classes Inevitable?

Explanations

In her book *Social Inequality,* Duberman (1976) says that even though the degrees of inequality in societies have varied, "in all types of societies, from the primitive hunting and gathering tribes to the highly industrialized democracies or communistic nations, inequality is unavoidable. True, total equality is unattainable, and to strive for it as a goal can only result in frustration and failure." (p. 20) Most people have been socialized to believe something like Duberman's conclusion. But is inequality inevitable? Must the poor and other classes always be with us?

What is the argument for the eternal existence of classes? Most people who make that argument present some version of the functionalist theory of inequality. According to this theory, those who have more money, power, and prestige than others, possess these things as rewards for contributing to the welfare of society. Doctors make more money because they contribute more to the survival of society than, according to this view, garbage collectors or assembly-line workers or most other people. Doctors and others must receive these rewards to compensate them for their rare skills, their long training to develop such skills, and the sacrifices they make. Many more examples could be given. The essence of the functionalist perspective is that those who receive higher rewards deserve them because they contribute more to the survival and well-being of society than other people do.

But neither class nor inequality are inevitable or necessary for the survival of a society. They arise because some people use power and coercion to benefit themselves. Given this, there are several arguments countering the functionalist point of view. First, it is not true that those who receive higher rewards (in money, prestige, and power) contribute more to the survival of society since many people in the ruling class inherit their wealth. There are also those who merely help the wealthy become wealthier. For example, an accountant, lawyer, or economist who helps a corporation reduce its taxes by manipulating tax loopholes is not only not contributing to the well-being of most people, he or she is causing harm by making other people pay the taxes corporations do not pay. Second, do doctors truly make more sacrifices than mine workers and many others, who may lose health or life in their jobs? Third, there is the question of inherited abilities. Most people have similar abilities and are capable of accomplishing many things—certainly there are more than 500,000 or so people who could become doctors given the opportunity.

Inequalities in Capitalist Societies

Throughout this and other chapters I have offered evidence of the inequalities in income, wealth, power, and prestige that exist in the United States. There are also life-style differences and ongoing struggles and conflicts between classes that attempt to reduce or to increase inequalities.

The degree of inequalities in capitalist societies varies somewhat. In some societies, workers have succeeded in modifying the economic system slightly and reducing some of the grossest forms of exploitation, injustice, and inequality. But all capitalist societies remain largely unequal, all are run by a strong ruling class. Sweden is a capitalist society that is reputed to have drastically reduced social inequalities. Heavy taxation supposedly redistributes money and resources from the upper classes to all people. Yet major inequalities persist: 0.3 percent (three-tenths of a percent) of "Swedish households own 50% of all shares in private companies." (*Guardian,* October 18, 1982:4). In 1987, the Central Bureau of Statistics of the Swedish government published a report that states that from 1975 to 1985 there was great progress in social equality in Sweden. It concludes that Sweden is the most egalitarian society in the world. I doubt that it is the most egalitarian, but certainly Sweden is more egalitarian than other capitalist societies. (See *Boston Globe,* May 20, 1987:4, and for inequalities in Japan, see Junkerman, 1983, and in Canada, Panitch, 1985.)

Inequalities in Socialist Societies

Although socialist societies have clearly reduced inequalities in such areas as income, they are still clearly class societies. Classes do exist, but the gaps between them have diminished and are narrower than in capitalist societies.

Let us first look at the Soviet Union and then examine other socialist societies. In societies where socialism arose before 1960 housing, medicine, and education are either free or cost a small percentage of a person's income. Food is subsidized and usually at stable prices (with a major exception of Poland in the last fifteen years). Compared to the United States, the material standard of living is low, but it has improved drastically from the presocialist years.

According to Lane (1982), the Soviet Union has no "private propertied class possessing great concentrations of wealth." (p. 52) People cannot own millions and billions of dollars worth of stocks, bonds, and other such property because the major means of production are owned by the government or by collectives (farms mostly). Thus, no property can be passed on from parents to children.

Theoretically parents cannot officially pass on top government and economic positions to their children. But children of top officials, factory managers, and top professionals do have clear advantages over other children—more education, more social contacts, and knowledge of how the system works, to name a few. As Lane points out, they begin life with more opportunities than do the children of peasants and workers. (pp. 153–157) The Chinese Cultural Revolution, 1966–1976, sought to eliminate the advantages of the children of top officials and others; it did not succeed. (See Liazos, 1982.)

Before examining the income inequalities in the Soviet Union, we should note that even the very top Soviet elite do not lead the kind of opulent lives the wealthy in the United States and elsewhere live. Lane thinks their life style is comparable to the average living standard in the United States.

According to Lane, Soviet writers justify existing wage and income differences as "necessary in modern society to reward achievement and innovation and to ensure that the most suitable persons are allocated to various roles." (p. 55) Despite that explanation, income differences are being reduced.

Soviet occupations are divided into three broad categories: nonmanual, manual, and peasant (farm). Excluding peasants, the official minimum wage in 1981 was 70 roubles a month, and the average in 1980 was 168.9 roubles. Following are some specific average wages for 1980 (Lane, 1982, p. 55):

Building (construction)	202 roubles
Transport	200 roubles
Education	136 roubles
Science	179 roubles
Administration (government offices, union offices, etc.)	156 roubles

A look at income ratios is even more revealing. Taking the income of skilled workers as 100, the U.S.S.R. and the United Kingdom (Britain) show the following ratios.

	U.S.S.R.	U.K.
Unskilled worker	83	73
Engineer	122	130
Teacher	61	116
Physician	89	161
Clerk	50	80

According to Lane, doctors, engineers, and others do much better than skilled workers in Britain, and considerably better in the United States, where a doctor makes at least four times what skilled workers make. A few individuals make considerably more than the monthly average income of 168.9 roubles.

Top ballet dancers	900 to 1,200 roubles
First Party Secretary	900 roubles
Industry directors	450 to 600 roubles

In addition, these people also receive some free goods and services. Altogether, Marquit (1978) estimates that 0.2 percent of those who work receive over 500 roubles a month. Large as these incomes are, however, they do not reach the 7,000 to 1 income ratios common in capitalist societies.

Income, education, and consumer goods are unequally distributed. High officials in government and industry, professionals, and others give their children more education, read more books and magazines, and exhibit other life-style differences. So there are classes, but relatively small income inequities diminish sharp class differences.

East European socialist societies resemble the Soviet Union. Class differences exist but are less pronounced than in capitalist societies. But they are real and working people resent them. Such class differences, plus a badly managed economy, led to the formation of the Solidarity union in Poland in the early 1980s. The fact that the military and the government crushed the union is a clear indication of class differences and conflicts. (For a history of Poland and Solidarity, see Starski, 1982; see also Sweezy, 1983 for a critique of the class inequalities in Poland.)

In the 1970s in Cuba and China income ratios were 5 to 1 to 3 to 1. That is, managers, doctors, and others made at most 3 to 5 times what the lowest paid worker made. Zimbalist (1975) found that in most Cuban factories and workplaces the income ratio varied from 3.5 to 1 to 2 to 1.

In Chapter 10 we shall see that in both capitalist and socialist societies power is held by a small ruling group. Even though socialist societies have reduced inequalities, classes and a ruling group exist. (See Szymanski, 1981; and Sweezy, 1980.)

Conclusion

Egalitarian societies have existed. But in size, economy, and life style they differ radically from industrial societies. Can we create egalitarian societies in our world?

The answer to this question has many parts. First, the future is not totally determined by the past and the present. Absence of egalitarian societies today does not prohibit their appearance in the future. We will never know if egalitarian societies are possible in our world unless we struggle to create them. They will not arise whole as if by magic. We learn from history that no change and improvement in social conditions has ever taken place without struggle, determination, and much suffering.

Second, we may not eliminate all inequalities, to be sure, but by aiming for egalitarian social conditions we will at least erase some of the most oppressive and unjust social conditions. We can be sure that without a struggle conditions will deteriorate and more injustice will appear.

Third, in capitalist and socialist societies, now and in the future, we must unite with others and work for a world without classes, turn away from a world where a few run the society as the expense of the many. Contemporary socialist societies have made some progress, but they still are a long way from a democracy and egalitarianism. The class struggle has only begun when the economy is taken away from the previous ruling class.

Let me make it very clear that the search for *equality* is not a search for *sameness*. It is often said that there can be no society in which all people are alike. There has not been, cannot be, should not be any such society. A careful study of egalitarian societies, such as the !Kung and the Mbuti, clearly shows that people vary in temperaments, interests, abilities, personalities, and in the amount of material goods they possess. The community acknowledges different abilities, skills, and judgments. People listen to the advice of wise and experienced women and men. This is hardly a world of automatons and robots. What does not exist are unequal opportunities to make a living. There is sharing and cooperation. The land is everyone's common property. All children begin their lives with equal chances to grow up, learn, and develop their capacities and abilities. Differences exist, but they are individual differences, not differences imposed on people by some pre-existing condition like what family they are born into.

Look at our society. You could like ballet; she could prefer baseball; he could prefer to make quilts; I could enjoy taking walks around lakes. You could speak French, she could speak Spanish, he could speak Chinese, and I could speak English. Differences abound. But these differences are matters of taste, choice, and personal history. They need not mean I am better than you, she is better than he. We could still express and retain these individual preferences in a world where material wealth is more equally distributed and where the opportunity to develop skills, talents, and abilities is equally open to everyone. Can we say now that our society provides the children of poor Appalachians or of blacks in urban ghettoes, the same equal opportunity as the children of doctors, corporation executives, or the Rockefellers? Can we justify morally, or even existentially, the death, illness, and suffering of millions of people so that a few others can live in decadent luxury?

We could be equal *and* different. With the essentials of life available to all of us, we could all enjoy nature, develop individual preferences, and live securely. That is equality. The world has known it. It does not today. With uneven success and many setbacks, people everywhere are struggling towards that equality.

Finally, unless we eliminate or drastically reduce class differences, within *and* between nations, we face a precarious future: as individuals, families, communities, societies, and humanity. In addition to reducing inequalities in material possessions, we also must eliminate power differences. As in the societies of our foreparents, there must be no individuals or groups who control and dominate the society.

Summary

Deeply embedded in our collective memories and consciousness are experiences of social class inequalities. A brief survey of inequalities in the 1980s shows they are widespread.

Traditionally, sociologists focus on money and life styles to define social classes. Marxists, on the other hand, focus on people's relationships to the means of production, power, and income-producing wealth in defining classes. Most sociologists list six classes: upper upper, lower upper, upper middle, lower middle, upper lower, and lower lower. A Marxist's list includes: ruling class, managerial class, working class, and the poor. The ruling class owns most of the wealth, and the ruling and the managerial classes receive the highest salaries.

A person's class membership affects all aspects of his or her life—self-image, family, health and illness, childhood and education, marriage, housing, crimes, and language. These and more are related to social class.

Class consciousness, class conflicts, and class struggles characterize capitalist societies. The upper classes benefit at the expense of the lower classes. Upper social classes seek to control the society for their own benefit. Lower classes are conscious (to some degree) of these inequalities and seek to change conditions. Class conflict is inevitable in any class society.

Functionalists argue that social classes exist because they benefit society and allow it to survive. Marxists argue that classes arose and persist because the upper classes use their power to create and perpetuate differences that benefit them. Today, class differences exist in capitalist and socialist societies although the differences between classes have been reduced considerably in socialist societies.

Complete social equality may not be possible in modern societies, but we cannot know if it is unless we struggle to attain it. At the very least, by struggling for equality, we will reduce existing inequalities.

Suggested Readings

Center for Popular Economics (1986). *Economic report of the people*. Boston: South End Press. A thorough and critical review and discussion of the effects of economic conditions in the 1980s on the working class, women, and blacks.

Domhoff, G. William (1983). *Who rules America now?* Englewood Cliffs, NJ: Prentice Hall. An update of Domhoff's *Who rules America?* (1967). He discusses the composition and power of the U.S. ruling class.

Fabricant, Michael & Kelly, Michael (1986, March-May). No haven for the homeless in a heartless economy. *Radical America, 20*(3), 23–25. Poverty and insufficient affordable housing have made more people homeless.

Gilbert, Dennis & Kahl, Joseph (1987). *The American class structure: A new synthesis* (3rd ed.). Chicago: Dorsey. A thorough review and discussion of theories and research on social classes.

Marcuse, Peter (1987, April 4). Why are they homeless? *Nation,* 426–428. He comes to the same conclusions as Fabricant and Kelly.

Oppenheimer, Martin (1985). *White-collar politics.* New York: Monthly Review. Oppenheimer explores the conditions and political prospects of professional, managerial, clerical, sales, and other white-collar workers.

Sweezey, Paul (1951, May and June). The American ruling class. *Monthly Review, 3*(1), 10–17 and *3*(2), 58–64. A concise Marxist statement of classes in the United States, and how the ruling class dominates politics and the economy.

CHAPTER 9

The Transformation of Work

As we noted previously in Chapter 3, people in pre-industrial societies worked only fifteen to twenty hours a week. We do not know how long or how hard peasants in early agricultural societies worked, but in more recent times they seem to have worked unceasingly in order to survive. Early industrial workers put in twelve- to fourteen-hour days, six to seven days a week. Most people now work about forty hours per week, but many people have to work longer and work part-time jobs to supplement their income, or their job (executive, lawyer, doctor) demands more than forty hours of work per week.

Most people do not enjoy their work. This becomes obvious when you read reports where workers speak for themselves. Terkel's *Working* and Pfeffer's *Working for Capitalism,* among many other works, leave no doubt that work is alienating. Also, most jobs do not pay enough for people to be able to reach the American Dream, and many sicken and kill people. For others, the problem is unemployment.

The Joy of Work

Work is more than survival. It can enrich us with a sense of accomplishment and fulfillment; it can be as much play as it is work; and it can satisfy our creativity and imagination. Rip Torn, the actor, told Terkel (1974) that "You work out of necessity, but in your work, you gotta have a little artistry, too." (p. 127)

Work that is not endless, that is performed for oneself and one's family and not corporate profits, that exercises but not exhausts muscles, that causes one to think for oneself and also carry out ideas, such work is liberating. It has existed and still exists, but it is becoming more scarce. In a capitalist society, the management controls jobs and work. Business managers change, eliminate, move, simplify, and routinize jobs, all for profit.

Let us look at some examples (Terkel, 1974). Many of us enjoy gardens; they add meaning to our lives. But millions of Americans still earn their living working the land, providing us with the very stuff of life. They make a meager living, however, a bitter commentary on capitalism, which pays the least to those who do the most necessary work. And the work is dangerous. The damp weather causes rheumatism, arthritis, and bad backs; pesticides cause respiratory diseases; and the intense summer heat gets depressing when you are faced with endless rows of lettuce and a hurting back.

Biffle (Terkel, 1975), who has worked the fields early in the morning picking onions, says, "Your body gets into a strong, smooth rhythm and you take pleasure in the economy and strength of your movements." (p. 270) But as the day wears on, and as you see how little money you make, tiredness, exhaustion, and soreness set in. After six hours of work and thirteen sacks of onions, Biffle made $4.55. Working in the fields as a hired hand, for the profit of landowners (individuals, corporations, conglomerates), makes the producing and gathering of food a physical and emotional drudgery.

But as Roberto Acuna (Terkel, 1974) points out, "Working in the fields is not in itself a degrading job." (p. 38) If the hours were shorter, and the pay and conditions better, it could be pleasant.

And indeed, farm work has been different. Camara Ley (1954) describes his boyhood experiences in an African village, working with the men in the fields.

The movement of the sickles as they rose and fell was astonishingly rapid and regular. They had to cut off the stalk between the last joint and the last leaf at the same time that they stripped the leaf. They almost never missed. This was largely due to the way the reaper held the stalks so as to cut them. Nonetheless, the speed of the sickle was astonishing. . . . (p. 58)

My young uncle was wonderful at rice-cutting, the very best. I followed him proudly, step by step, he handing me the bundles of stalks as he cut them. I tore off the leaves, trimmed the stalks, and piled them. Since the rice is always harvested when it is very ripe, and, if handled roughly the grains drop off, I had to be very careful. Tying the bundles into sheaves was man's work, but, when they had been tied, I was allowed to put them on the pile in the middle of the field. (p. 61)

"Sing with us," my uncle would command.

The tom-tom, which had followed as we advanced into the field, kept time with our voices. We sang as a chorus, now very high-pitched with great bursts of song, and then very low, so low we could scarcely be heard. Our fatigue vanished, and the heat became less oppressive. (p. 56)

Harried by customers and orders, a Greek pizza house owner once told me, with sadness and longing, "we used to dance in the fields" during the reaping of the harvest. Under the right conditions, work can be joyful and playful, as among the Tikopia (Firth, 1936):

As the turmeric is being cleaned the young people pick out and chew an occasional root; the small girl takes a special delight in this, not so much for its aromatic flavour as for the sight of the bright yellow saliva which she dribbles out into a little cup made from a roll of banana leaf. The whole atmosphere is one of labour diversified by recreation at will, and exhibits what even the cold-blooded objective scientist may be allowed to call touches of essential humanity, little humorous asides which, trivial in themselves, constitute nevertheless part of the flesh and blood of the native social relationships. Thus Pa Nukunefu as he digs the turmeric clears away the weeds before him and throws them to the side of the plot. Suddenly he takes a handful and tosses it out into the trees on the slope below him, so that the dirt from the roots sprinkles through the foliage on to the heads of his wife and daughter, who are working a little way down. They look up in some astonishment, see him grinning, and laugh too. (p. 94)

As these examples illustrate, anthropologists have shown that in many societies people work in groups, sharing their experiences, and fusing work, play, creativity, and sometimes religion, into one experience. The picking of lettuce is not in itself either liberating or degrading. Through the exercise of muscles and minds, we take necessity and infuse it with creativity, fun, play, sharing, and cooperation to increase physical survival and make for individual and social enrichment.

Work under Capitalism

People without Work

For millions of Americans, work is a problem because they have none. The money, self-respect, and routine that work provides do not exist for them.

The number of *officially* unemployed Americans has varied in the last four decades. Changing economic conditions determine whether unemployment increases or decreases. From 1950 to the mid-1960s, it was about 5 percent. It went below 4 percent in the late 1960s, between 5 and 6 percent in the early 1970s, and between 6 and 8 in the late 1970s. In the early 1980s, it increased steadily, to 10 percent in 1983, and then began to decrease until it reached 6.5 percent in 1987 and 5.4 in April 1988. The statistics are always at least twice as high for blacks (12.4 percent in April 1988, compared to 4.7 percent for whites), and for black teenagers they range from 40 to 50 percent. In certain regions and cities they range from 15 to 20 percent official unemployment rates. (See *Statistical Abstract,* 1977:387; 1982–1983:376; 1987:391; *Guardian,* June 3, 1987:3; Schor, 1988; Moody, 1988; Sherraden, 1987; and Williams & Kornblum, 1985.)

But these statistics hardly tell the story. Since government statistics are averages for the whole year, they hide much of the reality of people who are unwillingly idle. If we look at how many people were out of work for some period during all of 1981, for example, we see that 20 percent were unemployed (some for many weeks, others for a few weeks). The figure was 24 percent in 1982. In addition, the average duration of unemployment was 15 weeks in 1975, 19.4 weeks in 1983, and 26 weeks in 1984. (See *Guardian,* October 27, 1982:2; *Dollars and Sense,* September 1984:18; and Center for Popular Economics, 1986:32.)

Many people who want to work but cannot find jobs are excluded from these statistics. Among them are the following: people who have lost hope of finding a job and are not actively looking for one; people who work part-time but want and need full-time work (about 5 million in May 1988); those re-entering the work force (such as mothers who took time off to raise young children) but have yet to find a job; and people on welfare, prisoners, and older people whom employers will not hire. At any given time, the actual unemployment rate is at least twice the official rate. In early 1988, estimates of real unemployment ranged from 10.4 percent (Moody, 1988) to 12.4 percent (Schor, 1988). In many black neighborhoods, up to half of the people who want and need to work have no jobs. (See also *Dollars and Sense,* October 1986:18–19, and U.S. Department of Labor, 1983b.)

Part-time workers are highly exploited. Of the estimated twenty-four million people who worked part-time in the mid-1980s, at least a fourth wanted but could not find full-time jobs. Part-time workers have no seniority and can be dismissed at any time; they usually have no benefits such as pension and health insurance; and they receive low wages, in 1985 an average $4.50 an hour versus $7.80 for full-time workers. In addition, in 1985 only 5 percent of full-time workers were paid minimum wages, but 28 percent of part-time workers were (*Dollars and Sense,* July/August 1985:19; *Guardian,* October 15, 1986:3).

The effects of unemployment are devastating. They hit poor and working-class families the hardest, not because these people are more likely to be unemployed but because they have no financial resource to fall back on. Depression, lower self-esteem, illnesses, and suicides all increase. In various surveys, workers report they cannot sleep (20 to 50 percent of them); they smoke and drink more (12 to 25 percent); ulcers and hypertension also trouble many. In a thirty-year study, Brenner found that just a 1 percent rise in unemployment was "followed by a 4.3% rise in suicides, a 5.7% rise in homicides, and a 1.9% increase in overall mortality" from drinking (cirrhosis of the liver) and stress (heart disease) (*Dollars and Sense,* December 1982:9). For many Americans, the threat and reality of unemployment are ever present and affect body and spirit, family and community. In Chapter 5 we saw how communities are devastated when local plants close down or lay off thousands of people. Divorce and other family problems increase. (See Rayman, 1982; Nyhan, 1983b; Leff & Haft, 1983; Kelvin & Jarrett, 1985; and Marquis, 1986.)

We may think that unemployment benefits soothe the pain and lessen financial hardships. They do to some degree. But in 1987 only 35 percent received them. They received 35 to 40 percent of their working wages for twenty-six weeks (*Guardian,* July 15, 1987:9).

Many workers who lose their jobs, especially those over forty-five, will never find work again, or they will find work that pays much less than the jobs they lost. From 1981 to 1986, eleven million workers in various industries were laid off because of plant closings and mass layoffs. What happened to them? A recent U.S. Bureau of Labor Statistics survey found that 18 percent were still without work; many who have jobs work part-time; and 56 percent found jobs at the same or higher pay level. In short, 44 percent were unemployed or made less money (*Guardian,* July 15, 1987:9).

Some areas were especially devastated. Thirty thousand people left the Flint, Michigan, area largely because of layoffs from General Motors. Suicide, alcoholism, and other problems have increased. Many corporations close down their U.S. plants to move to other countries where labor is cheap and easily exploited, but in doing so they traumatize communities and families in the United States. (See Matthiessen, 1984, and Moore, M., 1987.)

With temporary exceptions, unemployment has been a permanent feature of the U.S. economy. It exists primarily for two reasons. First, the existence of millions of unemployed people tends to prevent most of those working from asking for higher wages since they can be replaced easily. Second, in their search for profits, corporations move to wherever labor is cheapest. When they move out of the United States to Mexico, Southeast Asia, or elsewhere jobs are often permanently lost in the United States.

Illness and Death

Many studies show that farm workers, blue-collar workers in factories as well as office workers face injury, illness, and death in their jobs (see Chapter 3 for some details). About twelve thousand people are killed on the job each year, and an estimated one hundred to two hundred thousand die from illnesses they contract at work. Finally, an estimated five to ten million a year become ill from fumes, pesticides, chemicals, electronic office machines, and other workplace hazards. Secretaries, production workers, and farm workers face these dangers—not employers and major stockholders of corporations. (See Berman, 1978; Claybrook, 1984; and *Guardian,* April 9, 1987:1, 8.)

We do not know the true extent of injuries, illnesses, and deaths because corporations underreport them to the Occupational Safety and Health Administration (OSHA). Government reports and news stories in 1986 and 1987 exposed massive and deliberate underreporting. In one shipyard in Rhode Island, injuries and illnesses of more than one hundred workers were not listed by the company on federal injury logs. An article in the *Guardian* (April 8, 1987:1, 8) reported that a meat-packing plant in Nebraska showed 160 injuries for a three-month period, "when the actual number, according to another set of company-maintained records, was 1,800." (See also *Boston Globe,* November 10, 1986:6; July 21, 1987:25, 30.)

Another reason we do not know the extent of illness in the workplace is the long period between exposure to dangerous chemicals and other conditions, and the onset of illness. Asbestos, for example, may take up to thirty years before it destroys lungs and results in death. Many years also lapse between exposure to radiation, chemicals, and other substances, and eventual illness and death (Ritzer & Walczak, 1986).

Let us now look at the dangers specific workers face. Pesticides, herbicides, and other sprays maim and kill many farm workers. *Food and Justice,* the monthly magazine of the United Farm Workers, continually exposes the high levels of these chemicals used on grapes and other fruits and vegetables. They endanger the worker and the consumer. Under present conditions farm work is backbreaking and exhausting. Amazingly, it was only in 1987, after many years of delays by corporate farmers and the government, that farm workers won the right to toilets and clean water while they work in the fields. Meanwhile, the editors of the *Wall Street Journal,* whose restrooms are large, spotless, and gold-plated, advised the farm workers to "rough it." (See *Labor Notes,* March 1987:4, and *Guardian,* February 18, 1987:9.)

Workers in many settings are exposed to dangerous substances. Mine workers breathe coal dust and most eventually get black lungs, becoming sick and old in their 40s and 50s. Workers exposed to asbestos, in shipyards and other places, eventually also have their lungs damaged. Ritzer and Walczak (1986) point out that "A large number of the one-half million people who have worked with asbestos can expect to contract cancer and other diseases. In a study conducted at a Bethlehem Steel shipyard, it was found that over 86 percent of the shipyard workers who worked with asbestos showed signs of lung damage." (p. 416) (See also Bale, 1983.)

There are many other dangerous substances. Vinyl chloride (used in making plastics), cotton dust, radiation, and lead, among many others, endanger the health of millions of workers. Let us look at some examples. In 1987, Chrysler Corporation was fined $1.5 million for safety violations. (OSHA imposes such large fines very rarely.) Two hundred and twenty-five workers had been exposed to dangerous levels of lead and arsenic. In a thermometer plant in Brooklyn, workers were exposed to very high levels of mercury. Many were poisoned while OSHA and New York state agencies did nothing. Workers in the nuclear industry continue to be exposed to lethal doses of radiation. (See *Boston Globe,* July 7, 1987:1, 10, and Dobie & Goodman, 1987.)

Firefighters who clean up toxic waste spills, and other workers exposed to many other substances, may suffer permanent damage to their reproductive organs and bear children with birth defects. Pregnant women who produced microchips were found to have very high rates of miscarriage and other problems. Microchip companies solved the problem by excluding them from such jobs. But men work there still. They are still exposed to the dangers. Women are discriminated against and men are endangered, but the companies do not remove the dangerous substances. (See Bernstein & Blitt, 1986; Barnett, 1986; and Bingham, 1987.)

Marshall (1987) summarizes the problems facing even unborn children:

> *The government estimates that 15 million to 20 million jobs in the United*
> *States expose workers to chemicals that might cause reproductive injury. Ac-*
> *cording to the National Institute for Occupational Safety and Health*
> *(NIOSH), 9 million workers are exposed to radiofrequency/microwave radia-*
> *tion, which causes embryonic death and impaired fertility in animals; at least*
> *500,000 workers are exposed to glycol ethers, known to cause testicular atro-*
> *phy and birth defects in animals; and some 200,000 hospital and industrial*
> *employees work with anesthetic gases and ethylene oxide, both linked to mis-*
> *carriage in humans.*
>
> *No one knows how often workers suffer miscarriage or infertility due to*
> *chemicals in the workplace, or how many of their children are born with de-*
> *fects, but in 1985 the Federal Centers for Disease Control called human re-*
> *productive failure a "widespread and serious" problem, and one of the ten*
> *most prevalent work-related diseases. (p. 532)*

Thousands of other workers, mostly women who are immigrants or illegal aliens, work in sweatshop conditions most people think no longer exist. An estimated 75,000 of them work in 3,000 sweatshops in New York, 1,000 in Los Angeles, and others elsewhere, sewing clothes. A *Dollars and Sense* (April, 1984:6) article describes a nineteenth-century scene in one clothing manufacturer's shop.

> *"Se necesitan operadoras—operators needed," says the sign outside the ware-*
> *house. Inside, the lighting is dim, the noise ear-shattering, the air stale and*
> *full of dust. Tangles of electrical cords hang from the ceiling and run under*
> *work tables covered with bundles of highly flammable cloth. Cartons of cut*
> *goods block narrow aisles littered with more scraps of fabric.*
>
> *Two dozen young Asian and Hispanic women on stools bend over their*
> *Suki or Singer sewing machines, pushing collars, yokes, or sleeves under the*
> *needle at incredible speeds. There are no needle guards. Many of the women*
> *tie scraps of cloth over their mouths to keep out the fine cloth powder blown*
> *by a $10 fan. A few children alternately work and play on the floor near their*
> *mothers.*

Even supposedly clean environments may be dangerous. The high technology and computer industry is an example. There are many toxic chemicals in production facilities. As we saw, women in microchip production have problems with pregnancies. In offices, new machines and poor ventilation threaten many workers, especially women. (See Garson, 1981; *Dollars and Sense,* September 1984:6–7; Hembree, 1985; and *Guardian,* March 12, 1986:6.)

In 1970 Congress enacted the Occupational Health and Safety Act (OSHA), which created an agency to monitor working conditions and to force companies to eliminate dangerous chemicals and other workplace hazards. OSHA has been largely ineffective, primarily because it did not have enough funding, personnel, or enforcement power to inspect workplaces and penalize violators. But it did have some limited effect, it seems. In the chemical industry, for example, there was a 23 percent decrease in occupational injury and illness from 1970 to 1980. This improvement, however, has not held. When Reagan took over in 1981, he decimated OSHA, cutting funding and staff by 25 percent and relaxing, or not enforcing, regulations that controlled cotton dust and various chemicals. Any regulation that might improve working conditions but would cost industry money has been abolished. (See *Guardian,* July 22, 1981:2; April 20, 1983:11; April 15, 1987:6; and Claybrook, 1984.)

Kellogg, Idaho, is just one example. Over two thousand smelter workers were given a choice: accept dangerous working conditions or lose your jobs. Even though the company had made a profit of $25 million in 1980, it refused to spend $880,000 to fix the problem. In 1981, OSHA gave the company an extension of five years before it had to reduce dangerous emissions. Because of high unemployment in the area, (20 percent) and because of OSHA's business bias, 2,100 people were forced to work in a dangerous environment. There is no better evidence that corporate profits are more important than workers' health (*Guardian,* October 7, 1981:2).

The Working-Class Majority

Most social scientists believe that in work and income most Americans now are middle class or white collar and that most American workers are becoming more skilled and more educated. It is true that people are more educated, at least in the number of years they spend in school. By requiring more years of schooling for certain jobs but leaving the jobs unchanged, it can be claimed that jobs require more education and skill. But for most people, in fact, jobs are becoming more routine and repetitive, requiring less use of their minds and creativity.

The claim that most workers are white collar is merely statistical and verbal manipulation. Let us examine Table 9.1. It appears that blue-collar and

TABLE 9.1
Employed Persons by Occupation, 1985 (in thousands)

Occupation	Number of Employees	Percent
White-collar workers	59,082	55.1
Managerial and professional	25,851	24.1
Technical, sales, and administrative support	33,231	31.0
Blue-collar workers	30,156	28.2
Precision, production, craft, and repair	13,340	12.5
Operators, fabricators, laborers	16,816	15.7
Service workers	14,441	13.5
Farming, forestry, and fishing	3,470	3.2

Statistical Abstract, 1987:385–86

farm workers comprise only 31.4 percent of the labor force, barely a third of the total. White-collar workers are 55 percent of the work force and service workers 13.5 percent. But in reality service workers *are* blue-collar workers, in pay and prestige. Levison (1974) argues that "janitors, porters, ushers, elevator operators, doormen, and even shoeshine boys . . . guards, watchmen, cooks, housekeepers, hospital and other attendants, barbers, police, and firemen" are no different from traditional blue-collar workers. (p. 22)

Even among the white-collar group it is obscuring reality to include clerk typists or key punch operators who do nothing but type all day long with doctors, lawyers, and managers. These people share more characteristics with factory workers than with professionals and managers, and they certainly get paid much less. Most sales workers also make little money and share little with professionals and managers.

Among the workers listed in white-collar and service occupations (almost 70 percent) are the following:

    402,000 licensed practical nurses
    5,682,000 sales workers
    779,000 computer equipment operators
    5,002,000 secretaries, stenographers, and typists
    215,000 telephone operators
    694,000 general office clerks
    652,000 police and detectives
    722,000 guards
    1,367,000 waiters and waitresses

These are only a few examples. Millions more work under conditions closer to the factory than to professional and managerial independence. A few of these workers, for example executive secretaries, are closer to management than to workers. But their number is small.

Supposedly, computers have added to the millions of white-collar workers. But the description Beryl Simpson, an airline reservationist, gives of her work, reveals little, if any, difference from a factory assembly line (Terkel, 1974).

> *They brought in a computer called Sabre. It's like an electric typewriter. It has a memory drum and you can retrieve that information forever. Sabre was so expensive, everything was geared to it. Sabre's down, Sabre's up, Sabre's this and that. Everything was Sabre.*
>
> *With Sabre being so valuable, you were allowed no more than three minutes on the telephone. You had twenty seconds, busy-out time it was called, to put the information into Sabre. Then you had to be available for another phone call. It was almost like a production line. We adjusted to the machine. The casualness, the informality that had been there previously were no longer there. The last three or four years on the job were horrible. The computer had arrived. (pp. 82–83)*

Secretarial work, especially in large organizations, is also being subdivided and organized into repetitive and minute tasks. In the past, a company, for example a bank, had twenty-five secretaries, each working for a different person. Under the new system only about half that number are still employed. No one, however, works for any one person. All the secretaries work for everyone. Each becomes a specialist. Some do typing only. They type from taped messages that are recorded on telephone answering machines. If I am an executive and I want a letter typed, I pick up the phone, call a number, and record a message at the other end. Then someone else types it. I may never see the person who types the message. The finished letter is brought to me by a messenger, and I sign it. The secretaries are chained to their typewriters and tape machines. Other secretaries only answer telephones, others only make appointments, and so on. Routine and impersonal jobs are replacing jobs that gave secretaries a variety of work and some room for creativity. Work becomes alienating, but company profits go up because fewer secretaries are needed (Braverman, 1974).

Many professional and technical occupations also are changing. People are supervised closely by others and perform routine jobs. Computer specialists, pharmacists, and social workers are being subdivided into more positions and are doing less skilled work. They approximate the working conditions of factory and office workers. Computer work began as highly skilled and independent work, but it has been subdivided into system analysis, programming, and coding (the last is fairly routine work). Table 9.2 shows salaries for analysts starting at $29,141, programmers at $20,832, and computer operators at $13,727. Pharmacists once were independent owners who dispensed drugs and advice. Oppenheimer (1985) points out that now, most pharmacists work for chains and do little more than "move drugs from a larger to a smaller container and type a label." (p. 141)

Social workers also are divided in three groups: those with a Master's degree who hold supervisory positions and practice therapy (and who are pressuring states to license practitioners thus excluding those at lower levels); those with a Bachelor's degree; and those with Associate's degrees who perform semi-clerical duties, for example dispensing public assistance (welfare). These three professions illustrate the general tendency to subdivide, deskill, and routinize work. (See Oppenheimer, 1985, and Szymanski & Goertzel, 1979.)

Pay and Prestige

We saw in Chapter 8 that most jobs pay much less than the income required for what most people, and the government, consider a comfortable life style. But since the mid-1970s, the real pay (discounting for inflation and considering what we can buy with a dollar) of most workers has declined.

Consider some of these statistics. The minimum wage was not raised from 1981 to 1987. Because of inflation, it was effectively reduced by 27 percent. In terms of purchasing power, it was at the lowest level in thirty

TABLE 9.2
Annual Incomes of Some Occupations (various years)

Chief executive officers (CEOs) of
seven corporations, 1984
(compensation from
salary, bonus, and stock gains)

Mesa Petroleum	$22,956,000
Humana Hospitals	$17,921,000
Toys "Я" Us	$11,070,000
Chrysler Corp.	$ 5,510,000
City National Bank	$ 3,170,000
Ralston Purina	$ 3,057,000
Sears, Roebuck	$ 2,131,000
Physicians (median earnings, 1984)	
Gross median earnings	$ 181,300
All incorporated physicians (median *net* earnings)	$ 119,000
All unincorporated physicians (median *net* earnings)	$ 78,000
Attorneys (average salaries, 1986)	
Level 1 (starting)	$ 31,014
Level 6 (highest)	$ 101,169
Engineers (average salaries, 1986)	
Level 1 (starting)	$ 27,866
Level 4 (largest group)	$ 42,677
Level 8 (highest)	$ 79,021
Computer fields (average salaries, 1986)	
System analyst 1 (lowest)	$ 29,832
System analyst 6 (highest)	$ 71,770
Computer programmer 1 (lowest)	$ 20,832
Computer programmer 5 (highest)	$ 42,934
Computer operator 1 (lowest)	$ 13,727
Computer operator 5 (highest)	$ 28,986
College and university faculty (average salaries, 1986)	
Public institutions	
Instructor (lowest)	$ 20,900
Professor (highest)	$ 42,300
Private institutions	
Instructor	$ 19,800
Professor	$ 47,000
Public school teachers (average salaries, 1986)	
Elementary	$ 24,800
Secondary	$ 26,100
Secretaries and typists (average income, 1986)	
Secretaries	
Level 1 (lowest)	$ 16,326
Level 5 (highest)	$ 28,051
Typists (only two levels are given)	
Level 1	$ 12,584
Level 2	$ 16,854
Average annual pay, 1985, for workers in	
Construction	$ 21,351
Mining	$ 31,326
Manufacturing	$ 23,859
Retail trade	$ 10,732
Government	$ 20,250
Services	$ 16,840
Median earnings for 52 weeks, 1987, of 6 million service workers	
(except private household and protective)	$ 11,180

Statistical Abstract, 1987:93, 126, 145; U.S. Department of Labor, 1986e, 1986g, 1987e; and
Byrne, 1985

years. Also, a few million workers are not covered even by this low minimum wage ($3.35 in 1987). The real hourly wages for workers fell 8.7 percent from 1973 to 1987. The real earnings of men twenty to twenty-four years of age dropped by 30 percent from 1973 to 1984.

Workers in many occupations have had significant wage cuts. Greyhound bus drivers saw their wages reduced by 30 to 40 percent from their 1983 levels. New airline flight attendants were hired at 40 percent less than new attendants had been hired in the past. And the standard wage of 175,000 meatpackers fell from $10.69 an hour in 1980 to $8.50 in 1985. With inflation of about 15 percent, the cut was even more severe. (See *Dollars and Sense,* April 1987:17, 22; July/August 1987:6; *Guardian,* April 9, 1986:5; June 17, 1987:5, *Labor Notes,* April 1987:4; Moody, 1987; and Kuttner, 1987b.)

Wages have been reduced but corporate profits have not. "Since 1980, real after-tax profits have grown an average 12.2% a year, compared with a pre-1973 average growth of 3.1%" (*Dollars and Sense,* May 1987:7). Meanwhile, workers were not less productive. In fact, there was a modest rise in productivity. If wages had risen according to productivity, in 1987 workers would have been making about $1,000 more a year. Thus, real wages have been reduced to increase corporate profits, not because corporations were losing money or workers were less productive (*Dollars and Sense,* May 1987:7–8).

Table 9.2 shows some specific and average incomes of different occupations in the mid-1980s. You notice that corporation presidents reward themselves handsomely. Managers and professionals receive less, but still much more than working-class people do. You will also notice that, once we get past system analysts, average annual incomes for all occupations, college professors to salespeople, range from the low teens to the low forties. It is on this basis that we can conclude that economically most people belong to the working class.

Keep in mind that we cannot list in Table 9.2 the *earnings* for wealthy people since they are in the form of dividends from stocks, bonds, and other investments, which are not public information. These earnings reach into the many millions of dollars. Also, the incomes are *national averages*. Incomes differ from region to region and workplace to workplace; some people make much more than others in the same occupation.

A survey conducted in Baltimore in the 1970s shows that most people do not rank workers with managers and professionals (Bose & Rossi, 1983). (Corporation presidents are missing from this list.) People were asked to rank the social standing (prestige) of many occupations, on a scale of 10 (highest) to 0 (lowest). The averages of all responses were multiplied by 10. We see in Table 9.3 that the prestige people attach to occupations relates to the income and class of that occupation.

TABLE 9.3
Prestige Ratings of Occupations in the United States

Occupations	Baltimore, 1970s	National, 1972–83
Physician	95.8	82
Lawyer	90.1	76
Electrical engineer	79.5	69
Accountant	71.2	57
Elementary school teacher	65.4	60
Social worker	63.2	52
Police officer	58.5	48
Carpenter	53.5	40
Office secretary	51.3	46
Telephone operator	46.2	40
Bus driver	—	32
Truck driver	—	32
Assembly line worker	28.3	—
Waiter/waitress	22.1	20
Garbage collector	16.3	17
Janitor	12.5	16

Bose and Rossi, 1983; and *General Social Surveys, 1972–1983: Cumulative Codebook, 1983*

The Transformation of the Working Class

The reduction in real average earnings of the U.S. working class is the result of a massive shift in the kinds of jobs created by U.S. corporations. The percentage of low-paying jobs has increased dramatically over the last four decades.

Tables 9.4 and 9.5, together, show the size and significance of the transformation of the U.S. economy. In Table 9.4 we see that jobs in category 1, which we could label blue-collar occupations, have decreased from about 50 percent of all jobs in 1949 to about 30 percent in 1987. If the percentage had stayed at 50, it would mean that in 1987 over 20 million more jobs would belong to this category. Category 2 includes white-collar and service jobs. They have increased by 16 percent. Government jobs have grown by 3.4 percent.

Table 9.5 interprets this occupational shift. Both in 1949 and 1987, category 1 positions paid much better than those in category 2. Indeed, most of the job increase in category 2 has been in retail trade, clerical, and service occupations, which, as we saw in both tables 9.2 and 9.5, pay 50 to 100 percent less than most blue-collar jobs do, especially those in union plants.

Therefore, millions of working-class families no longer have an income that can support the stable life style that developed in working-class cities and suburbs after World War II. In 1985 dollars, the median family income that was $14,832 in 1950 increased steadily to a high of $29,172 by 1973. Then, with small annual increases and decreases, in 1985 it decreased to $27,735.

TABLE 9.4
Employment by Industry, 1949, 1978, and 1987*
(in thousands and percent)

Industries	1949	1978	1987
Mining, construction, manufacturing, transportation, and public utilities	21,566 (49.5%)	30,240 (35.2%)	30,383 (29.8%)
Wholesale and retail trade, finance, insurance, real estate, services	16,330 (37.3%)	40,050 (45.5%)	54,677 (53.6%)
Government	5,856 (13.2%)	15,476 (20.3%)	16,966 (16.6%)
Total	43,754 (100%)	85,763 (100%)	102,026 (100%)

Monthly Labor Review, May 1979:73; May 1987:68
* Agriculture exluded.

TABLE 9.5
Average Weekly Earnings by Industry Division, 1949 and 1987

Industry Division	1949	1987
Mining	$65.66	$522.92
Construction	65.27	417.38
Manufacturing	53.12	402.87
Transportation and public utilities	—	460.60
Wholesale trade	40.80*	362.33
Retail trade	—	174.24
Services	—	270.48
Finance, insurance, and real estate	45.48	315.95

Monthly Labor Review, May 1980:77; May 1987:71
* In 1949, wholesale and retail trade were combined.

Family income doubled from 1950 to 1973, but it went down 9.5 percent from 1973 to 1985.

Younger families are suffering the most from these low-paying service, clerical, and retail jobs. According to Moody (1988), "A recent study by the Congressional Budget office showed that while the real income of families headed by a person 25 to 34 years old dropped 7 percent between 1973 and 1986, it dropped 43 percent for those headed by persons under 25" (p. 1)

For millions of families, even the lower 1985 income is only possible because both spouses work, in contrast to the 1950s and 1960s when family income came from the husband's blue-collar job. Increasingly, the husband works in a service occupation and the wife in a clerical or sales job. Sometimes their combined income is less than his alone had been. Most of the new jobs in clerical and sales occupations, and many in the services, have been filled by women. And women who are the main or sole supporters of their families find themselves in an even worse financial situation. Their income comes from only *one* job in category 2 occupations. (For a general discussion of these issues, see the sources below, and also Faux, 1983; Montgomery, 1985; and Vail, 1987.)

What has caused this massive shift away from manufacturing, blue-collar jobs? There are three possible explanations. One, productivity has increased. A worker produces more goods per hour now than he or she did in the past. Thus, fewer workers produce the same number of goods. Two, the United States exports fewer goods. Other capitalist societies have developed their economies and can compete better with U.S. companies in selling throughout the world today than they did before. The U.S. economy is no longer as dominant as it was during the two decades after World War II. Thus, we export fewer goods and we import more, which means fewer production jobs are available. Third, and probably most important, U.S. companies have been moving plants and exporting jobs to countries where they can pay workers much less than they pay American workers. Often, workers in poor countries make as much or less in a *week* as American workers receive for one *day*. U.S. companies export manufacturing jobs thus reducing the number of jobs in the United States. (See next chapter for more details on this issue.)

Let us now examine some recent developments in this occupational and class change. Stories and details on it appear in different types of publications. A short item in *Parade* (*Boston Globe,* August 12, 1984) magazine, which is an insert in many Sunday newspapers, noted in 1984 that according to a study by the U.S. Department of Labor "in the next 13 years, the largest number of new jobs will be for building custodians (779,000), cashiers (744,000), secretaries (719,000), general office clerks (696,000), and sales clerks (687,000). Relatively few of these jobs call for education beyond high school." (p. 12) Or, they could have added, pay very much.

A study (*Guardian,* December 31, 1986:6) sponsored by the U.S. Congress in 1986 concluded that since 1979, about 60 percent of new workers earned $7,000 or less a year. They hold sales, service, and clerical positions. During 1985, "the retail industry grew the most, adding 700,000 jobs over the last year alone. Within this category, for example, clothing stores hired 50,000 new employees even while employment at U.S. clothing manufacturers fell by 16,000. In the last year finance, insurance, and real estate added 300,000 workers. Consumer services like hotels swelled by 1,000,000 jobs . . ." (*Dollars and Sense,* October 1986:7).

From 1979 to 1986, factory employment decreased by two million jobs. Most of the new jobs, up to 90 percent by some estimates, were in services. This trend continued in 1987. *Labor Notes* (June, 1987) gives this estimate: "Two-thirds of all new jobs created during the first quarter [of 1987] were in the two lowest-paying job categories—retail trade and health and business services." (p. 4) In retail trades, the average income in 1987 was $9,060, almost $2,000 below the poverty level of $11,000 for a family of four. (See also *Guardian,* January 14, 1987:5; February 4, 1987:7.)

Let us look at new jobs created in two states. According to the *Guardian* (July 20, 1988:4), in Arizona, from 1980 to 1985, employers hired twelve cashiers for every computer programmer, and in Connecticut in 1987, the ration was fourteen to one.

Projections of job growth for the years 1978 to 1990 tell the same story. The 350,000 new computer programmers are far out-numbered by the 600,000 janitors and 800,000 workers in fast-food establishments (Pincus, 1984).

The rise of the computer bodes ill for most workers who use them, in pay, jobs eliminated, and working conditions. A *Dollars and Sense* (June, 1986:12) article succinctly describes how computers affect office work.

Low tech data and word processing involves simple and repetitive keyboarding procedures, and takes place in the "back offices" of banks, insurance firms, utility companies, and the form-processing offices of the government. Known as "system processing centers," these offices house rows of women lined up behind computer terminals. The rooms are fluorescent-lit, huge, and windowless. Amenities such as private space, free time, or telephones are few.

In economists' jargon, office automation is "labor-saving," a peculiar term which really means labor-displacing. By replacing "back office" workers with machines, employers can increase productivity while they cut down on labor costs. An example of a major time savings system is mail-processing, where a machine opens a letter and displays it on a screen. The video display terminal (VDT) operator then pushes a sequence of buttons, and selects the appropriate form letter response. This is then automatically inserted into an envelope and sent down a mail chute. One worker, using this machine, can answer thousands of pieces of mail in a day.

Indeed, computers and telecommunications systems allow office work to be performed in people's homes or even outside the United States. The work is performed there and transmitted to central corporate locations. Some people argue that a mother who can do office work at home can benefit by a flexible schedule and also care for her children. In fact, however, home workers are paid on a piecework basis, which is usually much less than workers on salary receive per hour. They also have no benefits such as health insurance and pension. They are exploited.

Computers also make it possible for the office work of a company in New York to be done on a Caribbean island, or anywhere else, and be transmitted back to New York by telecommunication. Berch (1985) cites some examples from the *Wall Street Journal*.

West Publishing Company, St. Paul, Minnesota, sends some material to South Korea, where non-English speaking workers key-punch complex legal documents into the firm's Westlaw data bank. Barbados workers earn $2.50 an hour keypunching data into American Airlines computers. The work was previously done in Tulsa, Oklahoma, by 200 workers who made $6.50 an hour.

> . . . *American's Barbados unit saved the airline more than $3.5 million in 1983, its first full year of operation. (p. 45)*

Computers and telecommunications are used to exploit workers both in the United States and other countries. (See also Fuentes & Ehrenreich, 1983.)

The trend is clear: Working-class jobs are changing and paying less.

Work and Alienation

We work during most of our awake hours. Work pervades our existence. Our experiences during those hours affect our bodies and spirits, our families, our communities. We work out of necessity, but joy and creativity are essential to our lives also. When work become a drudgery, we suffer.

Essential aspects of our humanity are taken away from us when work is routine, monotonous, and very specialized, when others dictate to us our every move, when we lose control over what we make or the service we provide, and when others profit by our labor. *Work alienation* is the lack of control over what we do and how we do it, the loss of control of what we produce, the separation of action from thought. We feel we are estranged from our work. More generally, alienation refers to the feeling of estrangement and separation from the surrounding community. This feeling results from objective conditions that cause alienation. (See Chapter 5 on community.)

Aspects of Jobs

Some of you may reflect on jobs you or people you know have had and realize that you liked these jobs. It is important that we clarify the aspects of any given job we like or dislike.

Money

Some jobs, for example, writing commercials, pay very well. People may like these jobs for that reason. But the work itself may be very alienating. Other jobs, such as auto worker, may pay enough to keep body and soul together, even to permit some comforts, but the work itself is destructive of body and mind. Liking the job because of the pay is not the same as finding the work itself fulfilling.

Prestige

Some jobs are considered prestigious, and people like them for that reason. Jobs such as president and manager are more prestigious than factory worker or dishwasher. People like jobs because of the prestige. The power to control the work of others seems to give prestige to these positions. The work itself, however, may be full of pressures and compromises and leave its scars on emotions and feelings.

Friendships

Many of us make friends where we work. We like some of the people we work with and look forward to seeing them regularly—even see them evenings and weekends. But these satisfactions are not intrinsic to the work itself; they arise despite the work and working conditions (such as rules that prohibit talking while on the job or that allow two minutes to go to the bathroom). When people say they like their job, they may mean that they have defied dehumanizing working conditions and created a humane setting despite all obstacles.

Work

Finally, of course, we may in fact like the work itself (often, again, despite all pressures to not become involved and creative). The work may allow us to think about what we do, to be creative, and to plan and control our day. There can be satisfaction in the quality of a product we make or the service we provide because we have control over it and can use our minds. Under capitalism, there are fewer and fewer such jobs every year, as the drive toward minute division of labor continues inexorably. Some people manage to find and create jobs they like, such as the mason and the firefighter (see Terkel, 1974). A few others leave the money and prestige of some jobs and seek work they find satisfying, many returning to farming, for example. (Such solutions are possible for a few, but if work is to become meaningful and enriching for all, the only solutions are collective and cooperative efforts in a socialist society. A few people going to Vermont to farm will not liberate the vast majority in factories and offices.)

Any given job may possess none, one, or more of these qualities. We should be clear on the reasons we like or hate any given job.

Historical Changes

Even in the brief history of the United States there has been a profound transformation in working conditions. A few studies of American communities in the 1920s and 1930s document the changes in work. At that time the transformation of work to its present form was almost complete, but people had a living memory of different conditions. Two of the best studies are *Middletown* (Muncie, Indiana, by Lynd & Lynd, 1929), and *Yankee City* (Newburyport, Massachusetts, by Warner, 1963).

Consider the statistics on self-employment. In the early 1800s, about 80 percent of working Americans were self-employed; after that, the figures decrease drastically: only 33 percent in 1870, 20 percent in 1940, 10 percent in 1970, and 8.5 percent in 1985. This means that people who were independent farmers, store owners, and craftsmen went to work for others. For most people today, working for others is all they have ever known. Instead of learning the skills of farming or of a trade over years, people can spend years in school and then get a job they can learn to perform in a few days.

The changes in the making of shoes provide a clear case study of what has happened to work over the last three centuries. This description is found in Warner's (1963) study of Newburyport, Massachusetts.

From Cobbler's Bench to Assembly Line

During the first years of the settlement of Yankee City and New England and in the earliest phase of shoemaking, families made their own shoes. The second phase of the first stage was characterized by the itinerant shoemaker who, owning his own tools, made shoes in the kitchen of his customer, using materials supplied by the customer. In the process, the shoemaker was assisted by his customer's family and received his compensation largely in the form of board and lodging. Many families in Yankee City and in the outlying communities, particularly those dwelling on the north bank of the river, became proficient in the art of shoemaking at this stage. They made their own shoes during the winter months, passing down the art in the home from generation to generation. This section of New England has, therefore, a strong tradition of shoemaking.

The next stage began (circa 1760) when the shoemaker set up a small shop and made shoes to order for his local customers. These shops were known as "the ten-foot shops," and the customer's order was known as "bespoke." During the first part of this period, the shoemaker still made the complete shoe, but his relation with the market became indirect. The entrepreneur appeared. He was a capitalist shoemaker, hiring workers in their homes to make boots and shoes for him to sell at retail or wholesale. In the second phase of the period the central shop developed where materials were sorted. The parts were cut in the shop, distributed and served in the homes, then collected and the soles joined to the uppers in the shop. Machines were used scarcely at all. The processes of shoemaking were divided, and workmen specialized in one or more operations. Jobs were thus defined within the industry; for the most part, the worker no longer faced his customers.

During this period the market remained local, and the interests of the merchant-master and the journeyman were the same. When improved land and water transportation brought about an expansion of the market, the merchant became an increasingly dominant figure. The bargain became one of price as well as quality, and the interest of the merchant to produce cheaply in order to undersell competitors began to conflict with the maker's desire to earn as much as he could from his labor. . . . In 1852 a sewing machine for stitching uppers was invented, and the following decade saw the mechanization of many other processes. This development intensified the split in interests between the owner-control group and the operatives; it also established the subordinate position of the latter, which they have occupied ever since. . . . The security of the workers as craftsmen was threatened by the new developments. The shoe workers did not make the machines they were suddenly forced to operate, and they had no way of predicting what jobs would next be mechanized. The owning group had in the machines an effective weapon to lessen the value of the worker's craftsmanship. (pp. 275–277)

Since the 1850s, the trend has been one of further subdivision of work, more routine tasks and less control by workers, and total control of the planning of the making of shoes by management. One need not romanticize the life of the cobblers in order to see that their work was more meaningful than that of the modern operatives in a shoe factory. (Having taken over total control of conception and planning, management moved production out of New England to cheaper labor markets, when workers unionized. Few shoe factories remain in New England.)

People resisted this drastic change in their lives. Working in factories, under the conditions and control of employers concerned only with profits, was not accepted readily by formerly independent people. There was much resistance. Indeed, many of the first people who worked in factories were forced into such work. In England, where industrialization began, most industries got their workers from prisons, workhouses, and orphanages. Indeed, Pollard (Braverman, 1974) says, "The modern industrial proletariat was introduced to its role not so much by attraction or monetary reward, but by compulsion, force and fear." (p. 66) Factory work was resisted by most people, and so early capitalists turned to captive populations. These conditions of slave labor were "the forerunner of the company town in the United States in the recent past as one of the most widely used systems of total control before the rise of industrial unionism." (p. 67)

The coming of industrial capitalism affected people's lives in many ways (Lynd & Lynd, 1929). People not only felt demeaned because of their work but their family life was also altered as parents began spending less and less time with their children. Ties with family, friends, and community were also weakened as companies relocated plants.

Over the last thirty years there have been further changes in the United States labor force. Industry is reducing the number of skilled jobs. Some are being automated; others are being moved overseas (as are many unskilled jobs). American workers are increasingly forced to take unskilled and service jobs, that pay much lower than skilled industrial jobs.

The Experience of Alienation

Philosophers, sociologists, and others have debated whether workers are really alienated. Many have questioned the Marxist claim that people find their jobs destructive and degrading. Some sociologists have concluded that most people are relatively happy with their jobs.

Both formal studies and informal observations reveal that work for many, if not most, people ranges from boring to profoundly alienating. Blauner (Braverman, 1974) comments, "The average worker is able to make an adjustment to a job which, from the standpoint of an intellectual appears to be the epitome of tedium." (p. 29) In short, workers learn to live with boring jobs. Other studies and reports also find profound alienation with work. Surveys reported in *Work in America* show such alienation. By asking people if they would choose the same job if they were starting their work life from the beginning, researchers found that except for professionals, most people would not do the same work again. Only 43 percent of white-collar workers and 24 percent of blue-collar workers would choose the same work.

Other, more personal accounts of workers reveal the meaning and feeling of alienation. Studs Terkel's *Working* unearths deep wounds and buried dreams.

> *This book, being about work, is, by its very nature, about violence—to the spirit as well as to the body. It is about ulcers as well as accidents, about shouting matches as well as fistfights, about nervous breakdowns as well as kicking the dog around. It is, above all (or beneath all), about daily humiliations. To survive the day is triumph enough for the walking wounded among the great many of us.*
>
> *It is about a search, too, for daily meaning as well as daily bread, for recognition as well as cash, for astonishment rather than torpor; in short, for a sort of life rather than a Monday through Friday sort of dying. Perhaps immortality, too, is part of the quest. To be remembered was the wish, spoken and unspoken, of the heroes and heroines of this book.*
>
> *For the many, there is a hardly concealed discontent. The blue-collar blues is no more bitterly sung than the white-collar moan. "I'm a machine," says the spot-welder. "I'm caged," says the steelworker. "A monkey can do what I do," says the receptionist. "I'm less than a farm implement," says the migrant worker. "I'm an object," says the high-fashion model. Blue collar and white call upon the identical phrase: "I'm a robot." "There is nothing to talk about," the young accountant despairingly enunciates. (pp. xiii–xiv)*

The workers themselves are no less eloquent in pouring out their feelings and thoughts:

> *Sharon Atkins, Receptionist*
> *The machine dictates. This crummy little machine with buttons on it—you've got to be there to answer it. You can walk away from it and pretend you don't hear it, but it pulls you. You know you're not doing anything, not doing a hell of a lot for anyone. Your job doesn't mean anything. Because you're just a little machine. A monkey could do what I do. It's really unfair to ask someone to do that. (p. 59)*

> *Eddie Jaffee, Press Agent*
> *The occupation molds your personality. Publicity does that to people too. Calling an editor on the phone, asking favors, can be humiliating. Being refused a favor disturbs me, depresses me. That's why I could never resign myself to being a press agent. Many are not aware they're being turned down. They wouldn't develop colitis like I did. That's the way I act, emotionally, with my gut. That's why I went to the analyst. (p. 128)*

> *Phil Stallings, Spot Welder at an Auto Plant*
> *I don't like the pressure, the intimidation. How would you like to go up to*

someone and say, "I would like to go to the bathroom?" If the foreman
doesn't like you, he'll make you hold it, just ignore you. Should I leave this
job to go to the bathroom I risk being fired. The line moves all the time. . . .

I don't understand how come more guys don't flip. Because you're nothing
more than a machine when you hit this type of thing. They give better care to
that machine than they will to you. They'll have more respect, give more attention to that machine. And you know this. Somehow you get the feeling that
the machine is better than you are. (Laughs.). . . .

Proud of my work? How can I feel pride in a job where I call a foreman's
attention to a mistake, a bad piece of equipment, and he'll ignore it. Pretty
soon you get the idea they don't care. You keep doing this and finally you're
titled a troublemaker. So you just go about your work. You have to have
pride. So you throw it off to something else. And that's my stamp collection.
(pp. 222–225)

Levison (1974) shows different working-class jobs present different problems. Some jobs, such as doormen and guards, "are simply dull or repetitive
without being physically arduous." (p. 58) Other jobs, such as garbage collecting and loading and unloading trucks, involve heavy, dirty work, but the
workers are not tied to an assembly line. Then there are the classic assembly-
line jobs, in the auto industry, electronics, textiles, canning, and so on. Here
the problems of alienation are the most severe. Next highest on the alienation
scale are skilled machine operators who are not tied to an assembly line. Truck
and bus drivers are in the same position as skilled factory workers. "Finally,
there are the skilled craftsmen, the carpenters, electricians, auto mechanics,
etc., who have considerable knowledge and whose jobs involve a good deal of
independent judgment." (p. 59) Levison concludes that despite these differences, most of these people are alienated from their work because they are
treated more like machines than like people.

But Levison is mistaken in one respect: alienation is not limited to
working-class jobs. Many middle-class workers experience alienation, and, as
Braverman shows, many white-collar jobs are becoming more like those in a
factory.

In contrast, there are some sociologists that claim most workers are
relatively happy with their work. Nettler (1976) has summarized most of the
surveys done over the last 25 years on workers' attitudes about their work. It
is said that in western industrial societies only one-eighth of the workers report
dissatisfaction with their jobs. Nettler summarizes one survey:

A more recent test of the "work-alienation" hypothesis is contained in the results of the Survey Research Center's 1971 poll of a representative sample of
American adults on the "quality of their lives." In keeping with the reviews by
Hoppock and others . . . 90 percent of the respondents say that it is "very
true" or "somewhat true" that their "work is interesting," 75 percent say that
"the pay is good," 93 percent find that their jobs give them "a lot of chances
to make friends," 81 percent that at work "the physical surroundings are
pleasant," and 77 percent that "the job security is good."

As regards self-fulfillment, 76 percent say that it is "very true" or "somewhat true" that "I have an opportunity to develop my own special abilities," and 79 percent that "I am given a chance to do the things I do best." (p. 181)

There are two possible explanations for this disparity between sociologists' points of view on work and alienation. First, the opposing conclusions rise out of different kinds of research. Those studies showing relative worker contentment use survey methods—a researcher sends out hired interviewers who ask workers prearranged questions. The setting does not allow for a gradual acquaintanceship of the two people talking, for reflection, for revelations of deep feelings. Books like *Working,* on the other hand, are the result of many long personal encounters. Terkel talked to the workers himself. He did not interview people; they just talked, sharing experiences and emotions. The setting (bars, homes, and so on) and the informality of the situation allowed for the surfacing of inner feelings. "The talk was idiomatic rather than academic. In short, it was conversation. In time, the sluice gates of dammed-up hurts and dreams were opened." (p. xxv) People explored their lives and unearthed buried feelings. "On one occasion, during the play-back of the tape-recorded talk, my companion murmured in wonder, 'I never realized I felt that way'." (p. xxiii)

The second explanation for the differing conclusions on worker alienation is equally significant. It refers to the difference between what people learn to endure because they see no other choice, and their intrinsic needs, what people would like to do if they could. Hobart Foote (Terkel, 1974), a utility man in an automobile factory, said of younger workers: "And those other people when they settle down one of these days, they'll be what we call old-timers. He'll want to work. Number one: the pay's good. Number two: the benefits are good." (p. 235) Foote meant he had learned to adjust to the work, to endure the humiliations he described, because he must; he had a family to feed. But he does not *want* to work. It is the difference between, as the Queen in *Alice in Wonderland* said, "I like what I get" and "I get what I like." Foote revealed what he really felt about his work when he said later that, after seventeen years, he had thirteen more before he could retire. "Thirteen more years with the company, it'll be thirty and out. When I retire, I'm gonna have me a little garden. A placed down South. Do a little fishin', huntin', sit back, watch the sun come up, the sun go down. Keep my mind occupied." (p. 239) He is like a person waiting for his prison sentence to end. What does it tell about a man's work when he spends the prime of his life waiting for work to be over? Does he want to work? Does the pay compensate for the destruction of his hopes and dreams?

Working and other books are also inspiring because of their abundant evidence that workers' dreams and hopes persist. Most people in *Working* expressed the desire to do something that is creative, freeing, useful, and meaningful. Sharon Atkins, a receptionist, wants to refinish furniture; Louis

Haywar, a washroom attendant, wants to write; everyone wants something more than a job. Nora Watson, in a few words, captured the essence of the problem missed by countless social-science research studies: "I think most of us are looking for a calling, not a job. Most of us, like the assembly line worker, have jobs that are too small for our spirit. Jobs are not big enough for people." (p. xxix)

Conception and Execution

At the center of alienation is the loss of control over what we do and how we do it. As human beings, we need to think, plan, and imagine the work we do and then carry it out. We need to conceive and to execute our work. So long as we retain control, we are engaged in a human activity. As soon as we begin to lose the thinking function and perform only the physical labor, we lose part of our humanity.

Capitalists have always sought to control the work process. Centralizing production in factories was the first step; employers later dictated to workers the methods they should use to carry out their work. However, it was not until Frederick Taylor, the father of so-called scientific management, that a detailed theory for the total control of workers' labor was developed. According to Braverman (1974), "Taylor raised the concept of control to an entirely new plane when he asserted as an *absolute necessity for adequate management the dictation to the worker of the precise manner in which work is to be performed*" (italics in original). (p. 90)

While working for Bethlehem Steel Company (around 1900), Taylor found that men loading pig iron averaged twelve-and-one-half long tons per man per day. But careful study, Taylor (Braverman, 1974) claimed, showed they could load forty-seven to forty-eight. The task was to persuade the men they could load the higher tonnage and "to see that the men were happier and better contented when loading the new rate. . . ." (p. 103) They chose Schmidt, a man who was strong and sturdy and "mentally sluggish" to be the first who would try to produce the higher rate. He was told that if he agreed to carry out his work exactly as he was told, his wages would increase from $1.15 a day to $1.85 (a 60 percent increase in pay for a 300 percent increase in production). Taylor (Braverman, 1974) continued the explanation:

> "Well, if you are a high-priced man, you will do exactly as this man tells you tomorrow, from morning till night. When he tells you to pick up a pig and walk, you pick it up and you walk, and when he tells you to sit down and rest, you sit down. You do that right straight through the day. And what's more, no back talk. Now a high-priced man does just what he's told to do, and no back talk. Do you understand that? When this man tells you to walk, you walk; when he tells you to sit down, you sit down, and you don't talk back at him. Now you come on to work here to-morrow morning and I'll know before night whether you are really a high-priced man or not."

Schmidt started to work, and all day long, and at regular intervals, was told by the man who stood over him with a watch, "Now pick up a pig and walk. Now sit down and rest. Now walk—now rest," etc. He worked when he was told to work, and rested when he was told to rest, and at half-past five in the afternoon had his 47½ tons loaded on the car. And he practically never failed to work at this pace and do the task that was set him during the three years that the writer was at Bethlehem. (pp. 105–106)

In a footnote, Braverman (1974) comments:

Georges Friedmann reports that in 1927 a German physiologist, reviewing the Schmidt experience, calculated that the level of output set by Taylor could not be accepted as a standard because "most workers will succumb under the pressure of these labors." Yet Taylor persisted in calling it "a pace under which men become happier and thrive." We should also note that although Taylor called Schmidt "a man of the type of the ox," and Schmidt's stupidity has become part of the folklore of industrial sociology, Taylor himself reported that Schmidt was building his own house, presumably without anyone to tell him when to stand and when to squat. But a belief in the original stupidity of the worker is a necessity for management; otherwise it would have to admit that it is engaged in a wholesale enterprise of prizing and fostering stupidity. (p. 108)

The total control of the work process continues, despite talk about humanizing the workplace. Most people, in factories and increasingly in offices, find that Taylorism is accepted and practiced implicitly as the method of organizing work under capitalism. Management controls and dictates each step of the work process. Scientific and technical knowledge, of course, is necessary. But when the owners, experts, and managers are the only ones possessing such knowledge, they control the workers and the work process. They can then dictate to the workers what they must do. Braverman goes on to explain that some division of work exists in every society, but nowhere is it carried to the extremes found in the capitalist division of labor, where both the degree of the division, and the conception and control of it by management, dehumanize workers. (See Terkel, 1974, Pfeffer, 1979, and Magdoff, 1982b for examples and discussions of work alienation.)

The Technological Imperative?

New machines and technology have been part of the alienating work process —for example, machines that workers operate, performing minute tasks hundreds and thousands of times daily. But the nature of this technological process has been confused by sociologists and popular writers, such as Toffler (1970), who state that technology is an impersonal force that cannot be controlled. The most workers can do is adjust to it.

This is another area of confusion, where the role of capitalism and profit seeking have been obscured. Warner's study of the shoe industry in New-buryport, Massachusetts is an example of the confusion. In one place Warner (1963) writes about the "inevitable advance of industrial technology," (p. 299) but a few pages earlier, he shows us that the technology described is not inevitable; it was planned by management to subjugate workers, lower wages, and increase profits.

> *Designers and engineers invent new and cheaper ways to make shoes and design machines to perform the new processes. Since the shoe-factory workers holding high-skilled jobs are a potential threat to management's control of shoe operatives, inventors apparently are encouraged to break down complex jobs into series of simple, easily standardized operations. An important result of their work, therefore, is to eliminate more and more of the skilled jobs from shoemaking, tending to accelerate the level of technological jobs in the shoe factory to a common low order of skill. (p. 292)*

Technology is neutral. It can be used to make jobs more productive, more creative, and less stressful. Or, it can be used to control and manipulate workers. It depends on who uses the technology, to what end, for whose benefits.

Today, computers illustrate both possibilities of technology. They allow for faster work and more complicated operations. Workers can use them to work fewer hours and perform better and more creative work. Workers such as systems analysts or writers use computers creatively, but corporations tend to use them to get more production out of workers, to simplify and routinize tasks, and to monitor and control people while they are on the job.

About two-thirds of the thirteen million video display terminal (VDT) users are monitored. Someone is keeping track of their work and actions almost every second of their working day. They "count keystrokes per second, track the number of operator mistakes, and time customer service transactions" (*Dollars and Sense,* July/August 1986:15). They also record when people turn a VDT on or off, and some even note how many times workers go to the bathroom. In addition, VDTs are programmed to "talk" with the workers. They can tell them to work faster, admonish them that they are "not working as fast as the person next to you," and even inform them that they have been fired. (p. 15) "Some messages are flashed so quickly that they're only subliminally received." The working days of "telephone operators, customer service representatives, airlines reservationists, . . . data entry workers" and others are constantly monitored (*Guardian,* May 21, 1986:2). This tightly controlled work situation can cause depression, anxiety, and fatigue. There is even some evidence that sick days increase when technology is only used to manipulate and exploit people.

Taylor's methods and philosophy still hold sway in today's workplace. Taylor got Schmidt to increase his production by 300 percent by controlling his every move and stretching workers' strength to the limit. Today, managers of new automobile assembly plants, built jointly by U.S. and Japanese corporations, talk about worker-management cooperation to increase production, which sounds good but which really only means they speed up the line. Workers are given less time than before to finish the same task, as cars parade by them endlessly on the assembly line. They are worn out by the increased pace of the work. But it is not the machines that dictate the speed of the assembly line; management puts pressure on the workers to increase profits. (See Itoh, 1984; Junkerman, 1987a; Slaughter, 1987; and *Dollars and Sense,* May 1987:9–11.)

Conclusion

Management does not control workers like robots. Sooner or later workers resist management control and exploitation (see Chapter 8). The conflict between owners and workers, between management and labor, began with the rise of capitalism and industrialism. It continues to this day.

Management seeks to monitor and control the movements of VDT workers, but workers and unions resist such monitoring. The Communications Workers of America have negotiated a contract, and the state of Wisconsin has enacted legislation, that forbid telephone surveillance without notice. In Sweden and West Germany laws allow only the measuring of group productivity, not individual measurement. Internationally, unions and other groups seek to stop the use of computers to record arrival and departure times, work breaks, and other information of worker activities. (See *Guardian,* May 21, 1986:2, and *Dollars and Sense,* July/August 1986:15.)

There is some evidence that people are attempting to improve their work and their working conditions. Environmentalists and workers have formed an alliance to remove chemical and other pollutants from workplaces. They argue that the environment is not only clean air and clean water but also a clean workplace, free of hazards and pollution. This effort is a class struggle between workers and management for better working conditions.

In the United States as elsewhere there is a struggle for control over the workplace and the work process. One of the demands of the Solidarity union in Poland in the early 1980s was that workers should decide what gets produced and how it gets produced. Some factories and offices are owned and run by workers; in other workplaces (in capitalist and socialist societies) workers are demanding that they take over some or all of the work processes. They want to decide the speed, quality, and nature of the goods they make or services they provide. There is an important difference between allowing workers to offer advice and to make suggestions, a management technique to placate unhappy workers but one it can choose to ignore, and real control of the work process without interference from management. The latter gives workers control over conception and execution; the former is only the appearance of change without any substance. (See Williams, 1982; Gibson, 1983;

Itoh, 1984; Compa, 1985; *Dollars and Sense,* March 1986:8–9; June 1986:12–14; and Junkerman, 1987a.)

Summary

Work has been and can be joyful and creative. Under capitalism, however, work presents many problems. For millions of people, work is a problem because they can find none. Unemployment devastates individuals, families, and communities. Millions of workers face illness and injury at work, and thousands die from accidents and illnesses they contract at work. In pay, prestige, and working conditions most people in the United States hold working-class jobs.

There has been a gradual and profound change in the nature of the working class since the 1940s. By the late 1980s, the majority of jobs are in the low-paying service, clerical, and sales occupations. Even two incomes from these jobs do not support a family adequately by current standards.

Most workers are alienated in their jobs because they have little or no control over the conception of their work. As computers and other new technology are making jobs even more alienating, workers seek to exert some control over their jobs.

Suggested Readings

Bale, Tony (1983, May/June). Breath of death: The asbestos disaster comes home to roost. *Health/PAC Bulletin,* 7–21. A history of asbestos uses and their effects on workers.

Berch, Bettina (1985, November). The resurrection of out-work. *Monthly Review,* *37*(6), pp. 37–46. Computers allow more people to work at home, but these workers receive low wages and no benefits.

Braverman, Harry (1974). *Labor and monopoly capital: The degradation of work in the twentieth century.* New York: Monthly Review Press. An outstanding discussion of work under capitalism.

Junkerman, John (1987, June). Nissan, Tennessee. *Progressive,* pp. 16–20. Automobile workers in a Nissan plant work under a speeded-up assembly line and more controls, not cooperation between management and workers.

Moore, Michael (1987, June 6). In Flint, tough times last. *Nation,* pp. 753–756. Since General Motors closed down plants in Flint, Michigan, people have suffered economic, social, and emotional devastation.

Pfeffer, Richard M. (1979). *Working for Capitalism.* New York: Columbia University Press. Pfeffer discusses his seven months in a factory, using the perspective developed by Braverman.

Ritzer, George & Walczak, David (1986). *Working: Conflict and Change* (3rd ed.). Englewood Cliffs, NJ: Prentice Hall. A textbook on the conditions, conflicts, and historical changes in work.

Terkel, Studs (1974). *Working: People talk about what they do all day and how they feel about what they do*. New York: Avon. The subtitle says it all. Most people are alienated from their work, but they long for meaningful and creative work.

Terminal crossroads: Office automation and the future of clerical work (1986, June). *Dollars and Sense*, pp. 12–14.

The new service economy: Where the jobs are and why? (1986, October). *Dollars and Sense*, pp. 6–8.

CHAPTER 10

The Ruling Class, Imperialism, and Democracy

In previous chapters I have discussed briefly the ruling class, its composition, and its control of the economy and of political institutions. Let us now examine in detail the composition and power of the ruling class, both in the United States and the world.

Power and Authority

Power is an elusive and contoversial concept. Weber (Wrong, 1979) defines it as "the chance of a man or a number of men to realize their own will in a social action even against the resistance of others who are participating in the action." (p. 21) Gerth and Mills (1954), following Weber, define power as "simply the probability that men will act as another man wishes. This action may rest upon fear, rational calculation of advantage, lack of energy to do otherwise, loyal devotion, indifference, or a dozen other individual motives." (p. 195) Taylor (1982) focuses on *incentives* in power relationships: "One of the ways in which one person can get another to pursue a course of action he would not otherwise have chosen to pursue is by affecting the incentives facing him, so that it is rational for him to choose this course of action. I call this the exercise of *power*. Power as a *possession* is the ability to affect incentives in this way." (p. 11) Rewards, penalties, or combinations of the two function as incentives. Finally, let us look at Wrong's (1979) definition: "Power is the capacity of some persons to produce intended and foreseen effects on others." (p. 2) This is a carefully chosen definition in which Wrong clarifies and amplifies his terms. Power is not only the actual exercise of control over others, but also its *potential* exercise. If I do not oppose my boss at a public meeting because I know (or think) he or she will fire me or penalize me for doing so, then my boss has the capacity and potential for power (of course, I may be mistaken about her or his will or ability to penalize me, and sometimes when we test reputedly powerful people we find out they are actually powerless). In short, to lay claim to power people must be effective and successful in their attempt to exercise it. Finally, power exists in relationships, and Wrong argues that, with few exceptions, the powerful are not totally powerful nor are the powerless completely powerless.

Power then is a relationship in which some individual or group has the capacity (or the perceived capacity) to direct and control the actions of other individuals or groups. It exists when the powerful can deprive the powerless of valued possessions and social positions, of their freedom, and ultimately of their lives.

The powerful usually go beyond the coercive and forceful exercise of their power and seek to legitimatize their superior social positions and their control of economic resources or political positions. In other words, power seeks to become *authority*. That is, people should obey and follow the commands, wishes, or advice of powerful people because they see their power as legitimate and justified. We should do as police officers, bosses, and teachers say not because they have guns, can fire us, or can fail us in the course but because we have come to believe their directives are justified, because they represent the law or they possess superior knowledge. Individuals and institutions are more effective and less troubled when they can translate power into authority. Naked coercion creates tension, instability, and restless subordinates. It is easier to keep poor people from rebelling by convincing them they are inferior and deserve to be poor, than it is to keep a large police force that must be constantly on guard. (Usually, the powerful must resort both to coercion and propaganda.)

There are many sources of power. Wrong discusses the possession of force and the use of manipulation and persuasion or propaganda. Equally important is the control or possession of scarce resources—land or other property. In industrial societies, we refer specifically to ownership and control of corporations. Occupying powerful positions, especially in government, or the ability to influence or control people who occupy those positions, also confers power. Other social positions, expertise and knowledge (or the reputation of their possession), and organization of a determined group of people, can also give power.

It is obvious that power, as a relationship, arises in many situations. Parents take away privileges (movies, dances, trips) from teenagers who return home past a designated time; teachers fail students who are late with their papers or who fail to follow a designated format; bosses penalize workers who are late or fail to follow regulations; judges imprison people who violate the law; corporations relocate plants when workers will not accept lower wages; and police and governments all over the world imprison, torture, and execute people who protest against conditions they perceive as unjust, exploitative, and destructive.

Power is everywhere—as is the resistance to it. In this chapter, we will focus largely on the power of the ruling class in the United States, whose control of the economy, government, and other institutions affects the lives of millions of people inside and outside its borders. This class seeks to dominate the society largely for its own interest, and strives to legitimatize that control. The ruling class and its institutions want to persuade people that the economic system is just and provides equal opportunities to all, thus it is legitimate. But not everyone is persuaded. The ruling class is locked in a struggle with those who are powerless and who protest their subjugation.

The American Ruling Class

The ruling class is not easy to study. For obvious reasons, its members do not want to be exposed. Except for the most powerful (such as the Rockefellers and DuPonts), members of this class are not highly visible. In addition, many who do not belong to the ruling class but who work for it are often taken as members. (In time, of course, some of these people, or their children, do enter the ruling class. It is always open to new members with ambition and ability, for such people strengthen the class.) In spite of these difficulties, it is still possible to study the ruling class, both through careful analysis of government documents, business reports, and other similar documents, and through talks with ex-members or close employees of the ruling class. A number of social scientists in the last forty years have closely studied this class.

The ruling class consists of those families whose members dominate the society's economic and political institutions and who control a highly dispro-portionate amount of the wealth. Athletes and entertainers may make a million dollars or more a year, but they are not in the ruling class (although some of their children may marry and integrate into it) because it is *power* that defines the ruling class. People who make major decisions that affect millions of others, such as what role the United States should play in a foreign war, are what is meant by the ruling class. This group controls most of the wealth and the major corporations and wields power within the government.

The entire ruling class does not have periodic conventions where it conspires to manipulate the society. Morris (1977) notes that small groups may meet on specific occasions, but the essence of ruling-class activity lies else-where: in the sameness of values, interests, and experiences.

How do we identify its members? They are white, mostly of northern or western European descent, and those who exercise the power are mostly men. Domhoff (1983) argues that ruling-class members are found in the *Social Registers* of different cities, in the membership lists of exclusive clubs, and alumni lists of certain private preparatory schools. Also, some may be missing from all these lists but still belong to the ruling class if they are on the boards of directors of major corporations, hold powerful corporate positions, or they marry someone who meets any of the above criteria. Usually, most members are found in more than one list (Hill, 1975).

How large is the ruling class? Domhoff (1983) estimates that at most one-half of 1 percent of the American population, or a little over a million in the 1980s, belong to it. But in terms of very rich and powerful people, the number is much smaller. If we consider directors and executives of large corporations, and add a few powerful politicians from Washington, we have only a few thousand. If we consider wealth, and set a lower limit of ownership of a million dollars worth of corporate stock, there were about 50,000 such adults in 1969. With inflation, the number of million-dollar stockholders has probably doubled by the 1980s.

We should also note those people who do not belong to the ruling class. Doctors, most corporate managers, other affluent professionals, and owners of small businesses are not members of that class. They do not occupy positions of power in the economy or the government; with few exceptions, they are not socially integrated into and accepted by ruling-class families, and with fewer exceptions their income and wealth do not suffice to lead the kind of life style these families lead.

The Institutions of the Ruling Class

All sociologists agree that people of the same class tend to intermarry, attend similar schools, have fun doing similar things, belong to similar organizations, hold similar values, and undergo a similar socialization process. The ruling class is no different. In fact, because there are fewer of them, and they have more resources, people in this class find it easier to form a cohesive, clearly defined class. They intermarry, are exposed to the same experiences, and spend much of their time with each other.

Ruling-class parents rarely raise their children. Nurses, governesses, and maids take care of their needs. From early in life, they learn that they are born to be waited on and to give orders to others. When they go to school, these children attend exclusive preparatory schools (of course, not all children in these schools are from the ruling class—many are prospective members or children of parents with high aspirations). These schools serve many functions. First and foremost, they introduce children from different parts of the country to each other. This begins life-long friendships and acquaintances. All people make friends in school; the rich are no different. Second, boarding schools continue the molding of ruling-class values and personality. Burnham (1978), who attended such schools, says:

> The final step in the care and training of the propertied class occurs in the boarding school, a fact that is so completely understood all over the country that parents from Lake Forest, Illinois, or Pebble Beach, California, automatically send their children East to school. . . .
>
> The first thing that strikes the visitor is the extraordinary richness of Foxcroft, visible in the tennis courts, gardens, stables, orchards, and servants, in the boxwood walks and 18th century brick house, in the classrooms, art rooms, photo labs, and dorms. . . .

We accepted the wealth as natural. We didn't even see it. Just as we accepted the grooms who brought our horses to us, already saddled and bridled, and the gardeners trimming the formal walks, clipping the hedges and mowing the grass. We did not speak when passing them, but grunted, eyes grounded in pride or shyness, as they touched their caps. (p. 16)

Despite many societal changes, old-school ties remain strong. Arnold (1978) cites the schools attended by people such as the Saltonstalls, Kennedys, and Roosevelts and shows the emotional and social significance people attach to their school friendships. Ted Kennedy is said to attend Graduates' Day at Milton Academy whenever he can.

Ruling-class children continue their education in exclusive colleges. Although not as many now attend Ivy League and similar colleges, many do, and the rest go to other top schools, major state universities, for example. Ten generations of Saltonstalls have graduated from Harvard (Arnold, 1978). And the Domhoff (1967) study of 476 top executives showed 86 percent had attended Yale, Harvard, or Princeton.

Ruling-class men and women also tend to marry each other. This fact is fairly well known, and hardly surprising. It is important to note, however, that a high rate of intermarriage within a group is the best evidence that a class exists.

In addition to meeting each other in business and government, ruling-class people have other ways to meet after they leave school. They meet at clubs, summer resorts, and charitable and cultural organizations and in such recreational activities as foxhunts, polo matches, and yachting.

Clubs and camps are especially important. These places offer people a chance to meet and exchange ideas. Domhoff (1974) studied two camp retreats still open only to ruling-class men. The list of the Bohemian Grove is an "all-star team of the national corporate elite." (p. 35) The people in these clubs and camps sit on the boards of directors of major corporations, in advisory groups for the government, and in the government itself. President Reagan has spent time at the Bohemian Grove. We should not underestimate the importance of these clubs, retreats, and other nonbusiness activities. People who have fun, play, and talk together become closer to each other. In these settings, deals are made and ideas explored. One can meet people of one's own class, some from distant places, to make class ties truly national.

The Ruling Class and the Economy

The ruling class owns much of the wealth and most of the stock of the top corporations. It also runs those corporations.

Income and Wealth

We saw in Chapter 8 that the ruling class makes the highest incomes and has the most wealth, especially income-producing wealth. Let us examine some data on income, wealth, stocks and bonds, and individual and corporate taxes.

In Table 10.1 we see that the distribution of the annual income has been highly uneven for decades. Fully 60 percent of the families make about a third of the income each year, with the poorest 20 percent making under 5 percent in 1986. On the other hand, the richest 20 percent, the managerial and ruling classes, consistently make over 40 percent (44 percent in 1986). The richest 5 percent make 15 to 17 percent. In Table 10.1 we also see that whereas the gap between the top and the bottom closed a little from 1950 to 1970, it began to widen again during the 1980s.

The gap between the middle class, not to mention the poor, and the wealthy is growing wider each year. Most people use all their income to meet their expenses, but those with the highest incomes can save. These savings are turned into investments that add yet more wealth to the already rich. Except for homes, cars, furniture, clothes, and other personal possessions, most people own little or no wealth. Many are in debt. Only a very few people are very wealthy.

A study (*Dollars and Sense,* April 1987) based on government data revealed that in 1983 one-half of a percent, one in two hundred households, owned 35.1 percent of the wealth (this was 25.4 in 1963). The next half percent owned an additional 6.7 percent (7.4 in 1963). Nine more percent owned 29.9 percent of the wealth (32.3 in 1963). In short, the top ten percent owned 71.7 percent of the wealth. The rest, 90 percent of the people, owned 28.2 percent. If we exclude the value of homes people own, and focus on other forms of wealth, Kloby (1987) points out that the distribution is even more uneven. The richest 10 percent own 83.2 percent of it, up from 71.7 percent, and the richest half of a percent own 45.4 percent, up from 35.1.

We will close this discussion of wealth by looking at the wealthiest individuals and families in the United States. A story in *Forbes* (October 27, 1986), a business magazine, documents the wealth of the 400 richest Americans. In 1986, it ranged from $180 million at the bottom to 4.5 billion at the

TABLE 10.1
Money Income of Families—Percent of Aggregate Income Received by Each Fifth and Top 5 Percent of Families 1950, 1970, and 1986

	1950	1970	1986
Lowest fifth	4.5	5.4	4.6
Second fifth	12.0	12.2	10.8
Third fifth	17.4	17.6	16.8
Lowest three fifths	33.9	35.2	32.2
Fourth fifth	23.4	23.8	24.0
Highest fifth	42.7	40.9	43.7
Highest 5 percent	17.3	15.4	17.0

Statistical Abstract, 1977:443; and *Dollars and Sense,* November 1987:22

top. Of the 400, 77 had fortunes of $500 million or more. In addition, "some major U.S. fortunes have already been so divided among heirs that no individual among them qualifies for the Forbes Four Hundred, yet the families either show enough cohesion or are widely enough thought of as families of great wealth to merit consideration as entities." (p. 250) These 92 families possess from $300 million to $10 billion, and include the Rockefellers, Kennedys, and DuPonts.

Most wealthy people have their assets in joint holdings with other family members. These arrangements, informally called "family offices," mean that the wealth of the family is managed by a financial advisor, who manages their estates, dispenses allowances to the younger generation, advises on investments, and so on. Wealth is concentrated in families more than it is on individuals (Domhoff, 1983).

Most of this wealth produces income in dividends, rents, and other earnings. Various studies from the 1950s to the 1980s show that 1 percent of the population owns from 50 to 70 percent of corporate stocks. For example, one study in 1972 showed that one-half of a percent of Americans owned 49.3 percent of corporate stocks, 52.2 percent of bonds, and 80.8 percent of trusts. The congressional study of wealth in 1983 showed that the richest one-half of a percent of families owned 35.6 percent of the real estate, 46.5 of corporate stock, 43.6 of bonds, and 58.2 of business assets. (See Domhoff, 1983; Gilbert & Kahl, 1987; and Kloby, 1987.)

The wealth of the richest families has been increasing partly because over the last three decades the tax laws have changed to benefit rich individuals and corporations. The federal policies and programs of the 1960s and 1970s that provided modest increases in benefits for poor people did not come from increased taxation of the richest people. They came from heavier taxes on the working class, both in income tax and social security tax. And the tax cuts of the early 1980s benefitted only the richest people. According to Albelda (1988), a 1988 study by the Congressional Budget Office showed that compared to 1977, in 1988 the richest 10 percent of households will pay almost *20 percent less* in taxes, whereas the poorest 10 percent will pay *20 percent more*. The richest 1 percent benefit even more by the tax cuts. Whereas in 1977 they "retained 7.2% of all after-tax household income," by 1988 they will "accumulate 11.5% of after-tax income." (p. 10)

Many rich people paid little or no tax at all. According to the Treasury Department, in 1986, 306 people who made $1 million paid no federal income tax. Another 29,800 people who made over $250,000 paid less than 5 percent, and 25,452 paid between 5 and 10 percent. Of the 260,000 people who made over a quarter million dollars, 122,000 only (fewer than half) paid more than 20 percent in federal income taxes. (See Ciancanelli, 1978; Navarro, 1987; Center for Popular Economics, 1986; *Dollars and Sense,* April 1985:6–7; July/August 1985:9; and *Boston Globe,* August 2, 1985:3.)

Corporations also have come to pay very low taxes. The decreases began in the 1950s. In 1950, corporate income taxes were 26.5 percent of federal revenues. They have decreased steadily since then: 23.2 percent in 1960, 17.0 in 1970, 12.5 in 1980, and 9.00 in 1985. (The rise in the size of the federal government's budget deficits parallels the reduction in corporate taxes, especially since the late 1970s.) It became a minor scandal that some corporations that had made healthy profits paid no taxes at all. From 1981 to 1983, 128 large and profitable corporations paid no federal income taxes. One of them, General Electric, earned $9.5 billion between 1981 and 1984 and paid no taxes. It even received $98 million in tax rebates. According to one study cited in the Center for Popular Economics (1986) report, various tax exemptions allowed to businesses in the middle 1980s amounted to over $100 billion a year. (See McDermott, 1982; Medlen, 1984; *Boston Globe,* February 13, 1985:3; and *Dollars and Sense,* November 1986:22.)

The 1986 revised federal tax code enacted should make little difference in income and wealth distribution. In individual taxes, it will make it impossible for a few wealthy people to avoid taxation entirely, and the six million of the poorest families will pay no tax at all. Some of the exemptions rich people had used are gone, but since the top rate decreased from 50 to 28 percent, the tax bite on people making over $200,000 will drop from the 22.5 percent rate they have been paying in fact (exemptions reduced it from 50 to 22.5 percent) to a projected 21.3 percent. Most people will receive few or no tax cuts. Thus, the tax changes passed by Congress and the president in the early 1980s, which gave the rich sizable deductions, will continue. The new tax code will perpetuate the old inequalities.

Corporations will lose some exemptions and will pay a little more tax. It should no longer be possible for a corporation to make a big profit and pay no taxes. But the increase in corporate taxes takes away only a fraction of the huge tax deductions corporations accumulated since the 1950s (*Dollars and Sense,* November 1986:6).

Control of Major Corporations

The ruling class controls most of the stock in corporations. Moreover, a few corporations control the economy, and these corporations are run by a few people. Tables 10.2 and 10.3 show that about two hundred corporations control most of the assets, sales, and profits in the industrial and manufacturing fields. In Table 10.2 we see that in 1985, 281 corporations, with assets of one billion dollars or more, held 67.2 percent of all assets and made 69 percent of all net profits. These percentages are a considerable increase from 1970, when about 50 percent of both assets and profits were held by the corporations. Table 10.3 reveals that of assets and sales of the largest five-hundred industrials, the largest one hundred held 70 percent of assets and made 70 percent of sales. In short, relatively few corporations dominate the manufacturing sector of the U.S. economy.

A very few corporations are very wealthy. According to the Boston Urban Study Group (1984a), fifty firms "own 36 percent of all manufacturing

TABLE 10.2
Manufacturing Corporation Assets and Profits by Asset Size, 1970 and 1985
(in millions of dollars)

	Number*		Assets		Net Profits	
	1970	*1985*	*1970*	*1985*	*1970*	*1985*
All corporations	197,807*	—	$578,234	$1,932,766	$28,572	$87,647
Corporations with assets of 1 billion or more	102*	281*	$282,320 (48.8%)	$1,298,720 (67.2%)	$14,832 (51.9%)	$60,431 (69%)

Statistical Abstract, 1987:519
* Actual numbers, not in millions

assets. The top ten industrial firms account for one-quarter of all assets." (p. 7) Of these ten, six are oil corporations, two are auto makers, and the other two are IBM and DuPont. In insurance, the five largest companies account for half of the life insurance business. In 1985, of 14,405 commercial banks, 518 of them (3.6 percent), with assets of $500 million or more each, held 65 percent of the assets. *Five* of them held 19 percent of bank deposits in 1983. (See *Statistical Abstract,* 1987:478, and Center for Popular Economics, 1986.)

Even more revealing are figures that show that in many industries, four or fewer corporations control most of the market for that product or service: 86 percent of breakfast cereals, 76 percent of aluminum, 72 of photography equipment, 80 to 90 percent of aircraft, 70 to 80 percent of tires and drugs, 60 to 70 percent of dairy products, and soaps and household products. In another area, 50 corporations control most of the media (newspapers, magazines, television, etc.) in the United States. There is little or no competition in most industries. Only a few giants sell the products or services in most industries, which keeps prices high. (See *U.S. News and World Report,* August 24, 1981: 69; Fusfeld, 1982; and *Dollars and Sense,* November 1984:6.)

These powerful corporations are controlled by boards of directors that make all the important policy and financial decisions. These boards constitute only a few thousand people. Indeed, many people sit on more than one board of directors, thus creating the possibility for all sorts of cooperation between

TABLE 10.3
Assets and Sales of Largest Industrial Corporations, 1985
(in billions of dollars)

Corporation	Assets	Sales
Largest 500	$1,519.4 (100%)	$1,807.1 (100%)
Largest 100	1,068.6 (70.3%)	1,264.1 (69.9%)
Second largest 100	224.8 (14.8%)	265.5 (14.7%)

Statistical Abstract, 1987:519

corporations in different fields, or even between those that are supposedly in competition with each other.

Consider some details. Domhoff (1967) found that in 1963, 53 percent of the 884 people on the boards of the top fifteen banks, top fifteen insurance companies, and top twenty industrials were members of the upper class (as he defines it; see earlier part of this chapter). These directors, in addition to making these companies' major decisions, also own enough stock in them to control them—this was the case in 141 of the 232 largest corporations. (For similar findings in 1968, see Useem, 1978; see also Domhoff, 1983:66–72.)

But the extent of the power of a few thousand ruling-class people becomes obvious when we look at the prevalence of interlocking directorates—two or more companies with a common director on their board. The following quote from a study by a Senate Committee reveals the extensive connections between corporations (*Boston Globe*, April 23, 1978):

> *A direct interlock occurs when two companies have a common director. An indirect interlock exists when two companies each have a director on the board of a third corporation.*
>
> *The study showed that 123 of the 130 corporations examined on average had some connection with about 65 of the other companies. The 13 largest firms not only were linked together but accounted for 240 direct and 5,547 indirect interlocks, each being attached to an average of more than 70 percent of the other 117 corporations.*
>
> *The 13 largest companies ranked by assets were American Telephone and Telegraph Co., BankAmerica Corp., Citicorp, Chase Manhattan Corp., Prudential Co., Metropolitan Life, Exxon Corp., Manufacturers Hanover Corp., J. P. Morgan and Co., General Motors Corp., Mobil Corp., Texaco, Inc. and Ford Motor Co.*
>
> *The study said the boards of Citicorp, Chase, Manufacturers Hanover, Morgan, Prudential, Metropolitan, AT&T, Exxon and GM "looked like virtual summits for leaders in American business."*
>
> *The study found that leading competitors in the fields of automotives, energy, telecommunications and retailing met extensively on the boards of their corporate customers and suppliers and also on the nation's largest financial institutions.*
>
> *The patterns of director interrelationships, the study said, implied a potential for antitrust abuse and possible conflicts that could affect prices, supply and competition, and could also have an impact on the shape and direction of the economy. (pp. 41, 45)*

This national condition of interlocking directorates may become clearer by looking at some specific cases. In a study of the twenty-four largest newspaper owning companies, Dreier (1982) found that all of them, especially the top four, are very closely connected with the largest U.S. corporations and other institutions of the ruling class. They have 196 interlocking directors with large corporations, are trustees of elite universities, and belong to various elite clubs.

Another example is Boston Edison Company. This company has four-teen directors—eight sitting on the boards of other large local businesses, the three major banks and the two biggest insurance companies. The First National City Bank, second largest in the nation, is interlocked with seven of the top ten industrials, six of the top fifteen insurance companies, two of the largest four retailers, and the two largest utilities. Finally, in his study of United States directors, Domhoff (1967) found "the 16 men studied were also directors of trustees for 20 major industrials, 18 banks, 11 insurance companies, 9 railroads, 8 utilities, 5 universities, and 3 charitable foundations." (p. 55)

The people who serve on the boards of directors are predominantly from the ruling class, with the rest from the upper reaches of the managerial class. They are all socialized in ruling-class institutions. Useem and Karabel's (1986) study of 2,279 senior managers of 208 major corporations concludes that the rise to top managerial levels "is facilitated by the possession of a bachelor's degree from a top ranked college, a master's degree in business administration from a prominent program, or a degree in law from a leading institution." (p. 184) Even more, when we compare people with similar educational credentials, we find that a ruling-class "background increases the likelihood of rising to the top ranks of corporate management." (p. 184) Those from the ruling class who have a law degree are most likely to belong to the formal and informal groups that control and connect corporations.

New Forms of Control

Capitalism, like any social system, changes through time. The ruling class is always looking for new ways to increase its power and wealth. Food and land had been two areas largely uncontrolled by the ruling class, but the situation is changing rapidly.

The increased production of specific foods by a few corporations is a major reason for the increase in food prices. Four corporations control the following percentages in these foods: 90 percent of the breakfast cereals; 70 percent of the dairy products; 65 percent of the sugar; and 80 percent of the canned goods. Campbell Soup *alone* controls 90 percent of the canned soup market. Zwerdling (1980) says, "In most food products—not many, most—two to four corporations already have seized control of the market. In this vast nation of 220 million people, only fifty manufacturing firms now control the means of food production." (p. 25)

In the late 1970s, large food corporations were buying out small and medium companies at a rapid rate. *Business Week* called these moves "The Great Takeover Binge." For example, Procter & Gamble was not in the coffee business until the early 1970s. It then bought out a regional company making Folger's Coffee and proceeded to spend millions of dollars on advertising, driving out of business many local coffee companies as it sought to catch up with Maxwell House in the national market. Consumers pay higher and higher prices in order to finance these takeovers and the advertising campaigns of huge corporations.

Zwerdling (1980) points to the list of food (and nonfood) products Procter & Gamble makes that shows the tremendous market control this one corporation has: Pringle's potato chips, Duncan Hines cake mixes, Crisco oil, Ivory soap, Crest, Charmin, Pampers, Tide, and Cheer. Another company, Beatrice Foods, has bought and now controls over four hundred companies—among them the makers of Canada Dry, Dannon yogurt, Sunbeam bread, Miracle White fabric softener, and Samsonite luggage. The Center for Popular Economics (1986) found that in 1950, the one hundred largest food corporations already controlled 46 percent of industry assets, but they controlled 75 percent in 1981.

The following history of one food industry giant, General Foods, illustrates corporate growth. The Postum Company began in 1891 with a coffee substitute. Soon after it was marketing cereals (Silverstein, 1984):

> Then the mergers began. In 1925 the company acquired the Jello Company. In 1926 it acquired Ingleheart Brothers, makers of Swans Down cake flour, and the Minute Tapioca Company. In 1927 came Franklin Baker, maker of coconut, Walter Baker, maker of chocolate, and Log Cabin, the syrup company. Meanwhile, Clarence Birdseye had returned from the Arctic, where he had seen Eskimos preserving meat by freezing it. He invented a commercial method for freezing foods and, in 1924, he founded the General Foods Company.
>
> In 1929, the Postum Cereal Company bought General Foods and took over its name. Later the company acquired Gaines dog food (1943), Kool Aid (1953), Good Seasons salad dressing (1954), and Open Pit barbecue sauces (1960), among many other companies in the United States and overseas. Today, General Foods produces all of the aforementioned products as well as coffee, including Maxwell House, Yuban, Sanka, Brim, Max Pax, Maxim, and General Foods International Coffees. (General Foods and Procter and Gamble now sell almost two-thirds of the ground coffee in the country. General Foods and Nestle sell over three-quarters of the instant coffee.) The company also sells many pet foods, including Gravy Train, Prime, Top Choice, and Cycle, as well as many breakfast drinks, among them Orange Plus, Start, and Tang. Also marketed by General Foods are Shake 'n Bake, Pop Rocks, Cool Whip, Stovetop stuffing, Hollywood chewing gum, Burger Chef fast foods, and other products in many countries, including France, Spain, Sweden, Brazil, Japan, and Australia. (p. 46)

Land and farmland are also increasingly being owned by fewer and fewer people. In the United States, 1 percent of the landowners own 48 percent of the land, and 5 percent of the owners own 75 percent of the land (*Dollars and Sense*, January 1982:19, and Center for Popular Economics, 1986). An increasing number of small farmers are losing or having to sell their farms. Family farms, a cherished ideal in American society, are rapidly disappearing. In 1940 there were 6.4 million farms, but only 2.5 million in 1978, and only 1.86 million farms with sales of $2,500 and over. The smallest 66 percent of the farms made only 9 percent of all farm sales in 1978, and only an average of 15 percent of their income came from farm sales. The largest 7 percent made 56 percent of all sales and derived 83 percent of their income from farming. In specific parts of the United States, notably California, large corporations have bought thousands of acres to grow lettuce and other products (*Dollars and Sense,* May/June 1982:13).

Government policies and international trade conditions have sharpened the crisis of the American farmers. In 1987, family farms were disappearing at the rate of two thousand a week. Banks and other financial institutions foreclosed on them because they could not meet debt or mortgage payments. Lower prices for their crops, higher prices for the materials they buy, and government policies that favor large corporate farmers meant that family farmers were losing money. Much of the foreclosed land was taken over and is now often farmed by insurance companies. Prudential owns 23,000 acres in Indiana and Hancock owns 220,000 acres. (See Lanner, 1985; *Boston Globe,* July 14, 1985: A21; *Guardian,* May 20, 1987:7; and Davidson, 1987.)

The surviving small and family farms are at the mercy of a few large corporations that buy their products cheaply or sell them expensive machinery. An article in *Dollars and Sense* (May/June 1982:14) stated: "The biggest winners are the agribusiness giants that surround the farm. 65¢ of every dollar the consumer spends on food goes to food processors, wholesalers, retailers, and other middlemen. The farmer gets 35¢ in return for the crop, but is lucky to be left with 15¢ after paying for production costs." With rising costs, rising interest rates, and lower profits (since agribusiness makes most of the profits) more and more farmers are leaving the land.

Throughout the United States large corporations own or control most of the land for mineral exploration and other uses. The Appalachian region is a classic case of land that is controlled by few outside corporations that pay little or no taxes to local communities and take out all the profits, thus leaving communities impoverished. In one West Virginia county, 76 percent of the land is owned by out-of-state corporations. A study released in the spring of 1981 documents the outside control and the exploitation. The survey of 20 million acres showed that the ten largest corporate and individual landlords owned two million of them. The mineral rights, which allow corporations to explore for coal, oil, and minerals are owned by a few outside corporations. Large oil companies are buying out more and more coal companies and other energy corporations. (See Egerton, 1981; Sherrill 1980, 1983; and for North Carolina, see *Dollars and Sense,* December 1986:12.)

These companies pay incredibly low property taxes, an average of 90 cents per acre. About 75 percent of the mineral owners paid an annual tax of 25 cents per acre! Many communities are organizing to demand higher tax payments, so they can finance better schools and other improvements. One community succeeded in raising a corporation's tax bill by 500 percent, from the original 14 cents per acre. (See Egerton, 1981, and *Dollars and Sense,* October 1981:13.)

Land, farmland, and food are becoming controlled, owned, and processed by fewer and fewer corporations.

Conglomerates and Multinationals

In the early days of capitalism, a company made one product and sold it mostly within its own nation. Within the last fifty years, conditions began to change, however, and now most major corporations are *conglomerates* (they make more than one product) and *multinationals* (they operate in two or more countries).

International Telephone and Telegraph (ITT) began in communciations, but through the years it has purchased many other companies. It sells insurance, rents cars, makes baked goods (Wonder Bread). It is involved in over one hundred goods and services. Ford Motor Company owns Philco (televisions); Chrysler owns land; Tenneco owns farms; oil companies buy coal, solar energy, and uranium companies; DuPont raises cattle; and on and on it goes. Corporations buy corporations in related and unrelated fields. For example, while U.S. Steel was closing steel plants because it would not invest money to modernize their equipment, it spent $6.6 billion to acquire Marathon Oil (which itself had acquired twenty-three other companies from 1916 to 1976). From its inception around 1900, U.S. Steel has bought out almost one hundred corporations. (See *Progressive,* June 1982:15; Nyhan, 1983a; and *Guardian,* May 9, 1979:6.)

Mergers and acquisitions have continued unabated in the early 1980s, concentrating wealth and power in the hands of fewer and fewer corporations. Sherrill (1983) summarizes the merger movement of 1981 this way:

> *Big business engaged in an orgy of mergers and acquisitions in 1981. More than $82 billion was spent on 2,395 mergers, an amount nearly 50 percent greater than the previous yearly high. And the orgy continued last year: U.S. Steel bought Marathon Oil for $6.6 billion; the INA Corporation and Connecticut General united in a $4.3 billion merger; Occidental Petroleum bought Cities Service for $4.1 billion; Norfolk and Western Railway and Southern Railway made a $1.7 billion merger; American General bought N.L.T. for $1.6 billion; R.J. Reynolds bought Heublein for $1.3 billion; Baldwin-United bought M.G.I.C. Investment for $1.2 billion; Smith Kline bought Beckman Instruments for $1.04 billion; Allied bought Supron Energy for $712 million; Coca-Cola bought Columbia Pictures for $630 million. Those are just a few of the largest mergers and acquisitions of the year in terms of dollars. (p. 338)*

In 1981, there were 2,395 mergers and acquisitions worth $82.6 billion ($23 billion in oil and gas). The value of mergers and acquisitions declined to $54 billion in 1982, but increased sharply to $122 billion in 1984 (a third of that, $43 billion, for 102 mergers and acquisitions in oil and gas). Clearly, big fish are swallowing little fish and are growing to enormous size. Larger companies are not more efficient, but their size and monopolies enable them to raise their prices, increase profits, and cost consumers more money. (See *Statistical Abstract,* 1987:524, and Silverstein, 1984.)

Conglomerates mean that only a few companies can increase their profits, markets, and influence over local and national governments. The larger they get, the more money they have, the more new corporations they can acquire, the more resources they have to compete against competitors. The 1890 and 1914 anti-trust laws of the United States were meant to stop corporate power by preventing corporations from buying other corporations in related and unrelated fields. But they have almost never been enforced, especially under the Reagan administration (Sherrill, 1980, 1983).

The Six-Gun and the Fountain Pen: Corporate Crimes

Toward the end of Woody Guthrie's song "Pretty Boy Floyd" appear the following lines: "As through this world I ramble, I see lots of funny men, some rob you with a six-gun, some with a fountain pen." Corporations rarely rob people with guns, but by fixing and raising prices, selling defective or useless products, lying in their advertising, exposing workers to dangerous working conditions, polluting the environment, and so on, they rob, injure, and kill many times more people than street criminals do. It is all done by management decisions, all carried out with the fountain pen, all for corporate profits, growth, and power. Corporate crime is pervasive. According to Rothschild (1985), one government attorney stated, "The incidence of corporate crime is 100 times what the authorities ever hear about." (p. 26)

Various studies confirm his statement. A study of crimes committed by the 582 largest publicly owned corporations from 1975 through 1976 found that 60 percent were sued by the government at least once, with an average of 4.2 times each. A 1982 report (Green & Berry, 1985) showed that 115 of the 500 largest corporations had been convicted "of at least one major crime or have paid civil penalties for serious misbehavior" during the previous decade. (p. 704)

Corporate crime causes enormous economic, environmental, and health damage. Explicit and implicit agreements to keep prices high (price-fixing) means the theft of billions of dollars a year from the public. Estimates of this theft vary from $30 to $260 billion, with most estimates at about $60 billion. The public is robbed in other ways. For example, Exxon was sued by the U.S. Department of Energy in 1978 for $10 billion. The company was charged with overcharging and pricing violations during the oil crisis of the early 1970s. In 1983, Exxon was ordered by a federal judge to refund customers $1.5 billion. Price gouging is also standard among drug companies. Brand name drugs and generic drugs are chemically identical; the brand name is no more effective. But the drug companies advertise their brands heavily, and sell them for two to ten times the price of the generic product. For example, the tranquilizer

Librium is sold at $9.46 per 100 tablets, while the generic product is sold for $1.10. (See Green, 1985, and Simon & Eitzen, 1986. For an account of the insurance "crisis" manufactured from 1985 to 1987 by the insurance companies to increase their profits, see Peck, 1986.)

Besides cheating consumers, corporate crimes cause illness and often death. When a corporation refuses to spend money to remove dangerous substances from a workplace or to dispose properly of dangerous chemicals, and instead dumps them in the ground, it causes illness and death (Simon & Eitzen, 1986).

Asbestos will serve as an example. The dangers it poses to workers began to appear in the scientific literature in the 1930s. Documents produced as evidence in jury trials against Johns Manville Corporation, which was the largest U.S. asbestos manufacturer, showed that Manville knew of these dangers. Yet they never told their workers the lethal dangers they faced. Over the years, 1.6 million workers were exposed to it. It was not until the early 1970s that they finally learned of the effects of asbestos. Workers began to sue the companies who had kept the findings of asbestos' effects a secret. But these corporations have used bankruptcy laws and other legal loopholes to minimize and avoid payments to sick workers. (See Bale, 1983, and Kuttner, 1986a.)

Faulty products also endanger consumers. Drug companies have sold drugs that they knew had dangerous side effects. Thalidomide, a sleeping pill given to pregnant women in the early 1960s, caused severe deformities to thousands of babies. It was sold in the United States *after* its effects were known to drug companies in Europe. The Dalkon Shield, an intrauterine device (IUD) for birth control, was marketed by Robbins in the 1970s. Over two million women used it in the United States. The company continued to sell it *after* it had received many reports of serious infections, miscarriages, permanent sterility, and even deaths. A lawyer whose client sued Robbins wrote them two letters explaining the dangers faced by women who used the Dalkon Shield, but never received a response. Robbins ignored other warnings and evidence of illness and death. It was not until 1984 that they agreed to warn women to stop using Dalkon. At least eighteen women died. Many others lost babies, became sterile, or were ill. (See Mintz, 1985a; for a story of an anti-arthritis drug that killed hundreds of elderly users, see Rothschild, 1986.)

The Ford Pinto, produced in the early 1970s, may be the most notorious case of a dangerous product. Ford management wanted to produce an inexpensive car to compete with the German Volkswagen, which enjoyed great sales. Normally, cars took four years from the initial planning to rolling off the assembly line. Ford wanted to reduce this time to twenty-five months. In the process, they designed a car with a gas tank too close to the rear bumper, and thus more likely to explode if the car was in a rear-end collision. The engineers knew about this defect. Documents show they pointed it out to management. But in order to correct this defect, they would need more time to redesign the car, and during this extra time Volkswagen would have the small-car market to itself. To avoid loss of potential business, Ford decided to build the defective car. Millions were produced and sold. Thousands of people were injured and an estimated five hundred to nine hundred people died when the cars exploded in rear-end collisions. Ford knew beforehand that people would die from these rear-end collisions. The deaths and injuries were preventable. But business dictated the production of a defective car. Other defective cars have been built and sold even as the companies knew of these defects. (See Simon & Eitzen, 1986, and Green & Berry, 1985.)

The Pinto case shows that corporations exist solely to make profits and to grow. They will break laws, cheat the public, and sell dangerous products to achieve these ends. Simon and Eitzen (1986) provide an excellent summary of how and why corporations commit crimes.

> *Corporations are formed to seek and maximize profits. All too often, the result is a blatant disregard for human and humane considerations.*
>
> *It is too simplistic to say that corporations are solely responsible for these dangers to individuals and society. In many cases, consumers insist on convenience rather than safety. They would rather smoke or drink diet cola with saccharin than have the government demand that they quit. Moreover, consumers typically would rather take an unknown risk than pay higher prices for products, which would pay for the cost of cleaning up the pollution. So, too, workers would rather work in an unsafe plant than be unemployed. But for the most part, these attitudes are shaped by corporate advertising and corporate extortion (threatened higher prices and unemployment if changes are enforced). Also, corporations are guilty of efforts to persuade us that the dangers are nonexistent or minimal when the scientific evidence is irrefutable. They also do everything possible to block efforts by the government and consumer groups to thwart their corporate policies. (p. 123)*

Let me end on a hopeful note. A few government officials and courts are beginning to say that corporate crimes *are* crimes and that corporations must be punished accordingly. Let us look at one case that was reported in the *Boston Globe* (June 15, 1985). An employee who "worked over tanks of cyanide solution used in the plant's recovery of silver from used photographic films" (p. 1) was poisoned and died from breathing cyanide fumes. It was shown in court that company executives knew that the fumes were life-threatening but chose to do nothing. Three executives were prosecuted and found guilty of murder. (For other discussions of corporate crimes, see Rothschild, 1985; Ermann & Lundman, 1987; and Greenfield, 1987.)

The Ruling Class, the Government, and Social Policies

We may assume that the ruling class will control the economy, but it is more difficult to accept their control over the government. After all, politicians are elected.

The following summarizes the research conducted in this area and shows the extent to which the ruling class controls politics. Different wings of the ruling class control both the Democratic and Republican parties. Both Republican and Democratic policies have favored corporations, created recessions and wars, and generally benefitted the ruling class. In both Democratic and Republican administrations, the ruling class has held top positions, and they have financed the campaigns of people who run for the House and Senate.

The Executive

Most social scientists agree that the executive branch of the federal government is the most powerful. The cabinet and other executive positions have been mostly the province of ruling-class men. Domhoff (1983) shows that from 1932 to 1964, the majority of secretaries of state, defense, and treasury (the most important cabinet posts) have come from the ruling class. In a more extensive study, Mintz (1975) found that of the 205 people who served in presidential cabinets from 1897 to 1973 nearly 90 percent belonged to the "social or business elite" (as she defines them), who are, at most, 1 percent of the population. Freitag (1975), who also covered the period from 1897 to 1973, found similar connections: 76.1 percent of all cabinet officers were interlocked with big businesses. These men had served on boards of directors of, or held major offices in, major corporations. Another 11.7 percent were unknown lawyers (possible interlocks) and 12.2 percent had no connections with business. The percentages are approximately the same for both Democratic and Republican administrations.

President Carter's cabinet and other top executive positions continued the same trend—no outsiders there. Carter's cabinet was indistinguishable from Nixon's. Carter's people came from corporate headquarters and top law firms: the twelve cabinet secretaries had seventy years in public office, thirty corporate directorships, and an average income of $211,000. Even newcomer Juanita Kreps, Secretary of Commerce and Labor in the Carter Administration, sat on eight boards of directors, including Eastman Kodak and the New York Stock Exchange. Deputy secretaries also come from similar backgrounds (Morris, 1977). Indeed we find that over two hundred of Jimmy Carter's top cabinet appointees graduated from Ivy League colleges, as did some of his White House assistants, such as national security adviser Zbigniew Brzezinski (*Intelligence Report,* 1978).

Although President Reagan's cabinet secretaries were somewhat more conservative than those who worked for Jimmy Carter, they come from similar class and business backgrounds. Before they joined the government, most of them were top corporate officials or corporate lawyers. For example, Donald Regan, former secretary of the treasury and chief of staff, was chairman of Merrill Lynch, a large stock brokerage firm, and William French

Smith, former attorney general, was a senior partner in a law firm whose clients are large corporations. Bechtal Corporation, a large construction firm, had three of its executives serving in the Reagan administration, among them Secretary of State George Schultz. Through the years, many former Bechtal executives have run the CIA and held other top governmental positions (Brownstein & Easton, 1983).

Congress and Legislation

A number of studies have shown that not only has the ruling class controlled legislation that is obviously beneficial to its interests (most notably tax policy), but it has also shaped much of the reform legislation since 1900. For example, legislation enabling workers to unionize arose in part from strikes and protests of the workers, but Domhoff (1978b) argues it was finally passed because some ruling-class people thought they could shape the nature of unions to be less militant, and thus stabilize capitalism and ruling-class control. (We should note here that, like any social group, the ruling-class is not entirely unified. Ruling-class people do not always agree on the policies that best serve their interests. But they agree much more often than they disagree.)

Most laws serve the interests of the ruling class. The enactment and enforcement of corporate, criminal, and other laws show a clear bias to corporate and ruling-class interests. Chambliss and Seidman (1982) examine this bias. Senators and members of Congress, the people who write the laws, generally do not come from the ruling class. Some Senators do (Ted Kennedy, Charles Percy, others), but more of them get wealthier while in and after they leave the Senate. Most people in Congress come from the professional (mostly lawyers), managerial, and business sectors, and their ideology and interests are closely connected to those of the ruling class.

In addition, both presidential and congressional candidates have been heavily financed by contributions from wealthy individuals, families, and corporations. The election reforms of the 1970s did limit direct contributions to candidates. But corporations, labor unions, and other groups are allowed to form Political Action Committees (PACs), solicit money from many individuals, and then donate it to candidates. Corporate PACs far outspend union PACs. By 1980, there were hundreds of large corporation PAC. They collect money from their top executives and build sizeable treasuries. Thus, even though it is no longer possible for a very few wealthy people to give millions to their favorite candidates, *as a group* the ruling and managerial classes still dominate campaign financing. The influence of the class, as a class, continues. For example, in 1985 business PACs contributed heavily to members of Congress who served on committees writing tax laws. Of the $16.7 million PAC contribution to their campaigns, $11.4, two-thirds, came from business PAC. In contrast, labor PACs contributed only $2 million. (See Miller, 1982; Nyhan, 1982; Massie, 1982; Domhoff, 1983; Gilbert & Kahl, 1987; and *Boston Globe,* July 16, 1985:6.)

Regulatory and Other Agencies

To control business and corporate abuses, Congress created various regulatory agencies. Contrary to popular belief, however, many of these agencies were considered desirable by corporate heads. One case in point is the meat packing industry. Large meat packing companies wanted the Food and Drug Administration created because it would drive out small businesses that could not pass standards, forestall stricter state regulations, and allow them to sell meat overseas. Many government agencies have developed close ties with those they are supposed to regulate—a relationship that rarely inhibits the business.

Here are a few blatant examples of ruling-class influence over a regulatory agency. On April 27, 1971, Henry Ford II and Lee Iacocca, top executives of Ford Motor Company, met with President Nixon and succeeded in stopping pending federal regulation that would have required air bags in all new cars. (We know these facts courtesy of the Nixon tapes.) Another example involves the Environmental Protection Agency (EPA). In the spring of 1983 two top EPA officials resigned because the press exposed their favoritism toward business interests. However, the EPA has always been sympathetic to the problems corporations face. Regulations to clean up the environment have been changed, postponed, or ignored when corporations have complained they could not (or did not want to) pay the costs. Reagan officials have been brazen and open in their corporate bias. For example, Dow Chemical Company was known to be dumping dioxin, a deadly chemical. A 1983 preliminary EPA report on its dangers was given to Dow, but the final report was much softer on Dow and dioxin. It seems clear that Dow lobbied top EPA officials, who apparently ordered the report's writers to modify it. Carter officials, however, were just as lax and failed to look vigorously for toxic waste sites. The administration ordered one official to stop investigating hazardous waste dumps and then demoted him. (See *Progressive,* April 1983; *Guardian,* February 23, 1983:6; and *Boston Globe,* March 19, 1983:1.)

William Ruckelshaus, who headed the EPA in the early 1970s, was reappointed by President Reagan after the bad publicity of business bias. But Ruckelshaus is not exactly pristine as far as ties to business. He came to the EPA in 1983 straight from his position as senior vice-president of Weyerhaeuser Company, a timber corporation that had been in conflict with the EPA and other agencies over its use of dangerous herbicides. It has also been reported that when Ruckelshaus was at Weyerhaeuser, he had called for easing clean air standards. He has also represented other corporations that have opposed environmental regulations that would affect their practices. Who regulates whom? one wonders. (See *Boston Globe,* March 19, 1983:1, and March 27, 1983:18.)

Ralph Nader and his associates have investigated such agencies as the Food and Drug Administration (FDA) and the Interstate Commerce Commission (ICC). These agencies have failed to regulate the corporations they oversee. Nader's group points out that some regulators have come to an agency after having worked in the industry the agency is supposed to be regulating, and even more of them leave their government posts for positions in the business they regulated. Government agencies cater to corporate wishes. The FDA acts slowly to protect consumer health and interests but responds quickly to business concerns. Following the Tylenol poisonings in 1982, drug corporations wanted to avoid loss of consumer confidence, strict local regulations, and competition from those companies that would not make new packages. With unprecedented speed, the FDA issued new packaging regulations after it was pressured by drug companies. These regulations were needed, to be sure, but the FDA is usually much slower in responding to similar demands when they come from consumers (*Progressive,* July 1983:10). Corporate influence over and access to federal regulatory agencies is widespread. Directly or indirectly, these agencies do not regulate to protect the consumer but serve the business world. (See Nelson, 1983; Powledge, 1984a; and *Guardian,* December 3, 1986:3, May 13, 1987:3.)

Repression of Political Protest and Change

As we saw in Chapter 4, the U.S. government has spied on people, infiltrated political groups, and violated many of the laws protecting freedom of speech. It does so to stop those who want to change the political and economic system. New police technologies, computerized systems that store information about protesters, and increased spying by the FBI and other agencies, are all meant to repress protest and change. Surveillance of protesters is not the work of over zealous or fanatic government officials. It is systematic, planned, and ongoing. It is government policy, not violation of it (*Guardian,* July 8, 1981:18). (See *Progressive,* May 1983:10–11; Cooper, 1983; Burnham, 1983; Donner, 1985; McGehee, 1985; Navarro, 1986b; and *Guardian,* March 4, 1987:6.)

Corporations engage in their own spying and political repression. People opposing the nuclear power industry have been harassed, some even shot at. Karen Silkwood, a former worker at Kerr McGee, has become a symbol and martyr for those opposing the nuclear industry. In 1974, she was driving to meet a *New York Times* reporter and a union official to hand them evidence of safety violations at the Oklahoma nuclear plant where she worked. Her car was forced off the road. She was killed, and her documents disappeared. The accumulated evidence seems to indicate that the nuclear industry was involved in her death. (See Solomon, 1980, and Kohn, 1982.)

Violence to suppress political and social dissent is used only as a last resort, however, since it exposes the inequalities and profit orientation of the system. It is preferable and more effective to shape what people think than it is to beat or kill them.

Corporations, schools, workplaces, the mass media, advertising, and other institutions try to socialize us not to question the economic and political institutions. We are told that we are fortunate we do not live in country X, where dissenters are jailed. But what about the spying and persecution of dissenters by the FBI, CIA, and other government and corporate agencies?

For example, for six years (from 1981 to 1986), the FBI spied on and harassed hundreds of individuals and groups opposed to U.S. government policies in Central America. No illegal activity by these groups was ever found by the FBI, yet the campaign against them continued. According to a *Guardian* (February 3, 1988:9) story, the harassment included "visits by FBI agents to the families and workplaces of activists, Internal Revenue Service audits, tampering with organizations' and individuals' mail, and over 100 break-ins aimed at the homes and offices of people working for peace in Central America." In addition, church and other groups working for peace in Central America were infiltrated by FBI agents, who sought to destroy these groups.

We should question whether or not we are *really* free.

Are we free to choose when corporations spend billions of dollars to persuade us to want their products? Are we free when we can only choose our transportation from a list of energy-wasting cars but have no good public transportation as a viable alternative? Are we free when our education hides from us the real history of class struggles, class conflicts, and political persecution? Are we free when working people have no chance of serving in Congress since it costs so much money to run for office, and only rich people and corporation PACs have the money to finance such campaigns? (See Chomsky, 1985, and Albert et al., 1986.)

Advisory Commissions, Social Clubs, and Open Doors

The evidence so far concerning how the ruling class dominates government has come from fairly public knowledge, accessible to interested people. More hidden, but equally important, are the advisory commissions and study groups, whose members come from the major corporations, and who recommend policy to Congress and the executive branch. The many ties between the people in these committees and social clubs and the open-door policy that invites corporations to present their problems to sympathetic government ears are elements of how the ruling class gets and keeps its power. People meet informally at parties and social clubs where many important decisions are discussed, sometimes even made. Political power is exercised quietly in informal settings (Burnham, 1978).

Consider a few details. Before it had to disband itself in 1973 because it would not make its meetings public, the Industry Advisory Council to the Department of Defense met regularly with defense officials to discuss mutual interests and concerns. For example, they discussed what weapons the department wanted and needed. On the IAC board were the presidents or chairmen of thirty corporations, all among the top one hundred military contractors—people who sell equipment and weapons to the Department of Defense (Roose, 1975).

The Council on Foreign Relations (CFR) is another important private advisory group. Here, top corporate leaders get together with academics, such as Henry Kissinger and others, to study and explore the problems of American capitalism in United States foreign relations. Many CFR positions eventually become government policy, and members serve the government in many ways. They are appointed to government posts, serve on special presidential commissions, become government advisors, testify before congressional commissions, write books and articles (Domhoff, 1974b, 1978b, 1983).

Domhoff (1983) has shown that there is a great overlap between the members of the federal executive policy groups, social clubs, and corporate directors and officials. In some cases, the same people occupy positions in all these institutions. In other cases, the same corporation has representatives in these institutions. But in all cases, these people are members of the ruling class or are its hired experts.

The executive branch invites corporate executives to drop in any time to discuss their problems, especially problems with the government. Such hospitality is not publicized, but it is assumed by all corporate leaders. It becomes known only when the government is forced to open its workings to public exposure.

The ITT hearings (Committee on the Judiciary, 1972) is one such occasion. In 1972, the Nixon administration was accused of receiving a donation to the Republican Party (a bribe) in exchange for dropping an antitrust case against ITT. The hearings exposed the extraordinary hospitality of government agencies. Corporation presidents and representatives repeatedly testified that all it took was a phone call for them to see a government official. The director of ITT's Washington office testified that he set up an appointment with Secretary of the Treasury John Connally explaining that such appointments "are not difficult to get. You call the secretary as a rule and get an appointment." (p. 951) Richard Kleindienst, who was an attorney in the Justice Department at the time, had told another ITT official, "Well, the door is always open." (p. 952)

Such relationships are not surprising. Government officials often come from the corporate world and return to it after their service is over. When in government, they deal with business people they know or whose basic perspective they share. So explicit conspiracies and deals, even though occasionally made, are not really the issue. It is simpler: shared interests, values, and views.

Local Politics

The discussion thus far has focused on the control the ruling class has over the national economy and government. But big business also controls the economy on a local level by buying out or forcing out of business local companies. Through their local plants, corporations can exercise considerable control over municipal and state politics. In Gary, Indiana, U.S. Steel avoids paying $30 million in annual taxes and receives other preferential treatment. It is so large and dominates the local economy so thoroughly that an implied threat to move out if it is taxed more than suffices to stop any change in its tax status. Major reforms in local politics can always be opposed by such powerful corporations. By laying off thousands of workers if they move, and by their wealth and influence, they exercise enormous power (Bybee, 1983).

In addition, there are local ruling classes, businesses and groups of families that dominate local economies and governments. Real estate firms, banks, and other financial institutions control money, jobs, and campaign contributions. Their influence shapes local tax decisions and other policies. Sociologists and political scientists have conducted a great deal of research on the existence, or absence, of local ruling classes. (Hunter, 1953, 1980; Gilbert & Kahl, 1987; Domhoff, 1983 argues for a theory of local power structures as "'growth machines"; Dahl, 1961, disputes Hunter and others who claim there are local ruling classes.)

Boston is an example of a city run by local and national corporations and real estate interests. There are large insurance companies, department stores for the rich and affluent, restaurants to serve all tastes, marketplaces with stores catering to many fancies, condominiums for the urban gentry. It is a booming city, according to the media image. But poverty, racism, displaced tenants, and low-paying jobs in insurance, retail sales, and services are the other Boston, the one where most people live. Corporations and real estate interests, which rarely make the news, run the city's economy and politics. In 1982, according to the Boston Urban Study Group (1984a,b), eighteen men (all *were* men) formed an inner circle of interlocking directorates. One man served on six boards of directors, one on five, six men on four, and the other ten on three boards each.

The Boston Urban Study Group's study of the ruling class explores in depth how it dominates the city's politics and economy.

> *A small and relatively invisible group of men run Boston. They are not elected by the voters, but their daily decisions shape the lives of millions of Boston area residents. Their power is based on the control of large institutions, money, and property. It endures no matter who the voters elect as mayor, city councillors, school committee members. Their collective power, when organized, is greater than that of the elected representative government.*
>
> *Boston's power structure is not headquartered in any one bank, corporation, or law firm. It is an interlocking network of businessmen who share the common purpose of making Boston a good place to do business. To promote this goal, they have formed a variety of business organizations through which they meet, exchange ideas, sponsor studies, lobby and influence politicians, and (whenever possible) present a "united front" to the public.*
>
> *The men who comprise Boston's power structure are not powerful as individuals. Their power derives from their positions at the top of the city's major banks, insurance companies, retailers and manufacturers, utilities, and law firms. These men control the enormous wealth of large corporations. (p. 6)*

The Ruling Class in Other Institutions

We have seen how the ruling class influences and controls the economy and the government. But education, the mass media, criminal justice, and the culture in general are also influenced and shaped by the ruling class.

Let us briefly examine charitable foundations as an example of this influence. Although there are over twenty thousand charitable foundations, a few large ones dominate the distribution of grants to higher education, medical research, and related areas. They fund research in the social sciences, the physical sciences, and trends and directions in education. These foundations, among them Ford, Carnegie, Mellon, and Rockefeller, have been created and funded from the corporate wealth of the ruling class. They influence and direct the kind of research that becomes fashionable and acceptable. For example, schools are offered grants for specific uses that shape the direction of higher education. Periodically, foundations sponsor reports on trends and directions in higher education that influence its course. The Carnegie foundation was instrumental in creating the climate that created the two-class system, community colleges for the lower classes and better education for the upper classes. This is not to say that foundations directly exploit people. But it is clear that their money enables the ruling class to shape ideas, research, and directions institutions should take. In short, they exercise power. By funding research in one area (acceptable to them) and not another, foundations use ruling-class wealth to direct the course of our society. (See Arnove, 1980; Domhoff, 1983; Spring, 1984; and Aronowitz & Giroux, 1985.)

Does the Ruling Class Rule?

This section summarizes and clarifies the argument that a ruling class exists. It also briefly presents the pluralist perspective that holds there is no ruling class.

The Power of the Ruling Class

Some people think that the name *ruling* class overstates the power of the class. It implies that they have total and absolute control of the society.

I make no such claim. I have taken the meaning of *rule* from two dictionary definitions. One of its noun meanings is (Random House College Dictionary, 1980) "the customary or normal condition, occurrence, practice, etc." (p. 1153) The first definition of rule as a verb states: "to control or direct; exercise dominating power, authority, or influence over; govern." Taking these definitions together, we can say that *the ruling class usually exercises dominant power, authority, or influence over the economy, the government, and some other major institutions.*

Read that definition carefully. It speaks of what *usually* happens. It refers to power, authority, and influence, not total control at all times. I use different verbs to refer to what the ruling class does: dominate, shape, control, direct, and influence. At different times, under different circumstances, the ruling class may have total control over events, or dominant but not total control, or a major influence, or some influence, or none at all. We need to study how much, if any, power the ruling class exercises in different historical settings. We cannot assume total control, if any control.

The ruling class does not always prevail, but it does so frequently, especially in areas and institutions that are important to people in that class. They often succeed in stopping what they perceive to be harmful to their interests. For example, during the 1970s there was a proposal in Congress to create a Consumer Protection Agency. Despite ample evidence that consumers do need protection from corporations (see discussion on corporate crime, above), the proposed legislation was not enacted. According to Domhoff (1983), the Business Roundtable, a policy group of corporate executives, played a major role in killing the proposal.

Ruling class and corporate groups also often modify and moderate laws that benefit the working class. For example, since the late 1940s, they have pressured Congress to enact legislation to weaken the power of labor unions. Congress has done so. Other legislation that would benefit the working class is not enforced vigorously. The Occupational Safety and Health Administration (OSHA) is a recent and obvious example. Since its inception in 1970, OSHA has never been funded fully to enable it to inspect working conditions in all business. In the 1980s, OSHA's funding has been reduced drastically. Also, penalties imposed on offending wealthy corporations amount to what would be pennies for us. (See Domhoff, 1983, and Claybrook, 1984.)

Nor does the theory that says there is a ruling class claim that all people and institutions of that class are in complete agreement on all policies at all times. There is frequent debate and disagreement about what is best for an industry or for the economy as a whole. Also, there is disagreement about some foreign policies. For example, although all ruling class institutions opposed the National Liberation Front in South Vietnam during the 1960s, they disagreed on whether the costs of winning the Vietnam war were prohibitive. In the late 1980s, there is an intense debate over the policies to reduce the huge foreign trade deficit of the U.S. economy. There are frequent disagreements. There are also differences in style and personality conflicts, as we can expect to happen in any group of people. But these are *family* fights. Mostly everyone agrees about the ends: a corporate economy in a capitalist society. Most of the time there is broad agreement on most policies.

The 1987 Iran/Contra Congressional hearings are a good example of a family fight. Nearly everyone in government and corporate institutions opposes the Sandinista government in Nicaragua. They merely disagree on the *means* of their opposition. The entire debate was about specific policies, styles of governing, and some personality conflicts. If it were not for the still strong anti-war sentiments of most people, the Reagan administration would have invaded Nicaragua. Because of that sentiment, the government and the CIA had to create and finance the Contras. It is over the means to oppose the Nicaraguan government, not over the principle of opposition to that government, that the disputes and the TV drama of the hearings revolved.

Domestically, the military budget and tax policies show that people and groups in the ruling class agree on basic principles but disagree on details. No corporation president, and only a rare politician or writer for the major news media, questions whether the United States needs such a huge military budget for the nation's defense. The debates in Congress, the press, and elsewhere are over specific weapons, missiles, airplanes, and programs, not over the size and purpose of the defense establishment.

The same general agreement prevails in tax policy debates. Conservatives, moderates, and liberals often engage in heated debates over specific tax proposals. Democrats criticize Republicans for tax laws that take too much from the working class and not enough from the rich. But under Democrats and Republicans alike, the tax burden on the working class has been increasing and the taxes paid by the rich decreasing, as we have just seen. Even a proposal by Jesse Jackson at the Democratic convention in July, 1988, that the Democratic party commit itself to a modest increase in taxes paid by the richest people, was rejected. Some Democrats and Republicans genuinely care for working people and want to create government programs to help them. But even they do not question the morality of the huge income and wealth of the ruling class and the wealthier managers. They just want to increase their taxes a little.

Nor does the theory of the ruling class refer to a committee of ten, or a hundred, or a thousand people who meet secretly to plot and manipulate the rest of us. Rather, it refers to a group, a class, that *shares common experiences, interests, and values.* Domhoff and others have shown that family, school, association, work, and other experiences tend to unite them, to breed certain expectations and relationships. As a class, they come to occupy, or to influence who occupies, the top positions in the economy and the government. The groups and institutions of the ruling class make, control, and influence the major decisions about what gets produced, and where, about large plants that move or close down, about loans and investments in the billions, about wars to be fought and liberation movements in other countries to be opposed, about long-term educational policies, and about major legislation. Major issues and conditions that do not affect the ruling class (abortion and prostitution are examples) are of no interest. Religious groups, civil liberty groups, and others debate and argue over these issues. The ruling class does not control every aspect of our lives. But it does control the economy and plays *the,* or *a,* major role in policies that affect the economy and its own power and wealth.

The ruling class may be consolidating and extending its control over the economy. According to Useem (1984), directors and managers of major corporations now are thinking more of what is best for the entire ruling class and the corporate economy as a whole, rather than what benefits a family, a corporation, an industry. Especially with the increase in interlocking directorates, a few men (men they are) can have a general overview of the long-term interests of the capitalist economy as a whole. Fewer and fewer corporations are owned soley by one or a few families, but most stock in major corporations is owned by only a few individuals. The directors and managers of these corporations are members of the ruling class, or the upper reaches of the managerial class. All of them have a vested interest in making the corporate economy profitable because it is corporate stock and profits that give the ruling class its wealth and power, that make its life style possible.

Members of the ruling class are not equally powerful. In the 1980s, at most a thousand corporations own most of the assets in the United States. Each corporation has ten to twenty directors (but remember many people serve on the boards of directors of two, three, four, and even more corporations) and a few top managers. It is estimated that ten to twenty thousand people run the American economy. Even fewer are very powerful, those who run the top twenty to thirty corporations. These few thousand people, along with a few thousand professionals and corporate lawyers, also run the executive branch of the U.S. government; they are very influential in elections and legislation; and they serve on advisory and study groups and commissions that promote and shape long-term social policies.

Let me close this discussion by making two points. We should not focus on ruling class *individuals,* on their personalities and characters. They do not rule as individuals. *The ruling class rules because its members occupy powerful positions in the economy, the government, and other institutions, or they possess resources to influence the people who occupy those positions.* No one individual is indispensable or all-powerful. The people in the ruling class are not evil, as individuals. Most of them probably love their children, spouses, friends, and relatives. It is the action of the whole class that exploits people, that causes misery and illness.

Lastly, whatever social scientists may believe about the nature or even the existence of a ruling class, most people have a notion (vague, imprecise, and undefined though it may be) that a small group holds most of the power. Daily conversations lead to that conclusion, and so do some polls. The *Boston Globe* (April 15, 1984:16) reported a Harris pole of 1,270 adults that showed that 74 percent believe "there is a small group in the United States—the so-called establishment—who are insiders and who run things in the country." Nineteen percent disagreed and seven percent had no opinion.

The Pluralist Perspective

Many political scientists, sociologists, and other social scientists do not think there is a ruling class, or any such group with a similar label. They argue that power is not concentrated in any one group or class. They believe instead that power is dispersed among many competing interest groups, that there are many centers of power, and that no one group always prevails. Society is composed of many, more or less equal, groups: corporations, business associations, labor unions, professional associations, universities, environmental groups, religious groups, occupational groups, racial and ethnic groups, the military, political organizations, youth and elderly groups, PTAs, women's groups—the list goes on.

As each group tries to influence government policies for its benefit, it has to compete with other groups for resources. There is only so much money and so many resources available. Compromise is necessary and inevitable. Each group obtains at least some of its goals some of the time, but no group wins all of the time. Thus, these relatively equal groups balance each other out.

The combined power of many groups prevents any one group from dominating. Most groups are strong enough to have veto power over proposed policies that would harm them and to get what they want.

Some pluralists argue that contrary to the ruling class theory, businesses and corporations are neither unified nor dominant. There are conflicts between business groups; oil versus coal corporations, importers of clothes versus U.S. textile manufacturers, and so on. Generally, much of the time corporations do not agree or act as one group.

Most, if not all, people belong to, or have their interests represented by, one or more groups. Therefore, generally and in the long run everyone has some power. No one group totally dominates and no one loses out completely. (See Dahl, 1982, for a recent statement of the pluralist perspective.)

Imperialism

Imperialism refers to the world economic, political, and military system in which wealth flows from the periphery (poor nations) to the center (rich and powerful nations) and benefits the corporations and ruling classes of the center nations. The extent and nature of the capitalist ruling class in the United States can only be understood in this context. The world capitalist system began to develop in the sixteenth century and is now being challenged by nationalist and socialist revolutions throughout the world.

Spain, Britain, Holland, France, and other European countries began to colonize and exploit nations throughout Africa, Asia, and Latin America. As the power of one increased the power of others waned. The United States began to exert its power in this capitalist system around 1900 and has been the dominant and central power since 1945. United States power is now slowly being challenged by other capitalist nations, Europe and Japan mostly, and by socialist revolutions everywhere.

With some oversimplification, we can divide the world into three groups. The capitalist system controls and dominates poorer countries. At the center of this system are most European countries, Canada, the United States, and Japan. As of 1986, 15 percent of the world's five billion people live in these countries. On the periphery of the system are the poorer, exploited, and dominated nations of the world. Generally, wealth flows from the periphery to the center. As of 1986, about 1.8 billion people (36 percent of the world's population) lived in Asia, 580 million (11.6 percent) in Africa, and 420 million (8.4 percent) in Latin America. Largely outside this world capitalist system lie the noncapitalist nations, with about 1.45 billion (29 percent) people in the USSR, China, Eastern Europe, Vietnam, Cuba, and other socialist nations. Although they have limited trade with capitalist nations, they are not controlled economically, politically, or militarily by the U.S., European, and Japanese ruling classes. (See Sweezy, 1979; Amin, 1980; Amin et al., 1982; and *Statistical Abstract,* 1987:814–817.)

The points below outline the essence of imperialism today:

■ The United States, Europe, and Japan dominate the world capitalist system. Wealth flows from the periphery to these nations at the center.

■ The economies of all capitalist nations are controlled by powerful ruling classes, with ruling classes of the center nations (especially the United States) being the most powerful.

■ The peripheral nations have their own ruling classes, which have allied themselves with the ruling classes of the center nations.

■ Thus, the poor people of Asia, Africa, and Latin America are exploited both by their own and outside ruling classes.

■ In the poorer periphery nations a few people (the ruling classes) live well, even extravagantly, but most people suffer materially; millions are starving.

■ Conversely, in the center nations there is less poverty, but some exists, and the working classes barely manage. They suffer in comparison to the wealth of the upper classes, and their lives and communities are controlled by the ruling class.

■ Class divisions and class struggles, then, exist in an international system. Poor people in periphery nations are waging struggles and revolutions to escape the world capitalist system.

■ Most people in the United States do not exploit the poor people in periphery nations; U.S. corporations do. Most Americans lose, they do not gain, in this imperialist world system. (For some recent discussions and data on imperialism, and policies poor countries should use to fight imperialism, see the following excellent papers, mostly in *Monthly Review:* Samatar, 1984; Buchanan, 1985; Chinweizu, 1985; MacEwan, 1985, 1986; Payer, 1985; Pool & Stamos, 1985; Chapman, 1987; Hoogvelt, 1987; Pollin & Zepeda, 1987; and *Dollars and Sense,* January/February 1987:14.)

Stages of Imperialism

For centuries the peoples of Africa, Asia, and Latin America have been exploited by European and North American business interests. Much of the profit that enabled early capitalist enterprises to grow and expand came from slavery and economic exploitation of the labor and resources of nonwhite people on these three continents. (See next chapter for more details.)

Historically, imperialism has gone through three stages.

1. *Colonialism,* in its classic form, was the military conquest and governing of societies. Land, labor, and resources were appropriated (stolen), enriching the ruling classes of the imperialist nations.

2. Classic colonialism became difficult to administer, and gradually colonies became independent (the United States was one of the first). But more recently, poorer nations have been exploited through *trade.* This neocolonialism involves buying minerals, food, and other raw materials at very low prices and then selling expensive manufactured products back to the poor nations.

3. Investment and loans constitute the latest form of imperialist exploitation. U.S., European, and Japanese corporations open plants in poor countries because the cheap labor and low taxes make higher profits. In addition, poor countries have been borrowing from imperialist governments and banks, and now are heavily in debt. The interest from these loans constitutes a large portion of the profits of many banks.

Neocolonialism

Corporations from the United States, Europe, and Japan invest in their group (the center of the imperialist system) and in the periphery nations. Today, most of these multinational corporations (MNCs) are based in the United States. Let us now examine the extent to which the U.S. economy and the large MNCs depend on poorer nations for mineral and other raw materials, and profit from trade, investments, and loans.

Minerals   Airplanes, appliances, cars, and other products depend on metals, fuels, and minerals. U.S. corporations largely (and increasingly) import these raw materials from poorer nations. They either own the facilities that drill and refine the oil, mine and process the minerals, or they buy them cheaply. The U.S. economy cannot operate without oil, copper, aluminum, and other raw materials, and the U.S. government has fought wars, sabotaged unfriendly governments, and threatened invasions to assure their availability.

Table 10.4 presents the percentage of each mineral U.S. corporations imported in 1960 and 1984. They show how deeply our economy depends on foreign sources of essential materials.

Investments   In 1960, U.S. corporations made 12.2 percent of their profits from foreign investments; by 1980, 23.8 percent of their profits came from $213.5 billion of foreign investments (45 percent of these were in Europe, 21 percent in Canada, and 25 percent in poorer countries). American MNCs depend heavily on foreign investments for their profits. For example, in 1972 only 9.8 percent of MNC invested capital was in foreign countries, but it

TABLE 10.4
Imported Minerals and Metals, as Percents of U.S.
Consumption, 1960 and 1985

	1960	1985
Petroleum*	17%	29%
Bauxite	74	97
Cobalt	66	95
Nickel	72	68
Zinc	46	69
Silver	43	64
Platinum	82	92
Manganese	89	100

Statistical Abstract, 1982–1983:724; 1988:661
* The petroleum percent increased to 36% in 1975, 43% in
1977, and has decreased since then to 29% in 1985.

brought 24.4 percent of total profits. (See *Dollars and Sense,* December 1981,
and July-August 1982; Edwards et al., 1978.)

U.S. corporations invest overseas because of the obvious profits. Cheap
labor, low taxes, and ununionized workers (many governments forbid unions)
attract investors. In Southeast Asia, Mexico, and elsewhere workers are paid
only 10 to 20 percent of what American workers make.

Many products sold to the U.S. market are manufactured overseas by
American MNCs. This is especially true of products that are labor-intensive.
For example, TVs sold by U.S. corporations here are made in Taiwan. Even
G.I. Joe toys, that all-American symbol, are made in Hong Kong (*Progressive,*
July 1983:4).

Loans   By holding the financial strings, corporations can directly control
countries politically and militarily. U.S. and European government agencies
(some of them international) have always loaned money to poor countries. But
more recently, U.S. banks have been lending heavily. Poor countries owe
about two-thirds of their debt to them (*Dollars and Sense,* December 1982:
10).

The debt is huge and increasing. According to the Center for Popular
Economics (1986), in 1985, poor, or developing nations had a total debt of
about $860 billion. Brazil owed over $100 billion and Mexico over $80 billion.
Latin America and Caribbean countries owed a total of $360 billion.

Mexico, Brazil, and other poor countries have borrowed heavily from
U.S. banks. Beginning in the middle 1970s, banks found fewer and fewer
profitable investments in the United States. They went out seeking countries
to loan money to. Some of them have over half of their loans in poor countries.
In 1980, 58 percent of the revenues of eight major U.S. banks came from
foreign sources. In 1985, Citicorp made 25 percent of its profits from interest
on Latin American loans. (See Moffitt, 1983; MacEwan, 1987; and *Guardian,*
February 25, 1987:14.)

Why did these countries borrow so heavily? What did they do with the money? They borrowed to shore up their sinking economies. From 1965 to 1984, what poor countries sell to the rich countries (minerals, crops, etc., except for petroleum) declined in value by 30 percent in relation to what they pay for the manufactured products they import from rich countries. For this and other reasons they borrowed. What happened to the money? Little of it benefitted the poor people in these countries. Some of it went to finance the military in countries like Brazil and Argentina. Some of it was taken by the rich and deposited in accounts in rich countries, especially in Switzerland. The economies of these societies have not grown enough to repay loans and interest—thus, the debt crisis of the 1980s. Many countries cannot even pay the interest on these loans. Those that do, in part or in whole, squeeze the money by lowering wages and living standards of their people. The poverty that had existed in these societies because of class inequalities is now worsening (Center for Popular Economics, 1986).

The Effects of Imperialism

Most people who live in the periphery nations of the capitalist system are exploited twice: once by their own ruling classes and again by the ruling classes of the United States, Europe, and Japan.

Thailand is a U.S. ally, one of the free world societies that lies on the periphery of imperialism. A United Nations survey (*Guardian,* January 12, 1983:10) found that two million Thai children under sixteen years of age work in factories. "Thousands of children, some as young as six years, are virutally sold into annual or lifetime work in farms, homes, factories, or brothels," according to the United Nations report. Out of 115 children that were sampled, 98 percent worked more than eight hours a day, and 32 percent over thirteen hours. The report notes that "52 percent of them worked 7 days a week. Their average wage was 55 cents a day, compared to the $3.25 a day legal minimum for adults."

In Latin America, 60 percent of the people live in extreme poverty. Even in Brazil, which for a while was touted as a country undergoing an economic miracle, there is much suffering. People live in shacks and slums. Millions of children live on the streets. The United Nations estimated that "Brazil has at least 10 million street children who have been abandoned or whose families cannot fully support them. Some social workers say 25 million is more likely" (*Boston Globe,* November 13, 1984:77). In a country of 120 million, that many abandoned children may be a quarter to a half of all children. In 1979, in Sao Paulo forty children a day died from poverty. About six hundred thousand children lived by begging, stealing, or prostitution. UNICEF estimates that throughout the world 280,000 children die each week from hunger and disease. (See *Boston Globe,* February 6, 1987:2; *Guardian,* June 20, 1979:12; January 28, 1987:18; Huebner, 1985; and Hoogvelt, 1987.)

Why are people hungry when the world produces more than enough food to feed everyone? One reason is that people's low wages do not enable them to buy enough food. Another reason, and one that is related to the first, is that much of the land in poor countries is owned by local ruling classes or foreign corporations (Del Monte is an example), which use it to raise cash crops for export (coffee, bananas, tomatoes). Corporations make large profits from these crops but the people within the countries have less land to grow the food they need to eat, such as rice, beans, lentils, and corn. (More data can be found in Lappé & Collins, 1977 and summarized in Liazos, 1982; see also *Guardian*, April 13, 1983:24, and Burbach & Flynn, 1980.)

As land is being taken over by the local ruling class and MNCs, people cannot make a living on their meager plots, so they migrate to the cities. But very few find jobs. Unemployment often reaches 40 to 50 percent, and those who work make very little. People resort to scrounging in garbage cans. Garbage collectors pick up dead bodies daily.

The huge debts that developing nations have incurred intensify people's suffering. These nations must often use a large portion of their income to repay loans and meet interest payments. When they cannot make payments, foreign banks and institutions offer more loans—on the condition that they "put their house in order." This squeezes the economies of these countries even further since wages must be lowered and food prices raised. Mexico experienced this squeeze in 1982, when it could not meet its payments. (See Magdoff, 1982a, and *Guardian*, January 19, 1983:17.)

When people find the will, they do rise up against imperialism and attempt to gain control over their lives. But this rebellion is often met with severe repression. Thousands of people in El Salvador who have supported land reform and human rights have been murdered. Thousands of blacks in South Africa who have demanded the right to participate in their government and work and travel freely have been killed and imprisoned. These are but two examples. There are hundreds more. But perhaps the only way we can begin to truly understand what it is like to be dominated by another nation or by people within our own country is to try to put ourselves in their place. Imagine you are a farmer who gets paid a $1.00 a day to work on land that is owned by a foreign corporation and that at night you must go home to your hungry family. There is no chance you will ever be able to work your own land or control your own fate. This is the true meaning of imperialism.

War and Nuclear War

The United States has engaged in colonialist and imperialist wars throughout its history. The government took land from the Indians or failed to stop settlers who did. In the 1840s, Mexico lost much of its land to the United States. Around 1900, the United States invaded and captured the Philippines, Puerto Rico, Cuba, and Hawaii. At various times during this century, United

States troops have interfered in the internal affairs of Latin American nations. In the 1950s, President Eisenhower used covert military actions to sabotage and overthrow governments the United States opposed, among them Iran and Guatemala. For most Americans Vietnam is still a vivid reminder of U.S. military intervention. But why have these actions taken place?

Protecting Corporate Interests

The explanations for such actions have been couched in terms of national security. U.S. administrations have claimed our political, military, and economic security have been at stake in each case. Since the rise of socialist states, the justification has been to stop communism from spreading. Vietnam in the 1960s and Central America in the 1980s are two examples.

Intervention in another country's internal conflict may have been partly justified at times. But the larger, continuing, and overriding reason for U.S. government military actions has been the expansion and protection of the economic domination of the ruling class. Chile is a clear example.

In 1970 the socialists won the election. Before and after that election the CIA (at the direct orders of U.S. Presidents) plotted to prevent the socialists' election and to overthrow them if they did win. Undisputed evidence has shown that ITT, which lost its business in Chile when the socialists took over, conspired with the CIA to overthrow the socialists. U.S. corporations regained most of their businesses after the Chile military, with CIA assistance, overthrew the government in 1973 (Petras & Morley, 1975).

There are various reasons for direct or indirect U.S. military action and CIA intervention: to provide new markets, to capture lands, to acquire cheap minerals and metals, and generally to provide a favorable climate for ruling class corporate interests. President Carter said that he would intervene militarily in the Middle East (and he pointedly did not exclude nuclear weapons) if he felt U.S. economic interests were threatened (for example, if unfriendly governments took over nations where U.S. oil corporations do business). In view of this, the question then becomes would the United States intervene if the governments (or socialist ones that may replace them) could not or would not repay their loans (Hulbert, 1982)?

El Salvador and Nicaragua are the latest examples of how the United States protects its investments. Only advisers were in El Salvador in 1988, but the U.S. government is training and financing the military regimes of the region and is financing the groups attempting to overthrow the socialist government of Nicaragua. Why? The possible loss of U.S. corporate investments, should socialist governments take over, is the main reason. According to an article in the *Guardian* (August 25, 1982).

> *U.S. direct investments in El Salvador—$100 million in holdings by 80 corporations—are small by U.S. standards. They pale in comparison to the $10.2 billion U.S. investments in Central America, like Del Monte's banana opera-*

tion in Guatemala, purchased from United Fruit in 1972 for a cool $20.5 million, or Gulf and Western's $300 million investment in sugar production in the Dominican Republic.

No one would argue that U.S. intervention in El Salvador is determined solely by economic interests. But the interests of U.S. corporations in El Salvador must be viewed in the context of several important regional and national trends. Over $1 billion of U.S. holdings in the Caribbean Basin are in manufacturing, the fastest growing sector for foreign investments. U.S. investments in El Salvador are almost exclusively in the manufacturing sector, and represent 10% of the Caribbean total, a significant portion of a growing market.

Although U.S. holdings in El Salvador are small in dollar amounts, the interests represented are among the largest in the world—Exxon, ITT, Standard Oil, and General Motors, to name a few. Most of the U.S. firms in El Salvador have holdings elsewhere in the region, and form a network of corporate and banking investments. Also, the rate of return on Caribbean Basin investments is extremely high—29.3% for 1980, in comparison with an average rate of return of 17.3% for U.S. foreign investments. Even small holdings in El Salvador produce large profits. (p. 8)

An additional, and equally important, reason given by the U.S. government is to stop the advance of anti-capitalist revolutions. Like Vietnam in the 1960s, the U.S. government wants to make an example of Central America. It wants to show it will not tolerate revolutions—even at the cost of supporting military regimes that slaughter civilians by the thousands, as in Guatemala and El Salvador. In themselves, neither Vietnam nor Central America represent huge economic interests for U.S. corporations, but if revolutions spread elsewhere then corporate interests would be threatened. The theory is that if Central America goes today, then Brazil, Mexico, and others could follow. If this should happen corporate economic interests would suffer. (See Sweezy & Magdoff, 1985c, 1986; Acharya, 1987; and Agyeman, 1987.)

(A note on Vietnam: After 1968, a number of corporate and ruling-class leaders called for a withdrawal of U.S.troops, disagreeing with other corporate and government leaders. Both groups wanted to stop social revolutions, but in time the group opposing the war concluded that the costs of the war—in money, lives, and popular opposition—was too high for whatever corporate and political interests there were to be gained. Resistance by the Vietnamese and U.S. citizens made the war too costly [Kolko, 1986].)

Military activities are in a sense *police* activities that protect corporate interests. Today, the United States has the largest military budget in the world, which acts as a sort of world capitalist police force.

The Current Scene

After Vietnam, U.S. military and CIA intervention waned. Thus, in the 1970s Angola and Nicaragua (and in its own way Iran) had revolutions that overthrew governments friendly to U.S. corporate interests, and the United States did relatively little to intervene. Public sentiment would not have supported more military intervention. But beginning in the late 1970s, the military budget received large increases. U.S. military units are being trained to stop revolutions. It has even been suggested that we could engage in a limited nuclear war.

The percentage of the federal budget allocated to the military is staggering. We must first subtract social security payments from the budget. They are made from funds collected through the social security tax to be paid for pensions to retired people and to disabled people. It is only funds from income, corporate, and other taxes that the President and Congress decide how to spend. From these funds, in 1980, 31 percent of the budget was spent on the military. By 1986, it had increased to 38 percent, or $265.8 billion.

Another $26.6 billion, 3.7 percent was spent on veterans' benefits and services, paying for past wars. If we look at the $777 billion total revenue receipts by the government in 1986, minus the $252 billion social security contributions, we find that over 55 percent ($292 of $525 billion) went to the defense and veterans' budgets.

On the other hand, the percent spent on human needs has decreased. For example, 12.7 percent of the budget was allocated to health, education, training, employment, and social services in 1980, 9.5 percent in 1986. Cuts in other programs benefiting the working class and poor were equally large. In addition to reducing spending on human needs, the larger military budget has also increased the annual deficit in the federal budget. From $74 billion in 1980 it grew to $203 billion in 1986. Interest paid on the accumulated federal debt increased from $52.5 billion (8.88 percent of the budget) in 1980 to $142.7 billion (14.56 percent of the budget) in 1986 (*Statistical Abstract*, 1987:293–294). Much of that interest is paid to the ruling class who own the bonds. Thus, the taxes paid by the working class go to finance a military whose primary reason for existence is the protection of corporate and ruling-class interests (Jobs With Peace, 1988).

After a brief hiatus, U.S. military presence and CIA sabotage are now expanding. In fact, U.S. military units and bases cover the world. In 1981, the United States had 1.5 million military personnel in 116 countries. There are four hundred major military bases (such as in Spain, the Philippines, and elsewhere) and three thousand smaller ones in every major world region, costing billions of dollars to operate (*Statistical Abstract*, 1987:787). Since World War II, the United States has given $110 billion in military aid to foreign countries. Police, militia, and two million foreign troops have been financed and trained by the United States to crush revolutions, not prevent foreign invasions.

The protection of corporate interests throughout the world is accomplished through various means. Political support, financing and training of the armed forces, and various CIA covert activities are available to the ruling classes of friendly governments. But such assistance, even when plentiful, does not always suffice, and friendly governments often seem ready to fall to local revolutionary groups. To meet these emergencies (and to prevent more

Irans and Nicaraguas) the Rapid Deployment force (RDF) was conceived in 1979 (Petras, 1980).

From its original size of fifty thousand, it grew to two hundred thousand and three hundred thousand. It is trained and equipped to fly quickly to any spot in the world where the local ruling class, supported by the United States, seems ready to fall. For example, various royal families, loyal to the capitalist world, rule the Middle East countries, rich with oil that flows to Europe, Japan, and the United States. They are not models of justice and democracy. Should local wars or revolutions break out, the RDF is ready to move in and protest these royal families and their allies—and thus the interests of corporations like Exxon and Mobil. But Klare (1981b) asks *is* Exxon worth dying for? General Maxwell Taylor thinks so. He wrote that "as the leading affluent 'have' power, we [the U.S.] may expect to have to fight to protect our national valuables against envious 'have-nots.'" (p. 156) But the "we" is only Exxon and the ruling class, not all Americans; and the "envious" poor of the world do not want our riches, they want to reclaim their countries and resources from their and U.S. ruling classes, and use them to lead a decent life. Petroleum profits go to Exxon stockholders and a few rich Arab families, they do not benefit most Arabs or Americans. In the meantime, the taxes paid by most Americans (and increasingly not paid by corporations) support a military that protects the economic and political interests of the ruling class. (See also Klare, 1980, 1981a.)

But CIA activities, RDF deployment, and other actions may not suffice to stop revolutions. One reason is cost. U.S. military spending is putting pressure on the economy. Public opposition to increases in the military and to the deaths of American soldiers (fifty-five thousand Americans died in Vietnam), are making it more difficult for the government to intervene. Another obstacle is the local revolutionary groups within countries. They are well organized and determined to escape poverty. They do receive some arms and money from friendly countries, but the leadership and fighting and most material support are local. It is a mistake to think foreign powers are instigating revolutions in poor countries. Poor people simply do not want to starve for U.S. corporations, nor do they want to die at the direction of the Soviets or Cubans. They will die, however, to save their children's and country's future (Burbach, 1982).

The U.S. government, through the CIA, is deeply involved in Central America. Poverty, suffering, and vast inequalities exist in all the countries of the region. A few rich people own most of the land and industries. Poor peasants and workers have been protesting against these conditions, some through strikes and demonstrations, some through revolutions. Local ruling classes and U.S. corporate interests oppose any change. The military and police forces, heavily financed and trained by the U.S. government through the CIA, have been trying to repress the people seeking justice and an end to poverty. Hundreds of thousands of people have been beaten, jailed, tortured, killed, or simply disappeared in El Salvador, Guatemala, and Honduras.

The Iran/Contra hearings in 1987 confirmed what many people already knew: the CIA conceived, organized, and financed the Contra forces that have been trying to overthrow the government in Nicaragua. That government has been the only one in Central America working to end poverty, educate all children, provide health care for everyone, and give land to the peasants. In 1979 the Sandinistas overthrew the Somoza dictatorship, long supported by the United States, and began to limit the power of the local ruling class and U.S. corporations. They have supposedly been setting a dangerous example since the country is run for all the people, not the few local rich and foreign corporations. Imperialism's logic dictates that such so-called dangerous examples must be crushed. Thus, the Contra forces had to be created and financed at any cost. This led to the secret manipulations to find support money since the U.S. Congress wavered between financing and not financing the Contras. While the Reagan administration has been conducting an illegal war to overthrow the Nicaraguan government, polls have been showing that two-thirds of those interviewed oppose U.S. financing of the Contras. (The following sources provided extensive documentation for the preceding discussion: Schlesinger, 1983; Burbach, 1984; *Boston Globe,* July 18, 1985:22; Armstrong, 1985; Chomsky, 1985; O'Brien & Thorkelson, 1985; Robinson & Norsworthy, 1985; Ryan, 1986; Hostetter, 1987; and Wise, 1987.)

Nuclear War

Chapter 3 discussed the development and spread of nuclear weapons. I argued that nuclear war is an extension of conventional war and arises out of the same motives and conditions: to control and dominate opponents.

Here I want to note that we can see nuclear weapons as the ultimate weapon in the defense of imperialism and ruling-class control. U.S. presidents have said that they might use nuclear weapons if and when U.S. interests (read: corporate interests) were threatened because the United States was losing a conventional war. President Carter made this point in reference to petroleum in the Middle East. (Authors discussed in Chapter 3, especially Klare, 1982, develop this point at length.)

The Effects of Militarism and Imperialism

The first and foremost effect of militarism and imperialism is death, injury, and destruction. Over fifty-five thousand Americans and over half a million Vietnamese died in Vietnam; many more were injured (physically, spiritually, emotionally). Agent Orange, a defoliant used in Vietnam, has caused illness and genetic damage to American and Vietnamese soldiers and civilians.

But there are many other costs. Militarism and wars cost money, which governments borrow or tax, and that leads to inflation. (Inflation in the 1970s was partly fueled by the cost of the Vietnam war.) Military spending also increases consumer demand (by the pay that goes to those who produce the arms) but does not increase the supply of goods we can buy (we can buy a car but not a tank). More money and the same number of goods mean higher prices.

There are other less visible costs. When money, scientists, and engineers are used to develop and produce arms, they are unavailable to produce civilian goods. The Japanese and Europeans, who spend much less on defense, use their resources to develop computers and other products they can sell; the United States builds arms that are wasted.

Also, as we've stated before, social programs in education, health, and other areas have been reduced as military spending has increased. In addition, the federal government has reduced its support of state and local programs. Local governments have been unable to make up the shortfall. "Collapsing bridges; students without teachers, books, or equipment; unprecedented numbers of people living in the streets; and [more] people trying to live on incomes well below the poverty level" have been some of the results (*Dollars and Sense,* July/August 1987:12).

Research has shown that money spent on military purposes usually creates fewer jobs than if it were spent on civilian uses. For example, one study from the Bay State Conversion Group (1982) estimated that a billion dollars in 1982 created jobs in the following areas:

Defense industry	18,000
Civilian industry	27,000
Armed services personnel	37,000
Government personnel (teachers, police, etc.)	72,000

According to another study, as military spending increased from 1981 to 1985, the United States lost 1,146,000 jobs. We need to start planning to convert arms production to civilian production, to save money, produce useful goods, decrease war tensions, and insure jobs for workers. (See Bay State Conversion Group, 1982; Gordon, 1986; *Progressive,* May 1987:46.)

State and Political Organization

Chapter 3 showed that in gathering and hunting and many horticultural societies power was not concentrated. This is not to say that everyone possessed exactly equal power, but no one person or group dominated the society. In the course of human evolution power became more concentrated as classes arose. According to Szymanski and Goertzel (1979), "the state emerged when societies developed social classes. The classes that monopolized wealth needed an armed force of some kind to protect their possessions. They needed a mechanism for controlling the ways in which this force was used, and for making sure that everyone played their appointed role in the social order. The state, then, originated as an instrument of oppression, and was used quite openly by those in power to advance their own interests." (p.197).

The State

A *state,* according to Webster's Dictionary (1961), is "A body of people permanently occupying a definite territory and politically organized under a sovereign government almost entirely free from external control and possessing coercive power to maintain order within the community." (p. 2228)

Weber (in Taylor, 1982) modifies this when he defines states as "human associations that successfully claim the monopoly of legitimate use of physical force within a given territory." (p. 4) That is, only governments can use physical force legitimately within states. Taylor (1982) modifies Weber's definition and argues no government can ever concentrate all power in its hands. Conversely, no society has existed in which power was completely equally dispersed.

Thus, a *state* is a central government that has concentrated power in its hands (but has no total monopoly of power) and that claims the sole right to use physical force to maintain order ("order" as defined by the government). In state societies, one person or a few people legislate. Government agents enforce the laws through police, courts, and prison systems. Citizens are not allowed to take the law in their hands.

Some important and controversial questions are raised about states. How do the top officials (or sometimes the one absolute ruler) who run the government of the state get their positions? Does anyone control or influence or elect them? If so, who? How? Who benefits by the rule of those who run the state?

To a considerable degree, states everywhere are controlled (directly and/or indirectly) by ruling classes. Even in the parliamentary democracies, there is only the appearance that the people rule and decide.

Capitalist States

There are four types of states today. Szymanski (1981) gives three variations of capitalism: a parliamentarian state (where the people elect legislatures), an authoritarian state, and a fascist state. A socialist state is the fourth type.

Parliamentary   The thirteen original colonies of the United States formed a very loose federation. Power was very dispersed. But soon merchants and large landowners realized that without an army, without a strong central government, without one money system, they could not control the nation. Thus, they called a constitutional convention and created a central government.

In the capitalist world of 1983 there were only about twenty-five states that had a parliamentary democracy. Only a few poor countries (India, Venezuela, one or two others) have such governments, and even these are unstable. Those twenty-five or so states are not true democracies. Despite the formal appearance of people choosing their leaders, the political and economic processes are largely controlled by the ruling class. The U.S. ruling class is more or less typical of the ruling class in parliamentary democracies. It occupies top government positions or finances the elections of those who do; it controls the few large corporations that dominate the economy; the government harasses, persecutes, and represses those who consistently oppose the control of the ruling class and the capitalist system. In times of extreme social crises, civil liberties, freedom of speech, and other democratic forms are suspended.

Authoritarian   Here, those who run the government are not elected. They are usually supported by the military. Generals run the government directly or appoint those who do. Opponents are repressed. Although opposition is formally banned and repressed, it is not totally crushed. According to Szymanski some differences in political opinion exist and arise. In addition to the use of force, authoritarian rulers also use ideological manipulation. They try to convince people that their rule is legitimate and justified. In the case of kings (now mostly disappeared), the justification is divine rule—God gave them the right to rule.

Fascist   Hitler in Germany and Mussolini in Italy are examples of fascist rulers. Fascist governments are more controlling and totalitarian than authoritarian ones. They usually arise in times of economic and political crisis, and they appeal to nationalistic, religious, and racist (antisemitic in Germany) sentiments to crush all opposition and consolidate their power.

Socialist States

All socialist states were created out of previously authoritarian societies. They arose in the midst of poverty, exploitation, and misery; after long and bloody struggles. The ruling classes do not willingly cede their power; they continue to oppose and sabotage new socialist governments (as in Nicaragua today). After years of hardship and hard work, many socialist societies have eliminated the poverty and suffering they inherited. Moreover, as we have seen, material inequalities have been reduced considerably, and most people enjoy at least the necessities of life.

But according to Sweezy (1980) this as about all that can be said about socialist societies. They have not created political democracies, and in this respect they resemble capitalist societies. All post-revolutionary societies have started as, or soon became, one party-states, "with the ruling party exercising a monopoly of political power." (p. 5) Ruling classes still exist but unlike capitalist ruling classes, they do not own or profit from the means of production. A socialist ruling class derives its power "from the unmediated control of the state and its multiform apparatuses of coercion." (p. 9) The top officials in government and economic enterprises are a self-perpetuating group, which enjoys more material benefits than do the rest of the people.

Socialist states vary in their degree of state control and centralization of power. Some maintain strict control over the society and attempt to repress all opponents, others allow some opposition. Many people gain improved living conditions and in various degrees support the new society, but other people are controlled by police forces. And, as in all societies, the state (or ruling class) controls the media and education, or the means by which the new generation is socialized to believe in the existing system. Since socialist governments arose in the midst of intense struggles and opposition from the previous ruling classes, they tend not to tolerate debates, disunity, or political opposition (Szymanski, 1981).

Many members of the socialist ruling class find themselves facing a dilemma. In theory and practice, they must reduce inequalities and provide everyone with the essentials of life (job, housing, food, medical care, clothes), but at the same time they have not given people real political power. Thus, people are guaranteed a job but they are powerless. They may not be afraid of losing work, but they have little control over their jobs, which gives them little incentive to work hard or well (unlike their capitalist counterparts). The economy does not grow fast or well, as a result. Should leaders give power to their people? Former Chairman Mao Zedong saw the same rise of a ruling class in China and struggled against this fundamental problem. The Cultural Revolution (1966 to 1976) was an unsuccessful attempt at finding a solution. We have yet to create a modern society that resembles those in the past where power was not concentrated. A ruling class may be an inherent part of the creation of a state.

Since 1985, a new openness—*glasnost*—has appeared in the Soviet Union. There is more freedom in the arts, the press, and politics. Many jailed political dissenters have been freed and television and newspapers openly discuss problems and abuses within the government and the economy. The reasons for and depth of this change are unclear, and its future course uncertain. But it is an encouraging development. (For two detailed discussions of the changes and their meaning, see the entire issue of the *Nation,* July 13, 1987, and Karol, 1987.)

Despite these problems of socialist societies, the political movement in the world today is toward socialism. The poor and the oppressed want to escape their poverty, suffering, and exploitation; they do not want to be slaves to the capitalist world system.

Who Benefits under Capitalism?

If we take as a given that there is a ruling class in America that controls the government and the economy, the question becomes could the class rule for the benefit of all people?

We cannot examine people's motives easily. But we can see their actions and the results of their actions. And these show clearly that the ruling class rules mostly for its own interests. They control most of the wealth. Most government decisions are favorable to the ruling class. Corporations shoulder only a small portion of the federal tax burden. The taxes paid by the working class finance the military, which protects ruling-class interests, subsidize huge contracts given to corporations, and pay for airports, shipyards, and other facilities that benefit mostly the corporations. The list is long, but the conclusion is clear.

The Shaping of Institutions

Any ruling class that holds power for a long period does more than occupy the leading government and economic positions. Through the years, it and its allies shape the political, economic, educational, and cultural spheres. As we saw in Chapter 4, the ruling class seeks to shape how we think and what we perceive as reality. Thus, even if the top positions in the government and the economy were occupied by factory workers, craftspeople, and other working-class people, not much would change if they had to play by ruling-class rules.

Let me give an example. The educational system, and the culture in general, have defined the American way as capitalism. Any challenges to the control of the ruling class are labeled "socialist" or "communist." These emotionally charged words make it difficult for most people to objectively examine the proposed change.

Thus, ruling-class power pervades the society. Ruling-class men (and it is almost entirely *men*) not only hold the decision-making positions in the economy and the government, but shape our social institutions and culture.

Challenges to the State

Both historically and presently we see evidence that the ruling class does not have total control over our lives. This and other books are proof that change and challenge are possible.

True democracy may not be possible in industrial societies, but this does not mean that the ruling-class power is never challenged, limited, and partially distributed more equally. Exploitation and poverty can be stopped, despite the existence of ruling classes. I hope and struggle for socialism without a ruling class, but until that day arrives, the elimination of hunger, poverty, and violent death are worthy goals.

Single individuals who resist and protest can rarely mount effective challenges to ruling-class power. Nevertheless, such challenges are important for three reasons: they can make some small changes; they symbolize dramatically that the ruling class is not in total control of our thoughts and actions; and they can inspire others who then act collectively to challenge power.

Mitchell, in *Truth and Consequences: Seven Who Would Not Be Silenced* (1981), describes seven average Americans who exposed, confronted, and challenged the powers of government agencies and corporations. Maude DeVictor, a counselor at the Veterans Administration, persisted in her research that showed that American soldiers who spread Agent Orange (a defoliant) in Vietnam are now suffering from severe illnesses and genetic damage that causes birth defects. Once she was able to trace that connection, she would not be silent about it. She publicized and discussed it, and inspired Vietnam Veterans and others to pursue the issue (the demand for medical treatment and benefits for victims of Agent Orange). She, and the other six people Mitchell includes, are people who ran serious risks by challenging powerful institutions, but who could not act otherwise. (See Gwaltney, 1986, for a similar book.)

The Solidarity union in Poland is an example of a large scale challenge to the ruling class in a socialist country. The working class in Poland has risen in protest many times against the ruling class, but its greatest challenge came in 1980, when it organized the Solidarity union (suppressed in December 1981). It inspired many people. It must be stressed that the Polish working class did not simply ask for more material goods and higher wages. Solidarity sought to limit (perhaps even eliminate) the power of the ruling class; it sought to give power to all people in all institutions. It was a struggle for a new society where power really was exercised by the people, not by a small elite. (See Sweezy, 1983a, and Starski, 1982.)

In capitalist societies too there are struggles against ruling classes and against the poverty and exploitation capitalism creates. Central America is one region of the armed resistance, but incipient and growing revolutions are everywhere. The power and control of the Chilean military is being challenged. As the supposedly all-powerful and invisible Shah of Iran (and other rulers) fell before, the military regime of Chile seems on its way out. Ten years of repression in Chile have not killed the dreams for justice, equality, and freedom (*Guardian,* June 1, 1983:17).

Returning to a personal and psychological level, we have seen many societies in which people are socialized not to covet power or try to dominate others. The !Kung curb the desire for power (Chapter 4), and native American societies practice noninterference in personal relations (Chapter 7). Power needs to be curbed at all levels: individual consciousness, social relationships, family and community life, and in government and economy. Even in the United States, people are calling for *economic democracy:* some unions and communities, some people who work in and are affected by the economic institutions are trying to take over economic decisions. Workers and communities are deciding whether cars or some other means of transportation should be manufactured and how they should be made. Decisions such as these affect all of us and cannot be left in the hands of corporation directors and managers whose primary concern is profit. (See Parenti, 1982; Moody, 1983; Boyte, 1984; Sweezy & Magdoff, 1985a; Riotta et al., 1987.)

Conclusion

As we think about the ruling class, and as we engage in the struggle to curb its power and create societies without concentrated power, we need to study history. We need to understand what issues and problems other societies and people have faced. We also must look at societies where no ruling classes have existed. From a limited study of power, I have come to four conclusions.

The first conclusion is that decisions are made and power is held by people. The decisions that affect our lives are not inevitable; they are not made by omnipotent, impersonal, and invisible powers that are beyond human control. Specific individuals and groups make decisions that affect all of us. For example, the triumph of the private car over public transportation (which pollutes the environment and affects community life) was the result of corporate and government decisions that favored the car. No God ordained that henceforth Americans will move by cars. Decisions and power are human creations; they can be made or unmade by other people.

The second conclusion is that we must realize ruling-class decisions and powers have created a *social system* that needs to be changed. It was not Ronald Reagan as an individual who caused havoc in millions of lives in the early 1980s. Replacing him will not change much. Most of his policies are just a continuation of already existing ones from previous administrations. The military and nuclear weapons direction began with Carter and even before, as did the business bias of OSHA, EPA, and other agencies. The entire structure of the economy and the government is the accumulated product of ruling-class decisions and actions over time. We must change the rules of the game, which favor the ruling class, not just the players. As the editor of the *Progressive* (December 1981:9) said, "It's not just a matter of getting rid of bad guys."

The third conclusion is that all past and present egalitarian groups, communities, and societies have been small. As Bodley (1983) makes clear the concentration of power and the rise of a ruling class are much more difficult in small groups.

> It has been suggested that a truly egalitarian society can only be maintained within a continuously interacting, face-to-face population of no more than approximately 250–500 persons which has common goals to pull it together. As population densities increase, not only do people have a more difficult time keeping track of their relationships simply because there are now too many to sort out, but the probability of conflict over everyday irritations becomes much more likely. Invariably, population densities greater than 500 in a single social unit either break up into antagonistic factions, and/or they become hierarchically ordered. (p.186)

Since we do not live in communities and societies of five hundred people, how can we translate this principle into our own context? Workplaces and functioning neighborhoods can be consciously arranged to be small, where all the people within that group make decisions together. Can such autonomous groups and communities, however, prevent the concentration of power on a national or international scale? In the United States, how could thousands of such small groups take power away from the ruling class? How could they jointly operate the entire society to prevent the re-emergence of a new ruling class? We have no answers to these questions. The answers, if they exist, lie in the future and must be made collectively by all of us and our descendants.

The fourth conclusion is best said by Frederick Douglass, a man born and raised a slave, a man who struggled against the degradations of slavery and who freed himself from it, first in spirit and then in body (in Quarles, 1969). As a free person, he engaged in a lifelong struggle to free the slaves, and when they were freed he continued to work for justice and the liberation of all people, black and white, men and women. His life exemplifies the dignity and beauty and achievements of humanity.

> If there is no struggle, there is no progress. Those who profess to favor free-dom, and yet deprecate agitation, are [people] who want crops without plow-ing up the ground. They want rain without thunder and lightning. They want the ocean without the awful roar of its many waters. This struggle may be a moral one; or it may be a physical one; or it may be both moral and physical; but it must be a struggle. Power concedes nothing without a demand. It never did and never will. . . . [People] may not get all they pay for in this world; but they must certainly pay for all they get. (p. 354)

Summary

Power is a relationship in which some individual or group has the capacity (or the perceived capacity) to direct and control the actions of other individuals or groups. The powerful, who usually seek to make their power legitimate, can deprive the powerless of valued possessions and social positions.

The American ruling class controls the economy, the government, and other institutions. As a class, it sends its children to exclusive schools for their socialization, and its members socialize and intermarry. It controls most of the wealth and major corporations and is expanding its control to new areas on an international level. In their search for power and profits, corporations often endanger the health and lives of their employees and the public.

The ruling class also controls the government. Most members of the executive branch come from the ruling class; congresspeople are influenced through campaign contributions and lobbying; regulatory agencies serve the interests of the industries they regulate; and advisory commissions and other groups that influence government policies are ruling-class institutions. People who protest against ruling-class power and control are repressed by corpora-tions and the government.

People in the ruling class are not unanimous in their thoughts and actions, but they share common interests and values. They also exercise various degrees of influence and control over the major institutions.

A world capitalist system began to develop around the 1500s. It has evolved from classic colonialism to neo-colonialism, which uses trade, invest-ments, and loans to control poor countries. In this system, wealth flows from the periphery (poor nations) to the center (the United States, Europe, and Japan to a smaller extent). Most large U.S. corporations, especially banks, derive much of their profit from investments in and loans to other countries.

Imperialism causes suffering and hunger in poor nations, heavy indebtedness, and eventually armed revolutions to stop the suffering and exploitation.

Historically, U.S. governments have fought wars to protect corporate interests throughout the world. Today, the United States has military bases in every major region of the world. The nuclear arsenal is the ultimate weapon to protect corporate interests. The Rapid Deployment Force of over three hundred thousand soldiers is a relatively new means to stop revolutions. This militarism takes human and financial resources away from human needs.

States are part of the evolution of human societies. Today there are capitalist states (parliamentary, authoritarian, and fascist) and socialist states. Through various mechanisms, ruling classes hold power in all of them, but in socialist societies the ruling class does not exploit the workers economically. Ruling classes generally attempt to shape all of the institutions.

Although some individuals and groups do challenge the ruling classes in all states, it is unclear whether true democracy is possible in modern industrial states.

In thinking about power, four issues are important: *people* not an omnipotent deity hold power and make decisions; we need to change the *systems* created by ruling classes, not only to replace individuals; past egalitarian societies were *small;* and no change can come without struggle.

Suggested Readings

Acharya, Amitav (1987, March). The Reagan doctrine and international security. *Monthly Review, 38*(10), 28–36. The U.S. government is becoming more militaristic and imperialistic.

Boston Urban Study Group (1984). *Who rules Boston?* Boston: Institute for Democratic Socialism. A few corporation directors and managers dominate politics and the economy of Boston.

Chomsky, Noam (1985, October). The bounds of thinkable thought. *Progressive*, pp. 28–31. Democratic systems have their own means of limiting thought.

Domhoff, G. William (1983). *Who rules America now? A view for the 80s.* Englewood Cliffs, NJ: Prentice Hall. Domhoff explores the social, economic, political, and organizational bases of the ruling class.

Gwaltney, John Langston (1986). *The dissenters: Voices from contemporary America.* New York: Random House. Social and political dissenters tell their stories.

Hoffman, Abbie (1987, May 2). Closing argument. *Nation*, pp. 562–563. A list of CIA activities in the last forty years against liberation movements throughout the world.

Kloby, Jerry (1987, September). The growing divide: Class polarization in the 1980s. *Monthly Review, 39*(4), 1–8. Class differences and income and wealth inequalities are growing wider in the 1980s.

Kolko, Gabriel (1986). *Anatomy of a war: Vietnam, the U.S., and the modern historical experience.* New York: Pantheon. An exhaustive history of the U.S. government's conduct of the Vietnam War.

Mintz, Morton (1985, November). At any cost. *Progressive,* pp. 20–25. Corporate greed led to the marketing of a lethal IUD (the Dalkon Shield).

Navarro, Vincente (1986). The Lincoln Brigade: Some comments on U.S. history. *Monthly Review, 38*(4), 29–37. The real history of labor unions and the working class is hidden and repressed.

O'Brien, Jim & Thorkelsen, Nick (1985, July-August). Myths and realities in Central America. *Radical America, 19*(4), 24–31. An outline of social, economic, and political conditions in Central America, and a history of U.S. interventions.

Simon, David & Eitzen, D. Stanley (1986). *Elite deviance* (2nd ed.). Newton, MA: Allyn and Bacon. A thorough documentation and discussion of crimes committed by corporations and the government.

Sweezy, Paul & Magdoff, Harry (1985, June). Lessons of Vietnam. *Monthly Review, 37*(2), 1–13. Review of a book by Richard Nixon that argues domination of poorer countries (imperialism) is vital to the U.S. economy (corporations).

Useem, Michael (1984). *The inner circle.* New York: Oxford University Press. A new class of directors and managers from large corporations has developed; it works for the interests of the corporate economy and the ruling class as a whole.

CHAPTER 11

The Oppressed Majority: Cultural and Racial Minorities

In 1973, a bus with eighty-six passengers was trapped by flood waters southwest of Delhi, India. Karim Kahn, a member of the lowest caste in India or what is called an "untouchable," waded to the bus with a rope he had tied to a truck (Alger, 1974). He told the passengers to hold onto the rope and pull themselves to safety. But the passengers belonged to higher castes and do not touch anything touched by untouchables. They refused to use the rope. They stayed in the bus and were swept away. Seventy-eight of them died.

Frederick Douglass (1969), an escaped slave, describes in his 1855 autobiography what a slave's existence was like. Slaveowners and overseers beat them frequently and savagely. They were controlled by fear that was instilled in them from childhood. Impudence was one of the offenses slaves committed that aroused the owners' wrath. Douglass writes, "This may mean almost anything, or nothing at all, just according to the caprice of the master or overseer, at the moment . . . . This offense may be committed in various ways; in the tone of an answer; in answering at all; in not answering; in the expression of countenance; in the motion of head; in the gait, manner and bearing of the slave." (p. 92)

Mangione (1981) grew up in an Italian neighborhood of Rochester, New York, in the 1910s and 1920s. His parents were from Sicily. Newspaper reports of crimes (especially murder and other violent offenses) often mentioned the Sicilian heritage of the accused criminals. His father sought to dissociate his family from any criminal labeling and forbad his sons to carry knives "because of the unpleasant association they had in the public mind with Sicilians. He enforced this rule so thoroughly that we eventually came to accept it as though it were a self-imposed one. And although it prevented us from joining the Boy Scouts, it gave us great satisfaction to tell non-Sicilians who wanted to borrow a knife from us that we never carried one." (p. 5)

Mangione's parents insisted that their children speak only Italian at home, and they followed many Italian customs and traditions. But as they grew older, the children experienced a severe conflict between their Italian family and the larger American culture. "It wasn't that we wanted to be Americans so much as we wanted to be like most people. Most people, we realized as we grew older, were not Sicilians. So we fretted inside." (p. 221)

The history of minority people is often one of exclusion, discrimination, violence, and exploitation. As an untouchable, Khan is forever forbidden from doing certain kinds of work, living in certain areas, and even associating with certain people—even if he is saving their lives. As a black slave in the antebellum South, Douglass was subject to mental and physical violence and made to live a less than human existence. Mangione was labeled and discriminated against merely because of his nationality.

This chapter examines the creation of minorities, the historical ties between minorities and economic exploitation, the relationships between majorities and minorities, the social conditions under which many minority groups live, and how people struggle to overcome discrimination and oppression.

The Creation of Minorities

Defining a Minority Group

Sociologically speaking, a minority is a group that is relatively powerless; experiences prejudice, stereotyping, discrimination, and exploitation; and over time, becomes conscious of being treated differently. A social minority is not necessarily a smaller numerical group in a community or a society. Women, blacks in South Africa, blacks in many American communities, and others compose a majority of the population, but they are still social minorities.

Minorities are *relatively powerless* in comparison to the majority group that controls them. They lack control over their lives in many areas. For example, in the nineteenth century husbands could commit their wives to mental hospitals almost at will; today, parents have legal control over their children; in South Africa, black people (a numerical majority) are forbidden to live in most cities. No group is ever totally powerless, but minorities are relatively powerless because their lives are controlled by others.

A group of people may be relatively powerless, stereotyped, discriminated against, and exploited, but may not be conscious that they are purposely singled out for such treatment. For a minority to exist in a sociological sense, it is necessary for its members to see that others treat them unequally. A *group awareness and consciousness* must arise. For example, old people have been discriminated against and stereotyped for many years, but their awareness as a minority group did not emerge until the 1970s. Certainly textbooks of the 1960s and before did not consider old people a minority. (This definition of minority was drawn from Kinlock, 1979; Luhman & Gilman, 1980; and Levin & Levin, 1982.)

Finally, the term *minority* may be inappropriate. According to Greg Williams (1985), it is numerically wrong. All the groups we call minorities in fact add up to a large majority. Also, minority is a negative label. It tends to denigrate the people in that group. We are, he said, a *majority,* an *oppressed* majority. I continue to use the term minority in order not to stray too far from common sociological usage, but I do so with some hesitation. We need to remember Greg Williams' argument.

Prejudice, Stereotyping, and Discrimination

Minority groups are subject to prejudice, stereotyping, and discrimination to a much greater degree than other groups within society.

Prejudice is the tendency to judge people, usually negatively, on the basis of a single characteristic (sex, race, ethnicity, religion, dress, age, etc.) and without knowledge of their individual abilities and character. According to Farley (1988), prejudice has three dimensions: "negative beliefs concerning what is true about a group . . . , disliking a group . . . , or wanting to discriminate against or show aggression toward a group. . . ." (p. 13) Stereotypes are related to prejudice. A *stereotype,* an exaggerated, simplistic and negative preconception about a minority, refers to the first dimension of prejudice. Here are some examples of stereotypes: Irish are quick-tempered; women are emotional; Jews are cheap and shrewd; blacks are lazy; Chinese are sly; Italians are passionate; and old people are forgetful.

Mangione (1981) relates a somewhat amusing but sad example of stereotyping. His grade-school teacher was convinced that all Italians were great painters. But despite his best efforts and his teacher's urgings, Mangione's landscapes "looked like scrambled eggs mixed with spinach." (p. 210) His teacher insisted that Mangione should be able to paint a simple landscape, and if he did not, it was because he failed deliberately. He could not be convinced that Mangione could not paint better, and in desperation he put him over his knees and whacked him twelve times, reprimanding him with " 'that will certainly teach you to paint a landscape when your teacher says you must.' It didn't." (p. 212)

The mass media and much of our culture perpetuate many stereotypes. Levin's and Levin's (1982) study of TV advertisements in the late 1960s shows many indirect stereotypes of Mexicans. The "Frito-Bandito" ad for Frito-Lay sent the message that Mexicans are sneaky thieves; the ad for Philco TV showing a Mexican asleep by a TV set implied Mexicans are lazy and always sleeping; and eight more commercials sent similar messages.

Some stereotypes, of course, contain an element of truth. Some women are emotional; some Italians are passionate; and some blacks have rhythm. Indeed, it may even be that as a whole women are more emotional than men, or that Italians are more passionate than the Irish, or that blacks have more rhythm than whites. Group differences do exist, but stereotypes go beyond merely describing general group differences. They label all members of a group, which prejudges individuals. They also exaggerate group differences. It may be that on the average women are more emotional than men, but averages are only that: a lumping of people of many different qualities together.

Another problem with negative stereotypes is that they can become self-fulfilling prophecies. By forbidding the Irish to study, the British made them ignorant; they created the stereotype they later attributed to the Irish. In the United States, slave owners made it illegal to teach slaves how to read and write and by doing so made slaves more ignorant in the context of this society. The truth in some stereotypes has been created by the oppressor group.

Prejudice and discrimination are often based on superficial differences. If someone looks different or acts differently, then they must be bad or undesirable in some way. Sociologically speaking, then, prejudice refers to the negative attitudes and beliefs we hold about someone who is different from us. It is the prejudging of a person without knowing anything about their abilities and qualities.

Discrimination differs from prejudice in that it refers to an *action* against a person, often because of a prejudice we may hold. For example, we may not hire a black person, a woman, or an older person because we believe they are too old, too emotional, or too lazy. In short, we deny people an opportunity because we think they possess negative qualities or lack positive ones. Most minorities are subject to prejudice and/or discrimination as part of their socialization and cultural conditioning.

Deutscher (1973) points out that prejudice and discrimination do not always accompany each other. A man prejudiced against women may or may not discriminate against them. He may be convinced that all (or most) women are too emotional to perform the job in his company, but when he faces a specific woman who applies for a job he may hire her either because it is against the law to discriminate or because he simply cannot turn away this specific woman in front of him. Attitudes and actions do not always coincide, as Deutscher (1973) has shown.

Many, perhaps most, prejudiced people do discriminate, of course. But at least some people who may discriminate are not necessarily prejudiced. For example, white real estate agents may not rent to black couples because they fear white renters will leave their buildings if black people move in, not because they hold prejudices against black people (of course, some agents may *say* they have no prejudices when in fact they do). In short, prejudice and discrimination are related but the relationship is not simple and direct.

A Note on Race

Skin color, facial features, and other racial physical traits have no intrinsic social, behavioral, or political significance. Such differences do exist, of course, (although they are becoming less pronounced), but they do not dictate how people should behave or how people should treat other people. They do not indicate or cause innate intellectual differences. They *are* only surface appearances. It is because of cultural differences between races, and because of economic exploitation of one race by another, that skin color has assumed any social significance. In short, skin color is a justification, an excuse for unequal treatment, used to justify the economic exploitation that precedes it.

Moreover, millions of people have mixed biological heritage. Most black Americans have some genetic ancestry from white people, and millions of people treated as white in America have inherited genes from black foreparents. A woman who thought of herself as white, and was treated as such by everyone, discovered that a Louisiana law classified her as black. Anyone with more than one-thirty second Negro blood and living in Louisiana in 1982 was black, and since one of her ancestors was a black slave in the late 1700s, she was considered legally black. The case illustrates that race is an arbitrary, useless, and harmful *social* creation. (See Ryan, 1981, and *Boston Globe,* September 14, 1982.)

A Historical and Economic View of Minorities

The creation of minorities is not solely due to a group's racial, cultural, or national differences. Minority groups are also created out of economic forces such as slavery or famine. Minorities have undoubtedly existed throughout the history of humankind, but minorities in the modern world were created around the sixteenth century when Europe began exploiting foreign lands and around the nineteenth century when United States imperialism began to spread. In recent history, blacks in Africa and the Americas, Indians in the Americas, and native peoples throughout the world have become minorities when their lands were colonized, their material resources taken away, and their labor enslaved or bought cheaply. Poor and landless Europeans (exploited by their own ruling classes) came to the United States in search of the promised land. Here they constituted a cheap and plentiful labor force; with their sweat, blood, and bodies, they and blacks built America and created fortunes for a few corporations and ruling-class families.

The following short histories of blacks, native Americans, and Irish examine their social and economic roles in the development of United States capitalism.

Minorities in the United States may be divided into voluntary and involuntary groups, according to their origin. Millions of people who belong to ethnic groups have emigrated from Europe and elsewhere to the United States to try to escape their poverty. These people are considered voluntary minorities. Involuntary minorities are those people whose ancestors were brought here as slaves, and those people whose lands have been conquered by force, Indians, Mexican-Americans, Hawaiians, Puerto Ricans, and others (Luhman & Gilman, 1980).

This distinction is somewhat forced, however. Starving Irish, landless Italians, and other poor people from Europe did not leave their families, communities, and cultures very willingly nor voluntarily. Parents and children, husbands and wives were separated, probably never to see each other again. Immigrants never forget the people and communities they leave behind. Immigration is a profoundly wrenching experience. It creates divided loyalties and emotions and leaves a permanent void for millions of people. (This is based not only on what I have read, but on my relatives and my own experiences.) Today people are leaving their countries for many reasons, but generally they are fleeing poverty, war, or political repression. As we will see later, many of the illegal aliens currently entering the United States are escaping from both economic hardship (brought about largely by capitalistic greed) and political violence (aggravated by misguided U.S. foreign policies).

Blacks

Slavery was crucial to the rise of capitalism, both because of the profits made from the slave trade, and because of the greater profits produced by cheap labor. When settlers came to the United States, slavery had not yet been instituted. The source of cheap, exploitable labor was instead white indentured servants from Europe. These were poor people and convicted criminals who had had their passage to America paid in exchange for a period of seven (sometimes more) years of labor owed to whoever had paid for their passage. At the end of the indentured period, they were free. From 1654 to 1683, ten thousand servants sailed from Bristol, England, for Virginia and the West Indies. Williams (1944) argues that the status of servants became worse in time, coming close to slavery.

But indentured servants apparently did not provide an adequate supply of labor for the plantations of the English colonies and the West Indies, nor was their servitude permanent. Native Americans were used for a time as servants and slaves, but they also did not solve the labor problem. They could not accustom themselves to slave work, and they could always run away to their native lands.

So merchants and plantation owners turned to Africa for cheap, plentiful, and permanent labor. According to some historians, slavery itself developed gradually. The first blacks from Africa used for labor were indentured servants. As commercial farmers needed more cheap labor, slavery and racist laws and beliefs to justify slavery, came into existence.

The profitability of slavery was obvious to contemporaries. Baron (1971) cites a nineteenth-century economist who put the economic argument this way:

> The most-approved judges of the commercial interest of these kingdoms have ever been of the opinion that our West Indian and African trades are the most nationally-beneficial of any carried on. It is also allowed on all hands that the trade to Africa is the branch which renders our American colonies and plantations so advantageous to Great Britain; that traffic only affording our planters a constant supply of Negro servants for the culture of their lands in the produce of sugar, tobacco, rice, rum, cotton, pimento, and all plantation produce,

so that the extensive employment of our shipping into and from our American colonies, the great brook of seamen consequent thereupon, and the daily bread of the most considerable part of our British manufacturers, are owing primarily to the labor of Negroes. (pp. 5–6)

Similarly, merchants in the United States profited immensely from the slave trade. According to Meier and Rudwick (1970),

Merchants in all sections of the mainland provinces participated in the slave trade, but pre-eminent were those from the Massachusetts and Rhode Island seaports. Rhode Island entered the slave trade much later than Massachusetts, probably around the beginning of the eighteenth century. By mid-century Newport and Providence surpassed their rivals in Boston and Salem. From then until the official closing of the slave trade in 1808, the traffic flourished in Rhode Island and formed the basis of some of the greatest fortunes in the State. (pp. 30–31)

Slavery was beneficial to merchants and large plantation owners. Slave labor in the sugar plantations of the West Indies resulted in the creation of a small class of rich whites, millions of exploited slaves, and the eventual destruction of a class of small white farmers. (Indeed, in the United States, black indentured servants and slaves staged periodic uprisings from 1663 on, sometimes together with poor whites.) After the slave trade and slavery were abolished by the British in the early nineteenth century, the plantation owners of the West Indies began importing cheap labor from other sources, chiefly from India (a colony of the British Empire). And British merchants continued to import sugar and other products from the slave plantations of Brazil and other places. Thus, slavery was not inherently connected to blacks. It was an economic institution of capitalism (Williams, 1944).

By its very nature as an institution, slavery engendered violence, cruelty, and death. Slaves were kept under control by long, brutal, and frequent whippings and beatings. Only *fear* could make slaves work, and their masters set out to inspire and keep that fear. Violence and fear are a part of all systems of oppression and control. Douglass' (1969) autobiography abounds with detailed accounts of brutal beatings. The whip, he writes, was used "with an unsparing hand." (p. 72) Douglass' master loaned him for a year to an overseer known as "Covey the Negro breaker." During his first six months there, he was "whipped, either with sticks or cowskins, every week. Aching bones and a sore back were my constant companions." (p. 214) Douglass recounts incident after incident of the brutality inflicted on slaves. He tells of one mother who was forcibly tied to a tree, despite her strong resistance, and savagely beaten. The owner "wielded the lash with all the hot zest of furious revenge. The cries of the woman, while undergoing the terrible infliction, were mingled with those of [her] children, sounds which I hope the reader may never be called upon to hear. When Nelly was untied, her back was covered with blood. The red stripes were all over her shoulders." (p. 94) A slave girl was assigned to care for the baby of her mistress. One night she fell asleep and did not awaken when the baby cried. The mother did, however. "Mrs. Hicks, becoming infuriated at the girl's tardiness, after calling her several times, jumped from her bed and seized a piece of fire-wood from the fireplace, and then, as she lay fast asleep, she deliberately pounded on her skull and breast-bone, and thus ended her life." Mrs. Hicks was never tried for the crime. Slaves did not have the protection of the law. (p. 125)

The Civil War freed the slaves in law but not in fact. There was a brief period when blacks made some legal gains, but the failure to provide them with an economic foundation (land and jobs) returned them to virtual slavery. A political compromise assured their fate: the Northern capitalists allowed the Southern plantation owners and the new industrialists to use blacks as cheap labor. Baron (1971) says plantation owners in the nineteenth century spoke of blacks as good and cheap workers. Most blacks became sharecroppers and were in constant debt to the owners of the land.

In the 1880s and 1890s the Jim Crow laws segregated blacks and denied them voting rights. These laws made blacks into virtual slaves. Lynchings, prisons, and chain gangs also contributed to the economic dependence of most blacks. The most subtle form of bondage was perhaps their socialization. Many blacks were socialized as obedient workers, which served to keep them slaves to an economic system.

After their emancipation most blacks were tenant farmers, worked for white people as servants, or had other menial, low-paying jobs. Tenant farmers rented land from white landowners. The rent was usually 50 percent of the crops they grew. What they kept was usually insuffient to make it through the winter, which forced them to buy goods on credit from stores owned by white landlords. Consequently, many were perpetually in debt and became virtual slaves.

Three developments eventually removed black people from tenancy and the rural South. One of these was the mechanization of farming, which made their labor unnecessary and displaced them from the land. Another was labor shortages during the two world wars, which created a demand for their labor in northern factories and other workplaces. The third development was the end of immigration in the 1920s, which meant the end of a large source of cheap labor. This mandated the search for a new source. Blacks became that source. But while blacks did get some industrial jobs, they were kept in the lowest job categories. Greer (1976) cites U.S. Steel Corporation officials who placed job quotas on blacks, keeping them out of many jobs in the 1930s:

> *When we got [up to 10 percent black] employed, I said [to the employment manager], "No more colored without discussion." I got the colored pastors to send colored men whom they could guarantee would not organize and were not bolsheviks. . . . It isn't good to have all of one nationality; they will gang up on you. . . . We have Negroes and Mexicans in a sort of competition with each other. It's a dirty trick, but we don't have the kind of work that will*

> *break a man down. . . . Negroes are nice, simple people. I don't approve of using them for skilled work—not that they couldn't do it, but we have enough competition within the skilled groups. Let the Negroes scramble for the un-skilled jobs. (p. 51)*

Black people continue to be exploited economically. (For some recent studies about black people, see Jones, 1981; Harris, 1982; Marable, 1983; Turner, Singleton & Musick, 1984; and Boskin, 1986.)

Native Americans

We do not have space here to give all of the details of the long and shameful history of the white people's relationship to the Indians. The list of crimes against them is long: the constant violation of treaties by the U.S. government, the massacres and persecution, the theft of their land, and the pervasive racism. The very statement that Columbus discovered America reveals a deep-seated racism that ignores the twenty thousand years of native tribal history.

Much of the racism against Indians, and their minority status, was the result of cultural conflicts between European materialism and the values of native peoples. As Sitting Bull said in 1877, "The love of possession is a disease" of European culture. But just as important is the fact that tribal peoples stood in the way of European capitalism ("progress," as it has been called). They had to be pushed aside.

Indian tribes welcomed and aided the early colonists, only to be attacked, massacred, and chased out of their own land. Although popular perceptions focus on violence by native tribes (which they sometimes used in retaliation and for defense), they were mostly the victims, not the perpetrators. Whole tribes were massacred, men, women, and children; others died by the hundreds and thousands as they were led on forced marches to new reservations; many starved when they lost their land. Andrew Jackson once said, "the only good Indian is a dead Indian," echoing popular sentiment. Massacres, starvation, and disease decimated tribes; some were entirely wiped out. (Details of torture and death are too gruesome to retell here. For more detailed descriptions see Jacobs & Landau, 1971; Marable, 1983; and many other sources, especially Rose's *Violence in America,* 1969, which contains a graphic account of the massacre of the Manhattan Indians after they sold the island.)

The Irish

The Irish were colonized by the English and have been exploited by them for many centuries. Indeed, they could be considered the first victims of European colonialism and imperialism. They were forbidden from speaking Gaelic and forced to speak English; Catholicism was repressed; all the best lands were taken by English settlers. For centuries, they were exploited culturally, politically, and economically. The peasants, according to Fallows (1979) were "caste-like serfs," near slaves. (p. 15) (See also *Guardian*, June 3, 1981:14.)

The potato famine of the 1840s was the direct result of the English taking the best land. The Irish peasants were forced to cultivate the least productive pieces of land, and to raise potatoes, the one crop that grew best and gave the most nutrition per acre. But the continued intensive cultivation of potatoes led to potato blight, a disease that ruined crops for some years. Famine followed. Somewhere between one and two million people died from starvation. Others left for England and America, beginning a long history of immigration that decimated families and communities.

They found work in America, but it was demanding and debilitating work. Men worked in factories and on construction. Women were usually domestics. The pay was low and unemployment frequent. They lived in crowded, filthy, and depressing slums. Violence, alcoholism, and family instability ruined the lives of many. They resisted the terrible working conditions and low wages with frequent strikes and occasional violence.

Ireland continues to suffer from its colonial legacy. It is still an economic colony. Half of its top one thousand corporations are owned by foreign corporations, mostly English. There is at least a 20 percent unemployment. Emigration continues. According to a *Guardian* (May 6, 1987) report, from a population of only 3.5 million people, 100,000 left from 1984 to 1986. (pp. 10–11)

It was the lands of the native peoples and the labor of slaves and immigrants that provided capital for expanding capitalism. Corporations and ruling class families built their fortunes on the backs of minorities. Gold (1965) has written that "America is so rich and fat, because it has eaten the tragedy of millions of immigrants"—and we might add blacks, Chicanos, and Indians. (p. 26) Miller's (1972) collection of biographies, autobiographies, and fiction from the history of the Irish, Italians, Jews, blacks, and Puerto Ricans shows that the extreme wealth of a few people and the comfort of others has been built from the labor, deprivation, and poverty of millions of our ancestors. They worked long hours for little or no pay; they worked in dangerous factories and construction. The expression "you haven't got a Chinaman's chance" came from the experience of Chinese workers who labored on the transcontinental railroad and who had many accidents and deaths because of extremely unsafe conditions. Immigrants were persecuted and stereotyped. They lived in poverty and slums. This too is the history of America, often hidden and glossed over. (See Jacobs & Landau, 1971, and Marable, 1983.)

Also generally ignored and minimized in history books is the violence visited upon most minority groups. Native Americans and slaves were not the only victims. Hundreds of freed blacks were lynched for merely looking at a white woman or for being accused of minor crimes. In the early 1900s, author Richard Wright and his family had to flee their home in the middle of the night after his uncle was killed by white people who were envious of his sucessful business. Immigrants may not have been as savagely violated as blacks and native people, but they too were victimized by frequent violence. The Chinese were stoned, beaten, and sometimes killed in periodic outbreaks of violence. The slightest rumor or incident sufficed to set off waves of terror and beatings. The Ku Klux Klan and various nativist movements opposed the presence of and terrorized not only blacks, but also Irish, Catholics in general, and Jews. To be sure, as Nelson (1967) points out, minorities themselves occasionally resorted to violence for protection or retaliation, but minorities have largely been the victims, not the perpetrators, of violence.

Economic Exploitation and Cultural Repression

In the preceding discussion we have seen that minorities have been and are exploited economically. We have also seen how their cultures have been and are scorned and repressed. But what is the relationship between economic exploitation and cultural repression?

Let us imagine two Irish people in the 1920s, one rich and the other poor. Let us further assume both are the children of parents born in Ireland, with memories of their ancestral land still echoing in their hearts. Let us also imagine they grew up together in the same neighborhood and were childhood friends. But now, they are both adults and find themselves in very different economic situations. Can they still be friends? Do their ethnic bonds and childhood experiences provide sufficient grounds to continue social interaction? Does the rich Irish person have more in common with the poor childhood playmate or with the rich people with whom he or she now has common economic interests? Whom does one consider one's social intimates and peers?

What about poor Irish people then or poor blacks today? Do they have more in common with the poor of other groups or with the more affluent people of their own group? Should poor and working-class Irish, Italian, Polish, black, Chicano, and Puerto Rican people today emphasize their common economic conditions that bind them together or their different ethnic cultures and histories that divide them? What dominates people's consciousness—ethnicity or class?

The historical records seem to show that cultural differences (ethnicity and race) have been more important to people than class similarities. For some writers, one tragedy in American history is the fact that people have been divided along ethnic and racial lines and thus been prevented from uniting to work together for common economic interests. (See Miller, 1972; Luhman & Gilman, 1980; and Steinberg, 1981.)

It is hard to deny that cultural identities and histories are important to our lives. I argue in Chapter 4 that our culture is equivalent to life itself. But historically culture, cultural differences, and race do not cause the existence of a minority group. They are merely the justifications and rationalizations used for the economic exploitation that precedes them. Stolen lands, enslaved bodies, and cheap labor happen first. The arguments and theories that supposedly explain the inferiority of the oppressed and seek to justify their exploitation follow. Slavery came first, then came theories of the so-called natural inferiority of black people. Once the need to justify exploitation arises, minorities are labeled, stereotyped, and systematically discriminated against.

Once prejudice, discrimination, labeling, and stereotypes arise, they do assume an existence of their own. Whites today have little or nothing to do with the direct economic exploitation of minority people, but as whites grow up they see and hear such claims as blacks are inferior, or Mexicans are lazy, or Asians are sly. Whites may then not rent to blacks, or not hire a Vietnamese, because of the stereotypes they have been socialized to believe. Socialization and cultural conditioning do play a significant role in the continued discrimination of minorities. In the past, the repression of the culture of ethnic groups was a significant event on its own terms—Americans *were* repelled by the Catholicism and other traditions of the Irish.

We should not forget, however, that there may be a difference between the elements that gave *rise* to a social condition and those that perpetuate it. Minorities largely arose because of the economic conditions that I have outlined above. They have been perpetuated both because of continued economic exploitation *and* because of the cultural conditioning of the so-called majority. The economic exploitation of some minorities, such as the Irish and the Italians, has abated along with much of the stereotyping and discrimination against them. This, however, is not true for other minority groups, such as blacks, Chicanos, Puerto Ricans, and native Americans. Many minority groups are still being exploited and discriminated against by corporations and the capitalist system. Members of many minority groups are still stereotyped and persecuted. Even minority groups that are racially, culturally, and ethnically close to the white-Anglo-Saxon-Protestant (WASP) majority are exploited economically if they happen to be poor or working class.

Martin Luther King, Jr., the black civil rights leader who was killed in 1968, came to the same view on class, economic conditions, and minorities. He realized that minorities suffer primarily from economic exploitation. The stereotypes and prejudice individual white people are taught, and later use to discriminate against blacks, contribute to black oppression. King struggled to end this discrimination. But eventually he concluded that capitalism and the corporate economy are the primary cause of the suffering of black people. Therefore, the economic system must change. King, like Jesse Jackson in the 1980s, argued that all people—all minorities, all working people, of all colors, ethnic groups, and ages, both women and men—need to unite. They need to understand their common interests and work for an economic system that benefits all people, not mostly the few who own the corporations. We need both changes: an end to individual prejudices *and* a different economic system. Later in this chapter I argue that racism and prejudice are harmful to most white people as well as to minorities. (See Kuttner, 1986b, and *Guardian,* January 21, 1987:1, 19.)

Majority-Minority Interactions

Historians and sociologists have found that a variety of social and political relationships develop when minority groups arise and exist within majority groups. Let us first examine how majority groups act and react towards minorities, and then look at how minorities have responded to the discrimination and oppression perpetrated against them by majority groups.

Majority Actions

Throughout history the group in power—the so-called majority—has acted on minority groups in several ways. The following briefly explains some of these actions.

Attempts to annihilate whole groups of people have occurred throughout human history—some have been more successful than others. When one group of people systematically and deliberately tries to destroy a racial, cultural, or political group it is called *genocide*. Jews in Germany and eastern Europe, native peoples in North and South America, and the Armenians in Turkey have been three targets of genocide. In these cases, the group in power, the majority, sought to either acquire the minority's wealth (land, businesses, etc.) or use the minority as a scapegoat for the ills (economic, social, etc.) of society.

Instead of genocide, majority members have used *expulsion* on members of a minority group. Greeks have expelled Turks and vice versa. Native Americans have been forcibly removed from their land reservations, and throughout South Africa blacks have been forcibly relocated into supposedly independent nations (black settlements surrounded by white South Africa). Since 1948, Israel has been trying to expel Palestinians (although the means have been indirect, the goal has been clear). By expelling a group, their land is taken over by members of the majority and their perceived alien culture banished. But history teaches us that minorities do not comply easily to or forget such expulsions.

The physical and social separation of a minority within a society is called *segregation*. Ethnic and racial minorities have been confined to neighborhoods and cities by law and custom. Houses have not been sold, mortgages have not been given, memberships to clubs have been denied, schools have been segregated—these and other actions have insured the physical and social separation of minorities. Old people in Boston still recall the signs in Boston establishments announcing that "No Irish or dogs need apply."

When a minority is allowed to incorporate itself into the society, but only on the majority's terms, this is called *assimilation*. Minority people are admitted into the social life and institutions of the society on the condition they abandon their culture and change their behavior, values, and life styles. American history can be seen as the continuing assimilation of minority groups into the dominant Anglo-Saxon culture. The dominance of English as the only language and the loss of most linguistic heritages is an obvious sign of assimilation of minorities.

Earlier in the twentieth century, some writers proclaimed that the equal mixture of English, German, Irish, Italian, black, and other cultures would produce an entirely new and unique people and culture. This was the *melting pot* ideology. Each group would make its contribution, but none would dominate, and a new people would arise. America would borrow from all its constituent groups and create a new group, unlike any one of its constituents. But this was never even a remote possibility. At most, there has been a gradual assimilation and the triumph of the English culture (which, of course, has changed over time, as most cultures change).

Over time, minority and majority groups intermingle and produce offspring, which carry the genes of two or more groups. This *amalgamation* often takes place over centuries, but it does always happen to some degree. Perhaps the most striking case of amalgamation (which does not necessarily mean social and cultural intermingling) today is the Jewish people in Israel. Those who came to Israel after centuries of living in European societies resemble the European host people, and those who came from Arab societies resemble Arab people. Indeed, there are social and economic tensions between European and Arab Jews in Israel (*Boston Globe,* December 30, 1982:9).

More recently, partly inspired by the civil rights movement of the 1950s and 1960s, some people have been trying to reclaim their ethnic identity. They want to be Americans *and* Italian or Irish or Polish. This concept of *cultural pluralism* is based on the belief that different cultures, races, and political groups can coexist in one society. While we may belong to ethnic groups (subcultures) with their own values, traditions, and customs, we also belong to one large culture. As indications of pluralism, there have been ethnic festivals, ethnic names revived (Sean instead of John, and other ethnic first names), and an assertion of pride in one's ethnicity. As valuable as it may be for some individuals, cultural pluralism cannot hide the economic roots, the history of minorities, or the domination of the English-American culture.

Minority Responses

The response of minority groups to their oppression ranges from the most self-destructive denial of their identity to liberating political actions. The following list reveals one of the most tragic aspects of American history. These are examples of the kinds of responses people make to economic exploitation and cultural denigration. People who respond this way deny their past and disassociate themselves from their physical and social identity. Since they are made to feel ashamed of who they are, they proceed to become different.

■ Many ethnic people have Americanized their last names, and African slaves were forcibly given European names.

■ Children have been given Americanized first names.

■ Ethnic foods, rich in garlic and other spices, have been given up for blander dishes.

■ Italians, Jews, and others have had their noses changed.

■ Asian people have had their eyes altered.

■ Black people have used hair straighteners, lotions to lighten their skin, and altered their appearance in other ways.

■ Many older people have plastic surgery and otherwise try to look younger.

Malcolm X (1965) describes *conking*, the painful process black people once used to straighten their hair.

> *The mirror reflected Shorty behind me. We both were grinning and sweating. And on top of my head was this thick, smooth sheen of shining red hair—real red—as straight as any white man's.*
>
> *How ridiculous I was! Stupid enough to stand there simply lost in admiration of my hair now looking "white," reflected in the mirror in Shorty's room. I vowed that I'd never again be without a conk, and I never was for many years.*
>
> *This was my first really big step toward self-degradation: when I endured all of that pain, literally burning my flesh to have it look like a white man's hair. I had joined that multitude of Negro men and women in America who are brainwashed into believing that the black people are "inferior"—and white people "superior"—that they will even violate and mutilate their God-created bodies to try to look "pretty" by white standards. (p. 54)*

To this day, within the black community lighter-skin blacks have more prestige. Many black people who talked to Gwaltney (1980) (a black anthropologist) reported this bias. A young black woman reprimanded a light black friend of hers for dating a dark black man, commenting "I didn't know you dealt in coal." (p. 81)

The following quotation captures all the shame some people feel about their ethnic and racial heritage. It shows how so many minority people come to accept the negative labels assigned to their groups, and how they internalize these negative images. This passage from Miller (1972) painfully shows how self-hatred corrodes the souls of many minority people.

> *I enter the parochial school with an awful fear that I will be called Wop. As soon as I found out why people have such things as surnames, I match my own against such typically Italian cognomens as Bianchi, Borello, Pacelli—the names of other students. I am pleasantly relieved by the comparison. After all, I think people will say I am French. Doesn't my name sound French? Sure! So therefore, when people ask my nationality, I tell them I am French. A few boys begin calling me Frenchy. I like that. It feels fine.*
>
> *Thus I begin to loathe my heritage. I avoid Italian boys and girls who try*

to be friendly. I thank God for my light skin and hair, and I choose my companions by the Anglo-Saxon ring of their names. If a boy's name is Whitney, Brown, or Smythe, then he's my pal; but I'm always a little breathless when I am with him: he may find me out. At the lunch hour I huddle over my lunch pail, for my mother doesn't wrap my sandwiches in wax paper, and she makes them too large, and the lettuce leaves protrude. (p. 33)

When poverty, discrimination and oppression grind down the spirits of minority people, some resort to violence and criminality against each other (most victims of black and poor street criminals are other black and poor people). Others resort to "alcoholism, promiscuity, and the misuse of religion" (Miller, 1972, p. 22).

In American history, new immigrant and minority groups have replaced earlier ones. Earlier minorities frequently forgot their own history of being discriminated against and proceed to discriminate against the new arrivals. Thus Irish forbade union membership to Chinese workers. Irish, Italians, and others have excluded black people from their neighborhoods. Such enmity between minorities has only helped corporations and the ruling class, and it has often been consciously encouraged by corporations to divide workers along ethnic and racial lines. (See Greer, 1976, and Miller, 1972.)

The choice of minority individuals or groups to change their behavior so they can blend in with the majority is termed *acculturation*. This is a somewhat less destructive version of identity denial. More or less willingly, minority people change their behavior and values to match those of the majority, and thus to be accepted into the economy and culture. Dress, language, cuisine, leisure-time activities, and general life style are some of the changes people make. Jews who move into WASP and Christian suburbs no longer practice the orthodox Judaism of their parents since it might seem too Jewish to their new Christian neighbors. Instead they practice conservative or reform Judaism. (See Philip Roth's excellent short story on this very point, "Eli the Fanatic," in his book *Goodbye, Columbus.*)

Some of Mangione's (1981) relatives and neighbors Americanized themselves. As they moved out of Mount Allegro to the suburbs, they "developed strange habits and tastes. They took to drinking fruit juices at breakfast and tea with supper. They wore pajamas to bed, drank whiskey with soda, and learned to play poker." (p. 207) Those who became *Americanos* were both envied and resented. They left their fellow Italians and were thought to put on airs, but they were also seen as successes as judged against the standards of the culture. The sons of poor Italians who became doctors or lawyers changed drastically.

As soon as they had established themselves, they married blonde American girls and moved as far as possible from their former neighborhoods. Some of them dropped the vowels from the end of their names, so that people would think they had always been American. They stopped associating with their relatives. Their wives got their pictures in society pages and, instead of having a raft of children, they bought wire-haired terriers and walked them around the block, like many other prosperous Americans. The only times they liked dealing with Italians was when it meant money in their pockets. (p. 223)

We said above that minorities are forced to live in segregated areas, apart from the majority. But at the same time neighborhoods, which are mostly Italian, Irish, Polish, Greek, or black are also partly a matter of choice. They may not like the poor, crowded, and dilapidated housing they occupy, but they appreciate living close to people who share the same language and customs. Indeed, early in their history, immigrants not only settled near people of their own ethnic group, but they found compatriots from the same village, town, or region. In a new, strange, and threatening land, ethnic enclaves are a haven of security and familiarity.

The above are all common responses of minority individuals and families. Rarely are they collective and organized group actions. In addition, minorities have also chosen from a number of alternative political and social actions.

Labor unions were among the first organized attempts to improve wages and working conditions. Even though at times unions themselves have discriminated against minorities, many unions represent struggles by Irish, Italian, and other workers to combat the power of their employers and increase their power. The history of unions is long and often violent—from the beginning employers used force and arms to defeat unions. (See Chapters 8 and 9 for a discussion of unions.)

In addition to unions, there are other forms of collective action. Nonviolent protests—marches, sit-ins, civil disobedience, and other tactics—have been used to awaken the conscience of the majority to stop discrimination. But some people, feeling frustrated from long suffering and no progress, have violently rebelled against their oppressors. Throughout American history slaves, Irish poor, blacks in large cities, and others have risen up against their owners, police, and employers.

But unorganized rebellion and spontaneous protest leads to little social change. Therefore, some people decide to engage in a long revolutionary struggle to take over the state and change the social, economic, and political system to end injustice and oppression. Still others seek to end discrimination and oppression without revolution. By organizing and participating in politics, groups seek a better deal for themselves. For example, political machines in American cities have opened political offices and jobs for many minority groups. Blacks have organized in many southern towns and now hold many public offices from mayor to police chief.

Finally, in many places in the world, minority people have concluded they can never attain full economic and cultural equality so long as they remain within the state in which they currently live. Many people in Quebec, Canada, in the Basque region of Spain, in Scotland and Wales, and some blacks in the United States, to name just a few, are seeking to form new nations, states, or societies, completely independent, politically, militarily, and economically, from the present state. In these separate states, they can practice their own culture and run their own economy.

Minority Groups in the United States

Now that we have defined minorities, looked at the history of some minority groups, explored some of the reasons for their rise, and outlined a number of relationships between majority and minority groups, we can turn to the conditions under which some contemporary U.S. minority groups live. (See Table 11.1 for population distribution of minority groups.)

Blacks, native Americans, and Hispanics have been considered minorities for some time, but it is only in the last two decades that social scientists have thought of the elderly, gays, and disabled people as minorities. Part of the reason for this recognition was due to people from these groups protesting discrimination, injustice, and stereotyping. Gays, the elderly, and the disabled experienced economic discrimination in varying degrees, by not being hired or being paid less because of their physical condition or because of their sexual preference. Certainly all three groups face general discrimination, are widely stereotyped, and often are powerless to control their lives.

The section on black people is the longest because they are the largest and still most discriminated against group. The conditions of native Americans and Hispanics are similar to those of black people, thus the sections on these two groups are short. (This discussion of blacks includes statistical data on

TABLE 11.1
U.S. Population, Various Groups and Years

Ethnic and Racial Groups	Population
White (1985)	202,478,000
Black (1985)	28,811,000
American Indian (1980)	1,420,000
Chinese (1980)	806,000
Filipino (1980)	774,700
Japanese (1980)	701,000
Asian Indian (1980)	361,500
Korean (1980)	354,600
Vietnamese (1980)	261,700
All other races (1980)	6,999,200
Spanish origin* (1985)	16,940,000
Chicano (Mexican-American) (1980)	8,700,000
Puerto Rican (in Puerto Rico) (1985)	3,282,000
Puerto Rican (in continental U.S.) (1980)	2,014,000

Statistical Abstract, 1982–1983:32; 1987:15, 17, 805
* People of Spanish origin may be of any race and include Mexicans, Puerto Ricans, Cubans, or others of Spanish/Hispanic origin.

Hispanics as a way of comparison and because the U.S. census often does not separate these two groups out.) I devote a little more space to the elderly, gay people, and disabled people because their conditions are somewhat specific to each group. We close this section with a brief mention of ethnic groups and recent immigrants. Chapter 12 discusses women.

Blacks

Income and Employment

The data below lead to two very clear conclusions: minority people (especially blacks) made some gains in income during the 1960s but have lost ground in the 1970s and 1980s; unemployment among blacks is twice that of whites.

Table 11.2 lists median family incomes in *1985* dollars and shows that black families in 1960 had a median income 55.3 percent of the median white income, both families gained in the 1960s, with black families gaining a little more, so by 1970 the black-white family income ratio was 61.3 percent. But through the 1970s both families' incomes declined, black incomes somewhat more, and by 1985 the ratio of black-white family incomes had decreased to 57.6 percent. Thus, the 1970s meant no progress for either black or white families, and the income gap between them widened.

The higher unemployment rate of blacks contributes to lower incomes for black families. But even if we compare families with wage and salary earners, we still find considerable differences. Median weekly earnings of families with wage and salary earners still reveal a significant black-white income gap, as we see in Table 11.3. When we compare all families with one or more wage or income earner, the ratio is 70.7 percent; with one earner, it is 69 percent; and with two or more earners, 81 percent.

In Table 11.4 we see that individual black and Hispanic workers, in addition to families, also have considerably lower earnings than white workers. Black and Hispanic workers have median weekly earnings less than 80

TABLE 11.2
Median Money Income of Families (in 1985 dollars), 1950 to 1985, by Race and Spanish Origin*

	White	Black	Black/White	Spanish Origin
1950	$15,935	$ 8,352	52.4%	—
1960	21,195	11,733	55.3	—
1970	28,358	17,395	61.3	—
1975	28,518	17,547	61.5	$19,090
1980	28,596	16,546	57.9	19,212
1985	29,152	16,786	57.6	19,027

Statistical Abstract, 1987:436

* Includes Mexicans, Puerto Ricans, Cubans, and others of Spanish/Hispanic origin.

TABLE 11.3
Median Weekly Family Earnings, by Number of Earners and
Race, 1987

	Median Weekly Earnings
White	
Families with wage or salary workers	$578
One earner	367
Two earners or more	750
Black	
Families with wage or salary workers	399
One earner	247
Two earners or more	605
Spanish	
Families with wage or salary workers	412
One earner	260
Two earners or more	581

U.S. Department of Labor, 1987d

TABLE 11.4
Median Weekly Earnings, by Race, Age, and Sex, 1987

	Median weekly earnings		
	Black	*Hispanic*	*White*
Total, 16 years and over	$291	$277	$370
16 to 24 years	205	209	235
25 years and over	307	300	402
Men, 16 years and over	318	299	433
16 to 24 years	211	212	250
25 years and over	344	326	477
Women, 16 years and over	263	241	294
16 to 24 years	197	203	220
25 years and over	277	255	313

U.S. Department of Labor, 1987a

percent those of white workers. The gap is most pronounced when we compare the black and Hispanic to white ratio for men twenty-five years and over, 72 and 68 percent.

The percentages below the official poverty level also reveal improvements in the 1960s but no change in the 1970s and 1980s. In 1959, 15.2 percent of all white families in the United States were below the poverty line, 8.0 percent in 1970, the same percent in 1980, and 9.1 percent in 1985. In comparison, in 1959, 48.1 percent of all black families were below the poverty level, 29.5 percent in 1970, and in 1980 and 1985 almost identical to

1970—28.9 and 28.7 percent (*Statistical Abstract,* 1982–1983:442; 1987: 444).

As we have seen, black families with one or more workers make 70 percent of the income of comparable white families. But the fact that more black people are unemployed lowers the ratio. When we compare *all* black families (those with workers and those without workers) with all white families, the ratio is 58 percent. First of all, more blacks than whites over sixteen years old are out of the labor force (the labor force includes those who work or are looking for work). In 1985, 70.8 percent of all black men and 77 percent of all white men were in the labor force, and 56.5 percent of all black women as opposed to 54.1 of all white women (*Statistical Abstract,* 1987:376).

Of those in the labor force, twice as many blacks as whites are usually unemployed. (See Chapter 9.) But these statistics are limited in what they reveal. As we saw in Chapter 9, they underreport the amount of actual unemployment. Specific black groups experience much higher unemployment. *Official* data for black youths (16 to 19 years old) show unemployment rates near 50 percent, compared to about 20 percent for white youths. In some cities, such as Gary, Indiana, and Montgomery, Alabama, unemployment reaches 80 percent for black youth. Even adult black males exceed 50 percent unemployment rates in some cities—60 percent in Liberty City, Miami, Florida, in 1982. According to one study quoted in the *Guardian* (December 31, 1986:7), in 1986 half of the 8.8 million black men of working age had no jobs. These are catastrophic rates, leading to poverty and wasted lives. (See *Guardian,* May 5, 1982:7.)

People without work suffer emotionally and financially, as we saw in Chapter 9. Millions of black men cannot find jobs. The cause of black poverty and economic hardship is the displacement of black men from the labor market. Millions of black women are single mothers because men cannot find jobs to help support their families. They are unemployed because discrimination and the economy deny them jobs. They want to work, desperately so, as Cottle (1979) shows when he described Ollie Sindon's problems in finding work, and as Valentine (1978) learned when she lived in a poor black neighborhood of Chicago. Those who do have jobs are paid increasingly lower wages. Male black high school graduates made an average of $11,444 in 1973, but by 1984, after adjusting for inflation, they were making $5,571, less than half of what they made in 1973. (See Joe, 1984; *Dollars and Sense,* April 1986:5–7; and Kuttner, 1987b.)

When there was a shortage of workers because white men went to fight a war in the 1940s, black people were given jobs and performed them well. Their education, skills, and motivation have not worsened since the 1940s—job opportunities have. Unemployment, lower pay, and discrimination in getting better jobs are at the center of minority life. Blacks and others benefit little when discrimination ends. They may be allowed to eat in restaurants, join clubs, and buy houses wherever they want, but this does little good if they can't afford to do these things. Gains in civil rights are largely hollow victories without the economic changes that make it possible for people to take advantage of the available equality.

Housing

Because of lower incomes and continuing discrimination, black people live in inferior housing and segregated neighborhoods. Large central cities have old, deteriorating, and segregated housing. More blacks live in these urban centers than whites. In 1970, 27.9 percent of all whites and 58.2 percent of blacks lived in central cities, and 24.6 percent and 57.2 percent did so in 1980. Blacks are also much more likely to rent than to own their dwellings, 46 percent owned their housing in 1983 versus 68 percent of all whites (*Statistical Abstract,* 1982–1983:21, 752, 757; 1987:712).

The worsening economic conditions of the 1980s are making home ownership more difficult. By 1983, only 40 percent of black "families and unrelated individuals" owned their own homes (60 percent of whites did). In the metropolitan Boston area, where only 23 percent of blacks (versus 55.7 for whites) owned their homes in 1986, the escalating prices of homes make it almost impossible for black people to buy homes. (See Center for Popular Economics, 1986: 27; and *Boston Globe,* August 25, 1986:1, 6.)

Realtors and banks discriminate against blacks and deny housing opportunities to those blacks who can afford better housing. Banks have selected areas in which they will not give mortgages to black applicants. This is called redlining. Blockbusting has been another popular tactic realtors have used. Once a few blacks move into an area, realtors frighten the white residents into selling at very low prices by claiming their homes will soon be worthless, and then selling these homes to black buyers at much higher prices. Realtors benefit, but white and black homeowners lose and neighborhoods remain segregated (Luhman & Gilman, 1980).

Occasionally a community will encourage black people to move in. But most communities have carefully and deliberately excluded blacks. Housing and community racial segregation continue. In metropolitan areas, blacks and other minorities are becoming more concentrated in central cities and excluded from suburban and other neighborhoods. *Racial polarity continues and increases.* Atlanta, for example, is a tale of two cities. Atlanta proper is black and poor, and the suburbs, where jobs and economic growth are moving, are white. (See *Boston Globe,* January 8, 1983:17; January 22, 1983:3; April 8, 1986:17; *Guardian,* April 2, 1986:5; and Beers & Hembree, 1987.)

Studies have exposed realtor discrimination. Minority people are shown only a few homes or apartments, are quoted higher prices, or are told a house has been sold when it is still on the market. In Milton, Massachusetts (adjacent to Boston), in 1986 seven real estate agencies pleaded guilty to charges of racial discrimination in their practices (*Boston Globe,* May 8, 1986:27). In Nassau County, New York, "of 78 homes visited by State investigators posing as prospective buyers, only three were shown to both black and white couples" (*Guardian,* April 2, 1985:5). Various studies have concluded that 70 to 80 percent of black prospective house buyers encounter bias.

Health and Health Care

Black people suffer from poorer health and receive less medical care than white people primarily because they are poor. We have seen in previous chapters that health care for poor people is not only inadequate, it is worsening. Many public hospitals are closing, funds for medicaid and other health care programs are being reduced.

A few statistics illustrate the effects of poverty, deprivation, discrimination, and low-quality health care on black people. In 1985, white males at birth were expected to live 71.8 years on the average, as opposed to 65.3 years for black males. For women, the expectancies were 78.7 for whites and 73.7 for blacks. Infant death rates per 1,000 live births were 43.2 for whites in 1940 and 9.7 in 1983, and 72.9 in 1940 and 19.2 in 1983 for blacks—twice as high as whites in 1983. Maternal deaths show even a greater difference in 1983—5.9 per 100,000 births for white women, 18.3 for black women. (See *Statistical Abstract,* 1982–1983:72, 75; 1987:69, 71, 74.)

The health of black people reflects the poverty and discrimination they face. Lower life expectancy, poor nutrition, higher infant death rates, more illness, and so on, result from unemployment and lower incomes. Inadequate or nonexistent medical care and poor diets lead to worse health (Krieger & Bassett, 1986).

Education

Blacks and other minorities, being mostly poor and working class, are victimized by the class biases of the educational system we have already discussed in Chapter 8. Basically, many studies, data, and personal experiences have shown that schools spend less money on black students, have traditionally segregated blacks in mostly, or all, black schools, and teachers have given black students inferior educations because they have expected less of them.

A number of studies and reports have found pervasive racism and labeling of black children as inferior, unintelligent, and lazy. In addition, teaching equipment and supplies have been generally inadequate or absent. These observations were made in the 1960s, but the conditions the authors reported do not seem to have changed. Black people may spend about the same number of years in school as whites (a median of 12.7 years of school completed for whites in 1985, 12.3 for blacks), but schools teach them less. Schools have not helped them find more jobs or better paying work. (See Ryan, 1981; Kozol, 1967; Herndon, 1968; and Hale-Benson, 1986, for the culture and learning styles of black children.)

Attitudes, Perceptions, and Daily Life

Black people live in two different worlds. They must in order to survive. They behave differently towards whites than they do with each other. At least that is the clear message they communicated to Gwaltney (1980).

Most blacks resent whites, some hate them. The comment by a black man who spoke with Gwaltney (1980) typifies this feeling. "Whitefolks have done me every kind of dirt they could think of doing. There is just nothing else you can do but hate them suckers! . . . Everything they do is rotten." (p. 59) Time and again Gwaltney was told by blacks that they cannot afford to trust whites; in order to survive, they must always be suspicious and on their guard. They must weigh carefully what they say and be on the lookout. Many whites are ignorant of the fact that black people consciously lead two lives, that they rarely act with whites as they do with each other. This is also true for other minorities. The Irish, according to Fallows (1979), dealt with the British by becoming "masters of deception and dodgers of the law." (p. 13)

Even in simple events like an approaching police officer whose intent is to help, blacks and whites experience different emotions. Hannah Nelson related the following experience to Gwaltney (1980).

> One time in rural Georgia a white woman and I were stranded in a ditch in her car. When some policemen came and helped us, she was relieved to see them but I was frightened. Now, I know many other black women who have had experiences something like that, and most felt just like I did. I didn't know what those policemen might do, but the white woman with me felt quite certain that they would help us. Well, I knew they would help her, but I didn't really think they would help me. I was very glad that the white woman was there with me because she was the only protection I felt I had at that time. (p. 6)

A recent *Time* magazine (February 2, 1987) poll showed clear differences in perceptions between black and white people. Fully 75 percent of blacks said they did not think black Americans have the same housing opportunities as whites; 47 percent of whites agreed with them, 48 did not. In education, 59 percent of blacks thought black people did not have the same opportunities as whites, but 73 percent of whites said they did. Finally, 71 percent of blacks said they thought they do not have equal employment opportunities, but 59 percent of whites said blacks do have such equality.

Harris (1987) reports some survey findings that he feels mean a large majority of white people are for racial equality. In 1965, 66 percent of whites said that black people are less ambitious than whites; only 26 percent thought so in 1985. Over three-quarters of white people support programs to help minorities and women.

But polls report what people *think*. They may tell us less about what people *do*. Browne (1986), a young black man from SANE, a peace organization, went to people's homes in Boston suburbs to ask for contributions to SANE. He met constant animosity. When they saw him through their windows, white people often never answered the door. One day in Lexington, he writes, "A police car passed me several times within 10 minutes. Finally, the police officer pulled up behind me in the car with the high beam lights on. 'What are you doing in this neighborhood?' he asked sternly. I explained. Not satisfied, he radioed the station to verify my name appeared on the list of those registered to canvass for SANE that evening. The radio dispatcher confirmed my story." (p. 15)

Despite such incidents he continued his work, until one day in Winchester someone opened the door and let loose a retriever to chase him. "The dog chased me the length of the street before it gave up and returned home. I quit that night." (p. 15)

Discrimination, prejudice, ignorance, and distrust remain. The economic conditions of black people (*and* whites and other minorities) need improvement. Attitudes must change. One source of ignorance and stereotypes is the continuing segregation. Most black and white people do not live near people of the other group, do not socialize with them, do not get to know them. That isolation must end.

Persisting Discrimination

Discrimination, prejudices, and stereotypes are still strong. They are *present* conditions, not past prejudices. They are found in cities, suburbs, schools, workplaces. They are practiced by many people of all ages, education levels, and incomes. The media ignore and stereotype blacks; employers discriminate against them; baseball will not hire blacks in managerial positions; housing discrimination is pervasive; violence against blacks still happens.

Civil Rights Laws   The *Boston Globe* (March 17, 1986:3) cited a 1986 report by the National Association for the Advancement of Colored People (NAACP) and the American Civil Liberties Union (ACLU) in 1986 that concluded that the government was not enforcing civil rights laws that prohibit discrimination against minorities, women, the elderly, and the handicapped. From the Federal government down, there is little or no effort to stop discrimination. The Institute for Social Research Newsletter (1985) reported a study on racial attitudes that concluded: "White America increasingly supports principles of racial equality, but is much less enthusiastic about specific methods for implementing them." In addition, Turner (1987) thinks there is no "outrage over discrimination that won't go away." (p. 17) Exclusion of and violent attacks against blacks usually stir no anger or action to stop them.

Employment   The conservative Commission on Civil Rights produced a study in 1982 that concluded blacks and women continue to experience employment discrimination. The Commission reported that blacks and women make less money and hold fewer desirable jobs. The reason for this is not because they have less education or fewer skills, but because the government does not enforce laws that give blacks and women equal access to jobs. (See *Boston Globe*, November 24, 1982: 3; and *Guardian*, December 8, 1982:3.)

Later studies have confirmed the commission's conclusions. The *Boston*

Globe's (January 20, 1984:1, 10) detailed investigations in 1984 and 1985 showed that the percentage of black people in most occupations was very low. Boston's population was 10 percent minority, but "of the 1,300 officials and managers who run Boston's major food stores, only 30 are minorities, the [Equal Employment Opportunity] Commission said. Of 2,200 clerical workers who work in these foodstores, only 50 are minorities." Colleges and universities did no better. No more than 1 or 2 percent of their faculty were black; only one college had as high as 8 percent black faculty. Little change had taken place from 1979 to 1984. In the high tech industries, 2 percent of officials and managers and 5 percent of all employees were black in 1984. The percentages were about the same in banking and other private corporations. For example, of employees in private corporations, 2.5 to 3 percent of professionals and managers were black, but 16 percent of service workers were black. A 1987 report concluded that sixty cities and towns in Massachusetts still have very few minorities in their police forces. (See *Boston Globe*, January 20, 1984:1, 10; November 11, 1985:1, 18; November 12, 1985:1, 12; and March 21, 1987:17–18.)

Sports organizations continue to hire very few blacks in managerial and office positions. In 1987, a racist comment by an executive of the Los Angeles Dodgers created a furor, but subsequent investigations showed how few blacks work in baseball after their playing days end. Whiteside (1987) notes that forty years after Jackie Robinson became the first black to play in major league baseball, and with about a quarter of the players black for fifteen to twenty years, "there are no black managers . . . and only a handful of coaches. . . . There are no black comptrollers, no black ticket managers, no black grounds crew chiefs . . ." and only three full-time black baseball writers. (p. 45) (Three blacks were managers for brief periods in the late 1970s, early 1980s.) Dupont (1987) talked with many former black players and found they had repeatedly been overlooked when jobs opened up. Some, including some former stars, had written many times inquiring about openings. Usually they received no reply at all. Football has never had a black head coach. In professional basketball, where 80 percent of the players are black, only four of the twenty-three head coaches were black in 1987.

Criminal Justice   Police harassment of black people has a long history. City after city has been rocked by black protests against police harassment and brutality. Police action often leads to the killing of unarmed black suspects. (See *Progressive*, September 1986:18; *Boston Globe*, February 1987:15; and *Guardian*, March 11, 1987:9.)

The *Boston Globe* (July 5, 1983:5) reported on a 1983 study of criminal sentencing in California, Texas, and Michigan that found that "for the same crime and with similar criminal records," whites, as compared to blacks and Hispanics, "are more likely to get probation, to go to jail instead of prison, to receive shorter sentences, and to serve less time behind bars than do minority offenders." The death penalty is also applied unequally. If you kill a black person, you are much less likely to be executed than if you kill a white person. It was reported in the *Boston Globe* (January 19, 1987:15) that

> *ninety-two percent of those executed in the United States since 1976 had killed whites while almost half of all homicide victims were black.*
>
> *A study in eight states between 1976 and 1980 showed that killers of whites were between four and eight times likelier to receive the death penalty than were killers of blacks.*
>
> *A 1983 study of Georgia sentencing showed that capital defendants who killed whites were up to 11 times likelier to receive the death penalty than were those who killed blacks.*
>
> *3,291 people have been executed since 1930; 54 percent have been blacks or members of other minority groups. Four hundred, fifty-five were executed for rape; 405 of them were black.*

Such biased sentencing by judges reflects the stereotype of minorities as more dangerous and criminal, and of minority victims as unimportant.

Violence   Violence against black people has become commonplace. The Justice Department found a 250 percent increase in reported racial attacks since 1981. In Cummings, Georgia, an interracial group of civil rights marchers was attacked by the Ku Klux Klan in early 1987. In Howard Beach (a section of New York City), a white neighborhood, three black men who entered a store to make a phone call were beaten and chased by a group of white men. One of the black men was killed by a car as he ran across a highway to escape. There was violence and threats against black people in the Los Angeles area. In Boston, an investigation concluded that black emergency medical technicians had been repeatedly harassed by their white co-workers, and the management had ignored their complaints. (See *Guardian,* August 6, 1986:6; January 14, 1987:1, 6; February 4, 1987:1, 9; February 25, 1987:18; and *Boston Globe,* December 26, 1986:34.) Blacks who have moved to white neighborhoods have been harassed and attacked. The *Guardian* (April 6, 1986:6) has also reported a long list of violence against blacks.

> *A sixty-six year old black woman was killed last June [1985] when someone threw a firebomb into her family's home in a predominantly white Cleveland neighborhood.*
>
> *In Philadelphia, homes owned by an interracial couple and a black family were besieged late last year [1985] by mobs screaming racist epithets, leading the mayor to declare a state of emergency in the area.*
>
> *A black mother and her eleven-year-old daughter were forced out of a Quincy, Massachusetts housing project after neighbors called them "niggers" and heaped garbage on their doorstep.*
>
> *In a single month last year, homes owned by blacks were firebombed in Chicago and Tacoma, Washington; a cross-burning occurred in East Meadow, New York; and acts of racist vandalism took place in Maplewood, New Jersey.*

Why all this violence? Much of the explanation lies in the government's refusal to enforce civil rights laws and to work to end discrimination. It encourages racism, even if only indirectly. The jury that found Bernard Goetz innocent of the subway shooting of four black youths only added to the racist climate (*Guardian,* February 25, 1987:18). Jordan (1987b), a black columnist for the *Boston Globe,* argues that he and other black men are often seen as potential criminals. As he was walking down the aisle of a department store one day, "about 20 yards down the aisle, a woman saw the man approaching and warned her friend, who had placed her pocketbook on a box, to 'pick up your pocketbook before it is stolen,' while giving the black man a stern look. . . . Other professional black men have also shared similar experiences, even when they were dressed like Wall Street bankers." (p. 17)

The numbers of black students attending college declined in the 1980s. At the University of Michigan blacks were 7.7 percent of the student body in 1976, but 5.2 percent in 1986. They feel isolated and alienated. Increasingly, they face harassment and discrimination. During 1986 and 1987 racist incidents took place at Columbia University, University of Massachusetts, University of Michigan, and Northern Illinois University, among others. (On most of these campuses, groups of black and white students organized protests against the harassment and violence.) (See *Guardian,* August 6, 1986:2; April 8, 1987:6; April 22, 1987:5; and *Boston Globe,* May 18–20, 1986; October 23, 1986:31, 34.)

Racism in the Media   There is considerable racism in the media. Johnson (1987) analyzed 3,215 stories on Boston radio and TV stations and in newspapers during one month in the summer of 1986. The *Boston Globe* (January 28, 1987:22) summarized some of his findings:

> *Coverage of the black community by white-owned news outlets disproportionately emphasized crime while giving scant coverage to stories on education, culture, and civic and business achievements that reflect the values and aspirations of Boston's black community.*
>
> *From June 9 to July 9, 1986, for instance, 70 percent of all stories from Roxbury and Mattapan in the city's major news outlets concerned either crimes or traffic accidents.*
>
> *85 percent of news items about the black community in the dominant media reinforced stereotypes of black Bostonians as drug pushers, thieves, troublemakers, fomenters of violence, and people mired in apathy.*

Racist messages in the media are indirect, subtle, and cumulative. They probably exist in most cities.

Network television also distorts the reality of black people's lives. Except for an occasional comedy series, black people have been largely absent. Movies also usually feature black stars only in comedy roles (Richard Pryor, Eddie Murphy). Part of the explanation for the invisibility of black people on television and the movies is the virtual absence of black screenwriters. Most scripts are written by white men under forty, according to one study reported in the *Boston Globe* (July 1, 1987). Black invisibility exists in other media. For example, only four children's books about black people were published in 1984 (*Guardian,* November 25, 1985:4). There was only one black editor for children's books (*Guardian,* November 12, 1986:20). Black people are either invisible in the media, or, when shown, the content stereotypes them. (See McDonald, 1983.)

Reverse Discrimination   Let us close this section with the much debated, but spurious, problem of *reverse discrimination*. Some people argue that unqualified blacks and women are given jobs and positions over qualified white men. Let us admit that this may happen on occasion, but there is no evidence that reverse discrimination is taking place on a large scale. On the contrary, the evidence cited above shows discrimination against blacks and, as we will see in Chapter 12, women continues. If reverse discrimination occurred to any great extent during the 1970s, how do we explain the *decline* in income, employment, and jobs blacks experienced in that decade? (See Ryan, 1981, and Luhman & Gilman, 1980.)

Preferred selection practices have always been used to help the disadvantaged. Traditionally, veterans have been given preference in government hiring with little objection being raised. Colleges chose students on criteria other than scholastic ability (geography, athletic ability, alumnae parents, and so on), yet only when blacks are admitted for similar considerations of representation do people object.

Native Americans

In 1980, there were about 1.4 million American Indians, Eskimos, and Aleuts in the United States. About half of them were living on reservations. In 1984, the reservations comprised a total of 53.5 million acres (down from 55.4 million in 1940), only 2.3 percent of the land. Indian lands were taken away long ago and are still being taken over by corporations, ranchers, and others.

Despite the barrenness of the land and poverty, native American tribes chose to live on reservations because they value their cultures and communities and want to survive not as isolated individuals in cities, but as whole cultures. Their relationships to each other and to the earth differ radically from the surrounding American culture. (I have given examples in previous chapters.) But they live in extreme poverty. In 1982, they had an average family income of $3,000 (the lowest in the United States) and a life expectancy of forty-six years. Unemployment and alcoholism ravage the lives of many. Health facilities (the responsibility of the federal government) are very limited. The schools run by the federal government provide limited and racist education. (See *Statistical Abstract,* 1982–1983:15, 224, 229; 1987:185; and a brochure from Native American Rights Fund, undated.)

We tend to think of the exploitation of native Americans as a past event.

But they are still struggling *today* to protect their few remaining lands from corporations, ranchers, and the government. For example, by treaty they are entitled to fish rivers and lakes for their livelihood. But people who fish for a sport, and those who want to use the rivers for commercial purposes, are constantly denying native Americans their treaty rights (and courts often will not enforce these treaties). We are now seeing resurgent racism—bumper stickers proclaiming "save a fish—spear an Indian." (See Faller, 1980; Thurtell, 1980; and Gebhart, 1980.)

Furthermore, the government, corporations, and organizations of ranchers and corporations continue to agitate for more Indian lands and the minerals under those lands. Coal, uranium, and oil lie under the barren reservations once given to tribes because they were considered worthless. Now they are coveted by corporations. In the Southwest, the government in 1981 was pushing to relocate 6,500 Navajos so Peabody Coal Company and others could dig out the estimated twenty-two billion tons of coal. These threats to Indian lands and cultures are present events, not past history. (See *Guardian*, June 17, 1981:9; Stillwaggon, 1981; Gedicks, 1983; and Winslow, 1983.)

Some Americanized Navaho, Hopis, and others seem willing to cooperate in the corporate theft of their lands and resources, but thousands of others are organizing, protesting, and suing in courts to protect and regain their lands. They are struggling, as they have for centuries, to survive and continue their cultures. (See Sullivan, 1983; for a history, see McLemore, 1983; Josephy, 1984; and *Dollars and Sense*, December 1985:14–16.)

Hispanics

Puerto Ricans

Puerto Ricans make up a large minority in many cities in the Northeast. They have been (within the last twenty years) one of the latest groups to migrate to cities in the United States. In 1980, there were 2 million Puerto Ricans in the continental United States, with about 1 million in New York City alone. With 3.2 million people in Puerto Rico itself, the Puerto Ricans in this country reprsent over one-third of all Puerto Ricans. An emigration of this magnitude results in profound social dislocations within the emigrant's own society and causes further dislocations in the receiving society. Why have Puerto Ricans left their native land in such numbers? How do they live in their new home? (See *Statistical Abstract*, 1982–1983:32; 1987:805.)

A brief look at Puerto Rican history explains the migration. The United States captured Puerto Rico from the Spanish in 1898 as part of its general imperialist expansion during the 1890s (Cuba, the Philippines, and other countries were also brought under its domination). Jacobs and Landau (1971) say that businesspeople and the federal government saw such expansions as "the only solution for internal economic problems of overproduction and insufficient markets for surplus commodities and capital." (p. 276)

Puerto Ricans became United States citizens in 1917, but they have not been allowed to govern themselves. Moreover, until 1948, when they took over their school system, educational content was controlled from the United States, and English was the primary language in schools—contributing in part to the general degradation of Puerto Rican culture. By the 1930s, the Puerto Rican economy was dominated by United States corporations. Much of the land was turned over to cash crops, primarily sugar, which forced people to pay higher prices for imported food. As a result, poverty became widespread.

To deal with this poverty, Operation Bootstrap was launched in the 1940s. Foreign corporations were encouraged to invest in Puerto Rico and provide jobs for people. The multinationals came not to provide decent jobs for people but because of a plentiful, cheap labor supply and large tax breaks from the government. A few rich people and a small middle class benefitted from Operation Bootstrap, but most people did not. Huge corporate profits now leave the island, minimum wages have been kept low, and unemployment remains high (21 percent in 1985, an official statistic that always underestimates real unemployment). (See *Statistical Abstract,* 1987:805.)

In 1940, 50 percent of the people in Puerto Rico worked in agriculture, but only 4.4 percent did in 1972. These displaced people who could not be absorbed into the Puerto Rican economy began migrating to New York City and elsewhere. They were running away. The promised land of New York was an escape from poverty, but it delivered less than it promised (Marden & Meyer, 1978).

Only about seventy thousand people had migrated to the United States by 1940. The increasing poverty in Puerto Rico, the demand for labor during the war, and the introduction of cheap air fares led to increased migration. In 1970, there were 1.43 million first and second generation Puerto Ricans in the United States and 2 million in 1980. Most Puerto Ricans live in New York and New Jersey, with smaller but increasing numbers in Connecticut, Massachusetts, California, Illinois, Pennsylvania, and Ohio.

Puerto Ricans have been doubly discriminated against. Unlike rural black migrants from the South, they do not speak English, and unlike European immigrants, they are seen as nonwhite. Generally, they have encountered all the prejudice, discrimination, and economic exploitation that have been the fate of all immigrants and minorities. The slums where Puerto Ricans live resemble those of the Irish, Italian, black, and other immigrants before them. Puerto Ricans work in low-paying unskilled or semi-skilled occupations, such as waiters and waitresses, workers in the garment industry, domestics, and other service jobs. In New York City, 50 to 60 percent are in manufacturing and processing industries and 30 percent in service occupations (Vander Zanden, 1983).

Chicanos (Mexican Americans)

The United States has a long history of exploitation and discrimination of Chicanos. One early chapter was the Mexican-American War in 1846. This war was opposed by some Americans then just as the Vietnam War was opposed in our day. Americans, however, won this war and annexed Mexican land.

From the beginning, Chicanos have been discriminated against in jobs, housing, voting, education, civil rights, organizations, and social activities. Their best lands have been taken away, and they have been forced to take low-paying jobs, first in agriculture and later in urban areas. In the nineteeth century, Chicanos were the Negroes of the Southwest. Although legally free, their lives were no better than those of the slaves in the South. Historically, they have been poorer than the poorest Mississippi blacks. Prejudice against them has been pervasive. Jacobs and Landau (1971) say that Chicanos have been portrayed as "treacherous, childlike, primitive, lazy, and irresponsible." (Vol. 1, p. 239)

In California in the nineteenth century, beatings and lynchings of Chicanos were frequent. Even though outright physical and social persecution has abated in the twentieth century, economic discrimination and exploitation continues. Jacobs and Landau point out that when corporate farming came to the Southwest early in this century, white tenant farmers were replaced by Chicano workers who provided very cheap labor. The Great Depression in the 1930s saw the deportation of hundreds of thousands of Mexican nationals but also of many Chicanos (American citizens). In this racist climate, Mexican-Americans were not treated as United States citizens.

Today, the Chicanos are this country's second largest minority, with 8.7 million people in 1980. Over three-quarters live in urban areas and about 45 percent live in central cities, the poorest areas in the United States. Most Chicanos live in Arizona, California, Colorado, New Mexico, and Texas.

Many still are farmworkers. Their battle to unionize themselves, which began in the 1960s and continues into the 1980s, has been long, bitter, and violent. Some people lost their lives during strikes. The unions have made modest gains in wage increases. Most Chicanos, however, now live and work in cities. Generally, they hold the lowest-paying jobs. Family income data reveal their economic condition. In 1985, Spanish origin families had a median family income of $19,027, 65 percent of white income (*Statistical Abstract,* 1987:436).

Tables 11.2, 11.3, and 11.4 provide more data on income and earnings of Hispanics (Puerto Ricans, Chicanos, Cubans, and others from Latin American countries).

Illegal Aliens

Illegal aliens are a very large but a somewhat invisible minority in the United States. They come from many places, mostly Mexico and other Latin American countries, to escape terrible poverty, war, and political persecution. Some are caught and expelled (over a million in 1985), most manage to escape detection (*Statistical Abstract,* 1987:164). No one knows how many are in the United States now. They do the menial jobs (farm work, cleaning, some factory work, restaurant work) that most Americans will not do at the prevailing low wages.

In 1987, a new immigration law went into effect. Following years of debate on the number, significance, and effects of illegal aliens on the economy, the law was passed in late 1986. It seeks to control and regulate the number of illegal aliens in the United States. Anyone who entered the United States in 1981 or before is allowed to stay here if they can prove to the Immigration and Naturalization Service (INS) that they have lived here continuously since 1981. Rent receipts, statements from employers, or some other document is necessary. But since they *were* illegal, many people purposely avoided records of any kind, making documentation very difficult. The law also allows new immigrant workers into the country (mostly from Mexico) if employers prove they cannot find American workers. Employers who hire workers without proper documentation of their U.S. citizenship are liable to penalities of up to $10,000.

No one can foretell if the law will stop the flow of illegal aliens looking for work in the United States, or escaping political persecution. Poor Mexicans who need work desperately will probably continue to cross the border. Some employers will probably risk fines to employ very cheap workers. Illegal aliens have been necessary to the economy in some U.S. regions; they will probably continue to be so. In addition, the law cannot be enforced. Unless millions of soldiers patrol the United States-Mexico border, people will continue to cross it, and they will continue to find work. According to the *Boston Globe* (August 22, 1988:1), preliminary investigations show that illegal aliens continued to enter after the law went into effect, and U.S. employers found ways to skirt the law and hire them. (See *Guardian,* February 4, 1987:6; May 13, 1987:5. Also see Cockroft's *Outlaws in the Promised Land* for an excellent history of Mexican immigrant workers in the United States.)

Somewhat related to the Puerto Rican, Chicano, and illegal alien minorities is their use of Spanish. There has been a movement seeking to make English the official language, forbid bilingual education, and forbid signs and directions in any language but English. California voters passed a referendum in 1986 making English the official language of the state. Twelve other states had joined California by 1987.

Proponents of U.S. English seek to make English the only official language of the United States. They seem to fear that we will become a divided society unless we speak one language. They ignore two historical facts. One, people in the United States have spoken many languages for centuries. We have been a multilingual society. Two, Puerto Rico and the Southwest became a part of the United States through colonial conquest (taken from Spain and Mexico). Many Spanish speaking people did not choose to enter the United States. Spanish is part of their heritage and culture. Taking Spanish away from them would be cultural genocide, reminiscent of the English forbidding the Irish to speak Gaelic and the slaveowners forbidding slaves from using their African languages. It is racist discrimination.

The Elderly

It has become obvious to many that old people have been a minority for a long time. At least in modern industrial societies they are relatively powerless, discriminated against and stereotyped, and sometimes exploited. Over the last two decades, moreover, they are becoming more and more conscious of their minority status and are working to overcome it (Levin & Levin, 1980).

It is more accurate to use the pronoun *we* instead of *they* since we do not age suddenly but go through an aging process that begins long before the age of sixty-five. Indeed, we reach our peak physical condition in our early twenties. From then on, aging begins, but at very different rates, depending on how we eat, work, and play. There is a general biological process of aging, but social conditions and life experiences also affect how we age. Aging is both a biological and social process. The aged as a separate social category is a new phenomenon (Crandall, 1980).

Today we live longer than people did in the past. In 1900, people over sixty-five were 4.1 percent of the population. They were 9.2 percent in 1960, 9.8 percent in 1970, 11.3 in 1980, and 11.9 in 1985. It is projected that in the year 2025 people over sixty-five will be about 19.5 percent of the projected three-hundred million Americans. Life expectancy has increased making older people a greater proportion of the population. (See Crandall, 1980, and *Statistical Abstract*, 1982–1983:8, 27; 1987:14.)

Life expectancy, in fact, has increased dramatically. People born in 1920 can expect to live an average of 54.1 years—54.4 for white men, 55.6 for white women, 45.2 for black men, and 45.2 for black women. (These low figures are partly the result of higher infant mortality rates. In the past, once people reached adulthood, they went on to live into their sixties and some into their seventies.) In 1983, the overall figure was 74.6 years—71.7 for white men, 78.7 for white women, 65.4 for black men, and 73.6 for black women (*Statistical Abstract* 1982–1983:71; 1987:71).

Very few old people, only 4 to 5 percent, live with their grown children. About 5 to 6 percent of the people sixty-five years and older live in institutions (but 20 percent of those over eighty-five do so). The rest live alone (about 30 percent) or with a spouse. Older women, since they live longer than men, are more likely to live alone. Most men sixty-five and older (79 percent) are married, but only 39 percent of women are. Widowed women thus live alone for many years. (See Crandall, 1980, and Curtin, 1972.)

Upon retirement, most people experience a decline in income. Some never had much income, and many have been homeless and poor for years. "Bag ladies" living in run-down hotels or on the streets, carrying all their possessions with them, are a common sight in most American cities.

The more affluent ones, however, are more likely to move to retirement communities in Florida, Arizona, and other warm climates. Some researchers find these communities lifeless, devoid of children and activities, and some old people who can afford them avoid them. Most old people stay in homes or apartments they have inhabited for some years. Some, especially poor and black, are forced to move by urban renewal or condominium conversion that take their homes or apartments. (See Jacobs, 1974; Crandall, 1980; and Curtin, 1972.)

Regardless of whether an older person is homeless, in an institution, or a resident of a retirement community, he or she is a member of a minority (*Dollars and Sense,* November 1980:6–7).

People's experiences in their later years—such as where they live, how well, alone or with people—are affected by their sex, class, and race, as we will see below.

Employment and Income

It is only recently that a specific age has signaled retirement. Throughout most of history, people have worked as long and as hard as their physical and mental powers allowed them. For example, in 1870, only 25 percent of the people who were sixty-five and older were retired; 40 percent were in 1950, and most are today, as Table 11.5 shows. Not only are fewer men over sixty-five working, but even men fifty-five to sixty-four years old are less likely to be working. People, especially men, retire earlier than in previous years.

For most older people, lower income accompanies retirement. Median monetary income of households for householders forty-five to fifty-four years old was $33,200 in 1985; for those fifty-five to sixty-four years old, $25,500; and for those sixty-five years old and older, $13,200 (*Statistical Abstract,* 1987:432).

TABLE 11.5
Civilian Labor Force Participation Rates by Sex and Age, 1960, 1975, 1985

	1960	1975	1985
Male			
20–24	88.1	84.5	87.3
25–34	97.5	95.2	93.7
35–44	97.7	95.6	94.3
45–54	95.7	92.1	90.4
55–64	86.8	75.6	62.6
65 and over	33.1	21.6	11.0
Female			
20–24	46.1	64.1	76.3
25–34	36.0	54.9	81.1
35–44	43.4	55.8	80.5
45–54	49.8	54.6	71.3
55–64	37.2	40.9	42.7
65 and over	10.8	8.2	5.5

Statistical Abstract, 1987:376

According to Crandall (1980), 58 percent of old people rely on social security for the largest part of their income. About 90 percent collect it, and about 25 percent supplement it with other pensions. In 1985, 26 million retired workers received an average monthly payment of $479—under $6,000 for the year (*Statistical Abstract,* 1987:350). Savings, current jobs, and rents are other sources of income. Most people manage with some difficulty. Many are in or very close to poverty, 42 percent according to Horn (1988). A few are well off.

Corporations and the government exploit old people. Most companies have no pension plans for their workers. Even those that do have them do not pay workers who leave the company before retirement age. The meager social security funds are paid for by workers—our contributions today support older retired workers. The government and corporations take no responsibility. The government created the so-called social security crisis of the early 1980s. Surely, if there is enough money for a destructive military weapons system, there can be enough money to support our parents and grandparents whose labors created the wealth of the country (and the wealth of the ruling class). (See all of *Dollars and Sense,* January/February 1988, for discussions of the economic and health conditions and problems of older Americans.)

Stereotypes and Discrimination

Everyday conversations and observations, television commercials, and other sources make it abundantly obvious that we fear getting old, and we fear old people. Women over thirty are urged to use lotions to hide the aging process, to have younger hands. This fear of aging especially oppresses women, but men too are not free of it. The old are to be avoided for they remind us of our impending fall from the grace of youth. (See Curtin, 1972, and Levin & Levin, 1980.)

Older people are largely absent from television. Various studies have shown that only about 2 percent of people in TV commercials, and also only 2 percent of drama characters on network television, are people sixty-five and older. Most commercials glorify youth and deny aging either by the absence of older people (ads for shaving creams always feature younger men) or by selling products that hide signs of aging. (See Levin & Levin, 1980, and Powell & Williamson, 1985.)

Other media also stereotype old people. Arnold (1986) did a content analysis of sixty-five children's books published from 1946 to 1985. Fifty of them (77 percent) contained one or more negative portrayals of the physical appearance of older people. In addition, the majority of elderly characters showed "anger, sadness, helplessness, worry, quarrelsomeness, and eccentricity in their behaviors." Such portrayals lessened only slightly over time (from 1946 to 1985).

The Gray Panthers of Greater Boston (1987) carried out a careful study of many media and concluded that they stereotype older people as frail, indecisive, and out-of-date. In addition, "Elders are rarely shown in the media working at jobs, teaching others their skills, having responsibility or making decisions in the workplace. . . . Children's books, nursery rhymes, cartoons and stories are filled with witches and demonic characters who are old and frightening. . . . Greeting cards are especially offensive. . . . Many of these cards insult, rather than celebrate, growing older."

Blomberg (1981), a twenty-two-year-old woman, visited various settings with a seventy-four-year-old woman friend. In all of them her friend's adulthood and responsibility were denied and insulted by people. When they stood together in front of a bank teller, her friend handed over a check to be cashed. The teller, however, ignored the old woman and turned to her young companion and asked, "Does she just want this check cashed?" A seventy-four-year-old person was deemed incapable of expressing her own wants. The old woman was treated similarly, as a helpless child, at a doctor's office, a post office, and a restaurant. None of these people meant to be insulting and denigrating; they were expressing cultural perceptions of old people.

Perceptions of old people's sex life deny their interest in and existence of sexual activity. Yet much research has shown that although people may not have sex as often after their fifties, the desire for and expression of sexuality continue. Some people, especially many older women, have no available partners, but many others continue to enjoy sex. Indeed, it is the widely held perception that older people do not (should not?) want or need sex that discourages many of them from expressing their interest and engaging in it. Physically and emotionally most older people are able to enjoy sex, but we discourage them. For example, most nursing homes socially and physically ban sexual activity among their men and women residents. (See Levin & Levin, 1980, and Crandall, 1980.)

Much senility is caused by biological aging, but researchers are finding that many old people suffer only from socially induced senility. They are ignored, paid little attention, and treated as if they have lost their capacity and ability for all activity and social interaction. In this way, the prophecy is fulfilled. We justify ignoring old people because they are senile, but the senility comes about because we ignore them and treat them as helpless children. (See Crandall, 1980, and *Boston Globe,* July 16, 1982:7.)

It is no wonder, then, that we tend to think workers in their fifties and sixties perform poorly, slowly, and unproductively. But studies of actual job performance by older workers clearly show that most workers over sixty-five years old perform competently and favorably compared to younger workers. They are more steady and conscientious than younger workers, and their knowledge, accuracy, and performance are as good as those of younger workers (Levin & Levin, 1980).

Yet older workers stay unemployed for longer periods than younger ones. Employers are hesitant to hire them. Television newscasters and weather forecasters (especially women) have been demoted or fired when they have shown signs of aging—in their forties. Most employers discriminate not only against people in their sixties but also against those in their fifties and even forties (Crandall, 1980).

The Social Creation of Old Age

There is a physical reality to aging. In every society people do change biologically, and some of their capacities do lessen. But this biological reality does not dictate that we must define people as inept, force them to retire, and treat them differently. Industrial societies have gradually created this new social category by the legal and actual treatment of older people as inherently different.

In all previous societies people did not retire at a given age. Individuals worked fewer hours and less strenuously as their own individual capacities changed. Some worked longer than others. Demos (1970) notes that the colonists at Plymouth Plantation in the seventeenth century did not retire. They worked until they died or until their strength waned. The Abkhasians today do not retire (Benet, 1974). People work into their seventies, eighties, and nineties—fewer hours, to be sure, but they work. Indeed, the Abkhasians do not fear old age primarily because they are given respect as old people, and they live secure lives in close families.

Industrialism has forced people to retire and become useless at specified ages. Our culture has developed fears and stereotypes of older people. These practices are not inherent to human societies. Although there is a certain sadness in waning strength and approaching death, societies vary widely in their responses to these existential realities. In fear, some isolate their members who are old and dying; others respect them, recognize their usefulness, and ease the pains of aging. It may be that earlier societies found the knowledge, experience, and wisdom of their older members necessary and useful for survival, and that today our "fast-changing" society makes their knowledge and skills obsolete. I doubt, however, that this is the main reason for our prejudice against and stereotypes of old people. At least as significant are our culture's and economy's materialistic values, profit seeking, and corporate domination. When profits are the sole motives of an economy, old people become obsolete. The obsolescence and fear then spread to the rest of the society. (See Minkler, 1987.)

Gays and Lesbians

Gay men and lesbians have existed in most, if not all, societies. In many of them, especially pre-industrial societies outside the West, they have been either tolerated or accepted fully. But in the West, they have been persecuted for centuries. The following passage from Balkan, Berger, and Schmidt (1980) gives us a glimpse into the history of this minority group.

> *In Old Testament ideology, homosexuality was considered the most sinful and pernicious form of criminal activity; as early as the sixteenth century, the*

death penalty was prescribed for people thought to be engaged in homosexual activities. Over the course of American history, lesbians and gay men have been, as Katz observes,

> *condemned to death by choking, burning, and drowning; they were executed, jailed, pilloried, fined, court-martialed, prostituted, fired, framed, blackmailed, disinherited, declared insane, driven to insanity, to suicide, murder, and self-hate, witch-hunted, entrapped, stereotyped, mocked, insulted, isolated, pitied, castigated, and despised . . . they have been castrated, lobotomized, shock-treated and psychoanalyzed.*

An early form of punishment for homosexuality involved burning at the stake, where gays were tied to the feet of alleged witches and burned, with faggots (wood) for kindling; hence, the label faggot. Death was the primary punishment for sodomy until the reform movement in 1776, led by Thomas Jefferson and other liberals, changed the laws. According to the new law, a man guilty of rape, sodomy, bestiality, or polygamy was castrated; a woman was punished by having a hole at least one-half inch in diameter cut through the cartilage of her nose. (p. 262)

When I arrived in the United States in 1955, and for the next ten to fifteen years, gay people were feared, condemned, and rejected. Millions of people kept their sexuality secret, in various degrees of fear, shame, guilt, anger, and confusion. But the climate of social change created during the 1960s by the civil rights, anti-war, and women's movements led to a movement for gay liberation also. Gradually, lesbians and gay men have become more open about their sexuality. There is more acceptance of them and some laws have changed. At least some politicians have discussed their gayness publicly, among them two U.S. Representatives from Massachusetts and a Boston City Councillor. Some people in entertainment and professional sports make no secret of their sexual orientation. As of 1986, twenty-six out of fifty states had legalized homosexuality. Finally, some cities and states have passed ordinances and laws prohibiting discrimination in employment, housing, and so on. But in some other places, notably Florida in 1977, such proposed laws were voted down by the voters or by legislatures.

Some researchers have estimated about 10 percent of the people in the United States are gay. In many cities, there are newspapers, clubs, advocacy groups, and other institutions for gay people. Although conditions have improved vastly since the 1950s, stereotypes, myths, homophobia (fear of homosexuals), harassment, and violence still haunt the lives of gay people. Many still hide their sexuality from friends, co-workers, and relatives. At the same time, many groups are working to change public ignorance and fears, and to stop discrimination.

There are many myths and stereotypes about gay people. I will discuss briefly three that are especially harmful. Many people fear that gay people seduce or molest children. All evidence from many studies shows this is untrue. (See Hammersmith, 1985, for a summary of these studies.) In fact, most child molesters are heterosexual men. Others believe that gay people are mentally ill. This belief is also wrong. All evidence shows that heterosexual and homosexual people are equally likely to be healthy or ill. Persecution and discrimination may cause some anxiety in gay people, but that is no symptom of illness; it is a condition imposed on them. Finally, people who have no gay friends assume that gay men act effeminately and lesbians act like men. With very few exceptions, it's a great misconception. It is impossible to tell people's sexuality by their dress or behavior. Many heterosexuals know gay people without ever suspecting their homosexuality.

According to Hammersmith (1985), *homophobia* is "both a negative attitude towards homosexuality and an element of fear of gay people, even fear of the very *discussion* of homosexuality." (p. 26) It stems from ignorance, stereotypes, a fear of change and differences, and our upbringing. Some statements by the Pope, the Moral Majority's pronouncements, the actions of many politicians, and the 1986 Supreme Court decision that allows states to keep sodomy illegal, have all contributed to the persistence of homophobia.

Homophobia is so strong in some people that they harass and attack gay people. A survey conducted by the National Gay and Lesbian Task Force in 1984 "found that 93 percent of the gay people in the sample reported either harassment, threats, assaults, arson or property vandalism because of their sexual orientation." A congressional committee held hearings on violence against gay people following many reports of attacks. In Boston and other cities in the late 1980s, there were many reported violent attacks. Some feel that the number of attacks may be even greater but that victims are hesitant to report them because they fear that it will stimulate more publicity and thus more harassment. (See *Boston Globe,* January 30, 1987:1, and *Guardian,* February 25,1987.)

Compared to in the past, gay people are now generally more open with others about their gayness. In some workplaces they need not be secretive. But many or most still do not reveal their sexual identity. According to the *Boston Globe* (May 6, 1986:43, 50), they "fear ridicule, contempt and even loss of their jobs if their sexual preference were revealed. . . . Most speak of the loneliness, anger and paranoia that are part of living a double life, the pain and pride they feel in being 'different'. . . . A closeted lesbian says the hardest thing is 'listening to people's craziness, the terrible things people say assuming no gay people are present.' " Even those who are openly gay find it difficult. Said one man: "Every time I tell someone I'm gay, my stomach goes kaboom, my heart starts pounding. It's always hard."

The AIDS epidemic of the 1980s may have worsened public attitudes about gay people. The initial association of AIDS only with homosexuality is gradually changing, but it has probably caused hostility against gay people. In time, as misconceptions disappear and we deal with AIDS rationally, that hostility should disappear. The claim that AIDS set back gay liberation may be a wish of the Moral Majority and others. Polls taken in 1985 and 1986 showed that most people have generally correct information about the spread of AIDS, and they do not wish to condemn and isolate people who have it. In a Harris (1987) poll, 80 percent of those interviewed "firmly said that AIDS victims should *not* be treated as lepers." (p. 168)

Like all minority groups, gay people can only overcome discrimination and prejudice by uniting to fight for changes. It is necessary to expose and attack myths and to demonstrate against politicians and others who discriminate against gay people. One such event took place on October 11, 1987, when five-hundred-thousand people went to a march in Washington that called for an end to legal and social discrimination against gay people and more money for research for treatment and a cure of AIDS. (See *Guardian,* February 25, 1987:7, and October 21, 1987:1.)

The Disabled

Ramps to buildings, handicapped parking spots, sidewalk ramps, and braille signs in elevators have made us somewhat aware that disabled people exist. But despite the prejudice and discrimination they encounter daily, we have not understood that the disabled are a minority. Even sociologists seem to ignore them. In the first edition of this text, I wrote only half a sentence about them. Ten introductory sociology texts published in 1985, 1986, and 1987 ignore the disabled. There is not a single entry for "disabled" or "handicapped" in the index of any of them. A quick scanning of the chapters on minorities reveals a similar silence on the handicapped.

My own consciousness of the disabled has grown slowly. It became even sharper when two students in wheelchairs were admitted to Regis College. They could not use the elevator in the main classroom building because the doors do not open wide enough. The electronic doors in the library usually did not work, and other doors could not be opened electronically. The two students were forced to depend on friends to accompany them and open the doors. The list of inconveniences and indignities was long. It was only when a group of faculty, the two students, and their mothers met and collected all the information of daily indignities they suffered that I became fully conscious of the disabled as a minority. I was dumbfounded and shocked when I heard that the electronic doors for the library had not worked for months and had not been fixed. Would any of us endure such inconvenience? Could we not see how outrageous this neglect was?

The limited awareness we do have was forced on us by the handicapped. They demonstrated, lobbied, and demanded public access. Ramps, handicapped parking, elevator buttons reachable by people in wheelchairs, and other changes came about only after the handicapped organized and demanded access and visibility. Until they protested, the rest of us were not upset that people in wheelchairs rarely went outside. We had not given these people a thought.

The handicapped have become conscious that they are a minority. In a Harris (1987) survey, 45 percent saw themselves as "a cohesive and disadvantaged minority much like blacks and Hispanics" (42 percent did not). (p.

199) The young did even more so. Seventy-four percent saw a "common identity" with other disabled people.

Disabled people face daily reminders of their condition. Zehring (1973) talks about her relationship with Bernard, a man who was on crutches because of cerebral palsy. He had had a "lifetime experience of prejudice, pain and abuse and endured a holocaust of rejections by doctors, therapists, psychiatrists, faith healers, relatives, strangers and the public at large." (p. 396) The disabled are ignored, stared at, pitied, considered unemployable, and discriminated in other ways. They also often go without affection. Bernard, like most handicapped people, lived a life without much physical touching. One day he asked an expecting female friend: "Listen. Most people don't let me near their kids, afraid I might rub off on them or something. Do you think maybe I could hold yours once in a while?" Zehring replied that she and the baby "would be delighted." (p. 397)

Bernard, despite his college education and other skills, often was unemployed. Employers repeatedly refused him jobs. Most disabled people who can and want to work experience similar discrimination. According to a Harris survey (1987), 78 percent of the disabled want to work, but 66 percent who are of working age have no jobs. Without an education and without a job most of the disabled live close to poverty, and it is very difficult for them to become independent. Equality is difficult to achieve.

Despite the increased mobility and accessibility of the disabled, they are a long way from full access to all public facilities. Their lives are still limited. In his survey, Harris (1987) found that "56% of all the disabled people report having real difficulty in getting around and attending cultural and sporting events. . . . While 78% of all adults went to a movie last year, only 36% of the disabled got out to see one. While 60% of all adults see live theater or a musical performance, no more than 23% of the disabled get to do it." (p. 195) It is not their physical conditions that limit the disabled, however. It is the *social* conditions that discriminate against them.

The media also ignore or stereotype disabled people. Until recently, no commercials included disabled persons. A few now do show them. Some television and movie stories are about disabled people, but their message is ambiguous. For example, some stories portray handicapped people whose determination and courage enable them to conquer their condition and lead a full life. But as Longmore (1985) states, the implied message is that the "disability is primarily a problem of emotional coping, of personal acceptance. It is not a problem of social stigma and discrimination." (pp. 35–36) The primary problem the disabled face is not their individual emotional adjustment; it is the discrimination and neglect from people and institutions around them. These stories ignore the social conditions of disability (Longmore, 1985:35–36).

The discrimination and bias against the disabled is very deeply ingrained in our minds. Even people who staunchly support the rights of black people, women, and other minorities do not realize they do or say things that oppress disabled people.

Among other demands, the disabled want full access to buses, trains, subways, and airplanes. A usual response is that wheelchair lifts for buses and other mechanisms that would lead to full access are too costly. But would the cost argument ever be made to deny civil rights to any other group? Can we imagine ever saying it would cost too much to provide black students with an education equal to white students, or girls to boys? Of course girls and blacks are often given inferior educations, but no one who believes in equality would ever justify that condition. How then can we make the cost argument to deny full public access to the disabled? (See Asch & Fine, 1984; Ervin, 1984; and O'Neill, 1984.)

Disabled people do suffer from physical conditions. But they suffer more from *social* conditions. O'Neill (1984) argues that "it is not the existence of disabilities but the way disabilities are viewed that prevents disabled persons from living full and independent lives. Government policies and public sentiments relegate the disabled to neglect, dependency, and marginality." (p. 22) Meaningful lives are possible for the disabled. Asch and Fine (1984) note that "in Sweden, national health care and a full range of social services enable parents of disabled children to easily partake in infant stimulation programs, integrated day care and schools, respite care, and a host of other services that contribute to their lives and their children's lives." (p. 54)

Since 1972, there has been a movement to set up Centers for Independent Living. There are 170 centers in the United States, England, Sweden, Germany, Japan, and Australia. They teach people to live independently and work for their rights. They teach daily skills, such as shopping, have seminars on sexuality and self-defense, and so on.

Disability is a social creation. In a society that did not fear, neglect, and discriminate against them, people would not be disabled. They would be people who are *different* and can lead meaningful lives. We could never argue that we cannot afford services needed for full access and mobility. We need to re-orient the use of our resources. Shall we spend them on the military and for the wealth of a few people or to meet all of our needs?

Recent Immigrants, Ethnic Groups, and Others

The social dislocations that followed the Vietnam war and its ending have created new immigrants. Since 1975, Vietnamese, Cambodians, and others have come to the United States. Many American cities have large concentrations of people from Southeast Asia. Because they are so recent, there are few population figures or studies on them. They are the latest of many groups to arrive here. In time we will know whether and how they will follow the historical experiences of Irish, black, Italian, Chinese, Japanese, and all the others.

Ethnic groups that were minorities once have overcome their minority conditions, but they still face some problems. Stereotypes of and prejudice against Jewish people persist. Italians are plagued by the Mafia and other stereotypes. Irish, Polish, and other groups suffer various indignities. Japanese, Chinese, Koreans, and other people from Asia also face some discrimination and stereotypes. These and other groups are discussed in most texts on ethnic and racial minorities.

Other groups can be considered minorities. The mentally ill are stereotyped, often powerless, and very much discriminated against. Children too are powerless and controlled, but they outgrow their condition. People with various physical conditions (short, fat, ugly, and others) also face some discrimination, ridicule, and ostracism.

Minorities in Other Societies

Racial, ethnic, and other minorities exist in most societies. Some are native to these societies, some are immigrants. Their minority status results partly from cultural conflicts, from ethnic, religious, and other differences. In most cases, however, the root of their oppression is economic exploitation by other groups. One of the most blatant cases of minority exploitation is in South Africa. Blacks in this country are the largest minority in the world. We will use the situation in South Africa as an example of minority repression in another society and then mention briefly some other groups in other countries.

Apartheid: Oppression in South Africa

Dutch settlers arrived in South Africa in 1652, and the British came in the late 1700s. They soon began to steal the land from native black peoples and in time enslaved many of them. Eventually slavery was abolished, but *apartheid,* the government's official policy of racial segregation, kept native people virtually enslaved. They were segregated, their movements were controlled and limited, they could not vote, and they were forced to work at very low wages.

After the Boer War between the Dutch and the English settlers between 1899 and 1902, South Africa became part of the British Empire. In 1961, in order to perpetuate apartheid, the white South African government left the British Commonwealth and South Africa became a republic. Under white rule, the best land is still owned by whites; blacks cannot vote or pass laws, and they are paid poverty wages (Mermelstein, 1987).

Social and Economic Conditions

Blacks in South Africa are a *numerical majority*. Of the thirty-three million people living in South Africa in 1986, twenty-four million (72 percent) were African (black); five million (16 percent) were white; 9 percent coloured; and 3 percent Asian, mostly from India. (See *Statistical Abstract,* 1987:817; Donaher, 1984, and Mermelstein, 1987. The numbers for blacks and white vary by 1 to 2 percent, depending on the year and source of information.)

Most black people in South Africa live in segregated townships outside cities. The rest live in ten so-called homelands, where more blacks continue to be forced to live. Homelands are fictitious nations recognized by no country except South Africa. The government forced blacks to move there. These lands are barren; little or nothing can grow on them. About 87 percent of the farmable land in South Africa is owned by whites.

There are few jobs in the homelands. Therefore, people must get work permits and find jobs in mines, factories, and other places outside their home-lands, often very far away. But the workers, mostly men, are not allowed to bring their families with them. Most visit home three to four times a year. The rest are gradually separated from their families.

The effect is devastating. Wives and husbands rarely see each other; children and fathers become strangers. The following is from an article in the *Boston Globe* (December 25, 1986:8) and graphically describes the kind of lives these people lead.

> *By bus, by train, sometimes even by foot, they stream back at Christmas to the rural enclaves where their wives and children are held hostage by a web of racial laws and social circumstances . . . In 30 years of marriage, Magalo reckons, he has spent a total of about 40 months at home rarely sharing more than a week at a stretch with Lucy and their four children.*
>
> *"Chistmas time, Easter time, a few weekends here and there—these are the days I am a husband and father," he said, adding, "My children, they seem as strangers to me."*
>
> *"Only at holidays do we become a whole family again," she said. "Only at holidays do our children ever see their father."*

Even more devastating is the poverty that plagues people in the home-lands. The men who work off the homelands get paid very little; what they manage to send home usually cannot support their families. In 1987, relief groups estimated that almost 3 million children were malnourished. Half a million were at "extreme" risk of starvation. About fifty thousand a year die from starvation or diseases related to starvation (*Boston Globe*, February 10, 1987:6).

Steiff (1985) says that blacks who live in townships (black communities outside but next to white cities) also endure extreme poverty. Neighborhoods are crowded. Houses are small, often shacks. Unemployment is high. Those who work make low wages, usually a quarter or less of what white workers are paid. Many receive the minimum of $40 a month, some even less.

Working conditions are abominable. For example, a U.S. business executive complained of the high cost ($100,000) of installing sprinklers in U.S. factories, and said, "Do you know what kind of fire protection system is required in South Africa? A bucket of sand" (*Labor Notes,* June 1987:4).

In August 1987, three hundred thousand black miners went on strike over wages and working conditions. They were paid only one-fifth (20 percent) of what white workers made (*Boston Globe*, August 11, 1987:8).

Medical care and health are very poor. There is one doctor for every three hundred thirty whites but one for every twelve thousand blacks. Life expectancy is 72.3 years for whites, 58.9 for blacks. (See *Guardian* supplement to March 19, 1986.)

The angry protests that began in 1984 have led to some cosmetic changes. But black and white people continue to live in two separate and unequal worlds. Intermarriage, illegal until 1985, is now allowed. The change is meaningless, however, since laws still forbid black and white people from living in the same areas. Schools are segregated. Those for black students receive much less money and fewer resources than do schools for whites. Black people still cannot vote. Black workers are exploited, receiving about one-fourth of what whites get paid.

A rigid pass system had existed until 1985. It required all blacks to carry an identity card that stated where they could and could not go. It was supposedly abolished in 1985 and replaced with a system that requires blacks, whites, coloureds, and others to carry the same ID. But the administration of the new pass law still discriminated against blacks since a different set of numbers is used for blacks than is used for whites. The system is computerized so that a person's place of work and home can be quickly located. Also, blacks are asked to show their IDs regularly and often, whites are not. It is an updated, sophisticated, and effective system. It controls black people as much as the old system did but seems fair on the surface.

The Struggle for Freedom

Black people have been protesting against these conditions. The African National Congress (ANC), the main organization fighting for black liberation, started in 1912. For years it employed legal and peaceful means, but there was no change in the apartheid system. Since the early 1960s, the ANC and other groups have become more militant in their tactics.

The struggle for freedom has intensified since the early 1980s. The ANC is banned from South Africa, but with the help from neighboring countries, the organization is organizing and training people for the revolution that seems inevitable. It is also campaigning in the United Nations and elsewhere to convince governments to criticize, isolate, and boycott the white South African government. Some of its leaders, Nelson Mandela being the most prominent, have been in South African prisons for years.

Millions of people are involved in the resistance spread throughout South Africa. Children boycott schools and demonstrate against inferior education and discrimination. Despite a strict law that regulates unions, black workers have formed and joined unions and often strike or demonstrate to protest low wages, working conditions, and apartheid in general. Whole towns organize boycotts of white businesses. The United Democratic Front (UDF) is a national coalition of many organizations working for change through boycotts, demonstrations, strikes, and other means. In every township there are local organizations, by block and by district, leading a constant attack on apartheid. Resistance is everywhere. (See Adams, 1980; Saul & Gelb, 1981; the entire issue of *Monthly Review,* April 1986; *Guardian,* January 21, 1987: 10–11; and Mermelstein, 1987.)

Government Oppression

The white government has reacted to the black resistance with extreme violence and oppression. It has imprisoned thousands of people, including thousands of children demonstrating for better education. Most have been tortured and some have died. The police and the army regularly shoot at, wound, and kill demonstrators and protesters. In 1960, sixty-seven protesters were killed in Sharpeville. In 1976, over a few months in Soweto and other places, troops killed at least 575 demonstrating students and their supporters. Since 1984, when protests intensified, there have been frequent shootings and killings. About two thousand people were killed from 1984 to 1986. When foreign television cameras and reporters recorded and communicated the violence to the outside world, the government restricted their movement and banned them from many areas. Soon there were few pictures and little news, so the foreign media lost interest. (See *Guardian,* December 24, 1986:1, 16; and April 8, 1987:10–11.)

The white government declared a continual state of emergency during the middle and late 1980s. It wanted to end protests by controlling public behavior. "Demonstrations, unfavorable news accounts, T-shirt slogans, . . . large funeral gatherings" for people killed by the police, and much else, were banned (*Boston Globe,* August 7, 1987:12). Violent repression continues while meaningless changes are made (the new pass law, permission of intermarriage, etc.). But the poverty, exploitation, and near-slavery of the black majority continue.

British, U.S., and other corporations have invested heavily in South Africa. They are essential to the South African economy. They make great profits because they pay low wages to their black workers. U.S. corporations had invested and loaned South Africa $14 billion by the mid 1980s—20 percent of total foreign investments. Under intense pressure, some U.S. corporations withdrew their investments, and the amount may be lower now. Investments in South Africa were twice as profitable in 1985 compared to investments in most other countries.

Since the early 1980s, the anti-apartheid movement has called for a total boycott of the white South African economy. The United Nations and some countries called for an end to buying from and selling to South Africa, no new investments there, and divestment (withdrawal) of foreign investments already in that country. Many countries have honored that strategy. In the United States, the Reagan administration argued against the economic boycott and divestment. But in 1985 Congress passed a bill (over President Reagan's veto) forbidding the new U.S. investments in South Africa and calling for some other measures to pressure the South African government. On many college campuses, in states, cities, and towns, groups are calling for divestment of college, state, or municipal holdings (stocks) in companies with investments in South Africa. Many institutions and governments did divest.

The South African government has insisted that no economic sanctions would force it to end apartheid. The economy has been affected to some degree, but we cannot tell in 1988 if or when the economic boycott will end the oppression of the black majority. (For the role of U.S. corporations and the anti-apartheid movement, see Danaher, 1984; Cordes, 1985; *Monthly Review,* April 1986; Razis, 1986; and Mermelstein, 1987.)

The control and exploitation of black South Africans is the most naked example of an oppressed minority today. What is indirect and hidden elsewhere is direct, open, and brutal there. South Africa reminds us of *the economic basis of minorities,* of the untold suffering and exploitation they endure.

Minorities Everywhere

Minorities exist on all continents. In Australia, the Aborigines who have lived there for thirty thousand years are strangers in their own land since their lands were stolen from them. Whites, who arrived only three hundred years ago, control and discriminate against them.

In Europe too we find minorities. In England, there are blacks and Asians from former English colonies. Discrimination against them has increased since the 1970s, including legislation to stop the immigration of more people from the British empire (Cashmore, 1987).

Guestworkers (foreign workers) from south and southeast Europe, north Africa, and other places began to arrive in Germany, France, Switzerland, and other northern European countries in the 1950s. They were needed to do jobs local people would not do because of low pay and prestige, or because there were labor shortages. (There were fewer guestworkers in the 1980s because the European economies needed fewer of them.) They could work but not settle permanently in these countries (except for those who married citizens of the country where they worked). They were permanent aliens, permanent minorities (*Guardian,* April 16, 1986:15).

In France, people from Algeria and other former French colonies have been encouraged to come and do mostly low-prestige and dirty jobs. Many people blame them for France's economic problems. Laws discriminating against them are proposed and sometimes passed, and some people attack and occasionally kill Algerians. (See Singer, 1985, and *Guardian,* April 14, 1985: 1; August 20, 1986:14.)

In Switzerland, most guestworkers come from South Italy. They compose about 25 percent of the work force. They live in segregated housing, hold the lowest paying and least prestigious jobs, and are isolated and avoided by the Swiss.

All over Europe, ethnic minorities make long-standing claims of cultural and economic discrimination. The Basques in Spain, the Brettons in France, and the Albanians in Yugoslavia are three of many examples.

Ethnic, racial, and other minorities exist all over Asia. The untouchables in India, the lowest of five castes, are still discriminated against. They are often attacked when they seek the equality guaranteed them by the law. In Israel, the Palestinians are a minority in their own land. Discriminatory laws and the police force are used to deprive them of freedom and equality. Like other minorities, they are relegated to the worst jobs. When they protest, they are jailed and sometimes their houses are destroyed. (See Glass, 1982; *Guardian*, May 27, 1987 special issue on the Palestinians; Turki, 1972; and Lie, 1987.)

Who Benefits by the Existence of Minorities?

In 1836, Frederick Douglass (1969), who was still a slave, worked in the shipyards of Baltimore. His wages were lower than those of the white workmen. Resenting him for keeping their wages low, the whites beat Douglass brutally. Years later, in 1855, Douglass gave an analysis of the way slavery and racism are used by the ruling class to divide blacks and whites and exploit both—an analysis that has not been equalled since.

> *The slaveholders, with a craftiness peculiar to themselves, by encouraging the enmity of the poor, laboring white man against the blacks, succeed in making the said white man almost as much a slave as the black slave himself. The difference between the white slave, and the black slave, is this: the latter belongs to one slaveholder, and the former belongs to all the slaveholders, collectively. The white slave has taken from him, by indirection, what the black slave has taken from him, directly, and without ceremony. Both are plundered, and by the same plunderers. The slave is robbed, by his master, of all his earnings, above what is required for his bare physical necessities; and the white man is robbed by the slave system, of the just results of his labor, because he is flung into competition with a class of laborers who work without wages. The competition, and its injurious consequences, will, one day, array the non-slaveholding white people of the slave states, against the slave system, and make them the most effective workers against the great evil. At present, the slaveholders bind them to this competition, by keeping alive their prejudice against the slaves, as men—not against them as slaves. They appeal to their pride, often denouncing emancipation, as tending to place the white working man, on an equality with negroes, and, by this means, they succeed in drawing off the minds of the poor whites from the real fact, that, by the rich slave-master, they are already regarded as but a single remove from equality with the slave. The impression is cunningly made, that slavery is the only power that can prevent the laboring white man from falling to the level of the slave's poverty and degradation. (p. 309)*

Others have seen a similar exploitation of ethnic conflicts. In the 1880s, some Irish writers argued that immigrants and other minorities must unite along class lines. They urged the workers not to compete against each other because of their different nationalities—otherwise, they would make no progress. But cooperation was not the case then nor is it now. Ethnic and racial conflicts have been common in our history (Miller, 1972).

Capitalism continues to play race against race, nationality against nationality, class against class. A few years ago, a meatpacking plant in Denver "closed down" and laid off all its workers. The largely Mexican work force had unionized, and at the time, members were making $10 an hour. The plant soon reopened, and the management hired Vietnamese and Cambodian refugees—paying them $5.25 an hour (*Guardian*, November 25, 1981:2).

Some social scientists have shown that racism and prejudice hurt both blacks and whites. Where racism of whites against blacks is greater, white workers make less money than do white workers in areas where racism is absent or lower. Michael Reich's (Bower & Hunt, 1981) studies show

> *where racial inequality increased . . . low and middle-income whites lost from it financially, while the upper 1 percent of white incomes increased and actually exceeded the losses of the white majority. Thus, the greater the extent of unionization and the more racially integrated is the union, the higher are white earnings and the lower are profits. The lower the percentage of the work force which is unionized and the less integrated it is, the more depressed are white wages and the higher are profit margins. (p. 248)*

Where there is general integration, integration of unions, and where white and black workers cooperate instead of white workers being prejudiced and keeping blacks away, then whites make higher wages. Where there is no interracial cooperation, no integration, white workers make lower wages and corporations make higher profits. (See Greer, 1976, and Frederickson, 1982.)

Racism causes white working people to blame black people for the good jobs they do not get and for other misfortunes. But the cause is not black people, it is the capitalist society, which engenders inequality and limits opportunities. For example, if all blacks in medical schools were replaced by whites, only 7 percent of the rejected whites would get in (Dreyfuss, 1978).

A final insight from Frederick Douglass (1969): not only are blacks and most whites hurt by racism, but "slavery is a greater evil to the master than to the slave." (p. 105) Douglass shows how slaveowner after slaveowner became cruel, suspicious, and unfeeling. They treated slaves in ways that were unnatural. To perpetuate slavery, they had to suppress much of their own humanity. When Douglass moved to Baltimore, his mistress there was kind and generous to him. But Douglass shows how, under the imperatives of slavery, she soon began to distance herself (she stopped teaching him how to read and write) and, although not brutal to him, no longer considered him as an equal human.

Slavery has ended. But racism today is no less harmful to us than slavery was. Not only economically, but in our daily relations with each other, in allowing racism to separate us and assure our common exploitation under capitalism, we all suffer. A few individual white workers may benefit in the short run by being given a job or a promotion over black workers, but the vast majority of white people do not benefit. Douglass hoped that someday blacks and whites would see their common interests and humanity; we progressed little toward that goal.

Singing the Spirit Home: Liberation and Justice

"Sing the spirit home" is a song composed and sung by Eric Bogle, an Australian folksinger. It tells the story of a black freedom fighter who was hung in a South African prison. Bogle pays homage to the courage, suffering, death, and resistance of the African people.

It is based on a true story told to Bogle by an eyewitness. A young black man, arrested and imprisoned for fighting apartheid, was taken from his cell before dawn and was being led to the gallows. He sobbed and screamed and weakened; "his legs would not support him so from the cell they dragged him." But he was not alone "in his final desperate hour" because "from the darkness of that prison came the sound of his brothers singing. . . . From the cells behind the shadows he heard the voices echo, as in love and pride and sorrow they sang his spirit home. 'Courage brother, /you do not walk alone;/we shall walk with you,/and sing your spirit home.' " His comrades' voices and song gave him strength and he walked to the gallows. He died with dignity. His death was not in vain; it was part of a long struggle for freedom and justice.

There is sadness, suffering, and tragedy here, but also courage, dignity, and hope. Both suffering and hope touch the lives of oppressed people. It is with a message of hope that I want to end this chapter.

People everywhere struggle for liberation. Sometimes, after there is no hope of change through peaceful means, people resort to revolution. During the 1970s, for example, black people in Zimbabwe fought a long war and finally overthrew the white government that had oppressed them for centuries.

There have been other individual and collective actions by minorities to defy their oppressors. Frederick Douglass (1969) was forbidden to educate himself. His mistress did begin to teach him reading and writing until she was reminded that it was dangerous to educate slaves. He persisted despite this. Secretly, he taught himself and other slaves. Education liberated his spirit and convinced him to resist slavery with all his power. After the overseer consistently beat him for six months, Douglass resolved to resist. One day he physically prevented the overseer from flogging him, over a three hour period, and thereafter he was never flogged again.

There are many instances where minorities have trained and armed themselves for protection from racist violence. The United League of Mississippi formed a secret armed police force that successfully drove a band of

KKK members out of black neighborhoods when they threatened violence. The KKK fled when they saw the armed black men (Marx, 1980).

There are many examples of successful struggles for freedom and justice. Erlich (1987) tells of poor Chicano women who led a strike for eighteen months, won, and protected their union and their jobs. Bond (1987) reported on other people who organized to boycott banks that did not give mortgages to poor and black people, and they changed the bank's practices. Finally, during the civil rights movement of the 1950s and 1960s women and men, young and old, blacks and many whites, waged years of struggle against segregation and discrimination. Much work remains to be done before blacks and other minorities can achieve equality and justice, but the civil rights movement erased much discrimination and showed us the way to freedom. It preceded and helped bring about the anti-war movement of the 1960s and later years, the women's liberation movement, and movements for equality by old people, gays and lesbians, the handicapped, and others.

Conclusion

This chapter has examined how the capitalist economic system created minorities. Their lands and labor have been used to enrich a few people in the majority.

Minorities arose and have persisted because of economic conditions. But once they arise, theories about their inferiority, which lead to prejudice and discrimination, appear and help perpetuate minorities. The children of the majority are socialized to fear, distrust, avoid, and discriminate against the minorities and their cultures. U.S. historians have focused on prejudice and the resulting theories of inferiority and on cultural differences as the causes of minority conditions. But they have paid little attention to the economic conditions that gave rise to minorities. Most historical accounts do not relate slavery and other minority conditions to capitalist economics. If we recognized this as the first and foremost reason for the existence of minorities, we would see that members of minority groups will continue to suffer poverty and discrimination.

The equation is simple: capitalism requires sources of cheap labor; minorities provide it. In order to change the equation, we need to change the system that requires many people to be exploited for the benefit of a few. But this is not all. We must also educate ourselves so that we and our children will lose our prejudices. We need to realize that discrimination and minority conditions hurt all of us, diminish the humanity in each of us. We must come to accept and respect cultural and racial differences, even to celebrate them.

Summary

A minority group is relatively powerless, faces prejudice, stereotypes, discrimination, and exploitation, and in time becomes conscious of being treated differently. Prejudice and discrimination may occur one without the other, but usually they exist together.

Whether they came to America voluntarily or as slaves, whether they were here originally or came later, all minorities arise out of economic conditions—poverty and exploitation. They are created to meet the economic needs of a few people in the majority group. The histories of black slaves and freed blacks, native Americans, and the Irish all show that minorities have been connected with economic exploitation and development. Violence has been common in the experience of all minorities.

Minorities may emphasize their common economic condition, their class, or their cultural differences. In the history of the United States, members of minorities have emphasized cultural differences over class similarities. Minorities arose because of economic conditions, and they continue because of economic conditions and because the majority children are socialized to notice and resent the cultural differences of minorities. Prejudice and discrimination against minorities are common and usually (but not always) exist together.

Historically, majorities have reacted variously to the minorities in their midst. Sometimes they have killed minorities; at other times, they have expelled them. When they have been allowed to stay minorities have often been segregated. Other majority reponses have allowed for varying degrees of acceptance and accommodation of minorities.

Minorities have responded variously to their condition. Some people have tried to deny and erase their identity, and others have engaged in self-destructive behavior and even discriminated against other minorities. Some have been acculturated while others have lived in neighborhoods with their own people. Finally, minorities have engaged in a variety of political strategies, from accepting their condition to trying to change it to separating from it.

Blacks, native Americans, and Hispanics still face prejudice and discrimination in income and employment, housing, health and health care, education, and the media. More recently, the elderly, gay people, and disabled people have become aware of their minority status. They too face stereotypes, prejudice, and discrimination.

Minorities exist in all countries, for economic and cultural reasons. One of the largest and most oppressed minorities in the world today are the South African blacks who live under the apartheid system imposed by the white government.

Prejudice, discrimination, and oppression obviously harm minority individuals and groups, but most majority people also suffer from the existence of minorities. Many minority groups and individuals, and some people from majority groups, are working to change the economic and cultural conditions that create and perpetuate minority groups.

Suggested Readings

Asch, Adrienne & Fine, Michelle (1984, July–August). Shared dreams: A left perspective on disability rights and reproductive rights. *Radical America, 18*(4), 51–58. Women have the right to control their bodies and lives, and the disabled need the same rights.

Beers, David & Hembree, Diana (1987, March 21). The two Atlantas: A tale of two cities. *Nation,* 357–360. Atlanta proper is black and poor; suburban Atlanta, where most jobs and growth are moving, is white.

Curtin, Sharon (1972). *Nobody ever died of old age.* Boston: Atlantic-Little, Brown. Old people suffer because of neglect and isolation, not old age.

Douglass, Frederick (1969, 1855). *My bondage and my freedom.* New York: Dover. A moving description of slavery, Douglass' escape, and his reflection of how slavery degraded both slaves and slaveowners.

Gwaltney, John Langston (1980). *Drylongso: A self-portrait of black America.* New York: Random House. Black people talk about their lives and white prejudice and discrimination. These are very reflective and often angry stories.

Jacobs, Paul & Landau, Saul (with Eve Pell) (1971). *To serve the devil* (2 vols.). New York: Vintage. A history of American minorities as told by the authors and historical documents.

Jones, James H. (1981). *Bad blood: The Tuskegee syphilis experiment: A tragedy of race and medicine.* New York: Free Press. Four hundred black men with syphilis were intentionally not treated by the U.S. Public Health Service, were not told they had syphilis, and were stopped from getting treatment elsewhere, so the doctors could study how syphilis affected their bodies.

Josephy, Alvin M., Jr. (1984). *Now that the buffalo's gone: A study of today's American Indians.* Norman, OK: University of Oklahoma Press.

Malcolm X (1965). *The autobiography of Malcolm X.* New York: Grove. A powerful story of the childhood, criminal youth, and adulthood of a respected black leader.

Mermelstein, David (ed.) (1987). *The anti-apartheid reader.* New York: Grove. Essays, speeches, and descriptions of the anti-apartheid movement in and out of South Africa.

Miller, Wayne (ed.) (1972). *A gathering of ghetto writers.* New York: New York University Press. Irish, Italian, Jewish, black, and Puerto Rican history in the United States as told by fiction writers.

National Urban League (1988). *The state of black America 1988.* New York: National Urban League, Inc. Papers by social scientists on education, employment, the black family, crime, the psychology of race, and civil rights.

O'Neill, Diane (1984, December). Silent no more. *Progressive,* pp. 22–24. Disabled people challenge policies and attitudes that limit their lives.

Wright, Richard (1966, 1945). *Black boy.* New York: Harper & Row. A powerful autobiography of Wright's childhood and youth in the South early in the twentieth century. He exposes the depth of discrimination and describes his resistance to it.

CHAPTER 12

Women, Power, and Equality

As of 1985, women made up 51.3 percent of the population in the United States—making them the largest minority group. For generations, women have been stereotyped and discriminated against. They have been relatively powerless, and they have been exploited materially and sexually. Before the late 1960s most sociology texts did not discuss women as a minority group. It took the women's liberation movement, which began in the late 1960s, to make people conscious of the minority status of women.

Socialization and Sex Roles

Biology, Socialization, or Both?

In Chapter 7 we discussed the case of the identical twin boy and girl who had the exact same biology but behaved very differently by the age of six.

We cannot deny the obvious biological differences in sexuality and size. But do these differences dictate that men and women will feel, think, or behave differently? If we could separate the role of biology from the role of culture and socialization, what would we find? If we found that some behavioral differences between men and women are biologically based, do we assume that the male traits are superior or that the traits are equal but different? Why should behavioral and biological differences mean inequality?

We already know that many behavioral differences between men and women are social creations, not biological imperatives. Margaret Mead (1935), for example, studied sex and temperament in three societies. In one, both men and women were nurturing, gentle, and nonaggressive. In another, both men and women were aggressive and competitive. And in the third, roles were reversed from the condition many people assume to be natural: women were productive and assertive, men were concerned with their appearance and with gossiping.

Women have always worked hard, physically and mentally. In Greek peasant society at one time, most of the agricultural labor was women's work, as it has been in many societies. In many societies today (especially socialist ones), women do physically demanding work. Moreover, even if we were to find most women incapable of performing certain strenuous tasks that most men can do, of what relevance is that in today's societies? Very few tasks now require strength and hard labor. Today, biology places few limits on us, if it ever did (Dixon, 1980).

Some traditional beliefs about women's physical state have been found to be only myths. For years women were excluded from marathon races (a little over twenty-six miles long) because experts did not think they could run and finish. Women tried in vain to enter the Boston Marathon in the 1960s. They were finally admitted in 1973. At that time women could not run the race under 3 hours (men ran it at about 2 hours and 15 minutes). Experts could not foresee women breaking the 3 hour barrier. When they did, two and a half hours was proclaimed as the next unpassable barrier. In 1983, Joan Benoit ran it at 2 hours and 22 minutes (the winning time for men in 1983 was 2 hours and 9 minutes). Socialization, lack of encouragement and training, and male stereotypes and discrimination are more of an obstacle than any biological trait women possess (*Guardian*, May 11, 1983:2).

My two daughters Melissa and Ariane have been physically strong all their lives. When they were slightly over the ages of four and two, they surprised me when they called to me from halfway up a pine tree. Melissa runs fast, goes hand-over-hand on parallel ladders faster than boys her age (she also did this earlier than all boys in her nursery school). I do not see my children as limited by biology. If at twenty they are not as strong and athletic, will biology be the explanation, or will socialization and lack of opportunities and encouragement be more accurate reasons for their athletic ability? Already, subtle and direct messages have directed them more to playing house than exercising their bodies. Also, as we shall see, in jobs and other aspirations it is not biology that dictates women's or men's fates. Women can be carpenters, and men can be nurses. Even the nursing of infants is no occupational barrier for women. In socialist societies today, nursing mothers bring their infants to day-care centers in or near their workplaces, and they receive two additional breaks (thirty to forty-five minutes each) to feed them. Social policies, stereotypes, and discrimination limit women and men, not biology.

Sex Roles

Although sex-role differences have become less pronounced since the turn of the century, they are stil clear and pervasive. The changes that have taken place are more in attitudes and perception than in actual behavior.

The three Middletown studies, two by Lynd and Lynd (1929 and 1937), and one by Caplow and his colleagues (1982) provide us with insights into the change and persistence of sex-role differences. In the 1920s and 1930s, the years of the first two studies, men were expected to support their families without any assistance from their wives (exceptions existed, of course). They were also expected to fix the car, do heavy work around the house and yard, and represent the family in contacts with social and political institutions. Women were expected to do the housework, raise the children, arrange the family's social life, and (for wives of professional men especially) partake in cultural and volunteer civic work.

These expectations continued until the late 1970s when Caplow's (1982) surveys for *Middletown Families* were carried out. His surveys showed that some of the traditional roles were slowly breaking down. More women were working, and more men were helping with the housework (at least in principle). In the survey, few people were willing to say that any task should be entirely the responsibility only of men or only of women. Fewer than 25 percent of all the men or women surveyed said that any major task should be the exclusive domain of one or the other sex.

Four roles are clearly sex stereotyped. Earning a living and repairing the home are men's duties, and housekeeping and childrearing are women's responsibilities. Disciplining older children and organizing family excursions are left to individual preference—to be shared equally or to be the task of men or women who are willing to assume the responsibility. Wives and husbands agreed on their own roles and on the roles of the other.

In Caplow's study some roles are seen as the primary but not exclusive responsibility of men or women. In reality, some roles are more exclusive than sentiments allow. They are more sex-limited and less shared than people say they should be. In 85 percent of the families husbands earn all or most of the family income, and 90 percent of the wives do all or most of the housework. Caplow's survey clearly shows that family sex roles have not changed nearly as much as people's perceptions of and attitudes about them have.

One apparent change, which in time may be significant, is in the attitude women have about the housework they are expected to do. Clean houses and great meals do not seem particularly prestigious in Middletown. The Caplow study presents one woman's attitude as typical: "I'm not a person who likes the role of housewife as far as dusting everything and waiting for the dust to pile up again and again. I have never liked staying home and doing housework. That's just not me. I'd rather be out doing something and so I enjoy working and just having a chance to be with other people." (p. 77)

The authors claim that Middletown men and women assign different personalities and psychological traits to each other. "In the main, women continue to be characterized as sympathetic, sensitive, and emotional; and men, as hardheaded, pragmatic, and analytical." (p. 82)

The Creation of Female Identity

Girls and women are either absent or stereotyped in books, in the mass media, in school, and in much of daily life. The result is that they learn to lower their self-esteem and expectations. As I noted in Chapter 7, sexist language in books and elsewhere teaches girls to use *he* to mean both male and female sex. By now, sexist language is obvious to most people, though most deny its significance or effect on people's self-image.

Most traditional fairy tales are stereotyped. Women seek their fulfillment in the eagerly awaited prince who will take them away on his horse. Once Cinderella meets and marries her prince there is no more to her story —her search in life is over, and her fate is supposedly happily sealed forever after.

Almost all children's books written over the last forty to fifty years are sexist. Their language (as all language) is male; girls and women are minor characters and are rarely featured in leading roles (one study found that prize-winning children's books have eleven pictures of boys for every one of girls, and a third of them have no females at all). When girls are shown, their actions, words, and jobs are stereotyped.

Dr. Seuss is a good example of the absence of women in children's books. When they were young I read to my daughters all but two or three of his many books. Only a minor story he wrote has a girl in a leading role. Girls and women are absent from most of his books. In *Green Eggs and Ham* there is no girl; in the two *Cat in the Hat* books the brother tells the story and interacts with the cat; his sister is a passive observer. The language is consistently sexist, pronouns are all masculine. Both my daughters enjoy Dr. Seuss. I have pointed out the sexism in all his books, not to diminish their pleasure, but to make them aware of the pervasiveness of sexism.

A few books today are free of sexism in language, action, and characters. But they have hardly begun to change the all-encompassing sexism in children's books. A trip to any children's library is a sobering experience. You will search long and mostly in vain for books populated by both sexes and free of the masculine pronoun.

Television and the mass media emulate children's books. Sexist advertising is blatant. Most TV newscasters are men, despite the increasing appearance of women. Studies have shown that about 75 percent of all TV roles are male, and men are shown as powerful and aggressive and women as attractive and sociable. (See Liebert et al., 1982, and Sapiro, 1986.)

Women, like all minorities, are affected by socialization and the environment that stereotypes and makes them invisible. People begin to think of themselves as they are portrayed, labeled, and treated. Feelings of inferiority and unworthiness become internalized and ingrained.

Banner (1983) notes, "The pursuit of personal beauty has always been a central concern of American women." (p. 3) Despite the progress made in the liberation of women, the pursuit of beauty still enslaves many women of all ages. Make-up and much else are still deemed necessary for women to be beautiful. Lurie (1981) sees clothing, even today to some degree, confining women's movement. There is now the added imperative to be slender and beautiful in mid-life and beyond. Older public women, actresses and others, remain forever young. They write books and promote exercise programs that promise eternal youth—at an enormous cost. According to Chapkiss (1986), "The over-forty beauties' insistence on energetic exercise seems to suggest that the older body, left to itself, is lazy, undisciplined, and out of control." (p. 10) Skin repair advertisements echo this message: "Over time your skin gets lazier and lazier. And it doesn't produce new cells as fast or as frequently as it once did. . . . Buf Puf Gentle promotes the rebirth of your skin. . . . Age-controlling cream by Estee Lauder . . . encourages all skin to do what young skin does on its own."

Girls and women are taught to be beautiful to please men. They also learn, through constant experience, to be tentative, apologetic, and defensive while talking with men. Men and women learn to talk differently. When couples talk, women ask three times as many questions as men, and they tend to make supportive statements. Even when they make declarative statements, they do so with a questioning tone. In talk, as in other areas, women learn not to be assertive.

Men, on the other hand, dominate discussions. They interrupt women constantly. In a study of eleven mixed-sex conversations, forty-six of forty-eight interruptions were of men interrupting women. Interruptions are much less frequent in same-sex conversations. Women's subordinate role in their talks with men reflects their general social subordination, one they are taught from early childhood. Maryann Ayim (Kohn, 1987) points out, "If females are more polite and less aggressive than males in their language practices, if they are more supportive and less dominant, this is hardly shocking, for it simply reflects the reality in every other sphere of life." (p. 38) Ideally, neither men nor women should be aggressive and interruptive; both should be supportive and polite, and assertive when others try to dominate. (See also Henley & Freeman, 1984, and Sapiro, 1986.)

Girls are raised to have more limited horizons. Daily life, the media, schools, and other institutions socialize girls and women to be and expect less. When she was three Melissa and I were sitting on the front steps. A yellow school bus drove by quickly. She turned to me and said, "Daddy, only men drive buses." This one was in fact driven by a woman (which I assume Melissa did not notice). Why did she say that? She had been on a bus only once or twice and had not read books with bus drivers portrayed in them. Could it be that since she had seen mostly male work roles on *Sesame Street* (the program she watched often) she came to an apparently obvious conclusion? Somehow, at three she had already been affected by the sexism all around her.

Freeman (1971) cites a study published in 1939 that uncovered the profound effects a sexist education and a sexist environment have on a girl's self-image. Young girls start school by speaking, reading, and counting better than boys. In early years they are better than boys, on the average, and receive better grades. But Freeman observed that "when they are asked to compare their achievements with those of boys, they rate boys higher in virtually every respect. Despite factual evidence to the contrary, girls' opinion of girls grows progressively worse with age while their opinion of boys and boys' abilities grows better. Boys, likewise, have an increasingly better opinion of themselves and worse opinion of girls as they grow older." (p. 211)

Subsequent research on this issue has provided more evidence that girls and women internalize a low estimate of their abilities. It cannot be otherwise. As a minority group, women need to struggle against the corrosive effect on the self that years of stereotypes, invisibility, discrimination, and negative labeling cause. (See also Goldberg, 1968, and Pogrebin, 1980.)

Sex Roles and Men

Frederick Douglass argued that slavery dehumanized both the slaves and the owners. The same is true for minorities and their oppressors. Sexism, the ideology and practice of denying equality to women, is harmful to both women and men. This chapter explores the oppression of women. But here, and again in the conclusion, we need to stress that men suffer from sexism too. The sex role system that assigns tenderness and nurturing to women denies them to men. To meet cultural expectations men repress their emotions; they do not cry or hug friends. They do not express fears or insecurities. Toughness becomes a shield under which men bury essential aspects of their humanity. Men repress their feelings. They find it difficult to have intimate friends. Men *do* things with their friends, but they cannot *share* emotions, feelings, fears, doubts, hopes. Rubin (1985) states that their "interactions are emotionally contained and controlled." (p. 60) She talked with women and men about their friendships and estimated that over three-quarters of the women had a best friend, someone with whom they could share their innermost feelings. Only a third of the men had such a friend, who was often a woman. If they ever did, most married men talked only with their wives about their emotional lives. *"At every life stage between twenty-five and fifty-five, women have more friendships, as distinct from collegial relationships or workmates, than men, and the differences in the content and quality of their friendships are marked and unmistakable."* (p. 60)

Life is a struggle to create meaning, to survive, to escape loneliness. That struggle becomes more difficult when over half of humanity are more antagonists than sharers. I do not mean that men and women are constant enemies. But the threat and reality of violence visited upon women by men, the implied mistrust so often under the surface, these create a situation that adds to our existential problems. Love, sharing, mutual trust, equality, and cooperation between men and women enrich lives and relieve loneliness. The absence of these qualities diminishes all of us, men and women. (See Lynd & Lynd, 1929;

Pleck, 1976; Pollner, 1982; Rubin, 1983, 1985; Freeman, 1984; and Sapiro, 1986.)

Anthropological Perspectives on Women

Anthropologists agree that in every society there is some division of labor between men and women, and that other sex-role differences exist, but agreement ends there. Many social scientists conclude that these differences mean women are naturally inferior to men, that men are the more powerful sex. Others, however, argue that in many societies women have not been considered inferior. Some of these studies explore the reasons for equality or inequality. Let us look at some specific societies and then at some general conclusions on the status of women.

The Debate on the Social Equality of Women

Since the early 1970s a lively debate on women's social status has been taking place in anthropology. Women's equality or inequality in past and present societies has become a controversial and important field of theory and research. Many writers have pointed out that anthropology has been a male-dominated field that has paid little attention to the lives and status of women. What are women's perceptions and lives like in different societies? Are women equal or unequal to men? Or as Leacock (1981) asks, Are they autonomous and in control of their lives, or are they controlled and exploited by men? An explosion of field research, re-examination of past ethnographies, and theoretical statements has forced us to realize that what had been ignored and taken for granted needs close examination and study. (Quinn, 1977, summarizes and examines much of this literature.) The debate can be stated concisely. Have women ever been equal to men? If so, in what types of societies? What social, political, and economic conditions contribute to the equality or inequality of women?

A related debate focuses on the fact that most anthropologists and historians, who have researched the various types of human societies, have been men. It seems clear that they paid little or no attention to women's lives, their private and social existence. By ignoring women's lives, have men anthropologists forced the conclusion that in all societies men's lives, roles, contributions, accomplishments, and power are more important and prestigious than anything women do?

Ironically, some of the women who pushed anthropology to begin studying the status of women still give credence to the conclusion that whatever men do is given higher social prestige and importance. Michelle Rosaldo's and Louise Lamphere's *Woman, Culture, and Society* (1974), considered by some anthropologists as the single most influential book of the 1970s on women and anthropology, joins in the chorus of universal male dominance.

Everywhere we find that women are excluded from certain crucial economic or political activities, that their roles as wives and mothers are associated with fewer powers and prerogatives than are the roles of men. It seems fair to say that all contemporary societies are to some extent male-dominated, and although the degree and expression of female subordination vary greatly, sexual asymmetry is presently a universal fact of human social life. (p. 3)

Women may be important, powerful, and influential, but it seems that, relative to men of their age and social status, women everywhere lack generally recognized and culturally valued authority. (p. 17)

Male, as opposed to female, activities are always recognized as predominantly important, and cultural systems give authority and value to the roles and activities of men. Contrary to some popular assumptions, there is little reason to believe that there are, or once were, societies of primitive matriarchs, societies in which women predominated in the same way that men predominate in the societies we actually know. . . . An asymmetry in the cultural evaluations of male and female, in the importance assigned to women and men with men always receiving the higher importance, appears to be universal. (p. 19)

Other women anthropologists have agreed with Rosaldo and Lamphere on the universal reality of male dominance and female subordination. For instance Hammond and Jablow (1976) note,

Everywhere woman's primary roles are determined by the structure of the family, and her activities are related to domestic life. The relegation of women to the domestic sphere would seem automatically to place them in a subordinate position. Public life, which confers power and authority, is the concern of men. Male activities, interests, and attitudes tend to dominate the values and ethos of every society. In effect, women do live in a man's world. (p. 6)

Evelyn Kessler (1976) came to similar conclusions: "It is universally true that women occupy a secondary status. Despite myths pertaining to Amazons, matriarchs, and the like, no anthropologist to date has ever found a culture in which women rule." (p. 12) Later, Kessler argues that women often do exercise *power* ("the ability to make others conform to one's wishes"), especially within the household, but rarely hold *authority* ("the legitimation of power by the society"), especially in the public domain, notably politics. (p. 54)

Other writers, men and women, and anthropology texts, echo in various degrees the conclusion that universally women have been subordinate and men dominant. Keesing (1981), Harris (1983), and Ember and Ember (1985), even though they clearly support equality for women and are critical of the male bias in anthropology, ultimately conclude that in no society have women been equal to men. Ember and Ember's summary statement is typical: "Although women generally have lower status than men, some societies seem to approach equal status for males and females." (p.155) The closest any of these writers comes to saying women are equal is to say they seem to *approach* equality in *some* societies.

Many writers have concluded that there is a universal higher evaluation of men's activities and roles. But *evaluating* human beings is not an objective phenomenon like evaluating trees or rocks or water. It is, by definition, subjective and judgmental. We need to ask *who* evaluates men's and women's roles—male anthropologists. How do we know if women's gathering or men's hunting is more prestigious? Do anthropologists draw their conclusions from asking and observing all men and all women? Do women agree with the lower evaluation of their roles? If they tell a male anthropologist they do but they are in the presence of the men, can we believe that they express their true thoughts and feelings?

Rosaldo (1974) also says that "the Nupe, then, came to see societies of female traders as societies of witches." (p. 34) Does the Nupe include both men *and* women? Or only men? Or some men and some women? Are the women traders not members of the Nupe society? Do *they* see themselves as witches?

It seems that what are reported as supposedly societal and cultural values and evaluations should more properly be labeled as male conclusions told to and reported by male anthropologists. Chiñas (1983) argues that most anthropologists have made two wrong assumptions: that "the sexes perceive their culture and their own sex's place in it in essentially the same way," and that "men and women share a common culture on similar terms." (p. 2) (See also Leacock & Sofa, 1986; O'Kelly & Carney, 1986; and for a guide to sources on *The Cross-Cultural Study of Women,* Duley & Edwards, 1986.)

Women in Six Societies

The following short discussions of women in six societies show that male dominance has been neither universal nor eternal. In many pre-industrial societies, women have been autonomous and equal to men.

!Kung

Most people who have studied the !Kung have concluded that women are equal to men. Draper (1975) summarizes some of the evidence:

> *In the hunting and gathering context, women have a great deal of autonomy and influence. Some of the contexts in which this egalitarianism is expressed . . . are: women's subsistence contribution and the control women retain over the food they have gathered; the requisites of foraging in the Kalahari which entail a similar degree of mobility for both sexes; the lack of rigidity in sex-typing of many adult activities, including domestic chores and aspects of child socialization; the cultural sanction against physical expression of aggression; the small group size; and the nature of the settlement pattern. (p. 78)*

Shostak (1981) opens her discussion of women and men by saying, "men and women live together in a nonexploitative manner, displaying a striking degree of equality between the sexes—perhaps a lesson for our own society.

!Kung men, however, do seem to have the upper hand. They more often hold positions of influence—as spokespeople for the group or as healers—and their somewhat greater authority over many areas of !Kung life is acknowledged by men and women alike." (p. 237)

As we have seen, !Kung fathers spend time with their children and provide more of their care than do fathers in many societies. In addition, "Men do not regulate women's schedules, do not tell them which foods to gather or where to go, and do not control the distribution of gathered foods. Women tell their husbands when they plan to be gone for the day, but this is as much a courtesy as a potential restraint, and it is what men usually do as well." (p. 241) The food women collect is their own, to use for their families or share with others as they see fit. Generally, !Kung women have high self-esteem. They go into the desert without men, where they use their extensive knowledge about hundreds of plants. They are strong, productive, and in control of their products and their lives.

Shostak (1981) found no rigid sex-role differences. Hunting is a male activity, but women do kill small animals they encounter on their gathering expeditions. And men do on occasion gather foods without causing comments or criticisms. There is no shame for men to perform tasks usually associated with women.

But Shostak (1981), although she does not see !Kung women as oppressed by men, concludes that the men "enjoy certain distinct advantages —in the way the culture values their activities, both economic and spiritual, and in their somewhat greater influence over decisions affecting the life of the group." For example, people are happy to see the women returning with the food they gathered (which provides more food than the men's meat) but they are delighted and celebrate when men return with the hunt they caught. Draper (1975) and others, however, have concluded that !Kung men and women are basically equal.

Mbuti

Turnbull's (1961) study shows sex-role differences exist among the Mbuti pygmies too. But unlike the !Kung, the hunt is a collective enterprise where women participate by chasing the animals into the net. Women have "a full and important role to play. There is relatively little specialization according to sex. Even the hunt is a joint effort. A man is not ashamed to pick mushrooms and nuts if he finds them, or to wash and clean a baby. A woman is free to take part in the discussions of men, if she has something relevant to say." (p. 154)

Agta

Eskioko-Griffin and Griffin (1981) studied some Agta groups (in northeastern Luzon, the Philippines) and found that women in this society hunt large animals as much as the men do. "Women not only hunt but appear to hunt frequently. Like men, some enjoy hunting more than others. . . . We have observed several combinations of hunting parties. Men and women hunt together or among themselves. Often sisters, or mother and daughter, or aunt and niece hunt together." In addition, "both Agta men and women fish. In fact, from early adulthood until the infirmity of old age all Agta fish." (p. 129)

Women, as much as the men, decide how to use and distribute their hunt. Women and men share equally in discussions and decisions that affect the family and the group. "Generally spouses discuss what work to do, what needs should be specified, and who will do what. Whole residential groups frequently together decide courses of action. Women are as vocal and as critical in reaching decisions as are men." (p. 136) The same rules and practices apply to men and women in all aspects of Agta life.

Navaho

The Navaho are sheepherders who live in the Southwest. Downs (1972) claims that "the female principle" is the norm among them. Women do not dominate men, but life revolves around women more than men. They organize the social life of the community. "Children, by and large, consider themselves as part of the descent group [larger extended family of sorts] of their mother." (p. 22) Generally, married couples go to live with the wife's mother. Women's opinions on "how and when work is to be performed is considered important and in many instances is *the* important factor in directing the activity" of the society. (p. 23) Women initiate relationships between the sexes, for example, girls select partners in dances and control courting behavior. (Leacock, 1981, comes to the same conclusion.)

Western Bontoc

The Tanulong and Fedilizan, two Western Bontoc subgroups, are horticultural people who live in Luzon, the Philippines. According to Bacdayan (1977), there is full equality between women and men.

> Sexual equality in these two groups can be seen in the following cultural conditions: the equal treatment of male and female children; the sharing of economic power between men and women in its domestic and public contexts; the full participation of women in the instrumental and expressive aspects of public life; and the freedom of women to form associations or ties with other people, so that they are neither confined to the homes nor isolated from others. (p. 274)

Let us look in some detail at the division of labor between women and men, or, rather, its relative absence.

In Bontoc culture there is "the performance of the same tasks by men and women in a pattern of work that brings the sexes together in the same working situation." (p. 270) Very few tasks are the province of one sex only. Most are shared by men and women or are open to either sex. Bacdayan estimates that 81 percent of the tasks are shared; these are the daily tasks of agricultural production and domestic work "by which the family or household is maintained." (p. 282) The 19 percent not shared are mostly seasonal tasks.

In agricultural work, the following are some jobs shared equally by men and women: preparation of the soil, planting, weeding the banks of the fields, watering, harvesting, planting vegetables, fertilizing, fencing, fixing dikes, and milling sugar cane. Ony men plow with animals and trap rats and mice. Only women sow seeds. Some jobs can be done by either sex but are performed usually by one sex. Women usually clear the padi dikes, plant and gather beans, and plant and dig up sweet potatoes. Erecting scarecrows, building walls, and hauling rice from the fields are usually male tasks.

In house-building tasks, only men construct roofs, prepare wood, and gather vines for binding. Both sexes gather thatch roofing, prepare the ground for building, and haul the material to the site. Men do the hunting, as well as gather mushrooms and trap birds.

In the household, men and women share the following: cooking, washing dishes, pounding rice, cooking breakfast, fetching water, babysitting, and feeding and counseling children. Men kill pigs and women weave cloth. Women usually keep floors clean, sew and wash clothes, keep the children clean, washed and cared for. Finally, the following domestic chores are usually male: splitting wood, distributing meat and cutting up meat for meals, and cutting children's hair. Most religious functions are shared equally.

Isthmus Zapotecs

Let us close by looking at a peasant society that Chiñas (1983) studied. The Isthmus Zapotecs live in Mexico. In many ways they are a traditional peasant society. Women are primarily housewives. When they have young children they stay home, but as the children grow older their mothers expand their activities. They process and sell some of the farm goods produced by their husbands (for example, they make tortillas). They do so at home, on the street, or in the marketplace. Even though their selling is important for family finances, they generally have a negative attitude towards it.

Boys and girls are raised differently. Boys have more freedoms, with few demands and responsibilities placed on them. Girls, on the other hand, start working early. By age seven, for example, they are expert shoppers. Except for shopping, they are restricted to the house after they reach the age of six. Girls cannot talk to or even look at boys when they are in public. If they do, any woman can report them to their mother. Girls and women seem to lead restricted lives. Virginity is expected for unmarried women.

Public office and other public roles are limited only to men. Women thought it was hilarious that a woman could hold public office. Women carefully control and divert male aggression, especially sexual male aggression (which Chiñas thinks is an important role). Girls are chaperoned and drunk men are cleverly manipulated and diverted.

Despite what seems to be clear inequality for women, Chiñas concludes that women are equal to men. Zapotec women are strong, proud, and productive. Chiñas interviewed fifty wives, and not one was a dependent "clinging-vine-type" wife. They have close bonds with each other, are not jealous of each other, and their roles and work are as important as the men's. Husband and wife form a "strong, egalitarian partnership with much of the actual burden of day-to-day responsibility and decision-making falling on the wife." (p. 87)

Different sex roles do not make women inferior, despite appearances. Zapotec women, according to Chiñas, are and see themselves as equal to men. (For peasant societies generally, see Hammond & Jablow, 1976; for Italian peasant societies, see Cornelisen, 1977; for Greek peasant societies, see Schein, 1971.)

Political, Economic, and Social Changes

Leacock and a few other anthropologists believe that the recent and present inequality of women in many societies is the result of changes that were introduced during European colonization.

Let us look at the !Kung again. Contact and conquest by outside companies and countries are making men more prominent and more powerful than women. Western societies tend to recognize men as spokespeople for the group, and thus enhance their position. Shostak (1981) adds that men are "the ones who learn foreign languages, who attend government meetings, and who speak out on behalf of the regional !Kung communities." (p. 245)

The !Kung have been encouraged, coaxed, and forced to leave their gathering and hunting life style and settle down to sedentary village life. Some believe that this is creating inequalities. Instead of moving about gathering food in the desert, women are housebound. The men, on the other hand, work the fields and have contact with the outside world. Once housebound, women train their daughters for the same role, while the boys follow and emulate their fathers. In the past, boys and girls played together in the desert, but as the society changes they become more separated very early (Draper, 1975).

Observations of gathering and hunting societies when they were first encountered by the West, and even later, revealed them to be very egalitarian. Power was dispersed. People were autonomous, and decisions were made collectively. Public and private spheres, family and community, were not sharply divided, so there was no public sphere for men to dominate, as they do in later societies. Men's and women's work roles were complementary. The role of each was respected and their contributions equally important (Leacock, 1981).

Leacock discusses at length the Montagnais-Naskapi of Labrador, Canada. When the French sent their armies, merchants, and Jesuits to supposedly civilize them in the early seventeenth century, the Naskapi were a very egalitarian society. The Jesuits disapproved of what they saw: men and women could not dominate each other; children could not be ordered by their parents; sex was guilt-free and prevalent. Despite their disapproval, the Jesuits did make careful observations, which give the unmistakable picture of an egalitarian society. The French (especially the Jesuits) introduced Christianity, new values, such as sex is evil and women should obey men, and an economy that focused upon men's work. Leacock (1981) notes that in time, "women lost their equal status when they lost control over the products of their work."

Fur trading and other activities eliminated much of the women's productive contribution to the society. The French chose men to be the spokespeople and official leaders. Thus, the Naskapi in 1950, when Leacock went there, had been changed by the impact of capitalism and Western culture over the last three centuries. But she still found women to be more equal to men than they are in many other societies. Old values, traditions, and institutions lingered on to some degree.

Other societies have undergone similar changes. It is a mistake to think that men have always dominated societies since the conditions for their domination have not always been present. In many societies, material changes and cultural values that were introduced and forced from the outside created gender inequality and male power where none had existed.

Conditions for Gender Equality

From 1984 to 1986 I researched the literature covering native societies that existed between 1500 and 1750 in the northeastern United States and southeastern Canada. From this research, I concluded that there are six basic social conditions that enable women and men to live and work together equally and cooperatively. Before these conditions can be met, however, a society must be egalitarian. Gender equality is possible and has existed only in egalitarian societies. Women are equal only when the many are not controlled and exploited by the few. Therefore, in order for a society to be egalitarian the following must exist.

■ Land and other resources needed for material sustenance are communally owned. Private ownership of personal items can exist but not the basic means of production and subsistence. The food and other goods people gather, hunt, raise, and make are for the direct use by the people within the group. They are not sold to others for profit.

■ There are no social classes and no great material differences within the society. Some people may make more or better pots, belts, or other material items than others, but vast differences in wealth do not exist and everyone has equal access to land and other resources.

■ Power is dispersed. Hierarchies and powerful rulers do not exist. People lead by persuasion and explanation, not by force and coercion. People do differ in abilities and interests, of course, but these do not entitle anyone to rule over others. Richard Lee's well-known paper, "Eating Christmas in the Kalahari" (Lee, 1984), illustrates superbly how the !Kung insure that better hunters do not become overly proud and haughty and do not come to dominate others. There is no better example of the egalitarian values of gathering-hunting and horticultural societies.

■ All people, children included, are free and autonomous. No one co-erces another, no one speaks for another. But this autonomy, this "inviolability of the individual," this ethic of non-interference co-exists with the learning and value of sharing, cooperation, and communal responsibility. People are not isolated individuals caring only for themselves. They share with each other, they cooperate and assume responsibility for the group.

■ Life is communal. People do not live in isolated nuclear families in the privacy of their own houses. Life is largely led, goods are produced, family and group life co-exist in common open spaces. Individuals and families do not withdraw in distinct and separate family spaces. They live in the common space of the group.

■ Finally, there is an emphasis on social relations, on being and sharing with others, not on accumulation of material possessions. People live simply. According to Shostak (1981), after their work is done, the !Kung have a lot of free time for "singing and composing songs, playing musical instruments, sewing intricate bead designs, telling stories, playing games, visiting, or just lying around and resting." (p. 10) Accumulation, profit, exploitation of others, and the exercise of power are absent. There are conflicts, periodic shortages, disagreements, fights, and death, but these are experienced in an egalitarian setting.

If an egalitarian society is achieved, then the following six conditions necessary for gender equality may be possible. They have existed in many societies, as we saw above in our brief look at six societies. They must exist in some form in any society we would consider egalitarian for women.

■ Women must make an equal and equally important contribution to the material sustenance of the society. This has meant that women procure as much food as men. This may mean gathering food or getting paid equally for the work they do. Other necessities such as clothing, housing, and other domestic necessities may be specifically assigned to one or the other sex.

■ Women must also share equally in deciding the use and distribution of the goods procured, raised, or made. (Keep in mind that the land and other means of production are owned communally by all people.)

■ Women are free to move about in public places. This must mean that they are free of male violence outside the home. (Societies such as the Zapotec and the Mundurucú cannot be considered fully sexually egalitarian since the women do not appear and move about in public as freely as the men do.)

■ Women must have control of their bodies and persons. They cannot be controlled by men, and they must be subject to the same standards that the men are. Specifically, women must be in control of their sexuality (premarital, marital, extramarital) as much as men and the same opportunities must be open to both. Menstruation must not be seen as defiling and dangerous, and women must be able to choose pregnancy or to end it. They must have as much choice in marriage as men do (and both must have a large degree of choice). Divorce must be available and resorted to by both in order to escape unhappy or oppressive marriages. And men must not use violence against women in their family.

■ Power and political life must be accessible to and shared by both sexes. (Again remember that in egalitarian societies chiefs cannot exist because power is dispersed. *All* women and all men must share equally in the making of all important decisions that affect the group.)

The five preceding conditions largely prevailed among the Montagnais, Huron, Iroquois, !Kung, Agta, Mbuti, and others. In these societies, men and women have fairly different functions and roles, but the work of each sex is absolutely necessary for survival and complements the work of the other. Men and women live as a cooperative whole. Their lives and contributions are equally necessary and equally prestigious. (See Turnbull, 1981, and Leacock, 1981.)

For us today and in the future, equality may require fully shared rather than complementary lives and roles. Choices, values, and economic and political conditions may not allow equality to develop while men and women lead largely separate lives. In the history of peasant and industrial societies, different roles and functions have meant inequality for women. Historically, women in these societies have not shared power with men. Women in the United States, for example, could not vote until 1920. Divorce laws, until only very recently, gave men the power over all possessions within a marriage. Women's income is still only 69 percent of that of men's. Women also still carry the heaviest domestic burden, even when they work outside the home. These inequalities contrast sharply with what we have seen in gathering and hunting tribes where women and men may have different tasks but they have equal power and status. For us, by necessity and choice, sex equality may mean shared lives in work, politics, housework, and raising children.

These five general conditions are essential to gender equality within the context of egalitarian societies. Others may add to, subtract from, or modify them. I cannot conceive of full gender equality without them. The first two—equally sharing in the production and distribution of goods—are absolutely essential conditions without which the other conditions for equality cannot arise. Women cannot have autonomy over their bodies and persons, and they cannot share in public decisions, if they depend on men for their material existence. I do not yet understand why in societies where women do meet these two conditions they are still limited in some of the others. Why, for example, do Mundurucú women have no freedom of movement? But I have not read of any society where women who do not fulfill the first two conditions do meet the others.

Where sex equality does exist women are strong, confident, assertive, and autonomous people. They are, as Shostak (1981) says of the !Kung

women, both "competent and assertive as well as nurturant and cooperative."
(p. 246)

Women in United States History

A brief historical account will help to clarify the place American women hold
in today's society and economy. History shows that women's place in our
society has changed in some ways but remained constant in others.

In colonial America, women's lives and work were more varied than
today. Men did most of the agricultural work and dominated some crafts, but
women did equally important work. In addition to the household chores, they
made shoes, soap, clothes, and many other items. This work was done with the
cooperation of their husbands, children, and other women. Thus, the woman
in the home was not isolated, and the husband was not gone all day as he is
today. Home and work were integrated and included the whole family.
Women typically developed many skills. Moreover, women were not entirely
excluded from outside occupations. Many women, especially widows, worked
in taverns and other businesses. Generally, before 1800, only a few middle-
class women were full-time housewives as we understand the term. The rest
worked very hard doing much more than housekeeping (Sacks, 1976).

We saw in Chapter 6 how industrialism changed the family in England.
Out of a society where women had been full and equal participants in agriculture and crafts, where parents and children formed an economic unit, there
gradually grew a new economic order. From 1750 on in England and from
about 1800 on in the United States, men began to have daily routines separate
from family life. At the same time, women became more dependent on men,
and more isolated with housework and childcare occupying their time (Oakley,
1974). Some women did work outside the home, mostly single and widowed
women. Most workers in the textile industry were women. For slave women,
freedom in 1865 meant little since they continued to work in the fields (as
sharecroppers) and in their former masters' houses as maids.

In the first half of the nineteenth century, most men were still working
on farms, so women and children were the only readily available labor supply.
At first, they were single women of Yankee settler families, but soon they were
immigrant women. But regardless of where these women came from they were
drawn into factories and manufacturing work from the very beginning of
industrialism.

By the late nineteenth century, most women were taken out of the paid
labor force, but poor immigrant women, black women, and widows still worked
in textile mills and other places. In 1900, 20 percent of the women over the
age of sixteen were in the labor force. (For more details on working women in
the late nineteenth century, see Baxandall, Gordon & Reverby, 1976.)

It is inaccurate to generalize about nineteenth-century women. The lives
of middle- and upper-class women differed drastically from those of working-

class and black women. Even their image was different. The women of the upper classes were seen as fragile, sick, and incapable of physical and mental straining. Working women, on the other hand, were not seen as fragile, nor as sick, even though they suffered from illness and deprivation. Working women were seen as sickening, as dangerous and polluting.

Medical arguments about the inherent weakness of women kept them from education and voting. Such arguments disqualified women as doctors, but qualified women of the upper classes as patients. The health care for the so-called fragile women was bed rest, surgery, and other treatments that incapacitated them. Rebellious women were kept in their place. Ehrenreich and English (1973) argue that the "cult of invalidism" was used as a way to control women of the upper classes. (p. 12) Poor women, on the other hand, suffered from real illnesses that went untreated.

In the early 1900s, more women entered the labor force. Although unions in general did not want women in their ranks because they would compete for men's jobs and lower wages, many women were active in some of the major strikes of that time. The demands of the capitalist economy began to create what were considered women's jobs. As corporations began to grow after 1890, they needed more clerical workers, and they turned to women for a plentiful and cheap source of labor.

Even though at this time fewer than 25 percent of women were in the labor force, the rest were not just keeping house. Many women (especially blacks) did farm work and some home manufacturing. Others took in boarders to supplement their income, and thus they had more washing, cooking, and cleaning to do. History has largely ignored women's monetary contribution to family survival.

Another major change in women's lives began to take place in the 1920s. In order to find markets for their goods, corporations began to advertise. Women were their major targets. Women became consumers while losing most of their role as producers. Home production declined drastically as clothing and other needs were manufactured in factories. (The desire for some products, of course, was created to increase corporate profits.) Women's role in society was very different from what it had been in colonial times.

The 1940s began the gradual but steady absorption of women into the labor force. Not only were working wives considered a blow to masculine self-esteem, but most jobs available to women were unpleasant and paid poorly, so women preferred housework. Most of the women who worked outside the home needed to for survival.

The labor shortages during World War II created and accelerated the trend of more women working. In 1940, 28.5 percent of the women were working, up from 23.6 percent in 1930. By the war's end, 36 percent of the women were in the labor force. During the war years wages increased, up to 40 percent higher for many women. The kind of women in the work force also changed. The number of working wives doubled, and black women began getting manufacturing jobs. In addition, women were now getting skilled, higher-paying jobs such as precision toolmakers, crane operators, lumberjacks, and drill press operators. (See Szymanski, 1976; Baxandall, Gordon & Reverby, 1976.)

Since the 1940s, working women have become more typical. Married women, many with young children, have been entering the labor force. At the same time, women have been limited to a few sex-segregated jobs, and their earnings (in relation to men's) have increased very slowly.

After the war, some women went or were sent back home. This was only temporary, however. The inflation of the late 1940s, the need for more money for families to buy the usual necessities and some new perceived necessities of the emerging consumer society, and other conditions began to make women regular workers. The percentage of women in the labor force has increased every year since the late 1940s. In 1987, 56 percent of the women were in the labor force as compared to about 76 percent of men. It is now normal for a married woman to hold a job outside the home. Many women must work because of increasing inflation and the consumption ethic created by advertising and corporate profits (Kessler-Harris, 1980).

Violence and Control

The Medical System and Women

Since its rise in the nineteenth century, the medical system in the United States has contributed to the socialization and oppression of women. In the nineteenth century, doctors viewed and treated upper-class and professional women differently than they did poor women. Ehrenreich and English (1973) contend that "affluent women were seen as inherently sick, too weak and delicate for anything but the mildest pastimes, while working-class women were believed to be inherently healthy and robust." (p. 12) As the same time, many working-class women were also seen as sickening, carriers of many diseases. In reality, they were simply sick, from poverty, poor nutrition, and long hours in factories and other workplaces.

Ehrenreich and English describe a veritable cult of invalidism that virtually imprisoned affluent women in their homes.

> *The affluent woman normally spent a hushed and peaceful life indoors, sewing, sketching and reading romances, planning menus and supervising servants and children. Her clothes, a sort of portable prison of tight corsets and long skirts, prevented activity any more vigorous than a Sunday stroll. Society agreed that she was frail and sickly. Her delicate nervous system had to be shielded as carefully as her body, for the slightest shock could send her reeling off to bed.*
>
> *The boredom and confinement of affluent women fostered a morbid cult of hypochondria—"female invalidism"—that began in the mid-nineteenth century*

and did not completely fade until the late 1910s. Sickness pervaded upper- and upper-middle-class female culture. Health spas and female specialists sprang up everywhere and became part of the regular circuit of fashionable women. And in the 1850s a steady stream of popular home readers by doctors appeared, all on the subject of female health. Literature aimed at female readers lingered on the romantic pathos of illness and death; popular women's magazines featured such stories as "The Grave of My Friend" and "Song of Dying." Paleness and lassitude (along with filmy white gowns) came into vogue. It was acceptable, even fashionable, to retire to bed with "sick head- aches," "nerves," and a host of other mysterious ailments. (p. 15)

Because women were thought of as delicate and weak, they were not allowed to pursue higher education, careers, or sexual activity. To cure their psychological problems (which of course stemmed from their oppression and virtual imprisonment), various treatments arose. Years of bed rest kept women imprisoned. But among the most punitive was the surgical removal of the clitoris.

Affluent women, argue Ehrenreich and English, were the perfect pa- tients: endless illness and almost unlimited bank accounts made them reward- ing to doctors. Thus, the medical system profited, but it did so by catering to and justifying the discrimination and oppression of women that arose in the nineteenth century.

Poor women, on the other hand, were exposed to sickness, exhaustion, and injury. Their poverty excluded them from the cult of invalidism. They had to work and could not afford to pay doctors for special treatments. Until they were on their deathbed, poor women were on their own with home remedies; only when death became imminent did doctors appear. Poor women were not only deprived of medical attention but they were also seen as the *cause* of disease and epidemics that frequently raged in the crowded slums of American cities. Doctors and the affluent classes believed poor women were a threat to public health (Ehrenreich & English, 1973).

Today, psychiatry and its ideology oppress women. First, women's real illnesses are often dismissed as unreal, as psychosomatic. A study of the American Medical Association reported in the *Guardian* (June 13, 1979) showed the sexist behavior of doctors: A team of researchers from the Uni- versity of California at Davis "examined the medical records of 52 married couples to find out how the doctors responded to such common complaints as backache, headache, dizziness, chest pain and fatigue—which may signal more serious illness. In all cases the doctors ordered more X-rays and diag- nostic tests for the men than for the women." (p. 10) Secondly, women are seen as dangerous to men. Mental illness, delinquency, and so on are attrib- uted to domineering or uncaring mothers. Ehrenreich and English (1973) point out that "The ambitious woman can be blamed for 'emasculating' men, and the devoted mother can be blamed for 'infecting' her sons with guilt and dependency." (p. 80) Pediatricians and psychiatrists warn working mothers that their children will suffer irreparable damage without constant mothering.

Either way, at work or at home, a mother runs the risk of neglecting or smothering her children.

Early in the twentieth century, doctors also succeeded in taking control of birth—a natural experience—and transforming it into an illness that they control. Women were routinely medicated and not told the disadvantages of the medication. Normal women were required to deliver in hospitals when they need not do so. Doctors had total control of the delivery process, which included medication, bed confinement, the lithotomy position, shaving the birth area, and so on. All these practices largely facilitated the doctors' control; they did not enhance the mother's comfort, her experience of the birth, or the baby's arrival and health.

Women's groups in the 1970s began to challenge the medical definition and treatment of birth. More women have become aware of the medical reality of birth today, which does not coincide with its biological and emotional reality. Thus women and parents have regained some control over the process. Natural deliveries, the presence of fathers, even deliveries at home are some examples.

But while women are struggling to liberate birth from medical control, doctors are finding new ways to regain and increase their dominance. Caesarean births have increased from 3.2 percent of all births between 1953 and 1962 to 5.5 percent in 1970, 10.5 percent in 1975, 18.0 percent in 1980, and 22.0 in 1986. This makes women passive observers and gives doctors total control over the process. (See Corea, 1980; Drummond, 1980; and *Boston Globe,* January 23, 1987:16.)

Finally, drug companies and doctors today oppress women by medicalizing their oppression. When women report depression, unhappiness, and other symptoms, which are often largely the result of sex roles, limited lives, social isolation, and general oppression and discrimination, doctors prescribe tranquilizers and anti-depressants. Social problems and conditions that cause the symptoms are ignored, and doctors merely treat the symptom with a pill. Drug companies advertise heavily in medical journals. One ad shows the "frowning countenance of an anxious woman," and then tells the doctor: "you've talked, . . . you've listened, . . . but here she is again. Looks like chronic anxiety—Looks like a case for Stelazine." Loneliness, tension, inability to fit in at school, unhappiness with an isolated life as the wife in nuclear families, all are seen as requiring the ingestion of pills. Women are seen as especially moody, neurotic, and psychologically weak. As a result, doctors give twice as many drug prescriptions for tranquilizers and other pills to women as they do to men. (See Kiefer, 1980; Hills, 1980; Fee, 1983; Leavitt, 1984; Freeman, 1984; and Sapiro, 1986.)

Reproductive Rights

Women in most societies have sought to limit the number of children they conceive or give birth to. Various contraceptive methods and abortion techniques have existed in most societies. Limiting births has been necessary for the whole society when resources were limited, but it has also been beneficial for the women who must raise the children. Spacing apart the birth of children by prolonging the nursing of infants and children, for example, has been common to many societies. (See Bodley, 1983; Gordon, 1981a; and Shostak, 1981.)

Reproductive rights include many aspects besides abortion. This issue is much broader and, some feel, is at the root of woman's equality. The forced sterilization of poor women (legal or through pressure) affects and controls women's lives. And the availability (or lack) of, distribution of, and education about contraceptives affect women (*and* men) as much as abortion does.

Gordon (1981a) claims that abortion and reproductive rights are aspects of an overall strategy for the equality of women. This strategy focuses on general changes toward equality for women. They must have equality at home and in the workplace. Their health concerns must be treated realistically and fairly. Women and men will enjoy sex more when it is freed from the fear of unwanted or unneeded children in a world much too overpopulated already.

Women's reproductive rights are endangered both by the medical system and working conditions. Doctors routinely perform hysterectomies. In 1984, eight hundred thousand women had hysterectomies, of which only 4 percent had cancer. And only 1 percent of removed ovaries were cancerous. The workplace presents a number of health threats (chemicals, microchips, etc.) that lead to sterility, stillbirths, and deformed infants (see Chapter 9 for details). (See Barnett, 1986; Bingham, 1987; and Marshall, 1987.)

New reproductive technologies are a new attack on women's control of their persons and bodies. Arditti (1985) points out that scientists are permitted "to arrange fertilization to occur outside the womb; to implant the embryo in a different womb from the woman who donated the egg; to freeze the embryo for storage until later implantation; to determine the sex of the embryo; to screen for genetic abnormalities during pregnancy and even to 'flush' embryos out of the womb so they may be transferred into another womb." (p. 9) The technologies exist already and more will surely follow. Their use has been expanded from women with fertility problems to women who have *no* problems.

Corea (1986) argues they have the potential to "distance women still further from our bodies, our selves." (p. 22) Patriarchal male institutions have the power to control pregnancy, birth, and women even more than they do now. Corea shows how new reproductive technologies affect all women and pose serious dangers.

When reproductive technologies are introduced, they are presented as solutions to the problems of a small number of women. Then, quickly, physicians expand the indications and enlarge the number of patients. In obstetrics, for example, electronic fetal monitoring was introduced for use on women in high-risk pregnancies. Now, in many industrialized countries, it is used in most cases. The same pattern is evident with ultrasound, amniocentesis, Caesarean section, and genetic testing and counseling.

This technological imperative is likely to prevail with in vitro fertilization, egg donation, sex predetermination, and embryo evaluation. In vitro fertilization was originally proposed for use only on women who were infertile because of blocked or absent fallopian tubes. But physicians quickly extended IVF so that now even fertile women married to men with low sperm counts are counted among IVF candidates. Indications for the procedure continue to grow.

Richard Seed says embryo evaluation may become part of routine prenatal care. Embryos would be flushed out of every pregnant woman and evaluated. Only "healthy" embryos would be transferred back into women; the others would be discarded. Some physicians have suggested that in the near future, people may use the sperm and eggs of other, genetically healthier people. (pp. 22–23)

One of the ironies is that despite their promises, some of these technologies work poorly. In vitro fertilization (IVF), for example, fails most of the time. In one survey, half of the fifty-four clinics who tried it "never sent a woman home with a baby." (p. 23)

Doctors and courts also intervene during pregnancies and deliveries. Many doctors are proposing that women whose diet and general life style do not meet the doctors' criteria of what is best for the fetus be forced to follow doctor's orders. A survey published in the *New England Journal of Medicine* (May 1987) found that "nearly half of the heads of training programs in maternal-fetal medicine across the country think that women who endanger the life of a fetus by refusing medical advice should be detained [held in jails and other places against their will]. More than a quarter advocate 'state surveillance' during the third trimester of pregnant women who don't seek medical care." (p. 8) These doctors ignore the fact that most pregnant women who seek no medical care are poor, uninsured, and cannot afford it.

Doctors are arrogant to order people to follow their advice when they have been wrong so often in the past. Lynn Patrow (*Boston Globe,* July 21, 1987:1) points out that "during the 1960s pregnant women were prescribed thalidomide, a sleeping pill that caused severe birth defects, and diethylstilbestrol (DES), a drug intended to prevent miscarriages that proved to be carcinogenic to unborn daughters." And by 1987, courts in eleven states had ordered women who wanted natural birth to undergo Caesareans because doctors had recommended them.

Women *and* men need to stop the male medical establishment and new reproductive technologies from taking over pregnancy and birth. The exploitation of poor women, in the United States and elsewhere, must also not happen. New technology makes it possible for the fertilized eggs of a (usually wealthy) woman to be implanted in the womb of another (usually poor) woman. If this is allowed to happen, we could be developing a class of breeders that will be exploited. (See Gordon, 1985, and Corea, 1986.)

This is no mere fantasy (or nightmare). It has already begun to happen. The controversy over surrogate motherhood, which became intense during the trial over custody of Baby M in 1987, exposed the exploitation of poor and minority women by other women. The legal, social, and moral issues of surrogate motherhood are many. It presents another threat to women's control of reproduction, and it can exploit poor women. (For excellent discussions of surrogate motherhood and the Baby M trial, see Pollitt, 1987, Goodman, 1987b, and *Guardian,* March 25, 1987:19.)

Modern contraceptives present various problems for women. First, new ones, like the pill, IUD, and so on, are usually tested on poor women, who are not told of the dangers they face by using them. Second, there is very little education about contraceptives. At least 25 percent of women thirteen to forty-four years old who are sexually active use no birth control. Ignorance about using birth control is especially severe for teenage women. Third, most research on contraceptives focuses on women. And fourth, drug corporations show little interest in doing research to develop safe, effective, and inexpensive new methods. The pill was widely used for some years, but more and more women are not using it since its side-effects became known.

A 1982 survey showed that of all women fifteen to forty-four years old, 27.2 percent were sterile (25.7 surgically sterile, 1.5 nonsurgically); 5.2 percent were pregnant or postpartum, and 4.2 percent were trying to conceive. Over a quarter, 26.9 percent, were neither sterile nor used contraceptives (19.5 sexually inactive, 7.4 active). The other 36.7 percent used nonsurgical contraceptives. About 42 percent of them (15.6 of 36.7 percent) used the pill. Of the rest, 4.0 used an IUD; 4.5 the diaphragm; 6.7 had partners who used the condom; and the last 6 percent used other methods. Some IUDs, as we saw in discussion of the Dalkon Shield, have been very dangerous. (See *Dollars and Sense,* January 1983:6–7; *Statistical Abstract*, 1987:66; and Mintz, 1985a, 1985b.)

Before we turn to the discussion of abortion, let us review some important points:

■ Abortion has been practiced in most societies. Historically, women have used herbs and other methods to abort unwanted fetuses.

■ It became illegal in the United States at various times in various states throughout the nineteenth century. It was not always illegal or always condemned by religious groups.

■ Today, most Americans want abortion legal. Some of them may not want it for themselves, but they do want other women to have that option.

■ In some future society at some future time, when contraception is more effective, and women and men are equal and free of economic worries, the need for abortion may not exist. Indeed, we should work towards such a society. But until that day arrives, abortion is important for many reasons. Among these are (a) it is part of the general demand for the equality and freedom of women; (b) it avoids financial and emotional catastrophe for women; and (c) in a world filled with poor and unwanted people, it does not add to their number.

The history of abortion is long and complicated. The most recent movement to make it available to all women began in the 1960s (although it has always been practiced secretly and illegally). According to Gordon (1981b), three conditions led to the social and political pressure to legalize abortion. One reason was the increase in teenage sexual activity without an increase in contraceptive use—thus leading to more pregnancies. Another reason was that single mothers and married mothers who needed to work had to limit the size of their families. The last reason is the absence of effective and safe contraception.

In 1973, the U.S. Supreme Court legalized abortion. Since then, various anti-abortion groups have sought to limit or abolish the availability of legal abortions. For example, some state laws required that single women under eighteen years of age needed parental permission to have an abortion. These and other restrictions were overthrown by a 1983 Supreme Court decision. However, the courts have let stand laws that limit or prohibit the use of public funds for abortion. In effect, poor women cannot have legal abortions if they cannot pay for them. Thus, as of 1983, abortion was legal only for those who could afford it.

Abortion has become generally more acceptable throughout the world. From 1967 to 1982, Francome (1984) states, "Forty countries extended their grounds [that allow abortion] and only three narrowed them." (p. 1) About two-thirds of the world's women live in countries where it is permitted "on request or on a wide variety of grounds." (p. 1) Ten percent live in countries that prohibit abortion totally.

The number of legal abortions in the United States has increased from 745,000 in 1973 to a million in 1975, and 1.5 million in 1979, where it stayed until 1983 (latest available data). In 1983, women fifteen to nineteen years old had 26 percent of the abortions; twenty- to twenty-four-year olds, 36 percent; twenty-five to twenty-nine year olds, 21 percent. Nineteen percent were married women (*Statistical Abstract,* 1987:69).

In the last few years, according to McDonnell (1984), some feminists have argued that there is a "moral ambiguity," an "ambivalent, paradoxical nature" to abortion. These writers are pro-choice and believe women must have access to legal and safe abortions. But, McDonnell argues in *Not an Easy Choice: A Feminist Re-examines Abortion* (1984), that abortion also has a "moral dimension." "Nobody *likes* abortion." It inspires "profound ambivalence." (p. 28) Many women who have had abortions, some of them feminists, have begun to talk about their "ambivalence and the complex web of feelings they have about abortion." (p. 29) We need to admit and discuss openly what many women who have abortions *feel* and *experience*. And they experience *grief*. They may have no regrets, but they may feel grief and loss nevertheless. They also feel torn between their feminist principles to nurture and protect life, and the ending of a potential life. Ultimately, abortion is a necessity, an option essential for women's equality, but it is no less morally ambiguous. (See also Harrison, 1980.)

Abortion and birth control also pose moral and social dilemmas because many poor and minority women have no choice but to use them. Population and birth control movements can be racist when they seek to limit the number of children minority women have. Women who really want to continue their pregnancies but their poverty forces them to have abortions have no choice. Real choices should exist for women who need to have abortions and for women who want to continue their pregnancies and have their babies.

Sexual Harassment

In the workplace and on the streets, most women experience sexual harassment. It is consistent and pervasive. Waitresses, secretaries, models, factory workers, and professionals all experience it. It includes staring, verbal abuse and obscene suggestions, touching, attempted and actual rape. It cannot be defined precisely and completely. Gordon (1981b) says, "Much of sexual harassment is embedded in innuendo, in body language, in rude gestures—gestures that will vary by culture, social group, class, and era, as well as by individual." (p. 8) Although it cannot always be proven that a gesture was meant to harass, it must be considered so if a woman feels harassment.

It may be that some of these experiences are not perceived as harassment. At least a few waitresses have told me that they are touched or pinched, and although they did not like it, they did not see it as a serious problem. In 1983, the *Boston Globe* (July 23–30) ran a series of stories about three waitresses who did mind. They worked in a restaurant in Massachusetts where the dress code required that they wear very short shorts, which, they argued, invited customers to make comments and to touch them. They went to court and argued that the uniform they were required to wear by their employer led to the harassment they experienced. They felt they should not be required to wear the shorts. The court agreed with them, and they won the right to the jobs without the required uniform.

Depending on the definition and perception of what constitutes sexual harassment, we may find more or less of it. Various surveys show that up to 70 percent of all working women experience it. Most women I have talked to have been recipients of suggestive and often openly sexual invitations, even to the point of total strangers standing in their way and inviting them to their car. The *Guardian* (December 12, 1979:2) reported on a survey of 150 government women workers, 93 of them said they had been harassed. "Some 73 had been the object of degrading remarks or jokes, 46 had been patted or touched, and 44 had received promises of special treatment from supervisors in exchange for sex. Nine women reported being sexually assaulted."

As women enter traditionally male occupations, they experience sexual harassment in that context, too. In a study of blue-collar women (welders, carpenters, mechanics, machinists, and others) who entered those fields in the 1970s, a third of women reported to Walshok (1981) that they had experienced harassment. "This one third did *not* include all the women who reported having to cope with the general 'tits and ass' conversation. . . . It pertained only to actions, invitations, or sexual language directed specifically at the woman worker." (p. 228) Many were physically intimidated by the touching and sexual propositions. The women found that in many instances "a candid rejection of a verbal overture, an angry response to an obscene innuendo, a slap or physically aggressive reaction to physical intimidation all resulted in changed behavior." (p. 239) One woman, for example, immediately slapped a man who grabbed her breast.

Walshok thinks that "there is probably more actual physical intimidation in blue-collar contexts and more verbal innuendo in white-collar contexts." (p. 240) She finds that sexual harassment is predictable for two reasons: most men think of women as sex objects, and when they have no "other common bases for interaction and discourse" they revert to the conventional ways of relating to women which means largely sexually. (p. 231) But when blue-collar women are able to establish relationships with men on a purely work basis or on the basis of other common interests, men do not relate to them in this traditionally stereotypic manner, they become peers, and men and women talk about their common work experience, or sports, or other mutual interests.

The rise and acceptance of the concept *sexual harassment,* the consciousness and awareness of it as a problem that should not be ignored, is an important gain towards the liberation of women. Gordon (1981b) says "that women are forced to accept the image of themselves as fair game in any public space—even if for the least serious of attacks, say, whistling from across the street—maintains and reinforces women's sense of belonging at home in the family, and hence of the most basic sexual division of labor, one of the biggest sources of sexual inequality." (p. 9) Men do not consciously plot and plan to keep women at home by whistling at, propositioning, touching, pinching, and verbally abusing individual women. But when men generally feel free to perform these acts they intimidate women away from public places and force them to lead primarily domestic lives. For this reason, sexual harassment, along with rape and physical abuse at home, oppress and limit women. The struggle for the liberation of women and men must lead to the elimination of these acts, for it is only then that men will be able to relate to women as whole people, not primarily as sexual objects.

Progress toward this goal was made in 1987 when the Massachusetts Supreme Judicial Court ruled that employers are responsible for the sexual harassment of women employees "even if the employer was unaware of the harassment " (*Boston Globe,* June 14, 1987:29). In effect, the ruling held that sexual harassment amounts to discrimination. The judge who wrote the majority opinion said: "A work environment pervaded by harassment or abuse, with the resulting intimidation, humiliation, and stigmatization, poses a formidable barrier to the full participation of an individual in the workplace."

(For discussion and cases of sexual harassment, see Freeman, 1984; Russell, 1984; Sapiro, 1986; and Junkerman, 1987b.)

Sexual Assault

Many girls and women are victims of sexual assault, the most violent form of sexual harassment. Sexual assault includes child sexual abuse and incest, attempted rape, and rape. They involve the violent exercise of male power over women, and of adults over children.

In Chapter 6, we discussed incest and sexual abuse. They seem to be more prevalent than researchers and the public had previously thought. Various studies estimate that one in seven girls have been abused by a friend, a relative, a sibling, or a parent (almost always a father). Such abuse leaves deep scars that take years to heal. After years of silence, some women are writing about their experience, their trauma, and the long struggle to become whole again. (See Randall, 1987, for a recent example. See also Russell, 1984, and *Guardian,* June 3, 1987:17.)

Rape is the expected consequence of a culture that glorifies and encourages male aggression, violence, control, competition, and toughness. Conversely, women are expected to be passive, helpless, and dependent on men. Boys and men are raised to tease, intimidate, and even attack girls and women. I have watched as six- and eight-year-old boys hit, threaten, and tease girls and parents find it cute or are surprised that the girls are offended and afraid. We expect boys to be aggressive. But in societies like the Arapesh, where women and men are gentle, nonaggressive, and nurturing, there is no rape. Male aggression is the precursor of rape. (See Balkan, Berger, & Schmidt, 1980; Mead, 1935, for the Arapesh; and Hill, 1980.)

Men who rape come from all classes, races, occupations, and educations. According to Hill (1980) a woman is most likely to be raped by a "friend, acquaintance, relative, coworker, employer, date, lover, former lover, husband—quite *normal* people." (p. 58) In at least 50 percent of rape cases the victim knows the perpetrator. But it is in cases where the victim does know her attacker that she will not report it, partly because she thinks no one will believe her, partly to protect his name.

Let us look at one rape incident that Karagianis (1981b) reported. On September 7, 1980, three doctors abducted a nurse from a party in Boston and brought her to an empty summer house in a nearby town. She knew them slightly and kept thinking they would come to their senses. But they did not. They undressed her and proceeded to rape her, engaging in "a series of lurid acts" over the next several hours. She eventually reported the assault, and they were tried.

Studies show that rape is widespread and committed by *normal* men. Hills (1980) reports a study carried out in the mid-1960s at a Midwestern university. Twenty-five percent of the men said "they had engaged in coercive physical attempts at intercourse to the extent that the [woman] cried, fought, screamed, or pleaded. Doubtlessly, few of these young men would conceive of themselves as having attempted rape." (p. 62) Perhaps even many of the women would not define these actions as rape. But they are, and they are bred in the same social climate that supports male aggression. (See Freeman, 1984, and Sapiro, 1986.)

The annual victimization survey of about one hundred thousand households, for people twelve and over, estimated that one hundred and eighty thousand rapes took place in 1984. Only about half were reported to the police, and there were sixteen thousand arrests. (I could find no data on how many were *convicted*.) (See *Statistical Abstract,* 1987:152, 155, 159, 163.)

Russell (1984) found a much greater incidence of rape when she interviewed 930 adult women in San Francisco in 1978. Here are a few of her findings:

> *Forty-four percent of the 930 women interviewed had been a victim of rape or attempted rape at some time in their lives.*
>
> *When wife rape is excluded from the calculation of prevalence, 41 percent of the women reported at least one experience of rape or attempted rape.*
>
> *Fifty percent of the women who had ever been a victim of rape or attempted rape reported more than one such experience.*
>
> *Only 9.5 percent (N = 66) of the nonmarital rapes and attempted rapes experienced by these women were ever reported to the police.*
>
> *Only 2 percent (N = 13) of the nonmarital rapes and attempted rapes resulted in arrests.*
>
> *Only 1 percent (N = 6) of the nonmarital rapes and attempted rapes resulted in conviction of the perpetrators. (p. 283)*

Hills (1980) gives several reasons for women not reporting rapes. Many wish to avoid the pain of reliving the experience through reporting it to the police (who often have no sympathy for the ordeal women undergo) and testifying during the trial. Indeed, they are made to feel as if the rape was their fault, as if they were "asking for it." Others feel a sense of futility, or guilt and self-blame, or shame. Some wish to protect the attacker whom they know.

In the 1970s and 1980s police, courts, and laws began to change. In the past many victims found police (mostly men) not only unsympathetic and unconcerned, but also found themselves being blamed for the crime. Police investigators seemed to relish forcing women to relive the experience by making them repeat the telling of it. Police departments now train officers (often women) to be sensitive to the victims' emotions, pain, and fright, and not to blame them for the attack. Laws have also been changed to make convictions more possible.

Three rape trials in Massachusetts in 1984 were another indication of a changing public attitude about rape. Traditionally, defense lawyers have argued that if a woman was known to have had sex with other men (was of supposedly questionnable character), or if she had consented to sexual contact initially, or even if she had been flirtatious, the man was not guilty of rape. Juries usually accepted this argument—not in these three cases. According to Goodman (1984) these convictions meant that if a woman says no, she *means* no. As a judge said: "No longer will society accept the fact that a woman, even if she may initially act in a seductive or compromising manner, has waived her right to say 'no' at any further time." (p. 13) In another case, a woman was raped by three men with whom she had had sex in the past. The judge said: "Sexual consent between a woman and a man on one occasion does not mean the man has access to her whenever it strikes his fancy." (p. 13)

It still takes courage for a woman to report her attacker and testify in court. The nurse who was raped by the three doctors was shocked when they were convicted. Co-workers apparently disapproved of her reporting the rape, she was left traumatized by the attack, and she left her job and later needed therapy. During the trial she felt as if *her* morality was on trial. But, she said, she had to report it, to protect other women (the three doctors were gynecologists). The men were convicted and sentenced to six months in jail. This was a light sentence considering that other violent crimes have sentences of five or more years. But the judge and lawyers could not bear to sentence doctors to such long sentences—somehow their status and profession mitigated the seriousness of their crime. But the victim's fear and degradation are no less because the attackers were doctors (Karagianis, 1981a, 1981b).

The most common rationalization for rape implies or claims that women who are raped are asking for it—they want to be raped. According to this argument, if a woman wishes not to be raped, she can resist. But in no other crime of violence (where there are knives or guns or many men are together) is the victim expected to resist. Many women are forced and beaten into submission. Gang rapes, for example, are common. But even if a woman is not beaten, what woman would ask to be so degraded? Consenting sexuality cannot ever be equated with the violence of rape. It is only male aggression and the myth of women as passive and sexual that allows men to believe (or say they believe) that women are asking to be raped. (For other myths explaining rape, see Hill, 1980; Balkan, Berger & Schmidt, 1980; and Schwendinger & Schwendinger, 1983.)

Rape and the fear of rape control and oppress women. They cannot move about as freely as men because they fear male aggression. Rape as social control helps perpetuate women's subordination.

In an attempt to struggle against and overcome the fear of rape and its oppression, women (six thousand in Boston in 1981) have organized "Take Back the Night" protests. In the 1980s these marches took place after dark. Women went through city streets reclaiming their right to be out at night without fear to their persons. After six men raped a woman customer in a bar in New Bedford, Massachusetts in early 1983 (while fifteen or twenty men watched and did nothing for two hours, some even cheering on the attackers), women immediately took to the streets to protest and to again defend their right to move wherever they want. (See *Guardian,* September 19, 1981:4; March 30, 1983:7.)

Women are more likely to escape attempted rapes when they are strong and assertive, not passive. Bart and O'Brien's (1985) study compared women who escaped attempted rapes with women who did not. The women who did were more likely to have been raised to be assertive, play sports, and have nontraditional expectations. When they were attacked, they screamed, yelled, and resisted much more than the women who did not escape.

Male Violence: Battered Women

Sexual harassment and rape are means of socially controlling women, keeping them subordinate. Violence at home—husbands hitting, beating, threatening, or injuring their wives—is a third means of social control.

During a basketball game between Boston and Philadelphia in May 1982, a Philadelphia spectator hung a banner that proclaimed, "Next to beating my wife, I love beating the Celtics" (the Boston team). The next day a *Boston Globe* sports writer reported the banner as a joke, calling it a "Hall of Fame Banner." The *Globe* subsequently published four letters from very angry readers, who were appalled at the apparent amusement of the writer.

The woman's movement has not only raised our consciousness about sexual harassment but it has also educated us about violence against women in the home. Some estimates of wife abuse may be exaggerated (one estimate gave 28 million cases a year). It is also probably true that wives are beaten no more today than in the past. But rather than making us complacent, we should be aghast at our past blindness when we overlooked so much violence and fear in the home. (See Schechter, 1982, and Caplow et al., 1982.)

What counts as abuse? Broken bones and bruised bodies do, certainly. But so should slaps and other physical force and intimidation. Depending on its definition, up to two million may be battered every year. In 1974, the Boston police received eighteen thousand calls reporting or complaining about wife-beating. These are not a few and isolated cases. Women are kicked, punched, cut with knives, broken bottles or razors, burned, and hit with belts. (See Schechter, 1982, and Balkan, Berger & Schmidt, 1980.)

Like sexual harassment and rape, battered women are found in all classes, races, and educational levels. They are not only found among the poor and working class. They may be less visible in affluent neighborhoods and suburbs, but they exist.

Many myths exist—in popular belief, in psychology and in sociology—about the causes of wife abuse. Some say women provoke their husbands. But the supposed provocation is often no more than refusing to submit to the whim and will of a husband. Other explanations also blame the victims as the direct or indirect instigators of the violence visited upon them.

The fundamental fact, however, is that a husband uses violence to impose his will on his wife. Wife beating has existed without much condemnation for centuries in the West. Indeed, it has almost been expected that men will control their wives by beating them, and that women will accept this beating as their lot in life. Pogrebin (1975) revealed this ingrained cultural expectation and acceptance by staging a series of fights between several couples. Bystanders intervened when men were being assaulted by other men or by women and when women hit women. No one interfered, however, when the male actors were hitting women actors. We may surmise that observers saw this as a marital dispute and felt that a husband has the right to hit his wife.

Men are raised to be aggressive and controlling toward women who are considered the legitimate subjects of their control and violence. Women are raised to be men's servants, to cater to their needs. Women are generally powerless and have few material resources. Thus, the culture of male violence and control and women's powerlessness and economic dependence combine to give rise to violence against women.

Studies have shown that women who had been beaten for years stay home for three reasons: (a) they are afraid that even if they leave their husbands will find and beat them; (b) they have no money to support them-selves and no place to go; and (c) they have a poor self-image, taught them by the culture that blames women and glorifies male aggression. Thus, we see again that women are beaten because of cultural traditions, socialization of men and women, and economic dependence.

!Kung women are not beaten by their husbands nor are they economi-cally dependent on them. Moreover, the culture disapproves of aggression and thus men are not socialized to control and beat women. Shostak (1981) says that life is also mostly public, in the presence of others, and "arguments between husbands and wives occur within sight of their neighbors. If a fight becomes physical, other people are always there and ready to intervene" (child abuse is rare for the same reason). (p. 239)

In addition to women's economic dependence and the male culture of aggression and control, the relative isolation of a family from community life also encourages wife abuse. Balkan, Berger, and Schmidt (1980) also argue that men who are frustrated in their jobs, who are powerless and failures in the capitalist culture of success, express their rage and frustration by beating their wives. There may be some truth to this argument, but we must still ask why they would take out their anger and rage against people who are not the cause of it. Is it not women's economic dependence and the culture that allows the violence against them?

Traditionally, police and courts did not intervene to protect abused wives. Indeed, they often blamed the women and assumed they deserved to be hit. Men were rarely arrested for assault. The women's movement led to some changes. They created more shelters for abused women (see below), and they struggled to create a new consciousness that abused women are victims who deserve legal protection. Public outrage about murdered women and successful lawsuits against police departments for not protecting them led some states and cities to institute procedures that require police to arrest men who assault their wives or lovers. The states of Connecticut and Pennsylvania and the cities of Seattle, Duluth (Minnesota), and Quincy (Massachusetts), among others, require police to arrest men who assault their wives. The *Boston Globe* (June 9, 1987) reported that in Duluth, mandatory arrest led to a "47 percent reduction in the number of repeat calls after the law was changed." (p. 1) In another *Boston Globe* (January 1, 1986) story a wife who shot her husband dead was not indicted. The grand jury concluded she did so in self-defense. He had abused her repeatedly for four years, and just before she shot him he had "punctured her ear-drum, fractured her nose, tried to choke her and left her with multiple bruises." (p. 19)

But much more change and education of the police are needed. The *Boston Globe* (November 3, 1986:18) reported that in Massachusetts, for example, in 1986, it took the murder of a woman by her husband, whom the court had refused to prohibit from going near his wife, to expose the general lack of enforcement of the domestic abuse prevention act. A report, written in December 1985 but kept quiet for months, concluded that the police and the courts had failed miserably in enforcing the law. Women who sought court protection because their husbands had slashed them with broken bottles, cut them with knives, kicked them in the head, burned them, beaten them unconscious, and so on, were berated by judges for wasting their time. In 1987, a woman was shot to death by her husband after failing repeatedly to get police protection. Six months before she was killed, she and her family filed six police reports that her husband had beaten her and kicked in the walls of her apartment. "Two days before her death, police took her telephone report that bricks were being thrown through her window at 1 A.M. and 6 A.M., but they did not send any officers to investigate" (*Boston Globe*, June 29, 1987:1).

Along with a new consciousness, the women's movement has also established shelters for battered women. There are approximately three hundred shelters in the United States. Some have been established and are run by women's groups, others by more traditional social agencies. But even these hardly suffice. In 1980, shelters in New York City had to turn away 85 percent of the callers seeking refuge. Similar lack of enough places for women who need them exists almost everywhere (Schecter, 1982).

These, then, are several causes of women's oppression that must be overcome for women to be truly liberated: the medical system must lose its power over women; women must gain full control of their reproductive rights; and sexual harassment, rape, and abuse at home must end.

Work and Politics

Women have become a permanent part of the labor force. But while more women than ever, in fact a majority of women, hold paying jobs, women receive much less pay than men and hold mostly sex-typed positions. They still shoulder almost all of the housework and are largely absent from top social, political, and economic positions.

Women in the Labor Force

Tables 12.1 and 12.2 leave no doubt that women have steadily become a permanent part of the work force. Whereas only 20 percent of women age sixteen years and over were working outside the home in 1900, 55.6 percent were in 1987, and 56.7 percent in 1988. In 1987, women comprised about 44 percent of the labor force. The increase in the percentage of married women who hold jobs or are officially unemployed (looking for work) outside the home has been even more dramatic, from 5 percent in 1900, to 25 percent in 1950, 55.6 percent in 1987, and 56.7 percent in 1988. More specifically, in 1987, 53.1 percent of married women with children under six held jobs, and so did 63.8 percent of those with children between the ages of six and seventeen (U.S. Department of Labor, 1987h, 1988).

By now, it is obvious that in fact and attitude women are no longer confined to the home. The working woman has become a permanent fixture of the social landscape. For women as well as for men, economic security, social satisfaction, and a positive self-image now require work outside the home. This is as true for middle-aged women who previously stayed at home to raise children as for young, unmarried women. Many women in their forties and fifties who no longer have children living at home and who may have lost their husbands either through death or divorce are now beginning to search for new ways to structure their lives. They are going back to school and looking for work out of both economic necessity and psychic survival. (See Jacobs, 1979; Rubin, 1979; and *Institute for Social Research Newsletter,* 1983.)

Women's Pay

The median weekly income of full-time, working women was 69 percent of the median income for full-time men in 1987. This discrepancy was around 60

TABLE 12.1
Labor Force Participation Rates by Sex (participants aged sixteen years old and over)

Year	Women	Men
1900	20.0%	85.7%
1920	22.7	84.6
1940	28.5	82.6
1950	33.9	86.8
1960	37.1	82.4
1970	42.8	79.2
1975	43.7	77.3
1980	51.5	77.4
1983	52.6	76.8
1987	55.6	76.0
1988	56.5	—

Szymanski, 1976; *Statistical Abstract,* 1987:376; and U.S. Department of Labor, 1983a; 1987f; 1988

TABLE 12.2
Labor Force Participation Rate of Married Women,
Husband Present

Year	Percent
1900	5.0
1940	17.0
1950	25.0
1960	32.0
1978	47.0
1983	52.0
1987	55.6
1988	56.7

Caplow et al., 1982:306, and U.S. Department of Labor, 1983a; 1987f

percent during the 1960s and most of the 1970s, and 65 percent in 1980. Table 12.3 shows that this earnings gap exists in all occupational categories (Center for Popular Economics, 1986:1).

Women have narrowed the earnings gap in relation to men partly because men's earnings have decreased. As we saw in chapters 8 and 9, more men now work in low-paying jobs than did a few years ago. Service jobs pay much less than manufacturing jobs do. The closing of the women/men earnings ratio has come about partly because men are making *less* money, not because women are making *more* money.

The figures above apply to *weekly earnings of full-time workers*. But during the course of a year, parental responsibilities force many women to work part time or take time off work. When we compare *yearly* incomes of all women who work with all men who work, women make much less than 69 percent of men's incomes. In 1984, women's median yearly income was 44 percent of men's, and a mean (average) 49 percent of men's. Fully 62.6 percent

TABLE 12.3
Median Usual Weekly Earnings of Full-time Wage and Salary Workers
by Occupation and Sex, 1987

	Women	Men	Women/Men Ratio
Managerial and professional	$433	$631	.69
Technical, sales, and administrative support	288	451	.64
Service occupations	198	292	.68
Precision production, craft, and repair	304	426	.71
Operators, fabricators, and laborers	224	336	.67

U.S. Department of Labor, 1987e

of women made under $10,000 during 1984, compared to 33.7 percent of men (*Statistical Abstract,* 1987:441).

Why do women make so much less money than men? There are at least three principal reasons. First, women are concentrated in less skilled and lower-paying occupations. Second, their socialization, training, education, and counseling direct them to certain low-paying jobs. Third, they tend to have fewer years of work experience. But even after these considerations are taken into account, at most only half of the gap is explained. Simply put, women get paid less even when they do the same work as men. In most professions and occupations, men make more than women who do the same work. (See Table 12.3.) The capitalist economy thus exploits women by limiting them to a few low-paying, stereotyped jobs and by paying them less even when they perform the same work as men.

In order to narrow the gap, women have begun to demand comparable pay for comparable worth. Let us look at one example. A woman who is the head of a municipal public library needs a graduate degree. She supervises fifty workers. A man who is the head of the city water department also needs a graduate degree. He also supervises fifty workers. They should make the same salary, but usually they do not. The man usually makes much more money. We can make many similar comparisons.

Why do men make more money in different jobs? Is their work that much more valuable? While it is difficult to measure comparable worth, it is necessary to examine and challenge traditional wage differences. How do we compare the value of the work performed by bank tellers and typists (almost all women) with the value of the work performed by machinists (almost all men)? Women lawyers may in time argue their comparable worth and make the same as men lawyers, but how can women prove their worth in occupations that are almost totally held by them?

Women clerical workers at Yale University unionized and went on strike in the fall of 1984. They won their main demand for comparable worth pay. Women in other workplaces are challenging traditional assumptions about the worth of men's and women's work. Although other changes are also necessary, comparable worth improves women's economic conditions. (See Amott & Matthaei, 1984; *Dollars and Sense,* May 1985:16–17; September 1986:9–11.)

Another reason women make less income is that they are largely non-union workers, such as secretaries, clerks, health workers, and maids. These people, however, have begun to organize and form unions. Union workers make much more money than those not in unions. In 1985, median weekly earnings of full-time workers was $347 for those in unions, but $262 (32 percent less) for those not in unions (*Dollars and Sense,* September 1986:22).

The Feminization of Poverty

Job and income discrimination is especially significant for women who support their families alone. Table 12.4 shows that when we compare married-

TABLE 12.4
**Families with Wage and Salary Earners,
by Type of Family, Median Weekly Wage, and Salary Earnings, 1987**

	Median Weekly Earnings
1. a. Families maintained by women	$313
b. Married couple families	639
a/b ratio	(.49)
2. a. Families maintained by women, one earner	267
b. Married-couple families, one earner (husband)	476
a/b ratio	(.56)
3. a. Families maintained by women, two or more earners	511
b. Married-couple families, two or more earners	767
a/b ratio	(.67)

U.S. Department of Labor, 1987g

couple families with families headed by women, the latter live very poorly. Study the table carefully. Except for female-maintained families with two or more earners, most of them make only about half of what married-couple families make. The reason they make so little is because the women who support these families hold service, clerical, and sales jobs—all of which are low paying.

Low wages, part-time jobs, former husbands who pay little or no child support, and shamefully low welfare payments have led to the feminization of poverty. Well over half of the poor are women and children. In 1985, 12.6 percent of all families fell below the poverty line. (The 1985 income of $11,000 as the upper level for an urban family of four, set by the government, is very low and excludes millions of families who live on the edge of poverty.) Of families with no husband, 33.5 were poor. Most significant, 53.6 percent of *families with no husband and children under eighteen years old* were poor. (*Statistical Abstract*, 1987:442, 443). (See also Handler, 1983; Stallard, Ehrenreich, & Sklar, 1983; Goldberg & Kremen, 1987; and *Guardian*, February 5, 1986:2.)

Divorce drives many women into poverty. Bader (1987) quotes from and summarizes Arendell's *Mothers and Divorce:*

> *"There are a lot of us women out here, and we need some attention. I work full time and bring home less than $10,000 a year, and four of us have to eat on that amount of money. We're not getting equal pay with the guys, even for the same work. And the union isn't even fighting for us. The guys work outside, so they get more than double what we get inside."*
>
> *Terry Arendell's new book gives voice to the thousands of formerly middle-class women whose families are economically devastated by divorce. Putting*

aside, at least for a moment, the emotional havoc of marital dissolution, the facts are staggering: middle-class women experience a 73% loss of income, while men experience a 42% increase in their standard of living within a year of divorcing. (p. 20)

Women's Occupations

Although there has been some movement of women into traditionally male occupations, most women still work in a few female jobs. A 1978 study by the U.S. Department of Labor shows 69 percent of working women holding "female" jobs, 21 percent nonstereotyped jobs, and 10 percent holding "male" occupations. In 1985, 62 percent worked in sales, clerical, and service work areas, 5.3 percent were elementary and secondary school teachers, and 1.8 percent were sewers and stitchers—the same 69 percent as in 1978. In Table 12.5, we see many jobs that are almost entirely male or female. By studying the table carefully, we see that over 90 percent of the secretaries, nurses, and bank tellers are women, and over 90 percent of the engineers, machinists, truck drivers, carpenters, and mechanics are men. There has been very little change from 1970 to 1985. (Bielby & Baron, 1986; *Guardian,* March 3, 1982:5–40; Grossman, 1980; and Nussbaum, 1981.)

Walshok (1981), in her book about blue-collar women (machinists, carpenters, mechanics, and other crafts) notes that most women do not work in nursing, teaching, social work, medicine, or similar professions. They are clerks, secretaries, and blue-collar workers, and if they change their traditional work roles, they are more likely to become skilled and craft blue-collar workers than doctors or lawyers. But as Table 12.5 shows, so far very few have entered those skilled blue-collar occupations.

Women are socialized and directed toward certain occupations. This socialization begins early in life. White and Brinkerhoff (1981) carried out a survey in Nebraska in 1979 to learn at what age boys and girls begin working and what they do. Over 80 percent do some household work at ages six to nine. Between fourteen and seventeen years of age, 75 percent hold paying jobs. But they do sex-typed work. As they get older, girls do kitchen work and boys yard work and take out the garbage.

Let us look at some details that White and Brinkerhoff provide:

| | *Ages 6–9* | |
	Boys	*Girls*
Outdoor	38%	21%
Kitchen	33	61
Housework	35	42

When we look at fourteen- to seventeen-year-olds, the division is sharper.

	Boys	*Girls*
Outdoor	80%	36%
Kitchen	22	72
Housework	28	79

The division of work around the house by gender is very pronounced by the mid-teens. Such socialization directs women to service and clerical occupations.

Those few women who applied to medical schools in the past were not discriminated against by admissions committees, according to Cole (1986). Rather, it was socialization that pushed women to nursing and other female occupations. Role models, books, teachers, parents, and many others discouraged women from applying to medical school. There has been some change in the last few years and more women are applying to medical schools. According

TABLE 12.5
Women as Percent of All Workers in Occupations, 1981 and 1985

	1981	1985
Secretaries	99.3	98.4
Dental assistants	97.9	99.0
Registered nurses	96.8	95.1
Sewers and stitchers	96.7	—
Bank tellers	94.0	93.0
Bookkeepers	91.2	91.5
Health Service	89.3	89.9
Cashiers	86.4	83.1
Waiters	85.1	84.0
Retail sales clerks	71.3	68.5
Teachers (except college and university)	70.6	73.0
Food service	66.5	62.5
Assemblers	52.7	—
Bus drivers [mostly school buses?]	47.3	—
College and university teachers	35.3	35.2
Sales reps—manufacturing	16.0	—
Lawyers, Judges	14.0	18.2
Physicians, Osteopaths	13.9	17.2
Lathe operatives	5.0	—
Engineers	4.3	6.7
Machinists	3.6	—
Truck drivers	2.7	2.1
Mechanical engineers	2.5	3.7
Carpenters	1.9	1.2
Mechanics	1.9	3.1
Data processing equipment repairs	.7	—

U.S. Department of Labor 1982b; *Dollars and Sense*, April 1982: 16; and *Statistical Abstract*, 1987:385–386 to one story in the *Boston Globe* (June 1, 1987), fewer women are entering nursing and more women are applying to medical school, 36 percent of all applicants in 1987, compared to 10 percent in 1967. (pp. 41–42)

Many of the women who become carpenters and mechanics have non-traditional childhoods. In Walshok's (1981) study many of the women came "from rural and small-town environments where they had freedom to come and go and [had] access to tools and 'outdoor' activities." (p. 248) But perhaps even more importantly, they were given responsibilities early in life—for themselves, for siblings, and for the household and even family business. Most also had mothers employed outside the home. These experiences, and later financial needs, allowed them to consider and apply for better-paying skill and craft positions.

But socialization is not the only reason women are concentrated in only a few occupations. A study by the U.S. Civil Rights Commission, released in November 1982, argues clearly and unequivocally that employer bias and discrimination explain women's (and blacks') confinement in low-paying and stereotyped jobs. There is a consistent and persistent job bias against women (*Boston Globe,* November 24, 1982:3).

For example, women still face discrimination in becoming firefighters. Chicago, Berkeley, and the state of Florida are among the very few places that recruit women for their fire departments. In 1986, out of 317,000 firefighters in the United States, only about 1,100 were women. (See *Guardian,* April 8, 1987:2, and *Statistical Abstract,* 1987:280.)

Sex discrimination is profitable for corporations. By paying the millions of secretaries, clerks, and others considerably lower wages than they pay men, they can make more profits. Thus, they have a vested interest in perpetuating sex-typed jobs and discrimination. Corporations did not create the sex stereotypes about women's work, but they are reinforcing and perpetuating them. By concentrating women in jobs that require passivity, nurturing, and caring of children and men, corporations are a primary cause in the continuing oppression of women. They do not want to pay women more money, and by keeping occupations mostly or all female (or male), they insure low pay. Historically, as occupations have become more male (such as secondary education) the pay has increased, and as they have become more female (secretarial, as compared to a hundred years ago), the pay has decreased (Szymanski, 1976).

Telephone operators are an example. The original operators of the 1880s were all men. Soon the companies switched to young, unmarried women whom they paid a third of what they had men. The men lost their jobs and the women were exploited (*Dollars and Sense,* June 1987:4).

Finally, many women's occupations are becoming more dangerous. As we noted in Chapters 3 and 8, new office equipment, such as video display terminals, word processors, and so on, are increasingly being linked to illness and disease. There is also psychological and emotional pressure on women as their work becomes more routine, mechanized, and controlled by others. The office has begun to resemble the factory (Chavkin, 1984).

Family Life

Women who work outside the house still do most of the housework. Personal observations and studies leave no doubt that working women now hold two jobs. A 1974 study in Sweden shows that working women on the average do at least three times as much housework as men (Adams & Winston, 1980). They spend over five times as much time on laundry, twelve times more time taking care of clothes, and three times more time cooking. Only with shopping do men approach equal amounts of time—1.56 hours for women and 1 hour for men.

In a 1978 Muncie, Indiana ("Middletown") survey the same conditions are revealed (Caplow et al., 1982). In 45 percent of the families, people report that the wife does all the housework; in 40 percent of the families, she does most of it; in only 8 percent do respondents say husbands and wives share it equally (I think observation would show that women actually still do most of it, even in these families); in 2 percent, the husband does more, and a third person does housework in 5 percent of the families. Most of these families report that they never argue about who should do the housework, about a third have "occasional arguments," and 5 percent "disagree frequently." Housework is still women's work, popular stories about househusbands and sharing notwithstanding. (For other studies that show working wives do most of the housework, see Spitze, 1986, and Ross, 1987.)

Despite new household technology, women do as much housework as ever. For example, washing machines mean that today women wash clothes much more often than their grandmothers did; they spend as much time on laundry as their grandmothers. Housewives spend about fifty hours a week on housework, working wives about thirty-five hours (Cowan, 1983).

Women who hold no outside jobs primarily identify themselves as housewives. Some say that they put their family over their own aspirations, jobs, careers, and interests. (These women often face severe identity crises in their forties when their children leave and, sometimes, their husbands). Even most working wives see themselves more as housewives than as workers. Clearly, as we see in Muncie, Indiana, the cultural expectation is that women are in charge of the house and do the cleaning, cooking, and other chores. The blue-collar women who talked with Walshok (1981) told her that for them their job is central to their lives. They identify more with their job, and their performance and competence in it, than they do with housework. Homemaking is no more material to them than it is to men. (See *Boston Globe*, April 2, 1981:41, and Jacobs, 1979).

How has family life been affected by women working outside the home? Clearly, the family has more money. But there are other benefits. Most women enjoy escaping from the house, even to routine jobs, because it provides them the social contacts and interaction that are missing when they are confined and isolated in their homes. According to Caplow and others (1982), since women began to enter the work force around 1900, "the family and other institutions have had time to adjust" and husbands and wives report no widespread unhappiness. (p. 100) Nevertheless, it is denying the obvious by saying there has been little or no effect. Working mothers, especially single working mothers, lead very hectic lives. They may, and most do, manage, but the burden of this management is on them. When husbands and wives return home in the evening, wives usually rush to prepare dinner, while husbands usually watch TV or read the papers. Women may learn to manage and endure, but do they prefer working two jobs? (See Rubin, 1976; Walshok, 1981; and Pleck, 1980.)

Government and other institutions have done little to relieve the burden of working mothers (fathers too, we should note). As we have seen in Chapters 6 and 7, child-care policy and facilities are very inadequate for the existing needs of working parents. (See Adams & Winston, 1980; *Guardian,* December 1, 1982:11; and Foreman, 1980.)

In a letter to the *Nation,* Durbin (1987) summarizes the complex and difficult lives of women who work and raise children.

> *Mothers in even the most liberated households are given the lion's share of responsibility for children. They accept it, as far as I can tell, because of the bond that has developed in those nine months and during the birth process, and because if they don't, who will? Today, society gives them little or no support, but plenty of hostility. If the mother worked before, she is looked down on if she doesn't return to work immediately. If she stays at home, she is wasting her education, or if she is a welfare mother, she is getting fat at society's expense. Good, reliable, loving child care is next to impossible to find, but any child care eats up most of what a mother earns. If she tries to make flexible work arrangements, she is not serious about her job. She doesn't get raises or promotions. If she expects the father home at reasonable hours to participate in nurturing, she is harming his career when he is trying to meet "his" new financial responsibilities. Besides, if she is breast-feeding, she is shutting him out. Let it be known, I am not dumping on the beloved father of my children; I believe our child-and-mother-hating society is placing those pressures on him, too. The Pope and the President and their right-to-life cronies want us to have children; they are not about to help us take care of them with any financial or emotional support. (p. 38)*

(For more discussion on the lives and choices of women who work and have children and families, see Pollitt, 1983; Borman, Quarm, & Gideonse, 1984; and Rivers, 1986.)

Power, Leadership, and Politics

Even though women have become a large part of the American work force, powerful leadership positions in corporations, educational institutions, unions, and politics are still largely held by males. Their continuing identity as housewives and the burden of job and housework provide little motivation and less time and energy for the demands of leadership.

In education, women make up a majority of teachers but not of principals—only 2 percent are women. School boards too are mostly male. While women are over 50 percent of the population, they are only 10 percent of school board members (Ballantine, 1983).

In politics, too, women are largely absent. Only four women have served as cabinet members in the last five administrations in Washington. In Congress, in 1986 only 22 of 435 Representatives were women, and only 2 of the 100 Senators were women. In 1986, 14.8 percent of state legislators were women, up from 8 percent in 1975 (*Statistical Abstract*, 1987:237, 241).

In unions, women make up 30 percent of the membership but only 5 percent of higher offices. In business, in 1947 women occupied 5 percent of the managerial and administrative positions. It was only 6 percent in 1981—"5 percent in lower and middle management and one percent in upper-level management"—while they made up over 40 percent of the work force (Leavitt, 1983, p. xi). (See *Guardian*, April 28, 1982:2; Leavitt, 1982; Ritzer & Walczak, 1986.)

There are many reasons for the exclusion of women from leadership positions—extra burden of domestic responsibility and discrimination are among the most salient. An additional one is the friendship ties men form in school and at work which exclude women. An example is the Bohemian Grove, an exclusive men's club on the West Coast where the most powerful ruling-class men (in business and politics) meet in a summer camp and socialize. (See Chapter 10.) A Grove policy excludes women, and the courts have allowed their exclusion to continue (*Guardian*, February 18, 1981:11).

(For the social and economic conditions of women before and during socialism in China, the Soviet Union, Cuba, East Germany, and other socialist societies, see Gordon, 1973; Davin, 1975; Diamond, 1975; Marquit, 1978; Randall, 1981; Molyneux, 1982; Goodman, 1985; and *Guardian*, February 11, 1987:10–11. They show that women have made great progress toward equality, but they need to struggle for many more changes before they can achieve full equality.)

The Future: Equality without Power

Women can be equal to men only in societies where all people are equal to each other. Only in egalitarian societies, societies without classes and power inequalities, can women be liberated. Only there can women and men struggle together to change sex roles and redefine family, work, and politics.

Roles

Male and female roles must change. Women need to be more assertive and men more gentle, cooperative, and caring. Neither men nor women should be aggressive, competitive, and controlling. Sex roles cannot change if only one sex changes. Men and women should copy the positive aspects of the other's role and shed their negative ones. Both sexes need to work, to do housework, to raise children, and to be assertive and nurturing.

Both sexes need to cry and express emotions. We learn from our children. Harrison (1974) relates a story a teacher told her about a girl who went to her doctor's office: "A little boy who was getting an injection was crying. The boy's father said, 'Boys have to be brave.' Jenny . . . said, 'I don't think boys have to be brave all the time, boys can cry.' The nurse humored her and said, 'That's right, honey, girls are really stronger, aren't they?' And Jenny said, 'No, girls aren't stronger; girls can cry and girls can be brave. Boys can cry and boys can be brave. It's what you feel like.' Jenny is seven." (p. 169)

Day care in itself is not freeing to women as a group. In all day-care facilities, in all societies, almost all (if not all) the staff who work there are women. Individual women may be relieved of some child care, but it is still women's work. Women are still seen as nurturers and caretakers. Women *and* men must care for children (at home and in day-care centers), women *and* men must clean, wash, iron, and cook. Sex roles need to be eliminated.

More and more women are attaining success in the corporate world by emulating the worst aspects of the male role. Jeannette Reddish Scollard, vice-president of a large corporation, wrote a book on how women should behave in order to succeed. Longcope (1983) says the book's message is "if the corporate Jack can be an impersonal bore, so can the corporate Jill." (p. 51) What does this mean? According to Scollard, all of a woman's (as now a man's) actions should be controlled and manipulated to cast a business-like image. "Almost nothing in the life of an executive woman is random. Every act is planned. Every minute is planned. Even fun and sleep are planned." (p. 51) Single women, for example, should never date carpenters, rock band performers, or salesmen below the vice-president level. Broadcast personalities and younger executives are acceptable dates.

Other hints lead to a perfect replication of the successful male executive: carry a briefcase, not a purse; wear understated clothes; befriend other women only after business hours; do not display family pictures; never admit to menstrual cramps; and learn to discuss sports and military affairs with men (who are socialized to play war-like games). Of course, the corporate woman can still be "feminine." She can do as Scollard does and rush home two or three days a week and cook her husband's favorite meal. This is surely a perverse form of equality. Both men and women remain slaves to a competitive, impersonal, and superficial existence. The road up the corporate ladder is not the road to women's or men's liberation.

Some popular movies of the late 1980s still show women in traditional, stereotyped roles. In *Fatal Attraction, Moonstruck,* and *Broadcast News,* among others, strong women are unhappy, in trouble, or psychopathic. According to Rapping (1988), "The nuclear family and old fashioned romantic love of the kind that leads to 'happily ever after' are presented as more or less unproblematic ideals. Independent women, for their part, are portrayed as seriously in trouble, in one way or another, for reasons that range from garden variety Freudian female neurosis to downright psychopathic evil." (p. 11)

Creating Sex Equality Today

Economic Equality

One of our goals should be for men and women to have equal work opportunities. There is absolutely no evidence, historical or contemporary, that shows women or men are unable to perform any task. Exploration of the traditional division of labor shows no physical, psychic, or temperamental superiority or inferiority in either sex that enables men or women to perform any task better than the other sex.

All jobs must be truly open to all women and men. Women should be able to become doctors, mechanics, carpenters, to hold any occupation. Conversely, men must also be able to be nurses, clerks, or secretaries. In a future ideal society, children will be raised without any gender-typed expectations and stereotypes. As adults, they will then be able to occupy themselves with whatever fits their temperaments, interests, and abilities regardless of their sex. Along the way we must come to understand that every job is equally important—whether it is raising food or making clothes or typing letters or ministering to others' physical or emotional needs. No job warrants higher prestige than any other job.

Along with equal opportunity goes equal pay for equal work. We need to begin now to reduce the huge income gaps between the very wealthy and the poor. We need to give women and men holding the same job equal pay and to institute the principle of comparable worth. The last is necessary because it will take decades before all jobs are truly open to all women, and working women need pay equity before that point.

Women cannot reach full equality in capitalist economies, where corporations depend on and exploit women workers. Occupational equality will eventually occur only where all jobs are considered equally necessary and valuable for the society's survival and thus rewarded equally, and where workers truly run workplaces for the common good, not individual profit. Certainly, women gain no equality when corporations promote a few women to top management positions and exploit the rest of their women workers with low salaries and wages (Moore & Marsis, 1985).

Sharing Power

A society where workers and people generally run workplaces and other institutions collectively, with no bosses, and where all jobs are equally open and actually occupied by women and men, surely this is a society where women share equally in deciding how the products of their labor will be used. But sharing power extends beyond the workplace. When women and men share housework, childrearing, and other roles (see below), women will also have autonomy and freedom within families, households, and communities. The !Kung, Montagnais, and other women do not need to become rulers and bosses in order to decide how the products of their work are to be used; they live in egalitarian societies where no one rules—or, where all rule. An economy and a society where workers' control and community control prevailed would allow women and men to determine what happens to them—how they eat, how they live, what they do.

Living without Violence

There is no doubt that in the United States today (elsewhere too) men use violence—implied, threatened, or actual—in the home and in public to control and dominate women. For the most part, women are economically dependent on men, and men and women are socialized to expect and accept male domination. The long history of patriarchy has sanctioned violence as one way for men to control women, inside and outside the home. Schechter (1982) says male violence is "an historical expression of male domination manifested within the family and currently reinforced by institutions, economic arrangements, and sexist division of labor within capitalist society." (p. 209)

Everyday observations and discussions with many women have made it clear to me that women simply do not have as much freedom of movement as men. Men may avoid certain places at certain times, but generally they may go anywhere they want at any time. As a woman student pointed out to me, when men do fear violence, they fear other men, not women.

Women will feel free to move about when they reach economic and occupational equality, when male socialization does not encourage violence and control, and when there is more social life in public places. Our examination of the !Kung and others shows the need for all three. Economic equality is obvious and is an absolute prerequisite. It exists among the few !Kung left. Socialization should be the same for both sexes (see below), as it is for !Kung children. And violence in the home and in public places ends when we reorganize our social life. When families do not lead isolated lives, men cannot beat women. When we populate the streets with many people, and when these streets are in communities where neighbors know and care about each other, women will feel safe to walk the streets.

Equal Political Participation

The traditional absence of women from politics and leadership positions in many societies may be solved by an equal number of women and men holding the few powerful roles in society. That would make a few women equal to a few men, but it would still leave most women and most men relatively powerless. The other alternative points to a society without leaders, run by all people participating daily in their neighborhoods, schools, workplaces, and other institutions. Worker and community groups would eventually give both men and women equal opportunity to enter political life.

Given the present way we are socialized, however, it is likely men would continue to dominate even these new forms of political and community participation. Sociological studies have revealed that there is an informal control mechanism at work in groups. Women in civil rights, anti-war, and other groups of the 1960s and early 1970s found that despite the egalitarian ideology of the groups, men dominated. Thus, constant awareness and vigilance are necessary to prevent male control. Children and adults must learn not to dominate, to let all people speak and participate equally in making group decisions. There is a tendency and a temptation for a few men, or even one man, to dominate in groups where no formal leadership exists. For gender equality, for equality of all people, it is necessary to constantly struggle against domination by a few men. The day may come when our children will be socialized in such a way that they will value the equal participation of every one in making decisions, but we need to be vigilant until that day arrives.

Autonomy of Person and Body

Economic equality, equal political participation, and freedom from male violence would make women more autonomous. But for women to be autonomous in their body and person, they need to engage in further struggles in the areas of sexuality, marriage, and divorce.

Premartial and marital sexuality have apparently become more frequent, more varied, and more satisfying for more people than they supposedly were in the last one hundred to two hundred years. This perception is probably justified. But problems persist, for women and men.

Some people within our society still hold the idea that sex is evil and something to fear. Other people, however, exploit sex to sell products and titillate. These people sell sex, promising more happiness than sexuality can deliver to people unhappy with meaningless work and social isolation. Pornography degrades women and leaves men unfulfilled. And at least for some women, guilt still haunts their sexual lives as the patriarchal double standard lives in their consciousness (Rubin, 1976).

These and other problems need to be addressed and discussed openly before women and men can lead satisfying sexual lives, where sex is a pleasurable human act but does not promise to provide the ultimate meaning for us. Meaningful work and a full social life are equally important.

Sex education and contraception are now more common and available, but millions of unwanted pregnancies still take place. Teenagers still do not talk much to their parents about sex and contraceptives. Although anthropologists have not discovered how, preindustrial peoples somehow prevented unwanted pregnancies. Women today control their bodies more than women did a few decades ago, but many still have unwanted babies because of fear, guilt, or ignorance. Safe, effective, and easily accessible contraception (for men too) should be a goal. In the early and middle 1980s, we have seen a resurgence of patriarchal and religious fundamentalism that seeks to deny women the right to control their bodies.

Since love does not insure marital happiness, and since male socialization and patriarchal attitudes still lead many men to dominate their wives, divorce is essential for female equality. We have seen that it has existed wherever women have been equal to men. Today divorces are easy to obtain, which means women can now leave unhappy marriages. They need not stay with men who dominate them economically, psychically, or physically. But divorce is partly hollow and meaningless for the equality of women so long as women are not economically autonomous. Statistics clearly show that divorced women face poverty or financial difficulties. Until the economy, child-care arrangements, and other institutions also change, divorce is only a partial guarantee of equality.

Sharing Lives

Biology   Men and women are more alike than they are different. Rubin (1975) notes that "far from being an expression of natural differences, exclusive gender identity is the suppression of natural similarities." (p. 180) It is a socially created reality that represses the male in women and the female in men. It is not physical strength and aggression that have allowed men to dominate, rather, it is their *verbal* aggressiveness. This characteristic has made it possible for men to hold decision-making roles. Verbal aggressiveness is a learned, not a biological, trait.

Socialization   If we accept the notion that aggressive verbal behavior is a learned trait rather than an inherent one, we must then examine how this trait is learned and how we may be able to change the learning process. Like the !Kung, boys and girls should undergo the same kind of socialization. While we work for economic and political equality, we must teach our children the same values irrespective of sex. Sex stereotypes must be erased at the same time we are trying to change the social realities that partly underlie those stereotypes. Changing children's literature to reflect women doing nontraditional work is insufficient if women *do* mostly female work.

Our focus tends toward changing *women's* roles and personalities. Women do need to become more assertive, strong, and confident, but men must also become more emotional, nurturing, and cooperative. Neither sex should be violent, aggressive, competitive, controlling, or power hungry—these values are oppressive.

Housework   It is not enough that women gain equality at work and in politics. Women should not have to shoulder all of the domestic responsibility. Nor is equality achieved when a few affluent couples free themselves from housework and childrearing by hiring full-time maids and paying them low wages. This exploits some women and does not liberate most of us (Hertz, 1987).

Sharing housework raises some important issues. First, how should we view domestic responsibility and work responsibility? Obviously, if a person is working sixty to seventy hours a week they can't share equally in taking care of children, cooking, cleaning, or other domestic work. We need to look at how much time we should devote to each of these responsibilities and see them as *equally* important.

Second, what is our life style like? Are we living in a house that is too large for us? Would living in a smaller house ease our family's domestic burden? Rather than having a big yard, we might choose to share a common playground that is cared for cooperatively.

Third, what does sharing housework mean? Even reduced housework would involve some cooking, cleaning, doing dishes, laundry, maintaining the house, shopping, some outside work, and child care. Would sharing mean some system where each adult performs about half of each task? For example, one person cooks and the other person washes the dishes. Or, would it mean that X number of tasks are divided in half, with each person choosing what they like to do, so long as the total housework of each person adds to about the same total hours over a specified period? If the latter, what would it mean if we found, say, that most men cook and most women wash the dishes or vice versa? Or if we found, as is the case now, that women do most of the childrearing and men fix the home (with men spending much less time at their tasks)? Is that role sharing? Is that a situation of different but complementary sex roles? There may be no problem with any individual couple where one prefers and is more skilled to cook, and the other enjoys washing dishes. But we should be concerned if cooking is seen as preferable and more prestigious, and becomes men's work, and women are left with what is seen as the drudgery of washing dishes. Individual choices are fine as long as each person feels they are doing what they chose to do.

Childrearing

Childrearing should not become the province of either sex. It is true that in no society have men ever shared it equally with women, although Bontoc men, !Kung men, and men in some other societies have participated in their children's lives more than men do in most other societies. There may have been good reasons why women did most or all childrearing. Women may prefer and enjoy it, but men in some societies, according to Turnbull (1981), have felt excluded and deprived to such an extent that they have ritually attempted to play the mother role. Men must *fully share* in raising the children. I cannot imagine not having fed, washed, rocked to sleep, changed and washed diapers, and all the other things I did for and with my daughters.

Men should share equally in childrearing not only because the burden shouldn't be solely on women but because men should share in the pleasures and joys of being with and watching their children grow up. Among my most treasured and tender pleasures have been seeing and participating in my daughters' lives: seeing their first steps, hearing their first words, sharing their excitement when they began to ride bikes, being nearby while they played with their friends and each other, reading them books, going for walks, and holding them for long periods while they slowly fell asleep. Such moments and experiences cannot be rushed during evenings and weekends. As a college teacher who could arrange his schedule, I was fortunate to be with my children more than most fathers are able (or willing?) to be.

Fathers and mothers need time and energy to care for their children, play with them, and also have some of their own free time. Some day care is necessary and desirable, but eight- to ten-hour days, five days a week is undesirable. Would adults want to be in institutions eight to ten hours a day? No matter how good—and they can be very good—day-care settings are, they are institutions. Even a full-time babysitter in one's home is a poor substitute for a parent. When parents must rush home from work to cook, eat, wash dishes, play with and take care of the children, there is no time to relax with each other. We need longer, unrushed time with our children and with ourselves.

Finally, if women and men can jointly raise children, the personality and value differences that now appear in boys and girls, women and men, may diminish. Since mothers now are the ones who feed and wash children, care for them, hold them when they cry, and listen to their troubles, boys and girls come to assume that only women nurture. Girls come to identify with their mothers, and boys who see their fathers' distant behavior come to believe that only women nurture. Thus boys distance themselves from their mothers, and from their emotional life, and become men who cannot feel. Girls identify with their mothers and nurturing, and by thus focusing on nurturing they deny assertiveness. The result is incomplete adult personalities in both sexes.

If women and men jointly, equally, and cooperatively raise their children the present gender differences should disappear. According to Rubin (1983), both girls and boys, men and women, would benefit if men were to share childrearing:

> *For boys, therefore, the connection to a male self would be more direct, defined positively by the primary identification with a male figure rather than negatively by the renunciation of the female, as is presently the case. Under such conditions, we would, I believe, see the disappearance of the kind of obsessive concerns about their masculinity that is now so common in men. And, since boys would not have to relinquish the only loved other [their mother] of their early lives, there would also be no need to develop the rigid defensive barriers against their own vulnerability and dependency that characterize men who have been raised by women alone.*
>
> *For girls, a primary attachment to and identification with both parents would mean that separation would be less fraught with conflict and confusion in childhood, and the development of a well-bounded and autonomous sense of self less problematic in adulthood. For both women and men, boundaries would be firm where necessary to maintain separation and permeable where unity was the desired result. For both, self and gender would be less rigidly and stereotypically defined and experienced—the artificial distinctions we now hold between masculine and feminine swept away by early childhood experiences that would permit the internalization of the best of both in all of us. (p. 204)*

The above theory may exaggerate the role of parenting in creating role and personality sex differences. Outside institutions—work, school, politics, religion—are equally important in shaping sex identities, and we need to change them too. But we must change the family environment, so children will see men and women sharing all work, in and out of the home, and all roles. It would make very little difference if a few couples were to share roles while most couples do not, while the economy discriminates against women, while media and schools perpetuate stereotypes. The children of these couples would only see their parents as exceptions. We need to change social conditions for all people. A man whose work requires long hours, whose self-image requires success and material wealth, who is bombarded by consumerist messages in a capitalist economy, can hardly devote much time to raising his children. Nor can a woman under the same pressures. We must all liberate ourselves from a sexist, capitalist, consumerist society so we can enjoy our children, each other, and the natural world around us.

Conclusion

Class and power differences, as well as inequalities in the status of women, appeared together in human history when societies evolved away from gathering and hunting. We cannot return to a gathering and hunting existence, but we should realize that unless we create societies that are more egalitarian, classless, where the exercise of power is distributed equally, we cannot hope to achieve gender equality. We will need, of course, to redefine sex roles. The struggle to eliminate the stereotypes of and discrimination against women will be a long one. We also need to redefine men's roles. They need to be less aggressive and less competitive, more nurturing and emotional.

Summary

Sex role differences between men and women are *socially* created. Although they exist in the United States, they are less sharply defined than in the past. To some degree, women and men lead separate social lives. Sexism lowers women's self-esteem and encourages men to repress their emotions; it is harmful to both women and men.

The issue of women's equality depends partly on how we define power and equality. It seems clear, however, that in societies where women make an essential and publicly recognized contribution to the survival of the society and where they exercise control over the products of their labor, they are equal to men. These are egalitarian societies (see Chapter 3), where members are equal to each other and where power is not concentrated. Western influences have changed the status of women in these societies.

In pre-industrial United States, women and men supported their families together by raising and producing all of the essential goods they needed. Industrialism took husbands out of this family environment and transformed wives into nonproducing housewives. By 1900, most women were out of the labor force. Since then, and especially since about 1950, women have entered the labor force, and today over 56 percent work outside the home.

Today, women in the United States are controlled by various means: by a medical system that defines and regulates women's health and illness; by denial of their reproductive rights; by sexual harassment, rape, and male violence.

Although women have joined the labor force as full-time and permanent workers, they are not equal partners in the labor force. They still face discrimination in pay, in the kinds of jobs they can get, and in job advancement. Moreover, they still do most of the housework, and they are excluded from most leadership positions.

Women have made considerable progress in socialist societies, especially when we compare their present status to the pre-revolutionary past. But even in these societies, they still do most of the housework and are excluded from top leadership positions.

Looking at the future, women cannot achieve equality by emulating men. We need to create egalitarian societies where men and women will change roles; men must become more nurturing and caring, and women must become more assertive—with neither sex being too controlling, competitive, violent, or aggressive.

Suggested Readings

Chiñas, Beverly (1983). *The Isthmus Zapotecs: Women's roles in cultural context* (2nd ed.). Prospect Heights, IL: Waveland. Despite the appearance of inequality, Zapotec women are equal.

Corea, Gena (1986, January). Unnatural selection. *Progressive*, pp. 22–24. New reproductive technologies present a new threat to women's control of their persons and bodies.

Draper, Patricia (1975). !Kung women: Contrasts in sexual egalitarianism in foraging and sedentary contexts. In Rayna Reiter (Ed.), *Toward an anthropology of women* (pp. 77–109). New York: Monthly Review Press. Women are equal to men when the !Kung live in the bush by gathering and hunting, but lose that equality when they settle down in villages.

Duley, Margot & Edwards, Mary (Eds.). (1986). *The cross-cultural study of women*. New York: Feminist Press. An extensive bibliography and outline for the study of women in many cultures.

Freeman, Jo (Ed.). (1984). *Women: A feminist perspective* (3rd ed.). Palo Alto, CA: Mayfield. Original essays that analyze women's social conditions and the progress they have and have not made in American society.

In pursuit of pay equity: the promise of comparable worth (1986, September). *Dollars and Sense*, pp. 9–11. Comparable worth will raise women's wages, but by itself, it will not eliminate poverty or women's low wages.

Leacock, Eleanor Burke (1981). *Myths of male dominance.* New York: Monthly Review Press. In egalitarian societies, women have led autonomous and equal lives with men.

McDonnell, Kathleen (1984). *Not an easy choice: A feminist re-examines abortion.* Boston: South End Press. While accessible and legal abortion is necessary for the equality of women, abortion also raises moral and emotional issues.

Moore, Richard & Farsis, Elizabeth (1985, January). Sisterhood under siege. *Progressive,* pp. 30–31. Corporations use feminism for profit and to cover their exploitation of women.

Pollitt, Katha (1987, May 23). The strange case of Baby M. *Nation,* pp. 667, 682–88. Surrogate motherhood raises questions of the exploitation of poor women, equality and choice for women, and similar issues.

Rubin, Lillian B. (1983). *Intimate strangers: Men and women together.* New York: Harper & Row. Rubin documents the immense difficulties women and men face when they seek to change sex roles, and concludes it will not happen until women reach full social equality *and* men share fully in raising children.

Sapiro, Virginia (1986). *Women in American society.* Palo Alto, CA: Mayfield. Sapiro summarizes and discusses much research on women's roles and social conditions in the United States.

Schechter, Susan (1982). *Women and male violence.* Boston: South End Press. A history of the women who founded the shelters for battered wives, and a theory that seeks to understand the social conditions that lead to male violence.

Shostak, Marjorie (1981). *Nisa: The life and words of a !Kung woman.* New York: Vintage. An outstanding portrait of Nisa's life and the lives of !Kung women generally, told through Nisa's words and Shostak's analysis.

Walshok, Mary L. (1981) *Blue-collar women: Pioneers on the male frontier.* Garden City, NY: Anchor Books. Walshok describes how some women entered blue-collar jobs, why they did so, and how they manage in traditionally male occupations.

Glossary

Acculturation.   The choice of minority individuals and groups to change their behavior so they can blend in with the majority.

Adult socialization.   Socialization after the childhood years, as we enter work roles, marry, and become parents.

Agents of socialization.   Family, school, peers, and others who participate in the socialization of children.

Amalgamation.   Biological intermingling of two or more racial groups.

Apartheid.   An official policy of racial segregation in the Republic of South Africa.

Assimilation.   Acceptance and incorporation of a minority group into the majority group, with the eventual disappearance of the minority as an identifiable group.

Authority.   Exercise of power that is seen as legitimate and justifiable.

Class conflict.   An inevitable condition in capitalist society, where one class can only benefit if another class loses. (Usually, the conflict is the sharpest between the ruling class and the working class.)

Class consciousness.   An awareness that social classes exist, that one belongs to one of these classes, and that the interests of one's class conflict with the interests of other classes.

Class struggle.   The deliberate organization of people within classes to change social conditions for their benefit.

Cohabitation.   An unmarried man and woman living together in one household.

Colonialism.   An early stage of imperialism when center nations exercised direct military and political control over colonies and exploited them economically.

Community.   A small group of people who have lived on the same piece of land for a long time, who share common values, beliefs, and activities and are in frequent contact, and among whom there is sharing, reciprocity, and relative social equality.

Conflict perspective.   Views society as sometimes being composed of co-operating groups that work to meet common goals and needs, but at other times sees society as composed of groups that dominate other groups for their own benefit. Human societies today, for example, are composed of groups in conflict over the use and distribution of limited resources and over appropriate social behavior.

Conglomerate.   A large corporation that makes two or more products or provides two or more services.

Content analysis.   A technique that carefully and systematically analyzes the content of books, magazines, newspapers, movies, television shows, and other forms of communication to uncover meaning and bias in the material.

Cultural diffusion.   The introduction of technology, customs, and other items into one culture from another culture.

Cultural imperialism.   The more or less forced change of a culture to standards of a more powerful society.

Cultural integration.   The ideal situation in a culture where values, roles, and norms fit together, and basic values are expressed in all social behavior.

Cultural manipulation.   In modern societies, the use of mass media by powerful corporations to induce people to buy and use their products.

Cultural pluralism.   Ethnic and racial groups maintain their identities yet co-exist and interact peacefully.

Cultural relativism.   An ideal that requires that we understand and examine another culture through its own standards and in its own context.

Culture.   The total way of life of a people, their values, customs, traditions, beliefs, norms, roles, skills, and knowledge.

Culture shock.   The emotional and even physical shock people experience when they encounter another culture.

Dependent variable.   A variable that is changed or affected by another one.

Discrimination.   Unequal treatment of members of a minority group.

Ethnocentrism.   The belief that one's own culture is superior to all other cultures.

Experiment.   A situation in which the researcher creates and controls a social situation and seeks to establish a causal relationship between an independent and a dependent variable.

Extended family.   A family composed of three or more generations living together in one household.

Family.   The human group that provides for procreation, care, and socialization of children, affords social and economic sustenance to its members, and once served as the basic economic and production unit of society.

Folkway.   A norm that states an expectation but whose violation has mild or no sanctions attached to it.

Functionalist perspective.   Views society as an organized and organic whole of interrelated parts, each part performing an indispensable function to benefit the whole society and enable it to exist.

Generalized other.   The internalized conception we have of the expectations of others and society in general.

Genocide.   The destruction of a community by killing or forcibly moving its people or by destroying the community's economic base.

Gentrification.   The process whereby rising real estate prices and related changes force the working-class or poor residents of a community to move out; they are replaced by more affluent and professional people.

Group marriage.   Two or more men married to two or more women.

Historical materialism.   The theory that a society's mode of production (its economy) influences and interacts with the family, politics, religion, education, other institutions, and the culture in general.

Hypothesis.   A tentative statement that proposes a relationship between two or more social conditions (variables), where A causes B.

Ideology.   A set of beliefs, ideas, and statements held by a group of people that explains and justifies their actions and interests.

Imperialism.   The world economic, political, and military system in which wealth flows from the periphery (poor and weak nations) to the center (rich and powerful nations) and benefits the corporations and ruling classes of the center nations.

Independent variable.   A variable that changes or affects a dependent variable.

Institution.   A stable form of social organization developed over time to meet some need or want. Within institutions, people have different functions and roles, and often some have authority or power over others.

Interactionist perspective.   Focuses on small-scale social interactions, on people's definitions of social situations, on people's interpretations of others' actions, and on people's response to this interpretation.

Labeling.   The identification of others (especially children) as people who possess certain traits and characteristics.

Law.   A written norm, with mechanisms for its enforcement and specific penalties.

Managerial class.   Doctors, lawyers, managers, other professionals, and business employees who work for the corporations of the ruling class or who provide professional services. They are the new middle class who rose with the coming of large corporations.

Marginal people.   People who leave their culture and later live in another. In time they relate to both cultures but belong fully to neither.

Melting Pot.   The ideology that out of the combination and melting together of all racial and ethnic groups in America there would arise a new kind of people and culture.

Minority.   A group that is relatively powerless, faces prejudice, stereotypes, discrimination, and exploitation, and in time becomes conscious of being treated differently.

Modified-extended family.   Adult married children who live in their own households near their parents. They socialize and share with their parents frequently, often daily.

Monogamy.   Marriage of one man to one woman.

More.   A norm equated with morality; condemnation and severe punishment follow its violation.

Multinational corporation.   A large corporation with branches in two or more countries.

Norm.   The appropriate and expected behavior in a given social situation.

Nuclear family.   A family composed of parents and their young children.

Observer effect.   The impact of researchers on the social settings they study; the new elements they introduce into the setting by the questions they ask, observations they make, or experiments they conduct.

Operational definition.   A statement of the specific meaning of a concept used in social research (for example, "upper class" is determined by X amount of money and Y years of schooling).

Participant observation.   Research in which a sociologist observes behavior in its natural setting and usually participates in the daily life of the people involved.

Patriarchy.   The oldest male has the most authority.

Peer group.   People of about the same age and status.

Polyandry.   Marriage of one woman to two or more men.

Polygamy.   Marriage of one person to two or more people of the opposite sex.

Polygyny.   Marriage of one man to two or more women.

Poor class.   The unemployed, those on welfare, and those working for minimum wages and who suffer both materially and socially.

Power.   A relationship in which an individual or group has the capacity (or the perceived capacity) to direct and control the actions of individuals or groups by depriving them of a valued possession, social position, and so on.

Prejudice.   The tendency to judge people, usually negatively, on the basis of a single characteristic (such as age, race, ethnicity, religion, dress, or sex) and without knowledge of their individual abilities and character.

Primary groups.   A group, such as the family, where people have an intimate, personal, stable, many-sided, and direct relationship.

Records of human behavior.   Data used by sociologists in their research, remnants of human behavior that exist independently of the researcher who organizes and interprets them.

Resocialization.   A new socialization in adult life that radically changes what a person became during his or her childhood socialization.

Role.   The expected behavior and rewards that accompany a status.

Role conflict.   The situation where the expectations of one role we play conflict with the expectations of another role(s).

Ruling class.   The highest class in a capitalist society; they own most of the wealth and control the economy and the government.

Sample survey research.   Sociological research that uses a representative sample of a group and asks questions through interviews or questionnaires, and usually attempts to test a hypothesis of a causal relationship between two or more variables.

Secondary group.   A group where relationships are impersonal, temporary, and practical.

Segregation. The separation of a minority group from the majority, in housing, education, and other areas.

Self-fulfilling prophecy. A social condition or kind of person that, though initially nonexistent, is created when people act as if it were true.

Sex role. The differing social expectations of boys and girls, men and women in any society.

Social class. A group of people who usuallly intermarry, have the same relationship to the means of production, share similar economic positions and political interests, and share common values and life styles (usually different from those of other classes). Classes exist in any society where inequalities exist and where two or more groups of families each share common characteristics.

Socialization. The process through which children acquire their culture and become fully human.

Social liberation (or sociology as liberation). The view that groups of people cooperate and struggle to create society and the norms and roles that organize social behavior.

Social mobility. The upward or downward social movement of a person, as compared to the social class of his or her parents and family.

Social structure. A fundamental assumption of sociology that society and social behavior are patterned, orderly, predictable, and organized, and that there is a social network composed of norms, roles, and institutions.

Sociological perspective. A way to view facts, conditions, people, and their relationships to each other; a way of perceiving and understanding the world around us.

State. The government or other ruling body that controls the society. It is usually a strong centralized government that claims monopoly over the use of force and laws to maintain order.

Status. A social position.

Stereotype. An exaggerated, simplistic, and negative preconception about a minority group.

Subculture. A group that both shares the culture of the society, and also has its own unique values and behavior.

Urbanization. The long social process that has led to most people living in or near large cities, and which is thought by some to have created social isolation and to have destroyed community.

Values. Cultural statements about ideals and desired social behavior.

Variable. Social characteristic that changes (varies), such as income and attitude.

Working class. The vast majority of Americans who work in factories, offices, and stores, and who have no power and who own no income-producing wealth.

Work alienation. The condition and feeling of powerlessness that results from having no control over the conception and process of what one does.

References

Abrahamson, Mark (1978). *Functionalism.* Englewood Cliffs, NJ: Prentice Hall.

Abrams, Herbert L., & von Kaenel, William E. (1981, November 12). Medical problems of survivors of nuclear war. *The New England Journal of Medicine,* pp. 1226–1232.

Acharya, Amitav (1987, March). The Reagan doctrine and international security. *Monthly Review, 38*(10), 28–36.

Adams, Carolyn, & Winston, Kathryn (1980). *Mothers at work.* New York: Longman.

Adams, Megan (1980, June). A bitter season in South Africa. *Progressive,* pp. 50–55.

Agee, James, & Evans, Walker (1941). *Let us now praise famous men.* Boston: Houghton-Mifflin, 1960.

Agyeman, Opoku (1987, May). Terrorism: A nonwestern view. *Monthly Review, 39*(1), 43–53.

Albelda, Randy (1988, April). Let them eat taxes: The growing tax burden on the poor. *Dollars and Sense,* pp. 9–11.

Albert, Michael; Cagan, Leslie; Chomsky, Noam; Hahnel, Robin; King, Mel; Sargent, Lydia; & Sklar, Holly (1986). *Liberating theory.* Boston: South End.

Alger, Norman (1974). *Many answers.* St. Paul, MN: West.

Alpert, Arnie (1987, April). Ten years after the Seabrook occupation: Continued resistance to poisoned power. *Peacework,* pp. 10–11.

Amin, Samir (1980, January). The class system of the contemporary imperialist system. *Monthly Review, 31*(8), 9–26.

Amin, Samir; Arrighi, Giovanni; Frank, Andre Gunder; & Wallerstein, Immanuel (1982). *Dynamics of global crisis.* New York: Monthly Review Press.

Amott, Theresa, & Matthaei, Julie (1984, September–October.) Comparable worth, incomparable pay. *Radical America, 18*(5), 21–28.

Anderson, Marion (1980). *Converting the work force.* Lansing, MI: Employment Research Associates.

Aptheker, Betinna (1982). *Woman's legacy: Essays on race, sex and class in American history.* Amherst, MA: University of Massachusetts Press.

Arditti, Rita (1985, November–December). Reproductive engineering and the social control of women. *Radical America, 19*(6), 9–26.

Arendell, Terry (1986). *Mothers of divorce: Legal, economic and social dilemmas.* Berkeley, CA: University of California Press.

Aries, Phillipe (1962). *Centuries of childhood.* New York: Vintage.

Armstrong, Robert (1985, December). War of attrition. *Progressive,* pp. 20–22.

Arnold, Alison (1978, February 9). Those old school ties remain strong despite changing society. *Boston Sunday Globe,* p. B3.

Arnold, Susan (1986). *Negative stereotyping of the elderly in children's picture books.* Student paper, Regis College.

Arnove, Robert F. (Ed.). (1980). *Philanthropy and cultural imperialism.* Bloomington, IN: Indiana University Press, 1982.

Aronowitz, Stanley, & Giroux, Henry A. (1985). *Education under siege: The conservative, liberal, and radical debate over schooling.* South Hadley, MA: Bergin and Garvey.

Asch, Solomon E. (1956). Studies of independence and conformity. *Psychological monographs, 70*(9) (Whole No. 416).

Asch, Adrienne, & Fine, Michelle (1984, July–August). Shared dreams: A left perspective on disability rights and reproductive rights. *Radical America, 18*(4), 51–58.

Babbie, Earl (1986). *The practice of social research* (4th ed.). Belmont, CA: Wadsworth.

Babson, Steve, & Brighman, Nancy (1975). *Why do we spend so much money?* (2nd ed.). Somerville, MA: Popular Economics Press.

Bacdayan, Albert S. (1977). Mechanistic cooperation and sexual equality among the Western Bontoc. In Alice Schlengel (Ed.), *Sexual stratification* (pp. 271–291). New York: Columbia University Press, 1977.

Bader, Eleanor (1987, February 18). Downwardly mobile and alone with the kids. *Guardian,* p. 20.

Bailey, Kenneth (1982). *Methods of social research* (2nd ed.). New York: Free Press.

Baldridge, J. Victor (1975). *Sociology.* New York: Wiley.

Bale, Tony (1983, May–June). Breath of death: The asbestos disaster comes home to roost. *Health/PAC Bulletin,* pp. 7–21.

Bale, Tony (1985, May–June). The great American health fortunes, 1984. *Health/PAC Bulletin,* pp. 18–25.

Balkan, Sheila; Berger, Ronald; & Schmidt, Janet (1980). *Crime and deviance in America: A critical approach.* Belmont, CA: Wadsworth.

Ballantine, Jeane H. (1983). *The sociology of education.* Englewood Cliffs, NJ: Prentice Hall.

Baltzell, E. Digby (Ed.). (1969). *The search for community in modern America.* New York: Harper & Row.

Balzer, Richard (1976). *Clockwork.* Garden City, NY: Doubleday.

Bane, Mary Jo (1976). *Here to stay: American families in the twentieth century.* New York: Basic Books.

Banner, Lois (1983). *American beauty.* Chicago: University of Chicago Press.

Barnett, Tracy (1986, July). Bad chemistry. *Progressive,* pp. 26–29.

Barnouw, Victor (1982). *Ethnology* (4th ed.). Homewood, IL: Dorsey.

Baron, Harold (1971, March–April). The demand for black labor. *Radical America, 5*(2), 1–46.

Bart, Pauline, & O'Brien, Patricia (1985). *Stopping rape: Successful survival strategies.* New York: Pergamon.

Bartholomew, Catherine (1987, April 18). Perils of teen call-in lines. *Boston Globe,* p. 15.

Bastian, Alan; Fruchter, Norm; Gittell, Marilyn; Greer, Colin; & Haskins, Kent (1985, Spring). Choosing equality: The case for democratic schooling. *Social Policy,* pp. 34–51.

Baxandall, Rosalyn; Gordon, Linda; & Reverby, Susan (1976). *America's working women.* New York: Random House.

Bay State Conversion Group (1982). *The case for economic conversion: Massachusetts.* Watertown, MA.

Beaud, Michael (1981). *A history of capitalism: 1500–1980.* New York: Monthly Review Press (American ed., 1983).

Becker, Howard S. (1986). *Writing for social scientists: How to start and finish your thesis, book, or article.* Chicago: University of Chicago Press.

Beers, David, & Hembree, Diana (1987, March 21). The two Atlantas: A tale of two cities. *Nation,* pp. 357–360.

Bellah, Robert; Madsen, Richard; Sullivan, William; Swidler, Ann; & Tipton, Steven (1985). *Habits of the heart: Individualism and commitment in American life.* New York: Harper & Row.

Bender, Thomas (1978). *Community and social change in America.* Baltimore: Johns Hopkins, 1982.

Benedict, Ruth (1934). *Patterns of culture.* New York: Mentor, 1959.

Benedict, Ruth (1938). Continuities and discontinuities in cultural conditioning. *Psychiatry, 1,* 161–67.

Benet, Sula (1974). *Abkhasians: The long-living people of the Caucasus.* New York: Holt, Rinehart & Winston.

Berch, Bettina (1985, November). The resurrection of outwork. *Monthly Review, 37*(6), 37–46.

Berger, Peter (1963). *Invitation to sociology.* Garden City, NY: Doubleday.

Berman, Daniel (1978). *Death on the job.* New York: Monthly Review Press.

Berns, Roberta M. (1985). *Child, family, community*. New York: Holt, Rinehart & Winston.

Bernstein, Dennis, & Blitt, Connie (1986, March). Lethal dose. *Progressive*, pp. 22–25.

Bielby, William, & Baron, James (1986, January). Men and women at work: Sex segregation and statistical discrimination. *American Journal of Sociology, 91*(4), 759–799.

Biffle, Christopher (1975, September 25). A ton of onions keeps you even. *Nation*, pp. 269–271.

Bingham, Eula (1987, June 12). Jobs and pregnancy. *Boston Globe*, p. 15.

Bird, Kai, & Holland, Max (1984, December 8). Europe: A hard rain falls. *Nation*, p. 609.

Birdwhistell, Ray (1970) *Kinesics and context*. Philadelphia: Pennsylvania University Press.

Blake, Phil (1974, December 7). Race, homicide, and the press. *Nation*, pp. 592–593.

Blau, Francine (1984). Women in the labor force: An overview. In Jo Freeman (Ed.), *Women: A feminist perspective* (3rd ed.) (pp. 297–315). Palo Alto, CA: Mayfield.

Blomberg, Helaine (1981, Fall). *Treatment of the elderly in contemporary American society*. Unpublished paper for a course on aging, Framingham State College, Framingham, MA.

Bodley, John (1982). *Victims of progress* (2nd ed.). Palo Alto, CA: Mayfield.

Bodley, John (1983). *Anthropology and contemporary human problems* (2nd ed.). Palo Alto, CA: Mayfield.

Bond, Patrick (1987, June). From divestment to reinvestment: Baltimore campaign links apartheid, redlining. *Dollars and Sense*, pp. 17–20.

Borman, Kathryn; Quarm, Daisy; & Gideonse, Sarah (Eds.). (1984). *Women in the workplace: Effects on families*. Norwood, NJ: Ablex.

Bose, Christine E., & Rossi, Peter H. (1983, June). Gender and jobs. *American Sociological Review, 48*(3), 316–330.

Boskin, Joseph (1986). *Sambo: The rise and demise of an American jester*. New York: Oxford University Press.

Boston Urban Study Group (1984a). *Who rules Boston?* Boston: Institute for Democratic Socialism.

Boston Urban Study Group (1984b). *Who's who in the Boston power structure?* Boston: Institute for Democratic Socialism.

Bowser, Benjamin, & Hunt, Raymond (Eds.). (1981). *Impact of racism on white Americans*. Beverly Hills, CA: Sage.

Boyte, Harry C. (1984). *Community is possible: Repairing America's democratic roots*. New York: Harper & Row.

Bradburn, Norman, & Caplovitz, David (1965). *Reports on happiness*. Chicago: Aldine.

Bradlee, Ben (1983, February 11). Long-term consequences feared as erosion strips farmland. *Boston Globe*, p. 2.

Brait, Susan (1981, November). For old people, a new kind of neglect. *Progressive*, pp. 30–34.

Bratt, Rachel; Hartman, Chester; & Meyerson, Ann (Eds.). (1986). *Critical perspectives on housing*. Philadelphia: Temple University Press.

Braverman, Harry (1974). *Labor and monopoly capital: The degradation of work in the twentieth century*. New York: Monthly Review Press.

Brecher, Jeremy (1972). *Strike!* San Francisco: Straight Arrow.

Breines, Wini (1981). The politics of sex and the family. In Scott G. McNall (Ed.), *Political economy* (pp. 24–25). Glenview, IL: Scott, Foresman.

Brenner, M. Harvey (1973). *Mental illness and the economy*. Cambridge, MA: Harvard University Press.

Bridenthal, Renate (1982). The family: The view from a room of her own. In Barrie Thorne (Ed.), *Rethinking the family* (pp. 225–239). New York: Longman.

Browne, Troy (1986, April 7). Fear and racism in the suburbs. *Boston Globe*, p. 15.

Browning, Frank (1981, September). Life on the margin. *Progressive*, pp. 34–37.

Brownstein, Ronald, & Easton, Nina (1983). *Reagan's ruling class*. New York: Pantheon.

Buchanan, Keith (1985, July–August). Center and periphery: Reflections on the irrelevance of a billion human beings. *Monthly Review, 37*(3), 86–97.

Burbach, Roger (1982, January). Central America: The end of U.S. hegemony. *Monthly Review, 33*(8), 1–18.

Burbach, Roger (1984, June). Revolution and reaction: U.S. policy in Central America. *Monthly Review, 36*(2), 1–20.

Burbach, Roger, & Flynn, Patricia (1980). *Agribusiness in the Americas.* New York: Monthly Review Press.

Burchett, Wilfred, & Alley, Rewi (1976). *China: the quality of life.* Baltimore: Penguin.

Burnett, Richard (1979, October). Illegal aliens come cheap. *Progressive,* pp. 44–46.

Burnham, Damian (1984, February). Dunkin' Donuts won't feed the hungry. *Progressive,* pp. 26–28.

Burnham, David (1983, April 30). Tales of a computer state. *Nation,* pp. 527, 537–541.

Burnham, Sophy (1978, April). Why the rich don't care. *The Washington Monthly,* pp. 11–19.

Butner, Marion (1983, March–April). Computerized big brother. *Science for the People, 15*(2), 6–12.

Bybee, Roger (1983, February). Corporate power at the local level. *Monthly Review, 34*(9), 57–62.

Byrne, John (1985, June 3). Who made what at the top in the U.S. business. *Forbes,* pp. 114–153.

Campbell, Angus (1975, May). The American way of mating. *Psychology Today,* pp. 37–43.

Camus, Albert (1960). *Resistance, rebellion and death.* New York: Knopf.

Caplow, Theodore; Bahr, Howard; Chadwick, Bruce; Hill, Reuben; & Williamson, Margaret Holmes (1982). *Middletown families.* Minneapolis, MN: University of Minnesota Press.

Case, John, & Taylor, Rosemary C. R. (Eds.). (1979). *Co-ops, communes, and collectives.* New York: Pantheon.

Cashmore, E. Ellis (1987). *The logic of racism.* London: Allen and Unwin.

Caudill, Harry M. (1963). *Night comes to the Cumberlands.* Boston: Atlantic-Little, Brown.

Center for Popular Economics (1986). *Economic report of the people.* Boston: South End.

Cerullo, Margaret, & Ewen, Phyllis (1982, January–April). Having a good time: The American family goes camping. *Radical America, 16*(1) and (2), 13–44.

Chambliss, William J. (1973, November–December). The saints and the roughnecks. *Society, 11*(1), 24–31.

Chambliss, William J., & Ryther, Thomas E. (1975). *Sociology: the discipline and its direction.* New York: McGraw-Hill.

Chambliss, William J., & Seidman, Robert (1982). *Law, order, and power* (2nd ed.). Reading, MA: Addison-Wesley.

Chandler, David L. (1986, December 29). Disasters bring a new sense of limits. *Boston Globe,* p. 55.

Chandler, David L. (1987, June 23). Maverick scientists encounter barriers. *Boston Globe,* pp. 1, 5.

Chapkis, Wendy (1986). *Beauty secrets: Women and the politics of experience.* Boston: South End.

Chapman, William (1987, June). Still without land. *Progressive,* pp. 26–28.

Chavkin, Wendy (Ed.). (1984). *Double exposure: Women's health hazards on the job and at home.* New York: Monthly Review Press.

Chernin, Kim (1982). *The obsession: Reflections on the tyranny of slenderness.* New York: Harper & Row.

Chesler, Phyllis (1987). *Mothers on trial.* New York: Seal.

Chinas, Beverly L. (1983). *The Isthmus Zapotecs: Women's roles in cultural context* (2nd ed.). Prospect Heights, IL: Waveland.

Chinweizu (1985, November). Debt trap peonage. *Monthly Review, 37*(6), 21–35.

Chomsky, Noam (1985a, January–February). Intervention in Vietnam and Central America. *Radical America, 19*(1), 49–66.

Chomsky, Noam (1985b, October). The bounds of thinkable thought. *Progressive,* pp. 28–31.

Ciancanelli, Penelope (1978). Politics and public school reform. In Union of Radical Political Economics (Eds.), *U.S. capitalism in crisis* (pp. 194–204). New York: URPE.

City Life (1983, February–March). The hotel workers: Rebirth of a union. *The Labor Page* (Boston, MA), No. 7, pp. 1–8.

Claffey, Charles E. (1982, August 9). Nuclear dump proposal and Utah's canyonlands. *Boston Globe*, pp. 1, 6.

Clawson, Dan; Johnson, Karen; & Schall, John (1982, September–October). Fighting union busting in the '80s. *Radical America, 16*(5), 45–64.

Claybrook, Joan (1984). *Retreat from safety: Reagan's attack on America's health*. New York: Pantheon.

Clinard, Marshal B., & Yeager, Peter C. (1980). *Corporate crime*. New York: Free Press.

Cockcroft, James D. (1986). *Outlaws in the promised land: Mexican immigrant workers and America's future*. New York: Grove.

Cole, Stephen (1986, November). Sex discrimination and admission to medical school. *American Journal of Sociology, 92*(3), 549–567.

Coles, Robert (1970). *Uprooted children*. New York: Harper & Row.

Coles, Robert (1977, September). The children of affluence. *Atlantic Monthly*, pp. 52–66.

Collins, Sheilla (1978, April 17). Class, family, forgiveness. *Christianity and Crisis, 38*(5), 82–88.

Committee on the Judiciary (1972). Hearings before the committee, U.S. Senate, 92nd Congress, second session—on the nomination of Richard G. Kleindienst, of Arizona, to be Attorney General (parts 1, 2, and 3). Washington, DC: U.S. Government Printing Office.

Commoner, Barry (1971). *The closing circle*. New York: Knopf.

Commoner, Barry (1976). *The poverty of power*. New York: Knopf.

Compa, Lance (1985, October). Fighting back. *Progressive*, pp. 32–34.

Connel, Thomas (1984, September). A tale of two studies. *Sanctuary*, pp. 10–11.

Conrad, Peter, & Kern, Rochelle (Eds.). (1986). *The sociology of health and illness* (2nd ed.). New York: St. Martin's.

Cook, Earl (1971). The flow of energy in industrial society. *Scientific American, 224*(3), 116.

Cook, Fred J. (1983, May 21). Big oil's stake in deregulation. *Nation*, pp. 630–632.

Cooley, Charles Horton (1962). *Social organization*. New York: Schocken.

Cordes, Helen (1985, September). Solidarity with a twist. *Progressive*, pp. 17–18.

Corea, Gena (1980, July). The caesarean epidemic. *Mother Jones*, pp. 28–35.

Corea, Gena (1986, January). Unnatural selection. *Progressive*, pp. 22–24.

Cornelisen, Ann (1976). *Women of the shadows: The wives and mothers of southern Italy*. New York: Vintage.

Cottle, Thomas (1979, October). A job for Ollie Sindon. *Progressive*, pp. 52–54.

Cowan, Ruth Schwartz (1983). *More work for mother*. New York: Basic Books.

Cox, Oliver (1976). *Race relations*. Detroit: Wayne State University Press.

Crandall, Richard C. (1980). *Gerontology*. Reading, MA: Addison-Wesley.

Croll, Elizabeth (1980). *Feminism and socialism in China*. New York: Schocken.

Curley, Jayme; Ladar, Sharon; Siegler, Anna; Stevens, Jane Greengold; & Matthews, Linda (1981). *The balancing act II: A career and a family*. Chicago: Chicago Review Press.

Curtin, Sharon (1972). *Nobody ever died of old age*. Boston: Atlantic-Little, Brown.

Dahl, Robert (1961). *Who governs?* New Haven, CT: Yale University Press.

Dahl, Robert (1982). *Dilemmas of pluralist democracy: Autonomy vs. control*. New Haven, CT: Yale University Press.

Danaher, Kevin (1984). *In whose interest? A guide to U.S.-South Africa relations*. Washington, DC: Institute for Policy Studies.

Davidson, Osha (1987, August). Farms without farmers. *Progressive*, pp. 25–27.

Davin, Delia (1975). *Women-work: Women and the party in revolutionary China*. New York: Oxford University Press.

Davis, Jennifer (1985, February). South Africa: The cycle is coming. *Progressive*, pp. 18–21.

Davis, Kingsley (1947, March). Final note on a case of extreme isolation. *American Journal of Sociology, 52*(5), 432–437.

Davis, Peter (1982). *Hometown: A portrait of an American community*. New York: Simon & Schuster.

Day, Samuel H. (1983, April). The new resistance. *Progressive*, pp. 22–30.

Degler, Carl (1974, December). What ought to be and what was: Women's sexuality in the nineteenth century. *American Historical Review, 79*, 1467–1490.

Dellums, Ron (1987, Spring). Comments on "Congressional sleepout." *Campaign News* (newsletter of Massachusetts Jobs with Peace), p. 1.

Demos, John (1970). *A little commonwealth*. New York: Oxford University Press.

Dennis, Werner (1984). *Amazon journey: An anthropologist's year among Brazil's Mekranoti Indians*. New York: Simon & Schuster.

Dennison, George (1969). *The lives of children*. New York: Random House.

Deutscher, Irwin (1973). *What we say/what we do*. Glenview, IL: Scott, Foresman.

Diamond, Jared (1987, May). The worst mistake in the history of the human race. *Discover*, pp. 64–66.

Diamond, Norma (1975). Collectivization, kinship, and the status of women in rural China. In R. Reiter (Ed.), *Toward an anthropology of women* (pp. 372–395). New York: Monthly Review Press.

Diamond, Stanley (1971, Spring). The rule of law versus the order of custom. *Social Research, 38*(1), 42–72.

Dinkins, David W., & Wackstein, Nancy (1986, Fall). Addressing homelessness. *Social Policy*, pp. 50–51.

Dixon, Marlene (1980). *Women in class struggle*. San Francisco: Synthesis.

Dobie, Kathy, & Goodman, Amy (1987, February). Playing with poison. *Progressive*, pp. 19–23.

Dobrin, Arthur (1980, May). An American prisoner of conscience. *Progressive*, pp. 35–39.

Domhoff, G. William (1967). *Who rules America?* Englewood Cliffs, NJ: Prentice Hall.

Domhoff, G. William (1970). *The higher circles*. New York: Vintage.

Domhoff, G. William (1974). *The Bohemian Grove and other retreats*. New York: Harper & Row.

Domhoff, G. William (1978a). *Who really rules?* New Brunswick, NJ: Transaction.

Domhoff, G. William (1978b). *The powers that be*. New York: Random House.

Domhoff, G. William (1981, January). Politics among the redwoods: Ronald Reagan's Bohemian Grove connection. *Progressive*, pp. 32–36.

Domhoff, G. William (1983). *Who rules America now: A view for the '80s*. Englewood Cliffs, NJ: Prentice Hall.

Donner, Frank (1985, October 12). The return of the red squads. *Nation*, pp. 329, 339–342.

Donzelot, Jacques (1977). *The policing of families*. New York: Pantheon, 1979.

Douglas, Pamela (1983, March). Harlem on the auction block. *Progressive*, pp. 33–37.

Douglass, Frederick (1969). *My bondage and my freedom*. New York: Dover.

Dowd, Doug (1982, December). The heart of the matter. *Monthly Review, 34*(7), 48–54.

Downs, James F. (1972). *The Navajo*. New York: Holt, Rinehart & Winston.

Downs, Peter (1986, July). Seeds of discontent. *Progressive*, pp. 30–34.

Downs, Peter (1987, January). Your money or your life. *Progressive*, pp. 24–28.

Draper, Patricia (1975). !Kung women: Contrasts in sexual egalitarianism in foraging and sedentary contexts. In R. Reiter (Ed.), *Toward an anthropology of women* (pp. 77–109). New York: Monthly Review Press.

Dreier, Peter (1982, February). The position of the press in the U.S. power structure. *Social Problems, 29*(3), 298–310.

Dreier, Peter (1982a, August 21–28). Dreams and nightmares. *Nation*, pp. 141–144.

Dreier, Peter (1982b, September). Renters' revolt. *Progressive*, pp. 16–17.

Dreier, Peter, & Atlas, John (1981, March). Condo mania: Across the country, it's pay up or move out. *Progressive*, pp. 19–22.

Dreyfuss, Joel (1978, January). The new racism. *Black Enterprise*.

Drummond, Hugh (1980, July). Playing doctor. *Mother Jones*, pp. 36–41.

Duberman, Lucille (1976). *Social inequality:*

Class and caste in America. Philadelphia: Lippincott.

Duboff, Robert F. (1974, September 11). For whom the polls toll. *Real Paper* (Boston), p. 9.

DuBois, Ellen (1982, January–April). Beyond the Victorian syndrome: Feminist interpretations of the history of sexuality. *Radical America, 16*(1) and (2), 149–154.

Duley, Margot I., & Edwards, Mary I. (Eds.). (1986). *The cross-cultural study of women.* New York: Feminist.

Dumanoski, Dianne (1983, February 23). An emerging alliance. *Boston Globe,* p. 6.

Dumanoski, Dianne (1988, June 28). World leaders call for drastic action to slow Earth's warming. *Boston Globe,* pp. 1, 13.

Dupont, Kevin Paul (1987, May 17, 18, 19). 40 years later. *Boston Globe,* pp. 1, 68, 69; 1, 38; 73, 81.

Durbin, Anna (1987, July 18/25). Mother courage. *Nation,* p. 38.

Eden, Philip (1986, May). The cancer of self-interest. *Monthly Review, 38*(1), 37–42.

Edwards, Richard C.; Reich, Thomas; & Weisskopf, Thomas E. (Eds.). (1978). *The Capitalist System* (2nd ed.). Englewood Cliffs, NJ: Prentice Hall.

Egerton, John (1981, June). Appalachia's absentee landlords. *Progressive,* pp. 42–45.

Egger, Daniel (1987, March 28). Chernobyl's cup runneth over: West Germany pours hot milk. *Nation,* pp. 392–396.

Ehrenreich, Barbara (1983). *The hearts of men: American dreams and the flight from commitment.* Garden City, NY: Doubleday.

Ehrenreich, Barbara, & Ehrenreich, John (1977, March–April). The professional-managerial class. *Radical America, 11*(2), 7–32.

Ehrenreich, Barbara, & English, Deirdre (1973). *Complaints and disorders: The sexual politics of sickness.* Old Westbury, NY: Feminist.

Elkin, Frederick, & Handel, Gerald (1984). *The child and society* (4th ed.). New York: Random House.

Ellsberg, Daniel (1981, September). Call to mutiny. *Monthly Review, 33*(4), 1–26.

Elshtain, Jean Bethke (1985, September). Invasion of the child savers. *Progressive,* pp. 23–26.

Ember, Carol, & Ember, Melvin. (1985). *Cultural anthropology* (4th ed.). Englewood Cliffs, NJ: Prentice-Hall.

Englebert, Michael (1983, March). Flight: Six Salvadorans who took leave of the war. *Progressive,* pp. 38–43.

Engler, Robert (1985, April 27). Technology out of control. *Nation,* pp. 488–500.

Erikson, Kai (1976). *Everything in its path.* New York: Simon & Schuster.

Erlich, Reese (1987, July). Victory on Cannery Row. *Progressive,* pp. 26–27.

Ermann, M. David, & Lundman, Richard J. (Eds.). (1987). *Corporate and governmental deviance* (3rd ed.). New York: Oxford University Press.

Ervin, Mike (1984, December). The new bigotry. *Progressive,* p. 24.

Estioko-Griffin, Agnes, & Griffin, P. Bion (1981). Woman the hunter: the Agta. In Frances Dahlberg (Ed.), *Woman the gatherer* (pp. 121–151). New Haven, CT: Yale University Press.

Etra, Donald, & Leinsdorf, David (1974). *Citibank.* New York: Grossman.

Ewen, Elizabeth (1985). *Immigrant women in the land of dollars: Life and culture in the Lower East Side, 1890–1925.* New York: Monthly Review Press.

Ewen, Phyllis (1977, May–June). Beauty parlor—a woman's space. *Radical America, 11*(3), 47–57.

Ewen, Stuart (1976). *Captains of consciousness.* New York: McGraw-Hill.

Fabricant, Michael, & Kelly, Michael (1986, March–May). No haven for the homeless in a heartless economy. *Radical America, 20*(3), 23–35.

Faller, Nancy (1980, September). Washington's fish war. *Progressive,* pp. 51–53.

Fallows, Marjorie (1979). *Irish Americans.* Englewood Cliffs, NJ: Prentice Hall.

Family Planning Perspectives (1986, May/June). Women in 30s experiencing record-high divorce; level expected to decline among younger women. *18,* 133–134.

Farley, John (1988). *Majority-minority relations* (2nd ed.). Englewood Cliffs, NJ: Prentice Hall.

Farrell, Michael P., & Rosenberg, Stanley D. (1981). *Men at Midlife.* Boston: Auburn House.

Farren, Pat (Ed.). (1983). *What will it take to prevent nuclear war?* Cambridge, MA: Schenkman.

Faux, Jeff (1983, November). What now, Willy Loman? *Mother Jones,* pp. 52–54.

Featherman, David (1979, March–April). Opportunities are expanding. *Society, 16*(4), 6–11.

Featherman, David, & Hauser, Robert M. (1978). *Opportunity and change.* New York: Academic.

Fee, Elizabeth (1983). *Women and health: The politics of sex in medicine.* New York: Baywood.

Ferguson, Thomas, & Rogers, Joel (1982, June 26). Neo-liberals and Democrats. *Nation,* pp. 767, 781–786.

Ferrey, Steven (1981, March 22). An Alaskan dilemma. *Boston Globe Magazine,* pp. 10ff.

Festinger, Leon; Riecken, Henry; & Schachter, Stanley (1956). *When prophecy fails.* New York: Harper & Row.

Firth, Raymond (1936). *We, the Tikopia.* Boston: Beacon.

Flanagan, Timothy; van Alstyne, David J.; & Gottfredson, Michael R. (Eds.). (1982). *Sourcebook of criminal justice statistics—1981.* Washington, D.C.: U.S. Government Printing Office.

Foreman, Judy (1980, November 16–20). US far behind in childcare policy for working parents. *Boston Globe.*

Foreman, Judy (1981, May 7). Survey boosts working women. *Boston Globe,* p. 49.

Foster, Douglas (1981, July). You are what they eat: A glowing report on radioactive waste in the sea. *Mother Jones,* pp. 18ff.

Foster, Douglas (1982, November). The desperate migrants of Devil's Canyon. *Progressive,* pp. 44–49.

Francome, Colin (1984). *Abortion freedom: A world-wide movement.* London: Allen and Unwin.

Frederickson, Mary (1982, November–December). Four decades of change: Black workers in Southern textiles, 1941–1981. *Radical America, 16*(6), 27–44.

Freedman, Tracy (1981, March 23). Leftover lives to live. *Nation,* pp. 624–627.

Freedman, Tracy, & Weir, David (1983, May 14). Polluting the most vulnerable. *Nation,* pp. 600–604.

Freeman, Derek (1983). *Margaret Mead and Samoa: The making and unmaking of an anthropological myth.* Cambridge, MA: Harvard University Press.

Freeman, Jo (1971, Spring). The building of the gilded cage. *The second wave,* 1:1. In Skolnick, J. A. and E. Currie (Eds.), *Crisis in American institutions* (pp. 198–218). Boston: Little, Brown, 1976.

Freeman, Jo (Ed.). (1984). *Women: A feminist perspective* (3rd ed.). Palo Alto, CA: Mayfield.

Freitag, Peter J. (1975, December). The cabinet and big business. *Social problems, 23*(2), 137–152.

Freudenberg, Nicholas (1984). *Not in our backyard! Community action for health and environment.* New York: Monthly Review Press.

Friedl, Ernestine (1962). *Vasilika: a village in modern Greece.* New York: Holt, Rinehart & Winston.

Friedl, John (1981). *The human portrait: Introduction to cultural anthropology.* Englewood Cliffs, NJ: Prentice Hall.

Fruhling, Larry (1986, October). Please don't drink the water. *Progressive,* pp. 31–34.

Fuentes, Annette, & Ehrenreich, Barbara (1983). *Women in the global factory.* Boston: South End.

Fullinwider, John (1983, February). The Sunbelt buckles: Neighborhood organizing in Dallas. *Dollars and Sense,* pp. 12–14.

Fusfeld, Daniel R. (1982). *Economics.* Glenview, IL: Scott, Foresman.

Gallagher, Art, Jr. (1961). Urbanizing influences on Plainville. In P. Olson (Ed.), *America as a mass society* (pp. 187–204). New York: Free Press, 1963.

Gallagher, Art, Jr., & Padfield, Harland (Eds.).

(1980). *The dying community*. Albuquerque, NM: University of New Mexico Press.

Gans, Herbert (1982). *The urban villagers* (2nd ed.). New York: Free Press.

Garson, Barbara (1975). *All the livelong day: The meaning and demeaning of work*. New York: Penguin, 1977.

Garson, Barbara (1981, July). The electronic sweatshop: Scanning the office of the future. *Mother Jones*, pp. 32–41.

Gebhart, Tim (1980, October). Who owns the Missouri? *Progressive*, pp. 44–45.

Gedicks, Al (1983, May–June). Resource wars in the Lake Superior region. *Science for the people, 15*(3), 12–18.

General Social Surveys, 1972–1983: Cumulative Codebook, 1983 (1983). Chicago: National Opinion Research Center, pp. 338–349.

Gerson, Joseph (Ed.) (1985). *The deadly connection: Nuclear war and U.S. intervention*. Philadelphia: New Society.

Gerth, Hans, & Mills, C. Wright (1954). *Character and social structure*. London: Routledge and Kegan Paul.

Gibbs, Lois (1981). *Love Canal: My story*. Albany, NY: State University Press of New York.

Gibson, Mary (1983). *Workers' rights*. Totowa, NJ: Rowan and Allanheld.

Gil, David (1975). Unraveling child abuse. *American Journal of Orthopsychiatry, 45*(4), 346–356.

Gilbert, Dennis, & Kahl, Joseph A. (1987). *The American class structure* (3rd ed.). Chicago: Dorsey.

Gitech, Lenny, & Daniels, Matthew (1985, April 30). Homophobia (Interview with Sue Kiefer Hammersmith). *The Advocate*, pp. 26–28.

Gitlin, Todd (Ed.). (1986). *Watching television*. New York: Pantheon.

Gitlin, Todd, & Hollander, Nancy (1970). *Uptown: Poor whites in Chicago*. New York: Harper & Row.

Glass, Ruth (1982, July–August). Divided and degraded: The downtrodden peoples of India. *Monthly Review, 34*(3), 101–127.

Goffman, Erving (1959). *The presentation of self in everyday life*. Garden City, NY: Doubleday.

Gold, Michael (1965). *Jews without money*. New York: Avon. (Originally published 1930)

Goldberg, Philip (1968, April). Are women prejudiced against women? *Trans-Action* (now *Society*), pp. 28–30.

Goldberg, Gertrude S., & Kremen, Eleanor (1987, Spring). The feminization of poverty: Only in America. *Social Policy*, pp. 3–14.

Goldfarb, Ted, & Wartenberg, Dan (1983, January–February). Fighting pesticides on Long Island. *Science for the People, 15*(1), 18–24.

Goodman, Ellen (1974, August 25). Belaboring the obvious. *Boston Globe*.

Goodman, Ellen (1979, November 27). A time for change . . . all in the family now. *Boston Globe*, p. 19.

Goodman, Ellen (1980a, September 16). Stop the presses? A breakthrough medical 'discovery.' *Boston Globe*, p. 11.

Goodman, Ellen (1980b, October 28). When lifestyle is on the stand. *Boston Globe*, p. 10.

Goodman, Ellen (1981, March 10). Uneasy silence on the campus. *Boston Globe*, p. 19.

Goodman, Ellen (1983a, January 11). The contrast is too great not to notice. *Boston Globe*, p. 19.

Goodman, Ellen (1983b, March 29). The phone lines that bind. *Boston Globe*, p. 19.

Goodman, Ellen (1984, March 27). A change in public attitude on rape. *Boston Globe*, p. 13.

Goodman, Ellen (1985, May 14). Housework? Soviet men say 'nyet.' *Boston Globe*, p. 15.

Goodman, Ellen (1987a, January 20). Pregnancy and jobs. *Boston Globe*, p. 13.

Goodman, Ellen (1987b, February 17). The word that's not mentioned in the Baby M case. *Boston Globe*, p. 15.

Good Tracks, Jim G. (1973, November). Native American noninterference. *Social Work, 18*(6), 30–35.

Gordon, Linda (1973, Fall). The fourth mountain: Women in China. *Working Papers, 1*(3), 27–39.

Gordon, Linda (1981a, Spring). The long struggle

for reproductive rights. *Radical America,* *15*(1) and (2), 75–88.

Gordon, Linda (1981b, July–August). The politics of sexual harassment. *Radical America,* *15*(4), 7–16.

Gordon, Linda (1985, November–December). Women's freedom, women's power: Notes for reproductive rights activists. *Radical America, 19*(6), 31–37.

Gordon, Linda, & Hunter, Allen (1977, November–1978 February). Sex, family and the new right: Anti-feminism as a political force. *Radical America, 11*(6)–*12*(1), 9–26.

Gordon, Michael (Ed.). (1978). *The American family in social-historical perspective* (2nd ed.). New York: St. Martin's.

Gordon, Suzanne (1983, February). The new corporate feminism. *Nation,* pp. 129, 143–147.

Gordon, Suzanne (1986, September). The case for conversion. *Progressive,* pp. 33–34.

Gough, E. Kathleen (1959). The Nayars and the definition of marriage. *Journal of the Royal Anthropological Institute,* 89, pp. 23–34.

Gough, E. Kathleen (1971, November). The origin of the family. *Journal of Marriage and the Family,* pp. 760–770.

Gould, Jay (1984, February). The future of nuclear power. *Monthly Review, 35*(9), 7–14.

Gould, Ray (1985). *Going sour: Science and the politics of acid rain.* Boston: Birkhauser.

Gratz, Roberta Brandes, & Fettman, Eric (1985, November 9). Iacocca's golden door: The selling of Miss Liberty. *Nation,* pp. 465–476.

Gray Panthers of Greater Boston (1987). Media watch project (brochure). Cambridge, MA.

Gray, Stan (1985, September–October). Sharing the shop floor: Women and men on the assembly line. *Radical America, 18*(5), 69–88.

Gray, Stan, & Berry, John (1985, June 8). White-collar crime is big business. *Nation,* pp. 689, 704–707.

Green, Mark (1982, January 6 & 13). Richer than all their tribe. *New Republic.*

Greenbaum, Daniel (1986a, November). Ozone redux. *Sanctuary,* p. 19.

Greenbaum, Daniel (1986b, December). Pesticide threats. *Sanctuary,* p. 21.

Greenbaum, Daniel (1987a, January). Appliance efficiency becomes law in Massachusetts. *Sanctuary,* p. 20.

Greenbaum, Daniel (1987b, January). Another Attleboro victory. *Sanctuary,* p. 20.

Greenbaum, Daniel (1987c, April). Contaminated water. *Sanctuary,* p. 19.

Greenfield, Jeff (1987, January 2). A year to bash the rich? *Boston Globe,* p. 15.

Greer, Edward (1976, September–October). Racism and U.S. Steel, 1906–1974. *Radical America, 10*(5), 45–64.

Greer, Edward (1982, October). Going 'bankrupt' to fleece the public. *Nation,* pp. 360–363.

Greif, Geoffrey (1985). *Single fathers.* Lexington, MA: Lexington.

Grossman, Rachel (1980, January–February). Woman's place in the integrated circuit. *Radical America, 14*(1), 29–49.

Gunther, Marc (1980, April). Goodbye to fair housing. *Progressive,* pp. 39–41.

Gutman, Herbert (1976). *The black family in slavery and freedom 1750–1925.* New York: Vintage.

Gwaltney, John Langston (1980). *Drylongso: A self-portrait of black America.* New York: Random House.

Gwaltney, John Langston (1986). *The dissenters: Voices from contemporary America.* New York: Random House.

Hahn, Steven, & Prude, Jonathan (Eds.). (1985). *The countryside in the age of capitalist transformation.* Chapel Hill, NC: University of North Carolina Press.

Hale-Bensen, Janice E. (1986). *Black children: Their roots, culture, and learning styles* (rev. ed.). Baltimore: Johns Hopkins University Press.

Halley, Jeffrey (1981). Culture in late capitalism. In S. McNall (Ed.), *Political economy* (pp. 135–155). Glenview, IL: Scott, Foresman.

Hammersmith, Sue Kiefer (1985, April 30). Homophobia. *The Advocate,* pp. 26–28.

Hammond, Dorothy, & Jablow, Alta (1976). *Women in cultures of the world.* Reading, MA: Cummings.

Handler, Peggy (1983, February–March). Can you live on an office worker's salary? *9 to 5, 12*(1), 1, 3.

Hansen, Paul (1984, September). Acid politics. *Sanctuary,* pp. 15–16.

Harding, Vincent (1984, July). A struggle for freedom. *Progressive,* pp. 75–79.

Hareven, Tamara (1979, Fall). A media myth: The American family. *Clark Now, 8*(4), 16.

Hareven, Tamara (1983). American families in transition: Historical perspectives on change. In A. Skolnick and J. Skolnick (Eds.), *The family in transition* (4th ed.) (pp. 73–91). Boston: Little, Brown.

Harlow, Harry (1959). Affectional response in the infant monkey. *Science, 130,* 421–432.

Harris, Louis (1987). *Inside America.* New York: Vintage.

Harris, Marvin (1974). *Cows, pigs, wars, and witches: The riddles of culture.* New York: Random House.

Harris, Marvin (1981). *America now: The anthropology of a changing society.* New York: Simon & Schuster.

Harris, Marvin (1983). *Cultural anthropology* (3rd ed.). New York: Harper & Row.

Harris, Michael (1981, February). Farewell, forests. *Progressive,* pp. 43–45.

Harris, William H. (1982). *The harder we run: Black workers since the Civil War.* New York: Oxford University Press.

Harrison, Barbara Grizzutti (1974). Unlearning the lie: Sexism in school. New York: Morrow.

Harrison, Barbara Grizzutti (1980). *Off center.* New York: Playboy.

Hart, Kathleen (1987, March). Is mother's milk safe? *Progressive,* pp. 32–34.

Hartman, Chester (1985, March). Why they have no homes. *Progressive,* pp. 26–27.

Hedman, Carl (1981, September–October). Adversaries and models: Alternative institutions in an age of scarcity. *Radical America, 15*(5), 41–51.

Hembree, Diana (1985, October). Dead end in silicon valley. *Progressive,* pp. 18–24.

Henle, Peter, & Byscavage, Paul (1980, April). The distribution of earned income among men and women. *Monthly Labor Review,* pp. 3–10.

Henley, Nancy, & Freeman, Jo (1984). The sexual politics of interpersonal behavior. In Jo Freeman, (Ed.), *Women: A Feminist perspective* (3rd ed.) (pp. 465–477). Palo Alto, CA: Mayfield.

Henry, Alan P. (1978, August 21). Inner city rebuilding: The wealthy move in, the poor get pushed out. *Boston Globe,* pp. 1, 9.

Henry, Jules (1941). *Jungle people.* New York: Vintage.

Henry, Jules (1963). *Culture against man.* New York: Random House.

Hentoff, Nat (1984a, May). The principals of censorship. *Progressive,* pp. 30–32.

Hentoff, Nat (1984b, July). The silencers among us. *Progressive,* pp. 33–36.

Hentoff, Nat (1986, May). Presumption of guilt. *Progressive,* pp. 24–26.

Herndon, James (1968). *The way it spozed to be.* New York: Bantam.

Hertz, Rosanna (1987). *More equal than others.* Berkeley, CA: University of California Press.

Hewitt, John P., & Hewitt, Myrna Livingston (1986). *Introducing sociology: A symbolic interactionist perspective.* Englewood Cliffs, NJ: Prentice Hall.

Hill, Judah (1975). *Class analysis.* San Francisco: Synthesis.

Hills, Stuart (1980). *Demystifying social deviance.* New York: McGraw-Hill.

Hodges, Michael H. (1987, Spring). Children in the wilderness. *Social Policy,* pp. 43–47.

Hoebel, E. Adamson (1960). *The Cheyennes: Indians of the Great Plains.* New York: Holt, Rinehart & Winston.

Hoffman, Abbie (1987, May 2). Closing argument. *Nation,* pp. 562–563.

Hoffman, William (1971). *David: Report on a Rockefeller.* New York: Dell.

Hollingshead, A. B. (1975). *Elmtown's youth and Elmtown revisited.* New York: Wiley.

Holt, John (1964). *How children fail.* New York: Dell.

Hoogvelt, Ankie (1987, May). IMF crime in conditionality. *Monthly Review, 39*(1), 23–32.

Hooks, Bell (1981). *Ain't I a woman? Black women and feminism.* Boston: South End.

Horn, Patricia (1988, January/February). Elders on the edge: Despite safety net, many fall into poverty. *Dollars and Sense,* pp. 8–9.

Hostetter, Doug (1987, January). In search of peace in El Salvador. *Peacework,* pp. 12–13.

Huebner, Albert L. (1985, June 22). Taking food from the poor's mouths. *Nation,* pp. 766–767.

Huer, Jon (1983). *The professional class.* Unpublished book.

Hulbert, Mark (1982, October 16). Will the U.S. bail out the bankers? *Nation,* pp. 364–366.

Humphreys, Laud (1975). *Tearoom trade: Impersonal sex in public places.* Chicago: Aldine.

Hunt, Morton (1974). *Sexual behavior in the 1970s.* Chicago: Playboy.

Hunter, Floyd (1953). *Community power structure.* Chapel Hill, NC: University of North Carolina Press.

Hunter, Floyd (1983, Winter). Women's wellbeing at midlife. *ISR Newsletter,* pp. 5–6.

Hyman, Herbert (1954). *Interviewing in social research.* Chicago: University of Chicago Press.

Iida, Yuka (1985). *Social interaction in the Back Bay and the North End.* Student paper, Regis College.

Institute for Social Research (1980). *Community power succession.* Chapel Hill, NC: University of North Carolina Press.

Institute for Social Research (1985, Autumn). Racial attitudes. *ISR Newsletter,* pp. 6–7.

Institute for Social Research (1985–1986, Winter). How families use time. *ISR Newsletter,* pp. 3–4.

Intelligence Report (1978, May 14). Carter and his Harvardians. *Parade (Boston Sunday Globe),* p. 18.

Itoh, Eichi (1984, March–June). Labor control through small groups: Japanese labor today. *Radical America, 18*(2)–(3), 27–38.

Iwanska, Alicja (1963). Without love for the land. In P. Olson (Ed.), *America as a mass society* (pp. 205–219). New York: Free Press.

Jackman, Mary R., & Jackman, Robert (1982). *Class awareness in the U.S.* Berkeley, CA: University of California Press.

Jackson, Anne, & Wright, Angus (1981, October). Nature's banner: Environmentalists have

just begun to fight. *Progressive,* pp. 26–32.

Jackson, Patrick G. (1983, March). On living together unmarried. *Journal of Family Issues, 4*(1), 35–59.

Jacobs, Jerry (1974). *Fun city.* New York: Holt, Rinehart & Winston.

Jacobs, Jerry (1984). *The mall: An attempted escape from everyday life.* Prospect Heights, IL: Waveland.

Jacobs, Paul, & Landau, Saul (with Eve Pell) (1971). *To serve the devil* (2 vols.). New York: Vintage.

Jacobs, Ruth Harriet (1979). *Life after youth: Female, 40, what next?* Boston: Beacon.

Jesuit Relations (1896–1901). *The Jesuit Relations and allied documents: Travel and explorations of the Jesuit missionaries in New France, 1610–1791.* (73 vols.). Cleveland: Burrows Brothers.

Jobs with Peace (1988). *Military spending and your federal tax dollar.* Boston, MA: Jobs with Peace Campaign.

Joe, Tom (1984, July 2). Prisoners of joblessness. *Boston Globe,* p. 15.

Johnson, Allen (1978, September). In search of the affluent society. *Human Nature,* pp. 50–59.

Johnson, Kirk A. (1987). *Media images of Boston's black community.* Boston, MA: William Monroe Trotter Institute, University of Massachusetts at Boston.

Johnson, Philip (1981, October). Fighting herbicides. *Progressive,* pp. 37–38.

Jones, Arthur (1982, July). Dorgan's complaint. *Progressive,* pp. 14–16.

Jones, James H. (1981). *Bad blood: The Tuskeege experiment: A tragedy of race and medicine.* New York: Free Press.

Joseph, Alvin M., Jr. (1984). *Now that the buffalo's gone: A study of today's American Indians.* Norman, OK: University of Oklahoma Press.

Junkerman, John (1983, May). The Japanese model. *Progressive,* pp. 21–27.

Junkerman, John (1987a, June). Nissan, Tennessee. *Progressive,* pp. 16–20.

Junkerman, John (1987b, June). Sexual harassment at Smyrna. *Progressive,* p. 19.

Kagan, Jerome. (1973, March 10). A conversation with Jerome Kagan. *Saturday Review.* In Judson R. Landis (Ed.), *Sociology* (4th ed.) (pp. 54–58). Belmont, CA: Wadsworth, 1980.

Kagan, Jerome (1976). Psychological requirements for human development. In Arlene Skolnick & Jerome Skolnick (Eds.), *Family in transition* (3rd ed.) (pp. 427–438). Boston: Little-Brown, 1980.

Kagan, Jerome (1978, August). The parental love trap. *Psychology Today,* pp. 54–61.

Kahn, Kathy (1973). *Hillbilly women.* Garden City, NY: Doubleday.

Kaku, Michio, & Axelrod, Daniel (1987). *To win a nuclear war: The Pentagon's secret war plans.* Boston: South End.

Kamerman, Sheila B. (1980, November). Child care and family benefits: Policies of six industrialized countries. *Monthly Labor Review,* pp. 23–28.

Karagianis, Maria (1981a, July 3). Guilty—but was it equal justice? *Boston Globe,* p. 11.

Karagianis, Maria (1981b, August 20). Raped nurse 'shocked' doctors were convicted. *Boston Globe,* pp. 1, 17.

Karol, K. S. (1987, July–August). Gorbachev's great gamble: An interview with K. S. Karol (conducted by Steve Wasserman). *Monthly Review, 39*(3), 11–23.

Keesing, Roger (1981). *Cultural anthropology* (2nd ed.). New York: Holt, Rinehart & Winston.

Kelley, Don Quinn (1982, November). What price freedom in America? *Monthly Review, 34*(6), 24–39.

Kelvin, Peter, & Jarrett, Joanne E. (1985). *Unemployment: Its social and psychological effects.* Cambridge, England: Cambridge University Press.

Kempe, Ruth S., & Kempe, C. Henry (1984). *The common secret: Sexual abuse of children and adolescents.* New York: Freeman.

Kenney, Michael (1988, August 17). In Poland, an environmental crisis. *Boston Globe,* p. 19.

Kenyatta, Muhammad I. (1983, March). In defense of the black family. *Monthly Review, 34*(10), 12–21.

Kessler, Evelyn (1976). *Women: An anthropolog-* ical view. New York: Holt, Rinehart & Winston.

Kessler-Harris, Alice (1981). *Women have always worked.* Old Westbury, NY: Feminist.

Kidd, Virginia (1970, September 3). Now you see, said Mark. *New York Review of Books,* pp. 35–36.

Kiefer, Tona (1980, December). The "neurotic woman" syndrome. *Progressive,* pp. 26–29.

Kimbal, Joseph (1970, April 27). Night thoughts of a police chief. *Nation,* pp. 290–292.

Kinloch, Graham (1979). *The sociology of minority group relations.* Englewood Cliffs, NJ: Prentice Hall.

Kitron, Uriel, & Schutz, Brian (1983, January–February). Alternatives in agriculture. *Science for the people, 15*(1), 25–30.

Klare, Michael T. (1980, July). Is Exxon worth dying for? *Progressive,* pp. 21–26.

Klare, Michael T. (1981a, February). An army in search of a war. *Progressive,* pp. 18–23.

Klare, Michael T. (1981b, Spring). Beyond the Vietnam syndrome: Renewed U.S. intervention in the Third World. *Radical America, 15*(1)–(2), 153–159.

Klare, Michael T. (1982, September 25). A nuclear freeze isn't enough. *Nation,* pp. 264–266.

Klare, Michael T. (1984, February 25). May the force project us. *Nation,* pp. 216–217.

Kloby, Jerry (1987, September). The great divide. *Monthly Review, 39*(4), 1–8.

Kluegel, James R., & Smith, Eliot R. (1986) *Beliefs about inequality: Americans' views of what is and what ought to be.* New York: Aldine de Gruyter.

Knox, Richard (1982, January 28). Research indicates risks in loneliness. *Boston Globe,* p. 11.

Kobrin, Frances (1976, February). The fall in household size and the rise of the primary individual in the United States. In M. Gordon (Ed.), *The American family in social-historical perspective* (pp. 69–81). New York: St. Martin's.

Kochis, Bruce (1986, September). AIDS and the mythmakers. *Progressive,* p. 16.

Koeppel, Barbara (1981, March). For rent, cheap, no heat. *Progressive,* pp. 23–25.

Koeppel, Barbara (1982, March). The migrants stoop, the growers conquer. *Progressive,* pp. 42–44.

Kohl, Herbert (1968). *36 children.* New York: Signet.

Kohl, Herbert (1987, May 9). Pushing kids away: What teen suicide means. *Nation,* pp. 603–606.

Kohn, Alfie (1987, May 4). Sex and status and a manner of speaking. *Boston Globe,* pp. 37–38.

Kohn, Howard (1982). *Who killed Karen Silkwood?* New York: Summit.

Kohn, Melvin (1977). Class and conformity (2nd ed.). Chicago: University of Chicago Press.

Kolko, Gabriel (1963). *The triumph of conservatism.* Chicago: Quadrangle.

Kolko, Gabriel (1986). *Anatomy of a war: Vietnam, the U.S., and the modern historical experience.* New York: Pantheon.

Kovel, Joel (1987, January). Class, power, and the state. *Monthly Review,* pp. 23–38.

Kozol, Jonathan (1988). *Rachel and her children: Homeless families in America.* New York: Crown.

Kranzberg, Melvin, & Gies, Joseph (1975). *By the sweat of thy brow.* New York: G. P. Putnam.

Krieger, Nancy, & Bassett, Mary (1986, July–August). The health of black folk: Disease, class, and ideology in science. *Monthly Review, 38*(3), 74–85.

Kristof, Nicholas D. (1981, August 13). Satellite data indicate peril to ozone. *Boston Globe,* p. 13.

Kumin, Maxine (1983, May 7). Carla: It's very hard to say I'm poor. *Nation,* pp. 561, 575–577.

Kurtz, Howard (1983, March 27). Ruckelshaus' business connections. *Boston Globe,* p. 18.

Kuttner, Bob (1985, December 27). A European plan that could ease housing crisis here. *Boston Globe,* p. 15.

Kuttner, Bob (1986a, January 6). When bankruptcy shields corporate negligence. *Boston Globe,* p. 15.

Kuttner, Bob (1986b, January 20). King's economic dream. *Boston Globe,* p. 15.

Kuttner, Bob (1986c, February 3). The tragedy was real, but the purpose of the mission was flawed. *Boston Globe,* p. 15.

Kuttner, Bob (1987a, February 9). Time to begin solving the housing problem that Reagan began. *Boston Globe,* p. 15.

Kuttner, Bob (1987b, June 15). The stakes are high for today's youths in Boston. *Boston Globe,* p. 11.

Lake, A. (1975, January). Are we born into sex roles or programmed into them? *Woman's Day,* pp. 24–25.

Landis, Judson R. (1986). *Sociology* (6th ed.). Belmont, CA: Wadsworth.

Lane, David (1982). *The end of social inequality? Class, status, and power under state socialism.* London: Allen and Unwin.

Lane, Harlan (1976a, Winter). The wild boy of Aveyron. *Horizon, 18*(1), 32–38.

Lane, Harlan (1976b). The wild boy of Aveyron. Cambridge, MA: Harvard University Press.

Lanner, Deborah (1985, February). High and dry. *Progressive,* pp. 28–32.

LaPiere, Richard (1934, December). Attitudes vs. actions. *Social Forces, 13,* 230–237.

Lappe, Francis Moore, & Collins, Joseph (1977). *Food first: Beyond the myth of scarcity.* Boston: Houghton-Mifflin.

Lasch, Christopher (1977, November 24). The siege of the family. *New York Review of Books.*

Lasson, Kenneth (1971). *The workers.* New York: Bantam.

Leacock, Eleanor Burke (1981). *Myths of male dominance.* New York: Monthly Review Press.

Leacock, Eleanor Burke, & Safa, Helen I. (Eds.). (1986). *Women's work: Development and the division of labor by gender.* South Hadley, MA: Bergin and Garvey.

Leavitt, Judith A. (1982). *Women in management: An annotated bibliography and sourcelist.* Phoenix: Oryx.

Leavitt, Judith W. (Ed.). (1984). *Women and health in America: Historical readings.* Madison, WI: University of Wisconsin Press.

Lee, Dorothy (1959). *Freedom and culture.* Englewood Cliffs, NJ: Prentice Hall.

Lee, Dorothy (1976). *Valuing the self: What we can learn from other cultures.* Prospect Heights, IL: Waveland.

Lee, Richard B. (1969, December). Eating Christmas in the Kalahari. *Natural History.*

Lee, Richard B. (1982). Politics, sexual and nonsexual, in an egalitarian society. In Eleanor Burke Leacock & Richard B. Lee (Eds.), *Politics and history in band societies* (pp. 37–59). New York: Cambridge University Press.

Lee, Richard B. (1984). *The Dobe !Kung.* New York: Holt, Rinehart & Winston.

Leff, Walli F., & Haft, Marilyn G. (1983). *Time without work.* Boston: South End.

LeMasters, E. E., & DeFrain, John (1983). *Parents in contemporary America* (4th ed.). Homewood, IL: Dorsey.

Lens, Sidney (1980, November). Reindustrialization: Panacea or threat? *Progressive,* pp. 44–47.

Lens, Sidney (1981, June). The postponed depression. *Progressive,* pp. 38–41.

Lens, Sidney (1982, August). Ban the bomb. *Progressive,* pp. 24–25.

Lenski, Gerhard, & Lenski, Jean (1978). *Human societies* (3rd ed.). New York: McGraw-Hill.

Lerner, Mary (1980, October). Sharecropper's daughter. *Progressive,* p. 66.

Levene, Susan (1985, January–February). Civil disobedience begins at home: The nuclear free Cambridge campaign. *Radical America, 19*(1), 7–22.

Levin, Jack, & Levin, William C. (1980). *Ageism: Prejudice and discrimination against the elderly.* Belmont, CA: Wadsworth.

Levin, Jack, & Levin, William C. (1982). *The functions of prejudice and discrimination* (2nd ed.). New York: Harper & Row.

Levine, James P. (1976, November). The potential for overreporting in criminal victimization surveys. *Criminology, 14*(3), 307–330.

Levins, Richard (1986, July–August). Science and progress. *Monthly Review, 38*(3), 13–20.

Levison, Andrew (1974). *The working class majority.* Baltimore: Penguin.

Lewis, Oscar (1951). *Life in a Mexican village: Tepoztlan restudied.* Urbana, IL: University of Illinois Press.

Lewis, Oscar (1959). *Five families.* New York: Basic Books.

Lewis, Sinclair (1920). *Main Street.* New York: New American Library, 1974.

Ley, Camara (1954). *The dark child.* New York: Farrar, Straus & Giroux.

Liazos, Alexander (1970). *Processing for unfitness.* Ph.D. dissertation, Brandeis University.

Liazos, Alexander (1972, Summer). The poverty of the sociology of deviance: Nuts, sluts, and perverts. *Social Problems, 20*(1), 103–120.

Liazos, Alexander (1974, Fall). Class oppression: The functions of juvenile justice. *Insurgent Sociologist, 5*(1), 2–23.

Liazos, Alexander (1976). *On sociological arrogance.* Unpublished paper.

Liazos, Alexander (1978, July). School, alienation, and delinquency. *Crime and delinquency, 24*(3), 355–370.

Liazos, Alexander (1982). *People first: An introduction to social problems.* Boston: Allyn and Bacon.

Liazos, Alexander (1986). *Before patriarchy: Social and sex equality.* Unpublished manuscript.

Lie, John (1987, January). The discriminated finger: The Korean minority in Japan. *Monthly Review, 38*(8), 17–23.

Liebert, Larry (1983, May 16). Kibbutz inspires communal housing plan in Calif. *Boston Globe,* p. 3

Liebert, Robert; Sprafkin, Joyce N.; & Davidson, Emily (1982). *The early window (2nd ed.).* New York: Pergamon.

Liebow, Elliot (1967). *Tally's corner.* Boston: Little, Brown.

Light, Donald R., & Keller, Suzanne (1982). *Sociology* (3rd ed.). New York: Knopf.

Linton, Ralph (1937, April). One hundred percent American. *American Mercury,* pp. 427–429.

Longcope, Kay (1983, December 13). Playing by the rules: One woman's formula for success. *Boston Globe,* pp. 49, 51.

Longmore, Paul K. (1985, Summer). Screening

stereotypes: Images of disabled people. *Social Policy*, pp. 31–37.

Lopate, Carol (1977, February). Daytime television. *Radical America, 11*(1), 33–51.

Luhman, Reid, & Gilman, Stuart (1980). *Race and ethnic relations*. Belmont, CA: Wadsworth.

Lupo, Alan (1986a, January 18). Fighting the speculators in Jamaica Plain. *Boston Globe*, p. 15.

Lupo, Alan (1986b, February 15). The reality behind hunger in Massachusetts. *Boston Globe*, p. 11.

Lupo, Alan (1986c, February 22). Framingham's poor. *Boston Globe*, p. 19.

Lupo, Alan (1986d, April 26). Desperate for housing. *Boston Globe*, p. 11.

Lurie, Alison (1981). *The language of clothes*. New York: Vintage.

Lynch, James (1977). *The broken heart: The medical consequences of loneliness*. New York: Basic.

Lynd, Robert S., & Lynd, Helen Merrell (1929). *Middletown*. New York: Harcourt, Brace.

Lynd, Robert S., & Lynd, Helen Merrell (1937). *Middletown in transition*. New York: Harcourt, Brace.

Lynd, Stoughton (1981, July–August). What happened in Youngstown: An outline. *Radical America, 15*(4), 37–48.

McCain, Nina (1983, June 8). From girlhood on, a devotion to taking care of children. *Boston Globe*, p. 2.

McCarthy, Colman (1983, March 5). Three days down and out in Chicago. *Nation*, pp. 257, 271–275.

McDermott, John (1982, August 21–28). The secret history of the deficit. *Nation*, pp. 129, 144–146.

MacDonald, J. Fred (1983). *Black and white TV: Afro-Americans in television since 1948*. Chicago: Nelson–Hall.

McDonnell, Kathleen (1984). *Not an easy choice: A feminist re-examines abortion*. Boston: South End.

MacEwan, Arthur (1985, February). The current crisis in Latin America. *Monthly Review, 36*(9), 1–18.

MacEwan, Arthur (1986, September). Latin America: Why not default? *Monthly Review, 38*(4), 1–13.

MacEwan, Arthur (1987, June). The money mandarins. *Monthly Review, 39*(2), 47–54.

McGehee, Ralph (1985, August). Back in the saddle again. *Progressive*, pp. 32–33.

McLaughlin, Loretta (1987, June 15). In Denmark, it's love the one you're with. *Boston Globe*, p. 11.

McLemore, S. Dale (1983). *Racial and ethnic relations* (2nd ed.). Boston: Allyn and Bacon.

McLuhan, T.C. (Ed.). (1971). *Touch the earth*. New York: Pocket Books.

McNall, Scott G. (Ed.). (1981). *Political economy*. Glenview, IL: Scott, Foresman.

Macionis, John C. (1987). *Sociology*. Englewood Cliffs, NJ: Prentice Hall.

Magdoff, Harry (1982a, April). International economic distress and the Third World. *Monthly Review, 33*(11), 1–13.

Magdoff, Harry (1982b, October). The meaning of work: A Marxist perspective. *Monthly Review, 34*(5), 1–15.

Makower, Joel (1982). *Office hazards*. Washington, DC: Tilden.

Malcolm X (1965). *The autobiography of Malcolm X*. New York: Grove.

Mangione, Jerre (1981). *Mount Allegro*. New York: Columbia University Press.

Mansbridge, Jane (1979). The agony of inequality. In J. Case & R.C. Taylor (Eds.), *Coops, communes and collectives* (pp. 194–214). New York: Pantheon, 1979.

Marable, Manning (1983). *How capitalism underdeveloped black America*. Boston: South End.

Marcuse, Peter (1987, April 4). Why are they homeless? *Nation*, pp. 426–428.

Marinelli, Janet, & Robinson, Gail (1981, December). No room at the bin. *Progressive*, pp. 23–27.

Marple, Gary A., & Wissman, Harry B. (Eds.) (1968). *Grocery manufacturing in the United States*. New York: Praeger.

Marquis, Christopher (1986, June). When the fires go out. *Progressive*, pp. 23–25.

Marquit, Erwin (1978). *The socialist countries*. Minneapolis: Marxist Educational Press.

Marshall, Carolyn (1987, April 25). An excuse for workplace hazard. *Nation,* pp. 532–534.

Marx, Andrew (1980, October). The United League of Mississippi. *Dollars and Sense,* pp. 12–14.

Marx, Karl, & Engels, Friedrich (1959). *Basic writings in politics and philosophy* (Lewis S. Feuer, Ed.). Garden City, NY: Anchor.

Massie, Robert (1982, May 8). Giving America the business. *Nation,* pp. 550–551.

Mattera, Philip (1979, September–October). Hot child in the city. *Radical America, 13*(5), 49–60.

Matthiessen, Constance (1984, October). Of cloth and steel. *Progressive,* p. 15.

Mayer, Milton (1984, February). Sunset in the east. *Progressive,* pp. 32–36.

Mead, George Herbert (1934). *Mind, self and society* (Ed. Charles Morris). Chicago: University of Chicago Press.

Mead, Margaret (1928). *Coming of age in Samoa.* New York: Morrow.

Mead, Margaret (1935). *Sex and temperament in three primitive societies.* New York: Morrow.

Medlen, Craig (1984, November). Corporate taxes and the federal deficit. *Monthly Review, 36*(6), 10–26.

Meier, August, & Rudwick, Elliott (1970). *From plantation to ghetto.* New York: Hill & Wang.

Melville, Keith (1983). *Marriage and family today* (3rd ed.). New York: Random House.

Mermelstein, David (Ed.). (1987). *The antiapartheid reader.* New York: Grove.

Merton, Robert K. (1957). *Social theory and social structure.* New York: Free Press.

Messenger, John C. (1969). *Inis Beag: Isle of Ireland.* New York: Holt, Rinehart & Winston.

Milgram, Stanley (1965, February). Some conditions of obedience and disobedience to authority. *Human Relations,* pp. 57–76.

Miller, Arthur (1982, October). Buying votes. *Progressive,* pp. 43–46.

Miller, Wayne (Ed.). (1972). *A gathering of ghetto writers.* New York: New York University Press.

Millman, Marcia, & Kanter, Rosabeth (Eds.).

(1976). *Another voice.* Garden City, NY: Doubleday.

Mills, C. Wright (1951). *White collar.* New York: Oxford University Press.

Mills, C. Wright (1956). *The power elite.* New York: Oxford University Press.

Mills, Diana (1982). *If I could have three wishes.* Unpublished paper for introductory sociology course, Framingham State College, Summer 1982.

Minkler, Meredith (1987, Winter). The politics of generational equity. *Social Policy,* pp. 48–52.

Mintz, Beth (1975, Spring). The president's cabinet 1897–1972: A contribution to the power structure debate. *Insurgent Sociologist, 5*(3), 131–148.

Mintz, Morton (1985a, November). At any cost. *Progressive,* pp. 20–25.

Mintz, Morton (1985b). *At any cost: Corporate greed, women and the Dalkon Shield.* New York: Pantheon.

Mitchell, Greg (1981). *Truth and consequences: Seven who would not be silenced.* New York: Dembner.

Mitchell, John H. (1982, June). Blues in the night. *Sanctuary,* p. 2.

Mitchell, John H. (1987, May/June). Embattled farmers. *Sanctuary,* p. 2.

Moffitt, Michael (1983, February). Global banking goes for broke. *Progressive,* pp. 20–24.

Molyneux, Maxine (1982, July–August). Socialist societies old and new: Progress towards women's emancipation. *Monthly Review, 34*(3), 56–100.

Money, John, & Erhardt, Anke (1972). *Man and woman, boy and girl.* Baltimore: Johns Hopkins University Press.

Montgomery, David (1985, November). America's working man. *Monthly Review, 37*(6), 1–8.

Montgomery, M. R. (1985, November 4). The dark side of an art exhibit from stately homes. *Boston Globe,* p. 15.

Montgomery, M. R. (1986, November 3). Clothes make, and unmake, the man. *Boston Globe,* p. 19.

Moody, Kim (1983, July). Going public. *Progressive,* pp. 18–21.

Moody, Kim (1987, May). Flight attendants at American Airlines fight two-tier wage system. *Labor Notes,* pp. 1, 10.

Moody, Kim (1988, July). Unemployment: The real story. *Labor Notes,* pp. 1, 10.

Moore, Michael (1987, June 6). In Flint, tough times last. *Nation,* pp. 753–756.

Moore, Richard W. (1987, May/June). The farm and the flood. *Sanctuary,* pp. 6–8.

Moore, Richard, & Marsis, Elizabeth (1985, January). Sisterhood under siege. *Progressive,* pp. 30–31.

Morris, Robert (1977, October). Jimmy Carter's ruling class. *Harper's,* pp. 37–45.

Morrissey, David (1983, February). A blast from the past. *Progressive,* pp. 32–37.

Mullin, James (1982, November). Saving the small bookstores. *Progressive,* p. 18.

Mumford, Lewis (1961). *The city in history.* New York: Harcourt, Brace, and World.

Murphy, Yolanda, & Murphy, Robert F. (1985). *Women of the forest* (2nd ed.). New York: Columbia University Press.

Nanda, Serena (1980). *Cultural anthropology.* New York: D. Van Nostrand.

National Urban League (1988). *The state of black America.* New York: National Urban League.

Navarro, Vicente (1985, July–August). The road ahead. *Monthly Review, 37*(3), 30–48.

Navarro, Vicente (1986a, July–August). What is socialist medicine? *Monthly Review, 38*(3), 61–73.

Navarro, Vicente (1986b, September). The Lincoln Brigade: Some comments on U.S. history. *Monthly Review, 38*(4), 29–37.

Navarro, Vicente (1987, June). The Rainbow Coalition and the challenge of class. *Monthly Review, 39*(2), 19–27.

Nelson, Harold (1967, Fall). The Defenders: A case of an informal police organization. *Social Problems, 14*(2), 124–147.

Nelson, Marcia (1985, March). Street people. *Progressive,* pp. 24–25.

Nelson, Robert (1983, April 2). Two, three, many Rita Lavelles. *Nation,* pp. 394–396.

Nettler, Gwynn (1976). *Social concerns.* New York: McGraw-Hill.

Newcomb, Paul R. (1984). Cohabitation in America. In Burt Adams & John Campbell (Eds.), *Framing the family* (pp. 483–492). Prospect Heights, IL: Waveland, 1984.

Nimmo, H. Arlo (1970, July). Bajau sex and reproduction. *Ethnology,* pp. 251–262.

Nisbet, Robert (1966). *The sociological tradition.* New York: Basic.

Norgren, Jill (1984). Child care. In Jo Freeman (Ed.), *Women: A feminist perspective* (3rd ed.) (pp. 139–153). Palo Alto, CA: Mayfield.

Norwood, Christopher (1980). *At highest risk: Environmental hazards to young and unborn children.* New York: McGraw-Hill.

Nyhan, David (1981, November 9). Out of work, some fill the void with drugs. *Boston Globe,* pp. 1, 11.

Nyhan, David (1982, August 2). PACs make waves on campaign trail. *Boston Globe,* p. 8.

Nyhan, David (1983a, January 31). In steel, making money always came first. *Boston Globe,* pp. 1, 4.

Nyhan, David (1983b, February 1). Unemployment halts good life in Pittsburgh. *Boston Globe,* p. 6.

O'Brien, Jim, & Thorkelson, Nick (1985, July–August). Myths and realities in Central America. *Radical America, 19*(4), 24–31.

O'Kelly, Charlotte, & Carney, Larry S. (1986). *Women and men in society* (2nd ed.). Belmont, CA: Wadsworth.

O'Neill, Diane (1984, December). Silent no more. *Progressive,* pp. 22–24.

Oakley, Ann (1974). *Woman's work.* New York: Vintage.

Oakley, Ann (1981). *Subject women.* New York: Pantheon.

Oliphant, Thomas (1982, November 23). US reportedly mulled plans to kill Allende. *Boston Globe,* p. 12.

Oliver, Chad (1981). *The discovery of humanity.* New York: Harper & Row.

Ollman, Bertell (1985, July 10). What is to be done? Little things. *Guardian,* p. 23.

Ollman, Bertell (1986, November). The meaning of dialectics. *Monthly Review, 38*(6), 42–55.

Olson, Philip (Ed.) (1963). *America as a mass society.* New York: Free Press.

Opie, John (1981, July). Draining America dry: What will we do when the water runs out? *Progressive,* pp. 20–23.

Oppenheimer, Martin (1985). *White collar politics.* New York: Monthly Review Press.

Orne, Martin T. (1962, November). On the social psychology of the psychological experiment. *American Psychologist, 17*(11), 776–783. In I. Deutscher (Ed.), *What we say/What we do* (pp. 184–200). Glenview, IL: Scott, Foresman, 1973.

Otten, Michael C. (1981). *Power, values, and society: An introduction to sociology.* Glenview, IL: Scott, Foresman.

Packard, Vance (1972). *A nation of strangers.* New York: McKay.

Panitch, Leo (1985, April). Class and power in Canada. *Monthly Review, 36*(11), 1–13.

Parachini, Allan (1982, November 29). Air bag rule dropped after Nixon met Ford executives, tape shows. *Boston Globe,* p. 3.

Parenti, Michael (1981, November). The high cost of empire. *Progressive,* pp. 16–17.

Parenti, Michael (1982, October). The left: Do we party? *Progressive,* pp. 23–26.

Parenti, Michael (1986). *Inventing reality: The politics of the mass media.* New York: St. Martin's.

Payer, Cheryl (1985, December). The case against debt relief. *Dollars and Sense,* pp. 8–9.

Peacework (1987, May). *Five years after the huge June 12 rally: Are we more secure from nuclear war, or less?,* pp. 1–6.

Pease, John (1981, November). Sociology and the sense of the commoners. *American Sociologist, 16*(4), 257–271.

Peck, Keenen (1983, May). Ad nauseam. *Progressive,* pp. 43–47.

Peck, Keenen (1986, April). The great insurance scam. *Progressive,* pp. 19–22.

Pell, Eve (1981, June 6). Libel as a political weapon. *Nation,* pp. 681, 698–700.

Pelletier, Wilfred (1970). Childhood in an Indian village. In Satu Repo (Ed.), *This book is about schools* (pp. 18–31). New York: Vintage.

Petras, James (1980, February). U.S. foreign policy: The revival of interventionism. *Monthly Review,* pp. 15–27.

Petras, James, & Morley, James (1975). *The United States and Chile: Imperialism and the overthrow of the Allende government.* New York: Monthly Review Press.

Pfeffer, Richard M. (1979). *Working for capitalism.* New York: Columbia University Press.

Pillemer, Karl A., & Wolf, Rosalie S. (Eds.). (1986). *Elder abuse: Conflict in the family.* Dover, MA: Auburn House.

Pincus, Fred L. (1980, August). The false promise of community colleges: Class conflict and vocational education. *Harvard Educational Review, 50*(3), 332–361.

Pincus, Fred (1984, Winter). From equity to excellence: The rebirth of educational conservatism. *Social Policy,* pp. 50–56.

Pinkney, Alphonso (1987). *Black Americans* (3rd ed.). Englewood Cliffs, NJ: Prentice Hall.

Pitcher, Evelyn Goodnough, & Hickey, Lynn (1983). *Boys and girls at play: The development of sex roles.* South Hadley, MA.: Bergin and Garvey.

Piven, Frances Pox, & Cloward, Richard W. (1982). *The new class war: Reagan's attack on the welfare state and its consequences.* New York: Pantheon.

Pleck, Joseph (1976). The male sex role. *Journal of Social Issues, 32,* 155–164.

Pleck, Joseph (1980, March). Conflicts between work and family life. *Monthly Labor Review,* pp. 29–32.

Pogrebin, Letty C. (1975, November). Do women make men violent? *Ms.*

Pogrebin, Letty C. (1980). *Growing up free.* New York: McGraw-Hill.

Pogrebin, Letty C. (1983). *Family politics: Love and politics on an intimate frontier.* New York: McGraw-Hill.

Pollak, Richard (1982, May 1). Covering the unthinkable. *Nation,* pp. 516–523.

Pollin, Robert, & Zepeda, Eduardo (1987, February). Latin American debt: The choices ahead. *Monthly Review, 38*(9), 1–16.

Pollitt, Katha (1983, January). The parent trap. *Mother Jones,* pp. 57–58.

Pollitt, Katha (1987, May 23). The strange case of Baby M. *Nation,* pp. 667, 682–688.

Pollner, Mildred (1982, Summer). Better dead than wed. *Social Policy*, pp. 28–31.

Polsgrove, Carol (1983, March). Not in my backyard. *Progressive*, pp. 22–27.

Polsgrove, Carol (1984, July). From Walden Pond to Love Canal. *Progressive*, pp. 20–21.

Pool, John C., & Stamos, Stephen C. (1985, March). The uneasy calm: Third world debt—the case of Mexico. *Monthly Review, 36*(10), 7–19.

Powell, Lawrence A., & Williamson, John B. (1985, Summer). The mass media and the aged. *Social Policy*, pp. 38–49.

Powledge, Fred (1982, June 12). Water, water, running out. *Nation*, pp. 703, 714–716.

Powledge, Fred (1984a, March 17). Dereg's deadly diet. *Nation*, pp. 314–318.

Powledge, Fred (1984b). *Fat of the land*. New York: Simon & Schuster.

Preston, Marilyn (1982, August 4). In search of America? Check the malls. *Boston Globe*, p. 22.

Prochnan, Bill (1982, November 24). Job bias persists at 'alarming' level, hiring study says. *Boston Globe*, p. 3.

Quarles, Benjamin (1969). *Frederick Douglass*. New York: Atherton.

Queen, Stuart; Habenstein, Robert W.; & Quadagno, Jill S. (1985). *The family in various cultures* (5th ed.). New York: Harper & Row.

Quigg, Catherine (1982, December). Leap of faith. *Progressive*, pp. 37–39.

Quinn, Naomi (1977). Anthropological perspectives on women's status. *Annual Review of Anthropology, 6*, 181–225.

Rabkin, Leslie (1976, February). The institution of the family is alive and well. *Psychology Today*, pp. 66–71.

Radin, Paul (1953). *The world of primitive man*. New York: Grove.

Randall, Margaret (1981). *Women in Cuba—twenty years later*. New York: Smyrna.

Randall, Margaret (1987). *This is about incest*. Ithaca, NY: Firebrand.

Randour, Mary Lou (1982, May). Women in higher education. *Harvard Educational Review, 52*(2), 189–202.

Rapping, Elayne (1980, November–December). Tupperware and women. *Radical America, 14*(6), 39–49.

Rapping, Elayne (1987). *The looking glass world of nonfiction TV*. Boston: South End.

Rapping, Elayne (1988, March 9). Fatal omission: Feminism. *Guardian*, pp. 10–11.

Rathje, William L. (1984). The garbage project. In David Hunter & Phillip Whitten (Eds.), *Anthropology* (pp. 70–76). Boston: Little, Brown, 1985.

Rayman, Paula (1982, July). The private tragedy behind the unemployment statistics. *Brandeis Quarterly, 2*(4), 2–4.

Razis, Vic (1986). *The American connection: The influence of United States business on South Africa*. New York: St. Martin's.

Redfield, Robert (1930). *Tepoztlán: A Mexican village*. Chicago: University of Chicago Press.

Redfield, Robert (1960). *The little community* and *Peasant society and culture*. Chicago: University of Chicago Press.

Reich, Michael (1981). *Racial inequality*. Princeton, NJ: Princeton University Press.

Reid, Robert Leonard (1982, March). Wilderness: Lusting after the last acre. *Progressive*, pp. 30–33.

Reiman, Jeffrey (1979). *The rich get richer and the poor get prison*. New York: Wiley.

Reiter, Rayna (Ed.) (1975). *Toward an anthropology of women*. New York: Monthly Review Press.

Rensberger, Royce (1983, April). Margaret Mead. *Science, 83*, 28–37.

Riotta, Gianni; Ireland, Doug; Stavis, Benedict; Orme, William A., Jr.; Brill, Julie; & Jackson, Gabriel (1987, April 11). Enemies of the state? *Nation*, pp. 453, 462–471.

Ritzer, George, & Walczak, David (1986). *Working: Conflict and change* (3rd ed.). Englewood Cliffs, NJ: Prentice Hall.

Rivers, Caryl (1980, September 23). Family statistics: A case of overkill. *Boston Globe*, pp. 18–19.

Rivers, Caryl (1986, January 3). The new stay-at-home mom. *Boston Globe*, p. 13.

Rivlin, Leanne (1986, Spring). A new look at the homeless. *Social Policy*, pp. 3–10.

Robertson, Ian (1981). *Sociology* (2nd ed.). New York: Worth.

Robinson, Jo Ann Gibson (1987). *The Montgomery bus boycott and the women who started it.* Knoxville, TN: University of Tennessee Press.

Robinson, William I., & Norsworthy, Kent (1985, December). Nicaragua: The strategy of counterrevolution. *Monthly Review, 37*(7), 11–24.

Rollins, Judith (1985). *Between women: Domestics and their employers.* Philadelphia: Temple University Press.

Roose, Diana (1975, Spring). Top dogs and top brass: An inside look at a government advisory committee. *Insurgent Sociologist, 5*(3), 53–63.

Rosaldo, Michelle (1974). Women, culture, and society: A theoretical overview. In Michelle Rosaldo & Louise Lamphere (Eds.), *Women, culture, and society* (pp. 17–42). Stanford, CA: Stanford University Press.

Rosaldo, Michelle, & Lamphere, Louise (Eds.) (1974). *Women, culture, and society.* Stanford, CA: Stanford University Press.

Rose, Arnold (1967). *The power structure.* New York: Oxford University Press.

Rose, Tom (Ed.) (1969). *Violence in America.* New York: Vintage.

Rosenbaum, Walter A. (1977). *The politics of environmental concern* (2nd ed.). New York: Praeger.

Rosenfeld, Stuart (1982, April). The new shape-up: Schooling workers to stay in line. *Progressive,* pp. 46–48.

Rosenhan, David L. (1973, January 19). On being sane in insane places. *Science,* pp. 250–258.

Rosenthal, Robert, & Jacobson, Lenore (1968). *Pygmallion in the classroom.* New York: Holt, Rinehart & Winston.

Ross, Catherine (1987, March). The division of labor at home. *Social Forces, 65*(3), 816–833.

Roth, Julius A. (1965, November). Hired hand research. *American Sociologist, 1*(1), 190–196.

Rothman, Robert A. (1987). *Working: Sociological perspectives.* Englewood Cliffs, NJ: Prentice Hall.

Rothschild, Edwin (1984, April 28). Don't let big oil get even bigger. *Nation,* pp. 508–509.

Rothschild, Matthew (1985, November). No place for scruples. *Progressive,* pp. 26–28.

Rothschild, Matthew (1986, June). Death by prescription. *Progressive,* pp. 18–22.

Rubenstein, Carin (1981, July). Alienation in supermarkets. *Psychology Today,* p. 19.

Rubin, Beth (1986, October). Class struggle American style: Unions, strikes and wages. *American Sociological Review, 51*(5), 618–631.

Rubin, Gayle (1975). The traffic in women: Notes on the political economy of sex. In R. Reiter (Ed.), *Toward an anthropology of women* (pp. 157–210). New York: Monthly Review Press.

Rubin, Lillian B. (1976). *Worlds of pain.* New York: Basic Books.

Rubin, Lillian B. (1979). *Women of a certain age: The midlife search for self.* New York: Harper & Row.

Rubin, Lillian B. (1983). *Intimate strangers: Men and women together.* New York: Harper & Row.

Rubin, Lillian B. (1985). Just friends: The role of friendship in our lives. New York: Harper & Row.

Rudolph, Richard, & Ridley, Scott (1986, March–May). Chernobyl's challenge to anti-nuclear activism. *Radical America, 20*(2)–(3), 7–22.

Russell, Bernard H.; Killworth, Peter; Kronenfeld, David; & Sailer,Lee (1984). The problem of informant accuracy: The validity of retrospective data. *Annual Review of Anthropology,* 13, pp. 495–517.

Russell, Bertrand (1961). *The basic writings of Bertrand Russell.* New York: Simon & Schuster.

Russell, Diana (1984). *Sexual exploitation: Rape, child sexual abuse, and workplace harassment.* Beverly Hills, CA: Sage.

Russell, Diana (1986). *The secret trauma: Incest in the lives of girls and women.* New York: Basic.

Ryan, Randolph (1986, December 6). A pattern

of deception and abuse. *Boston Globe*, p. 11.

Ryan, William (1981). *Equality*. New York: Random House.

Sacks, Karen (1974). Engels revisited: Women, the organization of production, and private property. In Michelle Zimbalist Rosaldo & Louise Lamphere (Eds.), *Women, culture, and society*. Palo Alto, CA: Stanford University Press.

Sacks, Karen (1976, February). Class roots of feminism. *Monthly Review, 27*(9), 28–48.

Sacks, Karen (1979). *Sisters and wives*. Westport, CT: Greenwood.

Sadker, Myra, & Sadker, David (1985, March). Sexism in the schoolroom of the '80s. *Psychology Today*, pp. 54–57.

Samater, Ibrahim (1984, October). From "growth" to "basic needs": The evolution of development theory. *Monthly Review, 36*(5), 1–13.

Sanders, William B. (1981). *Juvenile delinquency*. New York: Holt, Rinehart & Winston.

Sapir, Edward (1949). *The selected writings of Edward Sapir in language, culture, and personality*. David Mandelbaum (Ed.). Berkeley, CA: University of California Press.

Sapiro, Virginia (1986). *Women in American Society*. Palo Alto, CA: Mayfield.

Saul, John S., & Gelb, Stephen (1981, July–August). The crisis in South Africa: Class defense, class revolution. *Monthly Review, 33*(3), 1–156.

Scarlott, Jennifer (1986, March–May). Chernobyl, U.S.A. *Radical America, 20*(2)–(3), 12–15.

Schechter, Susan (1982). *Women and male violence*. Boston: South End.

Scheff, Thomas J. (Ed.). (1976). *Labeling madness*. Englewood Cliffs, NJ: Prentice Hall.

Schein, Muriel (1971, April). Only on Sunday. *Natural History*.

Schlesinger, Stephen (1983, January 1–8). Reagan's 'secret' war on Nicaragua. *Nation*, pp. 9–11.

Schneider, Karen (1983, June). Monroe doctrine, *Progressive*, pp. 38–39.

Schor, Juliet (1988, July/August). Eat the rich. *Zeta Magazine*, pp. 24–27.

Schorr, Alvin, & Moen, Phyllis (1979, March/April). The single parent and public policy. *Social Policy, 9*(5), 15–21.

Schrank, Jeffrey (1977). *Snap, crackle, and popular taste*. New York: Dell.

Schwendinger, Julia, & Schwendinger, Herman (1983). *Rape and inequality*. Beverly Hills, CA: Sage.

Scott, Donald M., & Wishey, Bernard (Eds.). (1982). *America's families: A documentary history*. New York: Harper & Row.

Shepard, Jon (1981). *Sociology*. St. Paul, MN: West.

Sherman, Howard J., & Wood, James L. (1979). *Sociology: Traditional and radical perspectives*. New York: Harper & Row.

Sherraden, Michael (1987, Winter). The myth of the youth labor shortage. *Social Policy*, pp. 12–13.

Sherrill, Robert (1980, October 25). Where is the cry of protest? *Nation*, pp. 413–415.

Sherrill, Robert (1983, March 19). The decline and fall of antitrust. *Nation*, pp. 321, 336–339.

Shostak, Marjorie (1981). *Nisa: The life and words of a !Kung woman*. New York: Vintage.

Shrader, William (1982, July). Demoralization in modern society: The experiential dilemma. *Contemporary Crisis, 6*(3), 267–283.

Sidel, Ruth (1982). *Women and childcare in China* (rev. ed.). New York: Penguin.

Silverstein, Brett (1984). *Fed up: The forces that make you fat, sick, and poor*. Boston: South End.

Simmel, Georg (1950). The metropolis and mental life. *The sociology of Georg Simmel* (Kurt H. Wolff, Trans. and Ed.). New York: Free Press, pp. 409–424.

Simmons, J. L., & McCall, George (1985). *Social research: The craft of finding out*. New York: Macmillan.

Simon, David, & Eitzen, D. Stanley (1986). *Elite deviance* (2nd ed.). Newton, MA: Allyn and Bacon.

Singer, Daniel (1984, March 10). Mitterand: Middle of the journey. *Nation*, pp. 273, 286–291.

Singer, Daniel (1985, September 28). France, racism and the left. *Nation,* pp. 279–281.

Skinner, Joseph (1985, December). Big Mac and the tropical forests. *Monthly Review, 37*(7), 25–32.

Skolnick, Arlene, & Skolnick, Jerome S. (Eds.). (1986). *Family in transition* (5th ed.). Boston: Little, Brown.

Skolnick, Jerone H., & Currie, Elliott (Eds.). (1976). *Crisis in American institutions.* Boston: Little, Brown.

Slater, Kelly (1986, November). After apple-picking. *Sanctuary,* pp. 7–9.

Slaughter, Jane (1987, April). Dissent grows at California GM-Toyota plant. *Labor Notes,* p. 3.

Smart, Mollie Stevens, & Smart, Laura S. (1976). *Families: Developing relationships.* New York: Macmillan.

Snell, Bradford (1973). American ground transport. In Jerome Skolnick & Elliott Currie (Eds.), *Crisis in American Institutions* (3rd ed.) (pp. 304–326). Boston: Little, Brown, 1976.

Snitow, Ann (1983, May 28). . . . And the rest are girls. *Nation,* pp. 679–681.

Snitow, Ann; Stansell, Christine; & Thompson, Sharon (Eds.). (1983). *Powers of desire: The politics of sexuality.* New York: Monthly Review Press.

Solomon, Norman (1980, January). Nuclear big brother. *Progressive,* pp. 14–21.

Solomon, Norman (1983, April 16). Europe, Russia, and the U.S. missiles. *Nation,* pp. 469–472.

Sonquist, John, & Koenig, Thomas (1975, Spring). Interlocking directorates in the top U.S. corporations. *Insurgent Sociologist, 5*(3), 196–230.

Spitze, Glenna (1986, March). The division of task responsibility in U.S. households: Longitudinal adjustments to change. *Social Forces, 64*(3), 689–701.

Spradley, James (1980). *Participant observation.* New York: Holt, Rinehart & Winston.

Spring, Joel (1984, April). From study hall to hiring hall. *Progressive,* pp. 30–31.

Stacey, Judith (1979, June). Toward a theory of family and revolution: Reflections on the Chinese case. *Social Problems, 26*(5), 499–605.

Stack, Carol B. (1974). *All our kin: Strategies for survival in a black community.* New York: Harper & Row.

Stallard, Karin; Ehrenreich, Barbara; & Sklar, Holly (1983). *Poverty in the American dream: Women and children first.* Boston: South End.

Starr, Paul (1979). The phantom community. In J. Case & R. C. R. Taylor (Eds.), *Coops, communes, and collectives* (pp. 245–273). New York: Pantheon.

Starski, Stanislaw (1982). *Class struggle in a classless Poland.* Boston: South End.

Statistical abstract of the United States (1977). Washington, DC: United States Department of Commerce, Bureau of the Census.

Statistical abstract of the United States (1979). Washington, DC: United States Department of Commerce, Bureau of the Census.

Statistical abstract of the United States (1982–1983). Washington, DC: United States Department of Commerce, Bureau of the Census.

Statistical abstract of the United States (1987). Washington, DC: United States Department of Commerce, Bureau of the the Census.

Steif, William (1985, February). Tales of apartheid. *Progressive,* pp. 22–24.

Stein, Maurice (1960). *The eclipse of community.* New York: Harper & Row.

Stein, Peter J. (Ed.). (1981). *Single life.* New York: St. Martin's.

Steinberg, Stephen (1981). *The ethnic myth: Race, ethnicity, and class in America.* Boston: Beacon.

Steiner, Stan (1976). *The vanishing white man.* New York: Harper & Row.

Sternglass, Ernest (1981). *Secret fallout.* New York: McGraw-Hill.

Stevenson, Paul (1982, October). Capitalism and inequality: The negative consequences for humanity. *Contemporary Crises, 6*(4), 333–372.

Stewart, Elbert W. (1981). *Sociology* (2nd ed.). New York: McGraw-Hill.

Stillwagon, Ellen (1981, November). Anti-Indian agitation and economic interests. *Monthly Review, 33*(6), 28–41.

Stoffel, Jennifer, & Phillips, Stephen (1986, April). Double jeopardy. *Progressive,* pp. 28–31.

Sullivan, Gail (1983, January–February). Ten years after: Letter from Wounded Knee. *Radical America, 17*(1), 75–80.

Sun Chief (1942). Sun Chief: The autobiography of a Hopi Indian (Leo Simmons, Ed.). Parts reprinted in J. Spradley and G. McDonough (Eds.), *Anthropology through literature.* Boston: Little, Brown, 1972.

Suomi, S. J., & Harlow, Harry (1972). Social rehabilitation of isolate reared monkeys. *Developmental Psychology, 6,* 487–496.

Swados, Harvey (1959). *The miners: Men without work.* In Philip Olson (Ed.), *America as a mass society* (pp. 232–243). New York: Free Press.

Sweezy, Paul (1951, May and June). The American ruling class. *Monthly Review, 3*(1), 10–17, *3*(2), 58–65.

Sweezy, Paul (1979, April). On the new global disorder. *Monthly Review, 30*(11), 1–9.

Sweezy, Paul (1980, November). Post-revolutionary society. *Monthly Review, 32*(6), 1–13.

Sweezy, Paul (1983a, January). The suppression of the Polish workers' movement. *Monthly Review, 34*(8), 27–30.

Sweezy, Paul (1983b, October). On socialism. *Monthly Review, 33*(5), 35–39.

Sweezy, Paul (1985, July–August). After capitalism—what? *Monthly Review, 37*(3), 98–111.

Sweezy, Paul (1986, September). Comments. *Monthly Review, 38*(4), 26–28.

Sweezy, Paul, & Magdoff, Harry (1980, April). U.S. foreign policy in the 1980s. *Monthly Review, 31*(11), 1–12.

Sweezy, Paul, & Magdoff, Harry (1982, September). Nuclear chicken. *Monthly Review, 34*(4), 1–11.

Sweezy, Paul, & Magdoff, Harry (1983a, February). The struggle to save social security. *Monthly Review, 34*(9), 13–16.

Sweezy, Paul, & Magdoff, Harry (1983b, June). Unemployment: The failure of private enterprise. *Monthly Review, 35*(2), 1–9.

Sweezy, Paul, & Magdoff, Harry (1985a, January). Four more years—of what? *Monthly Review, 38*(8), 1–12.

Sweezy, Paul, & Magdoff, Harry (1985b, March). What is Marxism? *Monthly Review, 36*(10), 1–6.

Sweezy, Paul, & Magdoff, Harry (1985c, June). Lessons of Vietnam. *Monthly Review, 37*(2), 1–13.

Sweezy, Paul, & Magdoff, Harry (1986, March). Questions for the peace movement. *Monthly Review, 37*(10), p. 1–13.

Sweezy, Paul, & Magdoff, Harry (1987, March). Vietnam and Nicaragua. *Monthly Review, 38*(10), 1–6.

Szasz, Thomas (1970). *The manufacture of madness.* New York: Harper & Row.

Szymanski, Albert (1976, Winter). The socialization of women's oppression. *Insurgent Sociologist, 6*(2), 31–58.

Szymanski, Albert (1978). *The capitalist state and the politics of class.* Cambridge, MA: Winthrop.

Szymanski, Albert (1981). The role of the state in society. In Scott G. McNall (Ed.), *Political economy* (pp. 156–188). Glenview, IL: Scott, Foresman.

Szymanski, Albert, & Goertzel, Ted (1979). *Sociology: Class, consciousness, and contradictions.* New York: D. Van Nostrand.

Tallmer, Matt (1981, November). Hooker's other Love Canals. *Progressive,* pp. 35–42.

Talmon, Yonina (1965). The family in a revolutionary movement—the case of the Kibbutz in Israel. In M.E. Nimkoff (Ed.), *Comparative Family Systems* (pp. 263–283). Boston: Houghton-Mifflin.

Tamir, Lois (1982). *Men in their forties.* New York: Springer.

Taylor, Michael (1982). *Community, anarchy, and liberty.* New York: Cambridge University Press.

Terkel, Studs (1974). *Working.* New York: Avon.

Thio, Alex (1986). *Sociology.* New York: Harper & Row.

Thompson, E. P. (1983, April 16). Peace is a third-way street. *Nation*, pp. 472–481.

Thompson, E. P., & Smith, Dan (Eds.). (1981). *Protest and survive*. New York: Monthly Review Press.

Thompson, Roger (1986). *Sex in Middlesex: Popular mores in a Massachusetts colony*. Amherst, MA: University of Massachusetts Press.

Thorne, Barrie (Ed.). (1982). *Rethinking the family*. New York: Longman.

Thorne, Barrie, & Luria, Zella (1986, February). Sexuality and gender in children's daily worlds. *Social Problems, 33*(3), 176–190.

Thurtell, Joel (1980, September). Troubled waters. *Progressive*, pp. 48–50.

Toffler, Alvin (1970). *Future shock*. New York: Random House.

Tonnies, Ferdinand (1887). *Community and society*. New York: Harper & Row, 1963.

Trausch, Susan (1981, December 29). The view from the top. *Boston Globe*, p. 27.

Turki, Fawaz (1972). *The disinherited: Journal of a Palestinian exile*. New York: Monthly Review Press.

Turnbull, Colin (1961). *The forest people*. New York: Simon & Schuster.

Turnbull, Colin (1962). *The lonely African*. New York: Simon & Schuster.

Turnbull, Colin (1981). Mbuti womanhood. In Frances Dahlberg (Ed.), *Woman the gatherer* (pp. 205–219). New Haven, CT: Yale University Press, 1981.

Turnbull, Colin (1983a). *The human cycle*. New York: Simon & Schuster.

Turnbull, Colin (1983b). *The Mbuti pygmies: Change and adaptation*. New York: Holt, Rinehart & Winston.

Turnbull, Colin (1984, June). Interview with Colin Turnbull. *Omni*, pp. 87–90, 124–134.

Turner, Jonathan H.; Singleton, Royce, Jr.; & Musick, David (1984). *Oppression: A sociohistory of black-white relations in America*. Chicago: Nelson-Hall.

Turner, Robert (1987, May 28). Where's the outrage over discrimination that won't go away. *Boston Globe*, p. 17.

Ulrich, David N., & Dunne, Harry P., Jr. (1986). *To love and work: A systematic interlocking of family, workplace, and career*. New York: Brunner/Mazel.

United Nations (1978). *Statistical yearbook*. New York: United Nations.

United States Department of Labor (1976). *The earnings gap between women and men*. Washington, DC: U.S. Department of Labor, Women's Bureau.

United States Department of Labor (1977). *Dictionary of occupational titles* (4th ed.). Washington, DC: U.S. Department of Labor.

United States Department of Labor (1983a). *Employment in perspective: Working women* (First quarter 1983). Washington, DC: Bureau of Labor Statistics, Report 683.

United States Department of Labor (1983b). *Workers, jobs, and statistics*. Washington, DC: Bureau of Labor Statistics, Report 698.

United States Department of Labor (1986a). *Employment in perspective: Women in the labor force* (Third quarter 1986). Washington, DC: Bureau of Labor Statistics, Report 733.

United States Department of Labor (1986b). *Employment in perspective: Minority workers* (Third quarter 1986). Washington, DC: Bureau of Labor Statistics, Report 735.

United States Department of Labor (1986c). *Employment in perspective: Minority workers* (Fourth quarter 1986). Washington, DC: Bureau of Labor Statistics, Report 737.

United States Department of Labor (1986d). *Employment in perspective: Women in the labor force* (Fourth quarter 1986). Washington, DC: Bureau of Labor Statistics, Report 738.

United States Department of Labor (1986e). *White-collar salaries, March 1986*. Washington, DC: Bureau of Labor Statistics, 86–325.

United States Department of Labor (1986f). *Half of mothers with children under 3 now in labor force*. Washington, DC: Bureau of Labor Statistics, 86–345.

United States Department of Labor (1986g). *Average annual pay by state and industry*.

Washington, DC: Bureau of Labor Statistics, 86–361.

United States Department of Labor (1986h). *Employment and earnings: Characteristics of families* (Third quarter 1986). Washington, DC: Bureau of Labor Statistics, 86–425.

United States Department of Labor (1986i). *Weekly earnings of wage and salary workers* (Third quarter 1986). Washington, DC: Bureau of Labor Statistics, 86–434.

United States Department of Labor (1986j). *Consumer expenditure survey, 1984*. Washington, DC: Bureau of Labor Statistics, 86–451.

United States Department of Labor (1987a). *Employment in perspective: Minority workers* (First quarter 1987). Washington, DC: Bureau of Labor Statistics, Report 739.

United States Department of Labor (1987b). *Employment and earnings: Characteristics of families* (Fourth quarter 1986). Washington, DC: Bureau of Labor Statistics, 87–43.

United States Department of Labor (1987c). *Weekly earnings of wage and salary workers* (Fourth quarter 1986). Washington, DC: Bureau of Labor Statistics, 87–44.

United States Department of Labor (1987d). *Employment and earnings characteristics of families* (First quarter 1986). Washington, DC: Bureau of Labor Statistics, 87–153.

United States Department of Labor (1987e). *Weekly earnings of wage and salary workers* (First quarter 1987). Washington, DC: Bureau of Labor Statistics, 87–165.

United States Department of Labor (1987f). *Employment in perspective: Women in the labor force*. Washington, DC: Bureau of Labor Statistics, Report 740.

United States Department of Labor (1987g). Employment and earnings characteristics of families (Second quarter 1987). Washington, DC: Bureau of Labor Statistics, 87–317.

United States Department of Labor (1987h). *Over half of mothers with children one year old or under in labor force in March 1987*. Washington, DC: Bureau of Labor Statistics, 87–345.

United States Department of Labor (1988). *Employment in perspective: Women in the labor force* (First quarter 1988). Washington, DC: Bureau of Labor Statistics, Report 752.

Urquhart, Thomas A. (1984, January–February). The ecosystem after. *Sanctuary* pp. 14–15.

Ursel, Jane (1977, January). The nature and origin of women's oppression: Marxism and feminism. *Contemporary Crisis, 1*(1), 23–26.

Useem, Michael, (1978, February). The inner circle of the American capitalist class. *Social Problems, 25*(3), 225–240.

Useem, Michael (1984). *The inner circle: Large corporations and the rise of business political activity in the U.S. and U.K.* New York: Oxford University Press.

Useem, Michael, & Karabel, Jerome (1986, April). Pathways to top corporate management. *American Sociological Review, 51*(2), 184–200.

Vail, David (1987, June). Uneven development downeast: The dark side of Maine's boom. *Dollars and Sense,* pp. 9–11.

Valentine, Betty Lou (1978). *Hustling and other hard work*. Chicago: University of Chicago Press.

Vander Zanden, James W. (1983). *American minority relations* (4th ed.). New York: Knopf.

Veevers, J. E. (1973, April). Voluntarily childless wives: An exploratory study. *Sociology and Social Research, 57,* 356–365.

Vidich, Arthur (1980). *Revolutions in community structure*. In Art Gallagher, Jr. & Harland Padfield (Eds.), *The dying community* (pp. 109–132). Albuquerque, NM: University of New Mexico Press.

Vidich, Arthur, & Bensman, Joseph (1958). *Small town in mass society*. Princton, NJ: Princeton University Press.

Vogeler, Ingolf (1981). *The myth of the family farm: Agri-business dominance of U.S. agriculture*. Boulder, CO: Westview.

Wald, Karen (1978). *Children of Che: Childcare and education in Cuba*. Palo Alto, CA: Ramparts.

Walsh, Joan (1986, September). Family ties: Feminism's new frontier. *Progressive,* pp. 21–23.

Walshok, Mary L. (1981). *Blue-collar women*. Garden City, NY: Anchor.

Walters, Eleanor (1982, February). Silent death: The misuse of medical x-rays. *Progressive*, pp. 33–37.

Warner, W. Lloyd (1963). *Yankee City*. New Haven, CT: Yale University Press.

Warner, W. Lloyd; Meaker, Marchia; & Eels, Kenneth (1960). *Social class in America*. New York: Harper & Row.

Wasserman, Harvey (1982, April). The industry that couldn't. *Progressive*, p. 66.

Wasserman, Harvey, & Solomon, Norman (1982). *Killing our own: The disaster of America's experience with atomic radiation*. New York: Dell.

Wasserman, Harvey, & Solomon, Norman (1983, January 1–8). New light on the dangers of radiation. *Nation*, pp. 1, 14–18.

Watch out for the rain (1982, January). *Sanctuary*, p. 12.

Watson, David L. (1953). *The study of human nature*. Yellow Springs, Ohio: Antioch.

Watson, Roy E. L. (1983, January). Premarital cohabitation vs. traditional courtship: Their effects on subsequent marital adjustment. *Family Relations*.

Weaver, Thomas C. (Ed.). (1973). *To see ourselves: Anthropology and modern social issues*. Glenview, IL: Scott, Foresman.

Weir, David, & Shapiro, Mark (1981). *Circle of poison*. San Francisco: Institute for Food and Development Policy.

Werner, Dennis (1984). *Amazon journey: An anthropologist's year among Brazil's Mekranoti Indians*. New York: Simon & Schuster.

West, James (1945). *Plainville, U.S.A.* New York: Columbia University Press.

Westhues, Kenneth (1982). *First sociology*. New York: McGraw-Hill.

Wettstein, Mike, & Gormican, John (1987, January). Steel workers on the line. *Progressive*, pp. 15–16.

Wexler, Richard (1985, September). Invasion of the child savers. *Progressive*, pp. 19–22.

White, Diane (1982, December 18). Taming the monster that's become Christmas. *Boston Globe*, p. 13.

White, Diane (1983, March 30). Food without thought. *Boston Globe*, p. 61.

White, Lynn K., & Brinkerhoff, David B. (1981, September). The sexual division of labor: Evidence from childhood. *Social Forces, 60*(1), 170–181.

Whiteside, Larry (1987, April 9). Racism still exists. *Boston Globe*, pp. 45, 48.

Whorf, Benjamin Lee (1941). The relation of habitual thought and behavior to language. In David W. McCurdy & James P. Spradley (Eds), *Issues in Cultural Anthropology* (pp. 50–67). Boston: Little, Brown, 1979.

Wilcox, Kathleen, Moriarty, Pia (1976, December). Schooling and work: Social constraints on equal educational opportunity. *Social Problems, 24*(2), 204–213.

Williams, Eric (1944). *Capitalism and slavery*. New York: Capricorn.

Williams, Greg (1985). Presentation at a conference of the April Actions Coalition, Cambridge, MA, November 23.

Williams, Mary (1982, November). The Weirton Steel that was and may yet be. *Progressive*, pp. 30–36.

Williams, Robin (1970). *American Society*. New York: Knopf.

Williams, Ted (1983, September). The sky as sewer. *Sanctuary*, pp. 13–16.

Williams, Ted (1984a, September). Waldsterben. *Sanctuary*, pp. 3–6.

Williams, Ted (1984b, November). The Attleboro swamp/mall. *Sanctuary*, pp. 8–11.

Williams, Ted (1985a, May/June). Undemocratic din. *Sanctuary*, pp. 14–15.

Williams, Ted (1985b, September). Banking on destruction. *Sanctuary*, pp. 4–6.

Williams, Ted (1986, September). The malling of Massachusetts. *Sanctuary*, pp. 8–10.

Williams, Terry, & Kornblum, William (1985). *Growing up poor*. Lexington, MA: Lexington.

Williams, Thomas R. (1982). *Socialization*. Englewood Cliffs, NJ: Prentice Hall.

Williams, Vicki (1982, February 5). Listen—for a change. *Boston Globe*, p. 15.

Willie, Charles V. (1981). *A new look at black families* (2nd ed.). Bayside, NY: General Hall.

Winslow, Art (1983, February 12). Speaking with forked tongue. *Nation,* pp. 177–179.

Wirbel, Loring (1980, November). Somebody is listening. *Progressive,* pp. 16–19.

Wirth, Louis (1938, July). Urbanism as a way of life. *American Journal of Sociology, 44*(1), 1–24.

Wise, Tim (1987, June). Iran/Contragate is only the tip of the iceberg—Christic Institute 'hidden policy' revelations. *Peacework,* pp. 3–5.

Wolf, Eric (1982). *Europe and the people without history.* Berkeley, CA: University of California Press.

Wooden, Kenneth (1976). *Weeping in the playtime of others.* New York: McGraw-Hill.

Work in America (1973). Report of a special task force to the Secretary of Health, Education, and Welfare. Cambridge, MA: MIT Press.

Worthy, William (1976). *The rape of our neighborhoods.* New York: Morrow.

Wright, Richard (1966). *Black boy.* New York: Harper & Row.

Wrong, Dennis (1961). The oversocialized conception of man in modern sociology. *American Sociological Review, 26,* 183–193.

Wrong, Dennis (1979). *Power: Its forms, bases and uses.* New York: Harper & Row.

Young, John, & Newton, Jan (1980). *Capitalism and human obsolesence.* Montclair, NJ: Allenheld, Osmun.

Young, Michael, & Willmott, Peter (1957). *Family and kinship in East London.* Baltimore: Penguin.

Zehring, Robin (1973, March 11). Two delicate conditions. *California Living Magazine (San Francisco Sunday Examiner and Chronicle).* In Judson R. Landis, (Ed.), *Sociology* (3rd ed.) (pp. 392–397). Belmont, CA: Wadsworth, 1977.

Zeitlin, Irving M. (1980). *The social condition of humanity: An introduction to sociology.* New York: Oxford University Press.

Zeitlin, Maurice (1978, June). Who owns America? *Progressive,* pp. 14–21.

Zeitlin, Maurice (Ed.). (1980). *Classes, class conflict, and the state.* Cambridge, MA: Winthrop.

Zimbalist, Andrew (1975, November–December). Worker participation in Cuba. *Challenge,* pp. 45–54.

Zinn, Howard (1980, June). A showcase of repression. *Progressive,* pp. 34–39.

Zinn, Maxine Baca, & Eitzen, D. Stanley (1987). *Diversity in American families.* New York: Harper & Row.

Zwerdling, Daniel (1975, January). The food monopolies. *Progressive,* pp. 13–17.

Zwerdling, Daniel (1978, December). Curbing the chemical fix. *Progressive,* pp. 16–25.

Zwerdling, Daniel (1980, March). The food monsters. *Progressive,* pp. 16–27.

About the Author

I was born in Llongo, Albania, in April 1941. I am the fifth of eight children (second of five who survived childhood and are still living) of Georgia and Theodore Liazos. My father and his male ancestors have lived in the village of Llongo for approximately four hundred years. The village is located in southern Albania, which is populated by Greek nationals who still carry on their language and customs.

In 1941, World War II was raging, with the Nazis shortly to conquer Albania. My earliest memory (1943 or 1944) is of hiding in the cellar with my family, protecting ourselves from German bombardments. The Albanian communist party fought the Nazis, and when the Nazis withdrew, Albania became a socialist society.

In 1947, when I was six, my brother Christos (then ten) and I left Albania and joined our paternal grandmother Afroditi Liazos and settled in Greece. We were very poor, as were most people in Greece then. Our home was one-third of a room in an old school building. It was used for housing people who had left the villages near the town of Ioannina because of the civil war in Greece. The poverty left me with deep impressions (which I discuss briefly in Chapter 8), but I also have fond memories of that period of my life. Since there were very few cars, we could roam and play in the streets freely. I remember friends with great fondness and nostalgia. And I remember the summer camps set under the olive trees by the sea and up in the mountains.

Our grandmother struggled to raise two young children in her old age. She did so with love, determination, courage, and a few eccentricities. In 1955, when she was seventy-five years old and no longer able to care for us, the three of us came to the United States. Aunts and other family in Worcester, Massachusetts, brought us over, and we lived with an aunt for two years.

From 1957 to 1964, as I attended high school and college (Clark University in Worcester), my grandmother, brother, and I had our own apartment. Even though I became an American citizen, I was filled with a longing for my family in Albania and my friends in Greece. I experienced some social isolation as I tried to fit into a strange new culture. I have only vague memories of the first six years of my life, but I have many vivid memories of my eight years in Greece and my first nine years in America.

From 1956 to 1962, I worked as a busboy and dishwasher in a restaurant in Worcester, and from 1962 to 1964, I worked in a factory cutting and shaping hardboard (pressed paper). In those eight years, I was in close contact with working class white people and poor black people. My life with them made a deep and permanent impression on me about the lives and problems of working people in the United States.

In 1964 I left Worcester to study sociology at Brandeis University. My grandmother first went to live with my brother and his wife near Philadelphia, Pennsylvania, and then returned to Worcester to live with one of her daughters (my father's sister). In May 1965, at the age of eighty-five, she died alone at 3:00 A.M. in a hospital room. I still cry when I think of the loneliness and aloneness of her last moments of life. All I write about family, culture, community, and social change has been permanently shaped by her life and death, and the sadness I still feel.

Later in 1965 I was married to Karen Judge. I continued my studies at Brandeis until 1968. While teaching part-time at Simmons College from 1967 to 1968, I studied an institution for emotionally disturbed adolescent boys. It became my dissertation, and I received my Ph.D. in sociology from Brandeis in June 1970.

I began teaching at Quinnipiac College in Hamden, Connecticut, in 1968. I stayed there until 1971. These three years were profoundly important to my personal, social, and political growth. I had been marginally active in the civil rights movement in Worcester in the early 1960s, and I had gone to some demonstrations against the Vietnam War. But while in New Haven, I joined AIM (the American Independent Movement), an organization that worked for civil rights, against the war, and for social equality for all Americans. My road to Marxism and socialism began there.

Two other experiences were important. During the writing of my dissertation on the boys' home (from 1968 to 1970), I read about one of the former residents who had died in Vietnam. It shook me and forced me to re-think my analysis of the institution and its function. I realized then that various institutions channel working-class people into limited lives and send boys to fight imperialist wars for the ruling class.

After three years of teaching a course on deviance at Quinnipiac College, I came to understand that sociology and the sociology of deviance focus on the crimes of the poor, but they ignore the crimes of corporations and the rich. A paper I wrote in 1971, "The Poverty of the Sociology of Deviance: Nuts, Sluts, and Preverts", discusses this understanding. It marked another step in my gradual but steady political awakening that led to *People First*, which was published in 1982.

Since 1971, I have been teaching at Regis College in Weston, Massachusetts. I have also taught evenings and summers at Middlesex Community College, Framingham State College, Northeastern University, and Clark University. In 1975, four colleagues, John Baumann, Jim Brady, Richard Quinney, Richard Speiglman, and I organized a study group of Marxist criminologists. It was at this time that my understanding of socialism and Marxism reached its maturity. This is not to say I have stopped thinking, growing, and changing but only that the foundation of my political consciousness was established and reached its maturity at this point. *People First*, three other papers I have written, this book, and my work with a number of political groups have been other steps in my social and political growth and practice.

In 1974 and 1976, my wife and I had two daughters, Melissa and Ariane. I have shared in their upbringing, and I have rich, warm experiences and memories of their childhood. As we raised them, I learned much about sex roles, sexism, and childhood in America. I read books to and with them. We visited and explored many places around greater Boston. In all seasons, we took walks through lovely New England woods. We played many games and watched *Sesame Street* and other television shows. I changed and washed their diapers, and I fed them when they were little. I told them bedtime stories and sang them lullabies as they fell asleep in my arms. I have sweet memories of their early years. Today, we continue to read together, tell stories, explore New England woods, but now we talk about social classes, wars, nuclear war, and other experiences of life.

In 1980, after thirty-three years of separation, I was able to visit Albania and meet my parents Georgia and Theodore, my brother Vangeli and sisters Kleoniki and Ifigenia with their families, and various other relatives. In Chapters 5 and 6, I recount some of my experiences and memories of those four weeks. My sense of family and community, and my appreciation of their significance, were enlivened and enriched during those twenty-eight days. That visit was a profound personal and emotional experience. The most rewarding part of it was the almost daily afternoon talks I had with my mother. I relived and was reunited with my family and my childhood self, a self long buried and repressed. I began to see that so much of me now was true of me as a child (this is discussed briefly in Chapter 7).

George Michelis, who came from Greece at the age of eighteen in 1968, shared an office with me at Regis from 1980 to 1984. He retained strong ties with his Greek heritage, and his singing and our frequent talks (mostly in Greek) awakened my Greek identity and culture. The discussion on culture owes much to our friendship and his influence on me.

My brother Chris and his wife Helena, and their sons Andrew and Teddy, together with our aunts and cousins have been a constant presence in my life, even during the years when I saw them infrequently. They have been the family, the continuity with the past, and the community we all need and seek but which is often fragile and problematic.

In 1981, my wife Karen and I separated. We were divorced in 1984. It was a difficult decision and a painful experience. Although Melissa and Ariane have been staying with me two days each week, and I see them on other days, I miss them terribly. They remain the most important people in my life, and we are very close.

From late 1981 to late 1984, I shared my life with a loving friend and companion. We talked about our lives and hopes and dreams, took walks through lovely woods and city streets, cooked together, and supported and encouraged each other. In late 1984, however, we ended our relationship. The different conditions and needs of our lives made it impossible to continue. Parting was sad and painful, but our time together was special and precious to both of us.

In August 1985, I went for a second visit to my family in Albania. With memories of 1980 still vivid, within a few days I felt at home, as if I had never left. Thus leaving home at the end of the month was more difficult than it had been in 1980.

I also visited Ioannina, the town where I grew up in Greece. So much of the town has changed, but a few sites from my youth still stand: the school where I spent six years, the yard where I played, my best friend's family store, and a few others. Memories engulfed me as I strolled through the streets in the quiet of the afternoon. (Greek stores still close from about 2:00 to 5:00 every afternoon.)

Two years later, in August 1987, my mother traveled to Athens, Greece, to visit a sister she had not seen in fifty-five years and a brother she had not seen in forty-five years. Melissa, Ariane, and I joined them for twelve days, days memorable and moving. We stayed with my friends George and Aleka, and their children Joanna and Harris. Thus, it was a reunion with family, friends, and a culture still part of me. Melissa and Ariane were happy to see their grandmother and to see and experience Greece.

Two events were especially meaningful. About 9:00 one evening, George and I went to an outdoor concert of Greek folk music. It was a cool, delicious night after a hot day. For part of the evening, three men and three women from Albania, all in their fifties and sixties, sang a few songs from the part of Albania where I was born. They are sad and melancholy songs, sung without instruments, recalling the home and family and community left behind. I began to cry and sob. I had not heard these songs since the early 1950s, when, lying on a straw mattress on the floor of the divided room we shared with another family, I would hear them sung by friends of that family, and I would cry. I had not thought of these sad songs and my tears for many years.

For three days, my mother, Melissa, Ariane, and I visited Ioannina, the town where I lived from 1947 to 1955. For years, I had had the fantasy that some day I would take my parents and my children to see the town and neighborhood where I grew up. It finally happened. My life felt complete and of one piece. I cannot describe the emotions I felt. Even though most of the buildings I knew were gone, including the buildings where I lived, and even though much of the culture has changed, the streets and some buildings are as I remembered them. Incidents, places, memorable events, friends, childhood games, daily routines, smells, joys and sorrows, reawakened within me and carried me back to my childhood. I don't know how much Melissa and Ariane could understand of what those days meant to me; they do not share the memories I hold. But they could see how touched and happy I was that I could share part of my childhood with them.

That visit to Ioannina left me with the need, longing, and determination to live there again for a few months, relive my youth, and write an autobiography of my life in Albania and Greece. It may happen in two, five, ten, or more years, but it must happen. The longing for home and the need to relive, understand, and interpret those years are very intense.

When I wrote this autobiography in 1984, I forgot a recurring dream I had for many years after I came to the United States in 1955. In the dream,

I was back in Ioannina, playing with my friends and walking the streets and yards I loved. But even as I dreamed this return home, I would say to myself, *while still in the dream*, that this *was* a dream, that it was not real. Thus I could not fulfill my wish to be home even in my dreams. I had forgotten this dream until I went back home in 1987. (I did visit Ioannina twice before, in 1969 with my former wife Karen, and in 1985, alone.)

Since 1982, I have become progressively more active in groups that work for peace, social and economic justice, and a nuclear-free world. I joined the Mobilization for Survival, a national organization that works for these goals. In 1983, I participated in a task force for a Nuclear Free Cambridge, which campaigned for a referendum to stop all nuclear weapons research in Cambridge, Massachusetts. It lost 59 to 41 percent. Since late 1984, I have been in various groups that seek to end the wars in Central America and the instigation of these wars by the U.S. government. In 1986, I worked intensively in the congressional campaign of Mel King's, a progressive black activist. Even though he lost the election, we established ties and friendships for future work for social and racial justice. In 1987, I joined with a few Watertown residents to work toward increasing the supply of affordable housing in our town. In 1988, I worked for the Jesse Jackson campaign. I saw that more people, many of them working class, were moved by his message for economic and social justice for all people. I continue to work for justice, for affordable housing, for peace in Central America and elsewhere, and the end of nuclear power and weapons. I feel hopeful.

Finally, a few words about my children and my inner and daily life. Melissa and Ariane are happy and growing young women of 14 and 12. It is a joy to watch them expand their horizons and identities. We are close. They continue to stay with me four days every two weeks and for part of their vacations. We bake cookies, see movies, and watch some television, still take walks through Walden Pond and other New England woods, laugh ourselves silly, debate and disagree. And I await impatiently the summer of 1989 or 1990, when I hope we can visit my family in Albania, and they get to meet their grandfather, aunts and uncles, and cousins.

At forty-seven, my life is generally happy and full. My favorite pastimes are bicycling and folk music. I first learned and began to bike in 1984, at the age of 43, and now I frequently ride the bikepaths along the Charles River. Folk music inspires me, soothes me, sometimes makes me cry, often it rekindles memories. I listen to and attend concerts of Greek, Irish, traditional and contemporary folk music, and music from many other places and times. I enjoy it because it celebrates and tells of historical events, social protests, family life, love and unfulfilled love, and dreams of peace and justice.

I feel an inner peace and tranquility. I am more patient and accepting, even as I feel angry and outraged at injustices, sufferings, and wars. I am at home in Watertown and the Boston area, even as I miss Greece and my family in Albania. I see that progress to peace and justice is painfully slow, but I am hopeful, and committed to the long search and work to achieve them. I will continue to seek inner and outer peace.

Index